ADVANCED

Visual Basic® 2010

FIFTH EDITION

Kip Irvine

Florida International University

Tony Gaddis

Haywood Community College

Addison Wesley

Boston   Columbus   Indianapolis   New York   San Francisco   Upper Saddle River
Amsterdam   Cape Town   Dubai   London   Madrid   Milan   Munich   Paris   Montreal   Toronto
Delhi   Mexico City   Sao Paulo   Sydney   Hong Kong   Seoul   Singapore   Taipei   Tokyo

Editorial Director:	*Marcia Horton*
Editor in Chief:	*Michael Hirsch*
Acquisitions Editor:	*Matt Goldstein*
Editorial Assistant:	*Chelsea Bell*
Managing Editor:	*Jeffrey Holcomb*
Senior Production Project Manager:	*Marilyn Lloyd*
Media Producer:	*Dan Sandin*
Marketing Manager:	*Yez Alayan*
Marketing Coordinator:	*Kathryn Ferranti*
Production/Operations Manager:	*Pat Brown*
Text Designer:	*Joyce Cosentino Wells*
Cover Designer:	*Suzanne Duda*
Cover Image:	*Shutterstock Images*
Project Management/Composition:	*Jogender Taneja / Aptara®, Inc.*
Printer/Binder:	*Bind-Rite Graphics*
Cover Printer:	*Lehigh-Phoenix Color*

Library of Congress Cataloging-in-Publication Data

Irvine, Kip R.,
    Advanced visual basic 2010 / Kip Irvine, Tony Gaddis.—5th ed.
      p. cm.
    ISBN-13: 978-0-13-231674-3
    ISBN-10: 0-13-231674-9
    1. Microsoft Visual BASIC.   2. BASIC (Computer program language)
    I. Gaddis, Tony.   II. Title.
    QA76.73.B3G32 2012
    005.13'3—dc22
                                 2011000246

10 9 8 7 6 5 4 3 2 1—BRR—15 14 13 12 11

Addison-Wesley
is an imprint of

ISBN 10:   0-13-231674-9
ISBN 13: 978-0-13-231674-3

*This book is dedicated to the memory of Barry Brosch,
my teacher and mentor.*

—Kip Irvine

*This book is dedicated to the memory of Ruth Young,
an inspiration and a role model for all who knew her.*

—Tony Gaddis

Brief Contents

Contents

Chapter 11 Web Services and Windows Presentation Foundation 555

Chapter 12 Reports, MDI, Interfaces, and Polymorphism 597

Appendix A Answers to Checkpoints 639

Advanced Visual Basic® 2010, Fifth Edition, offers instruction in Visual Basic .NET programming to those who have completed a semester course or equivalent in the same topic. After studying the book and completing the programming exercises (called Programming Challenges), students should be able to create small- to medium-size Windows and Web applications that use databases. They will also gain essential concepts in object-oriented programming, event-driven programming, and test-driven development.

Effective programmers must combine theory with practice in order to adapt to changing computing environments. This book does not cover the breadth of topics found in some professional reference books, but it provides a practical approach to programming and problem solving. The following features make it helpful in the classroom:

- A step-by-step learning method in which new ideas and concepts build on existing ones
- Tutorials in which students gain hands-on experience by working with the chapter topics
- Review questions (called Checkpoints) at the end of each chapter section
- Tips that provide advice for solving programming problems, sprinkled throughout the chapters
- A list of key terms at the end of each chapter
- Review questions and exercises at the end of each chapter
- Programming projects at the end of each chapter that reinforce the chapter material
- A companion website that contains sample programs and other support materials

Changes in the Fifth Edition

This edition of *Advanced Visual Basic 2010* offers many improvements. We place much more emphasis on object-oriented programming principles and software design than we did in the previous edition. The multi-tier application model (data, business objects, user interface) is a strong influence, as is programming with collections and components. Overall, the fifth edition provides an enhanced approach to designing, implementing, and testing well-constructed, maintainable, and extensible applications. Of particular note are the new sections on strongly typed collections, LINQ to Objects, LINQ to SQL, Unit Testing, Windows Presentation Foundation (WPF), and Windows Communication Foundation (WCF). The example programs were written in Visual Studio 2010.

Additional Materials

A primary selling point of a textbook lies in the quality of support given by the authors to adopting professors. The publisher makes excellent resources for this book available at www.pearsonhighered.com/irvine. The following materials are available to students and instructors:

- Online VideoNotes, narrated by Kip Irvine, which explain concepts and examples from the chapters
- A PowerPoint slide presentation for each chapter
- Example programs
- Online list of corrections to errors in the book

In addition, the following are available for professors:

- Answers to Review Questions and Exercises
- Solutions to Programming Challenges

Learning Objectives

Following are the learning objectives for this book, indicating the skills and knowledge that students may expect to attain:

- Master the use of .NET controls to create rich user interfaces
- Master the design and implementation of object-oriented multi-tier applications
- Master the design of manual and automated tests for desktop applications
- Master the use of .NET controls and exception handling to trap errors at the user interface level
- Master the displaying and updating of data in related database tables
- Master the creation of ASP.NET applications that contain multiple Web pages and databases
- Master the use of page-level state and session state in ASP.NET programs
- Be familiar with database constraints and database security
- Be familiar with creating and consuming Web services
- Be familiar with creating database-driven reports

Sequencing the Chapters

If your Advanced Visual basic course emphasizes Windows applications, we recommend that you complete Chapters 1 through 7 in sequence. For courses that cover Web programming, continue to Chapters 8 through 11. Chapter 12 (Reports, MDI, Interfaces, and Polymorphism) can be introduced any time after Chapter 4.

Chapter Descriptions

Chapter 1: Classes. Chapter 1 begins with basic concepts of classes and objects. Next, we show how to define classes, and enumerated types and structures, and how they are used in applications. We build a two-tier Bank Teller application that uses classes to simulate the basic operations of a software teller machine. The concept of multi-tier application design will continue to be a central theme throughout the book. We also introduce manual software testing as an important tool for validating program output.

Chapter 2: Input Validation and User Interfaces. Chapter 2 provides in-depth coverage of input validation and error handling. The ErrorProvider control is introduced as an ideal tool for input validation. Next, we review the ListBox, ComboBox, and CheckedListBox controls, and we show how to write code that deals with multiple selections. Following that, we show how to use the FlowLayout, WebBrowser, SplitContainer, and TabControl controls to create more creative user interfaces. The chapter finishes with the design and development of a software wizard and shows some of the power and flexibility of this type of application.

Chapter 3: Collections. Chapter 3 introduces some of the most useful and powerful collection classes in the .NET library, with the idea that collections of objects help to build concepts that can later be applied to databases. We show how to create and use ArrayLists, as well as strongly typed Lists and Dictionaries. The chapter finishes with examples that show how to search lists of objects, using Microsoft's new Language Integrated Query (LINQ) technology.

Chapter 4: Using SQL Server Databases. Chapter 4 focuses on the basics of displaying and updating databases using .NET controls. It shows how Visual Studio enables data binding, which is the connecting of the user interface directly to database components. The chapter also stresses basic database concepts; how to execute SQL queries; how to sort and filter database data; how to display data in a grid; and how to bind individual controls to database tables. After reading this chapter, students should be able to display and update database tables rapidly with almost no programming.

Chapter 5: Database Applications. Chapter 5 focuses on database programming, using the ADO.NET library. Students can think of it as an extension of the database concepts and database binding from Chapter 4. In Chapter 5, students can integrate their knowledge of multi-tier application design with objects and databases. The chapter concludes with an extended example application that schedules appointments for a home repair services company.

Chapter 6: Advanced Classes. Chapter 6 introduces structures, which are simple containers for variables, properties, and methods. Then the chapter demonstrates the building of components, also known as class libraries. Then the chapter introduces unit testing, the industry standard for automated testing of individual units of code. This is followed by a brief introduction to defining and using custom event types in classes. The chapter ends with inheritance, a fairly large topic that is a core topic in object-oriented programming.

Chapter 7: LINQ to SQL. Chapter 7 introduces LINQ to SQL, a powerful tool for querying and updating database data. LINQ to SQL offers the opportunity to use object-oriented programming techniques to view and update databases. Essentially, students work with databases in the same way that they did with in-memory collections in Chapter 3. They learn how to create entity classes that model database tables. They learn how to create selection queries that join multiple entity classes, using common linking properties. Students learn how to insert, update, and delete table entries.

Chapter 8: Creating Web Applications. Chapter 8 introduces the ASP.NET runtime environment and shows how to use Visual Studio to create Web sites. Students learn what happens when an ASP.NET page is processed by a Web server. Students learn about runtime events and about the different categories of controls available in ASP.NET applications, and they learn differences between HTML controls and ASP.NET controls. The chapter describes application and configuration files required by ASP.NET applications. Finally, the chapter shows how to create a simple Web application containing various types of buttons, labels, headings, and text boxes.

Chapter 9: Programming Web Forms. Chapter 9 introduces students to programming techniques in ASP.NET applications. They also learn about XHTML, cascading style sheets, menus, and validation controls. Students learn how to upload files to a Web site and send email from a Web site. They learn how to save page state information and how to save information when users switch between pages. Finally, the chapter shows how application cookies are created.

Chapter 10: Web Applications with Databases. Chapter 10 introduces master-detail pages, which let students create a consistent look across a Web site. Following that, the chapter shows how to use data-bound controls with databases. It examines some advanced use of the GridView control. The chapter shows a few basic techniques available in JavaScript, and finishes with a brief introduction to the Microsoft Ajax extension controls.

Chapter 11: Web Services and Windows Presentation Foundation. Chapter 11 helps students understand the basic technologies behind Web services and the types of applications that use them. Students learn how to create and consume Web services. Next, the chapter introduces Microsoft's exciting new Windows Presentation Foundation (WPF). WPF programs can be run from both the desktop and the Web. We show how to use ClickOnce technology, which greatly simplifies application deployment and installation.

Chapter 12: Reports, MDI, Interfaces, and Polymorphism. Chapter 12 introduces several important topics. First, its shows how to create reports for the desktop and Web, using Microsoft Report templates and the ReportViewer control. Next, it shows how to create Multiple-Document Interface (MDI) applications, which manage multiple client windows under a single parent window. Then we introduce advanced topics in object-oriented programming: interface types, abstract classes, and polymorphism. Although these topics are not heavily emphasized in Visual Basic applications, they can be important as programs grow in size and complexity.

Appendix A: Answers to Checkpoints. Students may test their progress by comparing their answers to the review questions at the end of each chapter section. These lists of review questions are called *Checkpoints*. Appendix A provides all the Checkpoint answers.

Appendix B: Optional Reference Topics. Appendix B contains a collection of optional reference topics. It shows how to calculate TimeSpan objects and how to format dates and times. It shows how to use the ListView control. Next is a guide to SQL Queries (SELECT, INSERT, DELETE, and UPDATE). Finally, it shows students how to write messages to the application log file. This can be a powerful tool for diagnostic and error reporting.

Acknowledgments

We wish to thank the following individuals for their contributions to this book:

- Matt Goldstein, Acquisitions Editor at Addison-Wesley, who was the driving force behind this book
- Chelsea Bell, Editorial Assistant at Addison-Wesley
- Jogender Taneja, my project manager at Aptara, did a great job of keeping the production moving, with quality work all the way and Marianne L'Abbate, the excellent copy editor

We wish to thank the following individuals who reviewed the current edition:

Evans Adams, Fort Lewis College
Patricia McDermott-Wells, Florida International University
David S. McDonald, Georgia State University
Rudy Lee Martinez, Austin Community College

We also wish to thank the following professors who reviewed earlier editions of this book:

Jeffery Allen, Indiana University Purdue University Indianapolis
Chuck Bailey, Kenai Peninsula College
Anthony Basilico, Community College of Rhode Island
Joni Catanzaro, Louisiana State University
Ronald Del Porto, Penn State University, Behrend
William Dorin, Indiana University Northwest
Dana Johnson, North Dakota State University
Melody Kiang, California State University, Long Beach
Bruce LaPlante, University of Wisconsin, Green Bay
Astrid Lipp, Georgia State University
Thomas McCullough, Hillsborough Community College
David McDonald, Georgia State University
Sally Field Mullan, College of DuPage
Theresa Nagy, Northern Virginia Community College
Adam Peck, Ohlone College
Anita Philipp, Oklahoma City Community College
Andre Poole, Florida Community College at Jacksonville
Ed Schott, Walsh University
Craig Van Lengen, Northern Arizona University

Lori Walljasper, Scott Community College
Sandy Wells, Gadsden State Community College

Kip Irvine
Tony Gaddis

About the Authors

Kip Irvine holds a Master of Science degree in Computer Science from University of Miami. He taught computer programming at Miami-Dade College for seventeen years, and he has taught at Florida International University since 2000. He has written programming textbooks for Addison-Wesley and Prentice-Hall, covering subjects such as Assembly Language, C++, Visual Basic, and COBOL. His books have been translated into Russian, Korean, Chinese, Polish, Spanish, and French. He briefly worked as a software developer in the industry.

Tony Gaddis taught computer programming languages, operating systems, and physics at Haywood Community College in North Carolina. He was selected as the North Carolina Community College Teacher of the Year in 1994, and received the Teaching Excellence award from the National Institute for Staff and Organizational Development in 1997. Tony has also provided training to companies and agencies, including NASA's Kennedy Space Center. He is a best-selling author of numerous computer programming textbooks for Addison-Wesley, covering topics such as Alice, Java, C++, C#, Visual Basic, and algorithms.

1 Classes

TOPICS

This chapter begins with basic concepts of classes and objects. Next, we demonstrate how to define classes and enumerated types, showing how they are used in applications. We build a two-tier Bank Teller application that uses classes to simulate the basic operations of a software teller machine. The concept of multi-tier application design will continue to be a central theme throughout the book. Finally, we introduce manual software testing as an important tool for validating program output.

1.1 Classes and Objects

CONCEPT: Classes are the basic elements of object-oriented programming, which in turn makes it possible for programmers to build rich, robust applications.

Object-oriented programming (OOP) is a way of designing and coding applications that focuses on the objects and entities in real-world applications. In this chapter, we present objects from a programmer's point of view. The more abstract concepts of object-oriented program and how they relate to the real-world of applications will not be emphasized here.

An **object** is a container for members such as properties, fields, methods, and events. It usually represents some entity in a problem that the application is designed to solve. If you were creating an automobile dealership application, for example, the entities might have names like vehicle, customer, salesperson, manager, and vehicle inventory. If you were creating a graphical user interface, the objects might be button, text box, list box, label, and radio button.

An object has **attributes** that may be thought of as common characteristics that apply to all objects of the same type. For example, a vehicle object might have attributes such as *make*, *model*, and *color*. An object also has **behaviors**, which represent the actions that can be carried out on the object. A vehicle object might have behaviors such as *start*, *stop*, and *turn*. An object may be able to raise **events**, which represent responses by the object to external actions. A Button object in .NET, for example, raises a *Click* event when the user clicks the button.

If you have already programmed in Visual Basic, you have used objects many times. In fact, buttons, check boxes, list boxes, and other controls are objects. But what you may not have known was that all of these objects were originally defined using classes.

Classes

A **class** defines which properties and methods can be applied to its objects. A class is defined using the Class keyword. For example, every form that you add to an application is defined by a class, such as the following:

```
Public Class Form1
End Class
```

Each control in the Visual Studio Toolbox window was defined by a class. The Button class, for example, contains definitions of properties, methods, and events that make it different from other classes. A TextBox control has properties named *Name, Text, Visible,* and *ForeColor*. All TextBox objects have these properties.

The **Microsoft .NET Framework** contains a large library of classes that make it possible to write applications for desktop computing, mobile applications, and the Web. The classes are grouped by similarity into namespaces to make it easier to find them. A **namespace** is a logical container that holds classes of similar types. For example, the *System.Collections* namespace contains classes related to building collections (arrays, lists, dictionaries, sets). The *System.Windows.Forms* namespace contains classes related to building desktop applications for Windows.

Creating Objects

If a class has been defined, you can create one or more objects of the class type. We sometimes call them *instances of the class*, or **class instances**. The following statement does this:

```
Dim freshman As New Student
```

The **New operator** tells VB to create an object in memory, and is required when creating an object (String objects are the exception to this rule). Or, you can separate this into two statements. For example, you might want to declare the variable at the class level in a Form:

```
Private freshman As Student
```

This variable does not reference any object at this point—it only has a data type. Then at some other point in the program's execution, you could create an instance of the class and assign it to the variable:

```
freshman = New Student
```

The = operator assigns the new object to the variable. We say that the variable contains a *reference* to the object.

Visual Studio Controls

Visual Studio creates instances of controls when you drag them from the ToolBox onto a form. For example, the following code was written to a form's designer file when a button was created and certain properties were set in the designer window:

```
Me.btnOk = New Button()
Me.btnOk.Location = New System.Drawing.Point(43, 48)
Me.btnOk.Name = "btnOk"
Me.btnOk.Size = New System.Drawing.Size(75, 23)
Me.btnOk.Text = "OK"
```

Notice how the first line uses the *New* operator to create an instance of the Button class. Then various property values are assigned to the button (Location, Name, Size, and Text).

The Nothing Keyword

The Nothing keyword indicates a null value, which results when a reference type variable has not been initialized. You cannot call a method or reference a property of an object that equals Nothing. The following statements, for example, would cause a runtime error:

```
Dim freshman As Student
freshman.PrintCourses()
```

If your code needs to know whether a variable has been initialized, you can compare the variable to the keyword Nothing.

```
If freshman Is Nothing Then
   ' must initialize the variable
   freshman = New Student
End If
```

Value Types and Reference Types

There are two general categories of Visual Basic data types: value types and reference types. A variable declared as a **value type** contains its own data in a single memory location. Value types include all the number types, such as Integer and Decimal, as well as Boolean. These types use a standard-size storage location.

A variable declared as a **reference type** does not directly hold its data. Instead, it points to (references) an object somewhere else in memory. Classes are reference types, as are Arrays. A **reference variable** is a variable declared using a reference type. When an object is created by invoking the New operator, the .NET runtime reserves space in memory for the object. The address of the object is stored in a reference variable. Doing this takes more processing time than for value types, but it allows .NET to reclaim the storage used by the object when it is no longer needed by the program.

Value Types

Value types do not require any initialization. As soon as you declare them, they have immediate storage. Variables of type Integer, Doubles, Boolean, and other standard types are value types. They are easy to use, consume little memory, and are the simplest to understand when using the assignment operator (=).

When you assign one value type to another using the assignment operator (=), a copy is made of the data in the variable on the right-hand side. The data is copied into the variable on the left-hand side. In the following example, *mCount* is copied to *temp*:

```
Dim mCount As Integer = 25
Dim temp As Integer = mCount
```

If a new value is later assigned to *temp, mCount* is not affected:

```
temp = 40       ' mCount still equals 25
```

However, not all variables work this way. When an object variable is assigned to another object, it's a little more complicated.

Reference Types

Whenever you create an instance of a class and assign it to a variable, your variable is a reference type. For example, the following code creates a `Person` object, assigns its reference to `P`, and assigns a value it its `Name` property:

```
Dim P As New Person
P.Name = "Fred Smith"
```

Figure 1-1 shows the relationship between `P` and the data it references. The data contained in the *Person* object is located in a special area of memory called the *managed heap*. P contains a reference to the data, not the data itself. If at any time in the future, the *Person* object is no longer needed, we can assign a value of Nothing to P:

```
P = Nothing
```

Figure 1-1 A reference type variable links to an object in memory

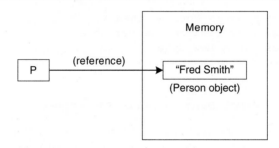

Assuming that no other references to the same *Person* object existed, a special utility in the .NET runtime called the *garbage collector* would eventually remove the object from memory.

In addition to objects, arrays are also reference types. Let's see what happens when reference objects are assigned to each other.

Strings

String objects are reference types, but they are a special case because their declarations do not require the New operator. Following are examples of String object declarations:

```
Dim strName As String
Dim strCity As String = "Miami"
```

Assigning Objects

The **assignment operator** (=) assigns an expression on its right side to a variable on its left side. It is common to use the assignment operator to assign one object to another. When you assign integers, for example, the value of the expression on the right side is copied into the variable on the left:

```
Dim Y As Integer = 25
Dim X As Integer
X = Y
```

After the above lines execute, X equals 25. But what if the variables X and Y are objects (reference types)?

```
Dim Y As New Account
Dim X As Account
X = Y
```

In this example, the contents of Y are not copied into X. Instead, the reference contained in Y is copied into X. Essentially, the variables X and Y now reference the same object.

Array Example

The following code creates an array of integers named *tests*, fills the array, and assigns the array to the variable named *scores*:

```
Dim scores() As Integer
Dim tests() As Integer = {80, 95, 88, 76, 54}
scores = tests
```

After this code executes, the same array is referenced by both scores and tests, as shown in Figure 1-2. The following code can be used to show that the two arrays share the same memory. By assigning a new value to scores(2), we automatically assign the same value to tests(2):

```
scores(2) = 11111
MessageBox.Show(tests(2).ToString())        ' displays "11111"
```

Figure 1-2 One array referenced by both variables

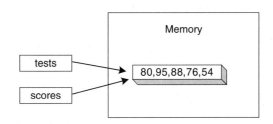

The message box shows that tests(2) equals 11111, as does scores(2). This type of dual reference can lead to a common type of programming error known as a **side effect**. Much like a medication that causes unwanted effects to a person, a software side effect changes variables in a way that can fool a programmer. Code containing side effects is very difficult to debug.

Using a Loop to Copy an Array

If you want to copy the contents of one array to another, you can use a loop to copy the individual elements. First, you reserve space in the scores array. Then you copy the data:

```
Dim scores(tests.Length - 1) As Integer
For i As Integer = 0 To tests.Length - 1
   scores(i) = tests(i)
Next
```

Figure 1-3 shows the result after copying the array. The following code shows that the two arrays do not share the same memory. When a new value is assigned to scores(2), the value of tests(2) is unchanged:

```
scores(2) = 11111
MessageBox.Show(tests(2).ToString())        ' displays "88"
```

Figure 1-3 Results after copying an array

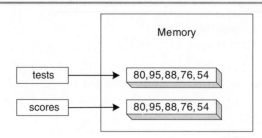

Using Object.Clone to Copy Data

Not all reference variables are arrays, so we need a more general way to copy the data from one reference type to another. This is where the Object.Clone method is useful. The `Clone` method copies the data from one reference variable to another. Using the same tests and scores arrays from the previous example, the following statement copies the array:

```
scores = CType(tests.Clone(), Integer())
```

Clone returns an Object, so the return value must be cast into an Integer array when *Option Strict* is in effect. The copy returned by *Clone* is called a *shallow copy* because it doesn't deal with the possibility that the elements in the array might be objects containing other reference types.

Here's another example, using two Person objects:

```
Dim P As New Person
P.Name = "George Smith"
Dim S As Person
S = CType(P.Clone(), Person)
```

Comparing Objects

All standard .NET objects can be compared for equality by calling the *Equals* method or by using the = operator. This is the case for strings:

```
Dim A As String = "abcde"
Dim B As String = "abcde"
If A = B Then ...          ' result: True
If A.Equals(B) Then ...    ' result: True
```

Another type of comparison is the *CompareTo* method, which compares two values X and Y:

- If X < Y, CompareTo returns a negative value
- If X = Y, CompareTo returns zero
- If X > Y, CompareTo returns a nonzero positive value

CompareTo is very useful because it is called automatically when you sort an array. You can call it yourself, as shown in the following examples.

CompareTo Examples

In the following example, result is assigned a negative value:

```
Dim A As String = "abcde"
Dim B As String = "abd"
Dim result As Integer = A.CompareTo(B)
```

In the following example, result is assigned a positive value:

```
Dim A As String = "abf"
Dim B As String = "abd"
Dim result As Integer = A.CompareTo(B)
```

In the following example, result is assigned zero:

```
Dim A As String = "abd"
Dim B As String = "abd"
Dim result As Integer = A.CompareTo(B)
```

Comparing Your Own Class Types

Your own classes, by default, will not use Equals and CompareTo effectively. For example, the following comparison of two Student objects is not useful. The call to Equals will return False, even though the students apparently have the same ID number:

```
Dim s1 As New Student(1001)
Dim s2 As New Student(1001)
If s1.Equals(s2) Then ...
```

Similarly, calling s1.CompareTo(s2) below is not meaningful:

```
Dim result As Integer = s1.CompareTo(s2)
```

This means that you cannot effectively sort an array of Students, at least not yet. In Chapter 3, you will learn how to implement the Equals and CompareTo methods in your own classes.

Checkpoint

1. What is a class, according to the definition in this chapter?

2. What is the term for an object that is declared using a class type?

3. A(n) ___ is a procedure or function that belongs to a class.

4. Unlike reference types, a variable declared with a(n) ___ type contains its own data and has immediate storage as soon as it is declared.

5. Assigning one reference type to another using the = operator leads to what type of potential error?

 Creating Your Own Classes

In future discussions, we will refer to a **user-defined class** (or a custom class) as a class that you design and build from scratch. In contrast, the .NET Framework already contains its own set of classes. You create a class in Visual Basic by coding a **class definition**. We will use the following general format when writing class definitions:

```
Public Class ClassName
   ' class members here
End Class
```

ClassName is the name of the class. The keyword Public is called an **access specifier**. The Public specifier tells VB that the class will be visible from all parts of your application. By visible, we mean that it will be possible to create objects that use this class name.

Follow these steps to add a class definition to a project:

1. Select *Project* on the menu bar, then select *Add Class*. The *Add New Item* dialog box, shown in Figure 1-4, should appear. Make sure that *Class* is selected in the Templates

pane. Notice that in the figure, the name *Class1.vb* appears in the Name text box. In this example, Class1.vb is the default name for the file that contains the code for the class, and *Class1* is the default name for the class.

Figure 1-4 Adding a class to a project

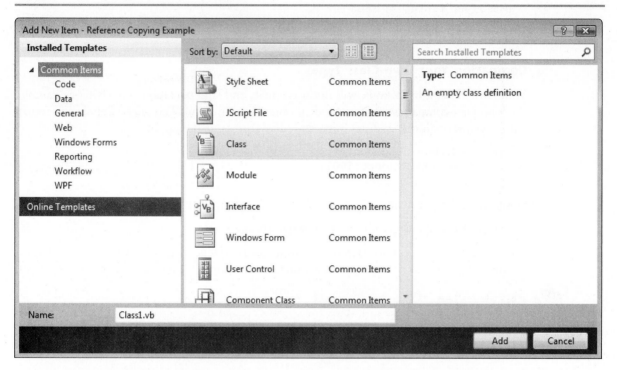

 TIP When adding a class to a project, the default class name will vary depending on the number of classes already in the project.

2. Change the default name displayed in the *Name* text box to the name you wish to give the new class file. For example, if you wish to name the new class *Student,* enter *Student.vb* in the Name text box.
3. Click the *Add* button. A new, empty class definition will be added to your project. The empty class definition will be displayed in the Code window, and an entry for the new class file will appear in the Solution Explorer window.

Adding a Class in Solution Explorer

You can also add a class to a project inside the Solution Explorer window. To do that, right-click on the Project name, select *Add,* and select *Class.* This is shown in Figure 1-5.

Class-Level Variables

A **class-level variable** is a variable that is declared inside a class but outside any methods in the class. This makes it visible to all methods in the class. A **local variable**, on the other hand, is declared inside a method and is visible only inside the method. You declare a class-level variable using the following general format:

```
AccessSpecifier name As DataType
```

Figure 1-5 Adding a class to a project inside the Solution Explorer window

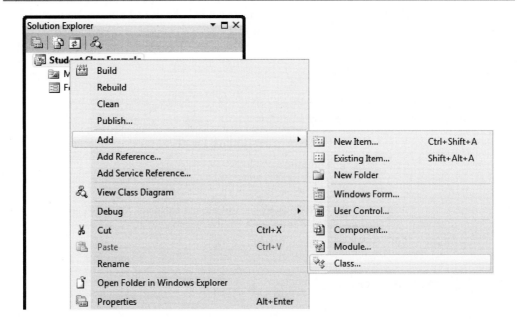

AccessSpecifier determines the accessibility of the variable. Fields declared with the Private access specifier may be accessed only by statements inside methods belonging to the same class. This is the normal way to declare a variable.

Name is the name of the variable, and *DataType* is the variable's data type. For example, the following code declares a class named Student. The class contains the variables mIdNumber, mLastName, and mTestAverage:

```
Public Class Student
    Private mIdNumber As String
    Private mLastName As String
    Private mTestAverage As Double
End Class
```

A class definition does not, by itself, create an instance of the class. It establishes a blueprint for the class's organization, which makes it possible for you to write other code that creates an object of this type.

Information Hiding

In object-oriented programming, the **encapsulation principle** says that you should bundle attributes and behaviors inside a class. Think of a class as a container that encapsulates everything inside for easy transporting and usage. The **information hiding principle**, which is closely related to encapsulation, says that certain class members should be visible only to methods inside the class. Usually, this applies to variables, which are labeled as Private. Many software engineers consider encapsulation and information hiding to be the same.

Hidden (private) members can be accessed only by other methods in the same class. This is a good idea because it leads to more reliable programs that are easier to debug.

A class-level variable could be declared Public, so code anywhere in an application could access it directly. But doing so would violate the information hiding principle. Instead, we use public methods and properties to define an interface, or public view of a class. Other information, such as variables, remain hidden by using the Private keyword.

Methods

A **method** is an action that implements some behavior of a class. You call a method by prefixing it with the name of a class instance. For example, a class named Account might have a method named ReadFromFile. First, we would have to create an instance of the Account class:

```
Dim savings As New Account
```

Then we would be able to call the ReadFromFile method:

```
savings.ReadFromFile("accounts.dat")
```

This is how the method could be declared in the Account class:

```
Public Class Account
  .
  .
  Public Sub ReadFromFile(ByVal fileName As String)
    '(code that reads the file here)
  End Sub
End Class
```

Shared Methods

Special methods, called *shared methods*, can be called using the name of the class. An example is the Array.Sort method that .NET provides for sorting an array:

```
Dim scores() As Integer = {62, 45, 89}
Array.Sort(scores)                          ' now: 45, 62, 89
```

Event handlers are also methods, but they have a special role—to respond to event messages passed to your application from the operating system. Every method in a class can access the class-level variables in the class.

ToString Method

All .NET classes support the **ToString method**, which returns a string representation of the data within the current class object. ToString is defined in the Object class, and all other classes inherit certain basic methods from the Object class. The method signature for ToString is:

```
Public Overridable Function ToString As String
```

Although we will provide a complete discussion of the concept of inheritance in Chapter 6, we can say here that **inheritance** is a basic concept of object-oriented programming. It means that one class can inherit attributes and behaviors from another class. In humans, for example, offspring inherit characteristics from their parents.

The Overridable keyword lets us know that we can override, or replace, the behavior of ToString by creating a version of this method in our own class. Here's how we would do that in the Student class:

```
Public Overrides Function ToString() As String
  Return mIdNumber & ", " & mLastName _
    & ", Test average = " & mTestAverage
End Function
```

Notice that the *Overrides* keyword must be used to let VB know that we want to override the ToString method that already exists in the Object class.

Properties

In Visual Basic, a **property** is a special type of method that uses the same member name for getting and setting a value. Whereas methods are the implementation of class behaviors, properties are implementations of class attributes. Button objects, for example, have a number of properties that are listed in the Properties window in Visual Studio. You have used properties since you began programming in Visual Basic. Now, you will learn how to add properties to your own classes. This is the standard format for a property definition:

```
Public Property PropertyName() As DataType
   Get
      '(code that returns data)
   End Get
   Set(value As DataType)
      '(code that assigns value to a class variable)
   End Set
End Property
```

PropertyName is the name of the property procedure and therefore the name of the property that the procedure implements. The parentheses following *PropertyName* are optional. *DataType* indicates the type of data, such as Integer or String. Notice that the procedure has two sections: a Get section and a Set section. The Get section holds the code that is executed when the property value is retrieved, and the Set section holds the code that is executed when a value is stored in the property. Properties are almost always declared with the Public access specifier so they can be accessed from outside their enclosing class module.

The following code defines a private field and its corresponding public property in the Student class:

```
class Student
   Private mLastName As String

   Public Property LastName As String
      Get
         Return mLastName
      End Get
      Set(ByVal value As String)
        mLastName = value
      End Set
   End Property
End Class
```

Auto-Implemented Properties

An **auto-implemented property** is a property that is defined by only a single line of code. You do not have to create a private member field to hold the property data. There are two general formats:

```
Public Property PropertyName As DataType
Public Property PropertyName As DataType = InitialValue
```

You can follow each property name with optional parentheses:

```
Public Property PropertyName() As DataType
Public Property PropertyName() As DataType = InitialValue
```

InitialValue is an optional value that you can assign to the property when it is created. When you declare an auto-implemented property, Visual Studio automatically creates a hidden private field called a *backing field* that contains the property value. The backing field's name is the property name preceded by an underscore character. For example, if you declare an auto-implemented property named ID, its backing field is named _ID.

The following are examples of auto-implemented properties that could be used in the Student class:

```
Public Property IdNumber As String
Public Property LastName As String
Public Property TestAverage As Double = 0.0
```

After learning about auto-implemented properties, why would anyone want to create the longer property definitions? In fact, the longer property definitions permit you to include range checking and other validations on data assigned to the property.

A ReadOnly property must be fully coded—it cannot be auto-implemented.

Getting and Setting Property Values

Before accessing a property, you must declare an instance of the class that contains the property. We could place the following statement anywhere in the program outside the Student class:

```
Dim freshman As New Student
```

The Set section of the property procedure executes when a value is assigned to the property. The following statement sets the value of LastName:

```
freshman.LastName = "Smith"
```

Therefore, the following statement inside the property procedure would execute:

```
mLastName = value
```

Conversely, the Get section of a property procedure executes when a program needs to have a copy of the LastName. Suppose that outside the Student class, we wrote the following statement, which copies the student's LastName value to a TextBox:

```
txtLastName.Text = freshman.LastName
```

Then the following statement inside the property procedure would execute:

```
Return mLastName
```

Input Validation in Properties

A property can be very useful when validating values assigned to it. In the following example, which implements the TestAverage property, the value assigned to the property must be between 0.0 and 100.0:

```
 1: Public Property TestAverage As Double
 2:    Get
 3:       Return mTestAverage
 4:    End Get
 5:    Set(ByVal value As Double)
 6:       If value >= 0.0 And value <= 100.0 Then
 7:          mTestAverage = value
 8:       Else
 9:          MessageBox.Show("Invalid test average.", "Error")
10:       End If
11:    End Set
12: End Property
```

Line 6 checks the range of the input value being assigned to the property. If line 6 equals *True*, line 7 assigns the input value to mTestAverage, the private class-level variable. If the input value is too large or too small, the mTestAverage variable remains unchanged, and line 9 displays an error message.

Object Initializers

Visual Basic provides a simple tool for declaring an object and assigning values to its properties. It is called an **object initializer**, and it is used in a couple of standard formats:

```
Dim VarName As New ClassName With {
   .Property = value [,.Property = value]...}
```

```
VarName = New ClassName With {
    .Property = value [,.Property = value]...}
```

VarName is the name of the variable. Dim can be replaced by Public, Private, or similar qualifiers. *ClassName* is the name of the class. *Property* is the name of a property. There is no rigid format as far as line breaks or property order.

The following statement declares and initializes a new Student object using literal values:

```
Dim aStudent As New Student With {
    .IdNumber = "1234",
    .LastName = "Smith",
    .TestAverage = 85.4 }
```

The following assigns a new object to an existing variable:

```
aStudent = New Student With {
    .IdNumber = "1234",
    .LastName = "Smith",
    .TestAverage = 85.4 }
```

The following statement creates and initializes a Student object using control values:

```
Dim aStudent As New Student With {
    .IdNumber = txtIdNumber.Text,
    .LastName = txtLastName.Text,
    .TestAverage = CDbl(txtAvg.Text) }
```

Assigning Object Variables

In our book *Starting Out in Visual Basic 2010*, we discussed well-defined rules for assigning values of standard data types to each other. You can assign an Integer expression to a Double variable, for example, because VB automatically expands the integer expression to type Double. There are similar rules for assigning class objects to each other, but they are definitely more restrictive. You can assign one object variable directly to another under the following specific circumstances:

1. The two variables have the same class type. A Student object, for example, can be assigned to another Student variable:

   ```
   Dim stu As New Student
   Dim Y As Student = stu
   ```

2. The two variables are of different types, but the variable on the left side is type Object. This is permitted because Object is a very general type that accepts any type of assignment:

   ```
   Dim stu As New Student
   Dim obj As Object = stu
   ```

In nearly all other cases, you must perform a cast from one type to another.

It is important to realize that the expression on the right side of the = operator might not be a variable; it might be a property name or method call. For example, a method named GetStudent returns a Student object, which cannot be assigned directly to a String variable:

```
Dim temp As String = GetStudent("12345")      'error
```

On the other hand, if we call the Student object's ToString method, it can be assigned to a string variable:

```
Dim temp As String = GetStudent("12345").ToString()      ' ok
```

Converting any object to a string is easy because all classes implicitly contain a ToString method. But if you want to convert to some other type, you will probably have to call the CType function.

Using the CType Function

The CType function casts (converts) an expression into a different type. This is the general format of CType:

```
CType(ObjectVal, TypeName) As TypeName
```

ObjectVal is a variable or expression that is to be converted. *TypeName* is the name of the type we wish to convert *ObjectVal* into. For example, the ListBox control's SelectedItem property returns an object. If you want to assign this object to a Student variable, you must call the CType function:

```
Dim selStudent As Student = CType(lstStudents.SelectedItem, Student)
```

The following, in contrast, would not compile (assuming that Option Strict is turned on):

```
Dim selStudent As Student = lstStudents.SelectedItem
```

Not all expressions can be converted. Suppose we were to try to assign a Student object to a BankAccount variable. No standard conversion exists for that, so VB throws an Invalid-CastException.

```
Dim stu As New Student
Dim bank As BankAccount = CType(stu, Student) 'error
```

Student objects and BankAccount objects have nothing in common, so we should not have been assigning them to each other anyway. Sometimes this type of error can be solved easily by calling a property or method in the class that returns the correct type of object. Perhaps the Student class contains a property that returns the student's bank account:

```
Dim bank As BankAccount = stu.SavingsAccount
```

There is more to learn about object assignments and conversions than we have introduced in this brief discussion. Once we have introduced the concept of inheritance in Chapter 6, we will revisit this topic.

Three-Tier Application Model

Most business applications today follow a basic design called the **three-tier application model**. Each tier contains classes that call methods in the tier below it, as shown in Figure 1-6.

Figure 1-6 Three-Tier Application Model

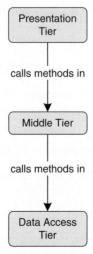

The **presentation tier**, also known as the *user services layer*, consists of all objects that interact with the user. Visual Basic uses a class to define a form, as well as the various controls on a form. When you write code inside the form of an application, your code belongs to the user interface tier. This includes, for example, all the event handler procedures, class-level variables, and other subprocedures in the form class.

The **middle tier**, also known as the *business logic tier* or *business services layer*, consists of classes that provide core information to the application, such as essential calculations and decision making. They often embody the business rules of an organization, which include operational principles that are common to multiple applications. These classes do not interact with the user. Instead, they contain methods and properties that are called by classes in the presentation tier.

The **data access tier**, also know as the *data services layer*, contains classes that interact directly with a data source. In later chapters, we will create classes for this tier that read and write to databases.

In Tutorial 1-1, you will create a two-tier application that uses a Windows form to call methods and properties in a class named Student. It contains a presentation tier and a middle tier.

Tutorial 1-1:
Creating a Student class

In this tutorial, you will create a two-tier application that uses a form to pass inputs by the user to the Student class. The form's class belongs to the presentation tier, and the Student class belongs to the middle tier. You will add controls to a form that permit the user to input a Student ID, last name, and test average. When the user clicks a button, your code will assign the input values to Student class properties. Finally, you will redisplay the Student object in a label. Figure 1-7 shows the form after the user clicks the *Save* button. Figure 1-8 shows the same form after the user clicks the *View* button.

Figure 1-7 After clicking the *Save* button

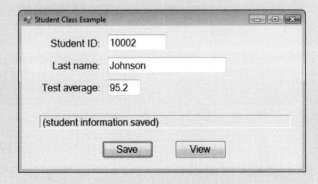

Figure 1-8 After clicking the *View* button

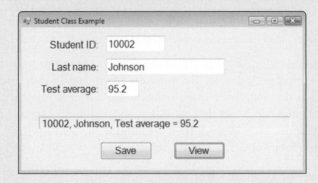

Tutorial Steps

Step 1: Create a new Windows application named *Student Class Example*.

Step 2: Next, add a class named Student to the project. Right-click on the Project name, select *Add*, and select *Class*. In the dialog window, select *Code*, select *Class*, and enter the class name as *Student.vb*. The items are marked in Figure 1-9 with arrows.

Figure 1-9 Adding a Student class to the project

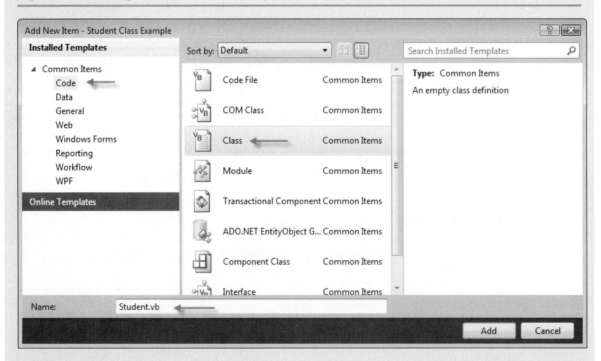

Step 3: Open the *Student.vb* file and replace its contents with the following class definition:

```
Public Class Student
    Public Property IdNumber As String
```

```
    Public Property LastName As String
    Private mTestAverage As Double

    Public Property TestAverage As Double
      Get
        Return mTestAverage
      End Get
      Set(ByVal value As Double)
        If value >= 0.0 And value <= 100.0 Then
          mTestAverage = value
        Else
          MessageBox.Show("Invalid test average.", "Error")
        End If
      End Set
    End Property

    Public Overrides Function ToString() As String
      Return IdNumber & ", " & LastName _
        & ", Test average = " & TestAverage
    End Function
End Class
```

The class contains auto-implemented properties named IdNumber and Last-Name. Because the TestAverage property requires range checking, it is implemented with explicit Get and Set sections.

Step 4: Open the startup form in design mode and add the named controls shown in Table 1-1. Also, add the labels shown earlier in Figure 1-7.

Table 1-1 Student Class example: named controls

Control Type	Control Name	Property Settings
TextBox	txtIdNumber	
TextBox	txtLastName	
TextBox	txtTestAverage	
Label	lblStudent	BorderStyle = Fixed3D, AutoSize = False
Button	btnSave	Text = *Save*
Button	btnView	Text = *View*

Next, you will write code in the startup form that copies the user's inputs to Student properties.

Step 5: Declare a Student variable at the class level:

```
Private objStudent As New Student
```

Step 6: Create the following Click handler for the *Save* button. You can omit the parameters from the btnSave_Click procedure because they are optional:

```
Private Sub btnSave_Click() Handles btnSave.Click
    objStudent.IdNumber = txtIdNumber.Text
    objStudent.LastName = txtLastName.Text
    objStudent.TestAverage = CDbl(txtTestAverage.Text)
    lblStudent.Text = "(student information saved)"
End Sub
```

This code copies values from the TextBox controls into the properties of the objStudent object. The additional label is added to provide a hint to the user.

 TIP A feature in Visual Basic named *relaxed delegates* lets you omit parameters in event handlers if the parameters are not being used inside the body of the handler.

Step 7: Create a Click handler for the *View* button that uses the Student.ToString method to display the Student object:

```
Private Sub btnView_Click() Handles btnView.Click
    lblStudent.Text = objStudent.ToString()
End Sub
```

Step 8: Save the project, and run the application with the following test:

Test

Input	Expected output
Enter an ID number such as "001234" and a student's last name, and click the *Save* button. Then click the *View* button.	You should see the same ID number and name that you entered. The test average will display as value 0.

Constructors

A **constructor** is a method that runs automatically when an instance of the class is created. In Visual Basic, a constructor is always named *New*. Constructors typically initialize class member variables to default values, but they can also be used to perform any required class initialization. If a class is connected to a network connection, for example, the constructor could be used to open a connection to a remote computer.

A **default constructor** is a constructor with no parameters. Let's create a simple one for the Student class that assigns a default values to the mIdNumber data member:

```
Public Sub New()
    mIdNumber = "999999"
End Sub
```

With this constructor in place, if a client program creates a new Student object, we know for certain what value the object's mIdNumber will contain.

Parameterized Constructor

A class may contain more than one constructor, so in addition to a default constructor, you may want to create a **parameterized constructor** (a constructor with parameters). Here is a parameterized constructor that assigns values to each of the Student class-level variables:

```
Public Sub New(ByVal pIdNumber As String, ByVal pLastName As String,
    ByVal pTestAverage As Double)
```

```
      mIdNumber = pIdNumber
      mLastName = pLastName
      mTestAverage = pTestAverage
  End Sub
```

Notice the arbitrary naming convention used here. Each parameter name has a "p" prefix and each class-level variable begins with "m".

When coding a constructor, do not use the same name for the parameters that you use for class properties. For example:

```
  Public Sub New(ByVal IdNumber As String, ByVal LastName As String,
    ByVal TestAverage As Double)

    IdNumber = IdNumber
    LastName = LastName
    TestAverage = TestAverage
  End Sub
```

The parameter names in this example hide the matching public property names. Always choose names for your constructor parameters that are different from the names of class-level variables and properties.

COMMON BUG: Reversing the asignment order in constructors

Beginners often have trouble writing assignment statements in constructors. Can you spot the errors in this code?

```
  Public Sub New(ByVal pIdNumber As String, ByVal pLastName As String,
    ByVal pTestAverage As Double)

    pIdNumber = IdNumber
    pLastName = LastName
    pTestAverage = TestAverage
  End Sub
```

The code compiles correctly, but the operands in the assignment statements are reversed. They copy the values from the properties to the parameters. The result is that the constructor does not work properly: The values passed to the constructor are not assigned to the class properties.

How Visual Basic Creates Constructors

If your class does not contain any constructors, Visual Basic creates an invisible empty default constructor for you. This is for convenience, so you can declare an object like this:

```
  Dim sophomore As New Student
```

But if you add a parameterized constructor to the class, a default constructor is *not* created automatically for you. Suppose this were the only one we had in the Student class:

```
  Public Sub New(ByVal pIdNumber As String, ByVal pLastName As String,
    ByVal pTestAverage As Double)
    ' (lines omitted)
  End Sub
```

Then the following statement would not compile:

```
  Dim objStudent As New Student
```

You might have a good reason for not permitting an object to be constructed unless it was assigned meaningful values. Decisions such as this one are based on the needs of the application. If your class has a parameterized constructor, and you also wish to create objects without passing any parameters, you must add a default constructor.

Constructors with Optional Parameters

An **optional parameter** does not require the calling method to pass a corresponding argument value. Sometimes you will want to create instances of a class using varying amounts of information. You can declare optional parameters in any method (including constructors) using the *Optional* keyword, as long as you assign each a default value. In the following example, the pLastName and pTestAverage parameters are optional:

```
Public Sub New(ByVal pIdNumber As String,
   Optional ByVal pLastName As String = "",
   Optional ByVal pTestAverage As Double = 0.0)

   IdNumber = pIdNumber
   LastName = pLastName
   TestAverage = pTestAverage
End Sub
```

Now, because the second and third parameters are optional, all of the following are valid ways of declaring Student objects:

```
Dim A As New Student("200103")
Dim B As New Student("200103", "Ramirez")
Dim C As New Student("200103", "Ramirez", 86.4)
```

There are two important rules to follow. Once a parameter is labeled optional, all subsequent parameters in the method's parameter list must also be labeled the same way. Second, all optional parameters must be assigned default values.

When the Visual Studio editor's Intellisense tool displays a method's parameter, optional parameters appear inside square brackets. Here is an example:

```
New Student(|
```
New(**IdNumber As String**, [pLastName As String = ""], [pTestAverage As Double = 0.0])

Tutorial 1-2:
Adding a parameterized constructor to the Student class

In this tutorial, you will add a constructor with three parameters to the Student class. The application will ask the user to input values, which are then passed to the Student constructor. Then the application will display the values stored inside the Student object.

Step 1:   In Windows Explorer, make a copy of the folder containing the *Student Class Example* project you wrote for Tutorial 1-1. Open the new project.

Step 2:   Change the caption in the form's title bar to *Student Class with Constructors*.

Step 3:   Add the following constructor to the Student class:

```
Public Sub New(ByVal pIdNumber As String,
   Optional ByVal pLastName As String = "",
   Optional ByVal pTestAverage As Double = 0.0)
```

```
        IdNumber = pIdNumber
        LastName = pLastName
        TestAverage = pTestAverage
    End Sub
```

Notice that the second and third parameters are optional.

Step 4: Edit the form's source code. First, change the declaration of objStudent to the following:

```
Private objStudent As Student
```

This statement declares a Student variable, but it does not create a student Object.

Step 5: Modify the btnSave_Click event handler so it contains the following code:

```
 1: Private Sub btnSave_Click() Handles btnSave.Click
 2:    Dim testAverage As Double
 3:    If Double.TryParse(txtAverage.Text, testAverage) Then
 4:       objStudent = New Student(txtIdNumber.Text,
 5:         txtLastName.Text, testAverage)
 6:       lblStudent.Text = "(student information saved)"
 7:    Else
 8:       lblStudent.Text = "Test average is not a valid number"
 9:    End If
10: End Sub
```

Line 4 calls the Student constructor, assigning values to the three class variables. If Double.TryParse fails to convert the test average, line 8 displays an error message in the lblStudent label.

Step 6: Save the application and test it twice, as follows:

Input	Expected output
Enter *200032, Johnson, 92.3* in the three text boxes and click the *Save* button.	The output should appear as in Figure 1-10.
Enter *100011, Adams, XX* in the three text boxes and click the *Save* button.	The output should appear as in Figure 1-11.

Figure 1-10 Sample output from Test 1

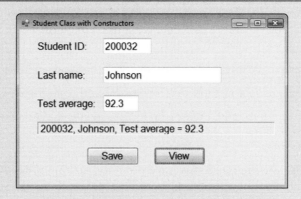

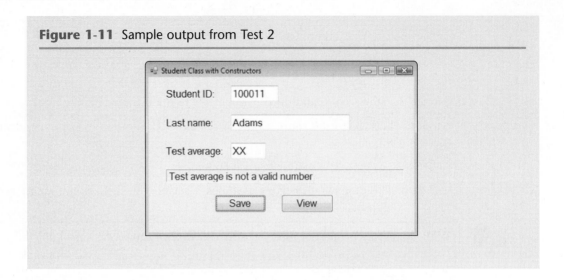

Figure 1-11 Sample output from Test 2

ReadOnly Properties

A **ReadOnly property** allows methods outside the class to get the current property value but not to change it. The *ReadOnly* qualifier must be added to the property declaration, and the *Set* statement in the property is omitted. For example:

```
Public ReadOnly Property Count As Integer
   Get
      Return mCount
   End Get
End Property
```

A ReadOnly property can prevent a client program from modifying the variable behind the property. Also, the value returned by a property might be calculated from internal data. A good example is the Count property in the Collection class, which returns a value indicating how many items are in the collection. You cannot directly change the value. You must either add or remove items from the collection before the value of Count changes. Here is an example:

```
Dim coll as New Collection
coll.Add("Joe")
coll.Add("Sam")
MessageBox.Show(coll.Count)       ' displays "2"
coll.Count = 20                   ' Error!
```

Example

Let's revisit the TestAverage property in the Student class that we have been using. Rather than letting callers set its value, we can calculate the value as the sum of all tests divided by the number of tests. To do this, we introduce a new class-level variable:

```
Private mTestGrades As New Collection
```

We then create a method that lets callers add test scores to the collection:

```
Public Sub AddTestGrade(ByVal grade As Double)
   mTestGrades.Add(grade)
End Sub
```

Now we rewrite the TestAverage property, making it ReadOnly. The For Each loop iterates through the collection, adding each test grade to testSum. Then the property returns testSum divided by the number of tests (contained in mTestGrades.Count):

```
Public ReadOnly Property TestAverage As Double
   Get
      Dim testSum As Double = 0.0
      For Each grade As Double In mTestGrades
        testSum += grade
      Next
      Return testSum / mTestGrades.Count
   End Get
End Property
```

The result is a more useful implementation of the student's test average than we had in the previous version of the Student class.

 TIP ReadOnly properties must be fully coded; they cannot be auto-implemented.

Shared Properties

A **shared property** belongs to the class in which it was declared, not to individual instances of the class. To put it another way, each instance of the class does not contain a separate copy of the property. Only one storage area is reserved for the property, and that storage area is shared by all instances of the class. For example, we can declare a shared property named `CollegeName` in the Student class:

```
Public Shared Property CollegeName As String
```

Having declared this property, a program could set the college name with a statement that uses the class name, followed by the property name:

```
Student.CollegeName = "Gaddis Technical Institute"
```

You can also create shared class-level variables. For example, the following variable could contain an integer that indicates the maximum credits for which any student can enroll:

```
Private Shared smMaxCredits As Integer
```

 Checkpoint

   6. List examples of access specifiers that were mentioned so far in this chapter.

   7. How is a class-level variable different from a local variable?

   8. Explain the principle of *information hiding*.

   9. Which type of property only contains a Get section?

  10. What two sections are contained in a property?

  11. What is the name of a constructor without any parameters?

  12. What are the three components of the three-tier application model?

 ## 1.3 Enumerated Types

An **enumerated type** is a list of symbolic names associated with integer constants. Its greatest value is in making a program more readable by giving names to what would otherwise be integers. Suppose, for example, that an application worked with four different account types, numbered 0, 1, 2, and 3. It might be difficult, when looking at program code, to recall which integer corresponded to each type of account. Instead, we could define an enumerated type that would provide this information:

```
Enum AccountType
    Checking
    Savings
    Trading
    Annuity
End Enum
```

The enumerated type defines, and therefore restricts, the set of values that can be assigned to variables of its type. Internally, the list of AccountType values are assigned the integer values 0, 1, 2, and 3.

 TIP When you press the dot after an Enum variable, Visual Studio's Intellisense tool shows a list of all the Enum values the variable can hold.

You do not use the *New* keyword when declaring an enumerated object:

```
Dim acct As AccountType
```

If you declare an AccountType object, only values from the prescribed list should be assigned to it:

```
acct = AccountType.Checking
acct = AccountType.Trading
```

The following statement is illegal because integers are not assignment-compatible with Enum types:

```
acct = 1
```

In specialized cases, you can assign an integer into an AccountType, but you should do that only when no other option is available. For example, suppose you were to read an integer from a TextBox, and the integer was supposed to indicate a type of account. The CType function must be used to cast the integer into AccountType:

```
Dim acct As AccountType
Dim N As Integer = CInt(txtAccountType.Text)
acct = CType(N, AccountType)
```

No cast is required to assign an enumerated type to an integer:

```
Dim N As Integer = acct
```

Using Boolean Expressions

Enumerated types are particularly useful when used in Boolean expressions that involve comparisons. For example, suppose we want to take a particular action if an account is an annuity:

```
If acct = AccountType.Annuity Then
    taxDeferred = True
End If
```

Such a statement is clearly easier to read than something like this:

```
If acctCode = 3 Then
    taxDeferred = True
End If
```

Similarly, the Select Case statement can go through a list of enumerated values and take a separate action for each possible value:

```
Select Case acct
   Case AccountType.Annuity
      lblResult.Text = "Plan payments for retirement"
   Case AccountType.Checking
      lblResult.Text = "Write checks to pay bills"
   ' etc.
End Select
```

In Tutorial 1-3, you will examine an application that uses an Enumerated type.

Tutorial 1-3:
Enumerated Account type

In this tutorial, you will examine and test an application that lets the user select an account type from a list box. Each time the user's selection changes, the selected index of the list box is converted into an AccountType object. Then, using a Select Case statement, a method selects an appropriate description to display for the account type. Sample program output is shown in Figure 1-12.

Figure 1-12 AccountType Enum Example program

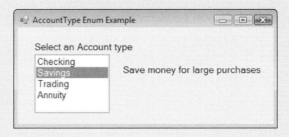

Step 1: Open the *AccountType Enum Example* project in the example program's folder for this chapter. In the code window of the startup form, notice the AccountType declared at the end of the file:

```
Enum AccountType
   Checking
   Savings
   Trading
   Annuity
End Enum
```

Step 2: Examine the remaining code, which is shown here:

```
 1: Public Class Form1
 2:    Private typeNames() As String = {"Checking", "Savings",
 3:    "Trading", "Annuity"}
 4:
 5:    Private Sub Form1_Load() Handles MyBase.Load
 6:       lstTypes.DataSource = typeNames
 7:    End Sub
 8:
 9:    Private Sub ShowDescription(ByVal acct As AccountType)
10:       Select Case acct
```

```
11:         Case AccountType.Annuity
12:            lblResult.Text = "Plan payments for retirement"
13:         Case AccountType.Checking
14:            lblResult.Text = "Write checks to pay bills"
15:         Case AccountType.Savings
16:            lblResult.Text = "Save money for large purchases"
17:         Case AccountType.Trading
18:            lblResult.Text = "Speculate in the stock market"
19:      End Select
20:   End Sub
21:
22:   Private Sub lstTypes_SelectedIndexChanged() _
23:      Handles lstTypes.SelectedIndexChanged
24:      Try
25:         Dim index As Integer = lstTypes.SelectedIndex
26:         ShowDescription(CType(index, AccountType))
27:      Catch ex As Exception
28:         lblResult.Text = ex.Message
29:      End Try
30:   End Sub
31: End Class
```

Line 2 declares a string array containing the AccountType member names. Line 6 assigns this array to the list box when the form first loads. When the user makes a selection, the SelectedIndexChanged handler (lines 22–30) executes. The index of the selected item is cast into an AccountType object on line 26 and passed to the ShowDescription method (lines 9–20). The Select Case statement shows each of the enumerated values in a way that is easy to understand.

Step 3: Run and test the application by selecting different account types in the list box.

Checkpoint

13. What is the primary advantage of using an enumerated type?

14. Can an integer be converted into an enumerated type?

15. Can an enumerated value be cast into an integer?

16. Why does the Select Case statement work well with enumerated type variables?

 Focus on Program Design and Problem Solving: Bank Teller Application

In this section, we will create a short two-tier application that simulates an electronic bank teller by letting the user look up an account, deposit funds, withdraw funds, and view the current balance.

Let's begin the design with a list of essential requirements:

1. Existing Account information (ID, account name, and account balance) will be stored in a data file.

2. The user must be able to input an account number and initiate a search for a matching account. If the account is found in the data file, the application will retrieve the name of the account holder and the account balance.

3. The user must be able to enter an amount of money to deposit. The application will show the updated account balance.
4. The user can enter an amount to withdraw, and the application will show the updated account balance.

In this version of the application, the updated account balance will not be written to the file. We will offer that task as one of the chapter Programming Challenges.

Background Information

Before we start to design this application, let's look at some helpful techniques.

Relative File Paths

The following code shows how to call the File.OpenText method to open a file for input, passing it a path to the file:

```
Dim infile As StreamReader = OpenText("c:\temp\accounts.dat")
```

An example of a file path could be just a file name (such as *accounts.dat*); or it might include a full path, such *as c:\temp\accounts.dat*; or it might contain a relative path such as *..\accounts.dat*. The *..* notation indicates that we must back up one directory level to find the data file. A compiled VB program is stored in either the *bin\Debug* folder or the *bin\Release* folder of a project. Therefore, if we place the accounts.dat file in the project's root directory, the path that we pass to the OpenText method must back up two directory levels. This is how the file path will be declared:

```
Private ReadOnly FILEPATH As String = "..\..\accounts.dat"
```

Reading Delimited Fields from a Text File

The StreamReader class has a method named ReadLine, which reads an entire line of input into a String variable:

```
Dim infile As StreamReader = OpenText(FILEPATH)
Dim entireLine As String = infile.ReadLine()
```

The data file in the Bank Teller application contains three items of information on each line, delimited by commas. Here is an example of a single line:

```
11111,George Baker,825.50
```

A lot of data files use this comma-delimited format. Usually, programs need to divide such a string into separate fields, each as its own string. Fortunately, the String.Split method divides a string such as this into an array of strings, using any delimiter character you choose. Let's assume that the string produced by calling ReadLine is stored in a string named *entireLine*. This is how we could call the Split method, passing it a delimiter character:

```
Dim infile As StreamReader = OpenText(mFilePath)
Dim entireLine As String = infile.ReadLine()
Dim fields() As String = entireLine.Split(","c)
```

As a result, the fields array contains the account ID (11111) in the first position, the account name (George Baker) in the second position, and the account balance (825.50) in the third position:

| 11111 | George Baker | 825.50 |

Incidentally, the notation `","c` creates a single character constant containing a comma. In fact, any character constant can be coded this way, such as the letter A: `"A"c`.

Detecting End of File

When reading from an InputStream, the easiest way to check for the end of a file is to inspect the EndOfStream property. This property will equal *True* if the end of the file has been reached. It is usually coded as the condition of a While loop:

```
Dim infile As StreamReader = OpenText(mFilePath)
While Not infile.EndOfStream

   infile.ReadLine()
   'etc.

End While
```

Account Class

The Bank Teller application will contain a class named **Account** that holds an account ID, account holder name, and the account balance. A property named **LastError** will contain a description of the last error that occurred while calling methods in the class. In addition, the class will have the following methods:

- *New(accountId)*—a constructor that receives an account ID and creates a new Account object.
- *GetData( )*—opens the data file and searches for the account ID. If the ID is found, the method reads the account name and balance from the file and returns *True*. If the ID is not found, the method assigns a message to the LastError property and returns *False*.
- *Deposit(amount)*—deposits an amount of money in the account.
- *Withdraw(amount) As Boolean*—attempts to withdraw an amount from the account. If the balance is at least as large as the amount being withdrawn, the method subtracts the amount from the account balance and returns a value of *True*. If the balance is too low, the method assigns an error message to the LastError property and returns a value of *False*.

Form1 Class

In the application's startup form, you will create the following event handlers:

- *btnFind_Click*—opens the account data file and searches for a record containing a matching account number. If a match is found, this method copies the account name and balance to Label controls on the form.
- *btnDeposit_Click*—reads the deposit amount from a TextBox control and passes it to the Account.Deposit method. Displays the account's updated balance in a Label.
- *btnWithdraw_Click*—reads the withdrawal amount from a TextBox control and passes it to the Account.Withdraw method. If the latter method returns *True,* this method displays the account's updated balance in a Label. If the Withdraw method returns *False,* an error message is displayed in a Label.
- *btnClose_Click*—closes the form.

User Interface Design

The user will interact with a single window containing text boxes, labels, and buttons. We wish to control the user's actions by disabling buttons until the appropriate account

Figure 1-13 Bank Teller application startup window

information has been located. Figure 1-13 shows the application's startup window, in which the user can enter an account number and click the *Find* button. The *Deposit* and *Withdraw* buttons are disabled. Figure 1-14 shows the same window after the user has entered an account number and clicked the *Find* button. Because the account was found in the input file, the account name and balance are displayed, and the *Deposit* and *Withdraw* buttons are enabled.

Figure 1-14 Bank Teller application after user's successful search for an account

Figure 1-15 shows the result when the user searches for an account that was not found in the input file. Any existing account information is cleared from the form, and the *Deposit* and *Withdraw* buttons are disabled. In Figure 1-16, the user has made a deposit into the account by entering a value into the text box and clicking the *Deposit* button. Notice that the account balance has changed.

In Figure 1-17, the user has made a withdrawal from the account by entering a value into the text box and clicking the *Withdraw* button. Notice that the account balance has changed. Table 1-2 lists the named controls on the startup form.

Figure 1-15 Bank Teller application after user's unsuccessful search for an account

Figure 1-16 Bank Teller application showing a deposit into the account (arrow added for clarity)

Figure 1-17 Bank Teller application showing a withdrawal from the account (arrow added for clarity)

Table 1-2 Named controls in the Bank Teller application

Control Type	Control Name	Property Values
Form	Form1	Text = *Bank Teller Application*
PictureBox	PictureBox1	Image = *logo.png*
GroupBox	GroupBox1	Text = *Select an action:*
TextBox	txtAccountNum	
TextBox	txtAmount	
Label	lblAccountName	BorderStyle = Fixed3D, AutoSize = False
Label	lblBalance	BorderStyle = Fixed3D, AutoSize = False
Button	btnFind	Text = *Find*
Button	btnDeposit	Text = *Deposit*
Button	btnWithdraw	Text = *Withdraw*
Button	btnClose	Text = *Close*

Tutorial 1-4:
Building the Bank Teller application

In this tutorial, you will complete the *Bank Teller* application. It consists of a class named Account and a single startup form.

Step 1: Open the project named *Bank Teller Start* from the chapter examples folder. The startup form has been created for you.

Step 2: Add a class named *Account* to the project.

Step 3: Add the following Imports statements to the *Accounts.vb* file, just above the class declaration:

```
Imports System.IO          ' StreamReader class
Imports System.IO.File     ' OpenText method
```

Step 4: Insert the following variable into the Account class that will contain the current account balance. In addition, create a read-only property that returns the value of mBalance.

```
Private mBalance As Decimal
```

Step 5: Insert the following auto-implemented properties:

```
Public Property AccountId As String
Public Property AccountName As String
Public Property FilePath As String
Public Property LastError As String
```

AccountName holds the name of the person who is the account holder. FilePath holds a string containing the location of the input file. LastError holds a string that contains the most recently generated error message by methods in this class.

Step 6: Insert the following constructor, which receives an account ID number:

```
Public Sub New(ByVal pAccountId As String)
   AccountId = pAccountId
   AccountName = String.Empty
   mBalance = 0.0D
End Sub
```

Step 7:   Insert the GetData method, which reads the data file and attempts to find a data set containing a certain account ID. If the ID is found, the method returns *True*:

```
 1: Public Function GetData() As Boolean
 2:   Dim infile As StreamReader = Nothing
 3:   LastError = String.Empty
 4:   Try
 5:     infile = OpenText(FilePath)
 6:     While Not infile.EndOfStream
 7:       Dim entireLine As String = infile.ReadLine()
 8:       Dim fields() As String = entireLine.Split(",","c)
 9:       If fields(0) = AccountId Then
10:         AccountName = fields(1)
11:         mBalance = CDec(fields(2))
12:         Return True
13:       End If
14:     End While
15:     LastError = "Account " & AccountId & " not found"
16:     Return False
17:   Catch ex As Exception
18:     LastError = ex.Message
19:     Return False
20:   Finally
21:     If infile IsNot Nothing Then infile.Close()
22:   End Try
23:   Return False
24: End Function
```

Line 5 opens the input file, using the file name and path in the FilePath property. If the file is found, OpenText returns a StreamReader that can be used to read all data from the file. Line 7 reads one line from the file, and Line 8 splits the line into an array of strings named *fields*. Line 9 compares the first field to mAccountId, which contains the ID we are looking for. If the IDs match, lines 10–11 assign the field values to AccountName and mBalance. Line 12 returns immediately with a value of *True*. On the other hand, if the While loop ends by reaching line 15, we assume that a matching Account ID was not found.

Notice in the code above that a *Finally* block is used to hold a statement that closes the input file (line 21). We know that the code in a Finally block is guaranteed to execute, even if an exception is thrown somewhere within the *Try* block. Even when a Return statement executes, the Finally block is still executed before control leaves the GetData function.

Step 8:   Add the Deposit and Withdraw methods to the class:

```
 1: Public Sub Deposit(ByVal amount As Decimal)
 2: ' Deposit the amount in the account by adding it
 3: ' to the balance.
 4:   mBalance += amount
 5: End Sub
 6:
 7: Public Function Withdraw(ByVal amount As Decimal) As
    Boolean
 8: ' Withdraw <amount> if the existing balance
 9: ' is at least as large as the amount.
10: ' Return False if balance is less than <amount>.
```

```
11:    If amount <= mBalance Then
12:       mBalance -= amount
13:          Return True
14:    Else
15:       LastError = "Balance is too low to withdraw the
             requested amount"
16:          Return False
17:    End If
18: End Function
```

On line 11, if the Withdraw method finds that the requested amount is greater than the account balance, it sets the value of LastError and returns *False* (lines 15–16). Later, when writing code for the user form, we will display the error message in LastError when the Withdraw method returns *False*. On the other hand, if Withdraw returns *True*, we know that the balance was updated so we can display the new value.

The Form1 Class

Next, you will write code inside the application's startup form.

Step 9: Open the code window for the startup form and insert the following code. The btnFind_Click handler is activated when the user clicks on the *Find* button after having entered an account number in a text box:

```
1: Private currAccount As Account
2: Private ReadOnly FILEPATH As String =
     "..\..\accounts.dat"
3:
4: Private Sub btnFind_Click() Handles btnFind.Click
5:    ' User clicked Find button to find an account.
6:    currAccount = New Account(txtAccountNum.Text)
7:    currAccount.FilePath = FILEPATH
8:    If currAccount.GetData() Then
9:       lblAccountName.Text = currAccount.AccountName
10:      lblBalance.Text = currAccount.Balance.ToString("c")
11:      btnDeposit.Enabled = True
12:      btnWithdraw.Enabled = True
13:   Else
14:      MessageBox.Show(currAccount.LastError, "Error")
15:      Clear()
16:   End If
17: End Sub
```

Lines 6–7 create a new Account and set its file path. Line 8 calls the GetData method to open the data file and attempt to locate the account information that matches the Account number entered by the user. If GetData returns *True*, lines 9–10 display the account name and balance. Lines 11–12 enable the *Deposit* and *Withdraw* buttons. If GetData returns *False*, line 14 displays the error message in the LastError property.

Step 10: Add the following *Clear* method, which removes the account name and balance and disables the *Deposit* and *Withdraw* buttons. It is called when the user enters an account number that cannot be found in the input file:

```
Private Sub Clear()
   lblAccountName.Text = String.Empty
   lblBalance.Text = String.Empty
```

```
      btnDeposit.Enabled = False
      btnWithdraw.Enabled = False
    End Sub
```

Step 11: Add the following Click handler for the *Deposit* button. It passes the amount entered by the user (in txtAmount) to the Account.Deposit method, and it retrieves and displays the account balance:

```
Private Sub btnDeposit_Click() Handles btnDeposit.Click
    ' The user has clicked the Deposit button
    Try
      currAccount.Deposit(CDec(txtAmount.Text))
      lblBalance.Text = currAccount.Balance.ToString("c")
    Catch
      MessageBox.Show("Please enter a numeric deposit amount",
      "Error")
    End Try
End Sub
```

Step 12: Add the following Click handler for the *Withdraw* button. It calls the Account.Withdraw method, passing it the amount entered by the user into the text box (txtAmount):

```
 1: Private Sub btnWithdraw_Click() Handles btnWithdraw.Click
 2:    ' The user has clicked the Withdraw button
 3:    Try
 4:      If currAccount.Withdraw(CDec(txtAmount.Text)) Then
 5:        lblBalance.Text = currAccount.Balance.ToString("c")
 6:      Else
 7:        MessageBox.Show(currAccount.LastError, "Error")
 8:      End If
 9:    Catch
10:      MessageBox.Show("Please enter a numeric withdrawal" _
         & " amount", "Error")
11:    End Try
12: End Sub
```

This code must deal with two kinds of errors. If the user enters a nonnumeric value, line 4 throws an exception and line 10 reminds the user to enter a numeric value. Or, if the user tries to withdraw more than the account balance, line 7 displays the error message stored in the LastError property.

Step 13: Add the following Click handler for the *Close* button:

```
Private Sub btnClose_Click() Handles btnClose.Click
    ' The user has clicked the Close button
    Me.Close()
End Sub
```

1.5 Manual Software Testing

We cannot stress enough how important it is to create programs that perform in the way they were intended. We all like to use reliable software, and often our lives depend on it. For example, the flight navigation system for an aircraft must not fail, nor should medical devices. There is a well-known case of software failure in a radiation therapy device, leading to severe consequences. (Look up *Therac-25* at *http://www.wikipedia.org* to read about this famous software failure.)

In this chapter, we divide software testing into two general categories: manual testing and automated testing. **Manual testing** is performed by a person (a tester) who manually enters a variety of inputs into an application. The tester compares the actual outcomes produced by the software to a set of expected outcomes. Manual testing is often associated with the term *black box testing*, where the tester is concerned only with the program's input and outputs. The tester cannot see the code inside.

Manual testing requires a lot of human labor, and therefore is expensive. **Automated testing** is performed by a computer program, which executes part or all of an application in a way that requires no manual intervention. This chapter will focus on manual testing, and Chapter 6 will introduce automated testing.

A **testing plan** is a list of tests that are to be run on an application to verify that the application works as expected. For each given user action or input value, the testing plan lists the expected output or action produced by the application. This chapter shows how to create manual testing plans for VB applications.

Requirements Specification

Before creating an application, we usually want to know what it is supposed to do. A **requirements specification** is a complete description of the behavior of an application. It should include a description of inputs and actions by the user, and how those inputs and actions affect the program's behavior. Here is a sample requirements specification for a program that inputs an integer and displays a corresponding color:

- The application prompts the user with a range of acceptable integer values.
- The user inputs an integer N.
- If the user inputs a noninteger value, the application displays an error message.
- If N is outside the range of acceptable values, the application displays an error message.
- If N is within the range of acceptable values, the application displays the name of a color that matches N from the following list: 0 = white, 1 = yellow, 2 = green, 3 = red, 4 = blue, 5 = orange.

This requirements specification will be used in Tutorial 1-5.

Tutorial 1-5:
Manually testing integer input

Software testing can get complicated when applications have a lot of inputs and outputs. In this tutorial, you will learn some basic techniques for creating manual tests. You will examine an application that asks the user to input an integer. The application will display a string by using the integer as a subscript into an array of strings. Then you will examine a manual testing plan for the application. The user interface is shown in Figure 1-18.

Step 1:   Open the project named *Manual Test* from the chapter examples folder.

Step 2:   Run the application, enter an integer, and click the *OK* button.

Figure 1-18 Application that uses an integer to find a color

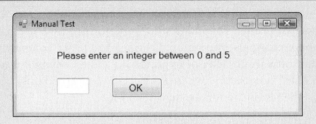

Step 3: Close the application and open the startup form's code window. Here is the source code:

```
1: Public Class Form1
2:    Private ReadOnly colors() As String = {"white",
3:      "yellow", "green", "red", "blue", "orange"}
4:
5:    Private Sub Form1_Load() Handles MyBase.Load
6:      lblPrompt.Text = "Please enter an integer " _
7:        & "between 0 and " _
8:        & colors.GetUpperBound(0).ToString
9:    End Sub
10:
11:   Private Sub btnOk_Click() Handles btnOk.Click
12:      Dim colorIndex As Integer
13:      If Integer.TryParse(txtInput.Text, colorIndex) Then
14:        If colorIndex < 0 OrElse colorIndex >
15:          colors.GetUpperBound(0) Then
16:          lblPrompt.Text = "The value is out of range"
17:        Else
18:          lblPrompt.Text = "You selected the color " _
19:            & colors(colorIndex)
20:        End If
21:      Else
22:        lblPrompt.Text = "Please enter an integer"
23:      End If
24:   End Sub
25: End Class
```

In Form_Load, line 6 initializes a Label control with a prompt that tells the user the range of values to be entered. You may recall that the GetUpperBound function returns the highest permissible subscript for a given array. In the OK button's Click handler, line 13 uses TryParse to convert the text box to an integer. If it fails, line 22 displays an error message. Line 14 checks colorIndex against a range of acceptable values. If colorIndex is within a valid range, line 19 uses colorIndex as a subscript into the colors array, to get the name of the color, as a string.

The requirements specification provides the basic structure of our testing plan because it mentions error handling for user input. Therefore, it is necessary to test the range of values entered by the user, and we must check for noninteger input. Each of the tests, shown in Table 1-3, has a specific output that we expect the application to produce.

Step 4: Run the application and perform the tests shown in Table 1-3 in sequence.

Table 1-3 Testing plan for the *Manual Test* application

Input	Expected output
"xx" or a blank string	*Please enter an integer*
−1	*The value is out of range*
0	*You selected the color white*
1	*You selected the color yellow*
2	*You selected the color green*
3	*You selected the color red*
4	*You selected the color blue*
5	*You selected the color orange*
6	*The value is out of range*

Example: Calculating Weekly Pay

Suppose you are about to create an application that calculates weekly pay. The requirements specification for this application is:

- The user enters the hours worked and the pay rate.
- Error messages are displayed if: (1) the user's inputs are nonnumeric, (2) the number of hours worked is less than or equal to 0 or greater than 60, or (3) the pay rate is less than 0 or greater than 999.
- The application displays weekly pay as the product of hours worked multiplied by the pay rate.

This is a fairly simple application to write, so we will leave that step as an exercise. But we do want to create a testing plan. When selecting inputs, we use values that should produce specific results. In the following table, the prompts to the user indicate valid ranges for the inputs. We begin by hand-calculating reasonable inputs and expected outputs for the testing plan.

Input	Expected output
hours = 10, rate = 45	*weekly pay = $450.00*
hours = 20.2, rate = 40.6	*weekly pay = $820.12*
hours = 60, rate = 999	*weekly pay = $59,940.00*
hours = 1.0, rate = 1.0	*weekly pay = $1.00*

You should also test the application with invalid inputs to make sure the correct error messages are generated. In our current example, inputs might be blank, nonnumeric, or out of range. Of course, the program must not throw an unhandled exception. The following entries should be added to the testing plan:

Input	Expected output
hours = *abc*, rate = 50.0	*Hours worked must be numeric*
hours = 22.5, rate = *xxx*	*Pay rate must be numeric*
hours = 0, rate = 40.6	*Hours worked is out of range*
hours = −20, rate = −40.6	*Hours worked and pay rate are out of range*
hours = 10, rate = −40.6	*Pay rate is out of range*
hours = 60, rate = 999.5	*Pay rate is out of range*
hours = 60.1, rate = 40.6	*Hours worked is out of range*

Summary

We cannot overemphasize the importance of testing your applications. Although you are not currently writing any flight navigation or medical equipment software, you might do that type of work in the future. Also, your current course grade might be improved if your programming assignments work correctly!

 Checkpoint

17. What type of testing is performed by an actual person interacting with an application?

18. What type of testing is performed by a computer program, with no human intervention?

19. Explain the purpose of a requirements specification.

20. What is the term used in this section for a table containing a list of user inputs and expected outputs?

Summary

1.1 Classes and Objects

- Object-oriented programming (OOP) is a way of designing and coding applications so that interchangeable software components can be used to build larger programs.
- A class is a program structure that defines an abstract data type. You create a class, and then create instances of the class. All class instances share common characteristics.
- Each control in the Visual Studio is a class. By that, we mean that it contains the properties, methods, and visual appearance that make it different from other controls.
- Each instance of a class can contain unique values in its class properties. For example, if you have two Button objects, each will have its own unique Name, Text, Width, and Height property values.
- A variable declared with a value type contains its own data, in a single location.
- A variable declared as a reference type does not directly contain its own data. Instead, it points to some other object in memory.

1.2 Creating Your Own Classes

- You create a class in Visual Basic by coding a class definition. It includes the Class keyword, the name of the class, an access specifier (such as Public), and a list of class members.
- A class-level variable is always declared inside a class, but outside any class methods or properties.
- The principle of *information hiding* says that most variables and even some methods must be hidden inside classes. The hidden variables and methods can be accessed only by other methods in the same class.
- Creating an instance of a class is a two-step process. First, declare an object variable; then create an instance of the class and assign it to the variable.
- A **property procedure** is a class member that defines a property. It has two sections: Get and Set. The *Get* section holds the code that is executed when the property value is retrieved, and the *Set* section holds the code that is executed when a value is stored in the property.

- Many desktop applications follow a basic design used widely in industry called the *Two-Tier Application Model*. Each tier consists of one or more classes. The presentation tier consists of classes that interact with the user. The middle tier, also known as the business logic tier, consists of classes that provide essential calculations and decision making. The data access tier contains classes that interact directly with data sources.

1.3 Enumerated Types

- An *enumerated type* is a named list of integer constants. It defines, and therefore limits, the set of values that can be assigned to variables of its type. You use the *Enum* keyword to define an enumerated type.
- When you press the dot after an enumerated variable, Visual Studio's Intellisense tool shows a list of values that the variable can hold.
- You can cast an integer value into an enumerated type, but you should do that only when no other option is available.

1.4 Focus on Program Design and Problem Solving: Bank Teller Application

- The Bank Teller application is a two-tier application that simulates an electronic bank teller by letting the user look up an account, deposit funds, withdraw funds, and view the current balance.
- Existing account information is stored in a data file. The user can input an account number and initiate a search for a matching account. The user can deposit funds and withdraw funds. If funds are withdrawn, the updated account balance is displayed.
- The application contains a class named Account that holds an account ID, account holder name, and the account balance.

1.5 Manual Software Testing

- Software testing can have critical importance, particularly when lives and finances are at stake.
- Manual testing is performed by a person (called a *software tester*) who manually enters a variety of inputs into an application. This person compares the actual outcomes produced by the software to a set of expected outcomes. Automated testing is performed by a computer program and requires no human input.
- A testing plan is a list of tests that are to be run on an application to verify that the application works as expected. For each given user action or input value, the testing plan lists the expected output or action produced by the application.
- A requirements specification is a complete description of the behavior of an application. It should include a description of inputs and actions by the user, and how those inputs and actions affect in the program's behavior.

Key Terms

access specifier
assignment operator (=)
attributes
auto-implemented property
automated testing
behaviors
class
class definition
class instance

class-level variable
constructor
data access tier
default constructor
encapsulation principle
enumerated type
information hiding principle
inheritance
instance

local variable	property
manual testing	property procedure
method	ReadOnly property
middle tier	reference type
Microsoft .NET Framework	reference variable
namespace	requirements specification
New operator	shared property
object	side effect
object behaviors	testing plan
object initializer	three-tier application model
object-oriented programming (OOP)	ToString method
optional parameter	user-defined class
parameterized constructor	value type
presentation tier	

Review Questions and Exercises

True or False

Indicate whether each of the following statements is true or false.

1. Strings are value types.

2. Private methods may be referenced only by other methods in the same class.

3. If a class named Account has a single constructor containing two required parameters, the following line will compile:

   ```
   Dim act As New Account()
   ```

4. A shared class-level variable must always be marked Private.

5. If the Employee class had a public property named IDSize, you would have to write an expression such as Employee.IDSize to access the property.

6. The controls in the Visual Studio toolbox represent classes.

7. When you drag a control onto a form, you are creating a class.

8. Integer is not a value type.

9. Instances of classes are reference types.

10. When you initialize a reference variable, use the New operator.

11. When the assignment operator (=) assigns one reference variable to another, the variables point to two different objects.

Short Answer

1. Suppose isFullTime is a Boolean variable. Is the following the best way to use it in an expression?

   ```
   If isFullTime = True Then ...
   ```

2. Which tier in a two-tier application is responsible for interacting with the user?

3. How are class behaviors implemented in Visual Basic?

4. In a two-tier *Student Registration* application, which tier would contain rules that decide if a student's grade average is high enough to enroll in classes during the current term?

5. How is a shared class variable different from a non-shared class-level variable?

6. Write code that creates a shared property named Color for a class named Window.

7. Show an example of declaring a method named MyMethod with a single reference parameter of type String. The method should not return a value.

8. What is the name of the principle that advocates keeping class-level variables private?

9. If a class-level variable is declared private, how can users of the class get and set the variable's value?

10. Create a constructor for a class named Hero that receives two Integer parameters: pStrength and pIntelligence. Make the parameters optional. The corresponding class properties are named Strength and Intelligence.

11. Which section (Set or Get) is omitted from a ReadOnly property?

12. Which Object method makes a shallow copy of a reference variable?

13. One way to create a class is to add a new class to a project from the Project menu. What is the other way to create a class?

14. Show how to declare a private, shared, class-level String variable named smDefaultColor.

15. What is the name of the type of constructor that permits callers to pass arguments?

16. Write a statement that opens a text file named *myfile.dat* for input, and returns a StreamReader.

17. Write a statement that reads a line of text from a StreamReader object named reader.

18. Which StreamReader property lets you know when there is no more data to read in the input stream?

What Do You Think?

1. Rather than using a loop with a subscript to copy one array to another, is it possible to use a For Each loop? If your answer is yes, write code that demonstrates your technique.

2. Why is it necessary to call the CType function when calling Object.Clone?

3. Why are shared properties useful in programs? Give an example.

4. Why do you think a middle tier class should not provide a user interface?

5. Why is it inconvenient for constructor parameters to have the same names as class-level properties or variables?

6. Why is a default constructor sometimes omitted in classes?

7. In the Bank Teller application in this chapter, how does the Account.Withdraw method let the caller know that the amount being withdrawn is larger than the balance? Can you think of a better way to signal this type of error?

Algorithm Workbench

1. Create a property that gets and sets a person's date of birth. Include appropriate error checking.

2. Create a constructor for a class named Investment that contains one required parameter and two optional parameters. You may choose any parameter names that seem appropriate.

3. Create an enumerated type named WindowColor that contains five colors. Then write a function that has a WindowColor input parameter. The function should display the color as a string in a Label control named lblWindowColor.

4. Suppose a string named *inputLine* contains "95.1\86.5\72.4." Write a single statement that divides this string into an array of three strings named *scores*.

Programming Challenges

1. **Bank Teller with Totals**

   Use the Bank Teller application shown in this chapter as a starting point for this exercise. Implement the following properties in the `Account` class:

   - TotalDeposits—the total amount deposited in this account
   - TotalWithdrawals—the total amount withdrawn from this account

   Add a button to the form that displays a message box containing the total deposits and total withdrawals, as shown in Figure 1-19. Display the two values in currency format. Reset the totals to zero when a new account is displayed.

   Figure 1-19 Showing total deposits and withdrawals in a message box.

   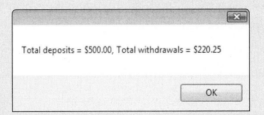

2. **Aircraft Takeoff Calculations**

   As we all know, conventional aircraft such as jets must reach a certain speed before they can take off. The required speed, known as *velocity*, enables lift, maneuverability, and safety requirements to be satisfied. Your job is to write an application that calculates how much time it will take for certain aircraft to reach their required takeoff velocity. You will also calculate how many feet of runway will be required. (Ignore the extra runway space normally required to allow an aircraft to safely abort a takeoff.)

   For each aircraft, you are given (1) its name, (2) its required takeoff velocity (feet/second), and (3) how quickly it accelerates (feet/second^2). Use the following arrays:

   ```
   Private ReadOnly Names() As String = {"A-747","A-737","C-150","D-240"}
   Private ReadOnly TakeoffVelocity() As Double = {250, 264, 270, 240}
   Private Acceleration() as Double = {33.5, 44.2, 37.1, 51.9}
   ```

   The names and values are, of course, fictitious. Create an Aircraft class that holds the corresponding information for one aircraft. It should have a ToString method that returns the aircraft name.

   In your startup form, create and fill an array of Aircraft objects. Then insert the array in a ListBox control. When the user selects an aircraft, your program should calculate and display the required takeoff velocity, the acceleration constant, the time required to take off, and the number of feet the aircraft will travel on the runway before leaving the ground. Format the output as a sentence, in the manner shown in Figure 1-20.

Figure 1-20 Aircraft Takeoff Calculations, sample output

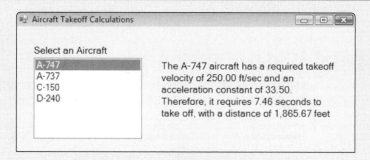

In the Aircraft class, create a property for each the following calculations:

TakeoffTime: Calculate the time it will take for the aircraft to reach takeoff velocity (t = time in seconds), a = acceleration, and v = velocity in ft/sec), using the following formula:

$$t = v/a$$

TakeoffDistance: Calculate the distance (d) traveled (in feet) before takeoff, using the following formula:

$$d = at^2$$

3. Training Workshops

Your company likes to present training workshops that help people in the information technology industry improve their skills. Your task is to write an object-oriented application that will let the company display and edit workshops.

There are several workshop categories: (1) application development, (2) databases, (3) networking, and (4) systems administration. You will create an enumerated type that matches these categories. A workshop consists of: (1) title, (2) length in days, (3) category, and (4) cost. Create a class named *Workshop* that holds this information, with a complete set of properties and a ToString method. It should also contain a public shared string array such as the following:

```
Public Shared CategoryNames() As String = {"Application development",
"Databases", "Networking", "System administration"}
```

Data File

When the application starts, it must read a list of workshops from a data file and store them in an array or collection. Each line in the file will be a different workshop, with the fields separated by the \ (backslash) character. Here is a sample line from the file:

```
0\3\800\Programming in Java
```

(Category = 0, Days = 3, Cost = $800, Title = Programming in Java)

Create a user interface that lets the user complete the following tasks:

1. Display all workshops in a list in the startup form, as shown in Figure 1-21.
2. Select a single workshop to display in detail format in a separate window, as shown in Figure 1-22. A combo box control should display a list of categories, with the workshop's actual category as the current selection. This window permits the user to modify the workshop fields and save all changes. If the user modifies a workshop, clicks the *Save and Close* button, and returns to the startup form, the workshop changes should appear in the list box.

None of the changes are permanent because you are not required to save the modified workshop list back to the data file.

Figure 1-21 List of training workshops

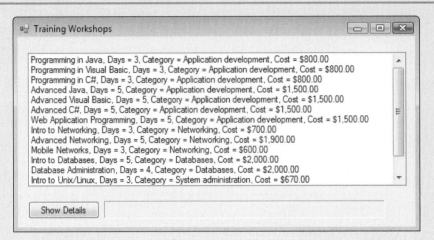

Figure 1-22 Viewing and editing a single workshop

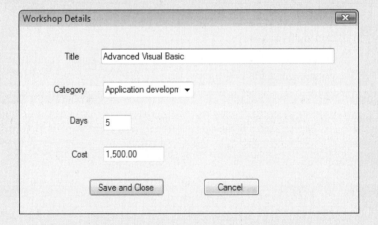

Implementation Suggestions

You can create a property of type Workshop in the *Workshop Details* form. Before displaying this form, assign the selected workshop (from the list box) to the Workshop Details form's Text property. When the form loads, copy the workshop property values into the text boxes and combo box.

Here are some suggestions for workshop titles, although you may add more of your own: Programming in Java, Programming in Visual Basic, Programming in C#, Advanced Java, Advanced Visual Basic, Advanced C#, Web Application Programming, Intro to Networking, Advanced Networking, Mobile Networks, Intro to Databases, Database Administration, Intro to Unix/Linux, Advanced Unix/Linux, and Windows Administration.

4. Investment Tracking

Create an application that tracks investments. Let the user type a ticker symbol into a text box, enter the number of shares, and set the purchase date. A sample is shown in Figure 1-23. In the example, the price per share was obtained from a data file that was read when the application started. The combo box contains a list of investment types.

When the user selects an investment type and clicks the *Confirm* button, the total purchase amount displays in the bottom right corner of the form.

Figure 1-23 After clicking the confirm button

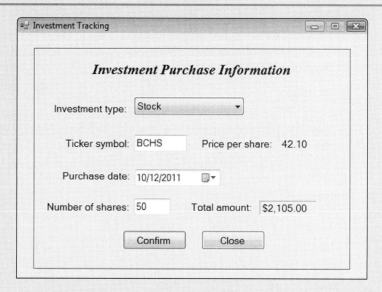

A *ticker symbol* is a short abbreviation that uniquely identifies the name of an investment such as a stock. The term *ticker* refers to the noise made by ticker tape machines that were once used to print stock prices.

Implementation

Define a class named *PriceType* with two properties: Ticker (string), and Price (Double).

Define an enumerated type named *InvestmentType* that lists four types of investments: stock, mutual fund, commodity, and money market.

Define a class named *Investment* containing the following public properties:

- Ticker symbol
- Investment type
- Purchase date
- Price per share
- Number of shares purchased
- Purchase amount (read-only)

The class should contain a shared collection of PriceType objects. Also, create a shared method in the Investment class that loads PriceType information from a comma-delimited text file (in real life, we would expect these values to change constantly). Each line in the text file should look like the following, in which the first value is the ticker symbol, and the second value is the current price:

```
AMB, 32.2
```

The file should contain at least ten lines like this, each with a different ticker symbol and price.

Create a method in the Investment class that receives a ticker symbol and returns the price of the investment associated with that ticker symbol.

User Interface Notes

As the user begins to type the ticker symbol into a text box, the application should search for the symbol and display the price per share. As soon as the ticker symbol matches an existing symbol in the collection, the price should appear in a label on the form. We suggest that you write an event handler for the TextChanged event of the TextBox control. When the user clicks the *Confirm* button, its click handler should create an Investment object and initialize its properties with values in the controls on the form.

5. **Client Billing**

Write an application that tracks the amount of billable time that the user spends on consulting projects. The application reads an input client file and appends information to a billing file, which it creates the first time it runs.

Startup Form

Figure 1-24 shows a sample of the main window. When the user begins working on a project, the client name is selected from a ComboBox control. In Figure 1-25, the user has clicked the *Start* button, so the billing timer is running. Notice that the *Start* button is disabled. In Figure 1-26, the user has clicked the *Stop* button. At that moment, the application shows the amount of elapsed time and writes a record to the billing file.

Figure 1-24 Client selected, before starting the billing timer

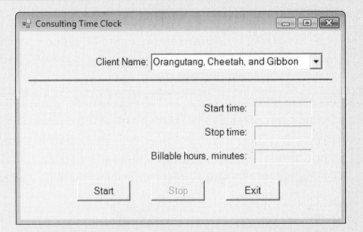

Figure 1-25 While the billing timer is running

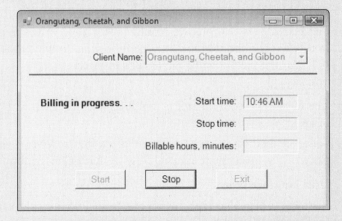

Figure 1-26 After stopping the billing timer

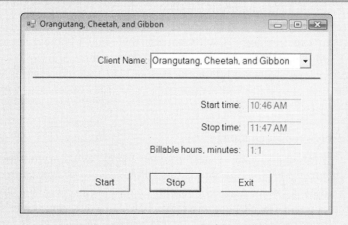

Coordinate the command buttons carefully to make sure the user cannot click out of sequence. The following table shows the two possible program states that affect the buttons. The program is in State 1 when it starts; after clicking the *Start* button, the program enters State 2. When the *Stop* button is clicked, the program returns to State 1.

State	Start	Stop	Exit
1	Enabled	Disabled	Enabled
2	Disabled	Enabled	Disabled

When the user clicks the *Start* button, display a status message *Billing in Progress ...* to show that the clock is running. Do not permit the user to select a different client while the clock is running. When the *Stop* button is clicked, display the stop time and the number of billable hours and minutes. The name of the selected client should appear in the window caption.

TimeClock Class

Create a class named TimeClock that encapsulates the time-related calculations performed by the program. Use a TimeSpan object to hold the difference between two DateTime values. The following table lists the TimeClock properties:

Name	Type	Attributes	Description
StartTime	DateTime	ReadOnly	
StopTime	DateTime	ReadOnly	
Elapsed	TimeSpan	ReadOnly	Duration between the starting and ending times
ClientName	String		

The following table lists the TimeClock methods:

Name	Return Type	Attributes	Description
StartClock	none	public	Begins the timing sequence
StopClock	none	public	Ends the timing sequence

BillingData Class

Create a class named BillingData to handle the client and billing files. Use the Visual Studio editor to create the client file. Insert at least five records in the client file before running the program. Each record in the client file contains a client name. Your program will create the billing file the first time it runs. Subsequent runs will append to the file. Each record in the billing file contains the following fields: billing date, client name, start time, stop time, and elapsed time. The following is a sample record:

```
02-01-2003,Jones and Smith,21:51,22:10,1:19
```

6. **Elevator Simulation**

Write an application that simulates the movement of a passenger elevator. Create a class named Elevator that holds the following information: current floor number, number of passengers on the elevator, and direction (up or down). Declare an enumerated type to represent the elevator direction. Most of your other code will be located in the startup form.

The simulated building contains eight floors. The elevator starts at the first floor and moves upward until it reaches the top floor; it then pauses for one cycle, and begins moving downward until it reaches the first floor. After one cycle, it begins moving up again. Each floor of the building is initialized with a random number of passengers (between 0 and 5). As the elevator stops at each floor and picks up passengers, the number of passengers inside the elevator increases. When the elevator reaches the end of its trip, all passengers leave the elevator, and the list of floors is filled with a new set of random passenger counts.

Use a Timer control to move the elevator to the next floor every two seconds. On each floor, display the number of people waiting for the elevator, as shown in Figure 1-27. Before moving to the second floor, the single passenger on the first floor will enter the elevator. In Figure 1-28 (a different simulation run), the elevator has arrived at the fourth floor with six passengers. After the three passengers on the fourth floor enter the elevator, it will contain nine passengers when it reaches the fifth floor.

Use a Panel control to display the elevator as it is moving up and down. To move the Panel up and down in the window, create a new Point object using *x* and *y* coordinates, and assign it to the Panel's Location property.

Figure 1-27 Beginning position of the elevator on the first floor

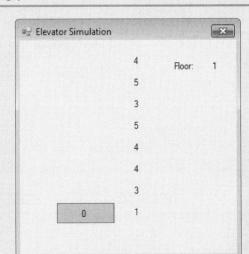

Figure 1-28 Elevator arrives at the fourth floor

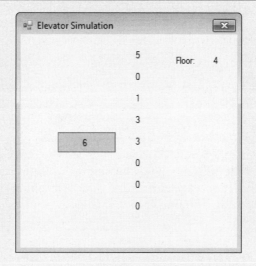

2 Input Validation and User Interfaces

TOPICS

This chapter provides in-depth coverage of input validation and error handling. The Error-Provider control is introduced as an ideal tool for input validation. Next, we review the ListBox, ComboBox, and CheckedListBox controls, which shows you how to write code that deals with multiple selections. Following that, we show how to use the FlowLayout, WebBrowser, SplitContainer, and TabControl controls to develop creative user interfaces. The chapter finishes with the design and development of a software wizard to illustrate some of the power and flexibility of this type of application.

2.1 Input Validation

Whenever possible, applications should do their best to detect and handle errors resulting from user input. Most of a programmer's efforts are often directed toward error detection and recovery. In our book *Starting Out with Visual Basic 2010*, we showed how to use Try-Parse, Try-Catch, and If statements to handle user input errors. In this chapter, we show two basic approaches to notifying the user when an error is detected:

- The StatusStrip control can display error messages in a label at the bottom of the form.
- The ErrorProvider control can use flashing icons to alert the user of an error. Then the user can see a more detailed error message when hovering over the control with the mouse.

Later in the chapter, we will review the topic of exception handling, and provide detailed information on how to handle multiple exception types.

The Char Data Type

The **Char data type** holds some useful tools for string manipulation and validation. Internally, a Char holds a single 16-bit Unicode character. The Unicode character format can represent a variety of international characters in most world languages.

A character constant is encoded between quotes, followed by a lowercase letter C. The following code stores the letter A in the variable named letter:

```
Dim letter As Char = "A"c     ' the capital letter A
```

The String class has a Chars property that you can use to get a single character from a given index position in a string. The following lines, for example, place the letter A in the variable named ch:

```
Dim temp As String = "ABC"
Dim ch As Char = temp.Chars(0)
```

Chars is a default property, so you can write the following equivalent statement:

```
Dim ch As Char = temp(0)
```

The Chars property is ReadOnly, so you cannot use it to modify a string. The following statement is not valid:

```
temp(0) = "X"c
```

The String class has a ToCharArray method to convert that builds a character array from a string:

```
Dim temp As String = "ABCDEFG"
Dim chars() As Char = temp.ToCharArray()
```

Shared Methods

Following is a list of the shared methods belonging to the Char class that you are likely to use:

- GetNumericValue(Char ch) As Double—returns the numeric value of ch
- IsControl(Char ch)—returns *True* if ch is a control character, such as a backspace, cursor arrow, Home, End, etc.
- IsDigit(Char ch)—returns *True* if ch is a decimal digit (0 to 9)
- IsLetter(Char ch)—returns *True* if ch is a letter
- IsLetterOrDigit(Char ch)—returns *True* if ch is a letter or digit
- IsLower(Char ch)—returns *True* if ch is a lowercase letter
- IsUpper(Char ch)—returns *True* if ch is an uppercase letter
- IsPunctuation(Char ch)—returns *True* if ch is a punctuation mark, such as a comma, semicolon, or period
- IsSymbol(Char ch)—returns *True* if ch is a symbol character, such as +, −, and *
- IsWhiteSpace(Char ch)—returns *True* if ch is a tab, newline, or space
- ToLower(Char ch)—returns the lowercase equivalent of ch
- ToUpper(Char ch)—returns the uppercase equivalent of ch

The classification of individual characters as punctuation and symbols varies from one language to another, but those values are generally known for the English language.

A shared method is called using the class name before the dot (.). For example, the following expression converts the contents of the Char variable named `letter` to lowercase:

```
Char.ToLower(letter)
```

The following code displays a message if the Char variable named input contains a decimal digit:

```
If Char.IsDigit(input) Then
   lblStatus.Text = "The character is a digit"
End If
```

Char methods can check for certain classes of characters. For example, the following code counts the number of letters and digits in a string:

```
Dim count As Integer = 0
For Each ch As Char in inputString
   If Char.IsLetterOrDigit(ch) Then
      count += 1
   End If
Next
```

You can use Char methods to validate keyboard input, as we show in the next section.

Working with TextBoxes and Strings

The **TextChanged event** associated with the TextBox control fires every time the user changes its contents. The event can also fire if a program statement modifies the Text property. For example, you might write code in a TextChanged handler to enable a button (the *OK* button) if the length of the Text is a certain size:

```
Private Sub txtPatientID_TextChanged() _
   Handles txtPatientId.TextChanged
   btnOk.Enabled = txtPatientId.Text.Length = 6
End Sub
```

There are many other ways you can filter or process the input string. You might convert all characters to uppercase, for example:

```
txtPatientId.Text = txtPatientId.Text.ToUpper()
```

KeyPress Event

The TextBox control also fires a **KeyPress** event each time the user presses a key while the input focus is on the control. You can use this event to filter out certain characters. For example, in the following event handler, we reject any character that is not a letter or digit:

```
Private Sub txtPatientID_KeyPress(ByVal sender As System.Object, _
   ByVal e As System.Windows.Forms.KeyPressEventArgs) _
   Handles txtPatientID.KeyPress

   If Not Char.IsLetterOrDigit(e.KeyChar) Then
      e.Handled = True
   End If
End Sub
```

By default, the e.Handled property equals *False*. This value means that the key will be processed and displayed normally. If you want to reject an input character, you must set e.Handled parameter to *True*. Then the character will not appear in the text box and it will not be added to the Text property.

Usually, when filtering a user's input, we permit him or her to press control characters such as the *Backspace* key or arrow keys. In the following code, line 5 exits immediately if a control character is found. This prevents any further filtering of the input:

```
1    Private Sub txtPatientID_KeyPress(ByVal sender As System.Object, _
2       ByVal e As System.Windows.Forms.KeyPressEventArgs) _
3       Handles txtPatientID.KeyPress
4
```

```
 5       If Char.IsControl(e.KeyChar) Then Exit Sub
 6
 7       If Not Char.IsLetterOrDigit(e.KeyChar) Then
 8          e.Handled = True
 9       End If
10 End Sub
```

If line 7 is reached, we assume that e.KeyChar is a displayable character. Then the character is filtered out if it is neither a letter nor a digit.

Displaying Messages with the StatusStrip Control

When signaling user input errors, it is possible to call the MessageBox.Show method. But this way of handling errors interrupts the user and forces her to close the message box. Generally, this approach should be avoided unless the error is so critical that it absolutely cannot be ignored.

A better way to display error messages is to alert the user without interrupting his actions. For example, you can display an error message in a label on a **StatusStrip control**. The user will see the error message, make a mental note, and fix the error when it is convenient.

You can find the StatusStrip control inside the *Menus & Toolbars* section of the Visual Studio Toolbox, as shown here:

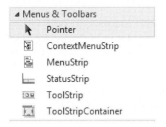

By default, the StatusStrip control docks along the bottom of the form. When you select the control with the mouse, as in Figure 2-1, an insert tool appears at the first available position. Click the arrow pointing downward to add a control to the strip. Although several types of controls are available, you will only need to add a ToolStripStatusLabel control to the strip in order to display messages for the user. A sample message, shown at runtime, appears in Figure 2-2. By changing its Dock property, you can attach the StatusStrip to any side of the form.

Figure 2-1 StatusStrip control, in design mode

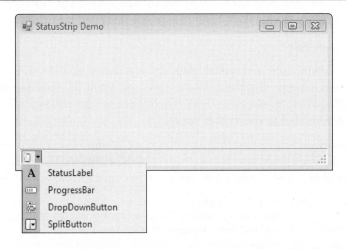

Figure 2-2 Message displayed in StatusLabel at runtime

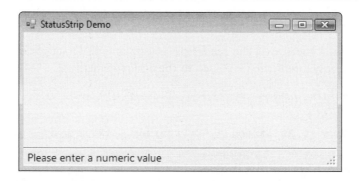

ErrorProvider Control

The **ErrorProvider control** provides a visual cue to the validation status of input fields on a form. It does not perform the actual validation—you must do that in your own code. But it displays a bright red icon next to fields that have been found to contain invalid data. In Figure 2-3, for example, the icon next to the text box was displayed by an ErrorProvider control. When the user hovers the mouse over the icon, a popup message appears much in the same way as a tool tip.

Figure 2-3 ErrorProvider control, with icon and popup message

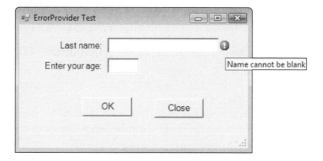

A single ErrorProvider control can validate all controls on the same form. The control can be found in the *Components* section of the Visual Studio Toolbox. The ErrorProvider is not visible on the form in Design mode, so when it is added to a form, it appears in the form's component area.

The best approach to using ErrorProvider is to write code in an input field's event handler that checks for invalid data. If an error is discovered, call the ErrorProvider's *SetError* method, passing it a reference to *sender* (the control being validated) and an error message string. This is the general format of SetError:

```
Provider.SetError(ControlName, Message)
```

Provider is the name of the ErrorProvider control. *ControlName* is the name of the control being validated, and *Message* is a string that will pop up when the user hovers the mouse over the error icon.

Last Name Input Example

The following example code is from the TextChanged event handler for a TextBox named `txtLastName`. If the box is blank, we pass an error message to the SetError method:

```
Private Sub txtLastName_TextChanged(ByVal sender As Object, _
    ByVal e As System.EventArgs) Handles txtLastName.TextChanged
```

```
If txtLastName.Text.Length = 0 Then
  errProvider.SetError(DirectCast(sender, Control),
     "Last name cannot be blank")
End If
```

In the code above, the *sender* parameter is type Object, so it must be cast into a Control object before it can be passed to the SetError method.

The ErrorProvider's GetError method returns the current error message associated with a control:

```
Dim st As String = errProvider.GetError(txtLastName)
```

Choosing Event Handlers

When implementing the ErrorProvider control, determine how and when you want the error checking to take effect. The *Leave* event is fired when the user moves the focus away from any type of input control. Examples are text boxes, list boxes, check boxes, and combo boxes. In a TextBox, if you want an event to fire each time the user types a character, write a handler for the TextChanged event.

You might implement the two types of checking by providing separate methods that handle both the Leave event and the TextChanged event. That would result in unwanted duplicate code. Instead, you can write a single event handler for multiple events. The following example handles both TextChanged and Leave events for the same control. Both event types use the same parameter list:

```
Private Sub txtLastName_Validate() _
   Handles txtLastName.TextChanged, txtLastName.Leave
```

In Tutorial 2-1, you will create an application that demonstrates the use of the ErrorProvider control.

Tutorial 2-1:
Using the ErrorProvider control

In this tutorial, you will create an application that prompts the user for his or her name and age. Your program will verify that the name field is not empty, and that the age field is numeric. An ErrorProvider control will be used to signal the user and display an error message on demand.

Step 1:   Create a Windows application named *ErrorProvider Test*.

Step 2:   Add an ErrorProvider control to the form and name it *errProvider*.

Step 3:   Add a StatusStrip control to the form. Edit the control and insert a Tool-StripStatusLabel named lblStatus.

Step 4:   Add the remaining controls listed in Table 2-1 to the form. The startup form is shown at runtime in Figure 2-4.

Step 5:   At the top of the form's code window, use ReadOnly strings to define error messages:

```
Private ReadOnly mNameMsg As String = "Name cannot be blank"
Private ReadOnly mAgeMsg As String = "Age must be a number"
Private ReadOnly mValidMsg As String = "All user input is valid"
```

Table 2-1 Controls in the ErrorProvider Test application

Control Type	Control Name	Properties
Form	(default)	Text: *ErrorProvider Test* Font.Size: 10pt
ErrorProvider	errProvider	
TextBox	txtLastName	Text: String.Empty
TextBox	txtAge	Text: String.Empty
Button	btnOK	Text: *OK*
Button	btnClose	Text: *Close*
Label	(default)	Text: *Last name:* TextAlign: MiddleRight
Label	(default)	Text: *Enter your age:* TextAlign: MiddleRight
StatusStrip	(default)	
ToolStripStatusLabel	lblStatus	Text: String.Empty

Figure 2-4 ErrorProvider Test user interface

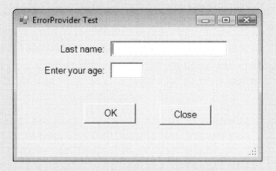

Step 6: Create the following methods that validate the age and last name fields:

```
Private Sub ValidateAge(ByVal ctrl As Control)
  If Not IsNumeric(txtAge.Text) Then
    errProvider.SetError(ctrl, mAgeMsg)
    txtAge.Focus()
  Else
    errProvider.SetError(ctrl, String.Empty)
  End If
End Sub

Private Sub ValidateLastName(ByVal ctrl As Control)
  If txtLastName.Text.Length = 0 Then
    errProvider.SetError(ctrl, mNameMsg)
    txtLastName.Focus()
  Else
    errProvider.SetError(ctrl, String.Empty)
  End If
End Sub
```

The methods shown above check to make sure the age is numeric and the last name is not blank. If an error is found, they call the ErrorProvider's SetError method, passing to it the control that caused the error along with an error message. They also call the *Focus* method, which sets the input focus to the input field that needs to be fixed.

 TIP When an ErrorProvider's message string is blank, the ErrorProvider icon disappears. This is a useful visual cue to the user that the input error has been corrected.

Step 7: Create event handlers for the txtAge and txtLastName controls. Each one handles both Leave and TextChanged events. And each one calls an appropriate validation method, passing to it a reference to *sender*, cast into a Control object:

```
Private Sub txtLastName_Validate(ByVal sender As Object,
  ByVal e As System.EventArgs) Handles txtLastName.Leave,
    txtLastName.TextChanged
  ValidateLastName(CType(sender, Control))
End Sub

Private Sub txtAge_Validate(ByVal sender As Object,
  ByVal e As System.EventArgs) Handles txtAge.Leave,
    txtAge.TextChanged
  ValidateAge(CType(sender, Control))
End Sub
```

Step 8: Create Click event handlers for the *OK* and *Cancel* buttons. The btnOK handler calls ValidateAge, in case the user has clicked the *OK* button without having visited the txtAge text box. The btnOK_Click event handler makes sure both error messages are blank before allowing the form to close:

```
Private Sub btnOK_Click() Handles btnOK.Click
  ' Enforce validatation of the Age input field
  ' in case the user tries to skip it.
  ValidateAge(txtAge)
  With errProvider
    If .GetError(txtLastName).Length <> 0 Then
      lblStatus.Text = mNameMsg
    ElseIf .GetError(txtAge).Length <> 0 Then
      lblStatus.Text = mAgeMsg
    Else
      lblStatus.Text = mValidMsg
    End If
  End With
End Sub

Private Sub btnClose_Click() Handles btnClose.Click
  Me.Close()
End Sub
```

Step 9: Save the project and run the application. Here are some suggestions for testing the application.

- Press the *Tab* key to move between the two blank text boxes. The Error-Provider icon will appear as soon as you move away from a blank text box. Hover the mouse over the icon to read its message.
- While the two text boxes are still blank, click the *OK* button. A message should inform you that the last name cannot be blank. Fix the last name

and click the *OK* button again. This time, the error message should say that age must be numeric.

- Type a name into the last name box and note that the ErrorProvider icon disappears.
- Enter a non-numeric value into the *Age* text box. Fix the error and watch the red icon disappear.
- Click the *Cancel* button, even when the input fields are empty. The form closes without performing any validation.

Summary

The ErrorProvider control offers a flexible way to deal with input errors, particularly because you can write your own methods to perform advanced types of validation.

Checkpoint

1. How many bits are used to represent a Char type object?

2. Which shared method in the Char class returns a specific character in a string?

3. Which shared method in the Char class tells you if a character is either a letter or a number?

4. How do you convert a character to uppercase?

5. How do you find out if a character is a control character, such as Backspace?

2.2 Exception Handling

In general terms, when any program encounters an error while running, we say that a run-time error occurred. In .NET and other environments like it, we can also say that the application threw an exception. The phrase **throwing an exception** seems a bit unusual, but it has always meant that some part of a program used the Throw statement to signal that it detected an error. Then another part of the program used the Catch statement to catch the exception.

Exceptions are objects. In other words, a program that throws an exception is really throwing an instance of one of the exception classes. All exception classes are related to the **System.Exception class**.

An exception is thrown when a program encounters an error severe enough to cause the program's behavior to become unreliable. The error must be resolved before the program can continue. If the exception causes the program to stop, we call it an **unhandled exception** or an **uncaught exception**.

Visual Basic performs what is known as **structured exception handling**. One part of a program detects and responds to specific exceptions. When an exception is thrown, the program may be able to recover from the exception and continue executing, or it may close in a controlled manner.

Handling Exceptions

Your programs will most often handle exceptions that were caused (thrown) because of invalid input by a user. A typical example is when you ask the user to enter a number, and instead he or she leaves the input field blank or types invalid characters. A statement such as the following can cause an exception to be thrown:

```
Dim age As Integer = CInt(txtAge.Text)
```

An exception can also be thrown when a program tries to open a data file that cannot be found, or when a program tries to divide by zero. Of course, these types of errors can often be avoided by calling TryParse, or checking a denominator's value before performing division. But other types of errors may be caused by circumstances outside the programmer's control.

Try—Catch—Finally Statement

Handling an exception is accomplished using a *Try—Catch—Finally* statement. An optional statement, Finally, is often used, too (see Figure 2-5). We will discuss the *exception-type* parameter in the next section. A structured exception handler begins with *Try* and *ends* with *End Try*. There are three blocks:

Figure 2-5 Syntax of the Try—Catch —Finally Statement

```
Try
    try-block
Catch [optional filters]
    catch-block
[additional Catch blocks]
    catch-block
[Finally
    finally-block]
End Try
```

1. The *Try* block starts with Try and ends just before the *Catch* keyword. The Try block contains code that might cause an exception to be thrown.
2. The *Catch* block starts with the Catch keyword and ends before the *Finally* keyword, or at the beginning of a new Catch block. The code in the Catch block executes when an exception is thrown. The Catch block is known as the exception handler.
3. The *Finally* block (optional) begins with Finally and ends at *End Try*. If no exceptions are thrown, the Finally block executes immediately after the last statement in the Try block. If an exception is thrown, the Finally block executes immediately after the last statement in the appropriate Catch block.

Figure 2-6 shows the alternate paths that may be taken through a Try—Catch—Finally statement, depending on whether an exception was thrown. Use the optional Finally block to release resources created inside the Try block or to perform any other type of cleanup.

Figure 2-6 Alternate execution paths

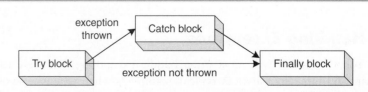

Integer Conversion Example

The following code attempts to convert the contents of a TextBox to an integer. It displays an appropriate message depending on the outcome:

```
Try
   Dim n As Integer = CInt(txtInput.Text)
   stsMessage.Text = "OK"
Catch
   stsMessage.Text = "That's not an Integer!"
End Try
```

Figure 2-7 shows the result when the user enters "xxx" into the text box and clicks the *OK* button.

Figure 2-7 Handling the exception

Catch Block—Optional Filters

What would happen in our exception test example if the user entered an integer outside the range −2,147,483,648 to 2,147,483,647? The message *That's not an Integer* would display, which is not quite appropriate. A preferred approach would be to catch two types of exceptions:

- InvalidCastException: Input string cannot be converted to an integer
- OverflowException: Conversion yields an integer that is either too large or too small

To do that, we create multiple catch blocks. And we create catch blocks that look for specific exception types by adding a filter expression to the Catch statement. Here is the general syntax:

```
Catch ObjectVar As ExceptionType
```

ExceptionType is the name of a class that is derived from the System.Exception class. *ObjectVar* is the name of a variable that references the exception object being caught. You can use the object variable to call System.Exception properties and methods. The most common ones are listed here:

- *Message*—Gets a message string describing the current exception
- *StackTrace*—Gets a string representation of the call stack when the exception was thrown, enabling you to trace the error through several method calls
- *ToString*—Returns a string representation of the exception, including the Message and StackTrace property values
- *GetType().ToString*—Returns a string containing the exception type

Examples

The following Catch block names a specific exception type and displays the Exception object's Message property:

```
Catch ex As InvalidCastException
   MessageBox.Show(ex.Message)
```

Let's return to our earlier integer conversion example and create Catch blocks for two specific exception types: InvalidCastException and OverflowException. We will also display the exception object's Message property in a label on a StatusStrip control:

```
Try
   Dim n As Integer
   n = CInt(txtInput.Text)
   stsMessage.Text = "OK"
Catch ex As InvalidCastException
   stsMessage.Text = "Please enter only digits"
Catch ex As OverflowException
   stsMessage.Text = "The number was out of range"
End Try
```

You may notice in the code above that the same object variable name (ex) was used in more than one Catch block. That is permitted because each variable is separate from the other. Figure 2-8 shows how the sample program responds when the user enters either "xxx" or a very large integer into the text box. Each message is customized to the particular type of error.

Figure 2-8 Handling specific exceptions

 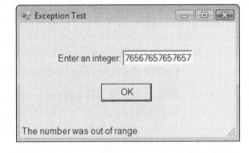

Using StackTrace and GetType

The following code displays a message box containing the Exception object's StackTrace property, with the name of the exception type in the title bar of the message box. The sample output is shown in Figure 2-9.

```
Try
   Dim n As Integer = CInt(txtInput.Text)
Catch ex As Exception
   MessageBox.Show(ex.StackTrace, ex.GetType().ToString)
End Try
```

Throwing Exceptions

When you create methods and properties that are called from other methods, you have the opportunity to throw exceptions. Throwing an exception is a powerful technique because it lets you signal that some data value is missing, inconsistent, out of range, or invalid. By throwing the exception, you are saying that you do not have enough information about the

Figure 2-9 Displaying a stack trace

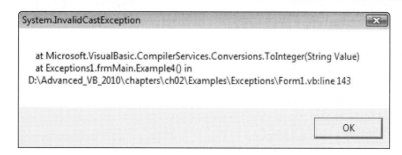

overall context of the application to resolve the issue fully. Suppose, for example, when working in an ice cream store, you discover that all the ice cream scoops are missing. Assuming that you cannot resolve the issue, you alert the manager. Essentially, you have *thrown an exception*. When the manager locates a scoop and gives you one, she has *caught the exception*. Now you can start eating ice cream again (and occasionally serve some to the customers).

You are likely to throw only two standard exception types from your own class code. Their names are self-explanatory:

- IndexOutOfRangeException
- ArgumentOutOfRangeException

It is possible to define your own exception classes, but that would be necessary only in applications more advanced than the ones presented in this book.

Payroll Example

Let's create a Payroll class with a property named HoursWorked, which should contain values between 0 and 80 (for a single week). If a value outside that range were to be assigned to the property, any other calculations based on this property would probably be incorrect. In those cases, we throw an *ArgumentOutOfRangeException* object:

```
Class Payroll
   Private mHoursWorked As Double

   Public Property HoursWorked() As Double
     Get
       Return mHoursWorked
     End Get
     Set(ByVal value As Double)
       If value < 0 OrElse value > 80 Then
         Throw New ArgumentOutOfRangeException
       Else
         mHoursWorked = value
       End If
     End Set
   End Property
End Class
```

We assume that the Payroll class does not directly interact with the user because it is a middle tier class. Therefore, catching the exception and displaying a message for the user cannot be done by the Payroll class. Instead, the exception would be caught and handled by a class in the presentation tier (a form).

Figure 2-10 shows what would happen if the calling code did not catch the exception we have thrown. The error message shown in the figure is a bit vague, so we might improve it by passing two parameters to the exception's constructor: the property name and a helpful message. The following code shows just the *Set* section of the revised property procedure:

```
Set(ByVal value As Double)
  If value < 0 OrElse value > 80 Then
    Throw New ArgumentOutOfRangeException("HoursWorked",
      "Must be between 0 and 80")
  Else
    mHoursWorked = value
  End If
End Set
```

Figure 2-10 Unhandled Exception as a result of an exception thrown by Payroll.HoursWorked

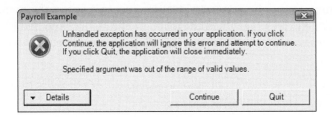

Now if the exception is not caught, the output shown in Figure 2-11 is more descriptive than in the previous figure.

Figure 2-11 Improved error message from the exception thrown by Payroll.HoursWorked

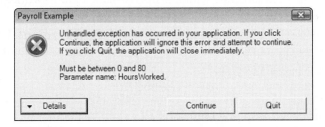

Handling a Thrown Exception

A method that assigns a value to the HoursWorked property can handle the potential thrown exception. The following is an example of how to do this:

```
Public Class PayrollForm
  Private myPayRoll As New Payroll

  Private Sub bntOk_Click() Handles bntOk.Click
    Try
      myPayRoll.HoursWorked = CDbl(txtHours.Text)
    Catch ex As Exception
      lblResult.Text = ex.Message
    End Try
  End Sub
End Class
```

You can see in this code that it is not necessary to be specific about the exception class because catching a basic Exception object will catch all other types of exceptions. When the code catches an exception, the message displayed in the label is easy to understand (see Figure 2-12). In our current example, the average user doesn't care that the property name is *HoursWorked*, but the name bears a close resemblance to the input field that the user was using at the time. We recommend that you customize your messages when throwing exceptions to make them more understandable to the user.

Figure 2-12 Exception caught in the PayrollForm class

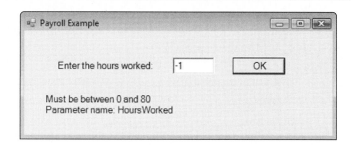

Summary

Think about exception handling from two points of view—how you throw exceptions in one part of your application, and how you handle them in another part. Understanding the appropriate places to do these two tasks will take some time, but it is well worth the effort. Here are a few guidelines that you may find helpful when using exception handling:

- Middle tier classes can detect errors, but they should not display any messages to the user. They tend to throw exceptions more often than they catch them.
- Presentation tier classes often execute other code that might throw exceptions. A form class will usually catch an exception and alert the user.
- If possible, try to prevent exceptions before they are thrown. The TryParse and IsNumeric methods are helpful in this regard.
- When a Try block contains multiple statements (and it usually does), not all statements in the block may be able to execute. If an exception is thrown partway through the execution of the block, control immediately transfers to the appropriate Catch block. The remaining statements in the Try block are skipped.
- Catch blocks should always begin with the most specific exception types and end with the most general. Once a Catch block is entered, no other Catch block can execute. In the following example, the Catch block for the Exception class is last. It catches all exceptions that have not yet been caught by the specific Catch blocks:

```
Catch ex As OverflowException
...
Catch ex As FormatException
...
Catch ex As Exception              ' catches all exceptions
```

- Throw predefined .NET exception types whenever possible. You can customize the Message property by passing a string to the exception's constructor.

Checkpoint

6. What type of exception causes a program to halt?

7. What action related to exceptions does a program take when it encounters invalid user input that might cause the program's behavior to be unreliable?

8. How can an application continue to run when an exception has been thrown?

9. Must a Catch block include an exception object variable?

10. Does the code in a Finally block execute regardless of whether an exception was thrown?

2.3 ListBox, ComboBox, and CheckedListBox

The ListBox, ComboBox, and CheckedListBox are not considered advanced controls. But there are techniques for using them that one might consider to be advanced. For example, we will show how you can use just one line of code to assign an array directly to the Items collection of a ComboBox control. We will also show how you can insert custom objects into a ListBox control.

To make this discussion as general as possible, we will use the term **list-type control** to include the ListBox, ComboBox, and CheckedListBox controls. As you are aware, these controls have many characteristics in common.

CheckedListBox Control

The CheckedListBox control has the same properties and behavior as a ListBox, except that it displays a check box next to each item (see Figure 2-13). Ordinarily, clicking once on an item selects it, and clicking a second time places a check in the item's check box. But if you set the *CheckOnClick* property to *True*, only a single mouse click is needed to check and uncheck each item.

Figure 2-13 CheckedListBox control

Multiple check boxes may be checked at the same time. The CheckedListBox has a property named *CheckedIndices*, which is a collection of the indexes of the checked items. Similarly, the *CheckedItems* collection contains the items that are checked.

Selecting Items

The *SelectedIndex* property returns the index position of the most recently selected item of a list-type control. Here's an example:

```
Dim index As Integer = lstNames.SelectedIndex
```

You can also use code to set the value of this property at runtime.

```
lstNames.SelectedIndex = 0        ' selects the first item
```

The *SelectedItem* property returns a reference to the item selected by the user.

```
Dim name As String = lstNames.SelectedItem
```

Selecting Multiple Items

The *SelectionMode* property of a ListBox can be configured to allow the user to make multiple selections. You can set it to each of the following:

- *None*—no items can be selected.
- *One*—only a single item can be selected.
- *MultiSimple*—multiple individual items can be selected by clicking the mouse on each item.
- *MultiExtended*—multiple individual items can be selected by holding down the *Ctrl* key, and a range of items can be selected by holding down the *Shift* key.

If a ListBox or CheckedListBox control allows multiple selections, the *SelectedIndices* property contains a collection of the indexes of the selected items. The following example loops through SelectedIndices:

```
For Each index As Integer in lstNames.SelectedIndices
Next
```

Similarly, the *SelectedItems* property is a collection containing all currently selected ListBox items:

```
For Each item As String in lstNames.SelectedItems
Next
```

The CheckedListBox control also has a *CheckedItems* property that is a collection containing all items checked by the user.

```
For Each item As String in lstNames.CheckedItems
Next
```

Items.AddRange

To insert an array into a list-type control, pass the array to the *Items.AddRange* method. For example, the following statement declares an array of strings named *colors* and adds it to a list box:

```
Dim colors() As String = {"Red","Blue","Green"}
lstColors.Items.AddRange(colors)
```

The same technique works with ComboBox and CheckedListBox controls.

Adding and Inserting Single Items

To append an item to the end of the Items collection in a list-type control, call the *Items.Add* method. For example:

```
lstColors.Items.Add("Purple")
```

To insert an item into the beginning or middle of a list-type control, call its *Items.Insert* method. Pass the index position where you want to insert. This is the general format:

```
ControlName.Items.Insert(index, item)
```

ControlName is the name of the control. For example, the following inserts "Yellow" into index 0 (at the beginning):

```
lstColors.Items.Insert(0, "Yellow")
```

Removing Items

The *Items.Remove* and *Items.RemoveAt* methods both erase one item from a list-type control. This is the general format for both methods:

```
ControlName.Items.Remove(item)
ControlName.Items.RemoveAt(index)
```

ControlName is the name of the control. Item is an object that exactly matches one of the items in the Items collection. Index is the index position where you wish to remove an item. For example, the following statement removes the color "Yellow" from the lstColors list box:

```
lstColors.Items.Remove("Yellow")
```

The following statement removes the item at index position 2:

```
lstColors.Items.RemoveAt(2)
```

If you pass an item to the Remove method that is not in the Items collection, nothing is removed. If you pass an index to the RemoveAt method that is out of range, an exception is thrown.

The *Items.Clear* method removes all items from the collection.

Inserting Objects into List-Type Controls

As we have shown, it is easy to insert an array into a list-type control. However, applications often use parallel arrays with related information. For example, you might have an array of drink names as strings that parallels an array of prices for those drinks. How could you insert both into a ListBox?

You can create a class that defines the objects to be inserted in the list. The class must have properties to hold the data, as well as a ToString method. For example, DrinkType is a class that contains the name and price of a drink:

```
Class DrinkType
  Public Name As String
  Public Price As Double
  Public Overrides Function ToString() As String
    Return Name
  End Function
End Class
```

DrinkType must contain a ToString method, which is called by the ListBox control when displaying the drink names.

To demonstrate, imagine a simple application that displays a list box containing the names of drinks. When the user selects a drink, the price of the drink appears. In Figure 2-14, the user interface shows how the price changes when the user selects different drinks.

First, let's define a couple of arrays of drink names and their corresponding prices:

```
Private ReadOnly Names() As String = {"Espresso", "Cappucino",
  "Latte", "Cortadito", "Cafe au Lait", "Chai Tea"}
Private ReadOnly Prices() As Double = {2.0, 3.5, 3.4, 1.5, 2.2, 1.5}
```

We certainly could have inserted only the drink names into a ListBox, and used its SelectedIndex to reference data in other parallel arrays. Let us consider, however, the advantages of using the DrinkType class. First, DrinkType objects can be passed easily as parameters between methods. Second, parallel arrays often become unsynchronized when new values are added or removed. We will not have that problem with an array or collection of DrinkType objects. Finally, DrinkType objects can easily be inserted into a database table.

Next, let's define an array named drinks that holds DrinkType objects:

```
Private drinks(5) As DrinkType
```

Figure 2-14 Displaying a list of drinks and prices

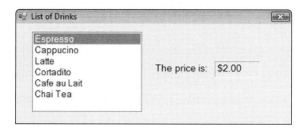

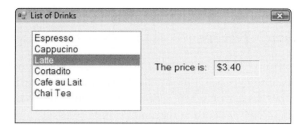

Next, the Form_Load event handler loops through the Names and Prices arrays and assigns their values to the objects in the drinks array:

```
1 Private Sub Form1_Load() Handles MyBase.Load
2    For i As Integer = 0 To Names.Count - 1
3       drinks(i) = New DrinkType
4       drinks(i).Name = Names(i)
5       drinks(i).Price = Prices(i)
6    Next
7    lstDrinks.Items.AddRange(drinks)
8 End Sub
```

Line 3 creates a new DrinkType object and assigns it to the current array position. Lines 4–5 assign the DrinkType properties, and line 7 copies the drinks array into the list box when the application starts.

In the SelectedIndexChanged event handler for the ListBox, we get the selected DrinkType object and copy its price to a label:

```
1 Private Sub lstDrinks_SelectedIndexChanged() _
2    Handles lstDrinks.SelectedIndexChanged
3
4    Dim aDrink As DrinkType = CType(lstDrinks.SelectedItem, DrinkType)
5    lblPrice.Text = aDrink.Price.ToString("c")
6 End Sub
```

The SelectedItem property of a list box returns a plain object, so it was cast it into a Drink-Type object on line 4. Then, on line 5, we were able to access the drink's Price field.

Summary

It is safe to say that connecting an object array to a list-type control can make your program code simpler. This is because each object may contain a number of fields, allowing you to keep all the information together. It is true that you have to invest some time in creating a class to hold the data. But as your programs become more object-oriented, this task will become natural, and you will find that classes make it easier to write advanced applications.

 **Checkpoint**

11. What is the purpose of the CheckOnClick property in the CheckedListBox control?

12. Which property of a ListBox contains the indexes of all the selected items?

13. Which ListBox property controls the way multiple items are selected?

14. Which ComboBox method fills the list from an array?

15. Which ComboBox method removes the item at index position 2?

2.4 Dates and Times

Many applications use date and time information. Some do scheduling of meetings, projects, appointments, and events. Other applications store information about events, such as when a stock was purchased or when a home was sold. The .NET framework provides several classes that make date and time manipulation very easy:

- DateTime
- TimeSpan
- DateTimePicker

First, we will start with the **DateTimePicker control**, which provides an easy-to-use interface for collecting or displaying date and time information. Then we will show some easy techniques for doing arithmetic with dates and times.

DateTimePicker Control

The DateTimePicker control provides an attractive and intuitive way to display and ask for date information from the user. You can use it to display either a date or a time, depending on how it is configured. Normally, when the user clicks the dropdown arrow, a month calendar drops down, as shown in Figure 2-15.

Figure 2-15 Dropdown month calendar in the DateTimePicker control

The DateTimePicker uses very little screen space until it is activated. The *Format* property controls the appearance of the date or time. Choices for the Format property are Long, Short, Time, or Custom. If Custom is selected, another property named *CustomFormat* is assigned a custom format string. Figure 2-16 shows examples of each of the standard formats, plus a custom format.

Figure 2-16 Sample formats for the DateTimePicker control

Custom Date/Time Formats

Custom date/time formats are somewhat hard to remember, but you can find ample documentation by looking for *Custom DateTime Format String* in MSDN help. Table 2-2 shows several sample custom format strings for displaying June 27, 2006, at 4:05 P.M.

Table 2-2 Sample date (June 27, 2006, 4:05 P.M.) displayed in custom DateTime formats

Custom Format String	Sample Display
`dd MMM, yyyy`	27 Jun, 2006
`MM/dd/yyyy, dddd`	06/27/2006, Tuesday
`dd.mm.yy`	27.06.06
`H:mm`	16:05
`h:mm tt`	4:05 PM

Other Properties

- The *MinDateTime* property limits the earliest date and time the user can select. The *MaxDateTime* property limits the latest date and time the user can select. In most applications, you will set these values to prevent the user from entering unreasonable dates.
- The *Value* property gets or sets the date and time assigned to the control. By default, the control displays the current date and/or time. You can set it to any value between MinDateTime and MaxDateTime. When the user selects a new date or time, the Value property tells you what the user selected.
- The *ShowUpDown* property, when set to *True*, prevents the dropdown month calendar from showing. Instead, the user must use the mouse to select individual parts of the date or time. He or she can type numbers or click on spin button arrows to change the values.
- The *ShowCheckBox* property determines whether to display a check box in the control. By selecting the check box, the user can indicate that the control has been selected. Use the *Checked* property set or get the value of the check box. A sample is shown here:

Date and Time Arithmetic

If you need to add a value to a DateTime object, there are couple of ways to do it. You can add individual months, days, hours, minutes, and seconds. None of these methods modifies the current DateTime object:

```
Function AddMonths( Integer ) As DateTime
Function AddDays( Double ) As DateTime
Function AddHours( Double ) As DateTime
Function AddMinutes( Double ) As DateTime
Function AddSeconds( Double ) As DateTime
```

Most of these parameters are doubles; for example, you can add 1.5 hours to a DateTime object.

Examples

The following adds 133 days to the current DateTime and returns a new value:

```
Dim later As DateTime = Today.AddDays(133)
```

The following adds 3.5 hours to the current DateTime and returns a new value:

```
later = Today.AddHours(3.5)
```

The following adds 60 minutes to the current DateTime and returns a new value:

```
later = Today.AddMinutes(60)
```

The following adds 30 seconds to the current DateTime and returns a new value:

```
later = Today.AddSeconds(30)
```

TimeSpan Objects

Another way to add or subtract from a DateTime is to use a TimeSpan object. You can add and subtract TimeSpan objects from a DateTime object:

```
Function Add( TimeSpan ) As DateTime
Function Subtract( TimeSpan ) As DateTime
```

A TimeSpan object can be constructed in a number of different ways. Here are four examples:

```
New TimeSpan( ticks As Long )
New TimeSpan( hours As Integer, minutes As Integer,
              seconds As Integer )
New TimeSpan( days As Integer, hours As Integer,
              minutes As Integer, seconds As Integer )
New TimeSpan( days As Integer, hours As Integer, minutes As Integer,
              seconds As Integer, milliseconds As Integer)
```

In the first version of the constructor, you pass the number of 100-nanosecond ticks. You are more likely to use the second and third versions. For example, the following creates a TimeSpan of 5 hours, 22 minutes, and 3 seconds:

```
Dim duration As New TimeSpan(5, 22, 3)
```

A TimeSpan can be added to a Date or DateTime object. Suppose an airline flight is due to take off on April 11, 2011, at 10:30 P.M. (22:30 military time). If the duration of the flight is 6 hours and 22 minutes, the following statements calculate the date and time of the flight's arrival:

```
Dim takeoff As New DateTime(2011, 4, 11, 22, 30, 0)
Dim duration As New TimeSpan(6, 22, 0)
Dim arrival As DateTime = takeoff.Add(duration)
```

Therefore, the arrival time equals 4/12/2011, at 4:52 A.M., assuming that the arrival airport is in the same time zone as the departure location.

Checkpoint

16. Which DateTimePicker property controls whether a date or time is displayed?

17. Which DateTimePicker properties limit the earliest and latest date and time the user can select?

18. Which method adds *N* days to a DateTime object?

19. Declare a TimeSpan object named *duration* that equals 2 hours, 30 minutes, and 5 seconds.

ToolStrip Control

The ToolStrip control is a customizable container that holds various types of other controls. You can use it to give your applications the look and feel of Microsoft software, such as Windows 7 or Microsoft Office. You can use it to create custom toolbars that support advanced layout features such as rafting, docking, and dragging by users. The ToolStrip replaces the older ToolBar control, with many improved editing features. Most important, you can insert buttons and other controls interactively at design time.

Adding Controls

When you add a ToolStrip control to a form, it attaches itself to the top of the form. Using the **Dock** property, you can cause the strip to attach to the top, bottom, left side, or right side of the form.

Controls placed on a ToolStrip respond to the same events they would respond to if they were placed anywhere on a form. To create a Click handler for a ToolStripButton, for example, just double-click the control in design mode.

In design mode, a dropdown list appears when you select the ToolStrip control with the mouse. An example is shown in Figure 2-17, with a list of available control types. You can insert buttons, labels, separators, combo boxes, text boxes, and progress bars to a ToolStrip. Once controls are in the ToolStrip, you can drag them to new locations with the mouse. If the **AllItemReorder** property of a ToolStrip equals *True*, the user can press the *Alt* key and drag an item from one ToolStrip to another at runtime. See an example in Figure 2-18. Each type of control has a corresponding .NET class (see Table 2-3).

Figure 2-17 Ready to add items to a ToolStrip control

Figure 2-18 The user can press *Alt* and drag an item to another ToolStrip

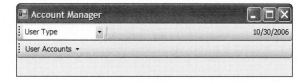

Table 2-3 ToolStrip Control types and their corresponding classes

Control Type	Class
Button	ToolStripButton
Label	ToolStripLabel
SplitButton	ToolStripSplitButton
DropDownButton	ToolStripDropDownButton
Separator	ToolStripSeparator
ComboBox	ToolStripComboBox
TextBox	ToolStripTextBox
ProgressBar	ToolStripProgressBar

Let's look at a few examples of ToolStrips that contain different types of controls. In Figure 2-19, the ToolStrip contains a ComboBox. It also contains a Label that displays the current date. To right-justify a control, set its *Alignment* property to *Right*. In Figure 2-20, the user is selecting from a DropDownButton.

Figure 2-19 ToolStrip with ComboBox selection

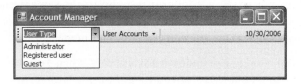

Figure 2-20 Selecting from a DropDownButton

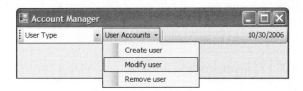

Choosing Between a MenuStrip or a DropDownButton

It can be argued that lists of actions to be carried out should be placed in menus rather than DropDownButton controls. This is a well-accepted point of view. On the other hand, Tool-Strips permit you to combine menu-like actions with lists of items, buttons, text boxes, and other controls. By making a variety of controls available in ToolStrips, Microsoft has implicitly endorsed a flexible approach to menu and toolbar design. Also, it can be pointed out that when lists of choices must be modified at runtime, it is much easier to change the contents of a DropDownButton or ComboBox control than to dynamically create and delete menu items.

When you first insert a ToolStripButton into a ToolStrip, the button is configured to display a graphic image. If you would rather have it display text only, change its *DisplayStyle* property to Text. If you prefer a combination of an image and text, set DisplayStyle to *ImageAndText*.

To change the image displayed by the button, select the *Image* property. The dialog window shown in Figure 2-21 will display. Click on the *Import* button to select a graphic image file and import it into your application. If your application already has a project resource file (containing strings, bitmaps, and so on), you can use items from it. Standard types of image files, including BMP, GIF, JPEG, WMF, and PNG, are supported.

Figure 2-21 Selecting a resource for a ToolStripButton's Image property

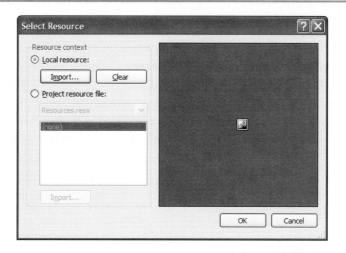

 TIP A good way to find out which images are available on your computer is to open Windows Explorer, click the *Search* button, and search for *Pictures and Photos*.

Scaling the Button Images

Each ToolStripButton has an *ImageScaling* property that determines whether the button image will be scaled (resized) to a standard image size. This property helps you create uniform button sizes in a toolbar. If you set ImageScaling to *None*, the button will expand to fit the size of the image you insert. In the ToolStrip control, the *ImageScalingSize* property controls the default image size for all buttons. Its default value is 16 pixels by 16 pixels, which is the typical size of a small toolbar button.

Figure 2-22 shows the *Items Collection Editor* window that lets you add and edit individual ToolStrip controls. All the controls are saved in the ToolStrip's Items property. Another way to edit a single control is to select it with the mouse and modify values in the Properties window.

Figure 2-22 Adding items to a ToolStrip control

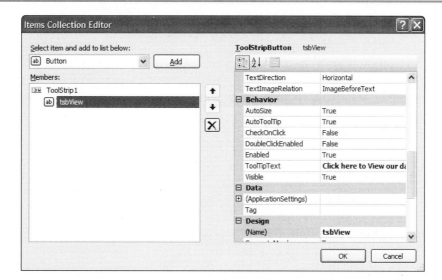

Design Tips

If you want to display a static list of selections that cause immediate actions, use a MenuStrip control. If you want to select from a list of items without necessarily causing an action, use a combo box (on the form or in a ToolStrip). In Microsoft Word, for example, ToolStrip combo boxes are used to select fonts and paragraph styles. The DropDownButton control is perhaps less common because it is a hybrid between a list and a button. For good examples on how to use toolbars, look at Visual Basic Express, Visual Studio, or Microsoft Office.

It's a good idea to assign a descriptive message to the ToolTip property of a ToolStripButton. The message appears when users hover the mouse over the control.

Each ToolStrip control should contain items relating to a single category. You can offer options to let the user hide and display individual toolbars. Visual Studio, for example, does this with the *View | Toolbars* menu command.

Tutorial 2-2:
Building the Coffee Shop application

In this tutorial, you will create a short application that lets the user purchase coffee. The application uses a ToolStrip control with various types of buttons and lists. Here is a simple description of the steps taken by the user to log in, purchase a drink, and log out:

1. The user logs in
2. The user selects a type of drink.
3. The cost of the drink, including tax, is displayed.
4. The user clicks the *Purchase* button.
5. The application confirms the purchase. The user can return to Step 2, or continue on to the next step.
6. The user logs out.

The focus in this application is on the user interface, so you will use program code to coordinate the visibility of various controls. Controls should appear only when their use is appropriate to the application needs.

Running the Application

The following sequence helps to show how the application coordinates the visibility of each control.

1. When the application starts up, only the *Account* dropdown button is visible (Figure 2-23).

Figure 2-23 Application startup

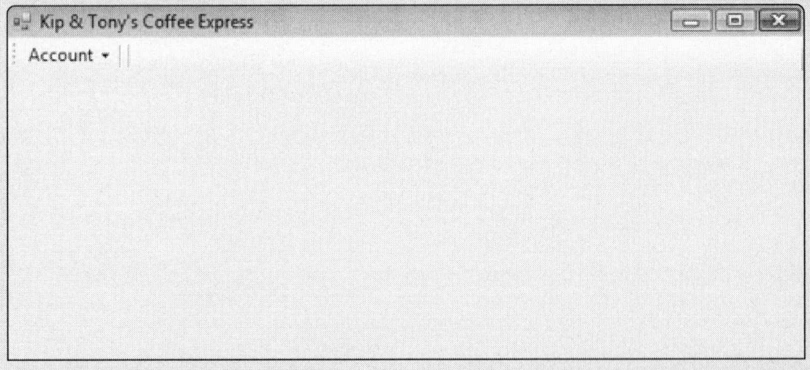

![Kip & Tony's Coffee Express window with an Account dropdown button in the toolbar]

2. When the user selects *Log in* from the *Account* button's menu, the login controls on the right panel appear (Figure 2-24).

Figure 2-24 User logs in

3. When the user clicks the *OK* button, the login controls disappear and the *Drink Type* combo box appears. In Figure 2-25, the user has selected a drink, so the price appears.

Figure 2-25 User selected a drink type and is ready to purchase

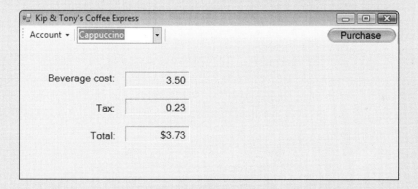

4. In Figure 2-26, the user clicks the *Purchase* button, causing a confirmation dialog to appear.

Figure 2-26 User has clicked the Purchase button

5. When the user selects *Log out* from the Account button list, the application returns to its original appearance (the same screen as when it started).

Hands-on Steps

Follow these steps to create the Coffee Shop application.

Step 1: Create a new project named *Coffee Shop*.

Step 2: You will find an image file named *purchase.gif* in the examples folder for this chapter. Copy it into your project folder.

Step 3: Add a ToolStrip control to the form.

Step 4: Add two Panel controls to the form, one on the left, the other on the right.

Step 5: Add a DropDown button to the ToolStrip and name it *btnAccount*. Set its DisplayStyle property to Text, and set its Text property to *Account*. Add the following values to its Items property: *Log In, Log Out*.

Step 6: Figure 2-27 is a guide to the locations of the controls. There are two Panel controls—the one on the left is named *pnlCost*, and the one on the right is named *pnlLogin*. Table 2-4 lists all controls and their properties. Using this information, add the remaining controls to the form.

Figure 2-27 Coffee Shop application in design mode

Step 7: Add the following code to the form class:

```
' Array to hold the prices of drinks.
Private ReadOnly mPrices As Double() = {1.75, 2.5, 3.5, 3.75}
Private ReadOnly mSalesTaxRate As Double = 0.065

Private Sub btnPurchase_Click() Handles btnPurchase.Click
  ' User has clicked the Purchase button.
  MessageBox.Show("Thank you!")
End Sub

Private Sub btnOk_Click() Handles btnOk.Click
  ' User has clicked the OK button to log in.
  pnlLogin.Visible = False
  cboDrinkType.Visible = True
End Sub
```

Notice in these lines that you can show or hide a group of controls that are located inside a Panel control. All you have to do is set the panel's visible property to *True* or *False*. Continue to add the following code to the form's class:

```
Private Sub mnuAccountLogin_Click() Handles
  mnuAccountLogin.Click

  ' User has selected Log in from the menu.
  pnlLogin.Visible = True
End Sub
```

Table 2-4 Controls in the Coffee Shop application main form

Control Type	Name	Property Values
Form	CoffeeShopForm	FormBorderStyle = FixedSingle
		Text = *Kip & Tony's Coffee Express*
ToolStrip		
ToolStripDropDownButton	btnAccount	Text = *Account*
		DisplayStyle = Text
		Items = *Log In, Log Out*
ToolStripSeparator		
ToolStripComboBox	cboDrinkType	Text = *Drink Type*
		Items = *Daily Brew, Espresso, Cappuccino, Latte*
		Visible = *False*
ToolStripButton	btnPurchase	Alignment = Right
		DisplayStyle = Image
		Visible = *False*
		Image = *(purchase.gif)*
Panel	pnlCost	Visible = *False*
Panel	pnlLogin	Visible = *False*
Label	lblCost	
Label	lblTax	
Label	lblTotal	
TextBox	txtUserName	
TextBox	txtPassword	
Button	btnOk	Text = *OK*
Label	(default)	Text = *Beverage cost:*
Label	(default)	Text = *Tax:*
Label	(default)	Text = *Total:*
Label	(default)	Text = *Username:*
Label	(default)	Text = *Password:*

```
Private Sub mnuAccountLogout_Click() Handles
   mnuAccountLogout.Click

   ' User has logged out from the menu.
   cboDrinkType.Visible = False
   pnlLogin.Visible = False
   pnlCost.Visible = False
   btnPurchase.Visible = False
End Sub
```

Step 8:   Next, add the SelectedIndexChanged handler for the Drink Type combo box:

```
1 Private Sub cboDrinkType_SelectedIndexChanged() _
2   Handles cboDrinkType.SelectedIndexChanged
```

```
 3     ' User has selected a drink from the combo box
 4
 5     Dim cost As Double = mPrices(cboDrinkType.SelectedIndex)
 6     Dim tax As Double = cost * mSalesTaxRate
 7     Dim total As Double = cost + tax
 8
 9     lblCost.Text = cost.ToString("n")
10     lblTax.Text = tax.ToString("n")
11     lblTotal.Text = total.ToString("c")
12
13     ' Show drink cost panel and enable Purchase button.
14     pnlCost.Visible = True
15     btnPurchase.Visible = True
16 End Sub
```

In the lines above, line 5 uses the selected index from the drink type combo box as a subscript into the mPrices array. That gives us the cost of the selected drink. On line 14, the panel showing the drink cost, tax, and total is made visible. On line 15, the purchase button is displayed.

Step 9: Save and run the application. Test it by logging in, selecting a drink, confirming the purchase, and logging out.

 ## Checkpoint

20. Name all the control types you can insert in a ToolStrip control.

21. Which ToolStripButton property determines whether the button will display an image, text, or both?

22. Once a button has been added to a ToolStrip, what property identifies the image to be displayed on the button?

23. Which ToolStripButton property determines whether the button image will be sized to the button's default size?

24. Which type of tool strip button displays a dropdown list when the button is clicked?

2.6 FlowLayoutPanel, WebBrowser, SplitContainer, and TabControl

In this section, we feature four specialized controls that were selected because of the unique features they bring to applications. The FlowLayoutPanel control is a general-purpose container into which you can insert any type of controls. The WebBrowser control lets users view HTML pages either on their local computer or from the Web. The SplitContainer control lets users change the sizes of panels at runtime, letting them use space on a form in the most effective way. The TabControl lets you create a form containing multiple pages, with only one page visible at a time. It is a great tool for creating software wizards.

FlowLayoutPanel Control

When you insert controls in a FlowLayoutPanel control, you do not position the controls with *x* and *y* coordinates. Instead, you treat the panel like a document that flows from one end to the other. When items reach the end of a line, they wrap around to the next line. Web pages follow this model, as do text editors. Normally, lines flow from left to right, but you can change that. Here are some essential properties:

- *Controls*—Collection of controls that have been added to the panel.
- *AutoScroll*—When this property equals *True*, scroll bars will appear when the panel content exceeds the displayable area.
- *FlowDirection*—Sets the flow direction to one of the following: LeftToRight, RightToLeft, TopDown, or BottomUp.
- *WrapContents*—Determines whether long lines are wrapped around or clipped at the boundary.

You can insert controls in a FlowLayoutPanel in design mode, of course. But the real value of this control is its ability to hold controls created dynamically, at runtime.

Creating Controls Dynamically

Sometimes you do not know what types of controls or how many controls you will need before an application runs. In such a situation, you need to be able to create controls dynamically (at runtime). For example, you could ask the user how many TextBoxes to create, or read an input file that determines the number of check boxes to display. You might want to create a photo album consisting of *N* PictureBox controls, where *N* is determined by the number of images in a disk directory.

You create a control at runtime by creating an instance of the control and setting any desired properties. All controls have default properties (which you can see in the Properties window), so you need to set only those properties that differ from the defaults.

First, you should create a panel to hold all controls you plan to create at runtime. The FlowLayoutPanel control is the easiest to use because you don't have to position the individual controls inside it. The following code, for example, creates a button and adds it to a FlowLayoutPanel named *LayoutPanel*:

```
Dim btn As New Button()
btn.Text = "Click here"
LayoutPanel.Controls.Add(btn)
```

If you also want to create a Click handler (or some other type of event handler) for your control, you can use the *AddHandler* statement to identify the address of a method in your program:

```
AddHandler btn.Click, AddressOf btn_Click
```

The Click handler itself would look something like this:

```
Private Sub btn_Click(ByVal sender As System.Object,
   ByVal e As System.EventArgs)
   ' (your code here)
End Sub
```

In this example, btn_Click must be declared with the standard parameter list for a button Click handler. In a Click handler, the *sender* parameter is a reference to the control that raised the Click event. But its data type is Control, so you may have to cast it into the type of control that generated the Click. For example, we assume our control to be type Button:

```
Private Sub btn_Click(ByVal sender As System.Object,
   ByVal e As System.EventArgs)
   Dim aButton As Button = CType(sender, Button)
End Sub
```

But it might just as easily have been a PictureBox or any control that is capable of generating a Click event.

If you would rather use a Panel control than a FlowLayoutPanel, you need to assign a Point object to the button's *Location* property that will determine the location of the control on the Panel's surface:

```
btn.Location = New Point(100, 50)
```

In Tutorial 2-3, you will create an application that builds an image album by creating PictureBox controls at runtime and adding them to a panel.

Tutorial 2-3:
Creating a simple image album

In this tutorial, you will create and display an image album by loading all images from a directory that is selected by the user. Because the number of images is not known at compile time, you will create a PictureBox array at runtime and insert the array items into a FlowLayoutPanel. Figure 2-28 shows a sample of the application while running. (The photos were taken by the authors.)

Figure 2-28 Image Album example

FolderBrowserDialog

In this tutorial, we introduce the **FolderBrowserDialog control**. It displays a list of folders and lets the user select one, as in Figure 2-29. Similar to the FileOpenDialog control, it does not appear until you call its *ShowDialog* method. This method returns an enumerated type that lets you know which button was clicked by the user. If it returns DialogResult.Cancel, the *Cancel* button was clicked. If it returns DialogResult.OK, the *Open* button was clicked. (There is no DialogResult.Open enumeration value.)

Figure 2-29 FolderBrowserDialog example

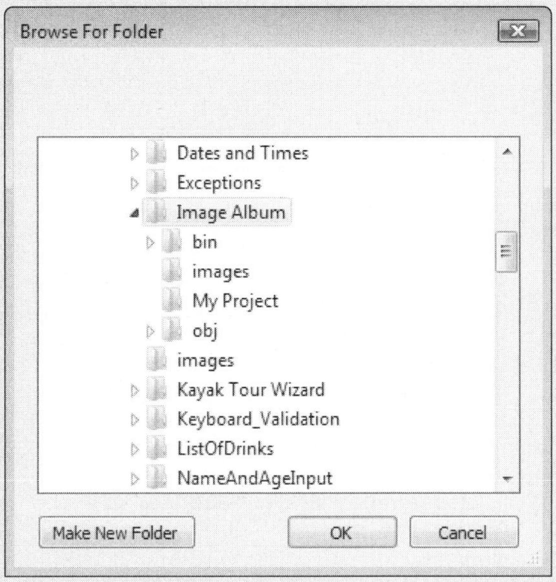

If you set the dialog's *SelectedPath* property to a folder path before calling ShowDialog, the dialog will position itself on the folder. After the user closes the dialog, you can query the SelectedPath property to find out what folder the user selected. Incidentally, the *Directory.GetCurrentDirectory* function returns the complete path to the application's EXE file directory.

Tutorial Steps

Step 1: Create a new application named *Image Album*.

Step 2: Create a folder inside your project directory that contains image files that are small enough so you can fit five to ten of them on a single window. If you want, you can use the *images* folder inside the Chapter 2 examples directory.

Step 3: Add a MenuStrip control with the following entries:

```
&File
    &Open
    E&xit
```

Step 4: Add a FlowLayoutPanel control named *FlowPanel* to the form, set its Dock property to *Fill*, and set AutoScroll = *True*.

Step 5: Add a FolderBrowserDialog control named *folderBrowser* to the form. This control will display a list of folders and let the user select a folder containing images.

Step 6: In the code window, add an *Imports* statement:

```
Imports System.IO
```

Step 7: Add the following declarations at the top of the class:

```
Private folderPath As String
Private pics() As PictureBox
```

The second variable is an array of PictureBox controls.

Step 8: Begin to create a Click handler for the *File | Open* command in the menu:

```
Private Sub mnuOpenFile_Click() Handles mnuFileOpen.Click
    ' The user clicked on the File | Open menu item.
  folderBrowser.SelectedPath = Directory.GetCurrentDirectory
  If folderBrowser.ShowDialog() = DialogResult.Cancel Then
    Return
  End If
  folderPath = folderBrowser.SelectedPath()
```

If the user cancels the dialog, the Return statement bypasses all remaining code in this method. The *SelectedPath* property of the FolderBrowserDialog control is set to the application's current directory before opening the dialog. Then after the dialog closes, the same property returns the directory path selected by the user.

Step 9: Get a list of files from the selected directory and store them in the *fileNames* array:

```
Dim fileNames As String() = Directory.GetFiles(folderPath)
If fileNames.Length = 0 Then
  MessageBox.Show("Unable to find any image files")
  Return
End If
```

Step 10: Next, your code will display the image directory name in the window title bar and set the PictureBox array size based on the number of image files in the directory:

```
Me.Text = folderPath
ReDim pics(fileNames.Length - 1)
```

Step 11: Now you are ready to write code that loads the images into the PictureBox controls and inserts the controls into the panel. This will complete the mnuOpenFile_Click method:

```
 1:    For i As Integer = 0 To fileNames.Length - 1
 2:       pics(i) = New PictureBox()
 3:       With pics(i)
 4:          .Size = New System.Drawing.Size(300, 200)
 5:          .SizeMode = PictureBoxSizeMode.Zoom
 6:          .Image = New Bitmap(fileNames(i))
 7:          FlowPanel.Controls.Add(pics(i))
 8:       End With
 9:    Next
10: End Sub
```

Line 2 creates a new PictureBox object. Line 4 sets the size (width, height), and line 5 sets the SizeMode property. The value named PictureSizeMode.Zoom causes the image to zoom to the size of the control. Line 6 uses the image file to create a Bitmap object and assigns the Bitmap to the Image property of the PictureBox. Line 7 adds the PictureBox to the FlowLayoutPanel's Controls collection.

Step 12: Save the project and run the application. When you load the images, resize the window and notice how the photos rearrange themselves within the FlowLayoutPanel.

This application runs out of memory when it tries to load a large number of full-size images. An improvement (requested in the end-of-chapter Programming Challenges) is to show only thumbnail images and let the user click an image to expand it to full size.

WebBrowser Control

You can use the **WebBrowser control** to view online Web pages or HTML documents on a local computer. In Figure 2-30, for example, the control is displaying the publisher's Web folder for books by Tony Gaddis.

Figure 2-30 Using the WebBrowser control

Methods and Properties

To load an HTML page into the WebBrowser control, call the *Navigate* method. Pass it a fully formed URL, beginning with a protocol specifier such as http://, file://, or ftp://. If you are using the file://protocol, include the complete path of the file.

Several other WebBrowser methods might easily be incorporated into a simple browser toolbar:

- *GoBack*—returns to the previously displayed page in the browser's history. Before calling it, check the CanGoBack property to see if moving backward is possible.
- *GoForward*—moves forward in the browsing history. Before calling it, check the value of the CanGoForward property.
- *Stop*—stops loading the current page.
- *Refresh*—reloads the current page.
- *Print*—sends the contents of the browser's document to the default printer.

The *DocumentText* property (a String) gets or sets the HTML content of the current Web page. The *Document* property (read only) returns an HtmlDocument object representing the Web page currently displayed in the WebBrowser control. You can use this object to access many HtmlDocument properties. Examples are images and links collections, all of the controls on the Web page (via the Forms collection), background and foreground colors, document title, and Url.

Events

The WebBrowser control fires some useful events that relate to browsing and moving between Web pages and HTML documents. The *Navigating* event fires just before the Web-Browser navigates to a new document. You can use this event handler to prevent the document from being opened or to redirect to a different document. The *Navigated* event fires when the WebBrowser has located a new document and has begun to load it. You can initialize a progress bar during this event handler and show the name of the page being loaded. The *DocumentCompleted* event fires when the WebBrowser has finished loading a document. You can use it to scan the contents of the page. A parameter named e **gives you access to the page's URL (address):**

```
lblStatus.Text = "Finished loading " & e.Url.ToString()
```

The *FileDownload* event fires when the WebBrowser has just finished downloading a file.

In Tutorial 2-4, you will create a simple Web browser application.

Tutorial 2-4:
Completing a Web browser application

In this tutorial, you will complete an application that contains a WebBrowser control. The user will be able to open other Web pages by clicking on the links that appear on the startup page. Also, the user will be able to open up HTML and GIF files on his or her local computer. Figure 2-31 shows an example of the finished application when it starts up. A home page is displayed in the WebBrowser control. The content shown in the browser is from an HTML file named *index.htm*.

Figure 2-31 Starting up the WebBrowser demo application

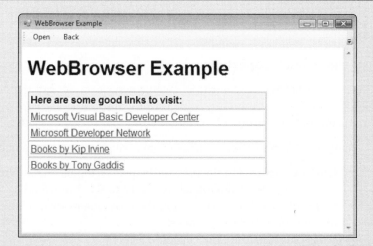

Tutorial Steps

Step 1: Open the *WebBrowser Demo* application from the chapter examples folder.

Step 2: The ToolStrip contains three controls: a button named *btnOpen*, a button named *btnBack*, and a label named *lblPageName*. The latter is currently empty, and because its AutoSize property equals *True*, you cannot see it in the ToolStrip.

Step 3: Open the startup form's code window and add the following code to the class:

```
Private Sub Form_Load() Handles MyBase.Load
  browser.Navigate(My.Application.Info.DirectoryPath & _
  "\..\..\index.htm")
End Sub

Private Sub browser_DocumentCompleted(ByVal sender As Object, _
  ByVal e As _
    System.Windows.Forms.WebBrowserDocumentCompletedEventArgs) _
  Handles browser.DocumentCompleted
  lblPageName.Text = "URL: " & e.Url.ToString()
End Sub
```

In this code, the DocumentCompleted event occurs after the WebBrowser has loaded the requested page. The code copies the page URL into a label on the ToolStrip.

Step 4: Continue by adding the following Click handler for the *Open* button on the toolbar:

```
1 Private Sub btnOpen_Click() Handles btnOpen.Click
2    With ofdOpenPage
3       .Filter = "HTML files | *.htm;*.html | GIF files | *.gif"
4       .FileName = String.Empty
5       .InitialDirectory = My.Application.Info.DirectoryPath
6       If .ShowDialog() = Windows.Forms.DialogResult.OK Then
7          browser.Navigate(.FileName)
8       End If
9    End With
10 End Sub
```

Line 2 identifies an OpenFileDialog object named *ofdOpenPage*. Lines 3–5 set the Filter, FileName, and InitialDirectory properties. Line 6 displays the dialog, so the user can browse through HTML and GIF files on the local computer. If a file is selected, it is displayed in the WebBrowser control on line 7.

Step 5: Add the following Click handler to the class:

```
Private Sub btnBack_Click() Handles btnBack.Click
  ' The user has clicked the Back button. Move backward one
  ' step in the browser history.
  browser.GoBack()
End Sub
```

Step 6: Save and run the application. Click on the hyperlinks in the homepage. If you are connected to the Internet, you should be able to navigate to the pages behind the three hyperlinks. Click the back button to return the previous page.

Step 7: Click the *Open* button, navigate, and select any HTML, JPEG, or GIF file on your computer. The file should display in the WebBrowser control.

SplitContainer Control

Some controls, like WebBrowsers, DataGridViews, and ListBoxes, occupy a great deal of space on forms. When you have more than one of these controls, you can use the **SplitContainer control** to divide the display area into separate panels. At runtime, the user can move the splitter bar between the panels to make one smaller and the other larger.

Figure 2-32 shows a simple mail client application that contains a SplitContainer. The left panel contains a TextBox, and the right panel contains two ListBoxes and a button. When the user passes the mouse pointer over the splitter bar, the cursor changes to indicate that the bar can be moved. Figure 2-33 shows the same mail client after the user has resized the window and moved the splitter bar.

Figure 2-32 Mail client with SplitContainer control

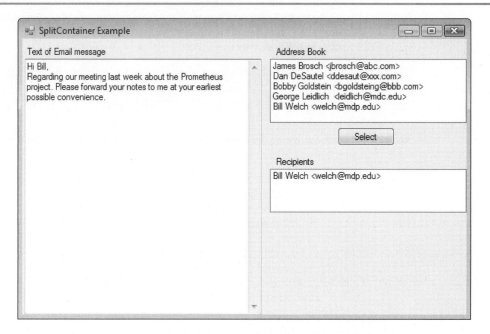

Figure 2-33 User has resized the window and moved the splitter bar

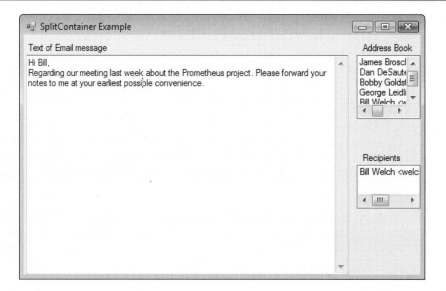

When inserting controls in each panel, the Anchor and Dock properties are important. Here are some guidelines to use, assuming the splitter moves in the horizontal direction:

- To attach a control to the bottom of the panel, set Dock to *Bottom*. You can still leave room at the top for other controls.

- To attach a control to the top of the panel, set Dock to *Top*. You can still leave room at the bottom for other controls.
- To place a control somewhere in the middle of a panel (neither top nor bottom), set the Anchor property to *Left, Right*.
- If the window is resizable, set Anchor to *Bottom* for any controls that need to move or expand downward when the bottom of the window is stretched.

You can do some other interesting things with splitters. There can be a minimum size for each panel. You can freeze the splitter bar. The **Orientation** property can be changed from *Vertical* (the default) to *Horizontal*.

SplitContainer with WebBrowser

The SplitContainer control opens up possibilities for designing forms in creative ways. In Figure 2-34, for example, a form contains a WebBrowser control in the upper pane of a SplitContainer. The lower pane contains a **RichTextBox control**, into which the user can write his or her notes and comments about the Web page shown at the top. The *Save* button can be used to write the notes to a file or database. The **BackColor** property of the lower pane was set to gray to make it easier for the user to see the location of the splitter bar.

Figure 2-34 Showing a WebBrowser and RichTextBox in a SplitContainer

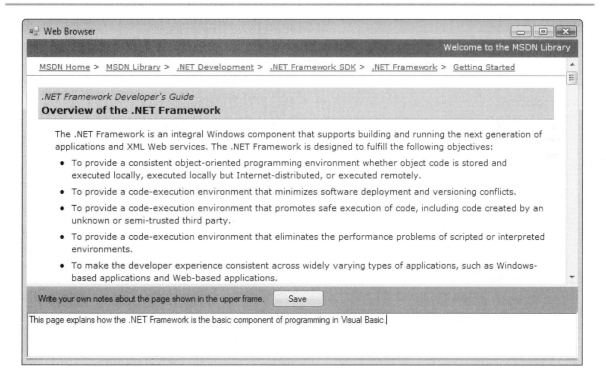

TabControl

The **TabControl control** provides a convenient way for you to divide a form into separate pages. Each page (a TabPage object) belongs to a TabPageCollection that is referenced by the control's *TabPages* property. Figure 2-35 shows the TabControl in design view, just after having been placed on a form. Two pages are placed in the control by default, but you can add more pages in design mode. To do that, open the *TabControl Tasks* menu, or select *TabPages* in the Properties window.

Figure 2-35 TabControl, in design view

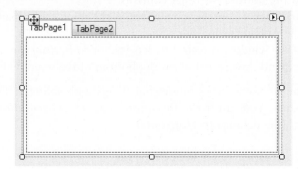

Only one page can be visible at a time. Each page is a container, so any controls on the page exist only when the page is visible. At runtime, if the user switches away from a page and returns to it later, the control settings on the page are retained.

The *SelectedIndex* property tells you the index of the tab that is currently visible. You can also make a particular page visible by setting the value of the SelectedIndex property to an integer between 0 and *TabPages.Count* – 1. The SelectedIndex property has built-in range checking, so if you attempt to assign to it a value that is out of range, no exception is thrown and no action occurs.

Another way to make a particular page visible is to call the *SelectedTab* method, which has three versions:

- SelectTab(String)—selects a page using the name displayed in the page's tab
- SelectTab(Integer)—selects a page using an index position (starting at 0).
- SelectTab(TabPage)—makes the specified TabPage the current tab.

The tabs appearing at the top of the control are part of the TabControl, but they are not part of the individual TabPage controls.

A *SelectedIndexChanged* event fires when the SelectedIndex property changes, indicating that a different page is visible.

TabPage Class

The TabPage class has a constructor that you can use to create a new page and add it to the TabPages collection. For example, the following statement adds a new page to myTabControl, with the caption *Events*:

```
myTabControl.TabPages.Add(New TabPage("Events"))
```

The text appearing in the tab above each page is set using the TabPage's Text property. The following statement, for example, changes the text for the first page in the TabPages collection:

```
myTabControl.TabPages(0).Text="Step 1"
```

Each TabPage fires an *Enter* event when it receives the focus, and a *Leave* event when the focus switches to another page. If you want, you can write an event handler for the Enter event that initializes the values of controls on the page.

 Checkpoint

25. Which WebBrowser control method opens a Web site?

26. Which WebBrowser method returns to the previously displayed Web page?

27. If you want to get a list of all the images on a Web page, which property must you access first?

28. Which event fires when the WebBrowser has finished loading a Web page document?

29. Which control can be used to divide the display area into two parts and allows the user to change the sizes of the two parts at runtime?

2.7 Focus on Problem Solving: Kayak Tour Scheduling Wizard

We would like to build a software wizard that guides customers of an imaginary kayaking outfitter company through the process of selecting one or more kayaking tours. An important aspect of selecting a kayaking tour is to make sure that the customer's level of skill and endurance are matched to the type of tour. This application asks questions that gather basic information from the user. Appropriate types of tours are suggested in a list, which the user can select according to his or her preferences. Finally, a list of available tours is displayed, allowing the user to select multiple tours. After the application is written, we will develop a manual testing plan that checks the inputs and outputs for consistency.

A **software wizard** (or *software assistant*) is a user interface that leads the user through a series of predescribed steps. In each step, the user may be given choices that influence subsequent steps. Wizards are particularly useful when completing tasks that are complicated or need to be completed in a specific sequence. One example that you have probably used is the *Database Connection Wizard* in Visual Studio.

In addition, wizards can be educational when they provide supplemental information and assistance at each step. Most wizards work best when they are short and simple and are limited to about five steps or fewer. Wizards with multiple execution paths may become too complex for the average person to follow.

The easiest way to construct a wizard is to use a TabControl. Each tab page represents a different step in the wizard. In Tutorial 2-5, you will create a wizard that helps the user select kayaking tours.

Walkthrough

When the application starts, the *About* window shown in Figure 2-36 is briefly displayed as a splash screen. This window can be redisplayed at any time by clicking a LinkLabel control at the bottom right side of the wizard window.

Figure 2-36 *About* window

In Step 1 of the wizard, shown in Figure 2-37, the user is asked about his or her experience level. In Step 2 (Figure 2-38), the user is asked about paddling endurance. In Step 3 (Figure 2-39), the user is shown a list of suitable types of kayaking tours. The user has selected three types of tours, and is about to click the *Next* button to continue. The user can also return to previous steps without losing any previous selections. If he or she returned to Step 1, for example, the *2 to 4 times* list box entry would still be selected.

Figure 2-37 Kayak Tour Wizard, Step 1 (experience level)

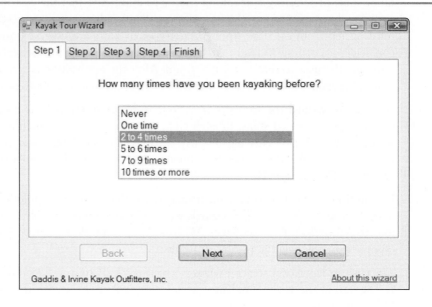

Figure 2-38 Kayak Tour Wizard, Step 2 (endurance level)

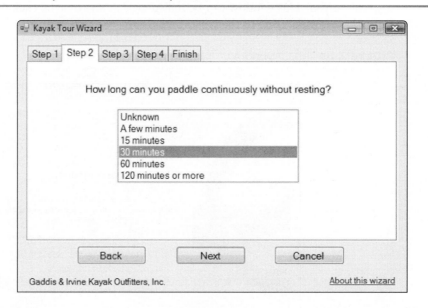

Figure 2-39 Kayak Tour Wizard, Step 3 (recommended tour types)

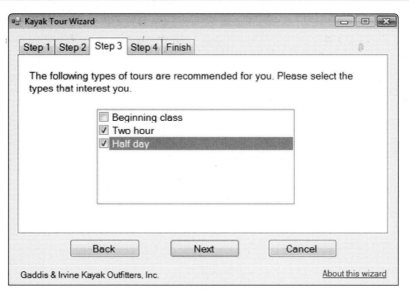

In Step 4 (Figure 2-40), the user is shown a list of upcoming tours that match his or her selected tour types. In our sample, the user has selected three tours and is about to click the *Next* button. In the final step (Figure 2-41), the user is shown a list of the tours he or she selected and asked to pay a deposit for each one.

Figure 2-40 Kayak Tour Wizard, Step 4 (available tours)

Figure 2-41 Kayak Tour Wizard, final step (selected tours)

In Tutorial 2-5, you will complete the *Kayak Tour Wizard* application.

Tutorial 2-5:
Completing the Kayak Tour Wizard application

In this tutorial, you will complete the *Kayak Tour Wizard* application. The user interface controls have been created for you so you can focus on the programming aspects.

Step 1: Open the project named *Kayak Tour Wizard—Start* from the chapter examples folder.

Step 2: Open the input data file, named *Tours.txt*. The first integer *N* identifies the number of tours, and also indicates the number of lines to follow. Each subsequent line begins with an integer, identifying the type of tour (0..5). Following each comma is the name of the tour:

```
14
0,Beginning Kayak Class
1,Garden Cove
1,Pennecamp Park
1,Rattlesnake Key
2,Garden Cove to Pennecamp
2,Largo Sound
3,Sunset Cove
3,Flamingo Park
3,Deer Key
2,Blackwater Sound
4,Little Blackwater Sound
4,Butternut Key Overnight
4,Whaleback Key Overnight
5,Multi-Day Ten Thousand Islands
```

When you look at the code listing later, you will see how the integer tour type relates to array variables in the program.

Step 3: Open the Design window for the main form. Click on each tab of the Tab-Control to examine its individual pages. Each page contains a Label and either a CheckedListBox or ListBox control. The ListBox on the last tab page (named *Finish*) has no border, and its SelectionMode property has been set to *None*. This was done because the user will not be called on to make a selection.

Step 4: Open the code view of the main form. Notice first that a class named *TourType* contains a tour name and a tour type. The variable named *Type* holds an integer between 0 and $N - 1$, assuming that there are N different types of tours:

```
Class TourType
   Public Name As String
   Public Type As Integer
   Public Overrides Function ToString() As String
     Return Name
   End Function
End Class
```

The class contains a ToString method because we plan to insert TourType objects in list boxes. When the items display in the list box, their ToString method is called automatically.

Next you will see three arrays of strings. The first array, ExperienceDescrip, contains the entries for the list box that asks for the user's level of experience. The second array, EnduranceDescrip, contains the entries for the list box that asks for the user's endurance level:

```
Private ReadOnly ExperienceDescrip() As String = {"Never",
"One time", "2 to 4 times", "5 to 6 times", "7 to 9 times",
"10 times or more"}
```

```
Private ReadOnly EnduranceDescrip() As String = {"Unknown",
  "A few minutes", "15 minutes", "30 minutes", "60 minutes",
  "120 minutes or more"}
```

You may wonder why we did not insert these lists into list boxes in design mode. The choice was made to do it this way because it is easier to modify string array variables if the values change in the future. Later, we will show an easy way to insert these arrays into their appropriate list boxes.

The third string array contains descriptions of the various types of tours.

```
Private ReadOnly TourTypes() As String = {"Beginning class",
  "Two hour", "Half day", "Full day", "Overnight",
  "Multi-day backcountry"}
```

The next two arrays, MinExperience and MinEndurance, are aids to decision making. At some point, we will have to write code that determines which types of tours are appropriate to which experience and endurance levels. The integers in these two arrays indicate the minimum acceptable levels for the tour types at the same index positions.

```
Private ReadOnly MinExperience() As Integer = {0, 1, 2, 3,
    4, 5}
Private ReadOnly MinEndurance() As Integer = {0, 2, 3, 4, 4, 5}
```

Table 2-5 shows how TourTypes, MinExperience, and MinEndurance are parallel arrays. For a customer to be advised to go on a half-day tour, for example, his or her experience must equal level 2 or higher, and his or her endurance must equal level 3 or higher.

Table 2-5 Parallel arrays: TourTypes, MinExperience, MinEndurance

TourTypes	MinExperience	MinEndurance
Beginning class	0	0
Two hour	1	2
Half day	2	3
Full day	3	4
Overnight	4	4
Multi-day backcountry	5	5

To understand the numeric experience and endurance levels, refer to the ExperienceDescrip and EnduranceDescrip arrays declared earlier. Table 2-6 shows how the level numbers match the descriptions in the ExperienceDescrip array. This array contains experience levels based on the number of times a person has been kayaking before.

Table 2-6 Experience levels

Experience Level	Description
0	Never
1	One time
2	2 to 4 times
3	5 to 6 times
4	7 to 9 times
5	10 times or more

Returning to the program listing, the last two variables to be declared are FilePath and Tours. FilePath identifies the path to the data file. (We discussed relative file paths in Section 1.5 of Chapter 1.) The Tours array holds a list of all the tours read from the input data file.

```
Private ReadOnly FilePath As String = "..\..\Tours.txt"
Private Tours() As TourType
```

Step 5: Create the *ReadTourList* method, which opens the data file and reads all the tour names into an array. (Omit the line numbers.)

```
1: Public Function ReadTourList() As Boolean
2:    Dim infile As StreamReader = Nothing
3:    Try
4:       infile = OpenText(FilePath)
5:       Dim count As Integer = CInt(infile.ReadLine)
```

```
 6:        ReDim Tours(count - 1)
 7:        For i As Integer = 0 To count - 1
 8:           Dim entireLine As String = infile.ReadLine()
 9:           Dim fields() As String = entireLine.Split(","c)
10:           Tours(i) = New TourType
11:           Tours(i).Type = CInt(fields(0))
12:           Tours(i).Name = fields(1)
13:        Next
14:        Return True
15:     Catch ex As Exception
16:        Return False
17:     Finally
18:        If infile IsNot Nothing Then infile.Close()
19:     End Try
20: End Function
```

Line 5 gets the number of kayak tours (named *count*) from the first line of the input file, and line 6 uses that value to resize the Tours array. Line 9 splits the input line into two array values (the fields array). Each element in the Tours array is a TourType object, so lines 11 and 12 assign values to its two fields (Type and Name).

Step 6:   Next, create the *Load* event handler for the form by typing in the following code;

```
1: Private Sub MainForm_Load() Handles MyBase.Load
2:     lstEndurance.Items.AddRange(EnduranceDescrip)
3:     lstExperience.Items.AddRange(ExperienceDescrip)
4:     If Not ReadTourList() Then
5:        MessageBox.Show("Cannot open file containing list of " _
6:           & "tours. Ending program now.", "Error")
7:        Me.Close()
8:     End If
9: End Sub
```

Lines 2 and 3 fill the lstEndurance and lstExperience list boxes by passing the array variables to the Items.AddRange method. Lines 5–7 display an error message and close the application if the data file cannot be read.

Step 7:   Insert the following Click handlers for the *Next* and *Back* buttons. They permit the user to move forward and backward through the pages of the Tab-Control by incrementing and decrementing its SelectedIndex property.

```
 1: Private Sub btnNext_Click() Handles btnNext.Click
 2:   If btnNext.Text = "&Done" Then
 3:      Me.Close()
 4:   Else
 5:      tabCtrl.SelectedIndex += 1
 6:   End If
 7: End Sub
 8:
 9: Private Sub btnBack_Click() Handles btnBack.Click
10:   tabCtrl.SelectedIndex -= 1
11: End Sub
```

On lines 2–3, the form is closed if the user has reached the last tab page (when the caption of the *Next* button becomes *Done*).

Step 8:   Next, you will create the ***UpdateTourTypes*** method. First, let's design the logic for this method in pseudocode:

clear the list box
if either the user's experience or endurance is missing, exit

```
for each type of tour, do:
  if the user's experience >= minimum required for the tour
       and the user's endurance >= minimum required for the tour,
       add the tour to the tour types list box
  endif
next
```

Now you can write the code. In lines 6–10, it gathers the experience level and endurance level from the list boxes in the first two pages:

```
1: Private Sub UpdateTourTypes()
2:  ' based on the customer attributes, create the list of
3:  ' eligible tour types (lstTourTypes).
4:
5:  lstTourTypes.Items.Clear()
6:  Dim experience As Integer = lstExperience.SelectedIndex
7:  Dim endurance As Integer = lstEndurance.SelectedIndex
8:  If experience < 0 OrElse endurance < 0 Then
9:     Return
10: End If
11:
12: For i As Integer = 0 To TourTypes.Count - 1
13:    If experience >= MinExperience(i) _
14:    AndAlso endurance >= MinEndurance(i) Then
15:       Dim tour As New TourType ' add object to the listbox
16:       tour.Name = TourTypes(i) ' name of the tour type
17:       tour.Type = i            ' tour type ID
18:       lstTourTypes.Items.Add(tour)
19:    End If
20: Next
21: End Sub
```

Line 12 begins a loop that determines which members of the TourTypes array can be inserted into the list box named lstTourTypes. Lines 13–14 verify that the user has sufficient experience and endurance to qualify for the type of tour located in the current position of the TourTypes array. Notice in particular a useful trick in lines 15–18, where a TourType object is inserted directly into the list box. Normally we insert strings into list boxes, but here we need to save both the name of the tour type as well as its tour type (an integer) for later use.

Step 9: Create a single SelectedIndexChanged event handler for both the lstExperience and lstEndurance list boxes. This event fires whenever the user selects a different experience or endurance level, so we have to update the list of tour types (on the third page of the TabControl).

```
Private Sub lstExperience_SelectedIndexChanged() _
   Handles lstExperience.SelectedIndexChanged,
      lstEndurance.SelectedIndexChanged

   UpdateTourTypes()
End Sub
```

Step 10: Next, you will create the *BuildTourList* method. Before writing the actual code, let's design the pseudocode for this method:

```
for each tour type selected by the user, do:
  for each actual tour, do:
    if the actual tour matches the tour type,
      add it to the list of possible tours
    endif
  next
next
```

This method loops through the list of items that the user has checked inside the lstTourTypes list box. The CheckedItems collection indicates which items were selected by the user. Now you can write the code:

```
 1: Private Sub BuildTourList()
 2:   lstPossibleTours.Items.Clear()
 3:   For Each item As TourType In lstTourTypes.CheckedItems
 4:     For Each tour As TourType In Tours
 5:       If tour.Type = item.Type Then
 6:         lstPossibleTours.Items.Add(tour)
 7:       End If
 8:     Next
 9:   Next
10: End Sub
```

A loop beginning on line 3 examines each member of the CheckedItems collection. As each item is examined, line 4 starts another loop that goes through the Tours array. Line 5 examines each tour to see if its type matches the tour type of the current member of the CheckedItems collection. Each matching tour is inserted into the lstPossibleTours list box.

Step 11: Create the *ShowSelectedTours* method. In the last page of the TabControl, it displays the list of tours selected by the user:

```
1: Private Sub ShowSelectedTours()
2:     lstSelectedTours.Items.Clear()
3:     For Each tour As TourType In lstPossibleTours.CheckedItems
4:     lstSelectedTours.Items.Add(tour)
5:   Next
6: End Sub
```

Lines 3–5 copy each checked item from the lstPossibleTours list box to the lstSelectedTours list box. Notice that each entry in the lstPossibleTours list is a TourType object.

Step 12: Next, you will create the SelectedIndexChanged event handler for the TabControl. This event fires when the user navigates from one page to another, either by clicking the tabs at the top of the control, or by clicking the *Next* and *Back* buttons at the bottom of the form:

```
1: Private Sub tabCtrl_SelectedIndexChanged() _
2:   Handles tabCtrl.SelectedIndexChanged
3:   'The user has moved to a new tab page
4:   btnBack.Enabled = tabCtrl.SelectedIndex > 0
5:   If tabCtrl.SelectedTab.Text <> "Finish" Then
6:     btnNext.Text = "&Next"
7:   End If
8: End Sub
```

On line 5, if the current tab is not the last tab, the caption (Text) is set to *&Next*.

Step 13: Create a handler for the lstAvailableTours list box. In other words, when the user changes the selection of the types of tours he or she wants to see, we rebuild the list of actual tours:

```
Private Sub lstTourTypes_SelectedIndexChanged() _
  Handles lstTourTypes.SelectedIndexChanged
  BuildTourList()
End Sub
```

Step 14: Create a Click handler for the *Cancel* button:

```
Private Sub btnCancel_Click() Handles btnCancel.Click
   Me.Close()
End Sub
```

Step 15: Create an Enter event handler for the last tab page. Its job is to build the list of selected tours and change the button at the bottom of the form to *Done*.

```
Private Sub Finish_Enter() Handles Finish.Enter
   ' If the user is on the last panel, build
   ' the list of selected tours.
   ShowSelectedTours()
   btnNext.Text = "&Done"
End Sub
```

Notice how several wizard pages were filled according to user selections on previous pages. In this application, for example, the list of tour types in Step 3 depended on the user's selections in Steps 1 and 2. This was accomplished by the *UpdateTourTypes* method. Similarly, the list of available tours in Step 4 depended on which tour types were selected by the user in Step 3. This was accomplished by the *BuildTourList* method.

Finally, verify that a Click handler exists for the *About this wizard* LinkLabel control:

```
Private Sub lnkAbout_LinkClicked() Handles lnkAbout.LinkClicked
   AboutForm.ShowDialog()
End Sub
```

Testing Plan

Step 16: Next, you will conduct the first series of manual tests of the Kayak Tour Wizard application. Carry out the following manual tests and verify the operation of the navigation buttons.

Input	Expected output
Start the application. In the *Step 1* tab page, click the *Next* button.	Step 2 is displayed.
Click the *Next* button.	Step 3 is displayed.
Click the *Next* button.	Step 4 is displayed.
Click the *Next* button.	The *Finish* step is displayed, and the *Next* button's caption has changed to *Done*.
Click the *Back* button.	Step 4 is displayed, and the *Done* button's caption has changed to *Next*.
Click the *Cancel* button.	The application ends.

Step 17: Carry out the second series of manual tests (shown in the table below) and verify the results.

Input	Expected output
In Step 1, select *Never*, and go to Step 2. Select *Unknown*, and go to Step 3.	The recommended tour type is *Beginning class*.
Select *Beginning class* and go to Step 4.	Step 4 displays *Beginning Kayak Class*.
Select *Beginning Kayak Class* and go to the step *Finish* step.	*Beginning Kayak Class* is listed, and the *Next* button's caption has changed to *Done*.
Go to Step 1, select *One time*, go to Step 2 and select *15 minutes*, and go to Step 3.	The recommended tour types are *Beginning class* and *Two hour*.
Select *Two hour* and go to Step 4.	The list of tours contains *Garden Cove, Pennecamp Park*, and *Rattlesnake Key*.
Select any two tours and go to the *Finish* step.	The tours selected in Step 4 are listed.
Go to Step 1, select *2 to 4 times*, go to Step 2 and select *30 minutes*, and go to Step 3.	The recommended tour types are *Beginning class, Two hour*, and *Half day*.
Select *Half day* and go to Step 4.	The list of three tours contains *Garden Cove to Pennecamp, Largo Sound*, and *Blackwater Sound*.
Go to Step 1, select *5 to 6 times*, go to Step 2 and select *60 minutes*, and go to Step 3.	The recommended tour types are *Beginning class, Two hour, Half day*, and *Full day*.
Select *Half day* and *Full day* and go to Step 4.	Six tours are listed: *Garden Cove to Pennecamp, Largo Sound, Blackwater Sound, Sunset Cove, Flamingo Park*, and *Deer Key*.
Select all tours and go to the *Finish* step.	All tours you selected are listed.
Click the *Done* button.	The application ends.

Summary

Software wizards such as the one presented in this tutorial are useful for end users because they simplify and organize tasks. At the same time, programming a wizard can entail quite a bit of debugging because you must control and organize the visible choices as the user moves from one step to another.

Chapter Summary

2.1 Input Validation

- Applications should do their best to detect and handle errors resulting from user input.
- When performing **input validation**, you will often use methods from the Char class. One use for Char methods is when scanning a string to look for certain classes of characters. Another way to use Char methods is when you are validating keyboard input.

- The TextChanged event associated with the TextBox control fires each time the user changes its contents. The TextBox control also fires a KeyPress event every time the user presses a key while the input focus is on the control.
- The StatusStrip control is the ideal container for displaying status and error messages to the user.
- The ErrorProvider control provides a simple way to validate input fields by displaying an icon and error message for any field containing invalid data.

2.2   Exception Handling

- When a program encounters an error while running, we say that an exception was thrown. Sometimes, the error is severe enough to cause the application's behavior to become unreliable.
- An exception is usually handled by alerting the user, retrying the operation that caused the error, or by terminating the application.
- Exceptions are objects. In other words, a program that throws an exception is really throwing an instance of one of the .NET exception classes.
- Most often, a program handles exceptions that were caused by a user's invalid input. When possible, try to prevent exceptions by checking all input.
- Handling an exception is accomplished using a Try—Catch—Finally statement.
- When a Try block contains multiple statements (and it usually does), not all statements in the block may be able to execute.

2.3   ListBox, ComboBox, and CheckedListBox

- ListBox, ComboBox, and CheckedListBox are collectively known as *list-type controls*.
- The CheckedBoxList control has the same properties and behavior as a ListBox, except with added check boxes next to each item.
- The CheckedListBox.CheckedIndices property contains a collection of the indexes of the checked items. Similarly, the CheckedItems collection contains the items that were checked.
- The SelectedIndex property returns the index position of the most recently selected item of a list-type control. The SelectedItem property returns the item selected by the user.
- The SelectionMode property of a ListBox can be configured to allow the user to make multiple selections.
- The SelectedItems collection contains all selected items. The SelectedIndices collection contains the indexes of all selected items.
- You can define a class and insert instances of the class into the Items collection of a list-type control.

2.4   FlowLayoutPanel, WebBrowser, SplitContainer, and TabControl

- The FlowLayoutPanel control is a general-purpose container into which you can insert any type of control.
- The WebBrowser control displays online Web pages and local HTML document files. To load an HTML page into a WebBrowser control, call the Navigate method.
- The SplitContainer control divides a form into panels. At runtime, the user can change the sizes of panels by dragging a splitter bar.
- The TabControl is a control that provides a convenient way for you to divide a form into separate pages. Each page (a TabPage object) belongs to a TabPageCollection stored in the property named TabPages.

2.5   Focus on Problem Solving: Kayak Tour Scheduling Wizard

- This application uses a software wizard to guide customers of the Kayaking Outfitter Company through the process of selecting one or more kayaking tours.

- A software wizard is an application that leads the user through a series of predescribed steps. In each step, the user may be given choices that influence subsequent steps. Wizards are particularly useful when completing tasks that are complicated or need to be completed in a specific sequence.
- In the *Kayak Tour Scheduling* wizard, the user is asked for his or her experience and endurance levels. A list of appropriate tour categories is displayed. The user selects one or more categories, and based on these selections, the wizard displays a list of matching tours. The user then selects individual tours, and a final report lists the selected tours.

Key Terms

catching an exception
Char data type
CheckedListBox control
DateTimePicker control
ErrorProvider control
Finally block
FolderBrowserDialog control
Input validation
KeyPress event
ListBox control
List-type control
ProgressBar control

RichTextBox control
software wizard
SplitContainer control
StatusStrip control
structured exception handling
System.Exception class
TabControl control
TextChanged event
throwing an exception
uncaught exception
unhandled exception
WebBrowser control

Review Questions

True or False

Indicate whether each of the following statements is true or false.

1. If an exception is thrown midway through a Try block, the appropriate Catch block executes immediately.

2. The IsDigit method is a shared method in the Char class.

3. After a Catch block executes, any remaining statements in the Try block are executed.

4. The Finally block always executes, whether or not an exception was thrown.

5. An exception must be caught inside the same method as the method throwing the exception.

6. Catch blocks should be sequenced so the most specific types of exceptions occur first, followed by more general exception types.

7. A Catch block does not have to declare an exception variable.

8. Only the first Catch block (in a series of Catch blocks) is permitted to catch an ApplicationException.

9. A separate ErrorProvider control is required for each TextBox on a form.

10. A Char data type holds a 16-bit Unicode character.

11. To convert a string to a Char array, call the MakeArray method.

12. The SetError method of the ErrorProvider method has a single parameter, which is a string.

13. The Leave event fires when the input focus moves away from a control.

14. An uncaught exception always causes an application to stop.

15. If an exception is thrown inside a Try block, all statements in the Try block execute anyway.

16. If an exception is thrown inside a Try block, all statements in the Finally block execute anyway.

17. When a Catch block finishes executing, execution resumes in the Try block where the exception was thrown.

18. The Finally block is optional.

19. The Items.Remove method of a ListBox receives an integer index parameter.

20. You cannot directly add a DateTime object to another DateTime object.

Short Answer

1. What do we call an exception that is never caught?

2. What type of exception should be thrown by methods in your own classes?

3. What type of exception is thrown when the format of an argument passed to a method does not match the format of the formal parameter?

4. Which exception property returns a string containing the sequence of method calls that led up to the exception being thrown?

5. Which control lets you divide a form into separate pages?

6. Which ErrorProvider method must be called to create a pop-up error message for a particular control?

7. Which Char method checks if a character is a member of the alphabet?

8. Which Char method converts a character to uppercase?

9. Which event handler is created when you double-click a TextBox control in design mode?

10. Which TextBox event fires each time the user presses a keyboard key?

11. Which control automatically docks at the bottom of a form and often contains a Label control?

12. Which control provides a visual cue to the validation status of an input field?

13. Which exception is thrown when an array subscript is out of bounds?

14. Which collection in the CheckedListBox control contains a list of the indexes of all checked items?

15. Which ListBox property must be modified to permit the user to select multiple items?

16. If you insert your own type of objects in a ListBox, which method in your class must be implemented?

17. Which control is shown in this chapter as a way for the user to select a date from a calendar-like display?

18. If you want to add 10 days to the current date, which DateTime method should you call?

19. What types of buttons can be added to a ToolStrip control?

20. If you want to display text in a ToolStripButton, which property must be set to *Text*?

21. Which control lets the user drag a vertical or horizontal bar between two panels?

22. Which WebBrowser method must you call when displaying a Web page?

What Do You Think?

1. Why might the user prefer to have all fields on a form validated at the same time?

2. Do you prefer that applications prevent you from making input mistakes, or would you rather make the mistakes and be notified later?

3. Do you think an OutOfMemoryException should be caught by application programs?

4. How might the Finally block be useful in a program that reads from a file?

5. What characteristics define a wizard-type application?

Algorithm Workbench

1. Suppose you want to create a wizard application to help the user set up a sprinkler system with a timer that would turn off and on at the same time each day. Make a list of the questions the wizard would ask the user.

2. Write a sequence of statements that set e.Cancel to *True* if a TextBox control named *txtZip* does not contain five decimal digits.

3. Write a statement that passes an error message to an ErrorProvider control named errProvider under the following condition: txtName.Text does not contain two words.

4. Show an example of creating a TimeSpan object from 3 hours, 10 minutes, and 0 seconds.

5. Get the current date and time, and add 3 hours and 10 minutes using the Date.Add method.

Programming Challenges

1. **Bank Teller with Totals**

   Extend the solution program you wrote for the *Bank Teller with Totals* program in the Programming Challenges for Chapter 1. Add the following error checking:

   - The Account.Deposit method must throw an ArgumentException if the *amount* parameter is less than zero. Pass a string containing "Deposit must be a positive value."
   - The Account.Withdraw method must throw an ArgumentException if the *amount* parameter is less than zero. Pass a string containing "Withdrawal must be a positive value."
   - The Account.Withdraw method must throw an ArgumentException if the *amount* parameter is greater than the current account balance. Pass a string containing "Insufficient funds for withdrawal."

   All exceptions must be caught by the main form, which displays the exception messages.

2. **Club Committee Organizer**

   Your student computer club needs to keep a record of which club members have joined committees. Your task is to write an application that will make the process easy. In Figure 2-42, the user is about to select the name of a committee from a combo box. Then in Figure 2-43, the user has selected several members from the general members list on the left side. The user is about to click the button containing an arrow pointing to the right, which will copy the selected member names into the *Current Members* list box. In Figure 2-44, the members have been copied, and automatically unselected from the list

Figure 2-42 Club Committee Organizer, selecting a committee

Figure 2-43 Club Committee Organizer, selecting several members

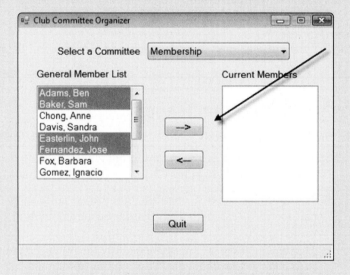

box on the left side. If the user should try to select and copy a member who already belongs to the committee list on the right side, nothing will happen. In Figure 2-45 the user has selected two committee members and is about to click the button with the arrow pointing leftwards. These members will be removed from the committee.

Both list boxes permit multiple items to be selected. Insert the following list of committees into the combo box: Activities, Community Services, Executive, Membership, Programming Team, Scholarship, Sports, Travel, Volunteer Tutoring. Make up your own list of at least ten names for the list box containing the general membership.

Error checking: Make sure the user selects a committee name before you permit members to be copied into the list box on the right side.

Figure 2-44 Club Committee Organizer, membership committee contains four people

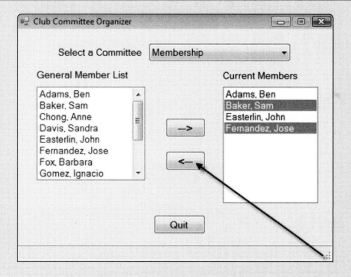

Figure 2-45 Club Committee Organizer, two members about to be removed from the committee

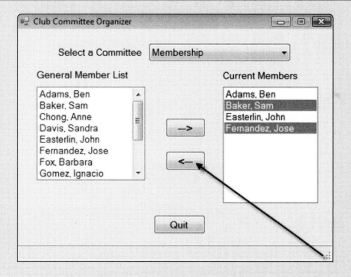

3. **Winter Sports Rentals**

A winter sports rentals store needs an application that will let the user (a store clerk) enter information about each customer's rental. The user should be able to select multiple equipment items, a rental duration, and insurance. Figure 2-46 shows a sample design, after the user has selected all items and clicked the *Calculate* button. Include a check box showing that a liability waiver was signed, and let the user input the deposit amount. Use a combo box to list the rental durations, but do not let the user type in an arbitrary duration. When the user clicks the *Calculate* button, the application should calculate the subtotal, tax, and balance due. Also, use a LinkLabel control (*Weather forecast*) to display a second form containing a WebBrowser control.

Figure 2-46 Winter Sports Rentals, prices calculated

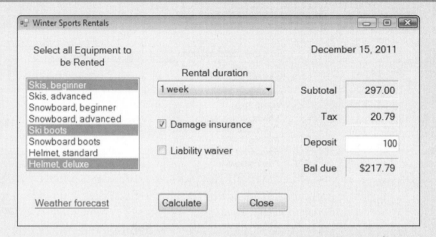

Figure 2-47 Winter Sports Rentals, showing weather forecast links

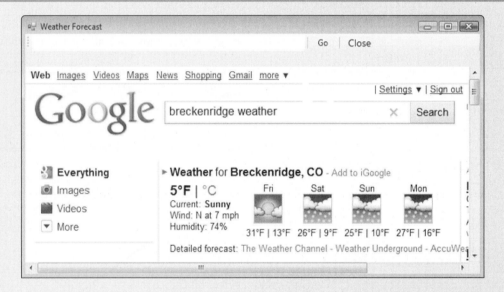

The form containing the WebBrowser control, shown in Figure 2-47, should display a series of links to weather forecasts for the area near the winter sports rental store. Place a ToolStrip container at the top of the form; it should contain a text box (for entering a Web address), a *Go* button to navigate to the address typed into the text box, and a *Close* button that closes the browser window. *Note: We do not endorse any particular Web search engine, so you may substitute another of your choosing.*

Error Checking: When the user clicks the *Calculate* button, make sure that at least one item has been selected from the equipment list box. Also, a rental duration must have been selected, and the Deposit amount must be a positive number. Use the ErrorProvider control to display all error messages.

The following rental durations should appear in the combo box: 1 day, 2 days, 3 days, 1 week, 2 weeks.

Calculations: Each equipment item has a rental rate based on different durations. Create a two-dimensional array containing all possible rental rates. Each row should contain the rental rates for a single item, using the different rental durations. The following first row of the array, for example, contains rental rates for *Skis, beginner:*

```
35,45,80,150,280
```

For this equipment, the rates are $35.00 for 1 day, $45.00 for 2 days, $80.00 for 3 days, $150.00 for a week, and $280.00 for 2 weeks. Damage insurance costs 10 percent of the total rental charge before taxes.

4. **Winter Sports Rentals Classes**

Using the *Winter Sports Rentals* program from Programming Challenge 3 as a starting point, make the following improvements:

- Create a class that holds all the rental rates. This class should contain a function named *GetRentalPrice* that returns a single rental price if passed the type of equipment and the rental duration. Inside the class, define an enumerated type for the type of duration (1 day, 2 days, etc.), and another enumerated type for the equipment type (skis, snowboard, boots, etc.). Use these enumerated types to define the parameter types for GetRentalPrice. For example:

```
Public Function GetRentalPrice( ByVal duration As DurationType,
    ByVal equip As EquipmentType ) As Double
```

- Also, create a readonly property that returns the cost of damage insurance (10 percent of the total rental charge before taxes):

```
Public Shared ReadOnly Property InsuranceCost(
    ByVal rentalAmount As Double) As Double
```

5. **Calculating Flight Times**

Imagine that you plan to apply for a programming position at an airline. Before interviewing, you need to have a good idea of how airlines calculate flight arrival times. Therefore, you will create a simple application that explores this concept. Your application will calculate the arrival time of any airline flight. The user selects the local departure date and time, the departure airport, and the arrival airport. Then the application calculates the local arrival date and time. It displays this information, along with the trip duration.

It is reasonable to assume that airlines use Coordinated Universal Time (UTC) when calculating departure and arrival times. (Appendix B explains how to convert between local time and UTC time, with examples.) Figure 2-48 shows information for a flight from Miami to Honolulu. The departure date is selected in a DateTimePicker control, and the

Figure 2-48 Information for a flight from Miami to Honolulu

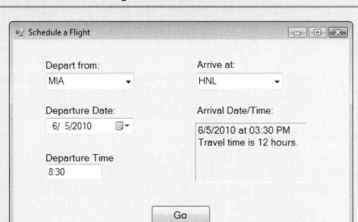

departure time is entered into a text box. When the user selects a departure airport, arrival airport, date, and time and clicks the *Continue* button, the arrival date and time appear on the right side of the form. Figure 2-49 shows information for an overnight flight from Honolulu to Miami. Notice that the arrival date is one day later than the departure date.

Figure 2-49 Information for a flight between Honolulu and Miami

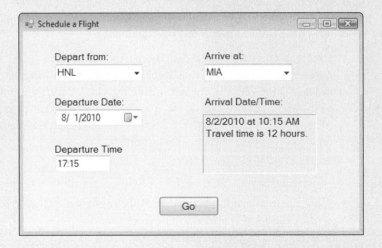

Implementation Notes

If the user clicks the *Continue* button without selecting departure and arrival airports, use an ErrorProvider control to signal the error. Do not let the program calculate dates and times until airports are selected. Create some application data, similar to the following:

```
Private airports As String() = {"MIA", "JFK", "HNL", "LAX", "DFW"}
Private utcOffsets As Integer() = {-4, -4, -10, -7, -5}
Private travelTimes As Double(,) = {{0, 3, 12, 8, 2.5}, _
    {3, 0, 14, 8.5, 3.5}, {12, 14, 0, 4.5, 8.5}, _
    {8, 8.5, 4.5, 0, 3.5}, {2.5, 3.5, 8.5, 3.5, 0}}
```

The *airports* array holds several airport identification codes. The *utcOffsets* array holds the UTC offsets of the corresponding airports. The *travelTimes* array holds the estimated travel time, in hours, between two airports and all the other airports. It is a two-dimensional array. Row 0, for example, represents the time to travel between MIA (Miami) and the following airports: MIA, JFK, HNL, LAX, and DFW. Row 1 represents the time to travel between JFK (New York) and the following airports: MIA, JFK, HNL, LAX, and DFW. The times listed here may very well be incorrect, so feel free to change them.

A suggested approach is to use three steps in your calculations: (1) Convert the local departure time into UTC time; (2) add the trip's duration, resulting in the UTC arrival time; and (3) convert the UTC arrival time into the arrival airport's local time.

6. **Simple Image Album**

The *Simple Image Album* application in Tutorial 2-3 has a fatal flaw—it runs out of memory when more than a small number of images are load into its array of PictureBox controls. Your challenge is first to display the images as thumbnails. Then, when the user clicks a thumbnail, your application will display the full-size image in a separate window. This means that you will have to add a click handler to each PictureBox control, but fortunately you can use the same handler for all the buttons.

CHAPTER 3

Collections

TOPICS

This chapter introduces some of the most useful and powerful collection classes in the .NET library, with the idea that collections of objects help to build concepts that can be applied later to databases. We show how to create and use ArrayLists, strongly typed Lists, and Dictionary objects. The chapter finishes with examples that show how to use Microsoft's new Language Integrated Query (LINQ) technology to search lists of objects.

3.1 ArrayLists

In the most general terms, a **collection** is any sequenced or unsequenced group of values. In a sequenced collection known as a **list,** the values retain their relative positions to each other. For example, we might refer to a *list of temperature samples* taken every hour during the day. Arrays can be considered lists. Another type of collection is a **set,** which does not have any particular sequence. We might refer to the *set of all people with green eyes*, for example, with the understanding that there is no particular ordering within that group. Another type of collection is often called a **Dictionary** or **map**, which associates keys with corresponding values. If you wanted to look up a student's academic transcript, for example, you would use his or her student ID as what is known as a *key*. The value associated with each key in the dictionary would be the student's transcript.

The .NET Framework has classes that implement different types of collections. In this chapter, we will present a few, such as ArrayList, List, and Dictionary.

There is a Visual Basic data type named *Collection* that was introduced in early versions of Visual Basic. It addresses a need for an array-type structure that can expand when new items are added. Also, it allows items to be stored with associated key values, which can be used in searches. In that sense, a Visual Basic Collection object is a dictionary. But the Collection type continues to have some drawbacks and has been overshadowed by newer classes in the .NET framework. For that reason, we will not use the Visual Basic Collection type from this point onward.

ArrayList Class

The most fundamental .NET collection is the **ArrayList class,** an expandable list-type collection that contains references to objects. ArrayList belongs to the *System.Collections* namespace. Like arrays, ArrayLists also permit subscripts to randomly access their elements. ArrayLists are more powerful and flexible than arrays in the following aspects:

- An ArrayList expands as new items are inserted, whereas an array does not.
- An ArrayList contains methods to find, insert, and remove items, whereas an array does not.
- You can insert different types of objects into the same ArrayList object.

Figure 3-1 helps to show some of the relationships between an ArrayList and the items it contains. Table 3-1 lists some of the most common ArrayList properties and methods.

Figure 3-1 Overview of ArrayLists

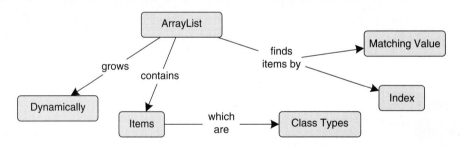

Table 3-1 Selected ArrayList properties and methods

Property or Method	Description
Add(element As Object)	Adds a new item to the end of the list
Clear( )	Removes all items from the list
Contains(element As Object) As Boolean	Returns True if the list contains the given item
Count( ) As Integer	Returns a count of the number of items in the list
Insert(index As Integer, element as Object)	Inserts an item into the list at a specified index position.
Item(index As Integer) As Object	Returns a reference to the list item at a specified index position
Remove(element As Object)	Removes the first occurrence of a specified item from the list
RemoveAt(index As Integer)	Removes the item at a specified index position

Creating an ArrayList

Use the *New* operator to create an instance of the ArrayList class. For example:

```
Dim customers As New ArrayList
```

You can also pass an array, an ArrayList, or any other object type that implements the ICollection interface to the ArrayList constructor. In the following code, for example, the ArrayList receives a copy of the scores array:

```
Dim scores() As Integer = {80, 66, 75}
Dim scoreList As New ArrayList(scores)
```

Adding and Inserting Items

One way to add items to an ArrayList is by calling the *Add* method. Here's an example:

```
customers.Add("Baker")
```

You can also use the *Insert* method to put an item into the list at a specified index:

```
scoreList.Insert(1,"Ramirez")
```

There is no limitation on inserting duplicate items, so if your application requirements disallow duplicate items, you should first test to see if the item is in the list.

Removing Items

The *RemoveAt* method removes an ArrayList item. You pass to it the index position of the item you want to remove. The following statement removes the customer at index position 2:

```
customers.RemoveAt(2)
```

The *Remove* method removes the first item that matches the item you pass as an input parameter. The following statement removes "Baker" from the customers ArrayList:

```
customers.Remove("Baker")
```

Finding Items

The *Contains* method returns a Boolean value indicating whether a certain value exists in an ArrayList. In the following example, the *found* variable will equal *True* if the value 66 exists in the ArrayList named *scoreList*:

```
Dim found As Boolean = scoreList.Contains(66)
```

The *IndexOf* method returns an integer that identifies the index position of an item. If the item is not found, the return value is −1. The following code calls IndexOf and displays a message if the customer name is not found:

```
Dim index As Integer = customers.IndexOf("Baker")
If index = -1 Then
   lblStatus.Text = "Customer not found"
End If
```

Retrieving and Replacing Items

The *Item* property returns a reference to an ArrayList element. You pass to the Item property an integer index between 0 and ArrayList.Count − 1. For example, the following code retrieves the value stored at index position 2 in the `customers` ArrayList:

```
Dim name As String = CStr(customers.Item(2))
```

Because the customers.Item(2) expression returns a plain Object data type, we must convert it into a String type before assigning it to the `name` variable.

Item is known as a *default property*, so the following statement implicitly gets the element at index position 2:

```
Dim name As String = CStr(customers(2))
```

You can use the Item property to replace an item in an ArrayList. The following lines show two ways to replace the item at index 2 with "Johnson":

```
customers.Item(2) = "Johnson"
customers(2) = "Johnson"
```

IndexOutOfRangeException

An *IndexOutOfRangeException* is thrown if you pass an index to the Item property that does not match the index of any item in an ArrayList. The following code example shows how to handle the exception:

```
Try
   Dim index As Integer = CInt(txtIndex.Text)
   Dim cust As String = CStr(customers.Item(index))
Catch ex As IndexOutOfRangeException
   MessageBox.Show(ex.Message)
End Try
```

The same rule applies when you call the *RemoveAt* method, which also must receive a valid index.

The Count Property

The *Count* property indicates the number of items stored in an ArrayList. The following code uses the Count property to display the size of the customers list:

```
lblInfo.Text = "The collection size is " & customers.Count
```

Loops

The preferred way to loop through an ArrayList is to use a *For Each* statement. During each loop repetition, the variable declared in the loop represents the current item value. The following code, for example, loops through scoreList and adds each score to a list box:

```
For Each score As Integer In scoreList
   lstBox.Items.Add(score)
Next
```

Similarly, the following code loops through the *customers* ArrayList and adds each element to a list box:

```
For Each cust As String In customers
   lstBpx.Items.Add(cust)
Next
```

In Tutorial 3-1, you will examine an application that builds an ArrayList of test scores.

Tutorial 3-1:
ArrayList of test scores

In this tutorial, you examine and test an application that has a Student class containing an ArrayList of test scores. As each test score is entered by the user, it is added to the list. A read-only property in the class calculates the test average. The class also contains a shared variable that holds the college name, with a corresponding shared property.

Figure 3-2 shows the application's output after the user has entered a student ID and name, and has clicked the *Save* button. Then, when the user enters a few test scores and clicks the *View* button, the sample output is the same as that shown in Figure 3-3. The user can continue to enter more test scores and click the *View* button as many times as necessary.

Figure 3-2 After clicking the *Save* button

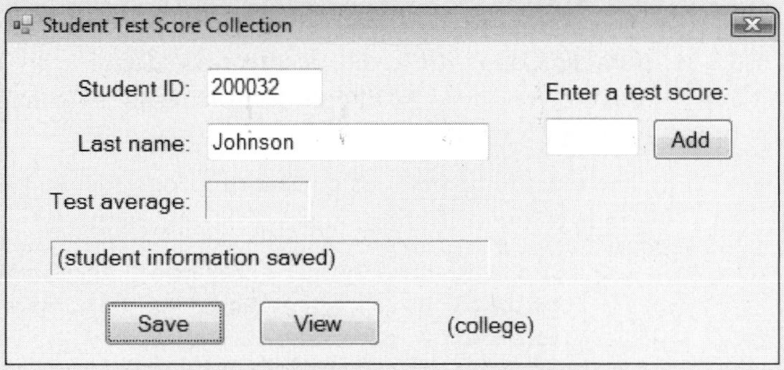

Figure 3-3 After adding two scores and clicking the *View* button

Tutorial Steps

Step 1: Open the *ArrayList of Test Scores* project in the chapter examples folder. The named controls used in this application are:

- TextBox controls: txtIdNumber, txtGrade, txtLastName
- Label controls: lblTestAverage, lblStudent, lblCollege
- Buttons: btnAdd, btnSave, btnView

Step 2: Open the Student class in the code editor and view the following code:

```
1: Public Class Student
2:   Public Property IdNumber As String
3:   Public Property LastName As String
4:   Public Shared Property CollegeName As String
5:   Private mTestScores As New ArrayList
6:
7:   Public ReadOnly Property TestAverage() As Double
8:     Get
9:       Dim testSum As Double = 0.0
```

```
10:        For Each grade As Double In mTestScores
11:          testSum += grade
12:        Next
13:        If mTestScores.Count > 0 Then
14:          Return testSum / mTestScores.Count
15:        Else
16:          Return 0.0
17:        End If
18:      End Get
19: End Property
```

The ArrayList is declared on line 5. Line 13 checks the value of mTest-Grades.Count, to avoid accidentally dividing by zero when no test scores have been added to the collection. Line 14 calculates and returns the test average.

The remaining methods consist of a constructor, a method to add a single test grade to the collection, and a ToString method:

```
Public Sub New(ByVal pIdNumber As String,
  Optional ByVal pLastName As String = "")
  IdNumber = pIdNumber
  LastName = pLastName
End Sub

Public Sub AddTestGrade(ByVal grade As Double)
  mTestScores.Add(grade)
End Sub

Public Overrides Function ToString() As String
  Return IdNumber & ", " & LastName
End Function
End Class
```

Step 3:   Open the code window for *MainForm.vb* and inspect the following code:

```
Public Class MainForm
  Private objStudent As Student
```

The Form_Load event handler sets the value of the CollegeName shared property in the Student class.

```
Private Sub Form_Load() Handles MyBase.Load
  Student.CollegeName = "My University"
End Sub
```

Step 4:   Find the Click handler for the *Save* button:

```
Private Sub btnSave_Click() Handles btnSave.Click
  objStudent = New Student(txtIdNumber.Text,
    txtLastName.Text)
  lblStudent.Text = "(student information saved)"
  btnAdd.Enabled = True
End Sub
```

This method creates a new Student object from the two text boxes. Notice how the *Add* button is enabled only after the user clicks the *Save* button. This is necessary to prevent the program from trying to add a test score before a Student object has been created. The *Add* button lets the user add test grades to the student's collection of scores.

Step 5: Find the Click handler for the *View* button, which displays the student (ID and last name), the college name, and the student's test average:

```
Private Sub btnView_Click() Handles btnView.Click
   lblStudent.Text = objStudent.ToString
   lblCollege.Text = Student.CollegeName
   lblTestAverage.Text = objStudent.TestAverage.ToString("n")
End Sub
```

Step 6: The Click handler for the *Add* button takes the test grade from the txtGrade text box and calls the Student.AddTestGrade method. This method adds the grade to the student's collection of grades.

```
Private Sub btnAdd_Click() Handles btnAdd.Click
   Dim testGrade As Double
   If Double.TryParse(txtGrade.Text, testGrade) Then
     objStudent.AddTestGrade(testGrade)
   Else
     MessageBox.Show("Test grade must be a number", "Error")
   End If
End Sub
```

Step 7: Test the application using the following testing sequence. Restart the application for each test.

Test 1

Input	Expected output
Enter *200032, Johnson,* and click the *Save* button. Next, click the *View* button.	The ID and name should appear in the label, and the test average should appear as 0.0. The college name should appear as *My University* on all tests.

Test 2

Input	Expected output
Enter any ID and name, and click the *Save* button. Enter a single test score (92.3), click the *Add* button, and click the *View* button.	The ID and name should appear in the label, and the test average should appear as 92.3.

Test 3

Input	Expected output
Enter any ID and name, and click the *Save* button. Enter the test scores 92.3 and 85.1, click the *Add* button, and click the *View* button.	The ID and name should appear in the label, and the test average should appear as 88.70.

Test 4	
Input	**Expected output**
Enter any ID and name, and click the *Save* button. Enter the test scores 92.3 and 85.1, click the *Add* button, click the *Save* button, and click the *View* button.	The ID and name should appear in the label, and the test average should appear as 0.00. (By clicking the *Save* button, you created a new Student and erased the existing collection of test scores.)

Test 4 was included to show how an unsuspecting user might click the *Save* button without realizing that it would erase all the test scores. For practice, decide how you would warn the user before erasing the scores.

Summary

The ArrayList class is a lightweight, powerful, and easy alternative to using arrays. It is the ideal container to use when a list must expand at runtime, or when you must search for items. So far, we have shown only how to create ArrayLists containing standard data types. In the next section, we will show how to create ArrayLists containing user-defined class types.

 Checkpoint

1. What is the subscript of the first element in an ArrayList object?

2. Which type of collection can more easily delete an element: an ArrayList or an Array?

3. Yes or no: Do ArrayList entries have key values?

4. Which ArrayList property returns a member of a collection at a given index position?

5. What type of exception is thrown if you pass an invalid index value to the Item method?

6. What is the preferred type of loop to use on an ArrayList?

3.2 ArrayLists of Custom Objects

You have seen how to create ArrayLists of standard data types, such as Strings and Doubles. Before long, you will also want to create lists containing instances of your own classes. Suppose we want to build a list of Student objects. The following tasks are commonly performed on lists:

- Loop through the list and display each student
- Search for a student
- Sort the list
- Remove a student from the list

We must create a new instance of the Student class each time we insert a new object, to avoid creating an ArrayList in which all items reference the same object. Also, the Student class needs to implement the Equals and CompareTo methods.

References and Copies

When an item in an ArrayList is a value type such as Integer or Single, the *Item* method returns a copy of the item. For example, the following code inserts an integer into an ArrayList named *numbers*:

```
Dim numbers As New ArrayList
numbers.Add(10)
```

Next, the following code retrieves the integer stored at index 0 and modifies its value:

```
Dim intNum As Integer = CType(numbers.Item(0), Integer)
intNum = 99
```

But *intNum* is only a copy of the item in the collection, so the item stored in the ArrayList at index 0 still equals its original value, 10.

But when an ArrayList item is a reference type, the Item method returns a reference to the object. The reference can be used to modify the object inside the list. To illustrate, we can create an ArrayList named *students* and insert a Student object:

```
Dim students As New ArrayList
students.Add(New Student("Johnson"))
```

Next, we use the Item method to obtain a reference to the same student:

```
Dim studentRef as Student = CType(students.Item(0), Student)
```

Next, we assign a new last name to the student reference:

```
studentRef.LastName = "Griffin"
```

By doing this, we have also modified the name of the Student object inside the ArrayList. That is because the Item method always returns a reference to an object in an ArrayList.

Common Error: Multiple References to the Same Object

Understanding how references work can really help you to avoid a common error when working with collections—that of storing multiple references to the same object. The following code (located inside the Click handler for a button named *Add*) shows the correct way to insert an object into an ArrayList:

```
1:   Private AllStudents As New ArrayList
2:
3:   Private Sub btnAdd_Click() Handles btnAdd.Click
4:      Dim objStudent As New Student(txtIdNumber.Text,
5:         txtLastName.Text, CDbl(txtAverage.Text))
6:      AllStudents.Add(objStudent)
7:   End Sub
```

Line 4 creates a new Student object, using values from the text boxes. Line 6 adds the student to the ArrayList. Next, let's look at similar code that contains a common bug:

```
1:   Private AllStudents As New ArrayList
2:   Private objStudent As New Student
3:
4:   Private Sub btnAdd_Click() Handles btnAdd.Click
5:      objStudent.IdNumber = txtIdNumber.Text
6:      objStudent.LastName = txtLastName.Text
7:      objStudent.TestAverage = CDbl(txtAverage.Text)
8:      AllStudents.Add(objStudent)
9:   End Sub
```

Can you see the error? A single Student object is created on line 2. Then, on lines 5–7, its properties are assigned values from text boxes. On line 8, the object is added to the

ArrayList. But each time the loop repeats, line 8 adds the same Student object to the ArrayList again and again. The ArrayList entries end up referencing the same object, as shown in Figure 3-4. So the lesson to be gained from this example is this: You must create a new instance each time you insert an object into an ArrayList.

Figure 3-4 When ArrayList members reference the same object

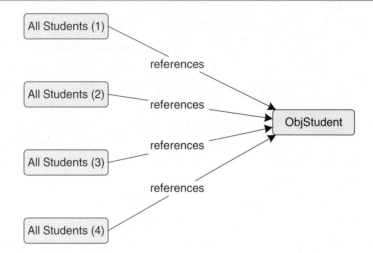

Comparing Objects with CompareTo

When you sort an array or ArrayList of custom objects, you must define how they will be compared, using a method named **CompareTo method**. This method has the following parameter list and return type:

```
Function CompareTo(ByVal obj As Object) As Integer
```

Given two objects A and B, CompareTo is called like this:

```
Dim result As Integer = A.CompareTo(B)
```

The return value of CompareTo when comparing two objects A and B is as follows:

- If A is less than B, `A.CompareTo(B)` returns a negative integer.
- If A is equal to B, `A.CompareTo(B)` returns zero.
- If A is greater than B, `A.CompareTo(B)` returns a positive nonzero integer.

If a class does not contain a CompareTo method, a list of instances of the class cannot be sorted. In common terminology, the objects are *not comparable*. To demonstrate, let's create the following Student class:

```
Class Student
   Public Property Id As String
   Public Property Name As String
   Public Sub New(ByVal pId As String, ByVal pName As String)
      Id = pId
      Name = pName
   End Sub
End Class
```

Next, we insert the students in an ArrayList and attempt to sort it:

```
Dim list = New ArrayList()
list.Add(New Student("2001", "Jones"))
list.Add(New Student("1004", "Thomas"))
list.Add(New Student("1050", "Adams"))
list.Sort()
```

Upon running the application, an unhandled exception like the one shown in Figure 3-5 says: *Failed to compare two elements in the array.* To put it another way, we failed to include a CompareTo method in the Student class. But before showing how to create a CompareTo method, we need to explain about Interfaces in .NET.

Figure 3-5 Attempting to sort an ArrayList

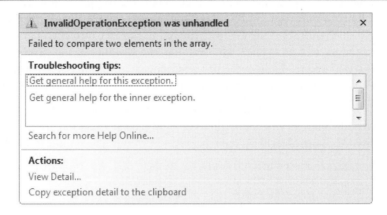

Interfaces

An **interface** defines a set of methods and properties that can be implemented by other classes. The classes that *implement the interface* are guaranteed to contain these methods and properties. When a class implements an interface, we learn something important about the class: We learn what it can do.

An interface is declared in much the same way as a class. For example, this is how .NET defines the **IComparable interface**:

```
Interface IComparable
   Function CompareTo(ByVal obj As Object) As Integer
End Interface
```

Notice that the *CompareTo* method does not contain a body—only the method signature, we call it, which is the line you see here. A **method signature** consists of the word *Sub* or *Function*, followed by the method name, parameter list, and return type (if it is a function).

If a class implements the IComparable interface, the class must contain a CompareTo method with the same signature as the one defined in the IComparable interface. Also, the CompareTo method in the implementing class must contain a body. Next, we'll show how the Student class can implement the IComparable interface.

CompareTo Example

Suppose we have created a Student class, and we want to compare Student objects by their ID numbers. Then our Student class will implement the IComparable interface. The shaded areas of the following code listing show which parts relate to the IComparable interface:

```
1:  Class Student
2:     Implements IComparable
3:     Public Property Id As String
4:     Public Property LastName As String
5:     Public Sub New(ByVal pId As String, ByVal pName As String)
6:        Id = pId
7:        LastName = pName
8:     End Sub
9:
```

```
10:    Public Function CompareTo(ByVal obj As Object) As Integer _
11:        Implements IComparable.CompareTo
12:        Dim S As Student = CType(obj, Student)
13:        Return Me.Id.CompareTo(S.Id)
14:    End Function
15: End Class
```

Line 2 states that this class implements the IComparable interface. Line 11 states that the CompareTo method in this class implements the CompareTo method specified in the IComparable interface. Line 12 casts the obj parameter into a Student object, allowing us to refer to the Id field on line 13. On that line, the Id value of the current student (identified by *Me*) is compared to the Id value of the student who was passed as the parameter to this method. (The *Me* qualifier is not required, but it helps to clarify which object is which.)

The CompareTo method looks very similar in every class that implements it. Only a few lines of code refer specifically to the type of objects being compared. For example, if we compared two Account objects by their balances, CompareTo would look like this:

```
Public Function CompareTo(ByVal obj As Object) As Integer _
    Implements IComparable.CompareTo
    Dim A As Account = CType(obj, Account)
    Return Me.Balance.CompareTo(A.Balance)
End Function
```

The shaded lines identify the code lines that are specific to this class.

If you think you will need to sort an ArrayList, every type of object you put into that ArrayList should be an instance of a class that implements IComparable. The same is true for an Array of objects. But IComparable is easy to implement and it's a great convenience. Although you rarely need to do so, it is also possible to define your own interface types. (Refer to Appendix B for details about interfaces.)

Related Topic: IList and IListSource Interfaces

It is possible to assign an Array, ArrayList, or List object to the DataSource property of a ListBox, but you cannot do it with most other types of objects. Any object assigned to the DataSource property must implement either the *IList* or *IListSource* interface. As it happens, the Array, ArrayList, and List classes implement IList, which contains methods named *Contains, Add, IndexOf, Insert, Remove,* and *RemoveAt*.

You can also assign a DataTable to the DataSource property of a ListBox because the DataTable class implements the IListSource interface. It turns out that IListSource is just a convenient wrapper for the IList interface. If you would like to see this information for yourself, open the *Object Browser* window from the View menu in Visual Studio, and search for IList, ArrayList, List, and IListSource.

Comparing Objects with the Equals Method

You learned in Chapter 1 that the Equals method compares all standard .NET types. It returns a value of *True* if the objects contain equal values. For the two strings shown below, the expression *A.Equals(B)* is *True*:

```
Dim A As String = "abcde"
Dim B As String = "abcde"
A.Equals(B)                    'True
```

But the Equals method is not automatically configured for your own custom classes. The following code examples compare two Student objects. Assuming that we have not created a custom version of the Equals method in the Student class, the expression *s1.Equals(s2)* is *False*.

```
Dim s1 As New Student(1001)
Dim s2 As New Student(1001)
s1.Equals(s2)                    'False
```

Naturally, it would be helpful to compare Student objects or other custom types in a useful way. We might want to search for Student objects in an ArrayList by calling the *Contains* or *IndexOf* methods, for example. In order to do that, we will have to override the Equals method in the Student class.

Overriding the Equals Method

To **override the Equals method** means to create an Equals method in your own class that has the same signature as the Equals method in the Object class. The signature of the Equals method is shown here.

```
Public Overrides Function Equals(ByVal obj As Object) As Boolean
```

The following Student class contains an Equals method that compares students by their ID numbers:

```
1:   Class Student
2:      Public Property Id As String
3:      Public Property LastName As String
4:
5:      Public Overrides Function Equals(ByVal obj As Object) As Boolean
6:         Return Me.Id.Equals(CType(obj, Student).Id)
7:      End Function
8:   End Class
```

Line 6 casts the obj variable into a Student object, and gets the object's Id property value. This value is compared to Me.Id, the ID of the current Student object. This Equals method returns *True* if two students have the same ID number.

You can select any properties, variables, or calculated values to be compared when implementing the Equals method. In general, you should choose a property or combination of properties that will uniquely identify each object. It is important that the class properties compared by the Equals method are either standard .NET types, or types that have themselves implemented the Equals method.

> **TIP:** If your class also implements the IComparable interface, it's a good idea for the Equals and CompareTo methods to use the same property for comparisons.

In Tutorial 3-2, you will examine an application that inserts Student objects into an ArrayList. The Student class contains an Equals method that compares ID numbers.

Tutorial 3-2:
Building an ArrayList of Student objects

In this tutorial, you will examine an application that creates an ArrayList of Student objects. The Student class will implement the Equals method.

Tutorial Steps

Step 1: Open the project named *ArrayList of Students* from the chapter examples folder.

Step 2: Run the application, input the following values into the text boxes, and click the *Add to Collection* button:

Student ID	10000
Last name	Smith
Test average	82.5

Step 3:   Enter two more students, using the following data, and click the *Add to Collection* button after each set of data has been entered:

```
10022, Jones, 90
20000, Ramirez, 79.5
```

Step 4:   Click the *View All* button. Figure 3-6 shows the expected output.

Step 5:   Next, you will search for a student by ID number. Enter *10022* into the TextBox in the lower left corner, and click the *Find by ID* button. The program should find the matching student and display it in the ListBox, as shown in Figure 3-7.

Step 6:   Enter a nonexistent student ID into the textbox at the bottom left corner of the form and click the *Find by ID* button. A message should say that the student was not found.

Figure 3-6 After inserting three Students into the collection

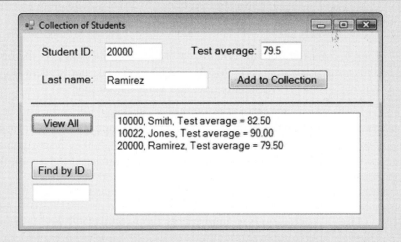

Figure 3-7 After searching for a student ID

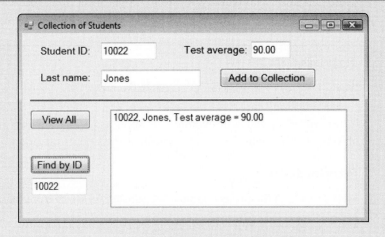

Step 7: Examine the source code for the Student class. It has Id, LastName, and TestAverage properties, a constructor, a ToString method, and an Equals method.

```
Public Class Student
  Public Property Id As String
  Public Property LastName As String
  Public Property TestAverage As Double

  Public Sub New(ByVal pId As String,
    Optional ByVal pLastName As String = "",
    Optional ByVal pTestAverage As Double = 0.0)
    Id = pId
    LastName = pLastName
    TestAverage = pTestAverage
  End Sub

  Public Overrides Function ToString() As String
    Return Id & ", " & LastName _
      & ", Test average = " & TestAverage.ToString("n2")
  End Function

  Public Overrides Function Equals(ByVal obj As Object) _
    As Boolean
    Dim other As Student = CType(obj, Student)
    Return Id = other.Id
  End Function
End Class
```

Step 8: Examine the source code for the MainForm Class. The *btnAdd_Click* method creates a Student and adds it to the collection. The *btnView_Click* method loops through the collection and inserts each item into a ListBox. The *btnFind_Click* method searches for a student ID and displays the matching Student in the ListBox.

```
1:  Public Class MainForm
2:     Private allStudents As New ArrayList
3:
4:     Private Sub btnAdd_Click() Handles btnAdd.Click
5:       Try
6:         Dim objStudent As New Student(txtIdNumber.Text,
7:           txtLastName.Text, CDbl(txtAverage.Text))
8:         allStudents.Add(objStudent)
9:       Catch
10:        MessageBox.Show("Invalid test average", "Error")
11:      End Try
12:    End Sub
```

Lines 6–7 create a student from the contents of the text boxes, and line 8 inserts the student into the *allStudents* ArrayList.

Step 9: Continuing in the same class, find the Click handler for the *View* button.

```
1:  Private Sub btnView_Click() Handles btnView.Click
2:     lstStudents.Items.Clear()
3:     For Each stu As Student In allStudents
4:        lstStudents.Items.Add(stu.ToString)
5:     Next
6:  End Sub
```

This method clears the list box and uses a *For Each* statement to traverse the ArrayList. Each student is inserted into the lstStudents list box.

Step 10: View the Click handler for the *Find* button.

```
1: Private Sub btnFind_Click() Handles btnFind.Click
2:    lstStudents.Items.Clear()
3:    Dim S As New Student(txtFindId.Text)
4:    Dim index As Integer = allStudents.IndexOf(S)
5:    If index <> -1 Then
6:       S = CType(allStudents(index), Student)
7:       lstStudents.Items.Add(allStudents(index).ToString)
8:       ' update the text boxes, to be consistent
9:       txtIdNumber.Text = S.Id
10:      txtAverage.Text = S.TestAverage.ToString("n")
11:      txtLastName.Text = S.LastName
12:   Else
13:      lstStudents.Items.Add("Student ID was not found")
14:   End If
15: End Sub
```

Let's look at some details in this code. Line 3 creates a Student object from the ID number in the txtFindId text box, and line 4 calls IndexOf to search for the student in the ArrayList. If the index returned by IndexOf is not equal to 1, line 6 gets a reference to the matching Student object in the list. Because the value returned by allStudents(index) is type Object, we must cast it into a Student type. Then, line 7 adds the student to the list box. Lines 9–11 copy the student's property values into the three text boxes on the form, so they will show the same data as the list box.

Summary

A great many applications build, search, and maintain lists of objects. The ArrayList class is an ideal tool for storing objects because of its rich set of methods and properties. Remember, if you want to call the Contains or IndexOf methods to search for objects, the class defining the items in the collection must override the Equals method.

 ### Checkpoint

7. If you plan to call the IndexOf method on an ArrayList containing custom objects, the class defining the objects must contain which method?

8. If you plan to sort an ArrayList containing custom objects, the class defining the objects must implement which interface?

9. True or false: In an ArrayList containing objects, the IndexOf method returns −1 if an item is not found.

10. In the tutorial that builds an ArrayList of students, how were the objects uniquely identified?

 ## 3.3 List and Dictionary Classes

The ArrayList class does not limit the types of items that may be inserted in a single list. Therefore, we say that ArrayList is a **weakly typed collection**. Although this may seem like an advantage because it offers the flexibility to create a collection containing various types of objects, it can lead to unintended runtime errors. For example, an application might throw an exception if a reference to one of the ArrayList members turned out to be a different type than expected. In that case, a call to the *CType* method could generate an invalid cast exception.

Invalid Cast Example

Let's look at an example of how the weak typing in an ArrayList can cause problems. In the following code, Student and Employee objects are inserted in the same ArrayList named *myList*:

```
Class Student
  '...
End Class
Class Employee
  '...
End Class

Sub Test()
  Dim myList As New ArrayList
  myList.Add(New Student)
  myList.Add(New Employee)

  ' The next line throws an exception.
  For Each item As Student In myList
    lstItems.Add(item.ToString())
  Next
End Sub
```

But when the code loops through the list with the *For Each* statement, an InvalidCastException is thrown. Figure 3-8 shows the resulting error message. Runtime conversion errors like this are difficult to catch during manual testing. The application might appear to work correctly during numerous tests. But at a later time, a certain sequence of inputs could cause the application to fail. There are workarounds, of course. You could surround every *For Each* statement with *Try* and *Catch* statements that would catch this type of conversion error. But doing so would require the inconvenience of extra work and planning. To avoid the type of conversion error we have been talking about, modern programming languages support strongly typed collections.

Figure 3-8 InvalidCastException

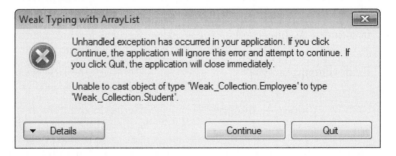

Strongly Typed Collections

A **strongly typed collection** is a collection that contains only a single type of object. The most common way to implement such a collection is through the use of *generic classes,* which can be found in the .NET *Systems.Collections.Generic* namespace. A **generic class** is a class that takes on a specific data type only when an instance of the class is created. From that point on in the application, the class is bound to the data type of its elements. (Another type of object can be inserted only if there exists an automatic conversion from that type to the type declared in the collection.)

Table 3-2 describes a few generic classes related to lists and dictionaries, which we demonstrate in this chapter. The .NET Library contains other generic classes, which you can read about in the online MSDN documentation at http://msdn.microsoft.com.

Table 3-2 Selected classes in the *System.Collections.Generic* namespace

Class or Structure	Description
List(Of Type)	A sequential list containing objects of the same type.
Dictionary(Of KeyType, ValueType)	A class that represents a collection of keys and values. The keys must all be unique. Each value is associated with a single key.
SortedDictionary(Of KeyType, ValueType)	A Dictionary class in which the keys are kept in sorted order.
KeyValuePair(Of KeyType, ValueType)	Represents a single Dictionary entry.

List(Of *Type*)

List(Of *Type*) is a class that holds strongly typed sequential collection of items. It is a useful substitute for the ArrayList class. It has nearly identical methods and properties as ArrayList, and it enforces strict type checking on the items you insert into it. Table 3-3 lists some of the more commonly used List properties and methods.

Table 3-3 Selected ArrayList properties and methods

Property or Method	Description
Add(item As *Type*)	Adds a new item to the end of the list.
Clear()	Removes all items from the list.
Contains(item As *Type*) As Boolean	Returns True if the list contains the given item.
Count() As Integer	Returns a count of the number of items in the list
Insert(index As Integer, item As *Type*)	Inserts an item into the list at a specified index position.
Item(index As Integer) As *Type*	Returns a reference to the list item at a specified index position.
Remove(item As *Type*)	Removes the first occurrence of a specified item from the list.
RemoveAt(index As Integer)	Removes the item at a specified index position.
Sort()	Sorts the list.
ToArray() As Array(of *Type*)	Returns a strongly typed array of objects from the ArrayList

Example: List of Integers

The following code declares a List(Of Integer) object and adds three integers to the list:

```
Dim intList As New List(Of Integer)
intList.Add(30)
intList.Add(10)
intList.Add(20)
```

The *Clear* method removes all items.

```
intList.Clear()
```

The *Item* property retrieves a reference to a list item, using an index to identify the item's position.

```
Dim X As Integer = intList.Item(1)
```

The *For Each* statement loops through a List. The following lines copy the List items to a ListBox:

```
For Each M As Integer In intList
  lstBox.Items.Add(M)
Next
```

The *Contains* method returns *True* if a matching value is found.

```
Dim found As Boolean = intList.Contains(20)
```

The *IndexOf* method returns the index position of a matching item, or −1 if the item is not found.

```
Dim index As Integer = intList.IndexOf(20)
```

The *Remove* method removes a matching item. If the value is not found, the statement has no effect.

```
intList.Remove(30)
```

The *RemoveAt* method removes an item at a given index position.

```
intList.RemoveAt(0)
```

The *Sort* method sorts the elements in ascending order.

```
intList.Sort()
```

The *ToArray* method returns an array containing the list items.

```
intList.ToArray()
```

The List class contains many other methods, which you can read about in the online MSDN documentation.

If You Want to Know More: Sorting with a Comparator

Sometimes, you may want to sort a List in a nonstandard way, such as sorting in descending order. Or, you might want to sort on some other property than the one used by the CompareTo method. To do so, you need to define a method called a **comparator,** which compares any two list elements based on your needs. The method must have this general format:

```
Public Function MethodName(ByVal val1 As Type,
  ByVal val2 As Type) As Integer
```

You can use any identifiers you like for *MethodName*, *val1*, and *val2*. The two parameters represent any pair of values that are compared during the sorting process. The *Type* in this general format must match the type of objects in the List.

Sorting functions always perform comparisons between pairs of arrays or list items. A comparator by itself, does not sort a list—you must still call the Sort method from the List class. You just need to tell the Sort method how you want the list items to be compared.

Student Comparator Example

Suppose we want to sort a list of Student objects. We will assume that the Student class already contains a CompareTo method that compares Students by their ID numbers. We might create the following list of Students and call the Sort method:

```
Dim stuList As New List(Of Student)
stuList.Add(New Student(1234, "Jones"));
```

```
stuList.Add(New Student(4023, "Baker"));
stuList.Add(New Student(5612, "Gonzalez"));
stuList.Add(New Student(1001, "Chong"));
stuList.Sort()
```

The list would now be sorted in ascending order by ID number:

```
1001    Chong
1234    Jones
4023    Baker
5612    Gonzalez
```

But we might also want to sort the list in ascending order by last name. To accomplish that, we would first create a comparator method that compares the LastName properties of the objects:

```
Public Function CompareNames(ByVal X As Student,
   ByVal Y As Student) As Integer
   Return X.LastName.CompareTo(Y.LastName)
End Function
```

Then we would sort the list by passing the address of the comparator to the Sort method:

```
studentList.Sort(AddressOf CompareNames)
```

After sorting, the list of students would be sorted in ascending order by last name:

```
4023    Baker
1001    Chong
5612    Gonzalez
1234    Jones
```

Dictionary(Of *KeyType, ValueType*)

The **Dictionary(Of *KeyType, ValueType*) class** maps a set of keys to a set of values. In other words, each key in the dictionary has a single value associated with that key. The keys must be unique, but the values need not be unique. A Dictionary is optimized for searching through a large number of keys. If you had 20 million items in a Dictionary, for example, the key of a single item would be found instantly. If you were to search for an item in an ArrayList, the search would take a good deal longer. We say that each Dictionary entry is a *pair*, consisting of a key and a value.

It's important to select a suitable property in your class to use as a Dictionary key. Look for a property whose value will be unique for every item you insert in the Dictionary. If you were inserting employees, for example, the ID property of the Employee class would probably be a good choice for a key. On the other hand, the LastName property would not make a good key because two employees might have the same last name.

The classes of dictionary keys must implement the IComparable interface, and they must override the Equals method. Therefore, it is easiest to use a standard .NET data type as a Dictionary key. Common choices are Integer and String. The associated values can be any data type, with no special restrictions.

Creating a Dictionary

When you declare a Dictionary object, supply the types of its key and value pair. The general format is:

```
Dim varName As New Dictionary(Of keytype, valuetype)
```

For example, the following code declares a Dictionary named *salaries*, using integers as keys and Decimals as the values associated with the keys:

```
Dim salaries As New Dictionary(Of Integer, Decimal)
```

Adding Entries to a Dictionary

The *Add* method adds a key/value pair to a Dictionary. The following lines, for example, add several employee IDs and salary values to the *salaries* Dictionary:

```
salaries.Add(3001, 50000D)
salaries.Add(2020, 45000D)
salaries.Add(3125, 64500D)
salaries.Add(2501, 32800D)
```

When inserting key/value pairs, their data types must match the data types used when declaring the Dictionary. That is why we call the Dictionary a *strongly typed collection*. The following statement would be incorrect because it tries to insert a string key and a salary of type Double:

```
salaries.Add("1002", 34000.2)
```

On the other hand, we can pass an integer as the second argument because integers are automatically converted to Decimals:

```
Dim N As Integer = 35000
salaries.Add("1002", N)
```

So to be more precise, the argument types must be *assignment-compatible* with the parameter types of the Add method.

The *Count* property indicates the number of Dictionary entries. The following statement assigns the count to a Label:

```
lblCount.Text = "There are " & salaries.Count & " entries"
```

The *Clear* method removes all entries from a Dictionary.

Looping Through Dictionary Entries

Each entry in a Dictionary is a **KeyValuePair** object, containing two properties: *Key* and *Value*. When you declare a KeyValuePair, you must be specific about the types of the key and the value. This is how we must declare it for the *salaries* Dictionary:

```
Dim entry As KeyValuePair(Of Integer, Decimal)
```

Then we can use the *entry* variable when coding a *For Each* statement. It holds the key and value of each Dictionary entry. The following code adds several entries to the *salaries* dictionary and then copies the entries to a ListBox:

```
salaries.Add(3001, 50000D)
salaries.Add(2020, 45000D)
salaries.Add(3125, 64500D)
salaries.Add(2501, 32800D)

For Each entry In salaries
   lstBox.Items.Add(entry.Key & "-->" & entry.Value)
Next
```

The loop produces the following output:

```
3001-->50000
2020-->45000
3125-->64500
2501-->32800
```

Finding, Modifying, and Removing Entries

You cannot use an integer index to access a particular position in a dictionary. To find a Dictionary entry, you must pass the key you want to find to the *Item* property. The following statement returns 45,000, the salary of the employee whose ID number is 2020:

```
Dim salary As Decimal = salaries.Item(2020)
```

If you try to get the value associated with a nonexistent key, the Item property throws a *KeyNotFoundException*.

If you assign a value to the Item property and reference an existing key, the Dictionary replaces the value associated with the key. For example, the following statement replaces the salary of employee 3001:

```
salaries.Item(3001) = 62000D
```

If you assign a value to the Item property and reference a key that is not in the Dictionary, a new entry is created and inserted. The following statement inserts a new entry in the Dictionary, assuming that the key 2025 does not already exist:

```
salaries.Item(2025) = 72000D
```

The **Remove** method removes the entry whose key matches the method's input parameter. Its general format is:

```
dictionaryName.Remove(key) As Boolean
```

If the key is found and the item is removed, Remove returns *True*. Otherwise, Remove returns *False*. For example, the following statement removes the entry whose key is 3125:

```
salaries.Remove(3125)
```

Extension Methods

Extension methods are a feature in .NET that let developers add new methods to existing classes. The Dictionary class has a large number of such methods associated with its Keys and Values collections. A few of the most common ones are listed in Table 3-4. Here are a few examples:

```
Dim average As Decimal = salaries.Values.Average()
Dim sum as Decimal = salaries.Values.Sum()
Dim minVal As Decimal = salaries.Values.Min()
```

Table 3-4 Sample extension methods in a Dictionary entry

Extension Method	Description
Values.Average	Returns the average of the values
Values.Sum	Returns the sum of the values
Values.ToArray	Returns an array containing the values
Values.Max	Returns the largest value
Values.Min	Returns the smallest value
Keys.Max	Returns the largest key
Keys.Min	Returns the smallest key

SortedDictionary Class

A **SortedDictionary** is a dictionary that maintains its keys in a specific order. Here is an example:

```
Dim orderedSalaries As New SortedDictionary(Of Integer, Decimal)
```

All of the methods and properties we discussed for the Dictionary class apply equally well to the SortedDictionary class.

You can pass an existing Dictionary object to the constructor of a SortedDictionary, as long as their key and value types are the same. For example, the following statement makes a copy of the *salaries* Dictionary when creating *orderedSalaries*:

```
Dim orderedSalaries As New SortedDictionary(Of Integer, Decimal)
    (salaries)
```

Tutorial 3-3:
Creating a text concordance

In this tutorial, you will create an application that builds a *concordance*, which is a catalog of words found in a document. The input file will be a text file containing words separated by spaces. The set of words will be saved as the keys collection in a Dictionary object, and each value associated with a key will be a List(Of Integer) containing the line numbers where the word was found in the input file. The Dictionary will be declared like this:

```
Private wordDict As New Dictionary(Of String, List(Of Integer))
```

When the application starts, the user will be able to select the *Open* command from the File menu, as shown in Figure 3-9. An OpenFileDialog control will appear and let the user select the input file. The file is read into a string list, and each word from the file is inserted into the dictionary. In Figure 3-10, the application is now ready to let the user search for a word. The user types in a single word and clicks the *Find* button to view a list of all lines from the file that contain the word (Figure 3-11). The file we have used as a sample contains the first ten chapters of *Moby Dick* by Herman Melville, available from the *Project Gutenberg* foundation (*www.gutenberg.org*). The performance of the program is excellent: It catalogs 4,256 words with no noticeable time delay. Searching for a single word is also instantaneous. If the user clicks the *All* button, the entire list of dictionary words appears in a multicolumn list box (Figure 3-12).

Before starting to create the application, we will briefly review the OpenFileDialog control, which was covered in our *Starting Out with Visual Basic 2010* book.

Figure 3-9 On startup, the user will select the input file

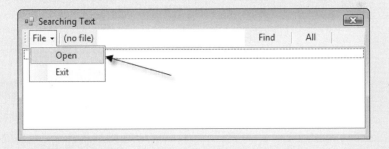

Figure 3-10 Input file loaded and ready to search for a word

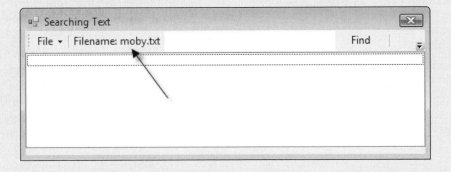

Figure 3-11 Displaying lines containing the selected word *whale*

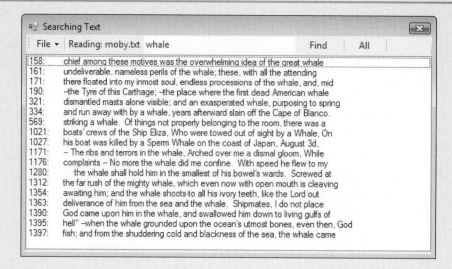

Figure 3-12 Displaying the entire dictionary

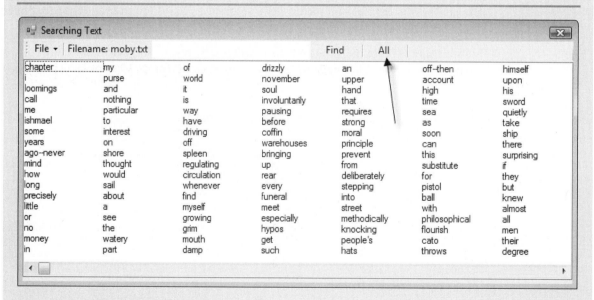

OpenFileDialog Control

The OpenFileDialog control lets the user select a file in a standard Windows dialog. It has an *InitialDirectory* property that allows the dialog to point to a particular directory when it opens. Let's assume that the control is named *ofdOpenFile*. The following statement assigns to it the application's current directory value, returned by the *GetCurrentDirectory* method:

```
ofdOpenFile.InitialDirectory = Directory.GetCurrentDirectory()
```

In addition, we can ask the dialog to display only certain types of files by setting the *Filter* property to a description, separated by a vertical bar from a wildcard name (*.txt):

```
ofdOpenFile.Filter = "Text files|*.txt"
```

The **ShowDialog** method displays the dialog window. The user clicks either the *Open* or *Cancel* button to close the dialog window. The method returns a **DialogResult** value that we can use to find out which button was clicked.

```
Dim result As DialogResult = ofdOpenFile.ShowDialog()
```

A simple If statement checks for the *Open* button (listed as *DialogResult.OK*).

```
If result = DialogResult.OK Then
```

If a file has been selected, the dialog's **FileName** property will now contain a complete path to the file.

The OpenFileDialog has an **OpenFile** method that opens the file selected by the user and returns a *System.IO.Stream* object. We can pass that object to the constructor for the StreamReader class, so the application can use the *infile* variable to read lines from the file.

```
Dim infile As StreamReader = New StreamReader(ofdOpenFile.
   OpenFile())
```

Filtering a String

When reading words from the input file in this tutorial, we want to remove any trailing punctuation marks such as commas and periods. We can define a string containing common punctuation characters and convert the string to a character array.

```
Dim filterOut As Char() = ("?':;.,!"" ").ToCharArray()
```

Later, when we have read a word from the file, we can call the *TrimEnd* method, passing it the character array that holds all characters that we want to trim from the string.

```
word = word.TrimEnd(filterOut)
```

So, a word like "Street;" would be converted to "Street".

We can also convert the input word to lowercase letters, making it easier to find matching words later on.

```
word = word.ToLower()
```

When examining a word, we might want to know if the first character is a letter. The Char class has a convenient method that returns either True or False.

```
If Char.IsLetter(word(0)) Then ...
```

Tutorial Steps

Step 1: Create a new application named *Concordance Builder*.

Step 2: Copy the file named *moby.txt* from the chapter examples folder into your project folder.

Step 3: Add the controls listed in Table 3-5 to the form. Refer again to Figure 3-9 for the control locations. The DropDownButton on the tool strip contains a *File* menu with two subitems: *Open* and *Exit*. The tool strip also contains a few separators, which are optional.

Table 3-5 Controls in the Concordance Builder application

Control Type	Control Name	Properties
Form		Text: *Searching Text*
ToolStrip		
ListBox	lstBox	ColumnWidth: *100*
ToolStripLabel	lblFileName	Text: *(no file)*
ToolStripTextBox	txtSearchWord	
ToolStripDropDownButton		
ToolStripMenuItem	mnuFileOpen	Text: *Open*
ToolStripMenuItem	mnuFileExit	Text: *Exit*
ToolStripButton	btnFind	Text: *Find*
ToolStripButton	btnAll	Text: *All*
OpenFileDialog	ofdOpenFile	

Step 4: Open the startup form's code window and add an Imports statement above the class, as follows:

```
Imports System.IO
```

Step 5: Inside the class, insert the following declarations:

```
Private infile As StreamReader
Private wordDict As New Dictionary(Of String, List(Of Integer))
Private rawText As New List(Of String)
```

The *rawText* variable holds all input lines from the file, so we can display these lines later in the list box when the user searches for a word.

Step 6: Add the *OpenInputFile* function, which returns *True* if a file was selected by the user. We have already discussed the mechanics of the OpenFileDialog.

```
 1: Private Function OpenInputFile() As Boolean
 2:    ' Displays an OpenFileDialog control and lets the user
 3:    ' select the input file.
 4:    With ofdOpenFile
 5:      .InitialDirectory = Directory.GetCurrentDirectory()
 6:      .FileName = "*.txt"
 7:      Dim result As DialogResult = .ShowDialog()
 8:      If result = DialogResult.OK Then
 9:        infile = New StreamReader(.OpenFile())
10:        lblFileName.Text = "Filename: " _
11:          & Path.GetFileName(.FileName)
12:        Return True
13:      Else
14:        Return False
15:      End If
16:    End With
17: End Function
```

Line 10 copies the filename from the OpenFileDialog control into a label on the tool strip. The call to *Path.GetFileName* returns just the filename after stripping off the long directory path.

Step 7:   Next, add the following Click handler for the *File | Open* menu command:

```
1:  Private Sub mnuFileOpen_Click() Handles mnuFileOpen.Click
2:    ' The user has clicked the File | Open menu item.
3:    If Not OpenInputFile() Then Return
4:
5:    ' Read each line and insert each new word into the
6:    ' dictionary. For each existing word, add its line
7:    ' number to the list for that word entry.
8:    Dim linenum As Integer = 0
9:    Dim filterOut As Char() = ("?':;.,!""").ToCharArray()
10:
11:   Do While Not infile.EndOfStream()
12:      Dim temp As String = infile.ReadLine()
13:      If temp.Trim().Length = 0 Then Continue Do
14:
15:      rawText.Add(temp)
16:      Dim words() As String = temp.Split(" "c)
17:
18:      For Each word As String In words
19:        word = word.TrimEnd(filterOut).ToLower()
20:        If word.Length > 0 AndAlso Char.IsLetter(word(0)) Then
21:          If Not wordDict.ContainsKey(word) Then
22:            wordDict.Add(word, New List(Of Integer))
23:          End If
24:          wordDict(word).Add(linenum)
25:        End If
26:      Next
27:      linenum += 1
28:   Loop
29: End Sub
```

This is a long method, so let's go through the code carefully. Line 3 calls OpenInputFile, and exits if the user canceled the dialog. Line 8 creates a variable named *linenum*, which will keep track of the line read most recently from the file. Line 11 repeats the loop until the end of the input file. Line 12 reads a complete line of input from the file, and line 15 adds the line to the *rawText* list we declared earlier. Line 13 skips the rest of the loop if a blank line is found and goes right back to line 11. Line 16 splits the input line into an array of words.

Line 18 begins a new loop whose job is to take each word in the array, trim it and convert it to lowercase (line 19), and make sure it is not blank and it begins with a letter (line 20). Then on line 21, we check if the word is already in the dictionary. If it is not, we add the word to the dictionary (line 22) and give it a new empty line number list. On line 24, we add the current line number to the list associated with the current word. Line 27 increments the line number, and the loop goes back to read another line from the file (line 12).

Step 8:   Add a Click handler for the *All* button, which displays all words in the dictionary.

```
Private Sub btnAll_Click() Handles btnAll.Click
  lstBox.MultiColumn = True
  lstBox.Items.Clear()
  For Each entry As KeyValuePair(Of String,
    List(Of Integer)) In wordDict
    lstBox.Items.Add(entry.Key)
  Next
End Sub
```

Notice how the code sets the MultiColumn property in the list box to display as many words as possible at the same time.

Step 9: Create a Click handler for the *Find* button. Its job is to look for the user's word in the dictionary and then pull out all matching lines from the *rawText* list.

```
 1: Private Sub btnFind_Click() Handles btnFind.Click
 2:    lstBox.MultiColumn = False
 3:    lstBox.Items.Clear()
 4:    If wordDict.ContainsKey(txtSearchWord.Text) Then
 5:      For Each lineNum As Integer In wordDict(
 6:        txtSearchWord.Text)
 7:        lstBox.Items.Add(lineNum & ":" & vbTab _
 8:          & rawText(lineNum))
 9:      Next
10:    Else
11:      lstBox.Items.Add("(word not found)")
12:    End If
13: End Sub
```

Line 4 calls *ContainsKey* to find out if the word (in txtSearchWord.Text) exists in the dictionary. This type of search executes very quickly. If the word is found, the following expression returns a *List(Of Integer)* object containing the line numbers where the word was found in the input file:

```
wordDict(txtSearchWord.Text)
```

Line 5 loops through the list of line numbers. Line 7 uses each line number as an index into the *rawText* List object, and inserts the text line into the list box. Finally, if the user's word is not found, line 11 displays a failure message in the list box.

Step 10: Finally, insert a Click handler for the *File | Exit* menu item.

```
Private Sub mnuFileExit_Click() Handles mnuFileExit.Click
  Me.Close()
End Sub
```

Step 11: Save the project and run the application. Open the *moby.txt* file from your project directory. Click the *All* button to display all words found in the file.

Step 12: Input a word into the text box that you would like to find, and click the *Find* button. You should see a list of the lines from the file that contain your word.

If you have another file you would like to search, repeat the process shown in Steps 11 and 12.

Summary

There is no limit to the ways in which lists and dictionaries can be combined. For example, you could create a list of dictionary objects. Each dictionary object might contain a key and an associated list (as we did in Tutorial 3-3). Each member of that list could be a Dictionary that holds yet another list.

The Dictionary class offers outstanding performance when you have a large number of items, or when you want to perform advanced operations on its data. Also, it does not require you to implement the Equals method in the class defining values inserted in the dictionary. The Dictionary keys, on the other hand, must be comparable.

Checkpoint

11. What is a weakly typed collection?

12. What is a generic class?

13. Which generic classes were described in this chapter?

14. When calling the List.Contains method, what restriction is placed on the class that defines the list elements?

15. Why is a comparator useful?

3.4 Language Integrated Query (LINQ)

Language Integrated Query (LINQ), is a query language built into .NET that can be used to display information from different types of data sources. For example, LINQ can query collections of objects (arrays, Lists, ArrayLists) in memory, databases, XML files, Excel spreadsheets, and so on.

A group of smart people at Microsoft had a good idea: If SQL is such a powerful language for searching (querying) databases, why not invent a similar type of language in .NET that can query many types of data, not just databases? And so, LINQ was born. In this chapter, we introduce a simple type of LINQ known as **LINQ for Objects.**

The simplest LINQ query revolves around four clauses: *From, Where, Select, and Order By*

- *From*—Identifies the data source, which can be object such as an array or List
- *Where* (optional)—Holds a Boolean expression that selects which values will be copied from the data source
- *Select*—Identifies the name of the field(s) that will be returned by the query
- *Order By* (optional)—Indicates how the results of the query will be ordered

The *From* and *Select* clauses are required.

Array Example

We will show how to use LINQ to query an array of integers. Let's begin with the following array declaration:

```
Dim intNumbers() As Integer = {4, 104, 2, 102, 1, 101, 3, 103}
```

The following LINQ statement returns all array values that are greater than 100:

```
Dim query = From item In intNumbers
   Where item > 100
   Select item
```

Let's take a closer look at the statement. First, notice that the statement begins with *Dim query*. We are declaring an object named *query* that defines a LINQ query, but we have not specified a data type. Visual Basic automatically determines the data type for the object, a technique known as **type inference.**

On the right side of the = operator is the query definition, which examines each item in the *intNumbers* array to see if the value is greater than 100, and if it is, to select the value.

```
From item In intNumbers
   Where item > 100
   Select item
```

Once the query has been defined, you can use it in different ways. You can loop through it, you can build another query from it, or you can pass the query to another method.

For example, the following code segment loops through the query (executing it) and adds each value to a list box named *lstResults*:

```
For Each intNum As Integer In query
   lstResults.Items.Add(intNum)
Next
```

Because the intNumbers array contains {4, 104, 2, 102, 1, 101, 3, 103}, our query will show the values 104, 102, 101, and 103 in the list box, in that order.

To sort the results of the LINQ query in ascending order, we can use the *Order By* operator, as shown here:

```
Dim query = From item In intNumbers
   Where item > 100
   Select item
   Order By item
```

LINQ uses operators such as *Where*, *Select*, and *Order By*, which are similar to operators in the SQL database query language. The operators are part of Visual Basic and can be checked by the compiler before the application runs. This makes it easier to know if you have made a mistake.

> **TIP:** **Anonymous types** are data types that are not explicitly declared anywhere in a program. Some expressions, particularly those created by LINQ queries, have types that can be determined only at runtime. So Visual Basic uses *type inference* to figure out the expression's type at runtime. You can create an anonymous type yourself, as we do in the following code:
>
> ```
> Dim aCustomer = New With {.Name = "Joe Smith",
>                           .Age = 22, .City = "Miami"}
> ```

Example: Selecting Even Integers from an Array

In this example, we query an array of integers, looking for the even values (evenly divisible by 2). Also, we sort them in ascending order:

```
Dim numbers() As Integer = {4, 3, 2, 1, 6, 9, 7}

Dim evensQuery = From num In numbers
   Where (num Mod 2 = 0)
   Order By num
   Select num
```

The expression *num Mod 2* returns the remainder after dividing num by 2. If the remainder equals zero, the number must be even. The values produced by evensQuery are {2, 4, 6}.

You can modify a query after it has been created. For example, the following statement reverses the order of the values generated by evensQuery:

```
evensQuery = evensQuery.Reverse()
```

What type of variable is evensQuery? It is defined as a strongly typed interface named *IOrderedEnumerable(Of Integer)*. The important point here is that the elements produced by this query "know" that they are Integers. We'll see how that matters when we start producing queries from lists of more complex objects, such as Students or Accounts.

Building a Query from an Existing Query

The *evensQuery* produced the even numbers {2, 4, 6}. We can build a second query that further limits the values produced by evensQuery. The following query named *evensLarge* produces just one value, 6:

```
Dim evensLarge = From num in evensQuery
   Where num > 4
   Select num
```

Extension Properties and Methods

An **extension method** is a method that returns a modified version of the output from a LINQ query. One such extension method is named *Count*.

```
evensQuery.Count()
```

It is important to realize that evensQuery does not contain actual data—instead, it is a variable that contains a query. You can modify the query, pass the variable as a parameter, or assign it to another variable. LINQ uses *deferred execution*, which means that a LINQ query does not execute until we actually use it. That might be when we fill a list box with the values or use the items in some other way.

In the following code, we copy the list of output values generated by *evensQuery* to a List-Box and then display the average value of the integers produced by evensQuery:

```
For Each number In evensQuery
   lstBox.Items.Add(number.ToString())
Next


' Display the average value of evensQuery.
lblAverage.Text = "Average = " & evensQuery.Average()
```

Querying a List of Objects

LINQ makes it easy to query lists and dictionaries of objects. In particular, you can refer to object properties by name. To show how this works, we will create a *List(Of Student)* and design LINQ queries that work with the list. We will assume that the following Student class has been defined, and it has a constructor with parameters:

```
Public Class Student
   Public Property Id As String
   Public Property LastName As String
   Public Property Status As Integer          'values: 1,2,3,4
   Public Property Gpa As Double              'grade point average
   Public Property Major As String
   'etc.
End Class
```

We can populate a List with Student objects, as follows:

```
Dim studentList As New List(Of Student)
With studentList
   .Add(New Student("1241", "Jones", 1, 3.2, "BIO"))
   .Add(New Student("1641", "Baker", 2, 3.9, "ENG"))
   .Add(New Student("1001", "Charles", 1, 2.6, "BIO"))
   .Add(New Student("2205", "Smith", 2, 3.1, "MTH"))
   .Add(New Student("1961", "Davis", 2, 2.2, "ENG"))
   .Add(New Student("2210", "Chong", 3, 2.4, "BIO"))
   .Add(New Student("1975", "Perez", 3, 4.0, "ENG"))
End With
```

The following LINQ query selects all students from *studentList* and sorts the results in ascending order by the Student.Id property:

```
Dim query = From aStudent In studentList
   Select aStudent
   Order by aStudent.Id
```

The following query selects all students from the list and sorts by Last name:

```
Dim query = From aStudent In studentList
   Select aStudent
   Order by aStudent.LastName
```

You can very easily assign a query's output to a DataGridView control, as shown in Figure 3-13. Just convert the query's output to a List and assign it to the DataSource property of the grid.

```
dgvStudents.DataSource = query.ToList()
```

If you want to display only some of each object's properties, you can list them in the *Select* clause, as follows:

```
Dim query = From aStudent In studentList
   Select aStudent.Major, aStudent.LastName
   Order By Major
dgvStudents.DataSource = query.ToList()
```

The result is a convenient listing of students by major, as shown in Figure 3-14.

Figure 3-13 Displaying a LINQ query in a DataGridView control

Id	LastName	Status	Gpa	Major
1001	Charles	1	2.6	BIO
1241	Jones	1	3.2	BIO
1641	Baker	2	3.9	ENG
1961	Davis	2	2.2	ENG
1975	Perez	3	4	ENG
2205	Smith	2	3.1	MTH
2210	Chong	3	2.4	BIO

List of Students — Sort by Select

Figure 3-14 Listing of students by major

List of Students — Sort by Select View

Major	LastName
BIO	Jones
BIO	Charles
BIO	Chong
ENG	Baker
ENG	Davis
ENG	Perez
MTH	Smith

Filtering the Rows

The *Where* operator in a LINQ query provides the filtering, or selecting of rows from a data source. You can use any combination of object properties, comparison operators, method calls, and compound operators. Let's look at some examples.

The following query selects only students with a grade point average (GPA) over 3.0 and sorts the results in descending order:

```
Dim query = From aStudent In studentList
   Select aStudent
   Where aStudent.Gpa > 3.0
   Order By aStudent.Gpa Descending
```

The following query selects only students with a GPA under 3.2 who are biology (BIO) majors:

```
Dim query = From aStudent In studentList
   Select aStudent
   Where aStudent.Gpa < 3.2 And aStudent.Major = "BIO"
   Order By aStudent.Gpa Descending
```

Rather than using constant values for comparison, you can use values in text boxes:

```
Dim query = From aStudent In studentList
   Select aStudent
   Where aStudent.Gpa < CDbl(txtGpa.Text) And
     aStudent.Major = txtMajor.Text
   Order By aStudent.Gpa Descending
```

We could write code that loops through studentList and perform the comparisons ourselves, of course. But LINQ does this type of work so much more easily. In Tutorial 3-4, you will look at various ways to query a list of students and to calculate useful statistics on the list.

Tutorial 3-4:
Performing LINQ queries on a list

In this tutorial, you will examine an application that uses LINQ queries to display, sort, filter, and calculate statistics on a list of students. The startup form has a menu with selections that let the user choose different sorts and filters. The results of the queries are displayed in a DataGridView control. Figure 3-15, for example, shows the output from a LINQ query that sorts by last name in descending order.

Figure 3-15 Sorting students by last name in descending order

Id	LastName	Status	Gpa	Major
2205	Smith	2	3.1	MTH
1975	Perez	3	4	ENG
1241	Jones	1	3.2	BIO
1961	Davis	2	2.2	ENG
2210	Chong	3	2.4	BIO
1001	Charles	1	2.6	BIO
1641	Baker	2	3.9	ENG

The *Statistics* form in Figure 3-16 displays statistics gathered from the list, using LINQ queries and extension methods. It shows the average GPA of all students, the range of GPA values from smallest to largest, and the average GPA of the major that was selected by the user from a list box. The list box itself is populated by a LINQ query.

Figure 3-16 Statistics form displays information about the student list

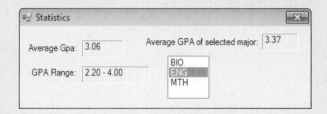

Tutorial Steps

Step 1: Open the sample project named *LINQ List of Students*.

Step 2: Examine the main menu items.

```
Sort by
  ID, ascending
  Last name, descending
Select
  Students with GPA > 3.0
  BIO majors with GPA < 3.2
View
  Statistics
```

Step 3: Open the code window and examine the following code:

```
Dim studentList As New List(Of Student)

Private Sub Form_Load() Handles MyBase.Load
  With studentList
    .Add(New Student("1241", "Jones", 1, 3.2, "BIO"))
    .Add(New Student("1641", "Baker", 2, 3.9, "ENG"))
    .Add(New Student("1001", "Charles", 1, 2.6, "BIO"))
    .Add(New Student("2205", "Smith", 2, 3.1, "MTH"))
    .Add(New Student("1961", "Davis", 2, 2.2, "ENG"))
    .Add(New Student("2210", "Chong", 3, 2.4, "BIO"))
    .Add(New Student("1975", "Perez", 3, 4.0, "ENG"))
  End With
End Sub
```

The studentList variable is declared as a List of Student objects.

Step 4: Examine the Click handler for the *Sort by / ID, ascending* menu item:

```
Private Sub mnuSortById_Click() Handles mnuSortById.Click
  ' Sort by ID, ascending
  Dim query = From aStudent In studentList
    Select aStudent
    Order By aStudent.Id
  ' Convert to List(Of Student)
  dgvStudents.DataSource = query.ToList()
End Sub
```

Step 5: Examine the Click handler for the *Sort by / Last name, descending* menu item:

```
Private Sub mnuSortByName_Click() Handles mnuSortByName.Click
  ' Sort by last name, descending
  Dim query = From aStudent In studentList
    Select aStudent
    Order By aStudent.LastName Descending
  dgvStudents.DataSource = query.ToList()
End Sub
```

Step 6: Examine the Click handler for the *Select / Student with GPA > 3.0* menu item:

```
Private Sub mnuSelectHighGpa_Click() _
  Handles mnuSelectHighGpa.Click
  ' Students with GPA greater than 3.0
  Dim query = From aStudent In studentList
    Select aStudent
    Where aStudent.Gpa > 3.0
    Order By aStudent.Gpa Descending
  dgvStudents.DataSource = query.ToList()
End Sub
```

Step 7: Examine the Click handler for the *Select / BIO majors with GPA < 3.2* menu item:

```
Private Sub mnuSelectBIO_Click() Handles mnuSelectBIO.Click
  ' BIO majors with GPA less than 3.2
  Dim query = From aStudent In studentList
    Select aStudent
    Where aStudent.Gpa < 3.2 And aStudent.Major = "BIO"
    Order By aStudent.Gpa Descending
  dgvStudents.DataSource = query.ToList()
End Sub
```

Step 8: Examine the Click handler for the *View / Statistics* menu item:

```
StatisticsForm.StudentList = studentList
StatisticsForm.ShowDialog()
```

Step 9: Run the application and verify that all queries based on menu items work correctly. Then stop the application.

Statistics Form

Step 10: Open the code window for the *Statistics* form. It contains a property that holds a reference to the list of students that was created in the *MainForm* class:

```
Public Class StatisticsForm
  Public Property StudentList As New List(Of Student)
```

Step 11: Examine the Form_Load event handler, which calculates the average GPA. Because we want only GPA values, the *Select* clause specifically identifies *aStudent.Gpa*:

```
Private Sub StatisticsForm_Load() Handles MyBase.Load
  'Calculate the average GPA.
  Dim GpaQuery = From aStudent In StudentList
    Select aStudent.Gpa
  lblAverageGpa.Text = GpaQuery.Average().ToString("n")
```

The extension method named *Average* returns the average value of all the values found by GpaQuery.

Continuing in the same event handler, extension methods are applied to the GpaQuery object to get the smallest (*Min*) and largest (*Max*) values returned by the query:

```
'Calculate the min and max GPAs.
lblGpaRange.Text = GpaQuery.Min().ToString("n") _
  & " - " & GpaQuery.Max().ToString("n")
```

Finally, the code fills the ListBox control with a single instance of each major. This is done first with a query (named *majors*) and then by calling the extension method named *Distinct*.

```
  'Fill the list box with major names.
  Dim majors = From aStudent In StudentList
    Select aStudent.Major
    Order By Major
  lstMajors.DataSource = majors.Distinct().ToList()
End Sub
```

Step 12: Examine the SelectedIndexChanged event handler for the ListBox.

```
Private Sub lstMajors_SelectedIndexChanged() _
  Handles lstMajors.SelectedIndexChanged
```

This method calculates the average GPA of students having the selected major, in two steps: First, it assigns a list of students who match the selected major to *majorQuery*.

```
Dim majorQuery = From aStudent In StudentList
    Select aStudent
    Where aStudent.Major = lstMajors.SelectedItem.ToString
```

Then, it uses majorQuery as the source for a second query that selects just the Gpa property of each student.

```
Dim gpaQuery = From aStudent In majorQuery
    Select aStudent.Gpa
```

Finally, when gpaQuery is assigned to the Label control, the *Average* extension method calculates the average GPA.

```
lblAvgGpaSelected.Text = gpaQuery.Average().ToString("n")
```

It is possible to combine the foregoing queries into a single nested query.

```
gpaQuery = From aStudent In (From aStudent In StudentList
    Select aStudent Where aStudent.Major =
    lstMajors.SelectedItem.ToString)
    Select aStudent.Gpa
```

Summary

This tutorial presented a few of the simplest types of queries available in LINQ for objects. It is worth noting that the types of operations performed on the data (min, max, average, select, sort) would require quite a bit of coding if LINQ were not used. Notice how easy it was to assign the results of the queries to a DataGridView control, just as you might do with an SQL Server DataTable.

Querying a Dictionary

You can perform LINQ queries on a Dictionary. Using the same Student class that we used in the previous examples, the following code fills the Dictionary with the same entries that we used for a List:

```
Dim studentColl As New Dictionary(Of Integer, Student)
With studentColl
   .Add(1241, New Student("1241", "Jones", 1, 3.2, "BIO"))
   .Add(1641, New Student("1641", "Baker", 2, 3.9, "ENG"))
   .Add(1001, New Student("1001", "Charles", 1, 2.6, "BIO"))
   .Add(2205, New Student("2205", "Smith", 2, 3.1, "MTH"))
   .Add(1961, New Student("1961", "Davis", 2, 2.2, "ENG"))
   .Add(2210, New Student("2210", "Chong", 3, 2.4, "BIO"))
   .Add(1975, New Student("1975", "Perez", 3, 4.0, "ENG"))
End With
```

Writing a LINQ query to process a Dictionary is a little different from writing a query for a List. Each entry in a Dictionary is of type *KeyValuePair*, which has two properties named *Key* and *Value*. The *Select* operator in a LINQ query needs to reference the Value property of the pair.

The following query selects all students from the Dictionary and sorts them by ID number:

```
Dim query = From aPair In studentColl
   Select aPair.Value
   Order By Value.Id
```

Because the expression *aPair.Value* returns a Student object, the *Order By* operator needs to use *Value.Id* to indicate the specific Student property for sorting the query results.

A simple alternative is to run the LINQ query on the *Values* collection of the Dictionary, which is itself a List. An example is shown here.

```
Dim query = From aStudent In studentColl.Values
   Select aStudent
   Order By aStudent.Id
```

Classes Containing Other Lists

One of the most powerful features of LINQ is its ability to access and search a list that may be inside another class. Suppose, for example, that a program declares a list of Account objects, as follows:

```
Dim accountList As List(Of Account)
```

Each Account contains an ID and a list of stocks.

```
Class Account
   Public Property ID As Integer
   Public Property Stocks As List(Of Stock)
End Class
```

A Stock object contains a Ticker symbol and a price.

```
Class Stock
   Public Property Ticker As String
   Public Property Price As Double
End Class
```

First, we can write a LINQ query that selects a single account that matches the ID number stored in a variable named *AcctIdToFind*.

```
Dim queryOne = From acct In accountList
   Where acct.ID = AcctIdToFind
   Select acct
```

Now that *queryOne* contains the selected Account object, we can call the *ElementAt* extension method to return a reference to the Account object and get its list of stocks.

```
Dim stockList As List(Of Stock) = queryOne.ElementAt(0).Stocks
```

Many programmers save space by combining all of this into a single query. Notice how parentheses must surround the first query before calling ElementAt:

```
stockList = (From acct In accountList
   Where acct.ID = AcctIdToFind
   Select acct).ElementAt(0).Stocks
```

Summary

LINQ has assumed an increasing level of importance in the .NET world over the past few years. Its greatest appeal is that it is designed to work directly with objects. Objects tend to be hierarchical in nature, so that a Student might reference a list of courses, each of which might then reference course catalog information. LINQ can save you a lot of coding time with its huge set of operators and extension methods.

 Checkpoint

16. What does LINQ stand for?

17. What are the three basic keywords in LINQ queries?

18. What data type is used when declaring a variable that holds a LINQ query?

19. What is an extension method?

20. When does a query execute?

Summary

3.1 ArrayLists

- The most fundamental .NET collection is the Collections.ArrayList class. It is the best replacement for the older Visual Basic Collection type, which has many limitations.
- The ArrayList class defines an expandable collection of references to objects.
- ArrayLists let you find, insert, and remove items; arrays do none of these tasks.
- The Add and Insert methods add new items to an ArrayList.
- The Remove and RemoveAt methods remove items.
- The Contains and IndexOf methods search for items.
- The Item property retrieves and replaces items.
- The Count property returns the number of items.

3.2 ArrayLists of Custom Objects

- When filling an ArrayList with instances of your own user-defined class, be sure to override the Equals method and implement the CompareTo method in your class.
- Always create a new instance of the user-defined class each time you insert a new object. You don't want to build an ArrayList in which all the items reference the same object.
- When an item in an array or ArrayList is a value type such as Integer or Single, the Item method returns a copy of the item.
- A reference to an item in an ArrayList can be used to modify the object that it references.

- An interface defines a set of methods and properties that can be implemented by other classes. The classes that implement the interface are guaranteed to contain these methods and properties.
- To *override the Equals method* means to create an Equals method in your own class that has exactly the same method signature as the Object.Equals method. You can select any property, variable, or method return value in your class to be compared when overriding Equals.

3.3 List and Dictionary Classes

- A *strongly typed collection* is a collection that contains only a single type of object.
- The most common way to create a strongly typed collection is through the use of generic classes, which can be found in the .NET Systems.Collections.Generic namespace.
- A *generic class* is a class that takes on a specific data type only when an instance of the class is created. From that point on in the application, the class is bound to the data type of its elements.
- The List(Of *ValueType*) class is a strongly typed List class.
- A *comparator* is a method that compares two list elements in a specific way.
- The Dictionary class maps a set of keys to a set of values. In other words, for each key in the dictionary, there is a single value associated with that key. The keys must be unique, but the values need not be unique.
- When you declare a Dictionary object, you supply the types of its key and value pair.
- Each entry in a Dictionary is a KeyValuePair object. It has two properties: Key and Value.
- A SortedDictionary is a dictionary that maintains its keys in a specific order.

3.4 Language Integrated Query (LINQ)

- LINQ, which stands for *Language Integrated Query*, is a query language built into Visual Basic that can be used to display information from different types of data sources.
- A query variable uses *type inference* to get its type based on the data returned by the query on the right side of the assignment operator.
- LINQ uses operators such as Where, Select, and Order By, which are similar to operators in the SQL database query language.
- LINQ operators are part of .NET and can be checked by the compiler before the application runs.
- LINQ provides many useful extension properties and extension methods that perform additional operations on queries.
- The Where operator in a LINQ query provides filtering, or selecting of rows from the data source.

Key Terms

anonymous types
ArrayList class
collection
comparator
CompareTo method
Dictionary(Of *KeyType*, *ValueType*) class
extension method
generic class
IComparable interface
interface
KeyValuePair
Language Integrated Query (LINQ)

LINQ for objects
list
List(Of *Type*)
map
method signature
override the Equals method
SortedDictionary
strongly typed collection
type inference
weakly typed collection

Review Questions

True or False

Indicate whether each of the following statements is true or false.

1. You must declare the size of an ArrayList when it is created.

2. An ArrayList can contain duplicate items.

3. If the ArrayList.IndexOf method does not find a matching item, it returns a value of zero.

4. If the ArrayList.Item property does not find a matching item, it throws an exception.

5. The ArrayList.Add method always adds the item at the end of the list.

6. When an item in an array or ArrayList is a value type such as Integer or Single, the Item method returns a copy of the item.

7. The CompareTo method in the Student class always has two Student parameters.

8. An interface defines a set of methods and properties that can be implemented by other classes.

9. The IComparable interface contains two methods.

10. The CompareTo method returns a Boolean result.

11. The Equals method always has a single Object parameter.

12. The Equals method always uses the Overrides keyword.

13. The List class can be used to create a strongly typed collection.

14. A generic class is often used to create a weakly typed collection.

15. The values in a Dictionary must be instances of a class that implements the CompareTo method, but the keys have no such restriction.

16. In a Dictionary, the values must be unique, but the keys need not be unique.

17. If you assign a value to the Item property and reference a key that is not in the Dictionary, a new entry is created and inserted.

18. The Dictionary class does not contain a Sort method.

19. A Dictionary automatically stores its keys in sorted order.

20. The OpenFileDialog control's OpenFile method returns a StreamReader object.

21. To get the application's current directory, call the Directory.GetCurrentDirectory method.

22. To get just the name of a file from a complete directory path, call the My.Application.GetFileName method.

23. To find out if a Dictionary has a certain key value, call the Contains method.

24. When you use LINQ to query a Dictionary of objects, you can refer to the object properties by name.

Short Answer

1. Why is it easier to insert a new item into index position 5 of an ArrayList than to do the same with an array?

2. If you want to sort an ArrayList containing Account objects, which interface must be implemented in the Account class?

3. If you want to call the Remove method in an ArrayList containing Account objects, which method must be implemented in the Account class?

4. Of the ArrayList methods and properties discussed in this chapter, which ones can throw an IndexOutOfRangeException?

5. What is the preferred way to loop through an ArrayList?

6. What common error is caused if you forget to use the New operator to create a separate object each time an object is inserted in an ArrayList?

7. Consider the following call to the CompareTo method:

```
Dim result As Integer = A.CompareTo(B)
```

What does result equal when object A is found to be less than B?

8. What happens if you call the Sort method on an ArrayList of Students, but there is no CompareTo method in the Student class?

9. Which generic class in this chapter has two data types in its definition?

10. Show how to declare a new List(of Student) objects named *stuList*.

11. What type of object is in each item of a Dictionary?

12. Show how to convert a List named *stuList* to an array of Student objects.

13. What type of method must you create if you want to sort a List of objects in a way that is different from the ordering implied by the objects' CompareTo method?

14. Write a definition of a Dictionary object named *myAccounts* in which the keys are strings and the values are Accounts.

15. Write a statement that adds a new entry to the Dictionary you created in Short Answer question 14.

16. What are the two properties of an item in a Dictionary?

17. If a String named *myLine* contains words separated by commas, show how to split it into an array of Strings named *words*.

18. Which Directory class method returns *True* when a certain key value is contained in its *Keys* collection?

Algorithm Workbench

Assume the following class declaration:

```
Public Class Account
    Public Property Id As String
    Public Property Name As String
    Public Property Balance As Double
    Public Property CreationDate As DateTime
    Public Property BalanceHistory As List(Of Double)
End Class
```

Assume that the following List contains a set of Account objects:

```
Dim accountList As New List(Of Account)
```

1. Write a LINQ statement that lists the accounts in ascending order by ID.

2. Write a LINQ statement that lists accounts created before 1/1/2005.

3. Write a LINQ statement that returns only the Name and Balance of the items in accountList.

4. Write LINQ statements that obtain the BalanceHistory of the account whose ID equals "10021." Assign the BalanceHistory property to a List variable.

Programming Challenges

1. Accounts Dictionary

Create an application that lists accounts from a Dictionary object. Create an Account class that contains an ID, name, and balance. Display the accounts in a ListBox, as shown in Figure 3-17. If the user enters new values, she or he can click on the *Add* button to add a new account to the dictionary. Or if the user clicks the *Replace* button, she or he can replace a dictionary item. Use exception handlers to catch errors caused by invalid input values, or an attempt to add a duplicate Account ID to the dictionary.

Figure 3-17 Adding an Account to the dictionary

```
┌─ Accounts Dictionary ─────────────────────────────────────[─][□][✕]─┐
│                                                                      │
│      Account ID:   [1041      ]        Accounts:                     │
│                                        ┌──────────────────────────┐  │
│                                        │ 1050, Jones, 800.50       │  │
│      Account Name: [Chong     ]        │ 1001, Adams, 750.18       │  │
│                                        │ 1020, Gonzalez, 1,800.21  │  │
│                                        │ 1032, Chong, 1,200.50     │  │
│      Balance:      [2300      ]        │                          │  │
│                                        │                          │  │
│         ┌────────┐   ┌─────────┐       │                          │  │
│         │  Add   │   │ Replace │       └──────────────────────────┘  │
│         └────────┘   └─────────┘                                     │
└──────────────────────────────────────────────────────────────────────┘
```

2. Stock Comparators

Write an application that sorts a List of *Stock* objects three different ways: by their ticker symbols (such as MSFT), their prices, and their price-to-earnings (P/E) ratios. The user can ask to sort in both ascending and descending order. Figure 3-18 shows the output after the user has clicked the *Sort by Ticker* button. In Figure 3-19, the list is sorted in descending order by stock price. In Figure 3-20, the list is sorted in ascending order by the P/E ratio.

Create a class named *Stock*, with the following properties: Ticker (String), Price (Double), Earnings (Double). Create a constructor that initializes these three values. Also, create a ReadOnly property named *PeRatio* that returns the stock's price divided by earnings.

In your startup form, create comparator methods and pass them to the List.Sort method.

Figure 3-18 Sorting in ascending order by ticker symbol

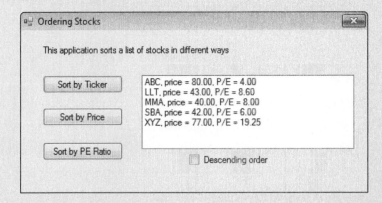

Figure 3-19 Sorting in descending order by price

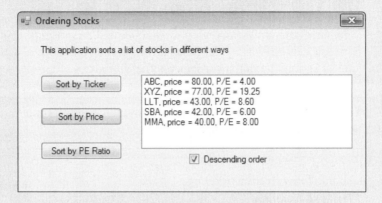

Figure 3-20 Sorting in ascending order by P/E ratio

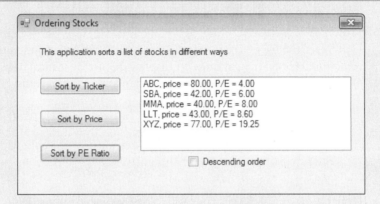

3. **Bank Teller Transaction Collection**

   Using the *Bank Teller* application presented in this chapter, build a list of transactions that you can display in a separate window. You should create a Transaction object and add it to a List or ArrayList inside the startup form class for the times when a user initiates a deposit or withdrawal. Add a button to the startup form that displays the transactions in a separate window called the *Transaction Log* form, shown in Figure 3-21.

Figure 3-21 Transaction Log window

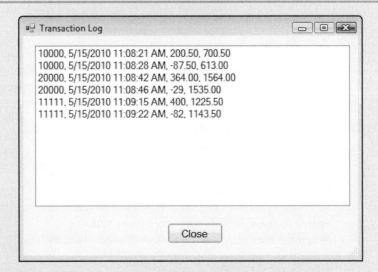

Create a Transaction class that holds information about a single transaction. It should contain the following properties: Account Number (String), TransactionDateTime, Amount (Decimal), and Balance (Decimal). The Balance property holds the account balance after the transaction was processed. A positive transaction amount indicates that a deposit was made. A negative amount indicates a withdrawal. The Transaction class should contain a constructor that initializes all properties, and a ToString method.

TIP: Pass the transaction list to the Transaction Log form before calling the Form.ShowDialog method.

4. **Bank Teller Transaction Log**

Using the solution program you wrote for Programming Challenge 3 as a starting point, modify it as follows. Log all transactions to a file. Transaction logging can be useful in a number of ways—when producing monthly account statements, for example, or when verifying and auditing account transactions. The log file should contain a separate printed line for each deposit and withdrawal transaction on customer accounts.

Replace the list of Transaction objects in the program's startup form with a single TransactionLog object. Continue to display the list of transactions in a separate window as before. But in the same button click handler, save the transaction log to a file by calling the TransactionLog.Save method.

TransactionLog Class

Create a TransactionLog class that is responsible for collecting transaction information and writing it to a text file. It should contain the following properties and methods:

Declaration	Description
ReadOnly Property Items() As Collection	Returns the collection of transactions stored inside the class.
Property FilePath() As String	Gets and sets the file path for the transaction log file.
ReadOnly LastError() As String	Displays the most recent error message that was generated by the class.
Sub Add(ByRef trans As Transaction)	Adds a new transaction to the log.
Function Save() As Boolean	Appends all logged transactions to the transaction file. Returns True if successful.

Internally, the TransactionLog class should use a List or ArrayList to hold the logged transactions. The *Save* method iterates over the collection and writes each transaction to a file. It must catch exceptions and set the LastError property if an exception is thrown.

5. **Club Committee Collections**

Using the Club Committee Organizer application that you wrote for Programming Challenge 2 in Chapter 2, make the following improvements:

- Create a class named *Committee* that contains a list of the students who are members of a single committee. The class should have a ReadOnly property that returns a reference to the class's internal collection variable.
- When the user selects different committees from the combo box, the application must remember which people were assigned to each committee. The only way to do this is

to store each list of names in a collection. Suppose the user adds Adams, Baker, and Chong to the Community Services committee, as in Figure 3-22. Next, the user selects another committee and adds some people to that one. If the user then returns to the Community Services committee, he or she should see Adams, Baker, and Chong in the list of current members.

In the startup form class, create a list of Committee objects. (Initialize the list with a loop in the Form_Load event handler.) When members are selected and copied into the committee list box, your code must add these members to the appropriate Committee object. Use the Committee list box's SelectedIndex property as a subscript that points to an element in the list of Committee objects.

Figure 3-22 Community Services contains three people

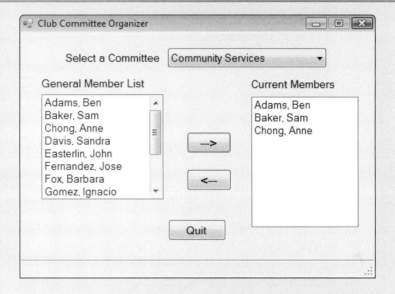

6. **FirstPlay Sports Rental**

Create an application named *FirstPlay Sports Rental* that keeps track of the inventory for a sports rental store.

Requirements Specification

- The user can input a new rental item and add it to the store inventory.
- The user can select an item's ID Number from a list and remove the item from the inventory.
- The user can select an item's ID Number from a list and display the item's properties.
- When the application starts, it reads an inventory list from a file (text format).
- When the application ends, it writes the inventory list back to the same file.

User Interface Details

Display a single sports rental item in a window, as shown in Figure 3-23. Each item has an ID number; a description; daily, weekly, and monthly rental rates; and the quantity on hand. When the application starts, it reads all item information from a file into a collection (implemented as a Dictionary) and copies the item ID numbers into a combo box on the form. The user can select an ID number from the combo box, and display or remove existing items. The user can also add new items to the collection. When the program ends, it writes the collection to the same file.

Figure 3-23 Preparing to add a new item

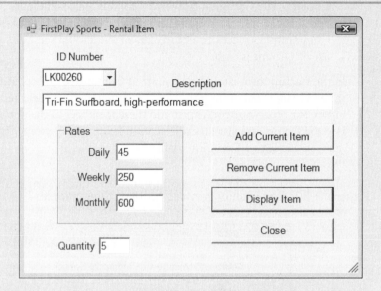

Startup Form

The application's startup form displays inventory items and lets users carry out each of the following actions:

- Input fields for a new rental item, and add that item to the inventory.
- Select an item's ID Number and remove the item from the inventory.
- Select an item's ID Number and display the item's properties.

When the form loads, the combo box should contain a list of all inventory ID Numbers.

Returning to Figure 3-23 for a moment, we see that it shows a new item about to be added to the store inventory. When the *Add Current Item* button is clicked, the button's handler creates a new Item object and passes it to the class that handles the store inventory. Figure 3-24 shows an example of searching for an item by ID Number. When the user clicks the *Display Item* button, the remaining item fields are filled in. When the user clicks the *Remove Current Item* button, the program confirms the operation with the user, as shown in Figure 3-25. If the answer is yes, the program removes the item identified by the ID Number.

Figure 3-24 Searching for an item selected by ID Number

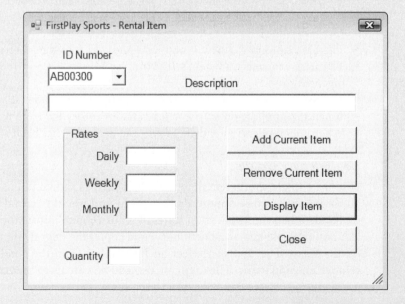

Figure 3-25 Confirm before removing an item

Classes

We suggest that the application define three classes: Item, Inventory, and InventoryFile.

- The Item class encapsulates a single inventory item.
- The Inventory class represents a collection that contains all items and provides methods for adding, finding, and removing items. Internally, it should hold the items in a Dictionary object.
- The InventoryFile class is responsible for reading the inventory data from a text file, and writing all Inventory data back to the file.

7. **Student Course Collection**

Create an application that collects information about students and the courses they have completed, and holds this information in collection, implemented as a List or ArrayList object. You can use Tutorial 3-2 as a starting point for this project. The main form, displayed when the application starts, should have the same fields as shown in the tutorial. A sample of the main form is shown in Figure 3-26.

In addition, do the following:

- Create a class named Course with the following properties: CourseId As String, Credits As Integer, Grade As Double.
- Add a class-level variable to the Student class that holds a list of courses.
- Create a new form named *Course Information* that contains the following input fields: course ID, credits, and grade. A sample is shown in Figure 3-27. The list box displays all courses in the student's transcript.

Figure 3-26 The main form, with the new *Course Information* button

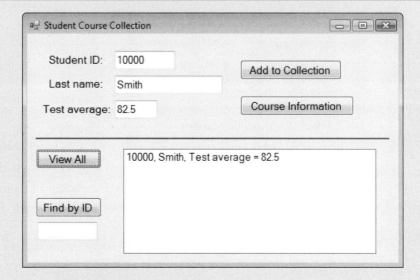

Figure 3-27 Sample *Course Information* form

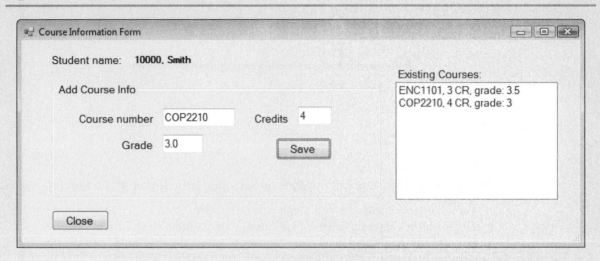

- On the main form, add a *Course Information* button. Use this button to display the Course Information form. The button should initially be disabled; it is enabled when the user clicks either the *Add to Collection* button or the *Find by ID* button.

Figure 3-28 shows the relationships between the classes and objects in this application.

Figure 3-28 Concept view of Student Course Collection

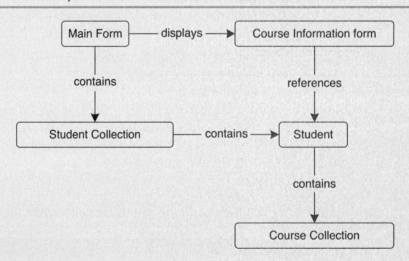

Input Requirements

The following input requirements are designed to prevent the program from throwing an exception or storing invalid data:

1. No two Student IDs can be the same.

2. No input fields can be blank.

3. The Grade field must be a positive numeric value between 0.0 and 4.0.

4. The course credits field must be a positive integer between 0 and 6.

5. A duplicate course number cannot be added to the list of courses.

6. Error messages must be specific, identifying exactly which field has a missing or incorrect value.

Each of these requirements is included in the testing steps that we have outlined for this programming challenge.

Suggestions

1. In the main form, create a class-level variable of type Student so it can be accessible to different event handlers. This will affect the event handlers for both the *Add* and *Find* buttons.

2. The Student class should have a ReadOnly property that exposes its ArrayList. This will be useful when your program needs to display the courses in a list box or add a new course to the list.

3. The Form_Load event handler for the Course Information form should fill the list box with the list of courses belonging to the current student. It should also clear all text boxes on the form.

4. Use the ErrorProvider control to display error messages.

Testing Steps

Bugs can be hidden in this application in quite a few ways. That is why we have created a detailed testing plan to help you verify that your application has satisfied the project requirements. The following table contains a sequence of manual testing steps that should (eventually) be completed without closing or restarting the program. If your program produces a response that does not match the expected output, you will probably need to halt the program, fix the error, and restart the test.

Input	On the main startup form, leave all fields blank and click the *Add to Collection* button.
Expected output	A message box says: *Student ID cannot be blank.*
Input	Enter 10000 as the Student ID and click the *Add to Collection* button.
Expected output	A message box says: *Last name cannot be blank.*
Input	Enter *Smith* as the last name value and click the *Add to Collection* button.
Expected output	A message box says: *Test average must be numeric.*
Input	Enter 82.5 as the test average and click the *Add to Collection* button.
Expected output	The *Course Information* button becomes enabled.
Input	Click the *Course Information* button.
Expected output	The *Course Information* window appears, showing the student ID and last name that you just entered. All input fields are blank.
Input	Input the following values for Course number, Credits, and Grade, respectively: *ENC1101, 3, 3.5.* Then click the *Save* button.
Expected output	The course information appears in the *Existing Courses* list box.
Input	Click the *Save* button, leaving all input fields blank.
Expected output	A red ErrorProvider icon blinks next to the course number input field. When you hover the mouse over the icon, the following message appears: *Course number cannot be blank.*
Input	Enter *COP3350* as the course number; leave the other input fields blank.
Expected output	A red ErrorProvider icon blinks next to the course credits input field. When you hover the mouse over the icon, the following message appears: *Credits must be an integer between 0 and 6.*
Input	Enter −2 as the course credits and click the *Save* button.
Expected output	The following message appears: *Credits must be an integer between 0 and 6.*

Input	Enter 4 as the course credits and click the *Save* button.
Expected output	A red ErrorProvider icon blinks next to the course grade input field. When you hover the mouse over the icon, the message says: *The grade must be a numeric value between 0.0 and 4.0.*
Input	Enter 6.0 as the grade value and click the *Save* button.
Expected output	An error message says: *The grade must be a numeric value between 0.0 and 4.0.*
Input	Enter 3.0 as the grade value and click the *Save* button.
Expected output	The *Existing Courses* list box contains the two courses you added.
Input	Click the *Save* button again.
Expected output	A red ErrorProvider icon blinks next to the *Save* button. The error message says: *Cannot add a duplicate course.* The contents of the list box do not change.
Input	Click the *Close* button.
Expected output	The *Course Information* window closes, and you are now back in the main startup form.
Input	On the main form, click the *Add to Collection* button.
Expected output	A message box pops up and says: *Cannot add a duplicate Student ID to the collection.*
Input	In the Student ID, Last name, and Test average fields, enter *20000, Jones, 87.2,* respectively, and click the *Add to Collection* button. Then, click the *View All* button.
Expected output	Both students (Smith and Jones) appear in the list box, with the same data values you have already entered.
Input	Click the *Course Information* button.
Expected output	The Course Information window opens, containing the following student ID and name values: *20000, Jones.* All input fields are blank.
Input	Input the following values for course number, credits, and grade, respectively: *COP2210, 4, 2.5.* Then click the *Save* button.
Expected output	The course information appears in the *Existing Courses* list box.
Input	Click the *Close* button.
Expected output	The *Course Information* window closes, and you are now back in the main startup form.
Input	In the text box at the lower left corner of the window, enter *19999* and click the *Find by ID* button.
Expected output	In the list box, a message says: *Student ID was not found.*
Input	In the text box at the lower left corner of the window, enter *10000* and click the *Find by ID* button.
Expected output	The text boxes fill with the following values: *10000, Smith, 82.50.* The student also appears in the list box.
Input	Click the *Course Information* button.
Expected output	The *Course Information* window appears, showing student ID *10000* and last name *Smith.* All input fields are blank. The list box displays information about the student's two saved courses: *ENC1101, 3, 3.5,* and *COP3530, 4, 3.0.*
Input	Input the following values, respectively, for Course number, Credits, and Grade: *MTH2005, 5, 3.0.* Then click the *Save* button.

Expected output	The new course you entered has been added to the courses in the list box.
Input	Click the *Close* button.
Expected output	The *Course Information* window closes, and you are now back in the main startup form.
Input	Close the main startup form.
Expected output	The application closes.

8. Students and Course Lists (LINQ)

Use a LINQ query to fill a DataGridView with a list of students. When the user selects a student in the grid, display all courses taken by the student in a separate grid. Use another LINQ query to fill the second grid. A sample is shown in Figure 3-29, in which Student 1001 (Charles) was selected when the user clicked the button on the left side of his row. The grid on the right fills with the list of courses taken by the selected student.

Figure 3-29 Displaying courses taken by a selected student

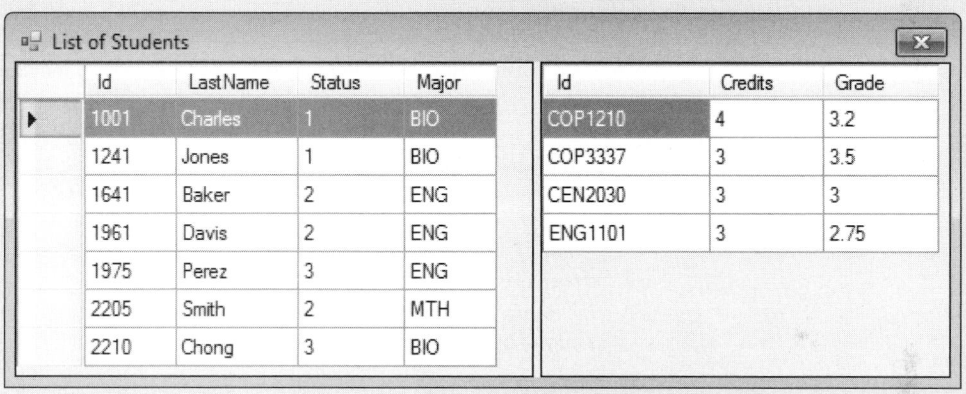

The two DataGridView controls should be inserted into panels belonging to a SplitContainer control. The user can drag the divider between the two panels to adjust their size. The SplitContainer's Dock property equals *Fill*, so the user can expand the form and create more space for the two grids. In the grid on the left, the RowHeadersVisible property should equal *True*, but in the grid on the right, the same property should equal *False*.

The Student class contains the following properties: Id (Integer), LastName (String), Status (Integer), Major (String), Courses (List(Of Course)). The Course class contains the following properties: Id (String), Credits (Integer), Grade (Double). All the student data must be read from a data file named *Students.txt*, supplied for you in the example programs folder for this chapter.

When the user selects a DataGridView row, a *SelectionChanged* event is fired. You can write code in the handler that gets the contents of the first column of the selected row, using the following expression: `dgvStudents.SelectedRows(0).Cells(0).Value`. Note, however, that the DataGridView fires SelectedItemChanged events when the form is being loaded, before the grid becomes visible. You will have to find a way to avoid responding to those events.

9. Cruise Selection Wizard

Selecting a cruise vacation can be tricky. We all have different preferences when it comes to details like the location of the cruise, the size of the ship, the average age of the passengers, and so on. Your job is to make this selection process easier. Create a wizard application that guides the user through selecting a cruise that suits his or her preferences. Create a class named Cruise that contains properties that represent the characteristics of a single cruise. Use the following: (1) size of ship, (2) geographical region, (3) formal versus informal attire, and (4) average passenger age. Next, create a class that contains a strongly typed List(Of Cruise) object. Use the constructor of this class to fill the list with cruise information.

User Interface

Ask the user for the relative importance of each cruise criterion, as shown in Figure 3-30. Next, ask the user for his or her individual preferences for each of the criteria. For example, in Figure 3-31 the user is asked for the ideal ship size; in Figure 3-32, the user is asked for an ideal geographical region; in Figure 3-33, the user is asked about the average age of the passengers with whom they would prefer to sail. In Figure 3-34, the user is shown a list of cruises, with a percentage next to each that shows the percentage similarity of the cruise to the user's preferred criteria. The user can select different radio buttons to filter the display so it shows cruises that meet various thresholds.

Figure 3-30 Cruise Selection Wizard, startup form

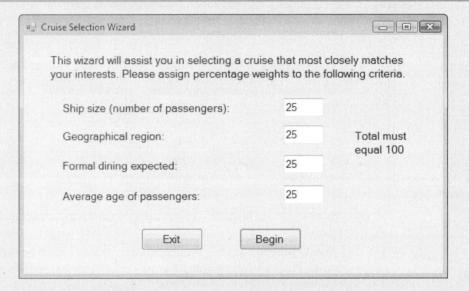

Figure 3-31 Cruise Selection Wizard, ship size

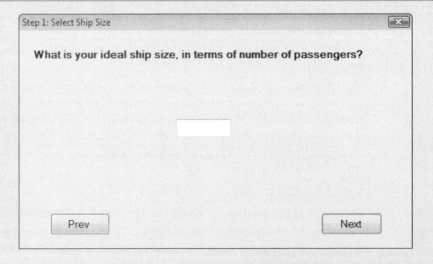

Figure 3-32 Cruise Selection Wizard, geographical region

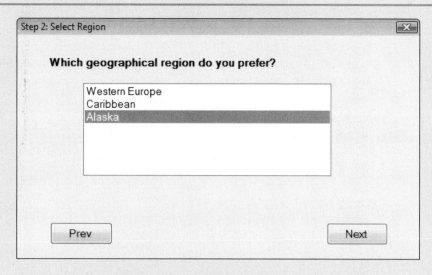

Figure 3-33 Cruise Selection Wizard, average age of passengers

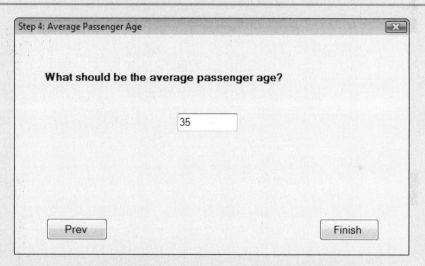

Figure 3-34 Cruise Selection Wizard, summary

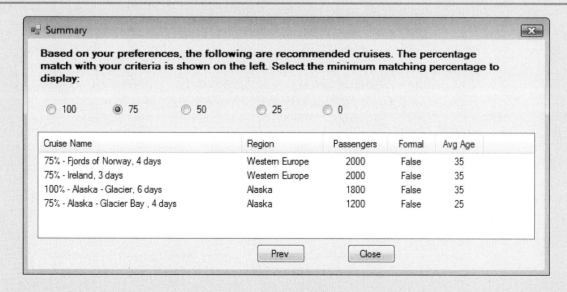

Use weighted criteria to help find the cruises that best match the user's preferences. Here is an example of the types of variables we used in our solution program:

```
NumPassengersWt As Single       ' Number of passengers
RegionWt As Single              ' Geographical region
FormalWt As Single              ' Formal attire expected?
AverageAgeWt As Single          ' Average passenger age
```

The algorithm for determining the percentage match of a cruise to the user's preferences must take into account the percentages the user assigned to the individual criteria. Let's call these percentages pc1, pc2, pc3, and pc4. The user's actual preferences can be called r1, r2, r3, and r4. For each cruise, let's say that it has characteristics c1, c2, c3, and c4. We will call **tp** the *total percentage match value* for this cruise:

```
tp = 0
if c1 = r1 then tp = tp + pc1
if c2 = r2 then tp = tp + pc2
if c3 = r3 then tp = tp + pc3
if c4 = r4 then tp = tp + pc4
```

Let's use an example, and the following table. Suppose the user has assigned the following values to the four preferences:

Preference	User's Preferred Value	Percentage Weight for Each Preference
size of ship (r1)	1500	pc1 = .25
geographical region (r2)	Alaska	pc2 = .45
formal versus informal (r3)	informal	pc3 = .20
average age (r4)	45	pc4 = .10

This sample user seems mainly concerned with the geographical region (45 percent) and the size of the ship (25 percent). We'll say that the ship size matches if it is within 500 feet of the user's preferred value. The age matches if it is within five years of the user's preferred age for the passengers. Next, let's look at a couple of sample cruises:

Cruise X holds 1,700 passengers, goes to Alaska, emphasizes formal wear, and has an average passenger age of 55. Its percentage match is 70 percent:

```
.25 + .45 + 0 + 0 = .70
```

Cruise Y holds 2,500 passengers, goes to the Caribbean, emphasizes informal wear, and has an average passenger age of 45. Its percentage match is only 30 percent:

```
0 + 0 + .20 + .10 = .30
```

Based on these two sample cruise evaluations, this user would be advised to select Cruise X because it has a higher percentage match value. But another user might place more emphasis on different criteria and produce a different set of percentages.

Suggested Classes

Cruise class—contains information about a single cruise, which in turn contains the following properties:

```
NumPassengers As Integer        ' number of passengers
Region As String                ' geographical region
Formal As Boolean               ' formal attire expected?
AverageAge As Single            ' average passenger age
```

CruiseCollection class—contains a List(Of Cruise) object, a constructor, and a read-only property that returns the list of available cruises.

4 Using SQL Server Databases

TOPICS

This chapter focuses on the basics of displaying and updating databases using .NET controls. We show how Visual Studio enables **data binding**, which is the connecting of the user interface directly to database components. We also discuss some basic database concepts, and show how to execute SQL queries, sort and filter database data, display data in a grid, and bind individual controls to database tables. After reading this chapter, you should be able to display and update database tables rapidly and with almost no programming.

4.1 Database Basics

A **database** is a collection of one or more tables, each containing data related to a particular topic. A **table** is a logical grouping of related information. For example, a database might have a table containing information about employees. Another table might list information about weekly sales. Another table might contain a store inventory. Let's look at a table named *Departments*, shown in Table 4-1, which contains information about departments within a company. Each **row** of the table corresponds to a single department. The sample table contains the ID number, name, and number of employees in each department.

Table 4-1 Table of departments

dept_id	dept_name	num_employees
1	Human Resources	10
2	Accounting	5
3	Computer Support	30
4	Research and Development	15

Each row of the table is also called a *record*. In the *Departments* table, the first row contains 1, Human Resources, 10. When discussing a table, we refer to their columns by name. In the *Departments* table, the columns are named dept_id, dept_name, and num_employees. Table columns are also called *fields*. Each table has a design that specifies the column's name, data type, and range or size. Table 4-2 describes the design of the *Departments* table. The SQL data types used in the table are *int* (integer) and varchar (string). The varchar type always has a maximum length count.

Table 4-2 *Departments* table design

Field	Type
dept_id	int (primary key)
dept_name	varchar (30)
num_employees	int

Primary Key

In the Departments table, the dept_id column is called a **primary key** because it uniquely identifies each department. In other words, no two departments can ever have the same dept_id value. Primary keys can be either numbers or strings, but numeric values are processed by the database software more efficiently. In the *Departments* table, the primary key is a single column. Sometimes a primary key will consist of two or more combined columns, called a **compound primary key**. The primary key's value is often generated automatically by the database server each time a new row is added to the table. This type of field is called an **auto-generated field**, or **identity field**. Generally, each new row's key value is generated by adding an integer to the value in the previous row.

SQL Server Data Types

We will be using Microsoft SQL Server databases. When you use Visual Basic to read a database, you must select variable types that match the type of data in the table. Fortunately, Microsoft SQL Server data types, .NET data types, and Visual Basic data types are similar. Table 4-3 shows a partial list of SQL Server data types, which are recognized by SQL Server when you pass parameters to database queries.

Designing Database Tables

Choosing Column Names and Types

A **database schema** is the design of tables, columns, and relationships between tables. Let's look at some of the elements that belong to a schema, beginning with tables. Suppose you want to create a database to keep track of club members. We might want to store each

Table 4-3 Comparison of common SQL Server and .NET data types

SQL Server Data Type	Compatible .NET Data Type
bit	*Boolean.* An unassigned numeric value that can be 0, 1, or a null reference. Can be assigned the values *true* and *false.*
datetime	*DateTime.* Date and time data ranging in value from January 1, 1753 to December 31, 9999 to an accuracy of 3.33 milliseconds.
float	*Double.* A floating point number in the approximate range $\pm10^{308}$.
int	*Int32.* Large signed integer. Visual Basic data type: Integer.
money	*Decimal.* Precise monetary values in the approximate range $\pm2^{63}$.
nvarchar	*String.* A variable-length stream with a maximum length of 4,000 Unicode characters.
real	*Single.* Floating-point number, in the approximate range $\pm10^{38}$.
smalldatetime	*DateTime.* Date and time data from 1/1/1900 through 6/6/2079, with an accuracy of 1 minute.
smallint	*Int16.* A signed integer between −32,768 and +32,767; Visual Basic data type: Short.
text	*String.* A variable-length stream of nearly unlimited size.
varchar	*String.* A variable-length stream with a maximum length of 8,000 non-Unicode characters.

member's first and last names, phone number, email address, date joined, number of meetings attended, and a field indicating whether the person is a club officer. Table 4-4 contains a possible design. Choosing the lengths of text fields involves some guesswork because we do not want to risk truncating individual field values. When in doubt, it is best to make fields a little larger than necessary.

Table 4-4 Sample design for the *Members* table

Column Name	Type
First_Name	varchar (40)
Last_Name	varchar (40)
Phone	varchar (30)
Email	varchar (40)
Date_Joined	DateTime
Meetings_Attended	smallint
Officer	bit (*Boolean*)

TIP: Although you can embed spaces in a column name, avoid doing so because it causes SQL queries to be more complicated.

Suggestions on Choosing Column Types

Table 4-5 contains some of the more common types of data you might be likely to insert in database tables. The table suggests types of database columns to use for each type of data.

Table 4-5 Recommended database column types

Type of Data	Recommended Column Type
Primary keys, unique identifiers such as ID numbers	int or smallint
Variable-length strings, such as names of people, departments, countries, companies, book titles, descriptions, and street addresses	varchar for 8-bit ANSI characters, or nvarchar for Unicode characters
Fixed-length strings, such as account numbers, and Social Security numbers	char or nchar (Unicode) type. This type pads all trailing positions in the field with blanks.
ANSI strings longer than 8,000 bytes, documents and other extended text	text
Financial values	decimal or money type, to avoid loss of decimal precision
Measured values as real numbers; ratios	float
True/False (logical) values	bit
Dates and/or times	datetime or smalldatetime, depending on how accurate you want to be
Image and document files	image

Avoiding Redundancy by Using Linked Tables

Well-designed databases keep redundant data to a minimum. When designing a table of employees, for example, it might be tempting to include the complete name of the department in which an employee works. A few sample rows are shown in Table 4-6. There are problems with this approach. We can imagine that the same department name appears many times within the *Employee* table, leading to wasted storage space. Also, someone typing in employee data might easily misspell a department name. Finally, if the company decided to rename a department, it would become necessary to find and correct every occurrence of the department name in the *Employee* table (and possibly other tables).

Table 4-6 *Employee* table with department names

Emp_Id	First_Name	Last_Name	Departments
1000	Ignacio	Fleta	Accounting
1001	Christian	Martin	Computer Support
1002	Orville	Gibson	Human Resources
1003	Jose	Ramirez	Research and Development
1004	Ben	Smith	Accounting
1005	Allison	Chong	Computer Support

Rather than inserting a department name in each employee record, a good designer would store a department ID number in each row of the *Employee* table, as shown in Table 4-7. A data entry clerk would require less time to input a numeric department ID, and there would be less chance of a typing error. Then one would create a separate table named *Departments* containing all department names and IDs, which is shown in Table 4-8. When looking up the name of an employee's department, we can use the department ID in the *Employee* table to find the same ID in the *Departments* table. The department name will be in the same table row. Databases make it easy to create links between tables such as *Employees* and *Departments*.

Table 4-7 *Employee* table with department ID numbers

Emp_Id	First_Name	Last_Name	Dept_Id
1000	Ignacio	Fleta	2
1001	Christian	Martin	3
1002	Orville	Gibson	1
1003	Jose	Ramirez	4
1004	Ben	Smith	2
1005	Allison	Chong	3

Table 4-8 *Departments* table

Dept_Id	Dept_Name	Num_Employees
1	Human Resources	10
2	Accounting	5
3	Computer Support	30
4	Research and Development	15

One-to-Many Relationship

- Databases are often designed using the relational model of data. In the **relational database model**, relationships exist between tables. A relationship consists of a common field value to connect rows from two different tables. In the relationship diagram shown in Figure 4-1, Dept_Id is the common field that links the *Departments* and *Employee* tables.

Figure 4-1 One-to-many relationship between *Departments* and *Employee* tables

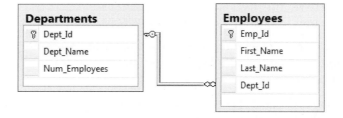

- In the *Departments* table, Dept_Id is the primary key. In the *Employee* table, Dept_Id is called a **foreign key**. A foreign key is a column in one table that references a primary key in another table. The column can contain duplicate values. Along the line connecting the two tables, the 1 and 8 symbol indicate a **one-to-many relationship**. A particular Dept_Id (such as 4) occurs only once in the *Departments* table, but it can appear many times (or not at all) in the *Employee* table. At first, we will work with one table at a time. Later, we will show how to pull information from two related tables.

Checkpoint

1. How is a table different from a database?

2. In a table of employees, what column makes a good primary key?

3. Which .NET type is equivalent to the bit column type in SQL Server?

4. Why would we not want to spell out the name of each person's department name in a table of employees?

5. How is a foreign key different from a primary key?

4.2   SQL SELECT Statement

Structured Query Language (SQL) was developed as a universal language for creating, updating, and retrieving data from databases. The American National Standards Institute (ANSI) has ratified different levels of standard SQL, which are followed to a greater or lesser degree by database vendors. ANSI standards are identified by their year of ratification and a level number. In this section, we introduce the most important of all SQL statements—SELECT. It is used to retrieve rows from database tables.

SELECT Statement

The **SELECT statement** retrieves rows from one or more database tables. The most basic format for a single table is as follows:

```
SELECT column-list
FROM table
```

The members of column-list must be table column names separated by commas. The following statement selects the ID and Salary from the *SalesStaff* table:

```
SELECT ID, Salary
FROM SalesStaff
```

In a Visual Basic program, the DataSet produced by this query would have two columns, ID and Salary. There is no required formatting or capitalization of SQL statements or field names. The following queries are equivalent:

```
SELECT ID, Salary FROM SalesStaff
select ID, Salary from SalesStaff
Select id, salary from salesstaff
```

As a matter of style and readability, you should try to use consistent capitalization. If field names contain embedded spaces, they must be surrounded by square brackets, as in the following example:

```
SELECT [Last Name], [First Name]
FROM Employees
```

The * character in the column list selects all columns from a table.

```
SELECT *
FROM SalesStaff
```

Aliases for Column Names

Column names can be renamed, using the AS operator. The new column name is called an **alias,** as in the following example that renames the Hire_Date column to Date_Hired:

```
SELECT
  Last_Name, Hire_Date AS Date_Hired
FROM
  SalesStaff
```

Renaming columns is useful for two reasons. First, you might want to hide the actual column names from users. Second, column headings in reports can be made more user-friendly if you substitute your own names for the column names used inside the database.

Creating Alias Columns from Other Columns

A query can create a new column from one or more existing columns in the same table. For example, we might want to combine Last_Name and First_Name from a table named *Members*. We can insert a comma and space between the columns, as shown here:

```
SELECT Last_Name + ', ' + First_Name AS Full_Name
FROM Members
```

Now the Full_Name column can be inserted into a ListBox or ComboBox. In general, when strings occur in queries, they must always be surrounded by single quotes. The + operator concatenates strings.

Calculated Columns

You can create new columns whose contents are calculated from existing column values. Suppose a table named *Payroll* contains columns named employeeId, hoursWorked, and hourlyRate. The following statement creates a new column named *payAmount*, using hoursWorked and hourlyRate:

```
SELECT employeeId, hoursWorked * hourlyRate AS payAmount
FROM PayRoll
```

Setting the Row Order with ORDER BY

The SELECT statement has an **ORDER BY clause** that lets you control the display order of the table rows. In other words, you can sort the data on one or more columns. The general form for sorting on a single column is the following:

```
ORDER BY columnName [ASC | DESC]
```

ASC indicates sorting in ascending order (the default) and DESC indicates sorting in descending order. Both are optional, and you can use only one at a time. The following clause orders the SalesStaff table in ascending order by last name:

```
ORDER BY Last_Name ASC
```

We can do this more simply as follows:

```
ORDER BY Last_Name
```

The following sorts the table in descending order by Salary:

```
ORDER BY Salary DESC
```

You can sort on multiple columns. The following statement sorts in ascending order first by last name; then within each last name, it sorts in ascending order by first name:

```
ORDER BY Last_Name, First_Name
```

For a more complete example, the following SELECT statement returns the first name, last name, and salary, sorting by last name and first name in the Members table of the Karate database:

```
SELECT
   First_Name, Last_Name, Date_Joined
FROM
   Members
ORDER BY Last_Name, First_Name
```

Selecting Rows with the WHERE Clause

The SQL SELECT statement has an optional **WHERE clause** that you can use to filter, or select zero or more rows retrieved from a database table. The simplest form of the WHERE clause is as follows:

```
WHERE columnName + value
```

In this case, *columnName* must be one of the table columns and *value* must be in a format that is consistent with the column type. The following SELECT statement, for example, specifies that Last_Name must be equal to Gomez:

```
SELECT First_Name, Last_Name, Salary
FROM SalesStaff
WHERE Last_Name = 'Gomez'
```

Character comparisons are case-insensitive by default, so the following WHERE clause is equivalent to the previous one:

```
WHERE Last_Name = 'gomeZ'
```

Because Last_Name is a string-type column, it must be assigned a string literal enclosed in single quotes. If the person's name contains an apostrophe (such as O'Leary), the apostrophe must be repeated:

```
SELECT First_Name, Last_Name, Salary
FROM SalesStaff
WHERE Last_Name = 'O''Leary'
```

Relational Operators

Table 4-9 lists the operators that can be used in WHERE clauses. The following expression matches last names starting with letters B . . . Z.

Table 4-9 SQL relational operators

Operator	Meaning
=	equal to
<>	not equal to
<	less than
<=	less than or equal to
>	greater than
>=	greater than or equal to
BETWEEN	between two values (inclusive)
LIKE	similar to (wildcard match)

```
WHERE Last_Name >= 'B'
```

The following expression matches nonzero salary values:

```
WHERE Salary <> 0
```

Bit Field (Boolean) Values

SQL Server stores Boolean values in columns that use the *bit* type. You can compare this type of column to bit constants such as 1, 0, 'True', and 'False'. A value of 1 indicates *True*, and 0 indicates *False*. Here are examples:

```
WHERE Full_Time = 1
WHERE Full_Time = 'True'
```

```
WHERE Full_Time = 0
WHERE Full_Time <> 'False'
```

Numeric and Date Values

Numeric literals do not require quotation marks. The following expression matches all rows in which Salary is greater than $30,000:

```
WHERE (Salary > 30000)
```

DateTime literals must be enclosed in single quotation marks:

```
WHERE (Hire_Date > '12/31/2005')
```

The following expression matches rows containing hire dates falling between (and including) January 1, 2005 and December 31, 2009:

```
WHERE (Hire_Date BETWEEN '1/1/2005' AND '12/31/2009')
```

Following is a complete SELECT statement using the WHERE clause that selects rows according to Hire_Date and orders them by last name:

```
SELECT First_Name, Last_Name, Hire_Date
FROM SalesStaff
WHERE (Hire_Date BETWEEN '1/1/2005' AND '12/31/2009')
ORDER BY Last_Name
```

LIKE Operator

The **LIKE operator** can be used to create partial matches with string column values. When combined with LIKE, the underscore character matches a single unknown character. For example, the following expression matches all Account_ID values beginning with X and ending with 4:

```
WHERE Account_ID LIKE 'X_4'
```

The percent sign (%) matches multiple unknown characters. We also call % a **wildcard symbol**. For example, the following matches all last names starting with the letter A:

```
WHERE Last_Name LIKE 'A%'
```

You can combine wildcard characters. For example, the following matches all First_Name values in the table that have *d* and *r* in the second and third positions, respectively:

```
WHERE First_Name LIKE '_dr%'
```

The character comparisons are case-insensitive.

Compound Expressions (AND, OR, and NOT)

SQL uses the AND, NOT, and OR operators to create compound expressions. In most cases, you should use parentheses to clarify the order of operations. The following expression matches rows in which a person was hired after 1/1/2005 and the salary is greater than $40,000:

```
WHERE (Hire_Date > '1/1/2005') AND (Salary > 40000)
```

The following expression matches rows in which a person was hired before 2005 or after 2010:

```
WHERE (Hire_Date < '1/1/2005') OR (Hire_Date > '12/31/2010')
```

The following expression matches rows in which a person was hired after 2005 and before 2010:

```
WHERE (Hire_Date > '12/31/2005') AND (Hire_Date < '1/1/2010')
```

The following expression matches two types of employees: (1) those who were hired after 1/1/2005 and whose salary is greater than $40,000, and (2) employees who are not full-time:

```
WHERE (Hire_Date > '1/1/2005') AND (Salary > 40000)
OR (Full_Time = False)
```

The following expression matches rows in which the hire date was either earlier than 1/1/2008 or later than 12/31/2010:

```
WHERE (Hire_Date NOT BETWEEN '1/1/2008' AND '12/31/2010')
```

The following expression matches rows in which the last name does not begin with the letter A:

```
WHERE (Last_Name NOT LIKE 'A%')
```

 Checkpoint

6. Write a SELECT statement that retrieves the pay_rate, employee_id, and hours_worked columns from a table named *Payroll*, and sorts the rows in descending order by hours_worked.

7. Write a SELECT statement that creates an alias named *Rate_of_Pay* for the existing column named *pay_rate* in the Payroll table.

8. Write a SELECT statement for the Payroll table that creates a new output column named *gross_pay* by multiplying the pay_rate column by the hours_worked column.

9. Write a SELECT statement for the Payroll table that returns only rows in which the pay_rate is greater than 20,000 and less than or equal to 55,000.

10. Write a SELECT statement for the Payroll table that returns only rows in which the employee_id column begins with the characters *FT*. The remaining characters in the employee_id are unimportant.

 ## 4.3 Using the DataGridView Control

The **DataGridView control** is a convenient tool for displaying the contents of database tables in rows and columns. Data binding is used to link database tables to controls on a program's forms. Special objects named **components** provide the linking mechanism. When you link a control to a database, a wizard guides you through the process. We will use the following data-related objects in this chapter:

- **Data source**—A data source is usually a database, but it can include text files, Excel spreadsheets, XML data, or Web services. It keeps track of the database name, location, username, password, and other connection information. Our data sources will be Microsoft SQL Server database files.

- **TableAdapter**—A TableAdapter pulls data from one or more database tables and copies the data into a DataSet. It can select some or all table rows, add new rows, delete rows, and modify existing rows. It can also delete, insert, or update table rows. TableAdapters use SQL queries to retrieve and update database tables.

- **DataSet**—A DataSet is an in-memory copy of data pulled from database tables. An application can modify rows in the DataSet, add new rows, and delete rows. Changes to DataSets become permanent when an application uses a TableAdapter to write the changes back from the DataSet to the database. DataSets can get data from more than one data source and from more than one TableAdapter.

- **DataTable**—A DataTable is a table inside a DataSet. It holds data generated by a TableAdapter's SELECT query. DataTables have a *Rows* collection that corresponds to database table rows. You can loop through the Rows collection and inspect or modify individual column values within each row.

- **BindingSource**—A BindingSource object provides a link between a DataSet and one or more controls on a form. We say that these controls are **data-bound controls**. If the user modifies the data in a control, the BindingSource can copy the changes to the DataSet.

Figure 4-2 shows the relationship among the data source, TableAdapter, DataSet, BindingSource, and application. Data from a data source travels across the path implied by these components to the DataSet and application. The DataSet contents can be modified and viewed by the application. Updates to the DataSet can be written back to the data source. The optional BindingSource provides data-binding capabilities to controls on forms.

Figure 4-2 Two-way data flow between a data source and an application

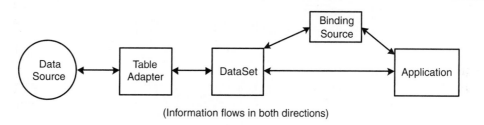

(Information flows in both directions)

Formatting Columns in a DataGridView

To modify the columns in a DataGridView control, open the *DataGridView Tasks* window, and select *Edit Columns* from the popup menu. Figure 4-3 shows the *Edit Columns* dialog window. To format a column, select a column name in the Listbox on the left side of the window, and select the DefaultCellStyle property from the list on the right. This causes the

Figure 4-3 Editing the column properties in a DataGridView

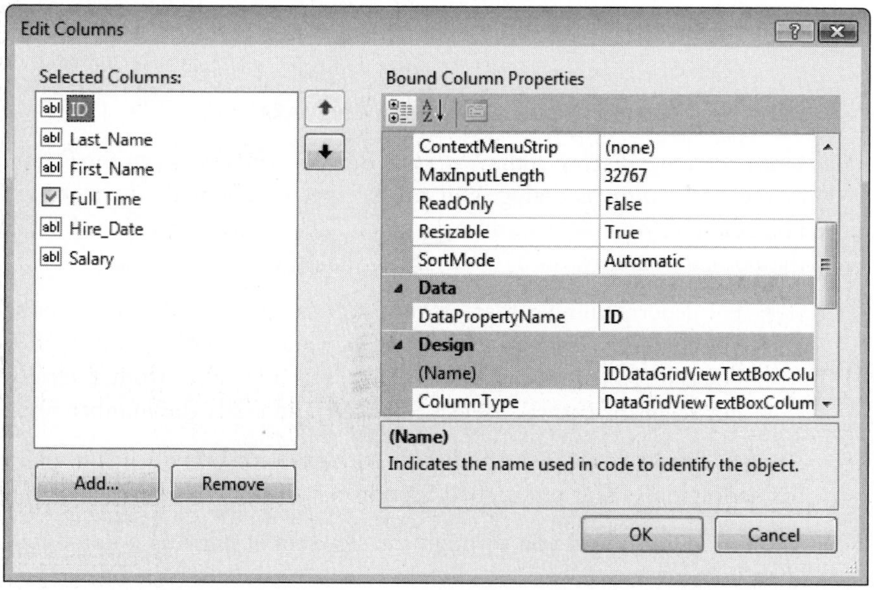

CellStyle Builder window to appear, as shown in Figure 4-4. In this window you can select the column's alignment (*TopLeft*, *MiddleRight*, and so on), padding, format, foreground and background colors, font, and so on. The preview feature at the bottom of the window shows standard column attributes, such as the font and foreground and background colors. It does not show the effect of the Format property.

Figure 4-4 The *CellStyle Builder* window

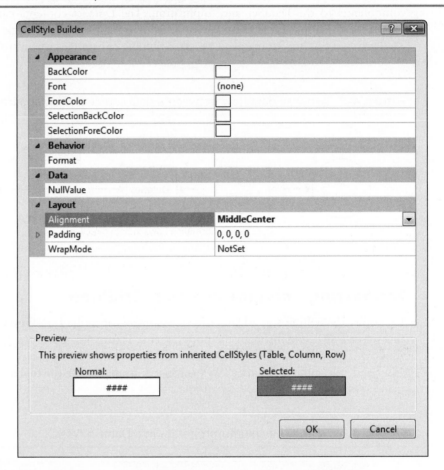

Selecting Numeric and DateTime Formats

Once you have displayed the *CellStyle Builder* window (from the DefaultCellStyle property) of the *Edit Columns* dialog, you can be specific about the formatting of the column data. For example, you might want to format a *DateTime* column as a short date. When you select the *Format* property, the *Format String* dialog window opens, as shown in Figure 4-5.

- For general number formats, select *Numeric* and select the number of decimal places.
- For currency formats, select *Currency* and select the number of decimal places.
- For DateTime formats, select *Date Time* and select from a variety of format samples.
- For scientific formats, select *Scientific* and select the number of decimal places.

Another option is to create a custom format string. If you would like to learn more about formatting dates and times, read Section B.1 in Appendix B.

Tutorial 4-1 will lead you through the steps for displaying a database table in a DataGrid-View control.

Figure 4-5 The *Format String Dialog* window, activated by the *CellStyle Builder*

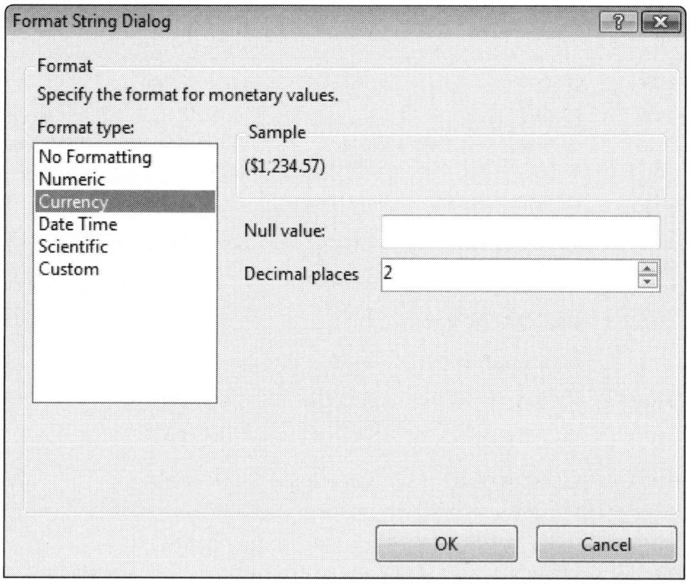

Format String Dialog	? ✕
Format	
Specify the format for monetary values.	

Format type:

No Formatting
Numeric
Currency
Date Time
Scientific
Custom

Sample

($1,234.57)

Null value: [ ]

Decimal places: [2] ⏶⏷

[OK]   [Cancel]

Tutorial 4-1:
Showing a database table in a DataGridView control

In this tutorial, you will display rows and columns from a table named *SalesStaff*, which is located in a database named *Company*. You will see how easy it is for users of your application to sort on any column, delete rows, and insert new rows. The *SalesStaff* table holds information collected about company sales employees. The table design is shown in Table 4-10, and sample rows are shown in Table 4-11.

Table 4-10 *SalesStaff* table design

Column Name	Type
ID	int (primary key)
Last_Name	varchar (40)
First_Name	varchar (40)
Full_Time	bit
Hire_Date	smalldatetime
Salary	decimal

Before you begin this tutorial, locate the *Company.mdf* file, which is located in the chapter examples folder.

Tutorial Steps

Step 1: Create a new Windows application named *SalesStaff 1*.

Step 2: Set the Text property of Form1 to *Company SalesStaff Table*.

Table 4-11 Sample rows in the *SalesStaff* table

ID	Last_Name	First_Name	Full_Time	Hire_Date	Salary
104	Adams	Adrian	True	01/01/2010	35,007.00
114	Franklin	Fay	True	08/22/2005	56,001.00
115	Franklin	Adiel	False	03/20/2010	41,000.00
120	Baker	Barbara	True	04/22/2003	32,000.00
135	Ferriere	Henri	True	01/01/2010	57,000.00
292	Hasegawa	Danny	False	05/20/2007	45,000.00
302	Easterbrook	Erin	False	07/09/2004	22,000.00
305	Kawananakoa	Sam	True	10/20/2009	42,000.00
396	Zabaleta	Maria	True	11/01/2009	29,000.00
404	Del Terzo	Daniel	True	07/09/2007	37,500.00
407	Greenwood	Charles	False	04/20/2008	23,432.00

Step 3: Drag a DataGridView control from the *Toolbox* window onto the form. Click the smart tag in the upper-right corner of the grid. You should see a small popup window named *DataGridView Tasks*, as shown in Figure 4-6.

Figure 4-6 *DataGridView Tasks* window

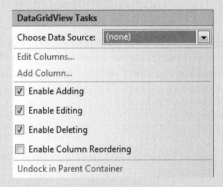

Step 4: Click the dropdown arrow next to *Choose Data Source*. In the dialog that appears (see Figure 4-7), click on *Add Project Data Source*.

Figure 4-7 Choosing a data source in Tutorial 4-1

Step 5: When the *Data Source Configuration Wizard* displays (see Figure 4-8), select the *Database* icon and click the *Next* button.

Figure 4-8 *Data Source Configuration Wizard*

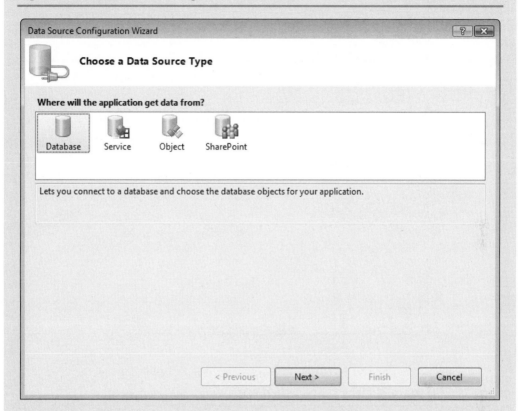

Step 6: The *Choose a Database Model* step appears next. Keep the default selection (Dataset) and click the *Next* button.

Step 7: The wizard asks you to choose your data connection. If you had an existing data connection, you could select it from the dropdown list. Because this is your first data connection, click the *New Connection* button (Figure 4-9).

Step 8: In the *Add Connection* window, if the *Data source* entry does not say *Microsoft SQL Server Database File*, click the *Change* button and select that option.

Step 9: Click the *Browse* button and locate the *Company.mdf* database in the chapter examples folder. Figure 4-10 shows an incomplete path to the *Company.mdf* filename because the actual path will be different on each computer.

Step 10: Click the *Test Connection* button. Assuming that the *Test Connection succeeded* message displays, click the *OK* button two times to return to the wizard, and then click the *Next* button.

Step 11: You will see the message shown in Figure 4-11, which asks if you want to copy the database file to the project directory. By answering *yes*, you can easily move your program and its database to another computer. When you hand in programming projects, having the database stored with the project is a good idea. Click the *Yes* button to continue.

Figure 4-9 Choosing your data connection

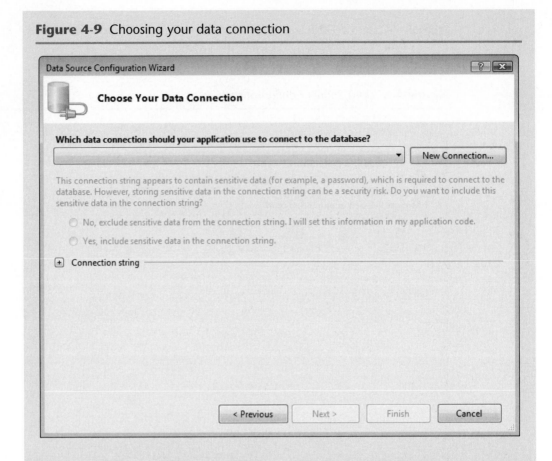

Figure 4-10 *Add Connection* window

Figure 4-11 Option to copy the database file to your project

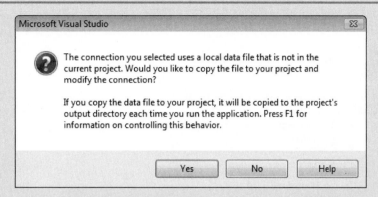

Step 12: Now you are given the option of saving the connection string to the application configuration file (see Figure 4-12). Leave the option checked and click the *Next* button to continue.

Figure 4-12 Saving the connection string to the application configuration file

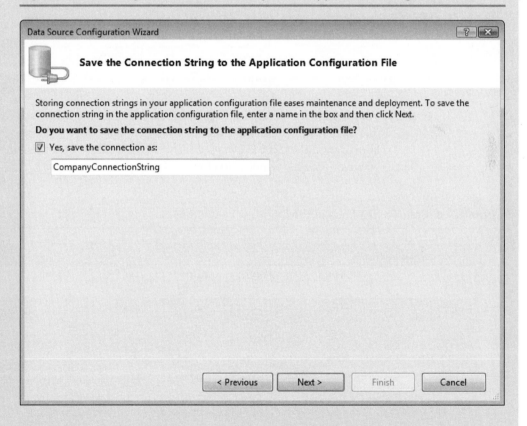

Step 13: Next, you are asked to select which database objects you want in your DataSet. Expand the entry under *Tables*, place a check next to *SalesStaff*, and change the DataSet name to *SalesStaffDataSet* (see Figure 4-13). Click the *Finish* button to complete the wizard.

Figure 4-13 Choosing database objects

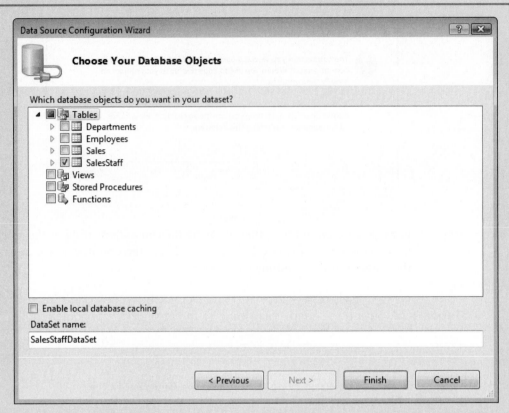

Step 14: You should see column headings in the DataGridView control (see Figure 4-14) that match the *SalesStaff* columns: ID, Last_Name, First_Name, Full_Time, Hire_Date, Salary. If the *DataGridView Tasks* window is still visible, click anywhere outside the window to close it.

Figure 4-14 Column headings in the DataGridView control

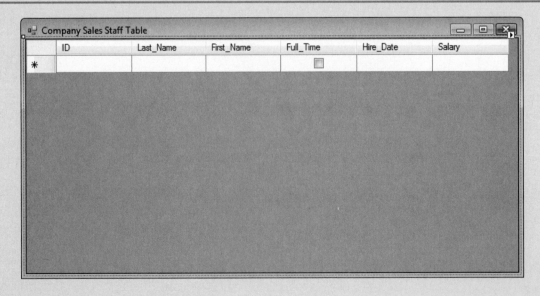

Step 15: Next, you will center the *Hire_Date* column. Select the grid's *Columns* property and open the *Edit Columns* window, which is shown in Figure 4-15. Select the Hire_Date column, and select *DefaultCellStyle*. This will display the *CellStyle Builder* window, shown in Figure 4-16. Select the *Alignment* property, and select *MiddleCenter* from its dropdown list. Click the *OK* buttons until the *Edit Columns* window is closed.

Figure 4-15 The *Edit Columns* dialog window

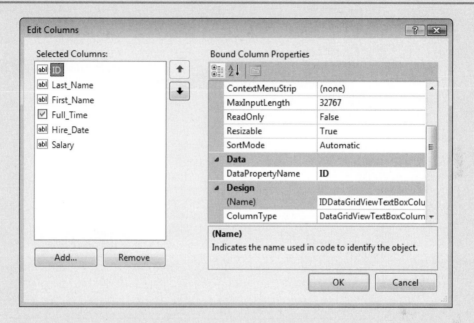

Step 16: Open the form's *Code* window, and inspect the code Visual Studio inserted into the form's Load event handler. It calls the **Fill** method from the SalesStaffTableAdapter, passing it the *SalesStaff* DataTable inside the SalesStaffDataSet DataSet.

```
Me.SalesStaffTableAdapter.Fill(Me.SalesStaffDataSet.SalesStaff)
```

This is how the grid gets its data: The TableAdapter pulls data from the database, using the *Fill* method. The Fill method holds an SQL query that determines which columns of which table will be used. The *SalesStaff* DataTable is a container that holds the data while it is being displayed by the DataGridView control.

Step 17: Save and run the application. You should see all the rows of the *SalesStaff* table, as shown in Figure 4-17.

Step 18: Currently the rows are listed in ascending order by ID number. Click the Last_Name column and watch the grid sort the rows in ascending order by last name. Click the Last_Name column again and watch the rows sort in descending order on the same column.

Step 19: Place the mouse over the border between two columns. When the mouse cursor changes to a horizontal arrow, use the mouse to drag the border to the right or left. This is how users can change column widths at runtime.

Figure 4-16 The *CellStyle Builder* window

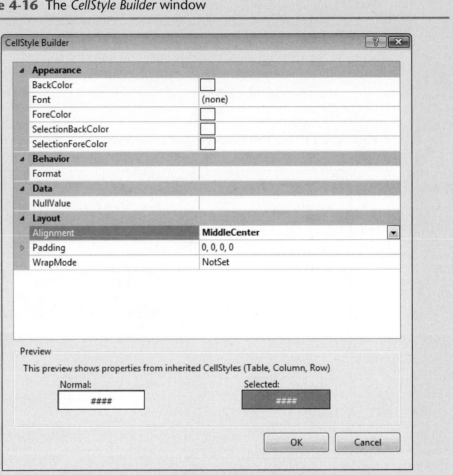

Figure 4-17 Running the application, displaying the *SalesStaff* table

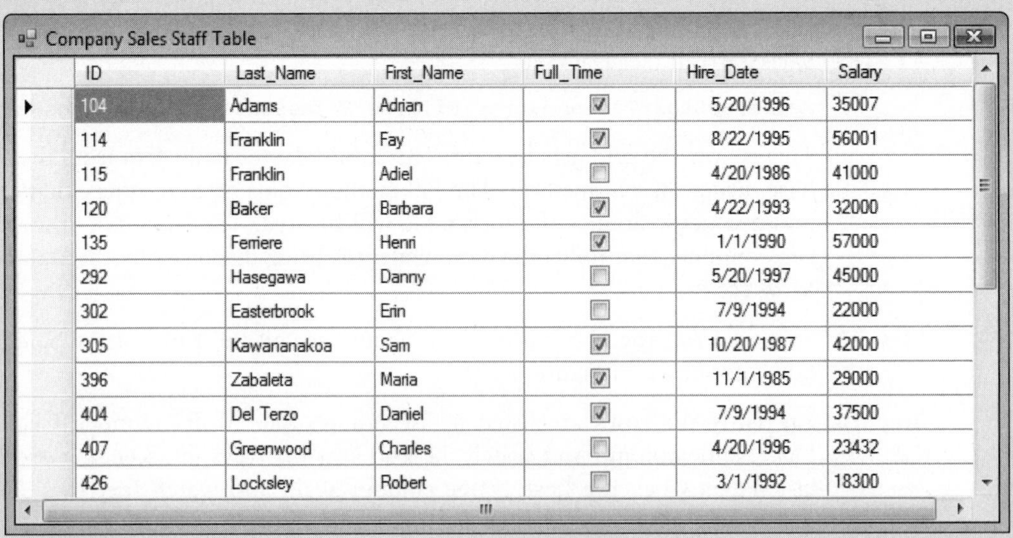

ID	Last_Name	First_Name	Full_Time	Hire_Date	Salary
104	Adams	Adrian	☑	5/20/1996	35007
114	Franklin	Fay	☑	8/22/1995	56001
115	Franklin	Adiel	☐	4/20/1986	41000
120	Baker	Barbara	☑	4/22/1993	32000
135	Ferriere	Henri	☑	1/1/1990	57000
292	Hasegawa	Danny	☐	5/20/1997	45000
302	Easterbrook	Erin	☐	7/9/1994	22000
305	Kawananakoa	Sam	☑	10/20/1987	42000
396	Zabaleta	Maria	☑	11/1/1985	29000
404	Del Terzo	Daniel	☑	7/9/1994	37500
407	Greenwood	Charles	☐	4/20/1996	23432
426	Locksley	Robert	☐	3/1/1992	18300

(Company Sales Staff Table)

Step 20: Try deleting a row. Click the button to the left of one of the grid rows. The entire row is selected (highlighted). Press the *Del* key and watch the row disappear. The row has been removed from the in-memory DataSet, but not the database.

Step 21: Next, you will insert a new row. Scroll to the bottom row of the grid and enter the following information in the empty cells: *847, Jackson, Adelle*, (check *Full-time*), *6/1/2011, 65000*. Press the *Enter* key to save your changes. (If you do not check *Full-time*, the program will throw an exception.)

Step 22: Sort the grid on the Last_Name column, and look for the row you inserted.

Step 23: Close the application and then run it again to verify that the changes you made to the DataSet were not saved in the database. The grid rows look exactly as they did when you first displayed the DataSet. Stop the program again.

Step 24: In Design view, notice the three components placed in the form's component tray by Visual Studio when you added the connection to the *SalesStaff* table.

- SalesStaffDataSet is the object that holds a copy of the database table in memory.
- SalesStaffBindingSource is the object that moves data from the dataset to the DataGridView control.
- SalesStaffTableAdapter is the object that copies data from the database into the dataset. As another option, it can save changes to the database. The TableAdapter contains the SQL statements that select, update, insert, or delete database table rows.

After completing Tutorial 4-1, we hope you see how easy it is to display database tables. The DataGridView control is an ideal tool for giving users a quick view of data. In our example, the column names and ordering were taken directly from the database table. As you learn more about the DataGridView control, you will be able to rename columns and change their order.

 Checkpoint

11. Using the application you created in Tutorial 4-1, explain how to change the formatting of the *Salary* column so it displays values in currency format.

12. The technique called _____ links database tables to controls on Visual Basic forms.

13. Which component pulls data from a database and passes it to a DataSet?

14. When changes are made to a DataSet at runtime, what happens to the database that filled the DataSet?

15. Which control displays DataSets in a spreadsheet-like format?

16. What type of component binds data from a DataSet to an application's controls?

 4.4 # Selecting DataSet Rows

In the previous section of this chapter, you learned how to display all rows of a DataSet using the DataGridView control. Applications often must select (or *filter*) only certain rows for display. Suppose, for example, you want to display only members of the company sales staff who are full-time. Or, you might want to display employees hired prior to 2005. You might want to display only those employees hired within the last five years whose salaries are less than $40,000. Using SQL queries and the tools in Visual Studio, almost any type of filtering is possible.

SQL

Structured Query Language (SQL) is a standard language for working with databases. SQL consists of several keywords. You use the keywords to construct statements known as **queries**. Queries are instructions submitted to a database, which then executes the queries.

> **TIP:** Although SQL is a language, you don't use it to write applications. It is intended only as a standard means of interacting with a database. You still need a general programming language such as Visual Basic to write applications with user interfaces.

Modifying the Query in a Data Source

To modify (edit) a query used in a data source, locate its DataSet schema file in the *Solution Explorer* window. Suppose you have created a data source named *SalesStaffDataSet*; then the DataSet schema file would be named *SalesStaffDataSet.xsd*. Double-click the filename to open the *Dataset Designer* tool, shown in Figure 4-18. The top line shows the table name (*SalesStaff*). The next several lines list the columns in the table, identifying the *ID* column as the primary key. The *SalesStaffTableAdapter* appears next, followed by a list of its database queries. By default, there is one query named *Fill, GetData()* that fills the DataSet when the form loads.

Figure 4-18 SalesStaffDataSet, in the *Dataset Designer* window

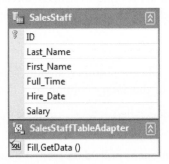

If you right-click the DataSet and select *Configure* from the popup menu, you can modify the currently selected query using the *TableAdapter Configuration Wizard*, shown in Figure 4-19. If the query text is simple enough, you can modify it directly in this window. If the query is more complicated, click the *Query Builder* button to display a *Query Builder* window. A sample is shown in Figure 4-20.

Query Builder

Query Builder is a tool provided by Visual Studio for creating and modifying SQL queries. It consists of four sections, called *panes*, shown in Figure 4-21.

- The ***diagram pane*** displays all the tables used in the query, with a check mark next to each field that will be used in the DataSet.
- The ***grid pane*** displays the query in a spreadsheet-like format, which is particularly well suited to choosing a sort order and entering selection criteria.

Figure 4-19 *TableAdapter Configuration Wizard*

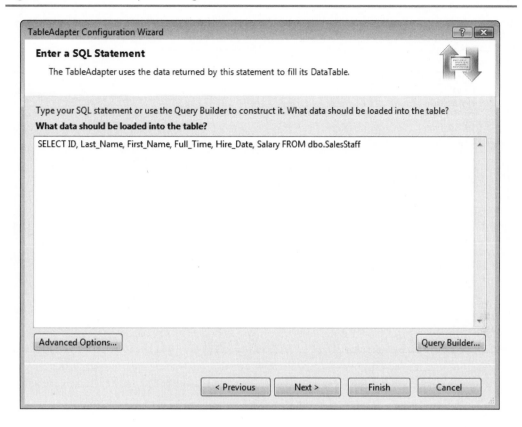

Figure 4-20 *Query Builder* window

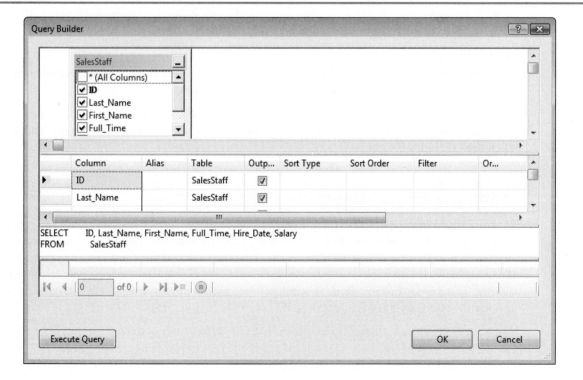

Figure 4-21 Sections of the *Query Builder* window

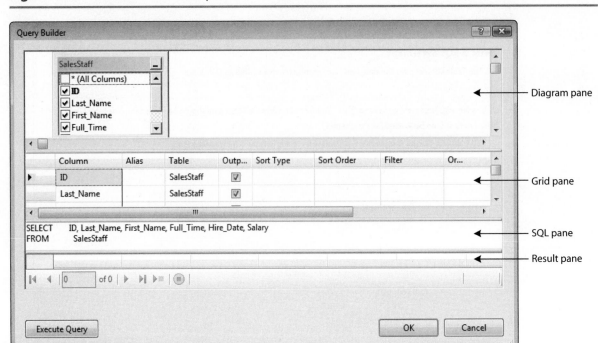

- The *SQL pane* displays the actual SQL query that corresponds to the tables and fields selected in the diagram and grid panes. Experienced SQL coders often write queries directly into this pane.
- The *results pane* displays the rows returned by executing the current SQL query. To fill the results pane, right-click in the *Query Builder* window and select *Run* from the *context* menu.

To remove and restore panes, right-click the window and select *Pane* from the popup menu. The menu allows you to check or uncheck individual panes.

To add a new table to the *Query Builder* window, right-click inside the diagram pane and select *Add Table* from the popup menu. To save the current query and close *Query Builder*, click the *OK* button.

Adding a SELECT Query to a DataGridView

If you want to add a SELECT query to a DataGridView control, the easiest way to do it is to use the TableAdapter attached to the grid. Suppose that the SalesStaffTableAdapter is attached to a DataGridView displaying the *SalesStaff* table from the *Company* database. Then in the form's Design view, you can right-click the TableAdapter icon and select *Add Query*. The *Search Criteria Builder* window appears, as shown in Figure 4-22. You could modify the query so it reads as follows:

```
SELECT ID, Last_Name, First_Name, Full_Time, Hire_Date, Salary
FROM SalesStaff
WHERE Salary < 45000
```

Figure 4-22 *Search Criteria Builder* window

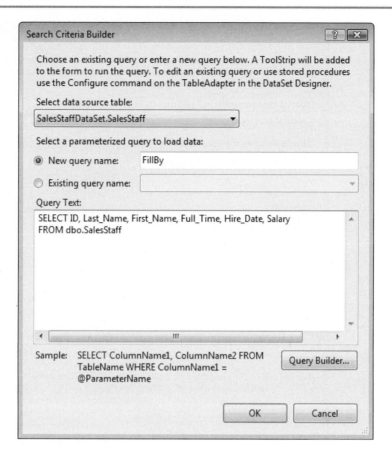

Figure 4-23 shows what the window looks like after adding a WHERE clause to the SELECT statement. You can give a name to the query, such as *Salary_query*. When you click the *OK* button, a ToolStrip control is added to the form, with a query button. When you run the application and click the *Salary_query* button on the ToolStrip, the results are shown in Figure 4-24. Only rows with salaries less than $45,000 are displayed.

> **TIP:** If you dock a grid inside a form and then add a ToolStrip control, the grid's title bar is covered up by the ToolStrip. To avoid this problem, set the grid's Dock property to *None*, drag the grid a bit lower on the form with the mouse, and resize it so it fits. Then set the grid's Anchor property to *Top, Bottom, Left, Right*.

If you add a query to a dataset and then later delete the query from the *DataSet Designer* window, you may find that your program will not run. If this happens, Visual Studio may have left behind some extra code that had been added to the designer file when the query was created. To work around this problem, select the *Rebuild <projectName>* command from Visual Studio's *Build* menu.

In Tutorial 4-2, you will create several queries that display rows in a DataGridView control.

Figure 4-23 Creating a query in the *Search Criteria Builder*

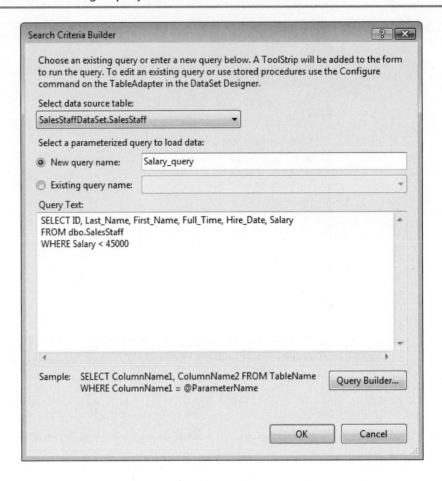

Figure 4-24 Dataset rows filtered by *Salary_query*

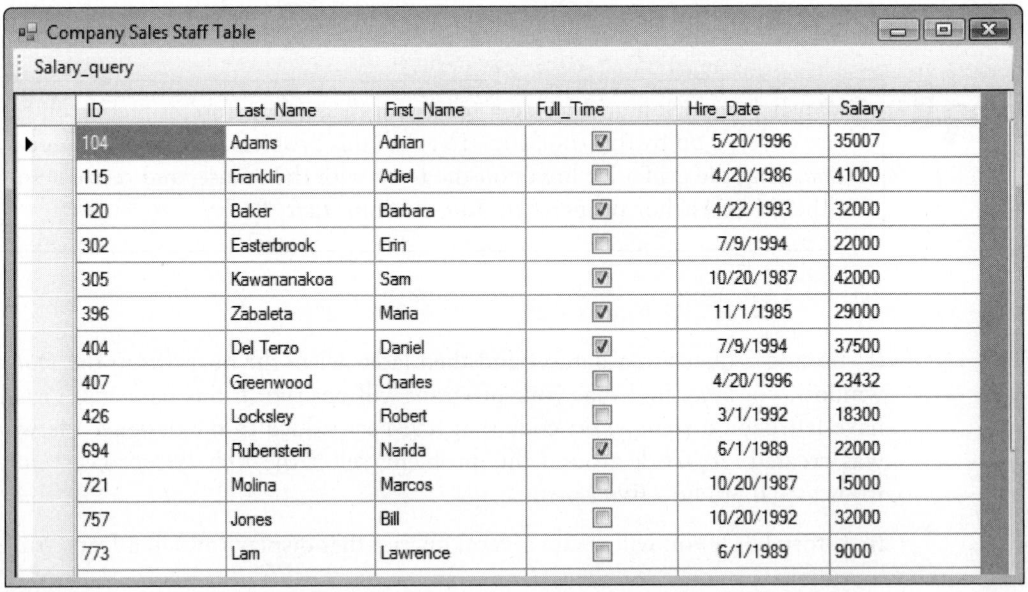

	ID	Last_Name	First_Name	Full_Time	Hire_Date	Salary
▶	104	Adams	Adrian	☑	5/20/1996	35007
	115	Franklin	Adiel	☐	4/20/1986	41000
	120	Baker	Barbara	☑	4/22/1993	32000
	302	Easterbrook	Erin	☐	7/9/1994	22000
	305	Kawananakoa	Sam	☑	10/20/1987	42000
	396	Zabaleta	Maria	☑	11/1/1985	29000
	404	Del Terzo	Daniel	☑	7/9/1994	37500
	407	Greenwood	Charles	☐	4/20/1996	23432
	426	Locksley	Robert	☐	3/1/1992	18300
	694	Rubenstein	Narida	☑	6/1/1989	22000
	721	Molina	Marcos	☐	10/20/1987	15000
	757	Jones	Bill	☐	10/20/1992	32000
	773	Lam	Lawrence	☐	6/1/1989	9000

Company Sales Staff Table

Salary_query

Tutorial 4-2:
Filtering rows in the *SalesStaff* table

In this tutorial, you will create several queries that change the way rows from the *SalesStaff* table are displayed in a DataGridView control.

Tutorial Steps

Step 1: Copy the *SalesStaff 1* folder you created in Tutorial 4-1 to a new folder named *SalesStaff 2*. You may have to close Visual Studio to release its lock on the database file.

> **TIP:** To copy a folder in Windows Explorer, right-click its name with the mouse and select *Copy* from the popup menu; right-click again and select *Paste* from the popup menu. The file will be named *Copy of <name>*, where *<name>* is the original folder name. Right-click the copied filename and select *Rename* from the popup menu. Type the new folder name and press *Enter*. (The same procedure works when copying files.)

Step 2: Open the project from the *SalesStaff 2* folder (the solution file will still be named *SalesStaff 1.sln*).

Step 3: Right-click the project name in the *Solution Explorer* window, and choose *Rename*. Rename the project *SalesStaff 2*.

Step 4: In the Design window for Form1, right-click the SalesStaffTableAdapter control in the component tray and select *Add Query* from the popup menu.

Step 5: In the *Search Criteria Builder* window, name the query *Full_Time*. Set its query text to the following:

```
SELECT ID, Last_Name, First_Name, Full_Time, Hire_Date, Salary
FROM SalesStaff
WHERE (Full_Time = 'True')
```

Step 6: Click the *OK* button to close the *Search Criteria Builder*.

Step 7: If your grid column headers are hidden behind the ToolStrip control, slide the grid downward to expose the column headers. Anchor it to the four sides of the form, using the Anchor property.

Step 8: Save the project and run the application. Click the *Full_Time* button and observe that only full-time employees are displayed. Close the application and return to Design mode.

Step 9: Let's look at the source code generated by Visual Studio when you added the Tool-StripButton. It calls a method named Full_Time, *using the* SalesStaffTableAdapter object. The argument passed to the method is the *SalesStaff* table inside the *SalesStaffDataSet* DataSet:

```
Private Sub Full_TimeToolStripButton_Click() _
  Handles Full_TimeToolStripButton.Click
  Try
    Me.SalesStaffTableAdapter.Full_Time
      (Me.SalesStaffDataSet.SalesStaff)
  Catch ex As System.Exception
    System.Windows.Forms.MessageBox.Show(ex.Message)
  End Try
End Sub
```

If an exception is thrown, a popup box displays the exception message. As an alternative, you can replace the call to MessageBox.Show with a statement that assigns a value to an ErrorProvider control.

Step 10: Now you will add another button to the ToolStrip that displays all table rows. Right-click the SalesStaffTableAdapter control, and select *Add Query*.

Step 11: In the *Search Criteria Builder*, name the query *All_Rows*, and keep the existing Query text. Click the *OK* button to close the window and create the query. Notice that a second ToolStrip has been added to the form, as shown in Figure 4-25.

Figure 4-25 *SalesStaff* table in a DataGridView, with two query buttons

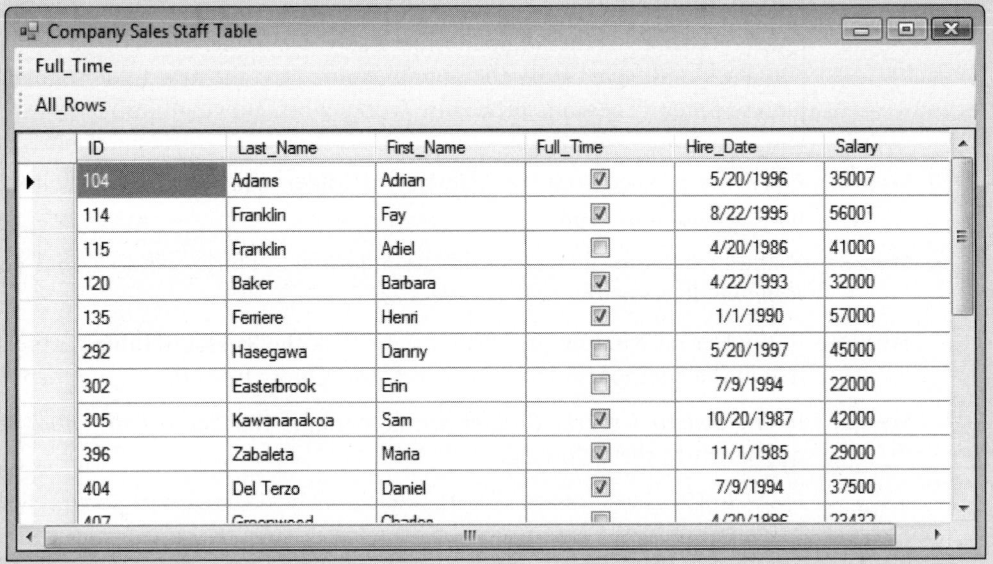

Company Sales Staff Table

Full_Time

All_Rows

ID	Last_Name	First_Name	Full_Time	Hire_Date	Salary
104	Adams	Adrian	☑	5/20/1996	35007
114	Franklin	Fay	☑	8/22/1995	56001
115	Franklin	Adiel	☐	4/20/1986	41000
120	Baker	Barbara	☑	4/22/1993	32000
135	Ferriere	Henri	☑	1/1/1990	57000
292	Hasegawa	Danny	☐	5/20/1997	45000
302	Easterbrook	Erin	☐	7/9/1994	22000
305	Kawananakoa	Sam	☑	10/20/1987	42000
396	Zabaleta	Maria	☑	11/1/1985	29000
404	Del Terzo	Daniel	☑	7/9/1994	37500
407	Greenwood	Charles	☐	4/20/1996	33432

Step 12: Again, you will need to adjust the top of the grid so the column headings are visible.

Step 13: Save the project. Run the application and click both query buttons. The display should alternate between displaying all rows, and rows containing full-time employees only.

Step 14: End the application and close the project.

In Tutorial 4-2, you saw how easy it was to create queries that select database rows. You can create any number of queries that filter rows on different columns and values. Later in this chapter, we will show how to use query parameters to modify search criteria.

It is possible to place both query buttons on the same ToolStrip if you do the following:

1. In Design mode, select one of the buttons and cut it to the Windows Clipboard (press *Ctrl-X*).
2. Select the other toolbar and paste the button (press *Ctrl-V*). Both buttons should be on the same ToolStrip.
3. Select and delete the empty ToolStrip.

4. Open the *Code* window and observe that the Handles clause has disappeared from the Click event handler associated with the button you copied. Add the Handles clause back to the method header. For example:

```
Handles All_RowsToolStripButton.Click
```

 Checkpoint

17. What does the acronym SQL represent, in relation to databases?

18. Why do SQL queries work with any relational database?

19. Write an SQL SELECT statement that retrieves the First_Name and Last_Name columns from a table named *Employees*.

20. How do you add a query to a TableAdapter in the component tray of a form?

21. Write a WHERE clause in SQL that limits the returned data to rows in which Salary is less than or equal to $85,000.

4.5 Data-Bound Controls

In this section, you learn how to bind data sources to individual controls such as TextBoxes, Labels, and ListBoxes. We call such controls **data-bound controls** because they update their contents automatically when you move from one row to the next in a DataSet. Data-bound controls can also update the contents of fields. You will learn how to bind a DataGridView to an existing DataSet. You will also learn how to use a ListBox control to navigate from one DataSet row to another.

Visual Studio Copies Database Files

When a new data source is an attached SQL Server file, the dialog window shown in Figure 4-26 pops up and asks if you want to copy the database file to your project. In general, making a local copy of the database is a good idea. The second paragraph, easily overlooked, reminds you that a fresh copy of the database will be copied to your program's output directory each time you run the application.

Figure 4-26 Copying a database file to the project folder

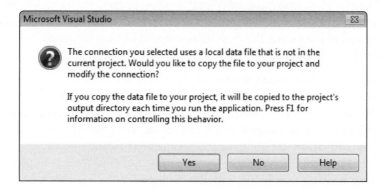

If you answer *Yes* to the dialog window, Visual Studio copies the database file to your project's root folder. Each time you build the application, the database is automatically copied to the project's output directory. This is the database file your application will display and update. Its location depends on how you run the program.

- If you run in Debug mode, the output directory is \bin\Debug.
- If you run without debugging, the output directory is \bin\Release.

Distributing a Compiled Database Application

Visual Basic makes it very easy for you to distribute a compiled application along with its database. The technique is called **xcopy deployment**. All you have to do is copy the application's EXE file and database files from the \bin\Debug folder, or from the \bin\Release folder. In Figure 4-27, for example, the application named *Insert Karate Payments* is bundled with the *karate.mdf* database file.

Figure 4-27 With Visual Basic, you can distribute a compiled application with its database

Name	Type
☐ Insert Karate Payments.exe	Application
🗔 karate.mdf	SQL Server Database Primary Data File

Modifying a Database Connection String

To modify a database connection string, right-click the entry named *My Project* in the *Solution Explorer* window. In the *Properties* window, select the *Settings* tab. The first line in the grid will probably be the database connection string. Click the button with the three dots in the Value column, as shown in Figure 4-28.

Figure 4-28 Modifying a database connection string

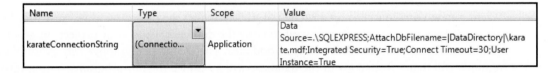

Name	Type	Scope	Value
karateConnectionString	(Connectio... ▾	Application	Data Source=.\SQLEXPRESS;AttachDbFilename=|DataDirectory|\karate.mdf;Integrated Security=True;Connect Timeout=30;User Instance=True

Renaming and Deleting Data Sources

You cannot rename a data source, for good reason: A data source represents the name of a DataSet class generated by Visual Studio. In fact, the DataSet class contains several other inner classes (classes declared inside classes). Renaming a DataSet class, all its related classes, and all objects using the class names would be next to impossible. Therefore, choose a name for your data source that you do not plan to change.

You can delete a data source easily: Select its *XSD* file in the *Solution Explorer* window and press the *Delete* key. However, if your program has one or more forms that contain BindingSources connected to the data source, be careful. After deleting the data source, you will not be able to open any forms in the *Designer* window that contain BindingSources. You will encounter an error message similar to the one shown in Figure 4-29. We recommend that you keep a separate backup copy of your project to protect yourself against errors from which it may be too difficult to recover.

TIP: Before deleting a DataSet, delete all BindingSource controls on your form that connect to the DataSet.

Figure 4-29 Error message generated by Visual Studio after a data source is deleted

The designer cannot process the code at line 26: Me.KarateDataSet = New DeleteMe.KarateDataSet() The code within the method 'InitializeComponent' is generated by the designer and should not be manually modified. Please remove any changes and try opening the designer again.
☝ Go to code

Instances of this error (1)
1. DeleteMe Form1.Designer.vb Line:26 Column:1   Show Call Stack

Binding the Data Source to a DataGridView Control

In Tutorial 4-1, you used the *DataGridView Tasks* window to guide you through creating a BindingSource, TableAdapter, and DataSet. If the project already contains a suitable data source, you can bind it to a DataGridView control just by dragging the *SalesStaff* table from the *Data Sources* window to the open area of a form. Visual Studio adds a custom navigation bar to the form, as shown in Figure 4-30.

Figure 4-30 After dragging the *SalesStaff* table from the *Data Sources* window onto a form

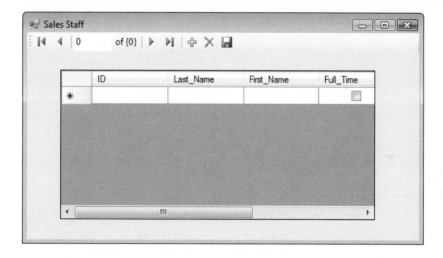

Once the grid has been bound to a DataSet, you can set its Dock property so it will always fill to the borders of the form. To do this, select the grid, display the *Properties* window, select the Dock property, and click the center docking button. The grid expands to fill the form. Figure 4-31 shows the *SalesStaff* table in a DataGridView with a toolbar at runtime.

Binding Individual Fields to Controls

If the *Data Sources* window contains an existing data source, you can easily create an individual data-bound control for each column by dragging a table from the data source onto your form. First, select *Details* in the dropdown list associated with the table, as shown in Figure 4-32. (The default control type is DataGridView, which we've already used.) When you drag the table name onto a form, a separate control is created for each field. As shown in Figure 4-33, a navigation toolbar is also added to the form. (You may have to wait a few seconds for the controls to appear.)

Sometimes data source column names such as First_Name contain underscore characters. When you bind the data source to controls, Visual Studio removes the underscores as it generates labels next to the controls.

Figure 4-31 After docking the grid in the center of the form (shown at runtime)

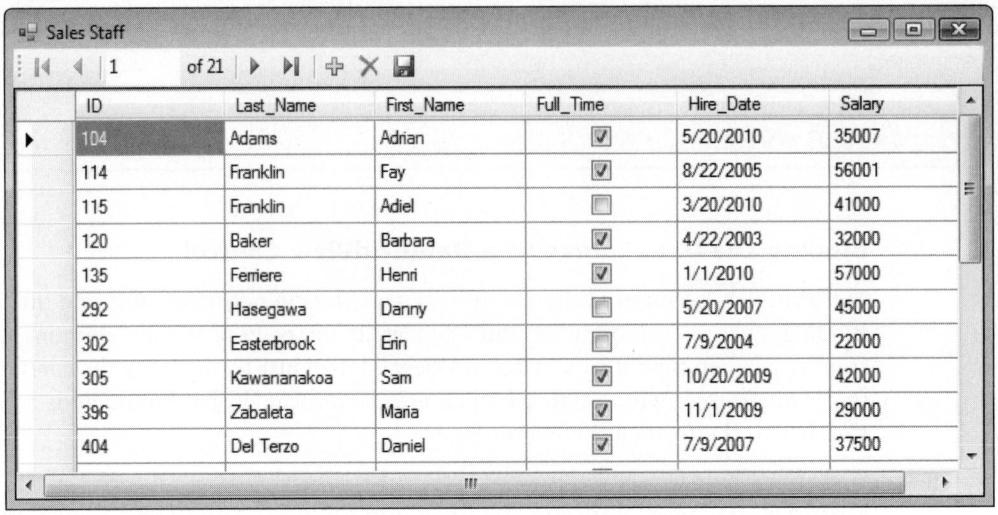

ID	Last_Name	First_Name	Full_Time	Hire_Date	Salary
104	Adams	Adrian	☑	5/20/2010	35007
114	Franklin	Fay	☑	8/22/2005	56001
115	Franklin	Adiel	☐	3/20/2010	41000
120	Baker	Barbara	☑	4/22/2003	32000
135	Ferriere	Henri	☑	1/1/2010	57000
292	Hasegawa	Danny	☐	5/20/2007	45000
302	Easterbrook	Erin	☐	7/9/2004	22000
305	Kawananakoa	Sam	☑	10/20/2009	42000
396	Zabaleta	Maria	☑	11/1/2009	29000
404	Del Terzo	Daniel	☑	7/9/2007	37500

Sales Staff — ◄◄ ◄ 1 of 21 ► ►| ✛ ✕ 🖫

Figure 4-32 Selecting a table's binding control, *Data Sources* window

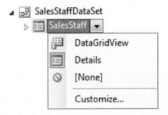

Figure 4-33 After dragging a data source onto the form

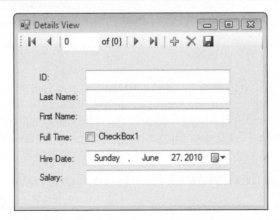

You may want to modify the appearance or properties of the controls. For example, if you want the Hire_Date column to display in *mm/dd/yyyy* format, set its Format property equal to *Short*.

By default, Text and Numeric database columns are bound to TextBox controls, *Yes/No* fields are bound to check boxes, and *DateTime* fields are bound to DateTimePicker controls. If you would prefer not to let the user modify a protected field such as ID, change the binding control type for individual fields in the *Data Source* window. For example, if you click the ID field in the *SalesStaff* table in the *Data Source* window, a list of control types displays (see Figure 4-34). If you choose the Label control type, a user can view the field but not modify its contents.

Figure 4-34 Selecting the control binding type for the *ID* field in the *Data Sources* window

Figure 4-35 shows a sample of the same form with a Label control for the *ID* field and with some customizing of the appearance of the other controls.

Figure 4-35 Displaying one row of the *SalesStaff* table in bound controls

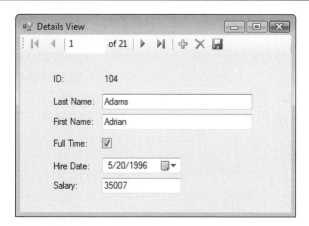

If you want to have only one or two bound controls from a data source, drag individual columns from the *Data Sources* window onto a form. To run and modify this sample program, see the *Binding_Example* program located in the Chapter 4 examples folder.

Introducing the *Karate* Database

The database we will use for the next set of examples is called *Karate (karate.mdf)*, designed around the membership and scheduling of classes for a martial arts school. A table named *Members* contains information about members, such as their first and last name, phone number, and so on. See Table 4-12.

Related to the *Members* table is the *Payments* table, shown in Table 4-13. It shows recent dues payments by members. Each row in the *Payments* table contains a Member_Id value that identifies the member (from the *Members* table) who made a dues payment. The

Table 4-12 The *Members* table from the *Karate* database

ID	Last_Name	First_Name	Phone	Date_Joined
1	Kahumanu	Keoki	111-2222	2/20/2002
2	Chong	Anne	232-2323	2/20/2010
3	Hasegawa	Elaine	313-3455	2/20/2004
4	Kahane	Brian	646-9387	5/20/2008
5	Gonzalez	Aldo	123-2345	6/6/2009
6	Kousevitzky	Jascha	414-2345	2/20/2010
7	Taliafea	Moses	545-2323	5/20/2005
8	Concepcion	Rafael	602-3312	5/20/2007
9	Taylor	Winifred	333-2222	2/20/2010

Table 4-13 The *Payments* table

ID	Member_Id	Payment_Date	Amount
1	1	10/20/2009	$48.00
2	2	02/20/2010	$80.00
3	6	03/20/2010	$75.00
4	4	12/16/2009	$50.00
5	5	04/11/2009	$65.00
6	3	02/16/2009	$75.00
7	8	03/20/2010	$77.00
8	8	02/27/2010	$44.00
9	6	04/20/2010	$77.00
10	5	01/16/2010	$66.00
11	8	05/11/2010	$77.00
13	6	02/20/2010	$77.00
14	7	07/16/2009	$77.00
15	1	03/11/2010	$44.00
16	3	03/28/2010	$43.00
17	4	03/27/2010	$44.00
19	9	02/20/2010	$44.00
22	9	03/20/2010	$55.00

relationship is shown by the diagram in Figure 4-36. The line connects the ID field in the *Members* table to the Member_Id field in the *Payments* table.

Binding Data Sources to List-Type Controls

ListBoxes and ComboBoxes are ideal tools for displaying lists of items and for permitting users to select individual items. All you have to do is set the following properties:

- The **DataSource property** identifies a data table that will provide the database data.
- The **DisplayMember property** identifies the column within the table that displays in the ListBox or ComboBox.

Figure 4-36 Relationship between the *Members* and *Payments* tables

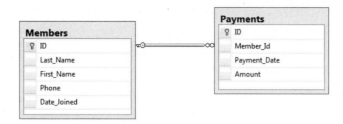

The ValueMember property identifies the column within the table that supplies an identifying value when an item is selected in the list box. The identifying value is returned in the SelectedValue property of the list box. Usually, the ValueMember property contains the name of the table's primary key field because that field uniquely identifies every table entry.

When you use the mouse to drag a table column from the *Data Sources* window onto a list box or ComboBox, Visual Studio automatically creates the necessary data components: a DataSet, a BindingSource, and a TableAdapter. When you click the smart tag at the top of a ListBox or ComboBox, a tasks dialog makes it easy to set the data-binding properties. A sample is shown in Figure 4-37.

Figure 4-37 Setting the data-binding options of a ListBox control

The data-bound ListBox or ComboBox is a great navigation tool. When the user selects an item in the list, the form's BindingSource repositions itself to the DataSet row that matches the selected value. All other fields bound to the same DataSet on the form are updated automatically with the current row's data. Tutorial 4-3 will show how this happens.

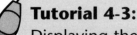

Tutorial 4-3:
Displaying the *Members* table in a ListBox

In this tutorial, you display the last names of members from the *Members* table in the *Karate* database. When the user clicks a member's name, the program displays the date when the member joined.

Tutorial Steps

Step 1: Create a Windows desktop application named *Member List*.

Step 2: Click *Add New Data Source* in the *Data Sources* window. (If you cannot see the *Data Sources* window, select *Show Data Sources* from the *Data* menu.)

Step 3: Follow the steps in the *Data Source Configuration Wizard* to create a connection to the *Members* table in the *karate.mdf* database file. Name the DataSet *KarateDataSet*.

Step 4: Set the form's Text property to *Member List*.

Step 5: Add a ListBox control to the form and name it *lstMembers*.

Step 6: Add a Label just above the list box and set its Text property to *Member Names*. Your form should look like the one shown in Figure 4-38.

Figure 4-38 *Member List* program with list box

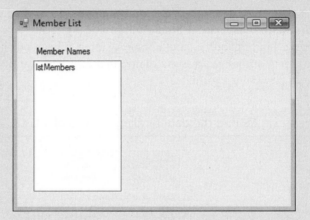

Step 7: Click the ListBox's smart tag, which causes the *ListBox Tasks* window to display, shown in Figure 4-39. Select the *Use Data Bound Items* check box.

Figure 4-39 The ListBox Tasks window

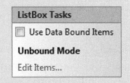

The ListBox Tasks window, shown in Figure 4-40, now contains several data-binding fields.

Figure 4-40 ListBox Tasks window

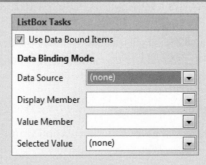

Step 8: Select the *Data Source* dropdown list, expand the *Other Data Sources* group, expand *Project Data Sources*, expand *KarateDataSet*, and select the *Members* table (shown in Figure 4-41). Notice that Visual Studio just added three components to the form's component tray: a DataSet, a BindingSource, and a TableAdapter.

Figure 4-41 Setting the list box's DataSource property

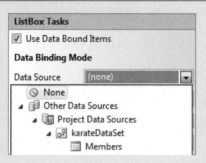

Step 9: While still in the ListView tasks window, set the list box's DisplayMember property to *Last_Name*.

Step 10: Save and run the application. The list box should contain the last names of members, as shown in Figure 4-42. Close the window and return to *Design* mode.

Figure 4-42 List box filled, at runtime

Step 11: Next, you will add a data-bound label to the form that displays the member's phone number. Click the *Phone* field in the *Data Sources* window, select *Label* from the dropdown list, and drag the *Phone* field with the mouse onto the program's form. Set the label's BorderStyle property to *Fixed 3D*.

Step 12: Save and run the program. As you click each member's name, notice how the current phone number is displayed. For a sample, see Figure 4-43.

Let's analyze what's happening here. When the user selects a name in the list box, the form's data-binding mechanism moves to the DataSet row containing the person's name. The Label control is data-bound to the phone number field, so it displays the phone number of the person selected in the list box.

Step 13: For each remaining field in the Data Sources window, select its dropdown list and choose the *Label* control type. Then drag each field onto the form. Set the BorderStyle property of each label to *Fixed 3D*. When you run the application, it should appear as in Figure 4-44.

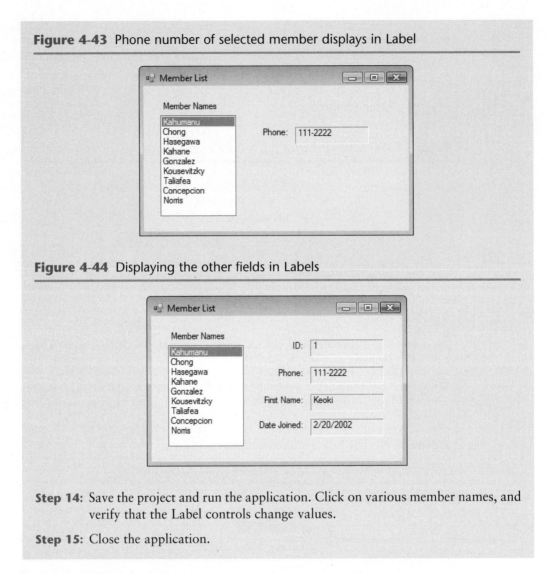

Figure 4-43 Phone number of selected member displays in Label

Figure 4-44 Displaying the other fields in Labels

Step 14: Save the project and run the application. Click on various member names, and verify that the Label controls change values.

Step 15: Close the application.

Adding Rows to DataTables

Using the NewRow Method

The DataTable class has two methods that help you add rows to tables in DataSets: NewRow and Add. The *NewRow method* creates and returns a new, empty row having the same structure as the other rows in the table. It is declared as follows:

```
NewRow() As DataRow
```

Here is a sample call to NewRow, using the Payments table in a DataSet named PaymentsDataSet:

```
Dim row As DataRow
row = PaymentsDataSet.Payments.NewRow()
```

Because NewRow returns a general DataRow type, the return value must be cast into a PaymentsRow type before we can reference any of the fields in the *Payments* table. The following lines redefine row and show how the cast is done:

```
Dim row As PaymentsDataSet.PaymentsRow
row = CType (PaymentsDataSet.Payments.NewRow,
  PaymentsDataSet.PaymentsRow)
```

Next, you can assign values to columns in the table. The column names are properties in the PaymentsDataSet.PaymentRow class.

```
With row
   .Member_Id = 5
   .Payment_Date = '5/15/2011'
   .Amount = 500D
End With
```

The last step is to add the new row to the table by calling the Add method from the Rows collection. This is how the method is declared:

```
Function Add(row As DataRow) As DataRow
```

Continuing with the same example, the following statement adds row to the *Payments* table:

```
PaymentsDataSet.Payments.Rows.Add(row)
```

Using the Rows.Add Method

The Rows.Add method also adds a row to a DataTable. When calling Rows.Add, pass it the new column values. The following code adds a new entry to the *Members* table of MembersDataSet:

```
MembersDataSet.Members.Rows.Add(15, Jones, Sam, 111-2222,
   '5/15/2010')
```

If the underlying database table's primary key is an auto-generated field, you should pass the value *Nothing* as the corresponding Add method argument. Here is an example from the Karate Payments table, in which the first column is auto-generated:

```
PaymentsDataSet.Payments.Rows.Add(Nothing, 5, '5/15/2011', 50D)
```

Updating a DataTable

Adding a row to a DataTable does not affect the database from which it was copied. If you want to copy your changes back into the database, call the **Update** method of the TableAdapter associated with the DataTable. The following statement, for example, writes all pending changes in the Payments table (in the PaymentsDataSet) back to the underlying database:

```
PaymentsTableAdapter.Update(PaymentsDataSet.Payments)
```

Because a DataSet can contain multiple tables, updating a DataSet causes all changes to its member tables to be updated. The following statement updates all tables inside the PaymentsDataSet:

```
PaymentsTableAdapter.Update(PaymentsDataSet)
```

Direct Insert Using a TableAdapter

To add a row to a database table, call a TableAdapter's **Insert** method. Pass it the required column values, ignoring auto-generated fields. In the next example, the PaymentsTableAdapter adds a new row to the *Payments* table, passing the ID, date, and payment amount:

```
PaymentsTableAdapter.Insert(5, '5/15/2011', 50D)
```

Removing a Row from a DataTable

Removing a row from a DataTable requires two steps. First, get a reference to the row you want to remove; second, call the **Rows.Remove** method, passing it the row reference. For example, the following code calls FindByID, passing it the ID of the payment to be removed. Then, the row object returned by FindByID is passed to the Rows.Remove method:

```
Dim row As DataRow = PaymentsDataSet.Payments.FindByID(36)
PaymentsDataSet.Payments.Rows.Remove(row)
```

In Tutorial 4-4, you will write a program that adds rows to a database table.

Tutorial 4-4:
Inserting rows in the *Karate Payments* table

In this tutorial, you will create an application that adds rows to the *Payments* table in the *Karate* database.

Tutorial Steps

Step 1: Create a new Windows application named *Insert Karate Payments*.

Step 2: In the *Data Sources* window, add a new data source, using the *Payments* table from the *Karate* database. Select the *karate.mdf* file located in the chapter examples folder. Name the DataSet *PaymentsDataSet*.

Step 3: When asked if you want to copy the database file to your project, answer *Yes*.

Step 4: Add three TextBox controls to the form with appropriate labels. One is named *txtMemberId*, another is *txtDate*, and the third is named *txtAmount*. Use Figure 4-45 as a guide.

Figure 4-45 The startup form in the *Insert Karate Payments* application

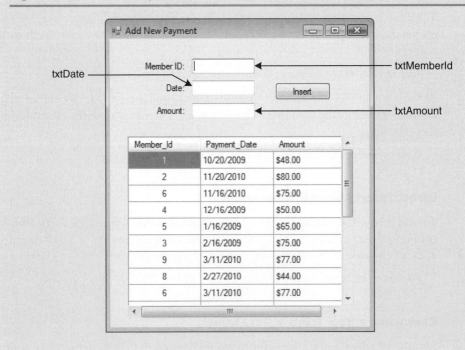

Step 5: Add a Button control named *btnInsert* and set its Text property to *Insert*.

Step 6: Add a DataGridView control to the form and set the following properties: Name = *dgvPayments*; BorderStyle = None; BackgroundColor = Control; ReadOnly = *True*; RowHeadersVisible = *False*; Anchor = Top, Bottom, Left, Right.

Step 7: Open the grid's *DataGridView Tasks* window and set its DataSource property to the *Payments* table of PaymentsDataSet.

Step 8: Select the grid's Columns property, which opens the *Edit Columns* window. Remove the ID column. The remaining columns are shown in Figure 4-46.

Figure 4-46 Editing the Columns property of the *dgvPayments* grid

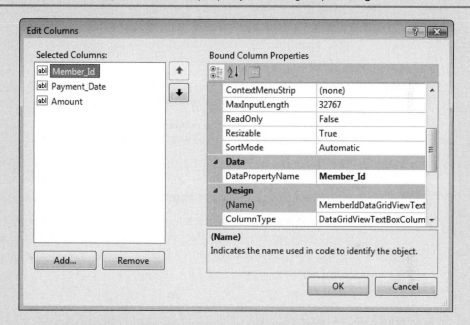

Step 9: Still in the *Edit Columns* window, select the Member_Id column, and open the DefaultCellStyle property in the right-hand list box. The *CellStyle Builder* window should appear.

Step 10: In the *CellStyle Builder* window, set the following properties: Alignment = MiddleCenter; ForeColor = Blue. Click the *OK* button to close the window.

Step 11: In the *Edit Columns* window, select the Amount column and open its DefaultCellStyle property.

Step 12: Open its Format property and select *Currency*. Click the *OK* button to close the dialog.

Step 13: Click the *OK* button to close the *CellStyle Builder* window.

Step 14: Experiment with the three columns, changing colors and formats as you wish. When you finish, click the *OK* button to close the *Edit Columns* window.

Step 15: Save and run the application. You should see a list of payments in the grid, as shown earlier in Figure 4-45. Then stop the application.

Step 16: Next, you will add code to the *Insert* button's Click event handler that lets the user create and save new payments. In *Design* mode, double-click the *Insert* button and add the following code to the button's Click event handler:

```
Try
  PaymentsTableAdapter.Insert(CShort(txtMemberId.Text),
    CDate(txtDate.Text), CDec(txtAmount.Text))
  Me.PaymentsTableAdapter.Fill(Me.PaymentsDataSet.Payments)
Catch ex As Exception
  MessageBox.Show(ex.Message, "Database Error")
End Try
```

We use a Try-Catch statement here to handle exceptions thrown by the database.

The code you added calls the TableAdapter's Insert method, passing to it the values of the three columns: member_Id, date, and amount. Each argument must be converted to a type that matches the appropriate DataSet column type. Then the Fill command is called so the user can see the new payment in the grid.

Step 17: Add the following lines to the form's Load event handler. As the comment says, we want the text box to display today's date:

```
' Set the text box to today's date.
txtDate.Text = FormatDateTime(Today, DateFormat.ShortDate)
```

Step 18: Save the project and run the application. Add a new payment, using a Member_ID value between 1 and 9. Verify that your payment appears in the grid after clicking the *Insert* button.

Step 19: Try to add a payment with a Member_ID equal to 152. This Member_ID does not exist in the *Members* table, so you should see an error message (shown in Figure 4-47) saying that you violated a foreign key constraint. The payment is not saved.

Figure 4-47 Error message displayed when the user attempts to add a payment row, using a nonexistent Member_ID

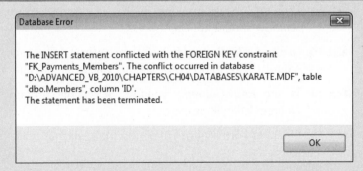

> **Database Error**
>
> The INSERT statement conflicted with the FOREIGN KEY constraint "FK_Payments_Members". The conflict occurred in database "D:\ADVANCED_VB_2010\CHAPTERS\CH04\DATABASES\KARATE.MDF", table "dbo.Members", column 'ID'.
> The statement has been terminated.
>
> OK

Step 20: Add a payment that uses an invalid date format or a nonnumeric value for the payment amount. When you click the *Insert* button, observe the error message generated by the database. Your programs should recover gracefully when users enter invalid data.

Step 21: Close the application.

If you run the program again without building the project, the payments you added during the previous run should appear. But if you build the project and then run it, the added payments will be gone. Whenever you build a database project, Visual Studio copies the database from the project's root directory to its executable directory, named *bin\debug*. When the application executes, it reads and writes the database in the executable directory.

Using Loops with DataSets

Techniques you've learned about loops and collections in previous chapters also apply to DataSets. You can iterate over the Rows collection of a DataTable using the *For Each* statement. Usually, it's best to create a strongly typed row that matches the type of rows in the DataSet.

The following loop iterates over the Payments table of the PaymentsDataSet, adding the *Amount* column to a total. The DataSet was built from the Payments table in the *Karate* database.

```
Dim row As PaymentsDataSet.PaymentsRow
Dim decTotal As Decimal = 0
For Each row In PaymentsDataSet.Payments.Rows
  decTotal += row.Amount
Next
```

In Tutorial 4-5, you will modify the *Karate Student Payments* application.

Tutorial 4-5:

Adding a total to the *Insert Karate Payments* application

In this tutorial, you will add statements that calculate the total amount of payments made by students in the karate school.

Tutorial Steps

Step 1: Open the *Insert Karate Payments* program that you created in Tutorial 4-4.

Step 2: Add a new button to the form. Set its properties as follows: Name = *btnTotal*; Text = *Total Payments*.

Step 3: Double-click the new button and modify its Click handler so that it contains the following code:

```
Dim decTotal As Decimal = 0
Dim row As PaymentsDataSet.PaymentsRow
For Each row In PaymentsDataSet.Payments.Rows
  decTotal += row.Amount
Next
MessageBox.Show("Total payments are equal to " _
  & decTotal.ToString("c"), "Total")
```

Step 4: Save the project and run the application. Click on the *Total Payments* button and observe the results. A sample is shown in Figure 4-48. (Your program's total may differ from the value shown in the figure.)

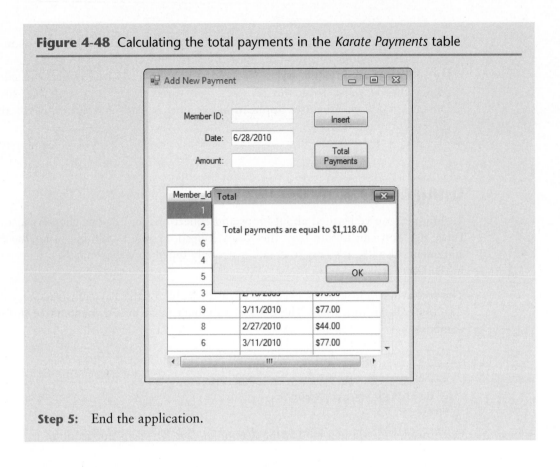

Figure 4-48 Calculating the total payments in the *Karate Payments* table

Step 5: End the application.

 Checkpoint

22. Which Visual Studio window displays the list of data sources belonging to a project?

23. The _____ *Configuration Wizard* is a tool you can use to create a connection to a database and select a database table.

24. If a certain DataTable already exists, what is the easiest way to bind it to a DataGridView control?

25. How do you bind a single DataTable column to a text box?

26. By default, which control binds to a DateTime field in a DataTable?

27. What is the menu command for adding a new DataSet to the current project?

4.6 **Focus on Problem Solving: Karate School Manager Application**

Suppose you are a black belt in the Kyoshi Karate School and you would like to create a management application with the following capabilities:

1. Displays a list of all members.
2. Permits the user to sort on any column, edit individual rows, and delete rows.
3. Adds new entries to the members table.
4. Finds a member by letting the user enter a partial last name.

5. Displays all payments, sorting on any column.
6. Displays a list of payments by one member.

Techniques for completing some of these tasks have been demonstrated in this chapter. Other tasks will require new skills that will be demonstrated along the way. Before beginning to write the application, you should consult with the application's potential users to clarify some user interface details. We will assume that users want the following:

- For requirement 1, use a DataGridView control.
- For requirement 2, set options that permit modifying and removing rows—the user will be able to sort by clicking on column headings.
- For requirement 3, create a data input form with TextBox controls and a DateTimePicker control.
- For requirement 4, let the user type a partial last name into a text box. Display a grid containing all members whose last names begin with the letters entered by the user.
- For requirement 5, join the *Members* and *Payments* tables and display the results in a DataGridView control.
- For requirement 6, display a list of member names (last name, first name) in a ComboBox control; when a member is selected by the user, fill a DataGridView control with payments by the member.

General Design Guidelines

Each form will have a *File* menu with a *Close* window option. A startup form will display a menu and a program logo. Each major task will be carried out on a separate form to allow for future expansion. When users see how easy the program is to use, they will surely request more features.

Before we start to create the application, let's look at the finished version to get a better idea of how the detailed steps fit into the overall picture. Professional programmers often create prototypes or demonstration copies of their programs. The prototype stage is where you can try different versions of the user interface, which requires some reworking, research, and discussions with customers.

The startup form, named *MainForm*, displays a program logo and a menu with three main menu items, shown in Figure 4-49. The startup form should be simple to avoid overwhelming

Figure 4-49 *Karate School Manager* startup form

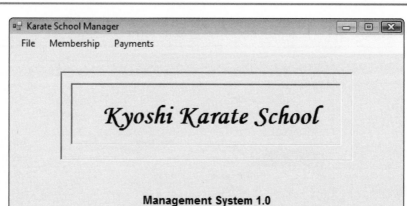

users with details. The menu makes it clear that our system handles two major types of functions: membership and payments. Here are the menu selections:

```
File
    Exit
Membership
    List All
    Find Member
    Add New Member
Payments
    All
    One Member
```

Membership Forms

To let users view a list of all members, we have provided the *All Members* form, shown in Figure 4-50. The grid allows users to sort on any column, select and delete rows, and modify individual cells within each row. If the user wants to save changes they've made back into the database, they select *Save changes* from the *File* menu.

Figure 4-50 *All Members* form

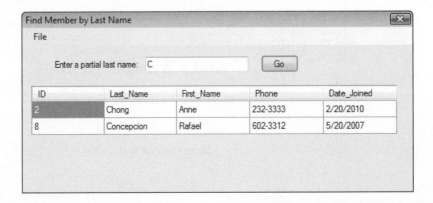

The *Find Member by Last Name* form, shown in Figure 4-51, lets the user enter all or part of a member's last name. When the user clicks the *Go* button or presses *Enter,* a list of matching member rows displays in the grid. We want name searches to be case-insensitive.

Figure 4-51 *Find Member by Last Name* form

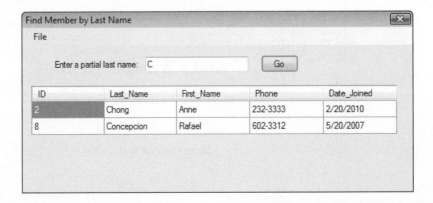

The *Add New Member* form, shown in Figure 4-52, lets the user add a new person to the *Members* table. After entering the fields and choosing a date from the DateTimePicker control, the user clicks the *Save and Close* button. If the user wants to close the form without saving the data, he or she selects *Close without saving* from the *File* menu.

Figure 4-52 *Add New Member* form

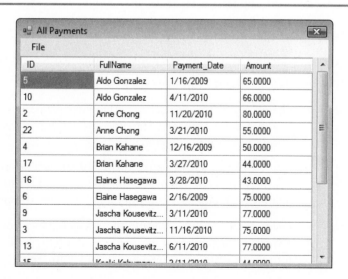

Payments Forms

Now we turn our attention to the *Payments* subsystem of our application. When the user selects *All* from the *Payments* menu on the startup form, the *All Payments* form shown in Figure 4-53 appears. The rows are initially ordered by last name, but the user can sort on any column by clicking on the column header (once for an ascending sort, twice for a descending sort).

Figure 4-53 *All Payments* form

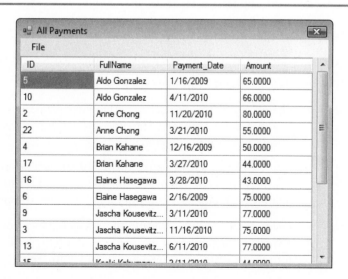

The *Payments by One Member form*, shown in Figure 4-54, lets the user select a member name from a ComboBox. The grid fills with the person's payment history.

Figure 4-54 *Payments by One Member* form

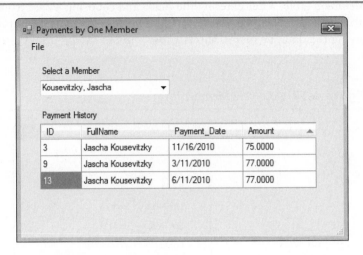

From the user's point of view, the program should be simple. By the time you finish creating it, you will know how to design a simple user interface, open multiple windows, create DataSets and connections, search for database rows in various ways, and perform simple configurations of the DataGridView control.

In Tutorial 4-6, you will create the startup form for the *Karate School Manager* application.

Tutorial 4-6:
Creating the *Karate School Manager* startup form

In this tutorial, the form will contain the name of the program, version information, and a *MenuStrip* control. This will always be the first form to open and the last form to close when the application shuts down.

Tutorial Steps

Step 1:   Create a new Windows application named *Karate School Manager*.

Step 2:   Rename the startup form to *MainForm.vb*.

Step 3:   Open MainForm and set the following properties: Size = *530, 275*; Text = *Karate School Manager*; StartPosition = CenterScreen; MaximizeBox = *False*; FormBorderStyle = FixedSingle.

Step 4:   Insert a Panel control on the form and set its Size property to *390, 115*. Insert another Panel control inside the first one and set its Size property to approximately *360, 80*. Set the BorderStyle property of both panels to *Fixed3D*.

Step 5:   Insert a Label control inside the smaller panel and set its Text property to *Kyoshi Karate School*. We used 26.25-point, bold, italic Monotype Corsiva font in the example shown earlier in Figure 4-49.

Step 6:   Add another label control near the bottom of the form and set its Text property to *Management System 1.0*. We used 11.25-point, bold Arial font in our example.

Step 7: Add a MenuStrip control to the form and insert the following menu items:

```
&File
   E&xit
&Membership
   &List All
   &Find Member
   &Add New Member
&Payments
   &All
   &One Member
```

Step 8: Double-click the *File / Exit* menu item and insert the following code into its Click event handler:
Me.Close()

Step 9: Save the project and run the application. Verify that the form closes when you click the *File / Exit* menu item.

You're done for now. Tutorial 4-7 will focus on adding the Membership subsystem to the application.

Tutorial 4-7:
Karate School Manager: Listing all members

In this tutorial, you will use a DataGridView control to list all members in the Karate school. A new data source will be added to the project, and the DataGridView will be bound to the data source.

Tutorial Steps

Step 1: Open the *Karate School Manager* project, if it is not already open.

Step 2: Add a new form named *AllMembersForm.vb* to the project. Set its MinimizeBox and MaximizeBox properties to *False*. Set its Text property to *All Members*.

Step 3: In *MainForm*, create a Click handler for the *Membership / List All* menu item and insert the following code:

```
AllMembersForm.ShowDialog()
```

Step 4: In the *Data Sources* window, select *Add New Data Source*. Create a connection to the *Karate* database. In the *Choose Your Database Objects* window, select the *Members* table and name the DataSet as *KarateDataSet*. Click the *Finish* button to save the DataSet.

Step 5: Place a DataGridView control on the *AllMembersForm* and name it *dgvMembers*. Anchor the grid to all four sides of the form. Set the following property values: BackGroundColor = Control, BorderStyle = None, RowHeadersVisible = *False*.

Step 6: On the same form, open the *DataGridView Tasks* window. In the *Choose Data Source* list, select the *Members* table from KarateDataSet. Check the

Enable Editing and *Enable Deleting* check boxes only. If the grid's column headings do not appear as shown Figure 4-55, edit the grid's Columns property and use the arrow buttons next to the column names list to adjust the column order.

Figure 4-55 Column layout for the *Members* table

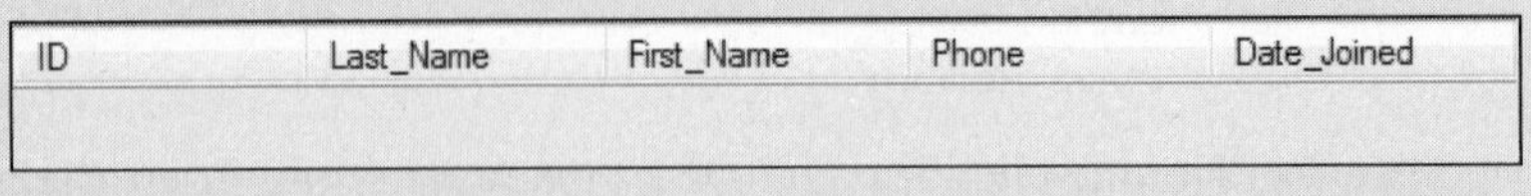

ID	Last_Name	First_Name	Phone	Date_Joined

Step 7: While still editing the Columns property, select the Date_Joined column and select its DefaultCellStyle property. Enter *d* into the Format property. (This format specifies the short date format, in the form *m/d/yyyy*.) Click the *OK* button twice to close the column editor.

Step 8: Add a *MenuStrip* control to the form. Add a *File* menu item, with one subitem: *Close*. In the *Close* item's Click handler, insert the Me.Close() statement.

Step 9: Save the project and run the application. From the *startup form* menu, select *Membership / List All*. You should see a list of members, as shown in Figure 4-56, which is similar to that shown earlier in Figure 4-50.

Figure 4-56 Listing all members

ID	Last_Name	First_Name	Phone	Date_Joined
1	Kahumanu	Keoki	111-2222	2/20/2002
2	Chong	Anne	232-3333	2/20/2010
3	Hasegawa	Elaine	313-3455	2/20/2004
4	Kahane	Brian	646-9387	5/20/2008
5	Gonzalez	Aldo	123-2345	6/6/2009
6	Kousevitzky	Jascha	414-2345	2/20/2010
7	Taliafea	Moses	545-2323	5/20/2005
8	Concepcion	Rafael	602-3312	5/20/2007
9	Taylor	Winifred	333-2222	2/20/2010

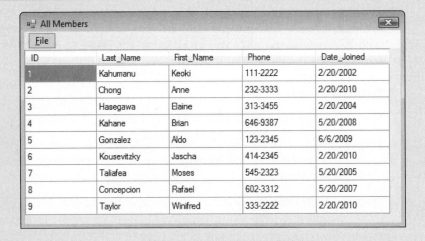

Step 10: End the application.

Using a BindingSource

A ***BindingSource*** object creates a connection between a DataSet and the data-bound controls on a form. The BindingSource is attached to the DataSet, and the form's other controls are attached to the BindingSource. As the user changes the contents of controls, the BindingSource updates the DataSet.

The BindingSource class has a *DataSource* property that exposes the DataSet to which it is bound. It also has methods that let you add new rows, edit rows, and cancel an editing operation in progress. Here are some of the more important methods in the Binding-Source class:

- *AddNew*—Adds a new row to the list.
- *RemoveCurrent*—Removes the current row from the list.
- *EndEdit*—Applies pending changes to the data source.
- *CancelEdit*—Cancels all changes.

When you bind a control to a data source, a BindingSource object is placed on your form inside the component tray area (shown in Design view). In Tutorial 4-7, for example, the DataGridView that displayed the list of members was bound to MembersDataSource. Visual Studio automatically created a MembersBindingSource object and set the following two important properties that bound it to the data source:

- *DataSource* = MembersDataSource
- *DataMember* = Members

The following are other important BindingSource properties:

- *Count*—Number of items in the list.
- *Current*—Returns the object at the current position of the list.
- *Filter*—An expression that filters the rows.

Let's look at some examples of these properties and methods. The following statement permits only those members who joined after 1/1/2005 to be displayed:

```
MembersBindingSource.Filter = "Date_Joined > '1/1/2005'"
```

The following statement adds a new empty row to the list of Members:

```
MembersBindingSource.AddNew()
```

The following statement removes the current row from the list of members:

```
MembersBindingSource.RemoveCurrent()
```

The following statement saves pending changes to the list of members back into Members-DataSource:

```
MembersBindingSource.EndEdit()
```

The following statement cancels all pending changes to the list of members:

```
MembersBindingSource.CancelEdit()
```

In Tutorial 4-8, you will add an *Add Member* form to the *Karate School Manager* program.

TIP: When you double-click a control in the design window for a form, an event handler procedure is generated for you. It always handles the default event for the control. But it is possible to write handlers for many other events on the same control. Here's how you select a different event so you can create a handler:

1. In the Design window, select the control with the mouse.
2. Select the *Events* button in the Properties window toolbar. It looks like a lightning bolt.
3. Double-click on the box to the right of the name of the property for which you wish to create a handler.

Tutorial 4-8:
Karate School Manager: Adding new members

In this tutorial, you will add a new form to the *Karate School Manager* program that lets users add new rows to the *Members* table. The form will use data binding and write its changes directly to the database.

Tutorial Steps

Step 1: Open the *Karate School Manager* project.

Step 2: Add a new form to the project named *AddMemberForm.vb*. Set its Text property to *Add New Member*. Set the following property values: MaximizeBox = *False*; MinimizeBox = *False*; FormBorderStyle = FixedDialog.

Step 3: In MainForm, locate the *Membership / Add New Member* menu item; double-click the item and insert the following statement in its Click event handler: AddMemberForm.ShowDialog()

Step 4: In the *Data Sources* window, locate the *Members* table under the KarateDataSet entry. Using the dropdown arrow to its right, select *Details* from the list.

Step 5: Drag the *Members* table onto the form. Visual Studio should automatically create data-bound fields and a ToolStrip named *MembersBindingNavigator*. Set the Format property of the DateTimePicker control to *Short*. Use Figure 4-57 as a guide.

Figure 4-57 Add New Member form in Design mode

Step 6: Delete the *MembersBindingNavigator* component from the form's component tray. Open the form's code window and delete the MembersBindingNavigatorSaveItem_Click method.

Step 7: Replace the code in the form's Load event handler with a statement that calls AddNew.

```
MembersBindingSource.AddNew()
```

The statement clears the form's input fields and waits for the user to enter data for a new member.

Step 8: Add a MenuStrip control to the form. Add a *File* menu item with one subitem: *Close*. In the event handler for the first item, insert a Me.Close() statement.

Step 9: Create a FormClosing event handler for the form and insert the following statement:

```
MembersBindingSource.CancelEdit()
```

This statement cancels any edit operation that might be in progress. The user might have opened the form, begun to fill in the fields, changed his or her mind, and decided to close the form.

Step 10: Rename the DateTimePicker control to dtp*Date*. Also, add the following line to the form's Load event handler:

```
dtpDate.Value = Today
```

This line is necessary to ensure that the date value will be saved in the database even if the user does not explicitly select a date.

Step 11: Add a button to the form named *btnUpdate*. Set its Text property to *Update*. Create a handler for the button. It calls EndEdit to complete the *add new row* operation. Then it calls Update to save the DataSet modifications to the actual database. Finally, it closes the form, as follows:

```
Private Sub btnUpdate_Click () Handles btnUpdate.Click
  Try
     MembersBindingSource.EndEdit()
     MembersTableAdapter.Update(KarateDataSet.Members)
     Me.Close()
  Catch ex As Exception
     MessageBox.Show(ex.Message, "Error")
  End Try
End Sub
```

Step 12: Save the project and run the application. Click the *Membership / Add New Member* menu selection and add a new member. Choose a member ID that does not appear when you list all members. If you're not sure, display a list of all members first.

Using Query Parameters

When SQL queries search for selected records in database tables, you don't know ahead of time what values the user might want to find. While it is possible to build a query from an existing SQL SELECT statement that contains the names of Visual Basic variables, the result is messy. Suppose, for example, that the user has entered a name in the txtLastName control, and you want to write a query that would locate all rows in the *Members* table having the same last name. You can build the following query:

```
Dim query As String
query = "SELECT ID, Last_Name, First_Name, Phone, Date_Joined " _
   & "FROM Members WHERE Last_Name = '" & txtlastName.Text & "'"
```

When typing code such as this, it is easy to make a typing mistake, and it can make your application more vulnerable to software exploits that attempt to access sensitive database data. A much better approach is to insert a parameter name directly into the SQL query. In the following example, a parameter named @Last_Name will be assigned a specific value at runtime:

```
SELECT ID, Last_Name, First_Name, Phone, Date_Joined
FROM Members
WHERE Last_Name = @Last_Name
```

When the TableAdapter's Fill method is called, we pass it a second argument. That argument value is automatically assigned to the query parameter:

```
MembersTableAdapter.Fill(Me.FindMemberDataSet.Members,
   txtLastName.Text)
```

If a query contains more than one parameter, the parameter values become additional arguments for the Fill method. The following query, for example, contains two parameters, @Last_Name and @Date_Joined:

```
SELECT ID, Last_Name, First_Name, Phone, Date_Joined
FROM Members
WHERE Last_Name = @Last_Name AND Date_Joined <= @Date_Joined
```

Notice how the call to the Fill method changes accordingly.

```
MembersTableAdapter.Fill(Me.FindMemberDataSet.Members,
   txtLastName.Text, txtDateJoined.Text)
```

WildCard Matches in SQL Queries

When searching for matching rows in a database table, you may not always know the exact value you're trying to find. SQL has a special keyword named LIKE that uses a *wildcard* character to perform partial matches. SQL Server uses the percent sign (%) character to match any string of characters. For example, the following WHERE clause returns all rows containing a name starting with the letter G:

```
WHERE Last_Name LIKE 'G%'
```

The database returns rows containing last names such as Gomez, Gonzalez, Green, and so on. By default, the LIKE operator is case-insensitive, so names in lowercase characters still match G%.

In Tutorial 4-9, you will create a form that lets users search using wildcard characters.

Tutorial 4-9:
Karate School Manager: Finding members by name

In this tutorial, you will create a form for the Karate School Manager application that lets users search for members using their last names. The query that performs the search will accept a partial string, so if users do not know the exact spelling of a member name, they can view a list of members with similar names.

Tutorial Steps

Step 1:   Open the *Karate School Manager* project.

Step 2:   Add a new form to the project named *FindMemberForm.vb*. Set its properties as follows: Text = *Find Member by Last Name*; MaximizeBox = *False*; MinimizeBox = *False*; StartPosition = CenterScreen; FormBorderStyle = FixedDialog.

Step 3: In *MainForm*, double-click the *Membership / Find Member* menu item and insert the following code in its event handler:

```
FindMemberForm.ShowDialog()
```

Step 4: Open FindMemberForm in Design view, add a MenuStrip control to the form, and create a *File* submenu with one selection: *Close*. In its Click event handler, insert the Me.Close() statement.

Step 5: Add a Label control, a TextBox named *txtLastName*, and a Button named *btnGo* to the form. Use Figure 4-58 as a guide. (The DataGridView control will be added in a later step.)

Figure 4-58 The *Find Member* form in Design mode

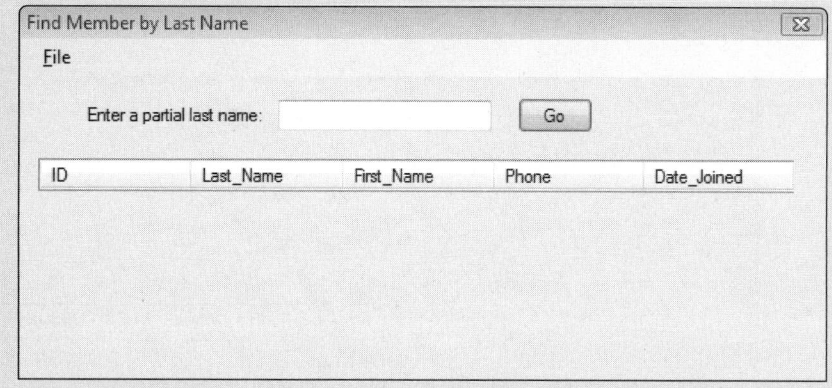

Step 6: Open the *KarateDataSet.xsd* file, right-click the MembersTableAdapter, select *Add*, and then select *Query*. Insert the following SQL query:

```
SELECT ID, Last_Name, First_Name, Phone, Date_Joined
FROM Members
WHERE (Last_Name LIKE @name + '%')
```

After creating the SQL query, click the *Next* button. In the *Choose Methods to Generate* step shown in Figure 4-59, select only the *Fill a DataTable* option and name the method *FindMember*. After you have finished adding the query, the MembersTableAdapter should appear as in Figure 4-60.

Step 7: Place a DataGridView control on the form and name it *dgvMembers*. Set its properties as follows: BackGroundColor = *Control*; BorderStyle = *None*; Anchor = *Bottom, Left, Right*; RowHeadersVisible = *False*.

Step 8: Using the smart tag in the grid's upper-right corner, set its data source to the *Members* table of KarateDataSet. Disable adding, editing, and deleting of rows.

Step 9: Next, you will add a call to the Fill method in the event handler for the button that activates the search. Double-click the *Go* button and insert the following code in its event handler:

```
' Perform a wildcard search for the last name.
Me.MembersTableAdapter.FindMember(FindMemberDataSet.Members,
    txtLastName.Text)
```

Figure 4-59 Selecting the names of the TableAdapter methods

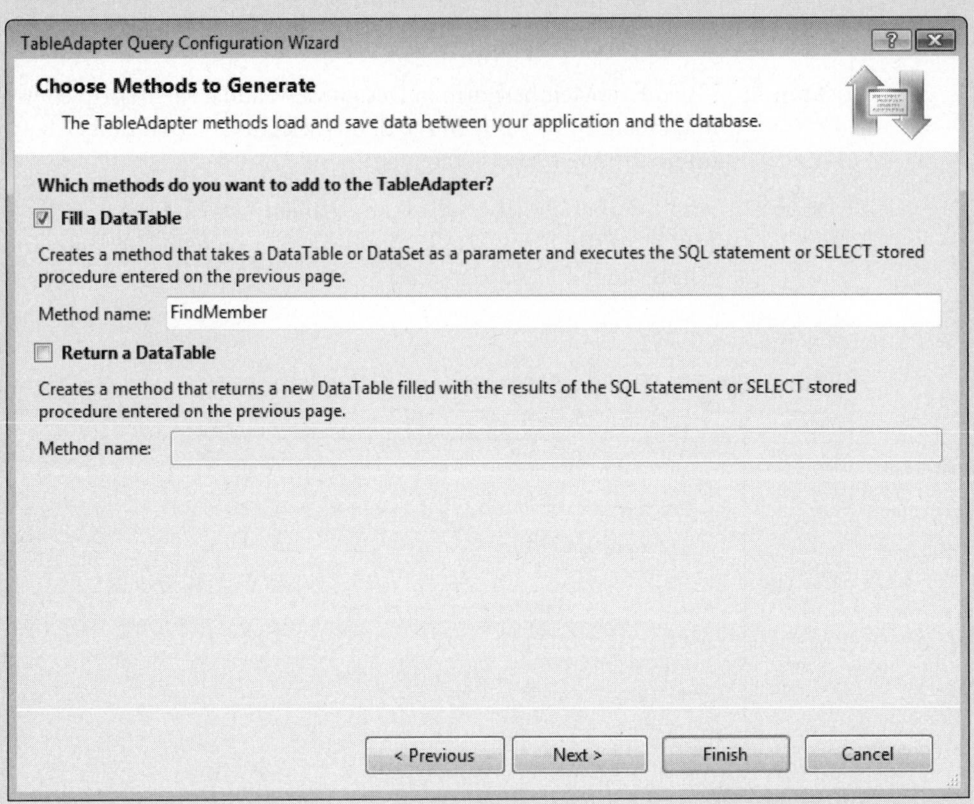
TableAdapter Query Configuration Wizard
Choose Methods to Generate
The TableAdapter methods load and save data between your application and the database.
Which methods do you want to add to the TableAdapter?
Fill a DataTable
Creates a method that takes a DataTable or DataSet as a parameter and executes the SQL statement or SELECT stored procedure entered on the previous page.
Method name: FindMember
Return a DataTable
Creates a method that returns a new DataTable filled with the results of the SQL statement or SELECT stored procedure entered on the previous page.
Method name:
< Previous
Next >
Finish
Cancel

Figure 4-60 The MembersTableAdapter, after adding the FindMember query

Members
ID
Last_Name
First_Name
Phone
Date_Joined
MembersTableAdapter
Fill,GetData ()
FindMember (@name)

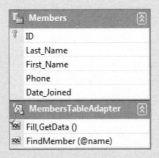

Normally, the Fill method has only one parameter—the DataSet's table. But here you pass a second parameter, which is the value to be assigned to the query parameter.

Step 10: Select the form with the mouse and set the Form's AcceptButton property to *btnGo*. This will allow the user to press the *Enter* key when activating the search.

Step 11: Remove any statements that might be inside the form's Load event handler. (You don't want the grid to fill with data until a member name has been entered.)

Step 12: Save the project and run the application. From the startup form, click *Membership / Find Member* from the menu. When the *Find Member* form appears, enter a partial last name, such as *C* or *Ch*, and click the *Go* button. Your output should look similar to that shown in Figure 4-61.

Figure 4-61 Finding a member by last name

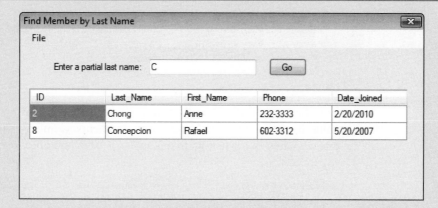

Step 13: Experiment with other partial last names, checking your results against the grid that displays all members.

In Tutorial 4-10, you will be able to track payments of membership dues for the *Karate* school.

Tutorial 4-10:
Karate School Manager: Listing all payments

In this tutorial, you will use the *Payments* table, which contains dates, member IDs, and payment amounts. It does not contain member names. You will join the *Payments* table to the *Members* table so you can display the member names along with the payments they have made. You will create a DataSet that contains the joined tables. The application will display the DataSet in a DataGridView control.

Tutorial Steps

Step 1: Open the *Karate School Manager* program if it is not already open.

Step 2: Add a new form to the project named AllPaymentsForm.vb. Set its properties as follows: Text = *All Payments*; MaximizeBox = *False*; MinimizeBox = *False*; StartPosition = *CenterScreen*.

Step 3: Add a MenuStrip control to the form, and create a *File* submenu with one item: *Close*. In the *Close* item's Click handler, insert the Me.Close() statement.

Step 4: In *MainForm*, double-click the *Payments / All* menu item and insert the following code in its event handler:

```
AllPaymentsForm.ShowDialog()
```

Step 5: Next, you will create a TableAdapter that joins the Members and Payments tables. This TableAdapter will be associated with a DataTable named *Payments*. Open the *KarateDataSet.xsd* file from the Solution Explorer window. Right-click in an open area of the designer window, select *Add*, then select *TableAdapter*.

When the TableAdapter Configuration Wizard starts, keep the same connection, and click the *Next* button two times. When you see the step entitled *Specify a SQL Select Statement*, insert the following SQL query:

```
SELECT Payments.ID,
  Members.Last_Name + ', ' + Members.First_Name AS FullName,
  Payments.Payment_Date, Payments.Amount
FROM Members INNER JOIN Payments
  ON Members.ID = Payments.Member_Id
ORDER BY Last_Name
```

This query joins the Members and Payments tables, using the common ID value found in the Members.ID and Payments.Member_Id columns. Also, it concatenates the last and first names of each member, using the following expression:

```
Members.Last_Name + ', ' + Members.First_Name AS FullName
```

Step 6: Click the *Query Builder* button, and in the Query Builder window, click the *Execute Query* button. If an error message appears, check your query's spelling and punctuation. Click the *OK* button to close the Query Builder window.

Step 7: Click the *Advanced Options* button. In the dialog window, shown in Figure 4-62, unselect the *Generate Insert, Update, and Delete statements* option. We're doing this because we generally do not update tables when they are joined together. Click the *OK* button.

Figure 4-62 Advanced Options window

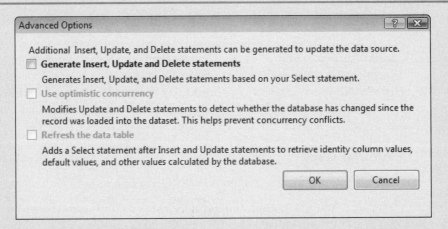

Step 8: Click the *Next* button. In the *Choose Methods to Generate* step, select only the *Fill a DataTable* option and name the method *AllPayments*. Also, unselect the third check box because you do not want to create methods that send updates directly to the database. Click the *Finish* button to close the wizard.

After you have finished adding the query, the PaymentsTableAdapter should appear as in Figure 4-63.

Figure 4-63 PaymentsTableAdapter, containing the AllPayments method

Step 9: Place a DataGridView control on the form and name it *dgvPayments*. Set its properties as follows: BackGroundColor = Control; BorderStyle = None; Dock = Fill, RowHeadersVisible = *False*.

Step 10: Click the smart tag of dgvPayments to open the *DataGridView Tasks* window. For the data source, choose the *Payments* table in KarateDataSet. Unselect the adding, editing, and deleting check boxes.

Step 11: Save the project and run the application. Display the *All Payments* window. Sample output is shown in Figure 4-64.

Figure 4-64 All Payments form

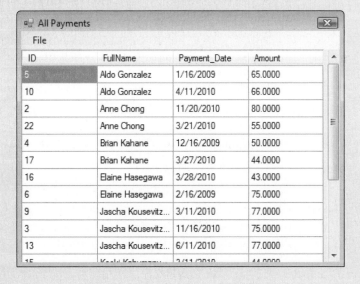

For extra practice, you may want to center the ID column and format the Amount column with two digits after the decimal point.

Step 12: Close the application.

In this tutorial you joined two database tables, using a relationship between the Members and Payments tables. You have seen how easily a DataSet can contain multiple TableAdapters. In Tutorial 4-11, you will complete the last requirement of the Karate School Manager application, which is to display payments by one member.

Tutorial 4-11:
Karate School Manager: Showing payments by one member

In this tutorial, you will create a form that displays a single member's payment history. A ComboBox control will present a list of first and last names. When the user selects a name, a DataGridView control will fill with payments made by the member.

Tutorial Steps

Step 1: Open the *Karate School Manager* program if it is not already open.

Step 2: Add a new form to the project named *MemberPaymentsForm.vb*. Set its properties as follows: Text = *Payments by One Member*; MaximizeBox = *False*; MinimizeBox = *False*; StartPosition = CenterScreen.

Step 3: Add a *MenuStrip* control to the form, and create a *File* submenu with one selection: *Close*. In the Close handler, insert the Me.Close() statement.

Step 4: In the *MainForm* form, double-click the *Payments / One member* menu item and insert the following code in its event handler:

```
MemberPaymentsForm.ShowDialog()
```

Step 5: Next, you will create a TableAdapter that displays member names. Open the *KarateDataSet.xsd* file from the Solution Explorer window. Right-click in an open area of the designer window, select *Add*, then select *TableAdapter*.

When the TableAdapter Configuration Wizard starts, keep the same connect, and click the *Next* button two times. When you see the step entitled *Specify an SQL Select Statement*, insert the following SQL query:

```
SELECT ID, Last_Name + ', ' + First_Name AS Name
FROM Members
ORDER BY Last_Name
```

Step 6: Click the *Query Builder* button, and in the Query Builder window, click the *Execute Query* button. If an error message appears, check your spelling and punctuation. Click the *OK* button to close the Query Builder window.

Step 7: Open the *Advanced Options* window and unselect the *Generate Insert, Update, and Delete statements* option. Click the *OK* button to close the window.

Step 8: Click the *Next* button. In the *Choose Methods to Generate* step, unselect the third check box because you do not want to create methods that send updates directly to the database. Click the *Finish* button to close the wizard.

Step 9: Rename the table and TableAdapter as shown in Figure 4-65. You rename by right-clicking on the gray bar and select *Rename* from the popup menu.

Figure 4-65 MemberNames DataTable and associated TableAdapter

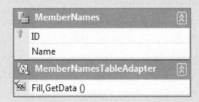

The next series of steps will be to bind a ComboBox control to the Member-Names table. When the user selects a member name, we want the member's ID to be available in the ComboBox's SelectedValue property.

Step 10: Add a ComboBox control to the form and name it *cboMemberName*.

Step 11: Open the *ComboBox Tasks* window. Select the *Use data bound items* option. Set its DataSource property to the MemberNames table in KarateDataSet. Set its DisplayMember property to *Name*. Set its ValueMember property to *ID*.

If you were to run the program now, you would see only a list of first and last names in this form's ComboBox. You need to add a grid to the form and use it to display payments made by the member selected in the ComboBox.

Step 12: First, you will create a query that selects members by ID number. Open the *KarateDataSet.xsd* file from the Solution Explorer window. Right-click the PaymentsTableAdapter, select *Add*, and then select *Query*. In the *Specify an SQL Select Statement* step, insert the following SQL query:

```
SELECT Payments.ID,
    Members.First_Name + ' ' + Members.Last_Name AS FullName,
    Payments.Payment_Date, Payments.Amount
FROM Members INNER JOIN
    Payments ON Members.ID = Payments.Member_Id
WHERE (Member_Id = @memberId)
ORDER BY Payment_Date
```

Step 13: Click the *Query Builder* button and, in the Query Builder window, click the *Execute Query* button. If an error message appears, check your spelling and punctuation. Click the *OK* button to close the Query Builder window.

Step 14: Click the *Next* button. In the *Choose Methods to Generate* step, select only the *Fill a DataTable* option and name the method *MemberPayments*. Click the *Finish* button, which closes the Wizard. You should see a new version of the PaymentsTableAdapter in the DataSet designer window, as shown in Figure 4-66.

Figure 4-66 Revised PaymentsTableAdapter

Step 15: Add a Label control to *PaymentsOneForm* just above the ComboBox and set its Text property to *Select a Member*. Add a second Label control below the ComboBox and set its Text to *Payment History*.

Next, you will add a grid to the form, and write code in the ComboBox's SelectedIndexChanged event handler that fills the grid with payments made by the selected member.

Step 16: Place a DataGridView control on the form and name it *dgvPayments*. Set its properties as follows: BackGroundColor = Control; BorderStyle = None; Anchor = Top, Bottom, Left, Right; RowHeadersVisible = *False*.

Step 17: Open the *DataGridView Tasks* window by clicking the grid's smart tag. Set the data source to the *Payments* table in KarateDataSet. Unselect the *Adding*, *Editing*, and *Deleting* check boxes.

Step 18: Double-click the ComboBox and insert the following code in its SelectedIndexChanged event handler:

```
If cboMemberName.SelectedIndex = -1 Then Exit Sub
' Get the Member_Id value associated with the selected
' member.
Dim member_Id As Short = CShort(cboMemberName.SelectedValue)
' Fill the payments grid, passing it the member ID.
PaymentsTableAdapter.MemberPayments(KarateDataSet.Payments,
    member_Id)
```

Step 19: Modify the Form_Load event handler so it is as follows:

```
Private Sub MemberPaymentsForm_Load() Handles MyBase.Load
    Me.MemberNamesTableAdapter.Fill(Me.KarateDataSet.
    MemberNames)
    cboMemberName.SelectedIndex = -1
End Sub
```

Step 20: Save the project and run the application. Select the *Payments / One Member* menu item. Select a member (Kousevitzky). Your output should be similar to that shown in Figure 4-67.

Figure 4-67 Displaying payments by one member

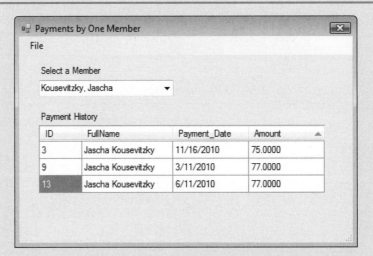

Summary

It is surprising how many simple steps are involved in creating a nontrivial application. The *Karate School Manager* application is tiny by professional standards. But it is expandable, and it even provides some usability for the customer.

If we continued to expand this application, eventually we would find that the large number of data sources, queries, and other data components would be overwhelming. For example, maintenance would be particularly difficult if the database table structure changed. Every form we have created has components and queries that match the existing database structure. A major problem of the application's design is that we have no clear separation of tiers, or layers, in this program. We have no separate layers for database access, user interface code, or business objects.

Fortunately, you will learn how to use database objects in Chapter 5. You will learn how to implement the three-tier approach to application design. As a result, you will be able to create applications that are expandable and maintainable.

Complete Source Code

The following is a listing of all the source code in the *Karate School Manager* application. Optional parameters have been removed from the event handler methods to preserve readability.

MainForm.vb:

```vb
Public Class MainForm
    Private Sub ExitToolStripMenuItem_Click() _
        Handles ExitToolStripMenuItem.Click
        Me.Close()
    End Sub

    Private Sub ListAllToolStripMenuItem_Click() _
        Handles ListAllToolStripMenuItem.Click
        AllMembersForm.ShowDialog()
    End Sub

    Private Sub AddNewMemberToolStripMenuItem_Click() _
        Handles AddNewMemberToolStripMenuItem.Click
        AddMemberForm.ShowDialog()
    End Sub

    Private Sub FindMemberToolStripMenuItem_Click() _
        Handles FindMemberToolStripMenuItem.Click
        FindMemberForm.ShowDialog()
    End Sub

    Private Sub AllPaymentsToolStripMenuItem_Click() _
        Handles AllPaymentsToolStripMenuItem.Click
        AllPaymentsForm.ShowDialog()
    End Sub

    Private Sub OneMemberToolStripMenuItem_Click() _
        Handles OneMemberToolStripMenuItem.Click
        MemberPaymentsForm.ShowDialog()
    End Sub
End Class
```

AllMembersForm.vb:

```vb
Public Class AllMembersForm
    Private Sub AllMembersForm_Load() Handles MyBase.Load
        Me.MembersTableAdapter.Fill(Me.KarateDataSet.Members)
    End Sub

    Private Sub CloseToolStripMenuItem_Click() _
        Handles CloseToolStripMenuItem.Click
        Me.Close()
    End Sub
End Class
```

AllPaymentsForm.vb:

```vb
Public Class AllPaymentsForm
  Private Sub CloseToolStripMenuItem_Click() _
    Handles CloseToolStripMenuItem.Click
    Me.Close()
  End Sub

  Private Sub AllPaymentsForm_Load() _
    Handles MyBase.Load
      Me.PaymentsTableAdapter.AllPayments(Me.KarateDataSet.Payments)
  End Sub
End Class
```

AddMemberForm.vb:

```vb
Public Class AddMemberForm
  Private Sub AddMemberForm_Load() Handles MyBase.Load
    MembersBindingSource.AddNew()
    dtpDate.Value = Today
  End Sub

  Private Sub CloseToolStripMenuItem_Click() _
    Handles CloseToolStripMenuItem.Click
    Me.Close()
  End Sub

  Private Sub AddMemberForm_FormClosing() _
    Handles MyBase.FormClosing
    MembersBindingSource.CancelEdit()
  End Sub

  Private Sub btnUpdate_Click() Handles btnSave.Click
    Try
      Me.MembersBindingSource.EndEdit()
      MembersTableAdapter.Update(KarateDataSet.Members)
      Me.Close()
    Catch ex As Exception
      MessageBox.Show(ex.Message, "Error")
    End Try
  End Sub
End Class
```

FindMemberForm.vb:

```vb
Public Class FindMemberForm
  Private Sub CloseToolStripMenuItem_Click() _
    Handles CloseToolStripMenuItem.Click
    Me.Close()
  End Sub

  Private Sub btnGo_Click() Handles btnGo.Click
  ' Perform a wildcard search for the last name.
    Me.MembersTableAdapter.FindMember(KarateDataSet.Members,
      txtLastName.Text)
  End Sub
End Class
```

MemberPaymentsForm.vb:

```vb
Public Class MemberPaymentsForm
  Private Sub MemberPaymentsForm_Load() Handles MyBase.Load
    Me.MemberNamesTableAdapter.Fill(Me.KarateDataSet.MemberNames)
    cboMemberName.SelectedIndex = -1
  End Sub
```

```
Private Sub cboMemberName_SelectedIndexChanged() _
  Handles cboMemberName.SelectedIndexChanged
  If cboMemberName.SelectedIndex = -1 Then Exit Sub
  ' Get the Member_Id value associated with the selected member.
  Dim member_Id As Short = CShort(cboMemberName.SelectedValue)
  ' Fill the payments grid, passing it the member ID.
  PaymentsTableAdapter.MemberPayments(KarateDataSet.Payments,
    member_Id)
End Sub

Private Sub CloseToolStripMenuItem_Click() _
  Handles CloseToolStripMenuItem.Click
  Me.Close()
End Sub
End Class
```

Checkpoint

28. In the *Karate* database, which table contains the dates when students joined the school?

29. In the AllPaymentsForm, which two database tables are required when filling the grid?

30. Which property of a DataGridView control lets you alter the order in which columns appear?

31. How does the MemberPaymentsForm obtain the ID number of the member selected by the user in the ComboBox?

32. What special keyword is used in the WHERE clause of a query when you want to search for partially matching strings?

Summary

4.1 Database Basics

- A database is a collection of one or more tables, each containing data related to a particular topic. A table is a logical grouping of related information. Each row of a table is also called a record. Table columns are also called fields.
- Each table has a design, which specifies each column's name, data type, and range or size. A database schema contains the design of tables, columns, and relationships between tables for the database.
- A primary key column uniquely identifies each row of a table. A primary key will sometimes consist of two or more combined columns.
- When you use Visual Basic to read a database table, you must select .NET and Visual Basic variable types that match the type of data in the table. A table at the beginning of this chapter correlates .NET data types to Microsoft SQL Server data types.
- Well-designed databases keep redundant data to a minimum. Always try to avoid having multiple occurrences of the same field contents in rows of a database.
- A relationship is a link or relationship that relies on a common field value to join rows from two different tables. The most common type of relationship is a one-to-many relation.

4.2 SQL SELECT Statement

- The SELECT statement retrieves rows from one or more database tables. The most basic format for a single table is SELECT *column-list* FROM *table*. In SELECT statements, column names can be renamed, using the AS operator. The new column name is called an *alias*. You can also create new columns whose contents are calculated from existing column values.
- The SELECT statement has an ORDER BY clause that lets you control the display order of the table rows.
- The SQL SELECT statement has a WHERE clause that you can use to filter, or select zero or more rows retrieved from, a database table. The LIKE operator can be used to create partial matches with Text column values. The NOT, AND, and OR operators can be used to create compound expressions.

4.3 Using the DataGrid View

- A data source connects a program to a database, text files, Excel worksheet, XML file, or other type of data.
- A BindingSource provides a link between a DataSet object and data-bound controls on a form.
- A TableAdapter pulls data from a database (or other data source) and passes it to your program.
- A DataSet is an in-memory copy of the data pulled from database tables.
- A TableAdapter's Fill method opens a database connection, reads data from a database into the DataSet, and closes the connection.

4.4 Selecting DataSet Rows

- Applications often need to filter, or select, certain rows when retrieving data from data sources. Filtering, or choosing rows to display in a DataSet, is done by creating a query. In SQL, the WHERE statement limits the rows retrieved from a database table.
- The *TableAdapter Configuration Wizard* and *Search Criteria Builder* can be used to modify queries.

4.5 Data-Bound Controls

- Using a data source, you can bind its fields to individual controls such as text boxes, labels, and list boxes.
- Data-bound controls update their contents automatically when you move from one row to the next in a DataSet.
- You can bind an existing data source to a DataGridView control by dragging a table from the *Data Sources* window to an open area of a form. Similarly, you can create separate data-bound controls, such as text boxes and labels, by dragging individual fields in the *Data Sources* window onto the open area of a form.
- ListBox and ComboBox controls have two important properties that are required when using data binding: The DataSource property identifies the table within the DataSet that supplies the data; the DisplayMember property identifies the column to be displayed.

4.6 Focus on Problem Solving: Karate School Management System

The *Karate School Manager* program has the following capabilities:

- Displays a list of all members.
- Permits the user to sort on any column, edit individual rows, and delete rows.
- Adds new rows to the *Members* table.
- Displays members having similar last names.

- Displays all payments.
- Permits the user to sort on any column.
- Displays a list of payments by a single member.

Key Terms

auto-generated field	foreign key
BindingSource object	identity field
components	LIKE operator
compound primary key	one-to-many relationship
database	ORDER BY clause
database schema	primary key
data binding	query parameter
data-bound control	relational database model
DataGridView control	SELECT statement
DataSet	Structured Query Language (SQL)
DataTable	TableAdapter
data source	WHERE clause
DataSource property	wildcard symbol
DisplayMember property	xcopy deployment

Review Questions and Exercises

True or False

Indicate whether each of the following statements is true or false.

1. A TableAdapter's Fill method receives a DataSet argument.

2. A DataSet may contain only a single TableAdapter.

3. A primary key can involve only a single column of a database table.

4. A DataTable column such as *Last_Name* can be bound to a TextBox or Label control.

5. The default type of control bound to DateTime fields is the TextBox.

6. The *Karate School Manager* program joins the *Members* table to the *Payments* table when searching for payments made by a single member.

7. The *Karate School Manager* program contains special event handling code that makes sorting in a DataGridView possible.

8. When the user makes changes to a DataSet, the changes are not permanent unless other measures are taken to write the DataSet back to a database.

9. In SQL Server, query parameter names always begin with the @ sign.

10. Query parameters are passed to DataSets as arguments when calling a TableAdapter's Fill method.

11. A DataSet is an in-memory copy of data pulled from one or more database tables.

12. Byte is an SQL Server table column type.

13. A .NET Double data type is equivalent to the SQL server *float* data type.

14. ValueMember is not a ListBox control property.

15. The MATCH keyword is used by SQL when performing wildcard matches.

Short Answer

1. Which property of a ComboBox control must be set before a program can use the SelectedValue property at runtime?

2. What type of relationship existed between the *Employee* and *Departments* tables in Section 4.1?

3. If the *Employees* table contains a foreign key named *dept_id*, is it likely that the values in this field are unique?

4. What type of string keeps track of the database name, location, username, password, and other connection information?

5. What happens when you drag a table name from the *Data Sources* window onto an open area of a form?

6. Write a statement that lets the SelectedIndexChanged event handler for a ComboBox exit when an entry has not yet been selected by the user.

7. Which property of a DataGridView control causes the buttons to the left of each row to appear?

8. Which database design tool describes the design of tables, columns, and relationships among tables?

9. Which control lets users select dates using the mouse?

10. What is another word for a database table row?

Algorithm Workbench

1. Suppose a database table named *Address* contains fields named *City* and *State*. Write an SQL SELECT statement that combines these fields into a new field named *CityState*.

2. Write statements that create and show an instance of a form named *AllMembersForm*. Be sure the user can click only in the form you have displayed and not in any other application window.

3. Write an SQL query that retrieves the *ID*, *Title*, *Artist*, and *Price* from a database table named *Albums*. The query should sort the rows in ascending order by *Artist*.

4. Write an SQL query that uses a query parameter to retrieve a row from the *Albums* table that has a particular *ID* value. Retrieve the *ID*, *Title*, *Artist*, and *Price*.

5. Write a statement that retrieves the value of an item selected by the user from a ComboBox named *cboMembers*.

6. Write a statement that fills a table named *Members* in a DataSet named *MembersDataSet*. Assume that TableAdapter is named *MembersTableAdapter*.

7. Write an SQL query that retrieves the ID, Last_Name, and First_Name from the Members table. You want only those rows having a Date_Joined value greater than or equal to the value of a query parameter.

Programming Challenges

1. Selecting Sales Staff

Create a program that lets the user select rows from the *SalesStaff* table. Fill a ComboBox control with the names (last, first). When the user makes a selection, the other controls on the form should display details about the staff member selected. A sample is shown in Figure 4-68. *Hint:* See the data-bound list box in Tutorial 4-3.

Figure 4-68 *Selecting* Sales Staff

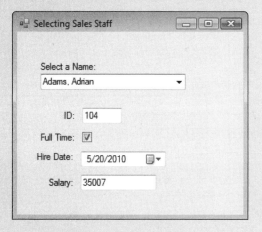

2. Sales Staff Salaries

Using the SalesStaff table in the Company database, let the user choose between lists of part-time versus full-time employees. Use radio buttons to display the choices. Display the average salary of the selected group in a label. A sample is shown in Figure 4-69. When the program starts, the *Full time* button is automatically selected. *Hint*: You can use a parameterized query, or create a separate query for part-time and full-time employees. When the user selects a radio button, call the Fill method that matches the appropriate query.

Figure 4-69 Displaying average salaries of full-time employees

3. *Karate* Member Dates

Create a program that uses the Members table of the Karate database. Let the user select a date from a DateTimePicker control. The program must display all members who joined before the selected date (see Figure 4-70). Use a parameterized query.

Figure 4-70 Finding the dates when members joined

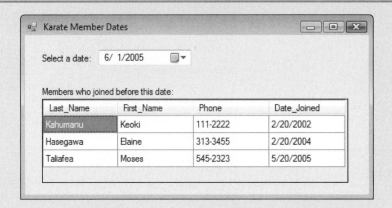

4. **Advanced *Karate* Member Dates**

   Enhance the program you created in Programming Challenge 3 by giving the user a choice between displaying members who have joined before a given date and members who have joined on or after the given date. Figure 4-71 shows members who joined before 6/30/2007. Figure 4-72 displays a list of members who joined on or after the same date.

Figure 4-71 Showing members who joined before the chosen date

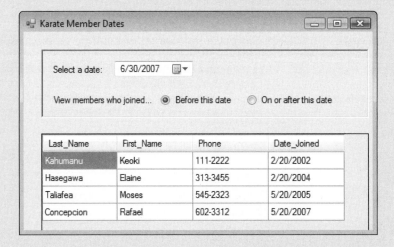

   You might want to create two queries, one for each type of search. At runtime, when the user switches between the radio buttons, the event handlers can call either of the two Fill methods that you created in the TableAdapter.

5. **Filtering the *Karate Members* Table**

   Tutorial 4-7 showed how to display the *Karate Members* table in a DataGridView control. In that same section of the chapter, a discussion about BindingSources explained how to assign a value to the Filter property when you want to limit the displayed rows. Here is the example we used:

   ```
   MembersBindingSource.Filter = "Date_Joined > '1/1/2005'"
   ```

   Create an alternative version of Tutorial 4-7 that displays a text box in a *ToolStrip* control just below the menu. When the user types in a filter expression and clicks the *Go* button, the filter expression is assigned to the Filter property of MembersBindingSource.

Figure 4-72 Showing members who joined on or after the chosen date

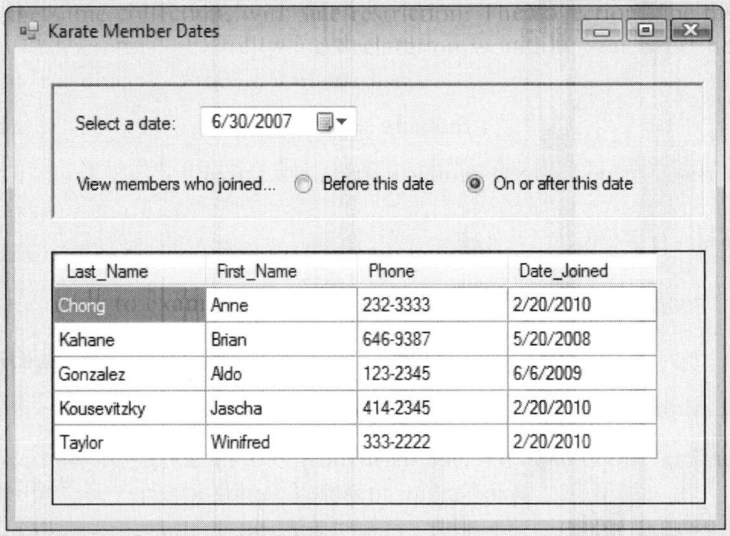
Karate Member Dates
Select a date: 6/30/2007
View members who joined... Before this date On or after this date
Last_Name First_Name Phone Date_Joined
Chong Anne 232-3333 2/20/2010
Kahane Brian 646-9387 5/20/2008
Gonzalez Aldo 123-2345 6/6/2009
Kousevitzky Jascha 414-2345 2/20/2010
Taylor Winifred 333-2222 2/20/2010

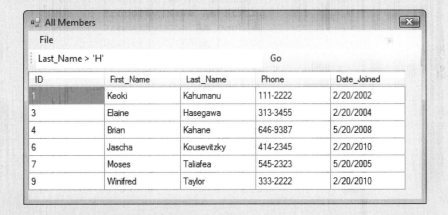

The rows appearing in the DataGridView change accordingly. An example is shown in Figure 4-73. Use a Try-Catch statement to prevent unhandled exceptions caused by incorrect filtering syntax.

Figure 4-73 Letting the user interactively filter the *Members* table

All Members
File
Last_Name > 'H'
Go
ID First_Name Last_Name Phone Date_Joined
1 Keoki Kahumanu 111-2222 2/20/2002
3 Elaine Hasegawa 313-3455 2/20/2004
4 Brian Kahane 646-9387 5/20/2008
6 Jascha Kousevitzky 414-2345 2/20/2010
7 Moses Taliafea 545-2323 5/20/2005
9 Winifred Taylor 333-2222 2/20/2010

6. **Editing and Deleting *Karate* Members**

   The DataGridView that displays all members in the *Karate School Manager* application has options checked that let the user edit and delete members. But when you run the application, these operations do not seem to be enabled. Your task is to enable those operations and find a way to write the changes to the underlying database. *Hint:* Call the TableAdapter's Update method.

CHAPTER 5

Database Applications

TOPICS

This chapter focuses on database programming, using the ADO.NET library, which is part of the .NET Framework. You may think of it as an extension of the database concepts and database binding from Chapter 4. Here, you are able to integrate your knowledge of multi-tier application design with objects and databases. The chapter concludes with an extended sample application that schedules appointments for an imaginary home repair services company.

5.1 Creating Databases

Server Explorer

The **Server Explorer** window in Visual Studio lets you view and manage connections to local and remote databases. From the *View* menu, select *Server Explorer* to open the window. In Figure 5-1, the Server Explorer window contains a connection to the *karate.mdf* database file we used in Chapter 4. A connection refers to a way of linking to the database so that you can modify its design and data. Each folder under a connection contains different types of objects associated with the database, as follows:

- The **Database Diagrams** folder contains graphical diagrams that show relationships between and among tables.
- The *Tables* folder contains all tables in the database.
- The *Views* folder contains a list of views, which are alternate ways of viewing the contents of tables; views often combine columns from different tables into what look like new tables.
- The **Stored Procedures** folder contains compiled SQL queries.
- The remaining folders are beyond the scope of this book and will not be discussed.

To add an existing database file to the Server window, right-click on *Data Connections*, select *Add Connection*, and browse to the file's location. (Server Explorer also lets you connect to a full version of SQL Server, either on the local machine or at a network location.) You can add multiple database connections to the Server Explorer window. It retains connections you created when other projects were open. You can display this window whether or not a project is open.

Figure 5-1 Server Explorer window, connected to the Karate database

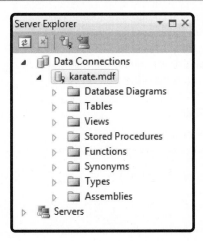

Creating a New Database

You can create a new database inside the Server Explorer window. Here's a quick summary of the basic commands you need to use:

- Open the Server Explorer window, right-click on *Data Connections*, and select *Create New SQL Server Database*.
- To add a table to an existing database, right-click the *Tables* folder below the database name and select *Add New Table*.
- To insert data into an existing table, right-click the table name and select *Show Table Data*.
- To modify a table's structure (called the *schema*), right-click the table name and select *Open Table Definition*.
- To rename a table, right-click its name and select *Rename* from the popup menu.

In Tutorial 5-1, you will create a database that will be used throughout the chapter.

Tutorial 5-1:
Creating an SQL Server Express database

Homeowners always need to have something fixed, and many companies offer a variety of home repair services. Managing appointments is a common task for the company, because they continuously update their customer list and appointment schedule. The company may also vary the types of repairs they offer. Therefore, our limited vision of the database needs of such a company includes a *Customers* table, a *RepairTypes* table, and an *Appointments* table. The Customers table will keep track of information such as customer ID, name, and phone. The RepairTypes table will include a description of each type of repair. The Appointments table will contain information about the type of repair being done, a description of the repair, licensing requirements, the customer's ID, and the scheduled date/time. Later in the chapter, we will create an application that displays and maintains this information.

In this tutorial, you will create the database, add a *Customers* table, and define a DataSet containing table adapters that connect to the database. Finally, you will display the Customers table in a DataGridView control.

Tutorial Steps

Step 1: Create a new Windows Forms project named *Repair Services*.

Step 2: Open the Server Explorer window. Then right-click on *Data Connections* and select *Create New SQL Server Database*.

Step 3: In the dialog window that appears, select *Computername*\SQLEXPRESS from the Server name dropdown list. (*Computername* is the machine name of your computer.) Then, name the database *RepairServices*. An example is shown in Figure 5-2. Click *OK* to close this window.

Figure 5-2 Creating a new database in Server Explorer

Step 4:   Expand the entries under the *RepairServices.dbo* entry under *Data Connections* in the Server Explorer window. Right-click the *Tables* folder and select *Add New Table*. This will display a table editor window, as shown in Figure 5-3.

Figure 5-3 Adding a table to the *RepairServices* database

Step 5:   Click under the *Column Name* heading and insert the database columns shown in Figure 5-4. Right-click the CustId column and select *Set Primary Key* from the popup menu.

Figure 5-4 Design of the *Customers* table

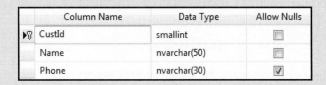

	Column Name	Data Type	Allow Nulls
🔑	CustId	smallint	☐
	Name	nvarchar(50)	☐
	Phone	nvarchar(30)	☑

Step 6:   Close the designer window and save the table. When prompted for a name, as in Figure 5-5, name it *Customers* and click the *OK* button to save the table name.

Figure 5-5 Naming the *Customers* table

Step 7: In the Server Explorer window, right-click the Customers table and select *Show Table Data*. In the window that appears, enter the data shown in Figure 5-6.

Figure 5-6 *Customers* table rows

CustId	Name	Phone
1000	Johnson, David	303-404-3333
1010	Smith, Linda	303-222-3333
1020	Chong, Susan	303-444-5555
1030	Kahane, Sam	303-555-4444
1040	Martinez, Maria	303-666-3333
1050	Ramirez, Jose	303-999-2222

Creating a DataSet

Next, you will create a dataset named *RepairServicesDataSet*.

Step 8: Open the Data Sources window and add a new data source that connects to the **Customers** table in your new database. If there is an existing database connection, use it rather than creating a new one. Name the DataSet as *RepairServicesDataSet*.

Step 9: In Solution Explorer, open the *RepairServicesDataSet.xsd* file. In the designer window, you should see the Customers table and the CustomersTableAdapter.

Next, you will display the Customers table in a DataGridView control, to verify that the data source was created correctly.

Step 10: Rename the project's startup form as *CustomersForm.vb*.

Step 11: Open the design window for CustomersForm and set its Text property to *Customers*.

Step 12: Add a DataGridView control named *dgvCustomers* to the form and attach it to the Customers table in RepairServicesDataSet. Set the grid's Dock property to *Fill*, and set other properties as you wish.

Step 13: Run the application. The customers table should appear as in Figure 5-7.

Figure 5-7 Displaying the *Customers* table in a DataGridView control

CustId	Name	Phone
1000	Johnson, David	303-404-3333
1010	Smith, Linda	303-222-3333
1020	Chong, Susan	303-444-5555
1030	Kahane, Sam	303-555-4444
1040	Martinez, Maria	303-666-3333
1050	Ramirez, Jose	303-999-2222

Summary

We hope you can see how easy it is to use the database tools in Visual Studio. In just a few steps, you were able to create a database and a table, and display the data on a form.

TIP: A quick way to add a new TableAdapter to an existing DataSet is to drag a table from the Server Explorer window onto the DataSet's design surface. You can also drag one or more columns from a table in the same manner.

Tutorial 5-2:
Adding the Appointments table to the RepairServices database

Any useful database requires more than one table to represent its data. In this tutorial, you will add an Appointments form that displays repair appointments in a grid. You will also add a table named *Appointments* to the RepairServices database. This table will contain the following information about scheduled repair appointments:

- *ApptId*—a unique ID number.
- *TypeId*—identifies the type of repair to be done.
- *Description*—a description of the repair.
- *Licensed*—true/false field that indicates whether a licensed repairperson is required.
- *CustId*—customer ID number.
- *Scheduled*—the date and time when the appointment is scheduled.

Tutorial Steps

Step 1: Open the *RepairServices Database* project from Tutorial 5-1.

Step 2: In the Server Explorer window, right-click the *Tables* folder under the database name and select *Add New Table*. This table will be named *Appointments*.

Step 3: In the editor window, add the columns shown in Figure 5-8. Then select the ApptId column and set its (*Is Identity*) property to *True* in the lower panel, as shown in Figure 5-9. Set Identity Seed to 1000, and Identity Increment to 1. Right-click the ApptId column and make it the primary key. Close the window and save your changes.

Figure 5-8 Design of the Appointments table

	Column Name	Data Type	Allow Nulls
🔑	ApptId	int	☐
	TypeId	smallint	☐
	Description	nvarchar(100)	☑
	Licensed	bit	☐
	CustId	smallint	☐
	Scheduled	smalldatetime	☐

Figure 5-9 Identity specification for the ApptId column

Identity Specification	Yes
(Is Identity)	Yes
Identity Increment	1
Identity Seed	1000

Step 4: In the Server Explorer window, right-click the Appointments table and select *Show Table Data*. Then input the data shown in Figure 5-10.

Figure 5-10 Contents of the Appointments table

ApptId	TypeId	Description	Licensed	CustId	Scheduled
1000	1	Replace 3 internal door frames	False	1000	10/1/2011 9:00:00 AM
1001	3	Repair wall next to kitchen	False	1020	10/1/2011 10:00:00 AM
1002	7	Replace tile in kitchen	False	1010	10/2/2011 11:00:00 AM
1003	4	Clean air conditioning coils	False	1030	10/2/2011 3:00:00 PM
1004	5	Install hot water pipe	True	1020	10/2/2011 2:00:00 PM
1005	6	Replace breaker switches	True	1040	10/3/2011 9:30:00 AM
1006	2	Repair refrigerator icemaker	False	1050	10/3/2011 10:00:00 AM
1007	8	Repair loose tiles on roof	False	1040	10/3/2011 1:00:00 PM
1008	9	Replace living room bay window	True	1030	10/4/2011 8:00:00 AM

Step 5: Add the Appointments table to the RepairServicesDataSet by dragging it from the Server Explorer window into the designer window for *RepairServicesDataSet.xsd*.

Step 6: Add a new form to the project named *AppointmentsForm.vb*. Set its Text property to *Appointments*. Add a DataGridView control named *dgvAppointments* to the form and attach it to the Appointments table in RepairServicesDataSet. Set the grid's Dock property to *Fill*.

Step 7: Change the application's startup form to *AppointmentsForm.vb*.

Step 8: Save the project and run the application. You should see the Appointments table in a DataGridView control. Close the application window.

Summary

The Appointments table is central to this application because we want to be able to display, create, and edit appointments. Two of the columns (TypeId and CustId) enable us to link to other tables with supplemental information. Fairly soon in this chapter, we will show how to create relationships between the tables. In Tutorial 5-3, you will create a table that lists the Repair types.

Tutorial 5-3:
Adding the RepairTypes table to the RepairServices database

In this tutorial, you will add a new table named *RepairTypes* to the RepairServices database. It will contain repair ID numbers that link it to the Appointments table.

Tutorial Steps

Step 1:   Open the *Repair Services* project from Tutorials 5-1 and 5-2.

Step 2:   In the Server Explorer window, right-click the *Tables* folder under the database name and select *Add New Table*.

Step 3:   In the *New Table* window, name the table *RepairTypes* and add the columns shown in Table 5-1. Close the window to save your changes.

Table 5-1 Design of the RepairTypes table

Column Name	Data Type	Length	Allow Nulls	Primary Key
TypeId	smallint	2	No	Yes
Description	nvarchar	20	No	No

Step 4:   In the Server Explorer window, right-click the RepairTypes table and select *Show Table Data*. Then input the data shown in Figure 5-11.

Figure 5-11 Contents of the RepairTypes table

TypeId	Description
1	Carpentry
2	Appliance
3	Masonry
4	Heat/Air
5	Plumbing
6	Electrical
7	Flooring
8	Roof
9	Window/Door

One-to-Many Relationships

A **one-to-many relationship** exists between two database tables when the primary key of one table links to a column called a **foreign key** in another table. For example, the Customers and Appointments tables have such a relationship, as shown in Figure 5-12. The infinity sign

Figure 5-12 One-to-many relationship between the Customers and Appointments tables

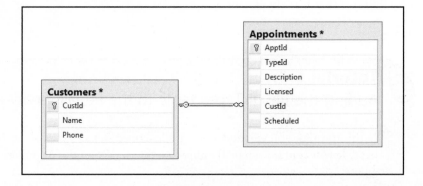

next to the CustId column of the Appointments table implies that the same customer ID can occur multiple times in this table. It is the *many* side of the relationship. The key symbol at the other end of the line touching the Customers table indicates that CustId is the primary key for that table. It is the *one* side of the relationship.

When a one-to-many relationship exists between two tables, the table on the *one* side is called the **parent table.** The table on the *many* side is called the **child table.** In our current example, Customers is the parent table and Appointments is the child table.

A one-to-many relationship is useful when applications need to find child table rows that match the rows in a parent table. Given a certain Customer ID, for example, we could find all Appointments pertaining to that customer. SQL Server can also join tables together, using columns defined in one-to-many relationsships.

Many-to-Many Relationships

Another type of relationship that links database tables is called a **many-to-many relationship.** This occurs when the linking column is a foreign key in both tables. Imagine, for a moment, that a table named *Employees* exists in our RepairServices database. Let us assume that multiple employees can be assigned to the same appointment, working together to get the job done. Also, we assume that multiple appointments can be assigned to the same employee. Clearly, we cannot create a one-to-many relationship between the Employees and Appointments tables. Therefore, a linking table is created that matches Employees to Appointments. Suppose employee number 105 has been scheduled to work on appointments 1002, 1004, and 1005. Also, suppose that employees 107 and 108 are scheduled for appointment 1004. We can create a table named *EmployeeAppointments* that contains the rows shown in Table 5-2. The table shows how each employee is assigned to each appointment.

Table 5-2 Design of the EmployeeAppointments table

EmpId	ApptId
105	1002
105	1004
105	1005
107	1004
108	1004

We will not add the Employee and EmployeeAppointments tables to our database at this time. But it should be possible to see that tables such as this can prove very useful in real-world applications.

Database Constraints

A **database constraint** is a rule that is inserted into a database by a database designer. A constraint helps to preserve the integrity of the data by preventing errors caused by the incorrect insertion, modification, and deletion of data. A constraint relieves individual application programs from having to verify the integrity of the data. Rather than inserting validation statements into every application that uses a database, it is more efficient to embed constraints in the database.

A **primary key constraint** requires that all values in a primary key are unique. If an attempt is made to add a table row containing a primary key value that already exists in the table, the database signals that a primary key constraint has been violated. The row is not added to the table. For example, if we were to add a new row containing CustId = 1030 to the Customers table, a primary key constraint would be violated and the message shown in Figure 5-13 would be displayed.

Figure 5-13 Primary key constraint violation

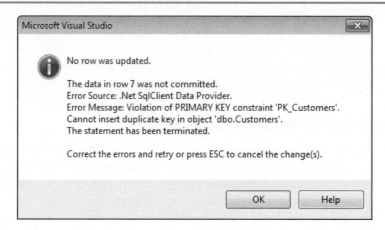

A **column check constraint** is a rule that defines whether data are valid when adding or updating an entry in a table. The constraint is applied to each table row. It may involve one or more column values. For example, values assigned to a Salary column could be required to be positive. Also the data types of the inserted data must match the data types of the table columns.

A **referential integrity constraint,** or **foreign key constraint,** applies to the relationship between two tables that have a one-to-many relationship. The parent table is required to contain a primary key value that matches each foreign key value found in the child table.

In Figure 5-14, for example, customer ID 1020 appears twice in the Appointments table (CustId column). Suppose an application updated the Customers table, changing 1020 to

Figure 5-14 Customers and Appointments tables

CustId	Name	Phone
1000	Johnson, David	303-404-3333
1010	Smith, Linda	303-222-3333
1020	Chong, Susan	303-444-5555
1030	Kahane, Sam	303-555-4444
1040	Martinez, Maria	303-666-3333
1050	Ramirez, Jose	303-999-2222

ApptId	TypeId	Description	Licensed	CustId	ScheduledAt
1000	1	Replace 3 internal door frames	False	1000	10/1/2011 9:00:00 AM
1001	3	Repair wall next to kitchen	False	1020	10/1/2011 10:00:00 AM
1002	7	Replace tile in kitchen	False	1010	10/2/2011 11:00:00 AM
1003	4	Clean air conditioning coils	False	1030	10/2/2011 3:00:00 PM
1004	5	Install hot water pipe	True	1020	10/2/2011 2:00:00 PM
1005	6	Replace breaker switches	True	1040	10/3/2011 9:30:00 AM

1022. If no constraints were in effect, the Appointments table would contain two (and possibly more) rows that could no longer link to the Customers table. In effect, the rows would become *orphan rows*. In a large database, errors like this might go undetected and cause serious data integrity problems. Similarly, if Customer 1020 were deleted from the Customers table, all rows in the Appointments table that contained CustId = 1020 would become orphans.

Another way to violate a referential integrity constraint is to add a new row to the Appointment table that includes a CustId value that does not exist in the Customers table.

Tutorial 5-4:
Creating relationships between the RepairTypes, Appointments, and Customers tables

In this tutorial, you will add two relationships to the RepairServices database: one connects RepairTypes to Appointments, and the second connects Customers to Appointments.

Tutorial Steps

Step 1: In the Server Explorer window, under the *RepairServices* database name, right-click the *Database Diagrams* folder and select *Add New Diagram*.

TIP: A message may pop up saying that Visual Studio needs to install an additional component. You can let it do that.

Step 2: The *Add Table* window should appear. Select the Appointments, RepairTypes, and Customers tables. Click the *Add* button, then click the *Close* button.

Step 3: Drag the mouse from the selection button just to the left of the CustId column in the Customers table to the selection button next to the CustId column of the Appointments table. When you release the mouse button, the *Tables and Columns* dialog window appears, as shown in Figure 5-15. Notice that Customers is selected as the Primary key table, and Appointments is selected as the Foreign key table. The CustId column is selected in both tables. If any of these values are different in your window, you can correct them now.

TIP: You might have to drag the mouse a couple of times before getting the line to appear between the tables. It's tricky. If you see a dotted line following the cursor as you drag the mouse, you are doing it correctly.

Figure 5-15 Creating a Relationship between the Customers and Appointments tables

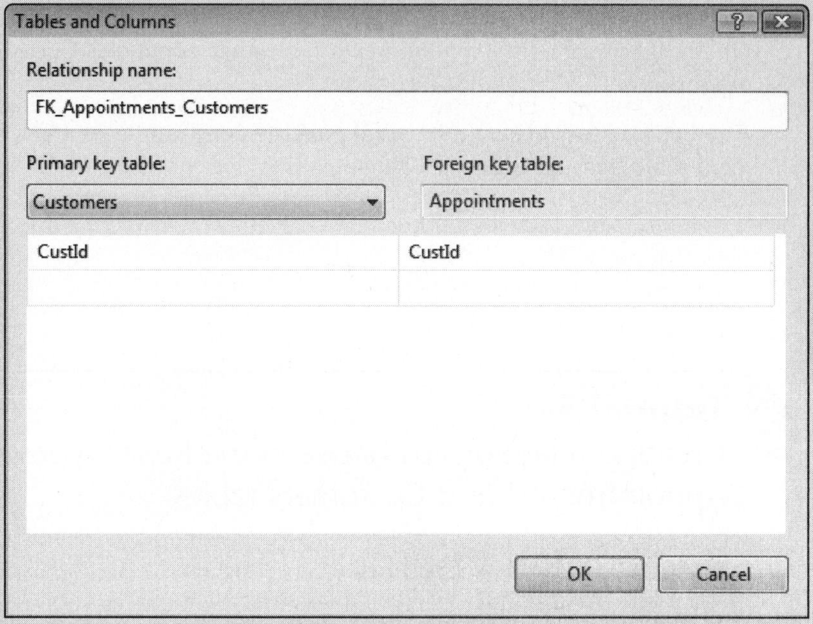

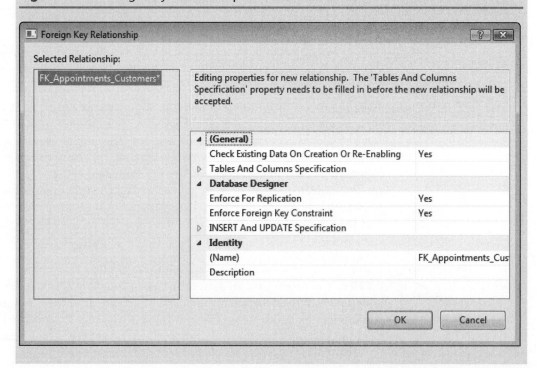

Step 4: Click the *OK* button to save the relationship. That should expose the *Foreign Key Relationship* window, shown in Figure 5-16. In here, you can modify specific options that control the table relationship. For example, the *Enforce Foreign Key Constraint* option equals *Yes*. That means the database will throw an exception if an application tries to delete a row from a parent table in such a

Figure 5-16 Foreign Key Relationship window

way that some child table rows would no longer be able to link to the parent table.

Step 5: Create another relationship between the RepairTypes and Appointments tables, using the TypeId field as the common link.

Step 6: Save the database diagram and give it a name, such as *Relationships*.

Step 7: Use the mouse to drag the RepairTypes and Appointments tables into the DataSet designer window. When you do that, lines indicating relationships should connect the tables, as shown in Figure 5-17. (The lines do not necessarily line up with the column names they represent.)

Figure 5-17 DataSet designer window

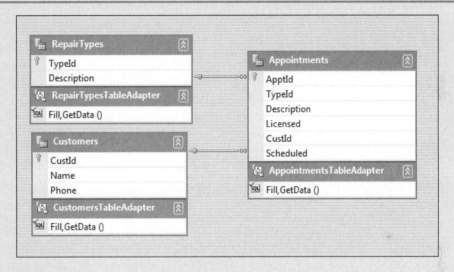

Summary

A **database diagram** is an essential tool for describing database table relationships and constraints. Database diagrams also provide a visual reference to the links between tables, which can help when the database grows beyond a few tables.

Copying a Database File

Rather than using a database directly connected to a server such as SQLEXPRESS, you may want to connect to a database file. It is possible, but you need to make a copy of the database first.

SQL Server Express stores its database files in a standard directory. You can find it by looking for the SQL Server installation directory. For example, on our computer, the *RepairServices.mdf* is located here:

```
C:\Program Files\Microsoft SQL Server\MSSQL.10.SQLEXPRESS\MSSQL\DATA
```

You can make a copy of the file. First, however, right-click the database in Server Explorer and select *Close Connection*. Or, you can close Visual Studio before copying the file.

TIP: If you're working in a college computer lab, the directory permissions might prevent you from directly accessing the data directory for SQL server. In that case, your instructor may be able to give you a copy of the database file.

In Tutorial 5-5, you will switch the database connection from SQL Server Express to a database file.

Tutorial 5-5:
Changing the database connection from the SQL Express server to a database file

If your application were to continue connecting to SQL Server Express to view and update the RepairServices database, all changes would be permanent. This could be a problem, for example, if you delete multiple appointments. For testing purpose, it's much better to work with a local database within your project directory, as we did in Chapter 4 with the Karate database. This tutorial takes you through the steps of fixing your database connection.

Tutorial Steps

Step 1: Close Visual Studio, so any existing connection to the server will be terminated.

Step 2: Locate the *RepairServices.mdf* file within your SQL Server data directory. Most likely, it will be in a path similar to *C:\Program Files\Microsoft SQL Server\MSSQL.1\MSSQL\Data*. You may have to ask your lab administrator or instructor for help. Copy this file to your Repair Services project directory.

Step 3: Open the *Repair Services* project in Visual Studio.

Step 4: In the Solution Explorer window, right-click the project name, select Add, and select *Existing Item*. Select the *RepairServices.mdf* file (to see the filename, you may have to change the filename filter to *All Files*). Click the *Add* button to close the dialog window.

Step 5: Double-click *My Project* in the Solution Explorer window. This will bring up the Project Properties window.

Step 6: Select the *Settings* tab and note the single entry in the window. Click inside the *Value* column and change it to the following single line:

```
Data Source=.\SQLEXPRESS;
AttachDbFilename=|DataDirectory|\RepairServices.mdf;
Integrated Security=True;User Instance=True
```

We have broken the line to fit on the printed page, but you should keep all this text in a single line when typing it into the settings.

Step 7: Save your changes to the project properties.

Step 8: Open the Server Explorer window and delete the old connection to the database. Create a new connection to the local database file. From now on, your project will use the local database file.

Summary

Visual Studio gives you some flexible options in how you connect to a database. It's a good idea for you to develop a practical working knowledge of how to create, delete, and modify database connections.

From this point on, you will be using the local *RepairServices.mdf* database file. A fresh copy of the file will be created every time you build the project. Any tables that were modified while running the application will be restored to their original values.

 Checkpoint

1. Which Visual Studio window lets you view and manage connections to databases?

2. How do you create a relationship between two tables?

3. In the RepairServices database, how are the Appointments and Customers tables related?

4. Which column connects the Appointments and RepairTypes tables?

5. If there were an Employee table in the RepairServices database, what would be the reason for creating an EmployeeAppointments table that connects the Employee and Appointments tables?

5.2 DataTables

A **DataTable** is an object that represents the contents of a table from a data source. The .NET DataTable class is used as the basis for creating more specialized DataTable types. When you add a data source to a project, Visual Studio creates a specialized DataTable class, such as CustomerDataTable or MembersDataTable.

A DataTable class describes a collection of rows and columns and is used to hold data from a database, XML file, or some other data source. A DataTable object contains a collection of columns, which describe the type of data in the table. It also has a collection of rows that contain the actual data.

Here are some of the most common properties in the DataTable class:

- *Columns*—A collection of DataColumn objects; each describes the name, type, and other characteristics of a column.
- *DefaultView*—A DataView object that lets you filter (select) the table rows or sort the rows on any column.
- *PrimaryKey*—An array of DataColumn objects that serve as the table's primary key; each row is guaranteed to hold a unique value in the column or columns.
- *Rows*—A collection of DataRow objects, each holding the data in each row of the table.

For a conceptual view, Figure 5-18 describes the Columns and Rows properties of a DataTable.

Figure 5-18 DataTable properties

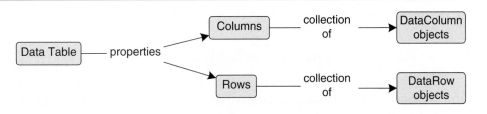

Binding Controls to a DataTable

If you want to display the contents of a DataTable on a form, you can bind it to a ListBox, ComboBox, or DataGridView control. Assign the table reference to the control's DataSource property. The following statement, for example, binds a DataTable object named customersTable to a DataGridView control named dgvCustomers:

```
dgvCustomers.DataSource = customersTable
```

Filtering and Sorting DataTable Rows

The DataTable class contains a *DefaultView* property. This property, in turn, has two important subproperties:

- *RowFilter* property—Holds a comparison expression that is similar to the WHERE clause in an SQL SELECT statement.
- *Sort* property—Identifies one or more columns to be used in the sort; also specifies the order as ASC (ascending) or DESC (descending).

You assign values to these properties in order to filter or sort the rows in a DataTable. The following statement, for example, sorts the rows of *customersTable* in ascending order by Name:

```
customersTable.DefaultView.Sort = "Name"
```

The following statement sorts *customersTable* in descending order by CustId:

```
customersTable.DefaultView.Sort = "CustId DESC"
```

The following statement restricts the table rows to those in which the Name field is greater than *M*:

```
customersTable.DefaultView.RowFilter = "Name > 'M'"
```

DataRow Objects

A **DataRow object** describes a row in a DataTable. You can add columns to a DataRow, fill the row with values, add the row to a table, and remove a row from a table. To construct an empty DataRow, call a DataTable's *NewRow* method:

```
Dim table As New DataTable
Dim row As DataRow = table.NewRow()
```

The *Item* property of a DataRow lets you get and set column values. Assuming that our table contains a column named Last_Name, the following statement assigns a value to the current row:

```
row.Item("Name") = "Johnson, Sam"
```

Item is the DataRow's default property, so you can shorten the previous statement:

```
row("Name") = "Johnson, Sam"
```

You can also refer to columns by their index positions, which begin at 0. The following statement assigns a person's name to the first column in the row object:

```
row.Item(0) = "Johnson, Sam"
```

The *ItemArray* property returns an Object array containing all the column values:

```
Dim columns As Object() = row.ItemArray
```

Strongly Typed DataTables

When you create a DataSet based on a database table, Visual Studio creates a set of custom classes. The custom classes match the structure of the tables in your DataSet. The

RepairServicesDataSet class, for example, contains an inner class (a class inside another class) named *CustomersDataTable*. It contains some useful methods and properties, such as:

- *AddCustomersRow*—A method that adds a new row to the table.
- *NewCustomersRow*—A method that returns an empty row having the same columns as the table.
- *RemoveCustomersRow*—A method that removes a row from the table.
- *FindByCustId*—A method that searches for a row using a customer ID number.
- *Count*—A property that returns the number of table rows.

Another inner class named *CustomersRow* contains properties that represent the different columns in the Customers table. You can use these properties to set column values in your program code:

- CustId As Short
- Name As String
- Phone As String

In addition, this class has a method named GetAppointmentsRows, which returns a collection of rows from the Appointments table that match the current row's customer ID number.

You will find, when writing code to view and update the RepairServices database, that having classes such as CustomersDataTable and CustomersRow greatly simplifies your work.

 Checkpoint

6. Which TableAdapter method usually returns a DataTable object?

7. Which DataTable property returns an object that can be filtered and sorted?

8. What types of objects are stored in the Columns property of a DataTable?

9. Which DataGridView property holds a reference to a DataTable when the table is displayed in the grid?

 # 5.3 Updating Databases Using SQL

In Chapter 4, you learned how to add, update, and delete rows from database tables, using data-bound controls. The database was modified by SQL queries working behind the scenes. Now is the time for you to learn how update operations are done in the SQL language.

- The **INSERT INTO** statement adds a new row to a table.
- The **UPDATE** statement modifies one or more existing table rows.
- The **DELETE FROM** statement deletes one or more rows from a table.

Inserting Table Rows

The SQL **INSERT INTO** statement inserts a new row into a table, using the following syntax:

```
INSERT INTO tablename
( field1[,field2[,...]] )
VALUES( value1,[,value2[,...] )
```

The following query inserts a row into a table named Payroll:

```
INSERT INTO Payroll (EmpId, PaymentDate, HoursWorked, HourlyRate)
   VALUES('1002', '1/15/2012', 47.5, 27.50)
```

All column names should be listed in the same order as the corresponding values. String and date literals must be enclosed in single quotes.

Query Parameters

INSERT INTO statements do not usually contain literal column values. Instead, query parameters are used so that values may be passed to the query at runtime. A parameter name must begin with the @ symbol. If possible, let each parameter name match the name of a table column.

The following statement inserts a row in the Payments table (Karate database) using three query parameters:

```
INSERT INTO Payments( Amount, Member_Id, Payment_Date )
   VALUES (@Amount, @Member_Id, @Payment_Date)
```

The primary key of this table is assumed to be an identity field, so there is no need to include its value in the INSERT statement. The database will generate a new primary key value each time a new row is inserted into the table.

Updating Table Rows

The SQL **UPDATE** statement modifies the contents of one or more rows in a database table. It has the following basic syntax:

```
UPDATE tablename
SET fieldname = newvalue
[ SET fieldname = newvalue ] ...
[ WHERE criteria ]
```

UPDATE has the potential to modify every row in a table. For example, the following query increases the values in the HourlyRate column of all rows in the Payroll table by 5 percent:

```
UPDATE Payroll
SET HourlyRate = HourlyRate * 1.05
```

Usually you want to update only certain rows, so you can include a WHERE clause with selection criteria. The following query, for example, increases the hourly pay rate for employees who were paid after the date stored in the @PaymentDate parameter:

```
UPDATE Payroll
SET HourlyRate = HourlyRate * 1.05
WHERE PaymentDate > @PaymentDate
```

If you want to update a single row, the WHERE clause must uniquely identify the selected row. Ordinarily, you would use an expression containing the table's primary key. For example, the following increases the hourly pay rate for a single employee whose ID number is specified by the @EmpId parameter:

```
UPDATE Payroll
SET HourlyRate = HourlyRate * 1.05
WHERE EmpId = @EmpId
```

We could also use a query parameter for the rate multiplier:

```
UPDATE Payroll
SET HourlyRate = HourlyRate * @RateMultiplier
WHERE EmpId = @EmpId
```

Karate Database Example

The following query updates the Payments table (Karate database). It sets Amount to the value in the @Amount parameter for the row in which the Payment_Id equals the value in @Payment_Id:

```
UPDATE Payments
SET Amount = @Amount
WHERE Payment_Id = @Payment_Id
```

Deleting Table Rows

The SQL **DELETE FROM** statement deletes rows from a table. This is the general syntax:

```
DELETE FROM tablename
[ WHERE criteria ]
```

Once a row has been deleted, it cannot be recovered. The following statement deletes all rows from the Payments table:

```
DELETE FROM Payments
```

The WHERE clause selects which rows to delete. The following code deletes all payments prior to the date in the @Payment_Date parameter:

```
DELETE FROM Payments
WHERE Payment_Date < @Payment_Date
```

The following statement deletes a single payment, assuming that Payment_Id is the primary key column:

```
DELETE FROM Payments
WHERE Payment_Id < @Payment_Id
```

Deleting Rows from Related Tables

Be careful when deleting rows from a table that participates in a one-to-many table relationship. For example, in the RepairServices database, a one-to-many relationship exists between the Customers and Appointments tables. Customers is the parent, and Appointments is the child. If we deleted a row from Customers whose CustId value matches any rows in the Appointments table, we would be left with appointments that had no matching customer rows. This deletion would violate a referential integrity constraint in the database, causing an exception to be thrown (see Figure 5-19).

Figure 5-19 Referential integrity constraint was violated

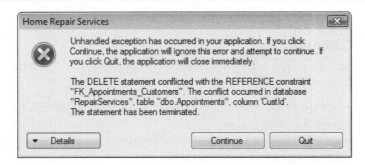

In Tutorial 5-4 we included referential integrity constraints when creating the DataTable relationships inside the DataSet designer window. Because we would like to be able to delete customers, we can use one of the following approaches:

1. We could mark the Customer row as inactive without physically deleting it. This would require us to add another column to the Customers table that might be named *Active*. Then we would have to modify all queries that use the Customers table, to make sure they include only active customers. This approach would require a significant amount of work.

2. An easier approach would be to delete the customer's appointments from the Appointments table before deleting the customer from the Customers table. That seems reasonable, although some companies might prefer to copy the affected appointments to an historical database before deleting them.

The situation for the Appointments table is different. You can delete its rows without any constraints. It is not the parent of another table, so no other tables depend on its data.

Summary

If you would like to learn more about the SQL language, there are many excellent books on the subject and many reference sources on the Web. First and foremost, the Microsoft MSDN library is a great reference. Go to **http://msdn.microsoft.com** and search for terms like *SQL Insert*, or *SQL Delete*, or *SQL Update*. Another excellent site is **http://w3schools.com/sql**.

 Checkpoint

10. Which SQL statement is used when adding new rows to a table?

11. Which SQL statement modifies one or more existing rows of a table?

12. If no WHERE clause is given in a DELETE FROM statement, how many rows are deleted?

 5.4 **Focus on Problem Solving: Home Repair Services Application**

Through the following series of tutorials (Tutorials 5-6 through 5-14), we will gradually build an application named ***Home Repair Services***. Its purpose is to enable company personnel to schedule repair services for residential customers. It will be a three-tier application, with a presentation tier made of windows forms, a middle tier containing three classes (Appointments, RepairTypes, and Customers), and a data access tier made up of DataSet classes. It will permit the customer to display appointments, search for appointments, create appointments, modify appointments, and display customers. As limited as it is, this application is designed to be expandable, so that it might include all of the features required by an actual company.

In Tutorial 5-6, you will create a middle tier class for this application.

 Tutorial 5-6:
Adding the Appointments class to the middle tier

In this tutorial, you will begin to create the Home Repair Services application. Your first task will be to create a middle tier class named *Appointments* containing a method that inserts new appointments into the database. You will also test this method from a new form that you add to the project.

Tutorial Steps

Step 1: Open the *RepairServices Database* project that you last worked on in Tutorial 5-3.

Step 2: Open *RepairServicesDataSet.xsd* from the Solution Explorer window.

Step 3: In the DataSet Designer window, right-click the AppointmentsTableAdapter and select *Properties*, as shown in Figure 5-20.

Figure 5-20 AppointmentsTableAdapter properties window

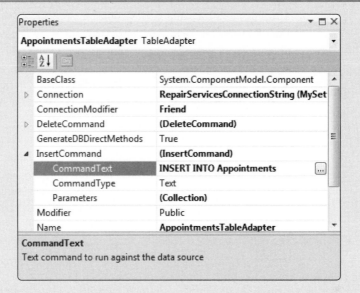

Step 4: In the Properties window, find the InsertCommand property and expand it so you can view its CommandText subproperty. Click on the button containing three dots to open the *Query Builder* window.

Step 5: Verify that the SQL query is the following, and change it if necessary:

```
INSERT INTO Appointments
   (TypeId, Description, Licensed, CustId, Scheduled)
VALUES (@TypeId,@Description,@Licensed,@CustId,@Scheduled)
```

Step 6: Add a middle-tier class named *Appointments.vb* to the project. In this class, declare the following class-level variables:

```
Private adapter As New _
  RepairServicesDataSetTableAdapters.AppointmentsTableAdapter
Public Shared Property LastError As String
```

The variable named *adapter* is an instance of the TableAdapter that you will use to carry out actions on the database. LastError will hold error messages generated by the TableAdapter methods.

Step 7: Create a new method named *Insert*.

```
1: Public Function Insert(ByVal typeId As Short,
2:    ByVal description As String, ByVal licensed As Boolean,
3:    ByVal custId As Short, ByVal Scheduled As DateTime) _
      As Boolean
```

```
 4:      ' Insert a new row into the Appointments table. Return
 5:      ' True if successful. If an exception is thrown,
 6:      ' LastError will hold an error message.
 7:      Try
 8:         LastError = String.Empty
 9:         adapter.Insert(typeId, description, licensed,
10:           custId, Scheduled)
11:         Return True
12:      Catch ex As Exception
13:         LastError = ex.Message
14:         Return False
15:      End Try
16: End Function
```

Line 8 clears any error message that might be left over in the LastError variable from a previous operation. Line 9 calls the Insert method from the AppointmentsTableAdapter class. If no exception is thrown, line 11 returns *True*, indicating success. On the other hand, if the call to Insert on line 9 throws an exception, ErrorMessage is assigned a string and the method returns *False*.

> **TIP:** There is one possible outcome that we are ignoring in the code for the Insert method. The call to adapter.Insert might not throw an exception, but it might somehow fail to insert a table row. It would complicate your code to check for this remote possibility, so you can leave the code as is.

Step 8: Add a Shared method named *CombinedDateTime* that receives a date and a time and returns a combined date/time value.

```
Public Shared Function CombinedDateTime(ByVal aDate As DateTime,
  ByVal aTime As DateTime) As DateTime
  Dim ts As New TimeSpan(aTime.Hour, aTime.Minute, 0)
  Return aDate.Add(ts)
End Function
```

It is not possible to directly add a time to a date, but you can add a TimeSpan object to it. The code above does just that. It is a shared method because it does not use any class-level variables in the Appointment class, and therefore does not require the user to create an Appointment object.

New Appointment Form

Next, you will create a *New Appointment* form, which will test the Appointments.Insert method. For the moment, we will not create a user interface.

Step 9: Add a new form named *NewAppointmentForm.vb* to the project. Set its Text property to *New Repair Appointment*. Add the following line of code to the form's class:

```
Private mAppointments As New Appointments
```

This line creates an instance of the middle-tier Appointments class inside the form, so we can call its Insert method.

Step 10: Add a button to the form, with the Text equal to *Save*. Insert the following code in the button's Click handler:

```
mAppointments.Insert(2,"Fix disposal",False,1020,
    #10/5/2011 9:00 AM#)
AppointmentsForm.ShowDialog()
```

The first statement insert a new appointment in the database. The second statement displays the complete list of appointments in a separate form, so you can verify that the appointment was created.

Step 11: Set the project's startup form to *NewAppointmentForm* and run the application. You should see the Appointments table appear in a grid, with the new appointment added to the end. A sample is shown in Figure 5-21.

Figure 5-21 Appointments table, with new row added

ApptId	TypeId	Description	Licensed	CustId	ScheduledAt
1000	1	Replace 3 internal door frames	☐	1000	10/1/2011 9:00 AM
1001	3	Repair wall next to kitchen	☐	1020	10/1/2011 10:00 AM
1002	7	Replace tile in kitchen	☐	1010	10/2/2011 11:00 AM
1003	4	Clean air conditioning coils	☐	1030	10/2/2011 3:00 PM
1004	5	Install hot water pipe	☑	1020	10/2/2011 2:00 PM
1005	6	Replace breaker switches	☑	1040	10/3/2011 9:30 AM
1006	2	Repair refrigerator icemaker	☐	1050	10/3/2011 10:00 AM
1007	8	Repair loose tiles on roof	☐	1040	10/3/2011 1:00 PM
1008	9	Replace living room bay window	☑	1030	10/4/2011 8:00 AM
1009	2	Fix disposal	☐	1020	10/5/2011 9:00 AM

If you should restart the application and click the button again, it would add another row with the same information to the Appointments table. Each appointment would have a different value in the ApptId column because that value is generated automatically by the database.

Step 12: When you're done, rebuild the project from the Visual Studio *Build* menu. That will reset the database to its original values.

Tutorial 5-7:
Creating the main startup form

In this tutorial, you will create a startup form for the Home Repair Services application. You will create a menu that displays all existing forms.

Tutorial Steps

Step 1: Add a new form named *MainForm.vb* to the project, and set its Text property to *Home Repair Services*.

Modify the project properties to make it the application startup form.

Step 2:   Add a MenuStrip control with the following menu structure:

```
File
   Exit
Appointments
   New
   View
   Appointment List
Customers
   View
```

As another option, you may want to rename the menu items to be more descriptive than the default names assigned by Visual Studio. For example, the names could be *AppointmentsNewMenuItem*, *AppointmentsViewMenuItem*, and so on.

Step 3:   Create a Click event handler for the *File / Exit* menu item, and insert a `Me.Close()` statement.

Step 4:   Create a Click event handler for the *Appointments / New* menu item, and insert the following statement:

```
NewAppointmentForm.ShowDialog()
```

Step 5:   Create a Click event handler for the *Appointments / View* menu item, and insert the following statement:

```
AppointmentsForm.ShowDialog()
```

Step 6:   Create a Click event handler for the *Customers / View* menu item, and insert the following statement:

```
CustomersForm.ShowDialog()
```

Step 7:   Run the application and test it as follows:

Input	Select *Appointments / New* from the menu.
Expected result	The *New Appointment* form displays.
Input	Close the *New Appointment* form, and select *Appointments / View* from the menu.
Expected result	The *Appointments* form displays, showing a grid that lists all appointments.
Input	Close the *Appointments* form, and select *Customers / View* from the menu.
Expected result	The *Customers* form displays, showing a grid that lists all customers.
Input	Close the *Customers* form. Select *File / Exit* from the menu.
Expected result	The startup form closes and the application ends.

Summary

It is useful to create a menu on the startup form so you can use it as a branching point to all the other forms in the application. Then, as you add each new form to the project, you will create a click handler for the appropriate menu item. In Tutorial 5-8, you will add more classes and methods to the application's middle tier.

Tutorial 5-8:
Adding classes to the middle tier

In this tutorial, you will add the **Customers** and **RepairTypes** classes to the Home Repair Services application's middle tier. These classes will provide important links to the CustomersTableAdapter and RepairTypesTableAdapter, which are part of the data access tier. You will also add methods that retrieve lists of repair types and customer names.

Tutorial Steps

Step 1: Add a new middle-tier class named *RepairTypes* to the project.

Step 2: Add the following class-level variable to the RepairTypes class:

```
Private adapter As New _
   RepairServicesDataSetTableAdapters.RepairTypesTableAdapter
```

Step 3: Create a ReadOnly property named *Items* that returns a DataTable containing all of the repair types.

```
1: Public ReadOnly Property Items() As DataTable
2:   Get
3:     Dim table As DataTable = adapter.GetData()
4:     table.DefaultView.Sort = "Description"
5:     Return table
6:   End Get
7: End Property
```

A middle-tier class gives you the opportunity to refine the data returned by a table adapter. In the Item method shown here, line 3 calls the table adapter's GetData method, which returns a DataTable containing all the repair types listed in the RepairTypes database table. Line 4 sorts the data by description, and line 5 returns the sorted table.

Step 4: Add a new middle-tier class named *Customers* to the project.

Step 5: Add the following class-level variable to the Customers class:

```
Private adapter As New _
   RepairServicesDataSetTableAdapters.CustomersTableAdapter
```

Step 6: Create a ReadOnly property named *Items* that returns a DataTable containing all of the Customers:

```
Public ReadOnly Property Items() As DataTable
  Get
    Dim table As DataTable = adapter.GetData()
    table.DefaultView.Sort = "Name"
    Return table
  End Get
End Property
```

Summary

Step by step, you are building up the classes in the middle tier. As you may have noticed, you do not have to invest very much time in these classes at the beginning. It is best to keep them short and wait until you need some new operation before adding more code. Building the classes in the middle tier should always be done before finishing the user interface in the presentation tier. Then the presentation tier will be able to call methods and properties in these classes. At this point, you have created all the necessary support for the *New Appointments* form.

Runtime Data Binding

Runtime data binding means to bind a control to a data source at runtime, using code statements. One example of this is to assign a DataTable object to the DataSource property of a DataGridView control. In Chapter 4, you used Visual Studio to create TableAdapter, BindingSource, and DataSet components on every form. But multi-tier applications automatically separate the presentation layer from the data components. Therefore, the best approach is not to fill a form with data component objects, but instead to perform runtime data binding.

If you want to fill a grid or list box using runtime data binding, do the following: Declare a variable in the form's code that is an instance of a middle-tier class. Then call a method from that class that returns a DataTable. Assign the DataTable to the DataSource property of a ListBox, ComboBox, or DataGridView control. In ListBox and ComboBox controls, you also need to set two other string properties:

- *DisplayMember*—The name of the DataTable column that will be displayed in the list.
- *ValueMember*—The name of the DataTable column that will provide a reference value when the user selects a member of the list. The reference value will be available in the SelectedValue property at runtime.

For example, let's assume that the variable *mRepairTypes* is an instance of the RepairTypes class. In that class, the Items property returns a DataTable object. We want the Description column of the table to display in the combo box, and we want the TypeId column to be returned in the combo box's SelectedValue property when the user makes a selection. This is the appropriate setup code, which would be in the Form_Load event handler of the form:

```
cboRepairType.DataSource = mRepairTypes.Items
cboRepairType.DisplayMember = "Description"
cboRepairType.ValueMember = "TypeId"
```

Formatting DataGridView Columns at Runtime

A disadvantage to runtime data binding is that it does not give you a chance to format DataGridView columns in design mode. There is a simple workaround: You can temporarily bind the grid to an existing data source just long enough to format the columns in design mode. Then, at runtime, you can still assign a DataTable to the grid's DataSource property.

On the other hand, if you just need to make only minor formatting changes to grid columns, you can assign values to each column's DefaultCellStyle property. This is done at runtime, usually in the Form_Load event handler. The following lines, for example, set column 2 to a numeric format, centered, with two decimal places, in a blue color:

```
With dgvCourses.Columns(2).DefaultCellStyle
   .Format = "n"
   .ForeColor = Color.Blue
   .Alignment = DataGridViewContentAlignment.MiddleCenter
End With
```

In the MSDN documentation, you can discover the other column formatting properties.

SelectedIndexChanged Event

If your Form_Load event handler assigns a value to the DataSource property of a ListBox or ComboBox control, a SelectedIndexChanged event is fired immediately, before the grid has been filled with data. If there is a handler for this event that responds to user selections, your program code might think that a selection has already been made by the user. Such a situation can cause an exception to be thrown. Here is a workaround: First, declare a Boolean variable that is initially set to *True*. Then set it to *False* at the end of the Form_Load event handler. Then in the SelectedIndexChanged event handler, process the event only if the

Boolean variable equals *False*. Here is an outline of the code we have described, using a ComboBox named cboCustomers:

```
Private formLoading As Boolean = True

Private Sub Form_Load() Handles MyBase.Load
  cboCustomers.DataSource = mCustomers.Items
    .

    .
  formLoading = False
End Sub

Private Sub cboCustomer_SelectedIndexChanged() _
  Handles cboCustomer.SelectedIndexChanged
  If Not formLoading Then
    ' OK to process the event
  End If
End Sub
```

In Tutorial 5-9, you will build the user interface for the *New Appointment* form.

Tutorial 5-9:
Adding controls to the *New Appointment* form

In this tutorial, you will add controls to the *New Appointment* form in the Home Repair Services application. This form permits the user to input appointment data and add a new row to the Appointments database table. Your code will call methods from three middle-tier classes: Customers, Appointments, and RepairTypes.

Tutorial Steps

Step 1: Open the design window for *NewAppointmentForm.vb*. Using the example in Figure 5-22 and the list of named controls in Table 5-3, add the necessary controls to the form.

Figure 5-22 New Appointment form

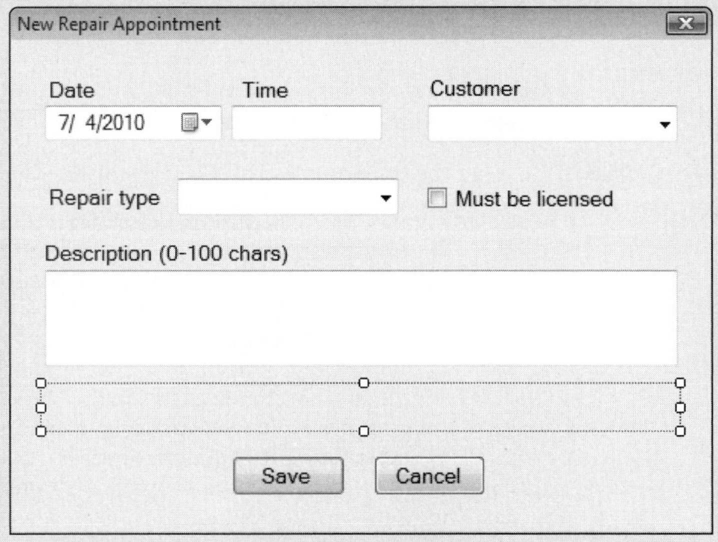

![New Repair Appointment form showing fields for Date (7/ 4/2010), Time, Customer dropdown, Repair type dropdown, Must be licensed checkbox, Description (0-100 chars) text area, and Save and Cancel buttons]

Table 5-3 Controls on the New Appointment form

Control Type	Control Name	Property Settings
Form	NewAppointmentForm	Text = *New Repair Appointment,* AcceptButton = btnSave CancelButton = btnCancel FormBorderStyle = FixedDialog MaximizeBox = *False* MinimizeBox = *False* Font.Size = 10
TextBox	txtTime	
TextBox	txtDescription	MultiLine = *True*
DateTimePicker	dtpDate	Format = Short
ComboBox	cboCustomer	
ComboBox	cboRepairType	
CheckBox	chkLicensed	Text = *Must be licensed*
Label	lblStatus	AutoSize = *False*
Button	btnSave	Text = *Save*
Button	btnCancel	Text = *Cancel*
ErrorProvider	errProvider	

The two combo boxes are important because they provide lists of customers and repair types. When the user selects values from these lists, their corresponding ID values will be saved in the new repair appointment. Next, you will add code to the form that calls methods from the Appointments, Repair-Types, and Customers classes in the middle tier.

Step 2: Open the form's code window and add new class-level variables so you now have the following:

```
Private mAppointments As New Appointments
Private mRepairTypes As New RepairTypes
Private mCustomers As New Customers
```

Each object declared here is an instance of a middle-tier class. This is a common pattern that will repeat itself in nearly every form.

Step 3: Create the following Form_Load event handler:

```
 1: Private Sub NewAppointmentForm_Load() Handles MyBase.Load
 2:    ' Fill the Repair Types combo box.
 3:    cboRepairType.DataSource = mRepairTypes.Items
 4:    cboRepairType.DisplayMember = "Description"
 5:    cboRepairType.ValueMember = "TypeId"
 6:
 7:    ' Fill the Customers combo box.
 8:    cboCustomer.DataSource = mCustomers.Items
 9:    cboCustomer.DisplayMember = "Name"
10:    cboCustomer.ValueMember = "CustId"
11: End Sub
```

The purpose of this code is to fill the two combo boxes with lists of customers and repair types. Line 3 calls the Items property from the RepairTypes class, which returns a DataTable that lists all the possible repair types. Lines 8–10 bind another combo box with a DataTable containing customer names and IDs.

Step 4: Create the following Click handler for the *Save* button. You may already have a Click handler, so replace it with this one:

```
 1: Private Sub btnSave_Click() Handles btnSave.Click
 2:    Dim Scheduled As DateTime
 3:    Try
 4:       Scheduled = Appointments.CombinedDateTime(
 5:          dtpDate.Value.Date, CDate(txtTime.Text))
 6:    Catch
 7:       errProvider.SetError(txtTime,
 8:          "Please enter a valid appointment time")
 9:       Return
10:    End Try
11:    Dim typeId As Short = CShort(cboRepairType.SelectedValue)
12:    Dim custId As Short = CShort(cboCustomer.SelectedValue)
13:    Dim licensed As Boolean = chkLicensed.Checked
14:    If mAppointments.Insert(typeId, txtDescription.Text,
15:       licensed, custId, Scheduled) Then
16:       Me.Close()
17:    Else
18:       lblStatus.Text = "Cannot Add Appointment. " _
19:          & Appointments.LastError
20:    End If
21: End Sub
```

Lines 4–5 call the utility method from the Appointment class that combines a date and a time, and assigns the result to the Scheduled variable. If the date conversion throws an exception, it will be caught on line 7, where the ErrorProvider control will display an error message.

Lines 11–12 get the repair-type ID and the customer ID from the two combo boxes, and line 13 gets the licensed value from the check box. Line 14 calls the Insert method in the Appointments class, passing all the required values. If the Insert method returns *False*, an error message is displayed by line 18. Finally, line 16 closes the form as soon as the appointment is saved.

Step 5: Add the following Click handler for the *Cancel* button, and save the project.

```
Private Sub btnCancel_Click() Handles btnCancel.Click
  Me.Close()
End Sub
```

Code Listing

Check the following complete code listing of the NewAppointmentForm.vb class, to make sure you haven't left anything out:

```
Public Class NewAppointmentForm
   Private mAppointments As New Appointments
   Private mRepairTypes As New RepairTypes
   Private mCustomers As New Customers
```

```
    Private Sub NewAppointmentForm_Load() Handles MyBase.Load
      cboRepairType.DataSource = mRepairTypes.Items
      cboRepairType.DisplayMember = "Description"
      cboRepairType.ValueMember = "TypeId"

      cboCustomer.DataSource = mCustomers.Items
      cboCustomer.DisplayMember = "Name"
      cboCustomer.ValueMember = "CustId"
    End Sub

    Private Sub btnSave_Click() Handles btnSave.Click
      Dim scheduledAt As DateTime
      Try
        scheduledAt = Appointments.CombinedDateTime(
          dtpDate.Value.Date, CDate(txtTime.Text))
      Catch
        errProvider.SetError(txtTime,
          "Please enter a valid appointment time")
        Return
      End Try
      Dim typeId As Short = CShort(cboRepairType.SelectedValue)
      Dim custId As Short = CShort(cboCustomer.SelectedValue)
      Dim licensed As Boolean = chkLicensed.Checked
      If mAppointments.Insert(typeId, txtDescription.Text,
        licensed, custId, scheduledAt) Then
        Me.Close()
      Else
        lblStatus.Text = "Cannot Add Appointment. " _
          & Appointments.LastError
      End If
    End Sub

    Private Sub btnCancel_Click() Handles btnCancel.Click
      Me.Close()
    End Sub
  End Class
```

Ready to Test

Step 6: Double-click on *My Project* in Solution Explorer and verify that the project's startup form is *MainForm*.

Step 7: Run the application. Select *Appointments / New* from the menu to display the *New Appointment* window. Input and save an appointment. From the main menu, select *Appointments / View* and verify that the appointment you added is now visible in the grid.

Step 8: Add a few more appointments and verify that they were saved.

Step 9: Close the application. Then rebuild the project from the Visual Studio Build menu to erase the appointments you added to the database.

Summary

After writing code for the *New Appointment* form, we hope that you are beginning to see how the classes in a three-tier application communicate with each other. For example, when creating a new appointment, the NewAppointmentForm class calls the Insert method in the Appointments class. To do that, the form must contain an Appointment object. Then the Appointments.Insert method calls the Insert method in the AppointmentsTableAdapter class. To do that, the Appointments class must contain a TableAdapter object. These steps are shown by a concept diagram in Figure 5-23.

In Tutorial 5-10, you will add the ability for users to search for appointments.

Figure 5-23 Communication between classes when adding a new appointment

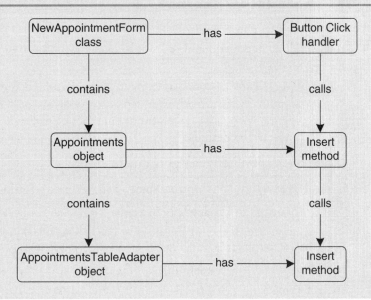

Tutorial 5-10:
Searching for appointments

In this tutorial, you will add searching capabilities to the Home Repair Services application. You will modify both the Appointments form and the Appointments class.

Tutorial Steps

Step 1: Open the *Appointments.vb* class and insert the following method, which returns all the rows of the Appointments table in the database:

```
Public ReadOnly Property Items As DataTable
   Get
      Return adapter.GetData()
   End Get
End Property
```

Step 2: Create the *GetByCustomerId* method, which returns a DataTable containing appointments for a single customer:

```
1 Public Function GetByCustomerId(ByVal custId As Short) As
  DataTable
2    Dim table As DataTable = adapter.GetData()
3    table.DefaultView.RowFilter = "CustId = " & custId
4    Return table
5 End Function
```

Line 2 gets all rows from the Appointments table, and line 3 applies a filter expression that limits the rows to a single customer ID. Line 4 returns the filtered table. This method is a good example of how code in the application's middle tier can enhance the methods that already exist in a TableAdapter. It was not necessary to create a separate query in the TableAdapter class.

AppointmentsForm Class

Step 3: Open the *AppointmentsForm.vb* class in the design window. Delete the data-binding components from the form, and delete all event handlers from the form's code window.

Step 4: Undock the grid and resize it to make room for a ToolStrip control at the top of the form.

Step 5: Add a ToolStrip control to the form and add the controls listed in Table 5-4. Optionally, you can insert separator controls between the ToolStrip items. Figure 5-24 shows the form at runtime, to give you a guide as to the placement of the buttons.

Table 5-4 Controls on the Appointments Form

Control Type	Control Name	Property Settings
DataGridView	dgvAppointments	BackgroundColor = Control
		BorderStyle = None
		Anchor = Top, Bottom, Left, Right
ToolStrip	(default)	
ToolStripButton	btnAll	AutoSize = *False*
		Size.Width = 50
		DisplayStyle = Text
		Text = *All*
ToolStripSeparator	(default)	
ToolStripLabel	(default)	Text = *Customer:*
ToolStripComboBox	cboCustomer	

Figure 5-24 The AppointmentsForm, shown at runtime

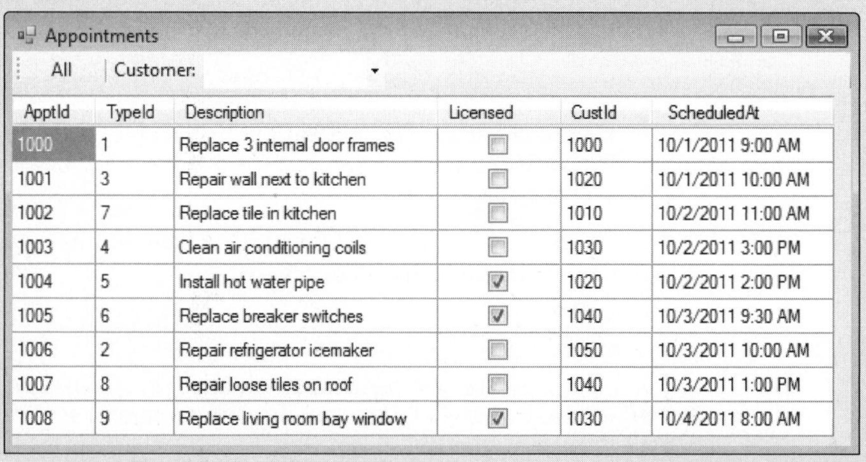

Step 6: Open the form's code window and add the following variable declarations:

```
Private mAppointments As New Appointments
Private mCustomers As New Customers
Private formLoading As Boolean = True
```

The first two variables are instances of middle-tier classes. The third variable will help us avoid responding to combo box events while the form is loading.

Step 7: Create a Click event handler for the *All* button and insert the following line of code, which fills the grid with all rows of the Appointments table:

```
dgvAppointments.DataSource = mAppointments.Items
```

Step 8: Run the application and test the *All* button in this form. It should display all appointments. Stop the application.

Your next task will be to let the user search for appointments by customer name.

Step 9: Create the following Form_Load event handler, whose job it is to fill the combo box with a list of customer names; it gets the list from the Items property of the Customers object:

```
 1: Private Sub AppointmentsForm_Load() Handles MyBase.Load
 2:    With cboCustomer.ComboBox
 3:       .DataSource = mCustomers.Items
 4:       .DisplayMember = "Name"
 5:       .ValueMember = "CustId"
 6:       .DropDownStyle = ComboBoxStyle.DropDownList
 7:       .SelectedIndex = -1
 8:    End With
 9:    formLoading = False
10: End Sub
```

Lines 3–5 initialize fields that help us display the list of customers in the combo box. (You wrote the same code in the NewAppointmentForm class.) Line 6 sets a property in the combo box that prevents the user from directly typing in a name at random. You can usually set this property in design mode, but because this combo box is on a ToolStrip, the Visual Studio Property window does not display the ComboBoxStyle property. Line 7 sets SelectedIndex to −1 so no customer name will be displayed when the form is first displayed. Line 9 sets formLoading to *False*, to indicate that the form has finished the loading process.

Step 10: Create the following SelectedIndexChanged event handler for the ComboBox control:

```
Private Sub cboCustomer_SelectedIndexChanged() _
  Handles cboCustomer.SelectedIndexChanged
  If Not formLoading Then
    Dim custId As Short =
      CShort(cboCustomer.ComboBox.SelectedValue)
    dgvAppointments.DataSource =
      mAppointments.GetByCustomerId(custId)
  End If
End Sub
```

The If statement checks the formLoading variable to see if this event was fired during the form's initial loading process. If the variable equals *True,* we do not perform any searches for appointments.

Step 11: Run the application, select *View* from the Appointments menu, and experiment by selecting different customer names from the combo box. An example is shown in Figure 5-25. Also, click the *All* button to verify that all appointments are displayed.

Figure 5-25 Displaying appointments for one customer

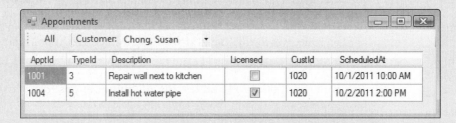

Code Listing

Check following complete code listing of the AppointmentsForm class to see if you've left anything out:

```
Public Class AppointmentsForm
    Private mAppointments As New Appointments
    Private mCustomers As New Customers
    Private formLoading As Boolean = True

    Private Sub btnAll_Click() Handles btnAll.Click
       dgvAppointments.DataSource = mAppointments.Items
    End Sub

    Private Sub AppointmentsForm_Load() Handles MyBase.Load
       With cboCustomer.ComboBox
          .DataSource = mCustomers.Items
          .DisplayMember = "Name"
          .ValueMember = "CustId"
          .DropDownStyle = ComboBoxStyle.DropDownList
          .SelectedIndex = -1
       End With
       formLoading = False
    End Sub

    Private Sub cboCustomer_SelectedIndexChanged() _
       Handles cboCustomer.SelectedIndexChanged
          If Not formLoading Then
            Dim custId As Short =
               CShort(cboCustomer.ComboBox.SelectedValue)
            dgvAppointments.DataSource =
               mAppointments.GetByCustomerId(custId)
          End If
    End Sub
End Class
```

Summary

You are starting to create code that can be reused (with small modifications) through the application. A great feature of the multi-tier design approach is that your application becomes easily expandable, with new types of searches and updates.

Copying a Class Within a Project

In the next tutorial, you will be asked to copy the NewAppointmentForm class and make changes to the copy. Here are the basic steps for copying a class:

1. Close Visual Studio, to detach it from its project files.

2. In the Solution Explorer window, right-click the name of the class you want to copy, and select *Copy* from the popup menu.
3. In the same window, right-click the project name and select *Paste* from the popup menu. After doing that, you will see a new file named Copy of *original filename*.
4. Rename this new file to a different name that matches the name of your new class.
5. Open the copied file in the code editor and change the name of the class.

In Tutorial 5-11, you will make a copy of the *New Appointment* form and modify the copy so it permits the user to modify existing appointments.

Tutorial 5-11:
Modifying existing appointments

In the Home Repair Services application, we want to permit the user to modify an existing appointment. In this tutorial, you will create a form that satisfies that need.

Tutorial Steps

Step 1: In the Dataset Designer window, right-click the AppointmentsTableAdapter and select *Properties*. Then expand the UpdateCommand property and select *CommandText*. The Query Builder window will appear.

Step 2: Replace the existing update query with the following:

```
UPDATE Appointments
SET TypeId = @TypeId, Description = @Description,
  Licensed = @Licensed, CustId = @CustId, [Scheduled] =
  @Scheduled
WHERE (ApptId = @ApptId)
```

This query updates the Appointments table by assigning new values to each of the fields in a single row. The ApptId column is not updated because it is the table's primary key. (Modifying a primary key could cause a referential integrity error in the database.) The *Scheduled* column name conflicts with an SQL language keyword, so the column name must be enclosed in brackets when you use it in a query.

Step 3: Open the *Appointments.vb* file and add the following *Update* method to the Appointments class:

```
Public Function Update(ByVal typeId As Short,
  ByVal description As String, ByVal licensed As Boolean,
  ByVal custId As Short, ByVal Scheduled As DateTime,
  ByVal apptId As Integer) As Boolean

  ' Update a row into the Appointments table. Return
  ' True if successful. If an exception is thrown,
  ' LastError will hold an error message.
  LastError = String.Empty
  Try
    adapter.Update(typeId, description, licensed,
      custId, Scheduled, apptId)
    Return True
  Catch ex As Exception
    LastError = ex.Message
    Return False
  End Try
End Function
```

This method is very similar to the Insert method you created in Tutorial 5-6. You may want to copy and paste your old code and change a few lines. There's one extra parameter (apptId), and in this version, you are calling the adapter's Update method rather than Insert. The comments are different, also.

Step 4: Add the *FindByApptId* method to the class:

```
1:  Public Function FindByApptId(ByVal apptId As Short) _
2:     As RepairServicesDataSet.AppointmentsRow
3:
4:     Dim table As RepairServicesDataSet.AppointmentsDataTable
5:     table = adapter.GetData()
6:     Return table.FindByApptId(apptId)
7:  End Function
```

Line 2 declares the return value as a specific type of DataRow, to enable the caller to access the database column names as object properties (you will see this when we create the form). Line 4 also declares a specific DataTable type. Line 5 calls the GetData method from the AppointmentsTableAdapter, which returns all rows of the Appointments table. Line 6 calls the FindByApptId method that was generated by Visual Studio. This method call returns a single row of the Appointments table, exactly what we will need when we display the appointment in a form.

 TIP: If the Appointments table were large, it could be argued that calling GetData is inefficient when all you really want is a single table row. In that case, the solution would be to add a new SQL query to the TableAdapter that selects only one row. This type of improvement would be easy to do any time in the future.

Build the *Modify Appointment* Form

Now you are ready to create the *Modify Appointment* form. The easiest way to do this is to make a copy of the *New Appointment* form and make a few changes to the copy.

Step 5: Make a copy of the *NewAppointmentForm.vb* class file and name it *ModAppointmentForm.vb*. Open its code window and rename the class to *ModAppointmentForm*. Rebuild the application from the *Project* menu.

Step 6: In the design window, rename the form's Text property to *Modify Appointment*.

Step 7: In the form's code window, add the following property, which will be initialized by another program just before it displays the *Modify Appointment* form:

```
Public Property AppointmentId As Short
```

Step 8: Add the following code to the end of the Form_Load event handler, which initializes the form fields to a single selected appointment:

```
1:  Dim row As RepairServicesDataSet.AppointmentsRow
2:  row = mAppointments.FindByApptId(AppointmentId)
3:  dtpDate.Value = row.Scheduled.Date
4:  txtTime.Text = row.Scheduled.TimeOfDay.ToString
5:  chkLicensed.Checked = row.Licensed
```

```
6:   txtDescription.Text = row.Description
7:   cboRepairType.SelectedValue = row.TypeId
8:   cboCustomer.SelectedValue = row.CustId
```

Line 2 gets a single row from the Appointment table by calling the Find-ByApptId from the middle-tier class. This row is a very specific type of DataRow object (see line 1). Your code must copy the row fields into the current form's controls. Fortunately, the row contains property names that tell us how to get the data. Line 3 gets the date portion of the Scheduled column, and line 4 gets the time portion of the same column. (The Scheduled column contains both a date and a time.)

Line 5 copies the Licensed field value (Boolean) to the chkLicensed check box. Line 6 copies the appointment description. Lines 7 and 8 copy the TypeId and CustId values directly into the SelectedValue properties of the two combo boxes. This will make the boxes display the currently selected type of repair and customer name, using values from the database row. For example, if the current row contains a CustId value of 1020, the customer combo box will select the name of the customer having that ID number.

Step 9: Modify the shaded lines below in the Click handler for the *Save* button:

```
 1: Private Sub btnSave_Click() Handles btnSave.Click
 2:   Dim Scheduled As DateTime
 3:   Try
 4:     Scheduled = Appointments.CombinedDateTime( _
 5:       dtpDate.Value.Date, CDate(txtTime.Text))
 6:   Catch
 7:     errProvider.SetError(txtTime, _
 8:       "Please enter a valid appointment time")
 9:     Return
10:   End Try
11:   Dim typeId As Short = CShort(cboRepairType.SelectedValue)
12:   Dim custId As Short = CShort(cboCustomer.SelectedValue)
13:   Dim licensed As Boolean = chkLicensed.Checked
14:   If mAppointments.Update(typeId, txtDescription.Text,
15:     licensed, custId, Scheduled, AppointmentId) Then
16:     Me.Close()
17:   Else
18:     lblStatus.Text = "Cannot update the Appointment." _
19:       & Appointments.LastError
20:   End If
21: End Sub
```

On line 15, the Update method in the Appointment class has one more parameter (AppointmentId) than the Insert method did. Line 16 closes the window right after the appointment is updated. Basically, as soon as the user clicks the *Save* button, the window closes.

Code Listing

Check the following complete code listing of the ModAppointmentForm.vb class to make sure you haven't left anything out:

```
Public Class ModAppointmentForm
  Private mAppointments As New Appointments
  Private mRepairTypes As New RepairTypes
```

```
      Private mCustomers As New Customers
      Public Property AppointmentId As Short

      Private Sub Form_Load() Handles MyBase.Load
         ' Fill the Repair Types combo box.
         cboRepairType.DataSource = mRepairTypes.Items
         cboRepairType.DisplayMember = "Description"
         cboRepairType.ValueMember = "TypeId"
         ' Fill the Customers combo box.
         cboCustomer.DataSource = mCustomers.Items
         cboCustomer.DisplayMember = "Name"
         cboCustomer.ValueMember = "CustId"

         ' Get the selected appointment and display in the form's
         ' controls.
         Dim row As RepairServicesDataSet.AppointmentsRow
         row = mAppointments.FindByApptId(AppointmentId)
         dtpDate.Value = row.Scheduled.Date
         txtTime.Text = row.Scheduled.TimeOfDay.ToString
         chkLicensed.Checked = row.Licensed
         txtDescription.Text = row.Description
         cboRepairType.SelectedValue = row.TypeId
         cboCustomer.SelectedValue = row.CustId
      End Sub

   ' The user wants to save the appointment.
   Private Sub btnSave_Click() Handles btnSave.Click
      Dim scheduledAt As DateTime
      Try
         scheduledAt = Appointments.CombinedDateTime( _
            dtpDate.Value.Date, CDate(txtTime.Text))
      Catch
         errProvider.SetError(txtTime, _
            "Please enter a valid appointment time")
         Return
      End Try
      Dim typeId As Short = CShort(cboRepairType.SelectedValue)
      Dim custId As Short = CShort(cboCustomer.SelectedValue)
      Dim licensed As Boolean = chkLicensed.Checked
      If mAppointments.Update(typeId, txtDescription.Text, _
         licensed, custId, scheduledAt, AppointmentId) Then
         Me.Close()
      Else
         lblStatus.Text = "Cannot update the Appointment." _
            & Appointments.LastError
      End If
   End Sub

   Private Sub btnCancel_Click() Handles btnCancel.Click
      Me.Close()
   End Sub
 End Class
```

Testing the User Interface

At this point, it is important for you to test the *Modify Appointment* form. Later, we will show you how to display this form from the applications main menu.

Step 1: Insert the following line of code at the beginning of Form_Load (it will be removed later):

```
AppointmentId = 1004
```

This line initializes the AppointmentId property to an ID that we know is in the database. The form will display the data for this appointment.

Step 2: Double-click on *My Project* in Solution Explorer and change the project's startup form to *ModAppointmentForm*.

Step 3: Run the application. You should see the *Modify Appointment* window, as shown in Figure 5-26. Change all of the column values and click the *Save* button. The window will close.

Figure 5-26 The Modify Appointment form at runtime

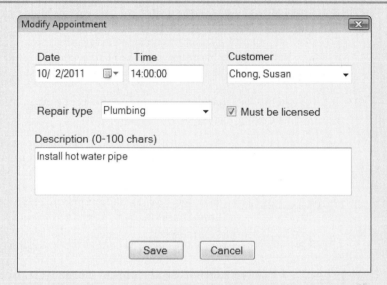

Step 4: Run the application again and verify that all the changes you made were saved.

Step 5: Remove the line of test code that you inserted in Step 1, and save the project.

This tutorial was an important step in learning how to display and edit a single database row. Although this type of editing could have been accomplished by using data-bound controls, that approach would violate the basic premise of multi-tier applications: The presentation layer (Windows forms) should not communicate directly with the database. In fact, the application you're writing now will show up as a Web application in a later chapter. A multi-tier design makes it easy to move an application from the desktop to the Web.

In Tutorial 5-12, you will launch the *Modify Appointment* window from another page.

Tutorial 5-12:
Selecting appointments to modify

In this tutorial, you will add a button to the Appointments form that lets the user launch the *Modify Appointment* window. You will add a second button that closes the Appointments window.

Tutorial Steps

Step 1: Open *AppointmentsForm.vb* in design mode.

Step 2: Set the RowHeadersVisible property of the DataGridView to *True*. (This will display a button to the left of each row in the grid, which can be used to select the row.)

Step 3: Add a ToolStripSeparator to the ToolStrip control. Then add a ToolStripButton control and set the following property values: Name = *btnEdit*, DisplayStyle = *Text*, Text = *Edit*.

Step 4: Add a ToolStripSeparator to the ToolStrip control. Then add a ToolStripButton control and set the following property values: Name = *btnClose*, DisplayStyle = *Text*, Text = *Close*.

Step 5: Create a Click handler for the *Close* button and insert a Me.Close() statement.

Step 6: Create a Click handler method for the *Edit* button and insert code to create the following method:

```
 1: Private Sub btnEdit_Click() Handles btnEdit.Click
 2:   If dgvAppointments.SelectedRows.Count > 0 Then
 3:     Dim apptId As Short = CShort(dgvAppointments.
 4:        SelectedRows(0).Cells(0).Value)
 5:     Dim frm As New ModAppointmentForm
 6:     frm.AppointmentId = apptId
 7:     frm.ShowDialog()
 8:     dgvAppointments.DataSource = mAppointments.Items
 9:   Else
10:     MessageBox.Show("Please select the appointment to edit")
11:   End If
12: End Sub
```

This code displays the *Modify Appointment* form. Line 1 verifies that a row was selected by the user. Line 4 gets the appointment ID value from the first cell in the selected row belonging to the grid's SelectedRows collection. (It is possible to select more than one row in a grid, although doing so would not be useful here.) Line 5 creates an instance of the *Modify Appointment* form, and line 6 assigns the appointment ID to the form's AppointmentId property. Line 7 displays the *Modify Appointment* form, and line 8 refreshes the grid with the complete list of appointments (to reflect the changes that were made).

Step 7: Double-click on *My Project* in Solution Explorer and change the project's startup form to *MainForm*.

Step 8: Run the application, select the *Appointments / View* menu item, click the All button, and select one of the grid rows. An example is shown in Figure 5-27.

Step 9: Click the *Edit* button, and the *Modify Appointment* window should appear. Make some changes to the appointment, and click the *Save* button. You should see the changes you made in the appropriate row of the grid.

Figure 5-27 Selecting an appointment from the grid in the Appointments form

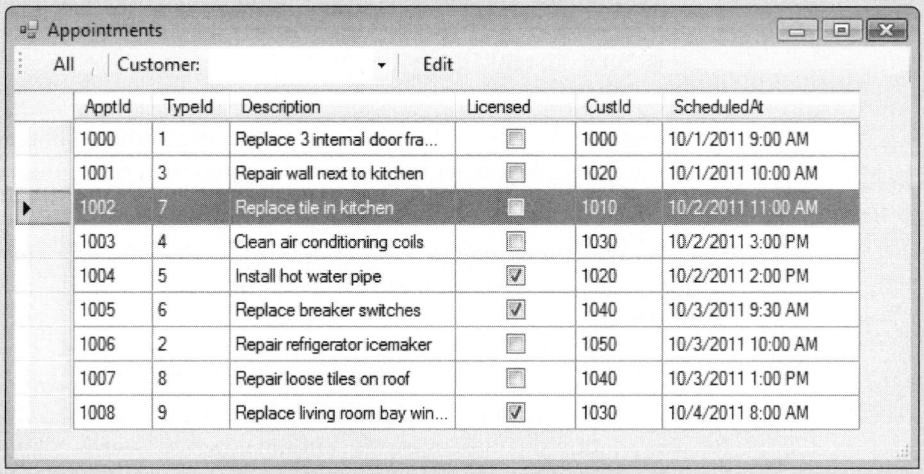

ApptId	TypeId	Description	Licensed	CustId	ScheduledAt
1000	1	Replace 3 internal door fra...	☐	1000	10/1/2011 9:00 AM
1001	3	Repair wall next to kitchen	☐	1020	10/1/2011 10:00 AM
1002	7	Replace tile in kitchen	☐	1010	10/2/2011 11:00 AM
1003	4	Clean air conditioning coils	☐	1030	10/2/2011 3:00 PM
1004	5	Install hot water pipe	☑	1020	10/2/2011 2:00 PM
1005	6	Replace breaker switches	☑	1040	10/3/2011 9:30 AM
1006	2	Repair refrigerator icemaker	☐	1050	10/3/2011 10:00 AM
1007	8	Repair loose tiles on roof	☐	1040	10/3/2011 1:00 PM
1008	9	Replace living room bay win...	☑	1030	10/4/2011 8:00 AM

Appointments — All | Customer: ▼ | Edit

Summary

The *Appointments* form offers some interesting possibilities. You could add a *Delete* button to the ToolStrip that would let the user delete a single appointment. Or, you could let the user search for appointments by their repair types. To do that, you might add another combo box to the tool strip that displays the RepairTypes table. Then you would write code that is similar to the code for the Customers combo box.

In Tutorial 5-13, you will add a *Delete* button to the Appointments form.

Tutorial 5-13:
Deleting an appointment

In this tutorial, you will make it possible for the user delete a selected appointment in the Home Repair Services application.

Tutorial Steps

Step 1: Open the *RepairServices.xsd* DataSet in the designer window.

Step 2: Select *AppointmentsTableAdapter* and open its Properties window.

Step 3: Expand the DeleteCommand property and open its CommandText subproperty. The default SQL query is very long because the code tries to match all of the columns. Replace it with a much simpler version that only matches the ApptId column with a single query parameter.

```
DELETE FROM Appointments
WHERE ApptId = @ApptId
```

Save your changes.

Step 4: Open the *Appointments.vb* file and add the following Delete method:

```
Public Function Delete(ByVal apptId As Integer) As Boolean
  Dim rowsAffected As Integer = adapter.Delete(apptId)
  Return rowsAffected > 0
End Function
```

The adapter.Delete method call returns a count of the number of rows affected by the query. We expect the count to be equal to 1, so the method returns *True* if at least 1 row was affected.

Step 5: Open the *AppointmentsForm.vb* file in the designer window, add separator, and then a *Delete* button to the ToolStrip at the top of the form, and name it *btnDelete*.

Step 6: Add the following Click handler for the *Delete* button:

```
 1: Private Sub btnDelete_Click() Handles btnDelete.Click
 2:    If dgvAppointments.SelectedRows.Count > 0 Then
 3:       Dim apptId As Short = CShort(dgvAppointments.
 4:          SelectedRows(0).Cells(0).Value)
 5:       If mAppointments.Delete(apptId) Then
 6:          dgvAppointments.DataSource = mAppointments.Items
 7:       Else
 8:          MessageBox.Show("Unable to delete this appointment")
 9:       End If
10:    End If
11: End Sub
```

Lines 2–4 were borrowed from the Click handler that you wrote earlier for the *Edit* button. They verify that a grid row was selected, and then they get the appointment ID from the first cell in the selected row. Line 5 calls the Delete method from the Appointments class and checks the Boolean return value. If an appointment was deleted, line 6 refreshes the grid by displaying all appointments. If the selected appointment was not deleted (because of an unknown error), line 8 displays an error message.

Step 7: Run the application, open the *Appointments* form, click the *All* button, select an appointment, and click the *Delete* button. The appointment should disappear.

Summary

Let's review the steps that were required to add the *Delete* operation to the Appointments window. First, you simplified the query in the TableAdapter's DeleteCommand property. Second, you added a Delete method to the Appointments class. Third, you added a *Delete* button with a Click handler to the Appointments form. Deleting an appointment was fairly easy because it is not the parent table in any table relationships. All you had to do was pass the ID of the appointment to be deleted to the Delete method.

Creating Queries That Join Tables

The columns in a table often hold numeric codes that are difficult for the end user to decipher. This is certainly the case with the Appointments table, which contains a customer ID and a repair type ID. No doubt, you have viewed this table more than once, trying to remember the meaning of these codes. Therefore, it's good to join tables together so the numeric codes can be replaced by user-friendly text values. Figure 5-28, for example, shows a join of the Appointments, Customers, and RepairTypes tables that leaves no doubt in our minds as to which customer has scheduled which type of repair. Some of the table columns, such as ApptId, CustId, TypeId, and Licensed are not shown, but that information is available elsewhere.

Figure 5-28 Tables joined together

Appointment List

Name	Description	RepairType	Scheduled
Chong, Susan	Repair wall next to kitchen	Masonry	10/1/2011 10:00 AM
Chong, Susan	Install hot water pipe	Plumbing	10/2/2011 2:00 PM
Johnson, David	Replace 3 internal door frames	Carpentry	10/1/2011 9:00 AM
Kahane, Sam	Clean air conditioning coils	Heat/Air	10/2/2011 3:00 PM
Kahane, Sam	Replace living room bay window	Window/Door	10/4/2011 8:00 AM
Martinez, Maria	Replace breaker switches	Electrical	10/3/2011 9:30 AM
Martinez, Maria	Repair loose tiles on roof	Roof	10/3/2011 1:00 PM
Ramirez, Jose	Repair refrigerator icemaker	Appliance	10/3/2011 10:00 AM
Smith, Linda	Replace tile in kitchen	Flooring	10/2/2011 11:00 AM

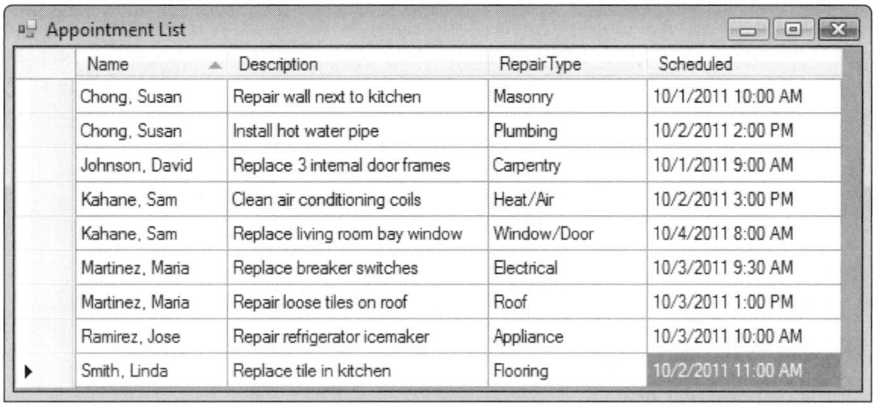

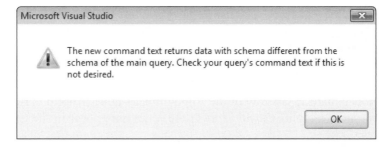

When you add a SELECT query to an existing TableAdapter, the query's columns should match the columns in the DataTable associated with the TableAdapter. For example, if we were to add a query to the AppointmentsTableAdapter that omits some columns, the message shown in Figure 5-29 would appear. Therefore, we would create a new TableAdapter with columns that match our query.

Figure 5-29 TableAdapter warning message

INNER JOIN Statement

The **INNER JOIN** operator in SQL joins two tables, using fields from each table that are expected to contain matching values. The joining process takes place in the part of the query that selects which tables will be used. For example, when you use only one table, it looks like this:

SELECT *field-1,…, field-n* FROM *tablename*

But if you have two tables, you have to identify which column in each table will link the tables together. For that, you use the INNER JOIN operator. Here is the general format:

FROM *table1* INNER JOIN *table2* ON *table1.key* = *table2.key*

The ordering of the names *table1* and *table2* is not important. The items labeled *key* can be the primary key or foreign key of the table. The idea is that the two columns contain essentially the same data. For example, the following query links the Appointments and Customers tables, using their common CustId column:

```
FROM Appointments INNER JOIN Customers
   ON Appointments.CustId = Customers.CustId
```

You may recall that we designed the RepairServices database so that the CustId column in each appointment matched one of the CustId values in the Customers table. That is how we could identify which customer had scheduled the appointment.

INNER JOIN returns only those rows in which the two tables have matching values. To illustrate this idea, let's use simplified versions of the Appointments and Customers tables, as follows:

Appointments Table

ApptId	Description	CustId
1000	Replace frames	1000
1001	Repair wall	1020
1002	Replace tile	1010
1004	Install pipe	1020
1005	Replace breaker	1040

Customers Table

CustId	Name
1000	Johnson, David
1010	Smith, Linda
1020	Chong, Susan

Let us consider the following query:

```
SELECT Description, Name, Customers.CustId
   FROM Appointments INNER JOIN Customers
   ON Appointments.CustId = Customers.CustId
```

When the query executes, it returns only rows that contain matching values in the CustId column:

Replace frames	Johnson, David	1000
Repair wall	Chong, Susan	1020
Replace tile	Smith, Linda	1010
Install pipe	Chong, Susan	1020

Notice that the last row of the Appointments table (ApptId = 1005) does not appear in the output because its CustId value (1040) does not appear in the Customers table.

Nested Join

A **nested join** is an SQL query that joins three or more tables. The FROM clause in the following query does this:

```
FROM Appointments INNER JOIN Customers
   ON Appointments.CustId = Customers.CustId
INNER JOIN RepairTypes
   ON Appointments.TypeId = RepairTypes.TypeId
```

First, the Appointments table is joined to the Customers table. Then the resulting table is joined to the RepairTypes table, using TypeId as the linking column.

Although the syntax for inner joins appears complicated, it should not trouble you. Visual Studio makes it very easy to join tables inside the Query Designer window. In Tutorial 5-14, you will add a new form to the project that displays a list of appointments, using data that was joined from three tables.

Tutorial 5-14:
Displaying a joined appointment list

In this tutorial, you will add a new form that displays the appointment list in an easier-to-read format. To do that, you will create a new TableAdapter that joins the Customers, RepairTypes, and Appointments tables.

Tutorial Steps

Step 1: Open the designer window for *RepairServicesDataSet.xsd*.

Step 2: Right-click in an open area of the window and select *Add*; then select *TableAdapter*. The *TableAdapter Configuration Wizard* window should appear.

Step 3: Click the *Next* button until you reach the *Enter a SQL Statement* panel. Click the *Query Builder* button.

Step 4: The *Add Table* window should appear. If it does not, right-click in the upper pane and select *Add Table*. Add all three tables to the query. Then place a check mark in each of the following columns, in order: Customers.Name, Appointments.Description, RepairTypes.Description, Appointments.Scheduled. The tables are shown in Figure 5-30.

Figure 5-30 Joining the Appointments, RepairTypes, and Customers tables

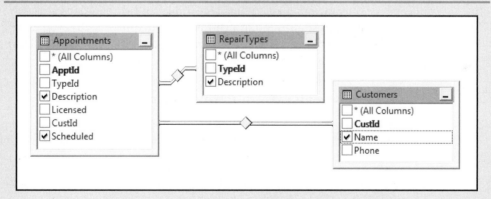

Step 5: Because there are two columns named Description in the query, you will need to find the place in the query that says *AS Expr1* and change it to *AS Repair-Type*. After doing so, the query should be the following:

```
SELECT Customers.Name, Appointments.Description,
    RepairTypes.Description AS RepairType, Appointments.
    Scheduled

FROM Appointments INNER JOIN Customers
    ON Appointments.CustId = Customers.CustId
INNER JOIN RepairTypes
    ON Appointments.TypeId = RepairTypes.TypeId
```

The formatting of the lines will be different in Query Builder, but that is not important. This query joins together the Customers, Appointments, and RepairTypes tables, using columns that are common to each pair of tables.

Step 6: Click the *OK* button to close the Query Builder window. In the Wizard window, click the *Advanced Options* button and unselect the *Generate Insert, Update and Delete statements* option. Click *OK* to save.

Step 7: Click the *Finish* button to save the query. You have just created a new TableAdapter.

Step 8: In the DataSet designer window, select the table named *DataTable1*, right-click, select *Rename*, and rename it to *AppointmentList*. Also, rename the TableAdapter to *AppointmentListTableAdapter*.

Add the AppointmentList Property to the Appointments Class

Step 9: Open the Appointments class and add the following *AppointmentList* property:

```
Public ReadOnly Property AppointmentList As DataTable
  Get
    Dim listAdapter As New RepairServicesDataSetTableAdapters.
      AppointmentListTableAdapter
    Return listAdapter.GetData()
  End Get
End Property
```

In this property procedure, you have declared an instance of your new type of TableAdapter. When your code calls GetData, it returns a DataTable containing all appointments.

Let's review what you have accomplished so far. You created a new TableAdapter, using an SQL query that joins all three tables in the database. Then you renamed the DataTable and TableAdapter classes to AppointmentList and AppointmentListTableAdapter. Finally, you added a new property to the middle-tier Appointments class that calls the GetData method from your new TableAdapter.

Add AppointmentListForm to the Project

In the next series of steps, you will add an *Appointment List* form to the project, insert a DataGridView in the form, write a Form_Load handler in the form, and then add a new entry to the Main form's menu that displays your new form.

Step 10: Add a new form to the project named *AppointmentListForm.vb*. Set its Text property to *Appointment List*.

Step 11: Add a DataGridView to the form and name it *dgvAppointments*. Set its Dock property to *Fill*. Right-click its smart tag and uncheck the Adding, Editing, and Deleting options.

Step 12: In the form's code window, add the following Load event handler:

```
Private Sub Form_Load() Handles MyBase.Load
  Dim mAppointments As New Appointments
  dgvAppointments.DataSource = mAppointments.AppointmentList
End Sub
```

Step 13: Open the MainForm class file and add a new entry to the Appointments menu: *Appointment List*.

Step 14: Create a click handler for the new menu item, and insert the following code:

```
AppointmentListForm.ShowDialog()
```

Step 15: Run the application, and select *Appointment List* from the Appointments menu. Your new form should appear as shown in Figure 5-31.

Figure 5-31 Displaying the Appointment List form

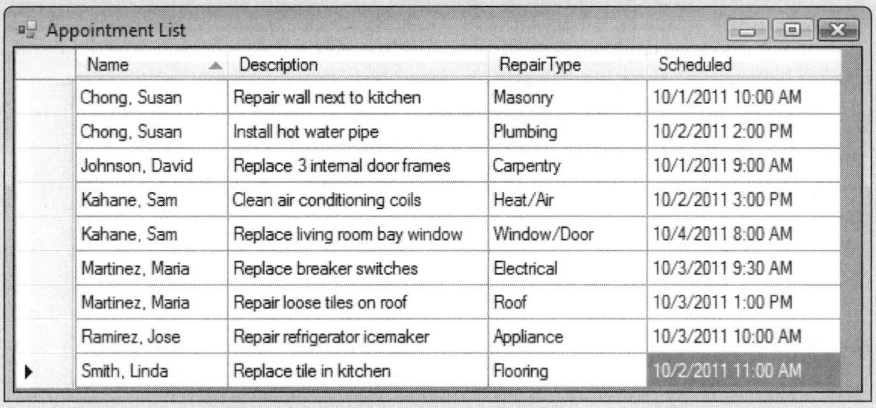

Name	Description	RepairType	Scheduled
Chong, Susan	Repair wall next to kitchen	Masonry	10/1/2011 10:00 AM
Chong, Susan	Install hot water pipe	Plumbing	10/2/2011 2:00 PM
Johnson, David	Replace 3 internal door frames	Carpentry	10/1/2011 9:00 AM
Kahane, Sam	Clean air conditioning coils	Heat/Air	10/2/2011 3:00 PM
Kahane, Sam	Replace living room bay window	Window/Door	10/4/2011 8:00 AM
Martinez, Maria	Replace breaker switches	Electrical	10/3/2011 9:30 AM
Martinez, Maria	Repair loose tiles on roof	Roof	10/3/2011 1:00 PM
Ramirez, Jose	Repair refrigerator icemaker	Appliance	10/3/2011 10:00 AM
Smith, Linda	Replace tile in kitchen	Flooring	10/2/2011 11:00 AM

By joining tables, you can combine their most useful columns to create an informative view of the database. Although the SQL JOIN query syntax takes some practice to master, you can rely on the Query Builder tool in Visual Studio to make joining an easy task.

Summary

5.1 Creating Databases

- The Server Explorer window in Visual Studio lets you view and manage connections to local and remote databases.
- When examining a database connection in Server Explorer, the *Database Diagrams* folder contains graphical diagrams that show relationships between tables. The *Tables* folder contains all tables in the database. The *Views* folder contains a list of views, which are alternate ways of viewing the contents of tables; views often combine columns from different tables into what look like new tables. The *Stored Procedures* folder contains compiled SQL queries.
- A one-to-many relationship exists between two database tables when the primary key of one table links to a column called a *foreign key* in another table. The table on the *one* side is called the *parent table*. The table on the *many* side is called the *child table*.
- A *many-to-many relationship* occurs between two database tables when the linking column is a foreign key in both tables. A third linking table must be created that has a one-to-many relationship with the first two tables.
- *Database constraints* are rules in a database that help preserve data integrity, preventing errors caused by the insertion of invalid data.
- A *referential integrity constraint*, or *foreign key constraint*, applies to the relationship between two tables. In a one-to-many relationship, the parent table is required to contain a primary key value that matches each foreign key value found in the child table.

5.2 DataTables

- The Server Explorer window in Visual Studio lets you view and manage connections to local and remote databases.
- A DataTable is an object that represents the contents of a table from a data source. The .NET DataTable class is used as the basis for creating more specialized DataTable types. When you add a data source to a project, Visual Studio creates a specialized DataTable class, such as CustomerDataTable, or MembersDataTable.
- The Columns property holds a collection of DataColumn objects; each describes the name, type, and other characteristics of a column.
- The DefaultView property holds a DataView object that lets you filter (select) the table rows or sort the rows on any column.
- The PrimaryKey property holds an array of DataColumn objects that serve as the table's primary key; each table row is guaranteed to hold a unique value in the column or columns.
- The Rows property holds a collection of DataRow objects, each holding the data in one row of the table.
- A DataRow object describes a row in a DataTable. You can add columns to a DataRow, fill the row with values, add the row to a table, and remove a row from a table.

5.3 Updating Databases Using SQL

- The INSERT INTO statement adds a new row to a database table.
- The UPDATE statement modifies one or more existing database table rows.
- The DELETE FROM statement deletes one or more rows from a database table.
- Be careful when deleting rows from a table that participates in a one-to-many table relationship. If you delete a row from the parent table, you may cause a violation of a referential integrity constraint.

5.4 Home Repair Services Application

- Tutorials 5-4 through 5-14 build the Home Repair Services application, whose purpose is to enable company personnel to schedule repair services for residential customers.
- *Home Repair Services* is a three-tier application, with a presentation tier made of windows forms, a middle tier containing three classes (Appointments, RepairTypes, and Customers), and a data access tier made up of the RepairServicesDataSet classes.
- *Runtime data binding* describes the assigning of a DataTable to the DataSource property of a control at runtime. To perform runtime data binding, you need to declare a variable in the form's code that is an instance of a middle-tier class. Then you call a method from the class that returns a DataTable.
- Many times, database table columns hold numeric codes that are difficult for the end user to understand. It's a good idea to join tables together, so numeric codes can be replaced by more descriptive text values.
- The INNER JOIN operator in SQL joins two tables, using fields from each table that are expected to contain matching values. INNER JOIN only returns rows in which the two tables have matching values.
- A nested join operation uses the result of joining two tables together to form another join expression. Using that principle, almost any number of tables can be joined in a query.

Key Terms

child table	DELETE FROM
column check constraint	foreign key
database constraint	foreign key constraint
database diagram	INNER JOIN
DataRow object	INSERT INTO
DataTable	many-to-many relationship

nested join
one-to-many relationship
parent table
primary key constraint

referential integrity constraint
runtime data binding
Server Explorer
UPDATE

Review Questions

True or False

Indicate whether each of the following statements is true or false.

1. Dragging a table from Server Explorer onto a DataSet design surface has no effect on the DataSet.

2. The ApptId column in the Appointments table uses an identity seed.

3. The Licensed column in the Appointments table holds Boolean values.

4. A database constraint limits the number of rows that can be added to a table.

5. It is possible to create table relationships in a database without enforcing referential integrity constraints.

6. A table's primary key must contain only a single column.

7. A DefaultView is an object that lets you filter and sort the rows of a DataTable.

8. The rows of a DataTable are usually a specialized type of DataRow.

9. The Insert method in a TableAdapter returns a Boolean value indicating whether the row insertion was successful.

10. The Delete method in a TableAdapter returns an Integer value indicating the number of deleted rows.

11. In the Repair Services application, the presentation-tier classes often called TableAdapter methods.

12. A SelectedIndexChanged event is fired when the DataSource property of a ComboBox is assigned at runtime.

13. The default TableAdapter query for deleting a single row from a table has a single query parameter for the primary key column.

14. When you write a query that joins two tables in a DataSet, you must create a separate TableAdapter with columns that match the query columns.

Short Answer

1. When you create a database in the Server Explorer window, where is the database data file stored?

2. How do you create a database in Server Explorer?

3. What type of relationship exists between the Appointments and Customers tables in the Home Repair Services application?

4. How is the *Data Sources* window different from the *Server Explorer* window?

5. Name at least four folders that are grouped under a database name in Server Explorer.

6. Which column joins the Customers and Appointments tables?

7. Which column joins the RepairTypes and Appointments tables?

8. In what type of relationship does a parent table participate?

9. Which table in a relationship contains a foreign key: parent or child?

10. In what type of relationship is a foreign key used as a linking field in both tables?

11. Name three types of database constraints mentioned in this chapter.

12. What types of objects appear in a database diagram?

13. If an application contains RepairServicesDataSet, what will probably be the fully qualified name of the TableAdapter class that holds the Customers table?

14. In the Repair Services application, what are the names of the middle-tier classes?

15. What is the definition of runtime data binding in this chapter?

16. Which ListBox properties are set when performing runtime data binding?

17. Which event fires when you assign a table to the DataSource property of a ComboBox or ListBox?

18. The DataTable class contains a method that lets you search by the primary key field. Suppose the primary key were named ID. What would be the name of the corresponding search method?

Programming Challenges

1. **Search for Appointments by Repair Type**

   Modify the Home Repair Services application as follows. In the Appointments form, add a combo box to the toolbar containing a list of repair types. When the user selects a repair type, restrict the list of appointments to those that match the selected repair type.

2. **Search for Appointments by Date**

   Modify the Home Repair Services application as follows. In the Appointments form, find a way for the user to search for appointments by date. For example, you could ask the user to enter a starting date and the number of days forward from the given date. Once he or she has made the selection, you can limit the list of appointments displayed in the grid to the chosen date range. If the ToolStrip seems too small to input all of the search information, you can use a button on the ToolStrip to display a small dialog window that gets the date information from the user.

3. **Add New Customer**

   Modify the Home Repair Services application as follows. Create a form that lets the user input a new customer. The CustId column in the database is not autogenerated, so you might want to use a query to get the list of IDs, find the highest one, and create a new ID that is larger. Do not permit any of the customer fields to be blank. Do not permit the new customer's phone number to be the same as an existing customer's phone number.

4. **Modify Customer**

   Modify the Home Repair Services application as follows. Create a form that lets the user modify an existing customer's name and phone number. Do not permit the customer ID field to be modified. When the user clicks a button to save their changes, the form must call an Update method in the Customers class, which in turn calls the TableAdapter's Update method.

5. **Training Workshops**

   Use the Programming Challenge 3 from Chapter 1 as a starting point for this challenge. This version will be a 3-tier application.

   1. Add an ID property to the Workshop class.

2. Create a database to replace the data file that was used for input in Chapter 1. In it, create a database table named *Workshops* that contains the workshop ID, category ID, number of days, cost of the workshop, and workshop title. Also in the database, create a Categories table that contains category ID and category description columns.

3. Create a DataSet containing table adapters based on the two database tables. In addition, create a TableAdapter that joins the two tables and contains the workshop ID, workshop category name, number of days, cost, and workshop description.

4. The Workshop class represents the middle tier. In this class, declare an instance of the TableAdapter class so you can call the TableAdapter methods. Provide properties and methods in the Workshop class that are called by your MainForm and DetailsForm classes.

5. Display the list of workshops in a DataGridView control, as shown in Figure 5-32. When the user selects a workshop in the grid, display the Worshop Details form, as shown in Figure 5-33. The combo box is filled from the Categories TableAdapter. The user must be able to modify a workshop in this window and save his or her changes. When the details form closes, the grid must be refreshed, so the user can see the changes he or she made.

Figure 5-32 Displaying the Training Workshops list

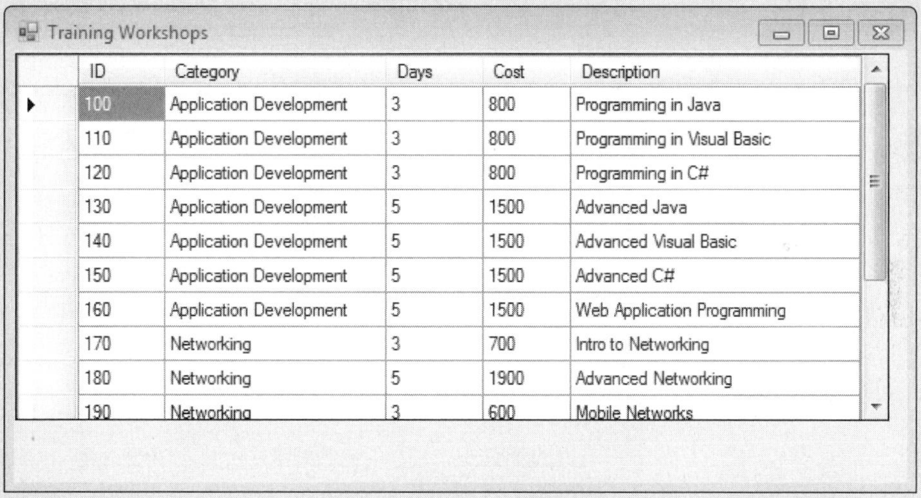

Figure 5-33 Displaying the Workshop Details form

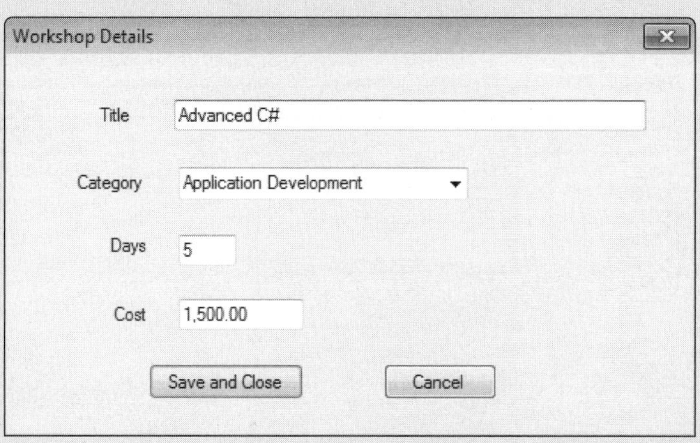

6. **Investment Tracking**

Use Programming Challenge 4 from Chapter 1 as a starting point for this programming challenge. In this version, create a database containing the following tables:

- Prices (ticker symbol, price)—holds the current price of each investment, identified by a unique ticker symbol.
- Investments (ID, ticker symbol, InvestmentType, price per share, purchase date, number of shares).

Choose column types that seem appropriate to you. The InvestmentType column should contain an integer that matches one of the enumerated InvestmentType values already defined in your program.

Create a DataSet that contains TableAdapters for the Prices and Investments tables. The existing classes named Investment and PriceType will exist as middle-tier classes.

When the user clicks the *Confirm* button, shown in Figure 5-34, collect the data from the form and call the Insert method in the Investment class, which will, in return, call the Insert method in the InvestmentTableAdapter class. In that way, the form's information will be inserted into the database. Then when the user clicks the *Show list* button, another form, shown in Figure 5-35, displays the current list of investments in a DataGridView control.

Figure 5-34 After clicking the confirm button

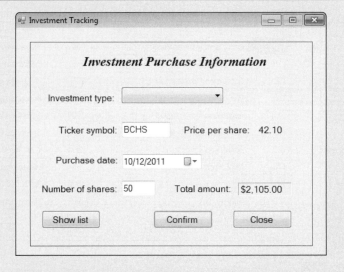

Figure 5-35 Showing the list of investments

ID	Ticker	Investment Type	PricePerShare	PurchaseDate	NumShares
100	BCHS	2	42	10/12/2011	50
102	XYZ	1	55	11/5/2011	20
103	DNGA	0	77	11/6/2011	35
104	FBNS	3	81.4	10/12/2011	22

CHAPTER 6 — Advanced Classes

TOPICS

In this chapter, we show how to define structures, which are simple containers for variables, properties, and methods. Then we explain how to create components, which are classes that are grouped for some common purpose into a library. Components have a valuable purpose in distributed computing because they can be located on different computers in a network. Then we introduce unit testing, the industry standard for automated testing of individual units of code. This is followed by a brief introduction to defining and using custom event types in classes. The chapter ends with inheritance, an essential topic in object-oriented programming.

6.1 Structures

A **Structure** defines a container into which you can include variables, properties, methods, and events. A structure might be thought of as a lightweight type of class. When you declare a structure variable, the .NET runtime doesn't have to allocate a separate area of memory and return a reference, as it does with classes. Instead, the structure occupies memory "in place," much like an Integer or Boolean.

Following are some differences between structures and classes:

- You can declare a structure variable without using the *New* operator.
- When you pass a structure to a method using the *ByVal* qualifier and the method modifies the structure's contents, the changes are not retained when the method returns.
- The assignment operator (=) copies the contents of a structure variable.
- If you compare two structure variables with the Equals method, they are compared using the values of their fields.

A well-known structure in .NET is *Point*, defined in the System.Drawing namespace. It appears in simplified form here:

```
Structure Point
   Public Property X As Integer
   Public Property Y As Integer
End Structure
```

Constructors

Structure types can contain constructors and other methods. Following is a constructor for the Point structure that initializes the X and Y properties:

```
Public Sub New(ByVal xVal As Integer, ByVal yVal As Integer)
   X = xVal
   Y = yVal
End Sub
```

If you want to call this constructor, you must use the *New* operator, as follows:

```
Dim p As New Point(10,20)
```

Structures as Method Parameters

Structure parameters declared *ByVal* behave just like integer parameters—in both cases, a copy of the structure or integer is passed to the called method. The method can modify the copy, but doing so will not affect the original. Let's consider the following code example:

```
Sub DoesNotModify(ByVal pPoint As Point)
   pPoint.X = 998
   pPoint.Y = 999
End Sub

Sub Example1()
   Dim P As New Point(10, 20)
   DoesNotModify(P)
   lblResult.Text = P.ToString
End Sub
```

In the code above, the method named *Example1* passes a Point object to the *DoesNotModify* method. The *pPoint* parameter is declared with the *ByVal* keyword, and the method modifies the X and Y properties of pPoint. When *DoesNotModify* returns, *Example1* displays P in a Label control. The output displays as *10, 20* because P was passed by value.

For a contrasting example in the following code, the *Example2* method calls the *ModifiesPoint* method, which declares *pPoint* using the *ByRef* keyword.

```
Sub ModifiesPoint(ByRef pPoint As Point)
   pPoint.X = 998
   pPoint.Y = 999
End Sub

Sub Example2()
```

```
    Dim P As New Point(10, 20)
    ModifiesPoint(P)
    lblResult.Text = P.ToString
End Sub
```

At the end of Example 2, P displays as *998,999* because it was passed by reference.

The same ByRef/ByVal behavior is true for Integers, Doubles, Boolean, and all other types considered to be *value types* in .NET. But if you were to declare Point as a class, it would be a *reference type*, and the variable named P would always be modified, whether or not the parameter was declared *ByRef* or *ByVal*. To test this idea, just change the word *Structure* to *Class* in the declaration of Point and execute the sample code.

Comparing Structure Objects

When you compare two structures using the = operator, they are considered equal if the values of their fields are equal. The following code, for example, finds the two points to be equal:

```
Dim p1 As New Point(10, 20)
Dim p2 As New Point(10, 20)
If p1.Equals(p2) Then
    lblResult.Text = "The points are equal"
End If
```

You cannot compare two structures using the = operator unless you define an overloaded = operator method inside the structure. Operator overloading is an advanced technique that will not be covered in this book.

Structure Array

An array of structure objects is declared just as you would any other array. For example:

```
Dim aShape(10) As Point
```

As an option, you can initialize each array element by calling its constructor. The following statement declares and initializes an array of two Point objects:

```
Dim aLine() As Point = {New Point(0, 5), New Point(2, 10)}
```

6.2 Components

Assemblies

A **.NET assembly** is an application building block. It represents a basic unit of deployment, consisting of types and resources that work together. To see a Visual Basic project's assembly information, open *My Project* in the Solution Explorer window, and click the *Application* tab. Figure 6-1, for example, shows the assembly information for a project named *ArrayLib* in this chapter.

In its simplest form, an assembly consists of a single .dll file, which contains the following parts:

- *Assembly manifest*—Contains information about the contents of the assembly itself.
- *Type metadata*—Contains information about the data types defined inside the assembly.
- *MSIL code*—The result of compiling the application source code.
- *Resources*—Such as bitmaps, icons, and strings.

You might imagine that a .NET assembly is like a published book. A book contains a table of contents (assembly manifest), a glossary (type metadata), chapters (MSIL code), and a collection of figures and tables (resources).

Figure 6-1 Assembly information for ArrayLib

Components

A **component** (also known as a **class library**) is a collection of related classes that belong to a single assembly and have been compiled and stored so they are easily available to other applications. Most companies that write software tend to recycle a great deal of their code in multiple applications. The same is true for computer consultants, who adapt and customize the same software application for multiple clients. In such situations, it would make no sense to insert duplicate copies of source code into each application. Imagine what would happen if a bug were found? Every single copy of the source code would have to be examined, fixed, and recompiled.

The primary advantage to using a component is that it makes it easier for you to reuse existing code. This advantage becomes even more important when a component contains detailed or tricky logic. If the component is debugged thoroughly, there is no need to write and debug the same code in every application that needs the same functionality. Over time, when new features and modifications are added to the component, a new version is distributed to all applications that use it.

Components fall into two general classes: (1) user interface components, such as Visual Basic controls, and (2) code components, such as those found in the middle tier or data tier. The former type of component is known as a *Custom Control* in .NET and is quite difficult to create. The latter type is easy to create, so we will demonstrate how in this chapter.

Using a Component in Visual Studio

Visual Studio has excellent support for components. You can create a component as a project, and then reference the component from other applications. We show how to do that in the following steps:

1. Create a *Class Library* project. In it, define one or more public classes.
2. With the solution name selected in Solution Explorer, add a *Windows Forms Application* project.
3. Add a reference from your new desktop project to the component.

TIP: The same component can be used by both Windows Forms applications and ASP.NET applications.

Component Versions

A component is compiled by Visual Studio into a DLL file (filename with .dll extension). Also known as a *dynamic link library*, this file could be used by any .NET application. If we were in the component sales business, we might sell the DLL file to other Visual Basic developers, who would plug it into their applications.

A component has a version number (such as 1.2.0) associated with it, which is very useful when it is modified at a future time. The component's developer increments either the major version number (first digit), the minor version number (second digit), or the service release number (third digit).

Given a current version number of 1.2.0, the new version number might be 2.1.0, 1.3.0, or 1.2.1, depending on the importance of the release. Over time, some clients might have multiple versions of the DLL file on their computer, so they would check each file's version number to find the one they wish to use.

TIP: When you add a component reference to your project, its version number will appear in the Properties window, under the name *Runtime Version*.

Tutorial 6-1:
Creating a component and referencing it from another application

In this tutorial, you will create a Class Library project containing a single class. Then you will create a Windows Forms application that references your component. Before starting this tutorial, make sure that the solution name is visible in the Solution Explorer window. If it is not, open the Tools menu, select *Options*, select *Projects and Solutions*, and select the *Always show solution* option.

Tutorial Steps

Step 1: First, you will create a blank Visual Studio solution. From the File menu, select *New*, select *Project*, select *Other Project Types*, select *Visual Studio Solutions*, and select *Blank Solution*. Save the solution with the name *Registration Library*.

Step 2: Next, you will create a class library project. From the File menu, select *New*, select *Visual Basic*, select the *Class Library* template as shown in Figure 6-2, and assign the name *RegistrationLib* to the library. Click the *OK* button to create the project.

Step 3: A class named *Class1.vb* is created for you. Rename the file to *Student.vb*. Open its code window.

TIP: Any classes in a library that you want to be visible to other applications should be declared Public.

Figure 6-2 Creating a component

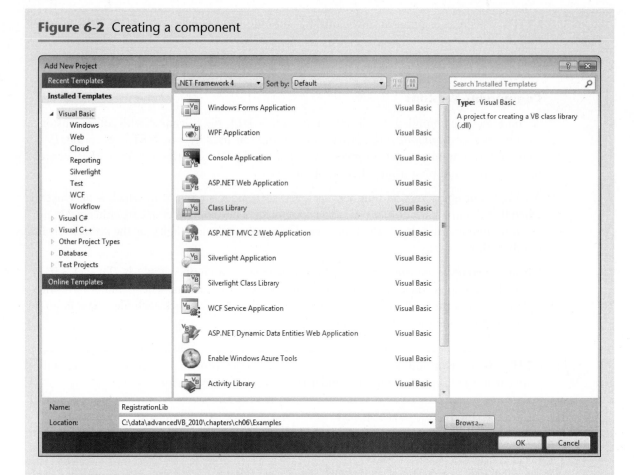

Step 4: Replace the code in the *Student.vb* file with the following:

```
Public Enum YearLevel
    LowerDivision
    UpperDivision
    Graduate
End Enum

Public Enum AcademicStatus
    Honors
    Normal
    Warning
    Probation
End Enum

Public Class Student
    Public Property Credits As Integer
    Public Property Level As YearLevel
    Public Property GradeAverage As Double
    Public Property Status As AcademicStatus

    Public Sub New(ByVal pCredits As Integer, _
      ByVal pLevel As YearLevel, _
      ByVal pGradeAverage As Double, ByVal pStatus As _
      AcademicStatus)

        Credits = pCredits
        Level = pLevel
```

```
        GradeAverage = pGradeAverage
        Status = pStatus
      End Sub
  End Class
```

Notice that we have used enumerated type declarations to make the meanings of the Level and Status properties clearer.

Step 5: Create a Windows Forms application named *Registration UI*. It will access the classes in the RegistrationLib library.

Step 6: Next, you will add a reference from this application to the RegistrationLib project. In the Solution explorer window of the current application, right-click the project name and select *Add Reference* from the popup menu. The Projects tab should be selected as in Figure 6-3, and the names of all projects in your current Visual Studio solution should be listed there. Select RegistrationLib and click the *OK* button.

Figure 6-3 Adding a reference to a component from an application

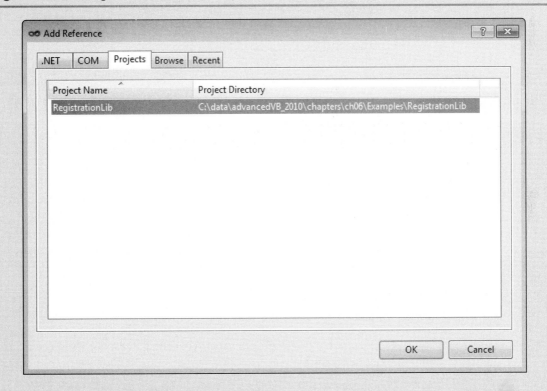

Step 7: Verify that the reference was added by opening the *My Project* window and selecting the *References* tab. Notice that the complete path of the file is displayed.

Step 8: Right-click the *RegistrationLib* reference and select *Properties*. Examine the properties window (shown in Figure 6-4). Notice in particular that it contains the directory path of the library's DLL file, and a runtime version number. If we were to release an update to our library, we would modify the runtime version number so programmers using our library would be able to verify that they were using the correct version.

Figure 6-4 Reference properties window

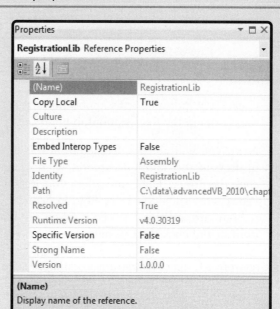

Step 9: Open the code window of the application's startup form and declare the following Student variable at the class level:

```
Private aStudent As New RegistrationLib.Student(10,
    RegistrationLib.YearLevel.LowerDivision, 2.75,
    RegistrationLib.AcademicStatus.Normal)
```

This statement calls the Student constructor, passing to it the four required parameters. Notice how the Student class name must be preceded by the RegistrationLib namespace. The same is true for the two enumerated types. Clearly, this type of coding gets tedious, so you can add an `Imports` statement to the form.

Step 10: Insert the following statement on the very first line of the code file:

```
Imports RegistrationLib
```

Step 11: Simplify the variable declaration by removing the namespace from each class and enumerated value.

```
Private aStudent As New Student(10, YearLevel.LowerDivision, 2.75,
    AcademicStatus.Normal)
```

Summary

This tutorial represented the first step in setting up a component that is accessed from another application. We simplified the process by creating both applications as projects within the same Visual Studio solution. You can also reference a component anywhere on your computer or on a network by connecting to a DLL file. In future tutorials, you will add another class to this component.

References Outside the Current Solution

Sometimes you may need to reference a component from outside a Visual Studio solution. In fact, you can reference a library anywhere on your computer or on a network. Here's what to do:

1. Create a new Windows Forms application in its own Visual Studio solution.
2. Right-click the project name and select *Add Reference*. The Add Reference dialog window will appear, as shown in Figure 6-5. Click the Browse tab. Use the browser tool to find the *RegistrationLib.dll* file, most probably located in the *bin\Debug* folder of the RegistrationLib project from Tutorial 6-1. Select the file and click the *OK* button to close the dialog.
3. Verify that the reference was added by opening the *My Project* window and selecting the *References* tab.

If a component's location changes, you must remove it from your project's references list. Then you can add it again, with the correct location. To remove a component reference from an application, open the My Projects window, select References, and select the component name from the list. Click the *Remove* button, or press the *Del* key. Then you can click the *Add* button to add the new reference.

In Tutorial 6-2, you will add another class to the RegistrationLib component.

Figure 6-5 Adding a reference to a component DLL file

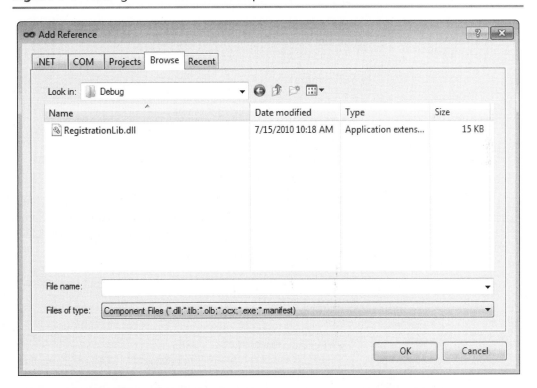

Tutorial 6-2:
Adding an Advisor class to the RegistrationLib component

In this tutorial, you will add a class named *Advisor* to the RegistrationLib component. This class will evaluate the number of college credits a student may take, based on criteria such as grade point average, student status, and student year level.

Tutorial Steps

Step 1: Open the solution file that you created in Tutorial 6-1. The file should be named *Registration Library.sln*. After opening the solution, verify that it contains two projects: (1) RegistrationLib, and (2) Registration UI. If either is missing, right-click the solution name, select *Add*, select *Existing Project*, and select the project's .vbproj file.

Step 2: Add a class named *Advisor.vb* to the RegistrationLib project.

Step 3: Insert the following declarations into the class:

```
Enum SemesterType
   Fall
   Spring
   Summer_A
   Summer_B
End Enum

Private Shared ReadOnly regDates() As String =
   {"Aug 15", "Dec 10", "April 15", "May 30"}
```

You have declared an enumerated type that lists each of the college-year semesters (these vary from one college to another). Also, you have declared an array of student registration dates, one for each semester.

Step 4: Insert the following shared method that returns a single registration date, based on the value of its SemesterType argument:

```
Public Shared ReadOnly Property RegistrationDate(
   ByVal semester As SemesterType) As String
   Get
      Return regDates(semester)
   End Get
End Property
```

The *Shared* qualifier is used throughout this class because users will not need to create an instance of the Advisor class.

Step 5: Create the following method named *MaxCredits*, which determines the maximum number of credits a student can take, depending on the student's situation (year in school, academic status, and grade point average):

```
Public Shared Function MaxCredits(
   ByVal aStudent As Student) As Integer
   With aStudent
      Select Case .Status
         Case AcademicStatus.Probation
            Return 6
         Case AcademicStatus.Warning
            If .Level = YearLevel.LowerDivision Then
               Return 6
            ElseIf .Level = YearLevel.UpperDivision Then
               Return 9
            ElseIf .Level = YearLevel.Graduate Then
               Return 7
            End If
         Case AcademicStatus.Normal
            If .Level = YearLevel.LowerDivision Then
               If .GradeAverage > 2.5 Then
                  Return 12
```

```
                    Else
                        Return 10
                    End If
                ElseIf .Level = YearLevel.UpperDivision Then
                    Return 18
                ElseIf .Level = YearLevel.Graduate Then
                    Return 14
                End If
            Case AcademicStatus.Honors
                If .Level = YearLevel.LowerDivision Then
                    Return 18
                ElseIf .Level = YearLevel.UpperDivision Then
                    Return 22
                ElseIf .Level = YearLevel.Graduate Then
                    Return 22
                End If
            End Select
        End With
        Return 0
    End Function
```

The MaxCredits method is a little long because it implements a series of hypothetical college rules regarding the advising of students. (We make no claim as to the validity of these rules.) In any event, this is precisely the type of code that we would *not* want to rewrite in each application related to student registration. Instead, we put this code in a component, test and debug it once, and use the component in as many applications as we wish.

If the rules shown in Step 5 were to change in the future, we could modify the component, test it again, and release it with a new version number.

Step 6: Add the *CanRegister* method to the class. It receives a Student object and returns a Boolean value that indicates whether or not the student can register. The Student object (named *aStudent*) contains a *Credits* property that indicates the number of credits the student would like to enroll in during the coming semester.

```
Public Shared Function CanRegister(
    ByVal aStudent As Student) As Boolean
    Return aStudent.Credits <= MaxCredits(aStudent)
End Function
```

The student can enroll in the desired number of credits as long as he or she does not exceed the maximum number of allowed credits for someone in his or her situation.

Step 7: Save and build the component.

In Tutorial 6-3, you will add code to the *Registration UI* application that calls methods in the Advisor and Student classes.

Tutorial 6-3:
Using the Advisor and Student classes

In this tutorial, you will add code to the *Registration UI* application that lets it call methods in the Advisor and Student classes belonging to the *RegistrationLib* component.

Tutorial Steps

Step 1: Open the solution file that you modified in Tutorial 6-2. The file should be named *Registration Library.sln*.

Step 2: In the *Registration UI* project, open the startup form and insert the named controls listed in Table 6-1 and displayed in Figure 6-6. You will also add descriptive labels.

Table 6-1 Controls in the Registration UI application

Control Type	Control Name	Properties
Form	(default)	Text: *Registration User Interface* Font.Size: 10pt
ComboBox	cboYearLevel	Items: *Lower division, Upper division, Graduate*
ComboBox	cboAcademicStatus	Items: *Honors, Normal, Warning, Probation*
TextBox	txtGradeAverage	
TextBox	txtCredits	
Button	btnCheck	Text: *Check*
Label	lblResult	AutoSize: *False* BorderStyle: *Fixed3D*

Figure 6-6 User interface for the Registration UI application

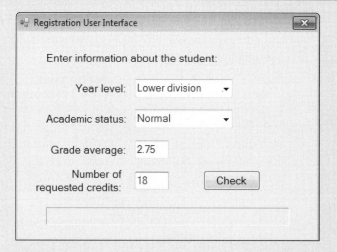

Step 3: Open the form's code window and delete the following statement:

```
Private aStudent As New Student(10, YearLevel.LowerDivision, 2.75,
    AcademicStatus.Normal)
```

Step 4: Create the following Click handler for the *Check* button:

```
1:    Private Sub btnCheck_Click() Handles btnCheck.Click
2:       Try
3:          Dim credits As Integer = CInt(txtCredits.Text)
4:          Dim level As YearLevel = CType(cboYearLevel.
```

```
 5:              SelectedIndex, YearLevel)
 6:          Dim gpa As Double = CDbl(txtGradeAverage.Text)
 7:          Dim status As AcademicStatus = CType(cboStatus.
 8:              SelectedIndex, AcademicStatus)
 9:
10:          Dim aStudent As New Student(credits, level, gpa, status)
11:
12:          If Advisor.CanRegister(aStudent) Then
13:              lblResult.Text = "The student can register!"
14:          Else
15:              lblResult.Text = "The student cannot register " _
16:                  & "for so many credits. Maximum = " &_
                    Advisor.MaxCredits(aStudent)
17:          End If
18:
19:      Catch ex As Exception
20:          lblResult.Text = "Please check all input fields"
21:      End Try
22: End Sub
```

Lines 3–8 collect Student field information from the form's controls. The combo boxes are set up so their SelectedIndex values exactly match the order of the YearLevel and AcademicStatus enumerated types. Line 10 creates a Student object from the values entered by the user. Line 12 calls the *CanRegister* method from the Advisor class in the RegistrationLib component. It is a shared method, so it can be invoked using the class name (as in Advisor. CanRegister).

If CanRegister returns *False*, lines 15–16 build a response message that includes the maximum number of credits the student is permitted to take. Notice that it calls *MaxCredits* to get this information.

Step 5: Run the application and enter the values shown in Figure 6-7. When you click the *Check* button, the output should appear as it does in the figure.

Figure 6-7 Testing the Registration UI application

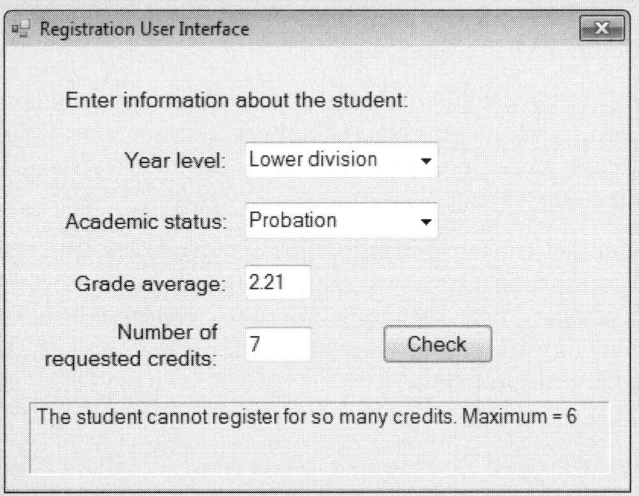

Summary

More testing needs to be done on this application to verify its accuracy. Rather than doing it manually, we will wait until later in this chapter to show how we can use automated testing to achieve the same result.

Checkpoint

1. What is a synonym for *component*?

2. What is the major advantage to using class libraries?

3. Which page in the *My Project* window identifies which components are used by an application?

4. Which statement in the code window of a client application simplifies references to component classes?

6.3 Unit Testing

In Chapter 1, you learned how important it is to test your software. Software engineers have found that testing is very effective when it is an integral part of the development process. One conventional approach to testing and debugging has been to begin testing at the end of a project after all code is written. But that approach can create a lot of stress and result in errors. Strict deadlines often force an application to be released before all defects are found. A test/debug cycle at the end of a project often follows this pattern:

1. A bug (also known as a *defect*) is found by a tester, and added to a list of known bugs.
2. A programmer attempts to reproduce all known bugs while stepping through the code with a debugger. This may take some time because the application is large, and many steps may be involved.
3. The programmer fixes all known bugs by modifying the project's source code.
4. The software tester tests the application again to verify that all known bugs are fixed. In doing so, the tester discovers new bugs that were caused when the code was modified in Step 3.
5. Steps 2–4 are repeated until (1) no more bugs are found, or (2) the product's release deadline has been reached.

Step 3 is often complicated by the fact that the programmer may have written the application code many months before and may not remember many details. This makes the code harder to fix. All too often, software is released with undiscovered bugs, leaving the customers to find them.

Naturally, developers using this approach may work extremely long hours near the end of a project. To complicate matters, managers may be tempted to add some last-minute features to the application to keep up with products released by competing companies. Many commercial software products are revised every few months, making this traditional testing model difficult to follow.

Continuous Software Testing

A fairly recent trend in software development uses a methodology known as **continuous software testing**, which requires programmers to test new code immediately, as soon as it is added to a project. Particularly when software must be created in short development cycles (to keep up with the competition), applications must be nearly defect-free all the time. Therefore, a significant amount of time is invested in testing while the application is being written. Then when a new version of the application is about to be released, its code has already been tested. Near the release deadline, some amount of manual testing must still be done, but fewer defects are found than if testing had begun at the end of the project.

> ***But don't well-disciplined programmers test their own code?*** Yes, many programmers manually test their own code, as you (hopefully) did in Chapters 1–5. At the same time, they may be under pressure to write more code that will move the product closer to a finished state. As a result, programmers usually do not redo a long sequence of manual tests every time they add a small amount of code to an application.

A central principle of continuous software testing is that you must rerun all existing tests as soon as you modify the application's source code. This type of testing is known as **regression testing**. But here's a basic problem—if regression testing were performed using manual tests, as you did in Chapter 1, a company would need an army of human testers to validate even a medium-size application. So it makes sense to let a computer do the testing instead, using a practice known as *automated testing*.

Automated Unit Tests

An **automated test** is a program that executes all or part of an application without input from a live user. There are different types of automated tests, but we will focus on just one type that is very easy to learn. A **unit test** is a method that executes and tests a single unit of code (such as a method) in an existing application. The unit test is designed to verify that the code being tested is working correctly.

Let's use an example from computer hardware. Desktop computers are assembled from different components such as motherboards, power supplies, memory chips, and a central processing unit (CPU). If you've tried this, you know how important it is that each component has already been tested. Then, when assembling the computer, you have only to do some final tests to verify that the components are compatible with each other (known as *integration testing*). Similarly, when creating a Visual Basic application, you can be sure that the TextBox, ListBox, and other controls have been used and tested by a great many people. That allows you to focus on your application code, without having to worry that the controls themselves might be defective.

Programmers usually write a series of unit tests at the same time they write the application that is being tested. They run the unit tests immediately, and if a test fails, they fix the application code before rerunning the test. In fact, when any new code is added to an application, all of the existing unit tests are run again to verify that the new code has not caused one of the tests to fail.

A central philosophy of unit testing can be expressed by the phrase *pay as you go, rather than paying at the end*. In other words, the time you invest in creating unit tests while developing an application saves you lots of testing and debugging time at the end of a project.

Unit Testing Basics

Unit testing falls under the general category of **white box testing**. This type of testing visualizes the application as a transparent box, permitting the tester to view all of the source code of the class being tested. In contrast, **black box testing** is used when the tester cannot view the source code of an application being tested. The application is like an opaque box into which one can only pass inputs and view outputs.

Each unit test is designed to test one particular code unit of an application. The unit being tested is usually a property or method. It is customary to create numerous unit tests for the same class.

When a unit test fails, it stops executing and returns immediately. In other words, it behaves as if it were throwing an exception. If the test contains any method calls following the point of failure, you will not know if they would have executed successfully. For that reason, each unit test should test just one method in the application being tested.

Unit tests do not run in any particular sequence. Each unit test should be independent of all other unit tests. Do not create dependencies between unit tests, so that, for example, the outcome of unit test B depends on the successful completion of unit test A.

Design your unit tests so they completely exercise your application's code. The goal is to have 100 percent code coverage of the class or method being tested. If the method contains nested If statements, for example, you should devise a unit test for each possible branch.

Unit tests are usually executed by a utility program known as a **test engine**. As it executes each test method, it reports the success or failure of the test in a visual display. It also stores information about which line of code was executing when the test failed, the time and date, and the data values that were being compared at the time. This information helps the person reading the output to pinpoint the source of the error that caused the test to fail. Some well-known test engines are *MBUnit*, *NUnit*, *JUnit*, and, of course, the Visual Studio test engine.

Unit Testing in .NET

Unit testing in .NET is supported by classes in the *Microsoft.VisualStudio.TestTools.UnitTesting* namespace. Visual Studio provides excellent support for unit testing. This is the basic working sequence you will follow:

1. Create a set of classes for your application that contain your program logic and basic operations. These classes are not forms, so they have no user interface.
2. Create a Visual Studio **test project**, which is automatically configured to run unit tests.
3. Add one or more unit tests to your test project. Each unit test identifies the class in your application that you wish to test. You can, if you wish, choose to test only certain methods and properties in the class.
4. Run the automated testing tool from the Visual Studio menu. You are shown a report that lists the outcome of each test—whether it completed as expected or it failed by producing the wrong output.

Creating a Test Project

To add a test project to the current Visual Studio solution, right-click the solution name, select *Add*, and select *New Project*. In the *Add New Project* window, which is shown in Figure 6-8, select *Test Documents* under the *Test Projects* heading. Select the Test Project template, give it a name, and click the *Add* button.

Running a Test

To run one or more unit tests, select the *Test* menu, select *Run*, and select either *All Tests in Solution* or *Tests in Current Context*. Before making the latter selection, you should select a test project, test class, or test method. The test output will appear in the *Test Results* window. A green circle containing a check mark will appear next to the name of each test method that passes.

Figure 6-8 Adding a Test Project to the current Visual Studio solution

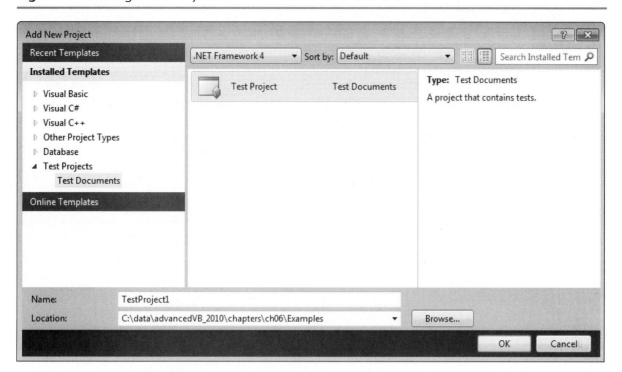

Running a Test in Debug Mode

To run a test in debug mode, wet a breakpoint inside the test that you wish to debug. Then, from the Test menu, select *Debug* and select *Tests in Current Context*.

Unit Testing Attributes

The .NET languages use **attribute names** to identify classes and methods that are unit tests. It does this so Visual Studio can identify and execute the tests when requested by the user. The two most common attribute names are TestClass and TestMethod:

- <TestClass()>—Identifies a class that contains unit tests.
- <TestMethod()>—Identifies a method that performs a unit test by executing methods in the application class.

These attribute names appear at the beginning of a class or method declaration. For example, the following statement declares a class for unit testing named AccountTest:

```
<TestClass()> Public Class AccountTest
```

The following statement declares a method that will be executed as a unit test:

```
<TestMethod()> Public Sub AccountConstructorTest()
```

A unit test method normally produces a Boolean return value that indicates whether the test passed or failed. It does this by calling one of the Assert class methods. For example, the following statement returns *True* if the values in the expected and actual variables were equal:

```
AreEqual( expected, actual )
```

Later in this section, we will talk about the Assert class methods in more detail. The AreEqual method is used 90 percent of the time. In Tutorial 6-4, you will create your first unit test.

Tutorial 6-4:
Creating a Unit Test project

In this tutorial, you will create unit tests for a class that finds the largest value in an array of integers. You will create two projects. The first will contain a class named *IntArray*, which performs operations on an array of integers. This is the class that will be tested. The second project will be a test project that contains a class named *IntArrayTest* that performs tests by calling methods in the IntArray class. When you tell Visual Studio to run the unit tests, it will execute each method in the IntArrayTest class. Figure 6-9 contains a diagram that expresses the relationships between these two classes.

Figure 6-9 Relationships between the IntArray and IntArrayTest classes

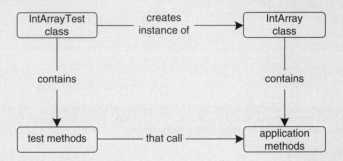

Tutorial Steps

Step 1: Create a Class Library project named *ArrayLib*.

Step 2: Add a class file to the library named *IntArray.vb*. It should contain a property that holds an array of integers, and a method named *GetLargest*.

```
Public Class IntArray
  Public Property Data As Integer()

  Public Function GetLargest() As Integer
    Return Data(0)
  End Function
End Class
```

When completed, the GetLargest method will return the element of the array that has the largest value. For now, it returns only the first element of the array.

Step 3: Next, you will create a test project named *ArrayLib Test*. In Solution Explorer, select the solution name, right-click and select *Add*, then select *New Project*. In the *Add New Project* window, select *Test Projects*, select *Test Documents*, and select the *Test Project* template in the middle pane. Name this project *ArrayLib Test* and click the *OK* button to close the dialog window.

Step 4: Next, you will add a unit test to the test project. In the Solution Explorer window, delete the existing .vb file inside the ArrayLib Test project. Then right-click the project name, select *Add*, and select *Unit Test*. The *Create Unit Tests* dialog will appear, as in Figure 6-10. Open up the tree below ArrayLib, expand the entries and find the *ArrayLib.IntArray* class. Select the *GetLargest* method and click the *OK* button to close the dialog.

Figure 6-10 Creating a unit test for the ArrayLib.GetLargest method

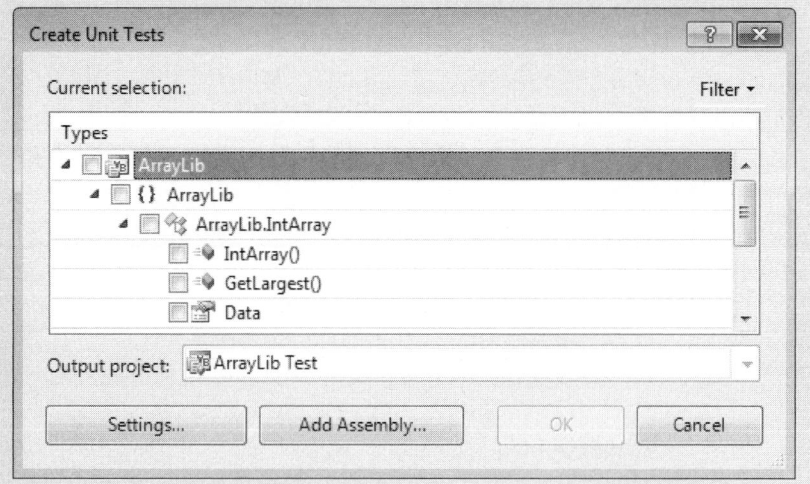

Step 5: Next, you will edit the IntArrayTest class that was just created by Visual Studio. Open its source file and edit the code until it looks like this:

```
1:  Imports Microsoft.VisualStudio.TestTools.UnitTesting
2:  Imports ArrayLib
3:
4:  <TestClass()> _
5:  Public Class IntArrayTest
6:
7:    <TestMethod()> _
8:    Public Sub GetLargestTest()
9:      Dim target As IntArray = New IntArray()
10:     target.Data = {40, 16, 12, 22, 0, -33}
11:     Dim expected As Integer = 40
12:     Dim actual As Integer = target.GetLargest
13:     Assert.AreEqual(expected, actual)
14:   End Sub
15: End Class
```

The *GetLargestTest* method passes an array of integers to the IntArray class, and then calls IntArray's GetLargest method to see if it returns the right value. Line 9 creates an instance of the IntArray class, which is the class we want to test. Line 10 creates an array of integers and assigns it to the Data property of the IntArray class. Line 11 sets *expected* to the largest value in the array, 40. Line 12 calls the IntArray.GetLargest method and stores the return value in the variable named *actual*. Line 13 compares the expected and actual values by calling the Assert.AreEqual method. At this point, the test will either pass or fail.

Notice the use of the TestClass and TestMethod attributes, which are required markers for unit tests. Each method labeled as such will be executed by Visual Studio's test engine.

Step 6: Build the project. Next, you will run the unit test.

Step 7: From the *Test* menu, select *Run*, and then select *All Tests in Solution*. You should see the *Test Results* window appear as in Figure 6-11, showing a green dot next to the GetLargestTest method name. The green dot indicates that the test passed, and the correct value was returned by the GetLargest method.

Figure 6-11 Showing the results for a single unit test

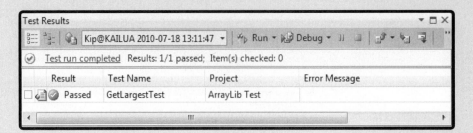

Summary

At this point, one might imagine that the GetLargest method was correct. Or, were we just lucky based on the arrangement of the numbers in the test array? You can inspect the test data and the GetLargest method to answer that question. In Tutorial 6-5, you will create more tests to determine whether GetLargest works correctly.

Tutorial 6-5:
Creating more unit tests for the IntArray class

Let us assume that the single test you created in Tutorial 6-4 for the GetLargest method was not sufficient to verify that the method worked correctly. In this tutorial, you will add more tests that properly test GetLargest and fix any defects you might find.

Tutorial Steps

Step 1: Open the IntArrayTest class and examine its test method.

```
<TestMethod()> _
Public Sub GetLargestTest()
    Dim target As IntArray = New IntArray()
    target.Data = {40, 16, 12, 22, 0, -33}
    Dim expected As Integer = 40
    Dim actual As Integer = target.GetLargest
    Assert.AreEqual(expected, actual)
End Sub
```

Step 2: Let's rearrange the values in the test array to see if the order matters when looking for the largest value. Make a copy of the method, rename it, and change the line containing the array. The shaded line in the following code needs to be modified:

```
<TestMethod()> _
Public Sub GetLargestTest_2()
    Dim target As IntArray = New IntArray()
    target.Data = {16, 40, 12, 22, 0, -33}
    Dim expected As Integer = 40
    Dim actual As Integer = target.GetLargest
    Assert.AreEqual(expected, actual)
End Sub
```

Step 3: Run all unit tests. A red circular icon should appear next to the new test in the Test Results window, as shown in Figure 6-12. Double-click the line containing this test, which will open the *Test Details* window, shown in Figure 6-13. Of particular importance are the error message, which explains why the test failed, and the stack trace, which contains a hyperlink that takes you to the statement in the source code that was executing when the test failed. Another interesting bit of information is the execution time, which can be useful if a test fails after running an unusually long time.

Figure 6-12 Showing the results for both unit tests

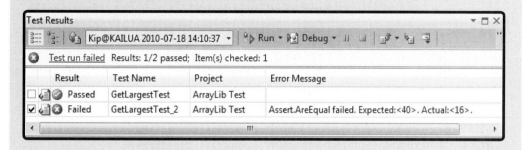

Figure 6-13 Test Details window

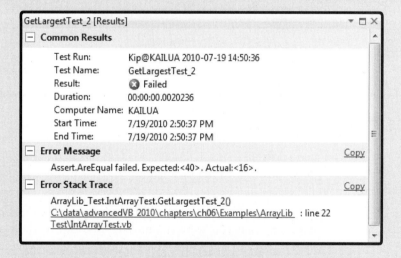

The test's error message indicates that the expected value was 40, but the GetLargest method returned 16. Clearly, the position of the number 40 seems to matter because the method fails to return the correct result when 40 is moved to the second position. Let's examine the code in GetLargest:

```
Public Function GetLargest() As Integer
  Return Data(0)
End Function
```

Of course, we must add more code to this method! This type of mistake is common because programmers often create an incomplete *stub* method when designing a class. They always *intend* to complete the code, but they often forget.

Step 4:   Revise the GetLargest method by writing some plausible-looking code:

```
Public Function GetLargest() As Integer
   Dim largest As Integer
   For i As Integer = 1 To Data.Length
      If Data(i) > largest Then
         largest = Data(i)
      End If
   Next
   Return largest
End Function
```

The loop iterates through the array, comparing each element in Data(i) to the variable named largest. Whenever a larger value is found in the current array position, it is copied into largest. As you may have noticed, it contains a bug.

Step 5:   Run the tests again. This time, both tests generate exceptions, as shown in Figure 6-14. You may already be able to identify the bug in this code, because it is very simple. But more complex methods in actual applications are often harder to fix, requiring you to trace them in the debugger.

Figure 6-14 Testing GetLargest after adding a loop to the method

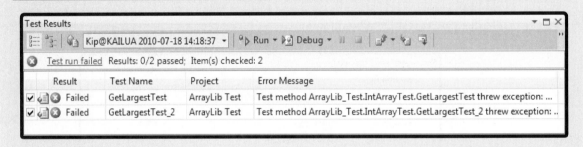

Step 6:   Set a breakpoint on the first line of GetLargest and run the tests in debug mode. This is how to do it: From the Test menu, select *Debug*, and select *All Tests in Solution*. When the debugger hits the breakpoint, inspect the value of *Data.Length*. It should equal to 6. Open a *Watch* window and insert the variables *i* and *largest*. Step through the code and watch the values change.

Notice that when $i = 6$, the program throws an *IndexOutOfRangeException*. Assuming that you were running the first test method (in which 40 was the first array element), notice that *largest* was never assigned the value 40. So it appears that the array index (i) should have started at 0 and ended at 5, which is the last position in the array. The length of the array could be different each time GetLargest is called, so let's end the loop at Data.Length − 1.

Step 7:   Revise the GetLargest method as shown:

```
Public Function GetLargest() As Integer
   Dim largest As Integer
   For i As Integer = 0 To Data.Length - 1
      If Data(i) > largest Then
         largest = Data(i)
      End If
   Next
   Return largest
End Function
```

Step 8: Run the tests again, see that they pass, and celebrate your success for a few seconds.

Are you convinced that you have thoroughly tested the GetLargest method? Perhaps not. Let's create some more tests that change the length of the array, reorder the elements, and include some duplicate values.

Step 9: Insert the following test methods and run the tests again:

```
<TestMethod()> _
Public Sub GetLargestTest_3()
   Dim target As IntArray = New IntArray()
   target.Data = {12, 16, 45, 12, 22, 0, -33}
   Dim expected As Integer = 45
   Dim actual As Integer = target.GetLargest
   Assert.AreEqual(expected, actual)
End Sub

<TestMethod()> _
Public Sub GetLargestTest_4()
   Dim target As IntArray = New IntArray()
   target.Data = {16, 40, -33, 40, 0, 12, 22, 0, 49}
   Dim expected As Integer = 49
   Dim actual As Integer = target.GetLargest
   Assert.AreEqual(expected, actual)
End Sub

<TestMethod()> _
Public Sub GetLargestTest_5()
   Dim target As IntArray = New IntArray()
   target.Data = {0, 0, 0, 1, 1, 1, 0, 0, 0}
   Dim expected As Integer = 1
   Dim actual As Integer = target.GetLargest
   Assert.AreEqual(expected, actual)
End Sub
```

All the tests pass, so we might be tempted to declare that GetLargest is correct. But it still contains a serious flaw, which further tests can uncover.

Step 10: Add a test for an array containing all negative integers. The largest value should equal −5.

```
<TestMethod()> _
Public Sub GetLargestTest_6()
   Dim target As IntArray = New IntArray()
   target.Data = {-5, -6, -33, -42, -10}
   Dim expected As Integer = -5
   Dim actual As Integer = target.GetLargest
   Assert.AreEqual(expected, actual)
End Sub
```

This test fails, with the following message: *Assert.AreEqual failed. Expected:<−5>. Actual:<0>.* If you trace the code in the debugger, you'll find that the Boolean condition in the If statement is never true, so *largest* remains equal its default value, 0.

```
If Data(i) > largest Then        ' Never equals True
   largest = Data(i)
End If
```

Therefore, largest was never explicitly initialized by our code, and it defaulted to the value 0. This is a common mistake when coding this algorithm. Let's fix it by initializing largest to the first value in the array.

Step 11: Revise the second line of GetLargest by initializing it to the value in the first array element:

```
Public Function GetLargest() As Integer
   Dim largest As Integer = Data(0)
   For i As Integer = 0 To Data.Length - 1
     If Data(i) > largest Then
        largest = Data(i)
     End If
   Next
   Return largest
End Function
```

We could also choose to change the starting value of i in the loop, but let's leave it for now.

Step 12: Run the tests again. All tests pass!

Step 13: Let's create what is known as a *degenerate test case* by passing an empty array. It's not clear what value the expected variable should contain, so you can set it to 0. Add the following test method:

```
<TestMethod()> _
Public Sub GetLargestTest_7()
   Dim target As IntArray = New IntArray()
   target.Data = {}
   Dim expected As Integer = 0
   Dim actual As Integer = target.GetLargest
   Assert.AreEqual(expected, actual)
End Sub
```

Step 14: Run the tests again and notice that the new test generates an IndexOut-OfRangeException. Of course, that makes sense when we look at the second line of GetLargest:

```
Dim largest As Integer = Data(0)
```

An empty array doesn't have a value at index position 0, so we cannot initialize *largest* to the first array element. Instead, we can initialize *largest* to the smallest value an integer could ever have, known as *Integer.MinValue* (defined in the .NET library). Then we will expect that value to be returned if the unit test passes an empty array to GetLargest.

Step 15: Revise the second line of the GetLargest method:

```
Public Function GetLargest() As Integer
   Dim largest As Integer = Integer.MinValue
   For i As Integer = 0 To Data.Length - 1
     If Data(i) > largest Then
        largest = Data(i)
     End If
   Next
   Return largest
End Function
```

Step 16: Modify the GetLargestTest_7 method by replacing the following line:

```
Dim expected As Integer = 0
```

with this line:

```
Dim expected As Integer = Integer.MinValue
```

Step 17: Run the tests again. Now, finally, all the tests pass. It appears that we've finally written and tested a completely bulletproof version of GetLargest.

What if the array passed to the Data property of the IntArray class were null (Nothing)? Then we could expect an exception to be thrown. But we won't fix that right now.

Summary

We hope that you can see from this tutorial that even the most trivial bit of code has the potential to contain undiscovered errors. The unit tests you created were able to uncover and fix the errors in the GetLargest method that may not have been obvious when reading the code. As a chapter exercise, we will ask you to add two more methods to the IntArray class (GetSmallest and GetMedian) and write accompanying sets of unit tests.

Grouping and Viewing Unit Tests

Visual Studio was designed to be easy for students to use, but it also has features that benefit professional developers. Developers can use tools to manage large numbers of unit tests and view the results of previous tests. They can also copy a test result to the Windows clipboard, paste it into an email message, and send it to another person on the development team.

Test List Editor

When you are testing more than one class, the *Test List Editor* is a useful tool for managing lists of tests and setting individual test properties. To display the window, select *Test* from the menu, then select *Windows*, and select *Test List Editor*. The window shown in Figure 6-15 has three selections in the left-hand pane. You can display lists of tests that have been predefined, tests that have not yet been added to a list, and all tests.

Figure 6-15 The Test List Editor window

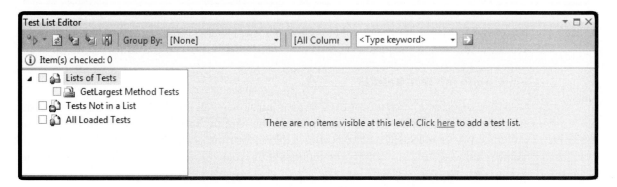

In the right-hand pane, you can click the hyperlink to add a new test. The *Create New Test List* window appears, and you can define a new list, as is being done in Figure 6-16. After defining a list, you can return to the *Tests Not in a List* pane and drag test names onto your new list, shown under the *Lists of Tests* heading. You can also select a group of tests and drag them all at once. Once you have assigned tests to lists, the list names will appear in the *All Loaded Tests* pane, shown in Figure 6-17.

Figure 6-16 Adding a new test list to the Test List Editor

Figure 6-17 Viewing all loaded tests

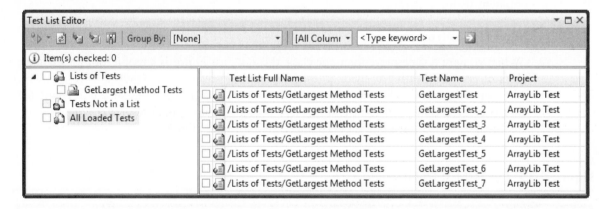

If you want to run only the tests belonging to a list, place a check mark next to a list in the Test List Editor, and then click the *Run Checked Tests* button on the editor's toolbar.

Viewing Prior Test Results

Visual Studio saves the results of each test for later review in the *Test Results* window. If you select the *All* option from the dropdown list in the window's toolbar, you can view all recent test runs. Figure 6-18, for example, shows all recent runs of the *GetLargestTest_6* method. You can double-click any test to get details about when the test was run, how it failed, and so on.

If you have grouped your unit tests into test lists, you can sort and group them by list name in the Test Results window, shown in Figure 6-19. Our example contains two test lists: *GetLargest Method Tests* and *MaxCredits Tests*.

All unit test results are stored in a file having the extension *.vsmdi*. You can find it in the *Solution Items* folder in the Solution Explorer window. You could run your tests and email this file to your class instructor, for example. The file can be opened in Visual Studio.

Figure 6-18 Viewing a test history

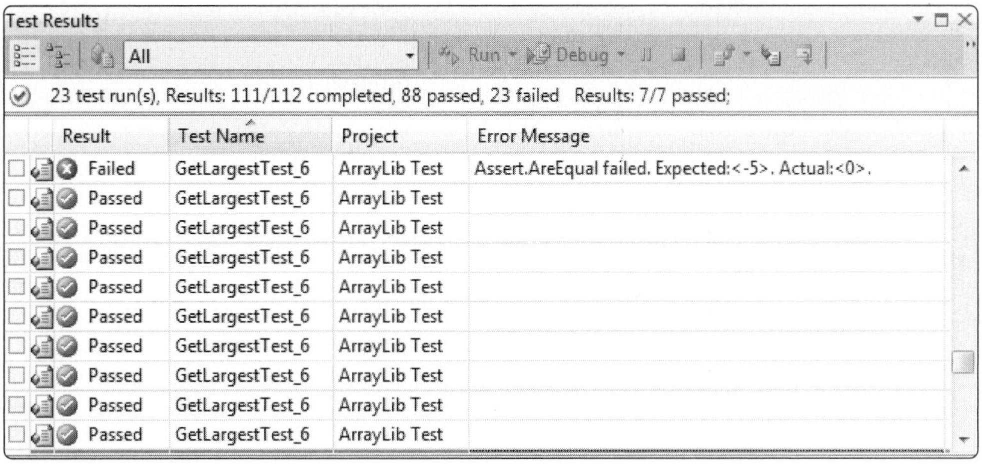

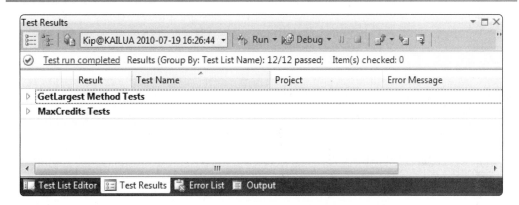

Figure 6-19 Viewing test results grouped by test list name

Assert Class Methods

An **assertion** is an expression that must be true for a program to continue. An assertion can be used to validate a method's input parameter, for example, if the parameter absolutely must conform to some requirement (such as being greater than 0). The designers of .NET unit testing framework decided to use assertions to signal whether unit tests pass or fail.

The **Assert class** contains a set of methods that are designed to execute within unit tests. You have already seen how the Assert.AreEqual method checks to see if two values are equal. Table 6-2 contains a list of the more commonly used Assert methods. These methods are shared (static) methods, so you call them using the Assert class name as the prefix, as in *Assert.AreEqual*. You cannot create an instance of the Assert class.

The Assert methods are overloaded with many different parameter lists. If you are comparing integers or strings, call AreEqual and pass it two values:

```
Assert.AreEqual(expected, actual)
```

Comparing Floating-Point Values

Comparing floating-point values for equality must be done in a special way because the computer's processor rounds the results of floating-point calculations. Values that should be equal frequently differ by a very small amount. Therefore, when comparing Single, Double, or Decimal

Table 6-2 Assert Class Methods

Method Name	Description
AreEqual(expected, actual)	Checks to see if *expected* is equal to *actual*. Fails otherwise.
AreEqual(expected, actual, diff)	Checks to see if the difference between *expected* and *actual* is less than or equal to *diff*. Fails otherwise.
AreNotEqual(expected, actual)	Checks to see if *expected* is not equal to *actual*. Fails otherwise.
AreNotEqual(expected, actual, diff)	Checks to see if the difference between *expected* and *actual* is larger than *diff*. Fails otherwise.
AreSame(expected, actual)	Checks to see if *expected* and *actual* refer to the same object. Fails otherwise.
AreNotSame(expected, actual)	Checks to see if *expected* and *actual* do not refer to the same object. Fails otherwise.
Fail(message)	Fails the assertion without checking any condition, passing a message.
IsFalse(boolExpression)	Checks to see if *boolExpression* is False. Fails otherwise.
IsTrue(boolExpression)	Checks to see if *boolExpression* is True. Fails otherwise.
IsNull(object)	Checks to see if *object* is null (Nothing). Fails otherwise.
IsNotNull(object)	Checks to see if *object* is not null (Not Nothing). Fails otherwise.

expressions, pass a third parameter to the **Assert.AreEqual method** that represents the maximum difference between the first two parameters that would still permit them to be considered equal. In the following example, if *expected* = 4.76 and *actual* = 4.77, the assertion succeeds.

```
Assert.AreEqual(expected, actual, 0.01)
```

But if *expected* = 4.76 and *actual* = 4.78, the assertion fails because their difference is larger than .01.

The **Assert.AreNotEqual method** is an assertion that fails if the first two parameters contain equal values. In the following example, if *expected* = 4.76 and *actual* = 4.77, the assertion fails because the values are just equal enough.

```
Assert.AreNotEqual(expected, actual, 0.01)
```

Comparing Object Values

If you pass objects to the AreEqual or AreNotEqual methods, the classes represented by these objects must override the Equals method. For example, we compare two Account objects in the following code:

```
Dim X As New Account(30024,"Smith")
Dim Y As New Account(10023,"Smith")
Assert.AreEqual(X, Y)
```

If the Account.Equals method were to compare accounts by their ID numbers, the assertion above would fail. On the other hand, if Account.Equals compared accounts by their names, the same assertion would pass. If you want to read more about overriding the Equals method, refer to Section 3.2 in Chapter 3.

Executing an Assert Method

This is how an Assert class method executes:

- If the assertion succeeds, the test method continues on to the next line.
- If the assertion fails, the test method throws an AssertFailedException, passing information about the values that were different. The test engine catches the exception and signals that the test has failed.

If a test method completes normally with no assertion failures, the test is flagged as successful by the Visual Studio test engine.

There is an important point to be made about Assert methods: If you call more than one of them within the same test method, the first one that fails will cause the test to fail immediately. No other Assert methods after that will execute, so you won't be able to tell which ones might have failed.

Adding Tests to an Existing Application

Developers are frequently called on to create unit tests for existing applications. Depending on how the code was structured, this may not be easy. Ideally, the existing code should be factored into methods that each focus on a single task. We say that such methods are *highly cohesive*.

If at all possible, each unit test should test only a single method in the application class. When a test fails, it is important for you to know exactly which application method failed to return the correct value. If you were to combine several method calls into a single test, the method calls past the failure point would not execute.

In Tutorial 6-6, you will test the Advisor.MaxCredits method of the RegistrationLib component.

Tutorial 6-6:
Testing the Advisor.MaxCredits method

Earlier in this chapter, we created a component named *RegistrationLib* that contained two classes: Student and Advisor. In this tutorial, you will create unit tests to verify the accuracy of the MaxCredits method in the Advisor class.

One of the realities of the software business is that as soon as an application is published, it becomes eligible for revision and improvement. We will assume that the *MaxCredits* method in the Advisor class must be revised, according to new criteria listed in Table 6-3. Therefore, we know that the existing application will not produce the correct output. In this tutorial, you will devise tests that identify changes that must be made to the MaxCredits method. Notice that many cells in this table are empty. They indicate that the particular property value is not used in the determination of MaxCredits.

Table 6-3 Revised registration criteria, RegistrationLib

Row Number	Academic Status	Year Level	Grade Average	Max Credits
1	Probation			6
2	Warning	LowerDivision	> 2.0	12
3	Warning	LowerDivision	≤ 2.0	6
4	Warning	UpperDivision	> 2.2	10
5	Warning	UpperDivision	≤ 2.2	8
6	Warning	Graduate		7
7	Normal	LowerDivision	> 2.5	16
8	Normal	LowerDivision	≤ 2.5	12
9	Normal	UpperDivision		18
10	Normal	Graduate		14
11	Honors		≥ 3.0	22
12	Honors		< 3.0	16

Tutorial Steps

Step 1: Add a default constructor to the Student class. This constructor will simplify the testing process by letting you create Student objects with only the properties needed for a particular test.

```
Public Sub New()
End Sub
```

Step 2: Next, add a Test Project named *Test RegistrationLib* to the current solution.

Step 3: In the test class, create a test method that tests the first row of Table 6-3, which relates to students on academic probation.

```
1: <TestMethod()> _
2: Public Sub MaxCreditsTest_Probation()
3:   Dim aStudent As New Student
4:   aStudent.Status = AcademicStatus.Probation
5:   Dim expected As Integer = 6
6:   Dim actual As Integer = Advisor.MaxCredits(aStudent)
7:   Assert.AreEqual(expected, actual)
8: End Sub
```

The expected value, 6, is taken from the Max Credits column of Table 6-3.

Step 4: Create the following test method, which tests for a lower division student with *Warning* status and a grade average greater than 2.0:

```
<TestMethod()> _
Public Sub MaxCreditsTest_Warning_LD_1()
  Dim aStudent As New Student
  With aStudent
    .Status = AcademicStatus.Warning
    .Level = YearLevel.LowerDivision
    .GradeAverage = 2.01
  End With
  Dim expected As Integer = 12
  Dim actual As Integer = Advisor.MaxCredits(aStudent)
```

```
    Assert.AreEqual(expected, actual)
End Sub
```

This test is based on row 2 of Table 6-3, so we set three properties for this student. When a test class contains a large number of tests, it is often useful to use a consistent naming scheme for the test methods. One approach is to number them consecutively. Another approach, which we have used, is to chose names that suggest what is being tested (*LD* for lower division students, *Warning* for students on academic warning).

Step 5: Add the following test method, which tests for a lower division student with *Warning* status and a grade average equal to 2.0:

```
<TestMethod()> _
Public Sub MaxCreditsTest_Warning__LD_2()
   Dim aStudent As New Student
   With aStudent
      .Status = AcademicStatus.Warning
      .Level = YearLevel.LowerDivision
      .GradeAverage = 2.0
   End With
   Dim expected As Integer = 6
   Dim actual As Integer = Advisor.MaxCredits(aStudent)
   Assert.AreEqual(expected, actual)
End Sub
```

Step 6: Run all the unit tests. The output, shown in Figure 6-20, shows that two tests passed and one failed.

Figure 6-20 Running the first three MaxCredits tests

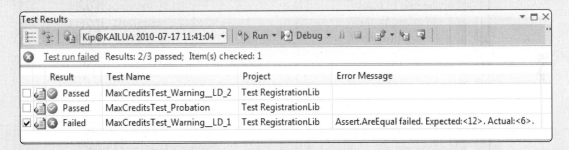

It seems that the *MaxCreditsTest_Warning_LD_1* test failed because it expected MaxCredits to return a value of 12 for a lower division student with a *Warning* status and grade average greater than 2.0. Instead, MaxCredits returned 6. Let's examine the relevant source code lines from the MaxCredits method in the Advisor class.

```
Case AcademicStatus.Warning
   If .Level = YearLevel.LowerDivision Then
      Return 6
```

Clearly, the code does not take the student's grade average into account. So let's revise the code in a way that is consistent with rows 2 and 3 of Table 6-3.

```
Case AcademicStatus.Warning
   If .Level = YearLevel.LowerDivision Then
      If .GradeAverage > 2.0 Then
         Return 12
      Else
         Return 6
      End If
```

Step 7: Run the tests again. They should all pass. Our new code worked, and we did not create errors in any existing code, as far as the tests show.

Step 8: Create the following test method, which tests for an upper division student with a warning status and a grade average greater than 2.2. It tests row 4 of Table 6-3.

```
<TestMethod()> _
Public Sub MaxCreditsTest_Warning__UD_1()
  Dim aStudent As New Student
  With aStudent
    .Status = AcademicStatus.Warning
    .Level = YearLevel.UpperDivision
    .GradeAverage = 2.21
  End With
  Dim expected As Integer = 10
  Dim actual As Integer = Advisor.MaxCredits(aStudent)
  Assert.AreEqual(expected, actual)
End Sub
```

Step 9: Create the following test method, which tests for an upper division student with a warning status and a grade average equal to 2.2. It tests row 5 of Table 6-3.

```
<TestMethod()> _
Public Sub MaxCreditsTest_Warning__UD_2()
  Dim aStudent As New Student
  With aStudent
    .Status = AcademicStatus.Warning
    .Level = YearLevel.UpperDivision
    .GradeAverage = 2.2
  End With
  Dim expected As Integer = 8
  Dim actual As Integer = Advisor.MaxCredits(aStudent)
  Assert.AreEqual(expected, actual)
End Sub
```

Step 10: Run all the tests. The new tests will fail, of course, because the MaxCredits method needs to be revised.

Step 11: Next, you will run the test in debug mode to discover which lines are producing the incorrect result. Set a breakpoint on the following line in the *MaxCreditsTest_Warning__UD_1* method:

```
Dim actual As Integer = Advisor.MaxCredits(aStudent)
```

Step 12: Run the test in debug mode. When the debugger stops at your breakpoint, step into the call to MaxCredits. You should reach the following lines, which show that all upper division students with warning status can take a maximum of 9 credits:

```
ElseIf .Level = YearLevel.UpperDivision Then
  Return 9
```

Step 13: Stop the debugger. Without reading beyond this point, look at rows 4 and 5 in Table 6-3, and decide how you wish to fix this error.

Step 14: Run the tests again. Did they all pass? If not, check the code you inserted against the following code, which distinguishes between students having different grade averages:

```
ElseIf .Level = YearLevel.UpperDivision Then
  If .GradeAverage > 2.2 Then
```

```
            Return 10
        Else
            Return 8
        End If
```

Step 15: Run the tests again, and verify that they all pass.

Summary

At first, it seems like a lot of work to create a different unit test for each set of inputs. It is fairly easy, however, to copy one of these methods to the Windows clipboard, paste the copy, and make minimal changes. Also, remember the essential philosophy of unit testing: *Pay as you go, rather than paying at the end.* In other words, the time you invest in creating unit tests saves you much more time at the end of a project when you would normally be stuck in a recurring cycle of find errors, fixing them, discovering new errors, fixing them, and so on.

At this point, you probably recognize a working pattern, which can apply to one or more tests:

1. Create and run a test.
2. If the test fails, locate and correct the code in the class being tested that caused the test to fail.
3. Run the test again.

We will ask you, in Programming Challenge 5, to create tests for all specifications in Table 6-3, and apply corrections to the MaxCredits method until all the tests pass.

Summary

All too often, programmers create complex applications without creating adequate unit tests. The potential number of errors in their code is so large that even counting them would be difficult. We have all used software that contains defects, and we know how aggravating that can be. In fact, few of us would be happy flying on an airliner whose flight control software contained defects.

Unit tests are not the only tool used in software testing, but they are the easiest to learn. They are also created by the people who know their code the best—the programmers.

Here's a good reason to learn about automated software testing: Many entry-level jobs are given to software testers. You may be fortunate enough to land a position that lets you develop your coding skills, and also learn to use industry-standard software testing tools.

 ## Checkpoint

5. What type of test executes all or part of an application without input from a live user?

6. What type of test executes test methods that run individual segments of an existing application?

7. What is the practice of rerunning all existing tests as soon as you modify an application's source code?

8. What type of testing technique permits the tester to view all of the source code of the class being tested?

9. What type of testing technique deals only with the application's inputs and outputs and does not permit the tester to see any of the application's source code?

6.4 Events

Events provide a signaling system for messages that must be broadcast to whomever is listening. For example, when you click the mouse on a button, the Windows operating system notices the click, creates a Click event, and adds it to an event queue. If an application is listening for events, and if the button was within the application's window, it handles the event.

In fact, Visual Basic applications handle many kinds of events, such as TextChanged, Load, Keypress, and Click. In regard to event handling, the following actions are important:

- A class **raises an event** when it wants to send a signal that something has happened
- Another class **handles an event** when it responds to the event

So far, you have written methods that handle events. Now we will show you how to create classes that raise events. You will learn how to define event types, raise events, and handle these events.

Delegates, Events, and Handlers

A **delegate** is a template that describes the return type and parameter list for a related group of event handler methods. For example, this is the delegate that .NET uses for button Click handlers:

```
Public Delegate Sub EventHandler(sender As Object, e As EventArgs)
```

Once a delegate has been defined, a class can define the types of events that it plans to raise. For example, this is the Click event type declared in the Button class; it is raised when a user clicks a Button control:

```
Public Event Click As EventHandler
```

Once an event type has been declared in the Button class, any class that contains an instance of the Button class can include event handlers. For example, the following is a Button.Click event handler for a button named btnOk; its parameter list conforms to the pattern described by the EventHandler delegate we saw earlier:

```
Private Sub btnOk_Click(ByVal sender As System.Object,
    ByVal e As System.EventArgs) Handles btnOk.Click
End Sub
```

The Handles keyword is important here because it ties the btnOk_Click method to a specific event from the Button class.

WithEvents Qualifier

When an object is declared, you must preface it with a *WithEvents* qualifier in order to permit it to raise events. This is the general format for a class-level variable that raises events:

```
Private WithEvents variableName As Type
```

When you put a Button control on a form, Visual Studio makes it possible for the button to raise events. This, for example, is how a Button control is declared in the form's designer code file:

```
Friend WithEvents btnOk As System.Windows.Forms.Button
```

The *WithEvents* qualifier means that btnOk can raise all events declared in the Button class, including the Click event.

TIP: By default, the designer source files for a program's forms are hidden. To make them appear, click the *Show All Files* button in the toolbar of the Solution Explorer window.

Another mouse event is *MouseHover*. A handler for this event uses the same delegate as the Click event, but it has a different Handles clause:

```
Private Sub btnOk_MouseHover(ByVal sender As Object,
    ByVal e As System.EventArgs) Handles btnOk.MouseHover
End Sub
```

Your own classes can raise events. You can use events to alert objects that an important field in your class has changed value, an operation has completed, or some other important action has taken place. In Tutorial 6-7, you will create a class that raises events.

Tutorial 6-7:
The WeatherStation Events application

In this tutorial, you will examine, test, and modify a short application that demonstrates the raising and handling of events related to a simulated weather station. The *WeatherStation* class simulates software attached to physical weather monitoring equipment. It detects four types of weather conditions: normal, rain, snow, and lightning. The class will raise a specific event for each of these conditions.

The application contains a startup form that tests the WeatherStation class. It declares a WeatherStation object, and it contains event handlers that respond to events raised by the object. Each event handler writes a message to the window, as shown in Figure 6-21. The form uses a Timer control to call the MonitorTheWeather method every 2 seconds.

Figure 6-21 User interface for the *WeatherStation Events* application

Tutorial Steps

Step 1: Open the *Weather Station Events* project from the chapter examples.

Step 2: Run the application, and notice that the weather station display changes. Close the application window.

Step 3: Open the source file for the WeatherStation class.

When adding events to a class, it's considered good style to select names that describe the types of events you want to raise. At runtime, when your class raises these events, other classes can listen and respond. The WeatherStation class defines a delegate named *WeatherEvent* that serves as a template for events that pass no arguments and return nothing.

```
Public Delegate Sub WeatherEvent()
```

Next, the class declares all events it can raise, each having type WeatherEvent.

```
Public Event Normal As WeatherEvent
Public Event Raining As WeatherEvent
Public Event Snowing As WeatherEvent
Public Event Lightning As WeatherEvent
```

Next, a random number generator is declared and is used by the ReadWeatherSensor method to simulate data returned by a physical weather sensor.

```
Private randGenerator As New Random

Private Function ReadWeatherSensor() As Integer
   Return randGenerator.Next(4)
End Function
```

When the ReadWeatherSensor method returns an integer between 0 and 3, the MonitorTheWeather method shown here uses the integer value to raise different events:

```
Public Sub MonitorTheWeather()
   Dim sensorValue As Integer = ReadWeatherSensor()
   Select Case sensorValue
     Case 0
       RaiseEvent Normal()
     Case 1
       RaiseEvent Raining()
     Case 2
       RaiseEvent Snowing()
     Case 3
       RaiseEvent Lightning()
   End Select
End Sub
```

Step 4: Open the source code for the MainForm class. First, it declares a WeatherStation object using the WithEvents keyword so it can generate events.

```
Private WithEvents myStation As New WeatherStation
```

When the user clicks the *Start* button, the Timer control is enabled and begins to generate a Tick event every 2 seconds:

```
Private Sub btnStart_Click() Handles btnStart.Click
   Timer1.Enabled = True
End Sub
```

Each time the Timer control generates a Tick event, MonitorTheWeather is called in the WeatherStation class:

```
Private Sub Timer1_Tick() Handles Timer1.Tick
   myStation.MonitorTheWeather()
End Sub
```

The next four methods handle events raised by the WeatherStation object. Each event is raised by the MonitorTheWeather method.

```
Private Sub myStation_Normal() Handles myStation.Normal
   lblEventDetected.Text = "The weather is normal"
End Sub

Private Sub myStation_Lightning() Handles myStation.Lightning
   lblEventDetected.Text = "A Lightning storm is in progress"
End Sub

Private Sub myStation_Raining() Handles myStation.Raining
   lblEventDetected.Text = "Rainfall has been detected"
End Sub

Private Sub myStation_Snowing() Handles myStation.Snowing
   lblEventDetected.Text = "It has begun to snow"
End Sub
```

> **Step 5:** (Optional) Add a new event named *Tornado* to the WeatherStation class and make the necessary changes so Tornado events can be raised and handled by the application. When you are done, run and test the application.

Summary

Events and event handlers are powerful tools that can process events that happen in a more-or-less unpredictable way. As we have seen, applications sometimes need to respond to input from a physical sensor. In other applications, your code might initiate an operation, such as playing a sound file, not knowing how long it will take to finish. If your application needs to know when the sound has finished playing, the system can raise an event. The .NET controls in the toolbox raise a wide variety of events that signal actions such as a mouse click, key press, and form load. Being able to raise events in your code gives you the same power as the .NET controls.

 Checkpoint

10. When a class wants to signal that some event type action has taken place, it _____ an event

11. A template that describes the return type and parameter list for a class of event handler methods is a(n) _____.

12. When an object is declared, you must preface it with a(n) _____ qualifier to permit the object to raise events.

13. What events are raised by the *Weather Station Events* application in Tutorial 6-7?

 ## 6.5 Inheritance

In object-oriented programming, **inheritance** refers to a parent-child relationship between two classes. It enables classes to build on properties, methods, and events in existing classes. Some examples of classes that exhibit this relationship suggest that the second name is a more specific type than the first name.

```
Person — Student
Account - CheckingAccount
Message — EmailMessage
Vehicle — Automobile
```

The **Inherits keyword** in Visual Basic identifies an inheritance relationship between the class being defined (called the **derived class**) and another class (called the **base class**). Figure 6-22 shows how any number of derived classes can inherit from the same base class. The reverse, by the way, is not true—a derived class cannot inherit from more than one base class.

 NOTE: Other programming languages (such as Java) refer to a base class as a *superclass* and a derived class as a *subclass*.

Figure 6-22 One or more derived classes inherit from a base class

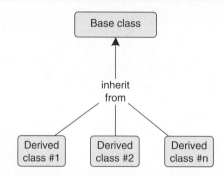

This is the basic syntax of declaring a derived class in Visual Basic:

```
Class derivedClass
    Inherits baseClass
```

A class that defines a Windows Form, for example, inherits from the Form class in the System.Windows.Forms namespace:

```
Public Class MainForm
    Inherits System.Windows.Forms.Form
```

Accessing Members

Unless members of a base class are declared *Private*, they are accessible to methods in any classes derived from the base class. This concept is described in Figure 6-23, in which the base class makes some of its members visible to the derived classes. By members, we mean variables, properties, methods, events, and even types such as enumerated types, and structures or classes declared inside the base class.

Figure 6-23 Accessing base class members

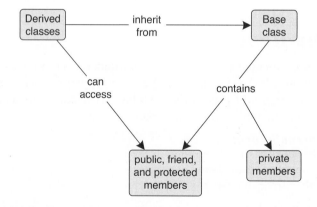

Access Modifiers

Before starting to create derived classes, let's review the various member access modifiers. Table 6-4 lists all access modifiers from most permissive (Public) to least permissive (Private). If no access modifier is used, methods and properties are Public. If a field is declared using Dim, it is automatically Private.

```
Class Demo
    Dim mCount As Integer              'Private
    Property Count As Integer...       'Public
    Sub Print()...                     'Public
    Class Inner                        'Public
```

```
    ...
    End Class
End Class
```

Table 6-4 Access modifiers

Modifier	Description
Public	No restrictions on access to the member.
Protected Friend	Union of Protected and Friend access.
Friend	Accessible to classes located within the same assembly (compiled unit) as the declared member.
Protected	Accessible from within the declaring class and classes that inherit from the current class.
Private	Accessible only from within the declaring class.

Creating a Derived Class

A derived class definition must include the **Inherits keyword.** The following indicates that the SalariedEmployee class inherits from the Employee class:

```
Class SalariedEmployee
    Inherits Employee
```

All classes implicitly inherit from the Object class, so it is not necessary to use the Inherits keyword to reference the Object class.

Heroes and Villains Example

Let's create a set of classes representing characters in a computerized role-playing game. We can look for characteristics identifying the following types of characters: Hero, Villain, and Wizard. This will be called the *Heroes* application, with outlines of classes shown in the following code listing:

```
Class Person

    Public Property Name As String
End Class

Class Hero
    Inherits Person

    Public Property Ability As String
End Class

Class Villain
    Inherits Person

    Public Property BadDeeds As ArrayList()
End Class

Class Wizard
    Inherits Person

    Public Property Specialty As String
End Class
```

A diagram of the class relationships is shown in Figure 6-24. It uses arrows pointing from derived classes toward Person, the common base class. Although Object is the implicit base class of Person, it is usually not shown in diagrams such as this one.

Figure 6-24 Hero class hierarchy

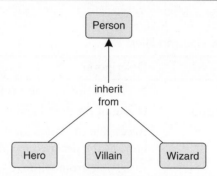

Hero, Villain, and Wizard objects implicitly contain the Name field declared in Person, as well as fields declared in their own classes. The following code is from a test program that illustrates the additive nature of inheritance. A Hero has a name and ability.

```
Dim H As New Hero
H.Name = "Superman"
H.Ability = "Invincible"
```

A Villain has a name, along with a list of bad deeds.

```
Dim V As New Villain
V.Name = "Evil Witch"
V.BadDeeds.Add("Casts spells")
V.BadDeeds.Add("Turns princes into frogs")
```

A Wizard has a name and a specialty.

```
Dim W As New Wizard
W.Name = "Merlin"
W.Specialty = "Wisdom"
```

Inheritance with Constructors

When a derived object is constructed, its base class constructors execute before the object's own constructor executes. When a Hero is constructed, for example, the compiler automatically calls the default constructor for Person. If the Person class has a parameterized constructor, the first statement inside Hero's constructor must explicitly call the Person class constructor. In the following example, the *MyBase.New* statement passes the name parameter to the Person class constructor:

```
Class Person
   Sub New(ByVal pName As String)
     Name = pName
   End Sub

   Public Property Name As String
End Class

Class Hero
   Inherits Person

   Sub New(ByVal pName As String, ByVal pAbility As String)
     MyBase.New(pName)
     Ability = pAbility
   End Sub

   Public Property Ability As String
End Class
```

Inherited Properties and Methods

In the same way that fields are inherited, properties and methods are also inherited by derived classes. The following statements show that a Hero can access any public member of the Person class:

```
Dim H As New Hero("Batman", "Speed")
lblOutput.Text = H.Name
```

But a Person object cannot access a public member of the Hero class.

```
Dim P As New Person("Joe")
lblOutput.Text = P.Ability        ' Error!
```

Assigning Object References

Object references can always be assigned upward in the inheritance hierarchy from a derived type to a base type. This is called an **upward cast**.

```
Dim P As Person
Dim H As New Hero("Aquaman", "Swims")
P = H
```

The compiler will not let you assign a base type directly to a derived type.

```
Dim P As New Person("Joe")
Dim H As Hero
H = P                    'error
```

If such an assignment were permitted, a programmer might be tempted to reference a member of Hero using an object that was, after all, just a Person. It is possible to satisfy the compiler using a **downward cast**, accomplished by calling CType, as follows:

```
Dim P As New Person("Joe")
Dim Z As Hero = CType(P, Hero)
```

The Common Language Runtime throws an exception if it discovers P holds a reference to a Person, not a Hero.

Downward casts are legitimate and useful in certain situations when you know a variable of a base type holds a reference to a derived type. The following example uses a valid cast:

```
Dim P As Person = New Hero("Aquaman", "Swims")
 .
 .
MessageBox.Show(CType(P, Hero).Ability)    'OK
```

To be on the safe side, we recommend that you surround downward casts with a Try-Catch block.

Overriding and Overloading

The terms *overriding* and *overloading* can easily be confused with each other.

- To **override a method** is to replace a base class method with a derived class method having the same signature. Properties can also be overridden.
- To **overload a method** is to create a new method having the same name as an existing method in the same class or a base class. The new method must have a different parameter list.

Table 6-5 lists the modifiers that relate to overriding methods and properties. A method or property must be declared Overridable before it can be overridden in a derived class. A method or property that overrides another method must be declared with the **Overrides keyword**.

Table 6-5 Modifiers related to method overriding

Modifier	Description
Overridable	Property or method *can* be overridden in a class derived from the current class.
Overrides	Overrides an existing property or method in a base class.
NotOverridable	Property or method *cannot* be overridden (default).
MustOverride	Property or method *must* be overridden in a class derived from the current class. (Only a prototype is used in the declaration.)

Tutorial 6-8:
Student Inheritance application

In this tutorial, you will examine a simple application that creates a collection of both undergraduate and graduate students. There will be a Student class (for undergraduates) and a GradStudent class. Figure 6-25 shows the startup form after the user clicked the *Create Undergrad Students* button. Figure 6-26 shows the same form after the user clicked the *Create Grad Students* button.

Figure 6-25 Displaying undergraduate students

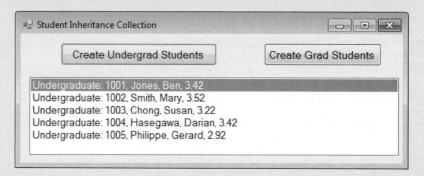

Figure 6-26 Displaying graduate students

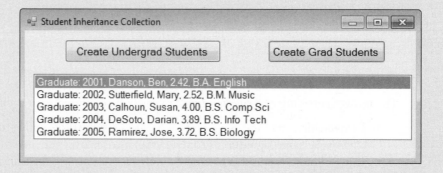

Strongly Typed Collections

Strongly typed collections are specific about the type of objects you can insert. If you declare a List(Of String), you cannot insert Students, Accounts, Integers, or any other type of objects into the list. But they do allow objects related by inheritance to be inserted in the same collection, with one restriction: The collection type must identify the base class. Therefore, the following declaration would let you insert both Student and GradStudent objects in the *allStudents* list:

```
Private allStudents As New List(Of Student)
```

On the other hand, the following declaration would permit you to insert only Grad-Student objects in *gradList*:

```
Private gradList As New List(Of GradStudent)
```

Now you are ready to examine the code in the tutorial's sample program.

Tutorial Steps

Step 1:   Open the *Student Inheritance* project from the chapter examples folder.

Step 2:   Examine the code in the Student.vb file. First, a public enumerated type defines the types of status a student might have.

```
Public Enum StatusType
    Unknown
    Undergraduate
    Graduate
End Enum
```

The Student class appears next, containing ID, Name, Gpa, and Status properties.

```
Public Class Student
    Public Property ID As String
    Public Property Name As String
    Public Property Gpa As Double
    Public Property Status As StatusType

    Private ReadOnly StatusName As String() =
        {"Unknown", "Undergraduate", "Graduate"}

    Public Sub New(ByVal pID As String,
      ByVal pName As String, ByVal pGpa As Double,
      ByVal pStatus As StatusType)

      ID = pID
      Name = pName
      Gpa = pGpa
      Status = pStatus
    End Sub

    Public Overrides Function ToString() As String
      Return StatusName(Status) & ": " & ID & ", " _
        & Name & ", " & Gpa.ToString("n")
    End Function
End Class
```

GradStudent Class

Step 3:   View the *GradStudent* class (GradStudent.vb file), which inherits from the Student class. Notice that this class contains one new property, PreviousDegree.

```
Public Class GradStudent
    Inherits Student
```

```
        Public Property PreviousDegree As String

        Public Sub New(ByVal pID As String,
          ByVal pName As String, ByVal pGpa As Double,
          ByVal pStatus As StatusType,
          ByVal pPreviousDegree As String)

          MyBase.New(pID, pName, pGpa, StatusType.Graduate)
          PreviousDegree = pPreviousDegree
        End Sub

        Public Overrides Function ToString() As String
          Return MyBase.ToString() & ", " & PreviousDegree
        End Function
    End Class
```

The GradStudent constructor has five parameters, four of which are passed to
the Student class constructor by calling *MyBase.New*. Notice that the
ToString method in this class overrides the ToString method in the Student
class. It doesn't have to duplicate the existing code, however, because it calls
MyBase.ToString before appending the value of PreviousDegree.

MainForm Class

Step 4: Open the MainForm.vb class file. It declares a List(Of Student) object at the
class level.

```
Public Class MainForm
    Private allStudents As New List(Of Student)
```

The Click handler for undergraduate students creates students and adds them
to the List. Then it connects the List to the ListBox.

```
Private Sub btnStudents_Click() Handles btnStudents.Click
    allStudents.Add(New Student("1001", "Jones, Ben", 3.42,
      StatusType.Undergraduate))
    allStudents.Add(New Student("1002", "Smith, Mary", 3.52,
      StatusType.Undergraduate))
    allStudents.Add(New Student("1003", "Chong, Susan", 3.22,
      StatusType.Undergraduate))
    allStudents.Add(New Student("1004", "Hasegawa, Darian", 3.42,
      StatusType.Undergraduate))
    allStudents.Add(New Student("1005", "Philippe, Gerard", 2.92,
      StatusType.Undergraduate))
    lstBox.DataSource = Nothing
    lstBox.DataSource = allStudents
End Sub
```

Notice how, when modifying the DataSource of a ListBox, you must first set it
to Nothing and then assign it your array or collection. Otherwise, the listbox
contents do not change.

Next is the Click handler for creating graduate students. It creates GradStudent
objects, adds them to the List, and displays the list in the ListBox. Each object
has one additional parameter: the student's previous degree.

```
Private Sub btnGradStudents_Click() Handles btnGradStudents.Click
    allStudents.Add(New GradStudent("2001", "Danson, Ben", 2.42,
      StatusType.Graduate, "B.A. English"))
    allStudents.Add(New GradStudent("2002", "Sutterfield, Mary",
      2.52,
```

```
        StatusType.Graduate, "B.M. Music"))
    allStudents.Add(New GradStudent("2003", "Calhoun, Susan", 4.0,
        StatusType.Graduate, "B.S. Comp Sci"))
    allStudents.Add(New GradStudent("2004", "DeSoto,
        Darian", 3.89,
        StatusType.Graduate, "B.S. Info Tech"))
    allStudents.Add(New GradStudent("2005", "Ramirez,
        Jose", 3.72,
        StatusType.Graduate, "B.S. Biology"))
    lstBox.DataSource = Nothing
    lstBox.DataSource = allStudents
  End Sub
End Class
```

Step 5:   Run the application and click on both buttons. The list is not cleared, so each time you click, a list of students will be appended to the existing list.

Summary

In actual college databases, the enrollment records of graduate and undergraduate students exhibit numerous differences. By having separate classes, you can specialize each according to an application's needs. For example, undergraduate students might have an activity fee that is not required for graduate students. Or, graduate students might have to track the dates of their candidacy and qualifying exams. These differences can be explored in Programming Challenge 6.

Inheriting common members from base classes helps to reduce the amount of duplicate code you must write. Inheritance improves consistency of member names and common operations throughout a class hierarchy. Before inheritance was introduced into programming languages, programmers had to duplicate all variables, methods, and other members in each class.

Checkpoint

14. Can more than one class inherit from a single base class?

15. Are base class methods accessible from a derived class?

16. Which keyword identifies a class as being derived from another class?

17. To _____ a method is to replace a base class method with a derived class method having the same signature.

Summary

6.1 Structures

- A structure defines a container into which you can place variables, properties, methods, and events. A structure might be thought of as a lightweight type of class.
- Because a structure occupies memory "in place," much like an integer or Boolean, it is known as a value type.
- When a structure parameter is declared with the ByVal qualifier, a copy of the structure is passed to the method at runtime.

- The assignment operator (=) copies the contents of a structure variable.
- If you compare two structure variables with the Equals method, they are compared using the values of their fields.

6.2 Components

- A component (also known as a class library) is a collection of related classes that have been compiled and stored so that they are easily available to other applications.
- The primary advantage to using a component is that it makes it easier to reuse existing code.
- Components fall into two general classes: (1) user interface components, such as Visual Basic controls, and (2) code components, such as those found in the middle tier or data tier.
- A component is compiled by Visual Studio into a DLL file (filename with .dll extension). Also known as a *dynamic link library*, this file could be used by any .NET application.

6.3 Unit Testing

- Software engineers have found that testing is very effective when it becomes an integral part of the development process.
- The traditional approach to testing and debugging has been to wait until the end of a project.
- The continuous software testing approach is to run tests on all newly written code during the development of a project.
- Regression testing is the running of a set of tests on existing code.
- An automated test is a program that executes all or part of an application without input from a live user.
- A unit test is an automated test that executes and tests a single unit of code (such as a method) in an existing application. It falls under the category of white box testing.
- When a unit test fails, it stops executing sequentially and returns immediately.
- Unit tests do not run any particular sequence. Each unit test should be independent of all other unit tests.
- Unit tests are typically executed by a utility program known as a *test engine*. As it executes each test method, it reports the success or failure of each test in a visual display.
- The *Microsoft.VisualStudio.TestTools.UnitTesting* namespace provides the .NET support for unit testing.

6.4 Events

- A method raises an event when it wants to send a signal that something has happened.
- Another method handles an event when it responds to the event.
- A delegate is a template or pattern that is used to classify event handlers.

6.5 Inheritance

- Inheritance in object-oriented programming means the ability of classes to specialize the properties, methods, and events of base classes.
- Inheriting common members from base classes helps to reduce the amount of duplicate code in an object-oriented program or code library. Inheritance improves the consistency of member names and common operations throughout a class hierarchy.
- When a derived object is constructed, its superclass constructors must execute before the object's own constructor executes.
- To override a member is to replace a base class member with a derived class member having the same name and signature.
- To overload a method is to create a new method having the same name as an existing method in the same class or a base class, but with a different signature.

Key Terms

Assert.AreEqual Method

Assert.AreNotEqual Method

Assert class

assertion

attribute name

automated test

base class

black box testing

class library

continuous software testing

delegate

component

derived class

downward cast

handle an event

inheritance

Inherits keyword

.NET assembly

overload a method

override a method

Overrides keyword

raise an event

regression testing

test engine

test project

unit test

upward cast

white box testing

Review Questions

True or False

Indicate whether each of the following statements is true or false.

1. When declared using ByVal, structure parameters behave just like integer parameters.

2. The assignment operator (=) cannot be used to copy a structure unless the operator is overloaded inside the class.

3. If you compare two structures using the Equals method, they are compared according to the values of their fields.

4. You can compare two structures using the = operator, even if you do not overload this operator in your structure definition.

5. A Visual Studio project can create a reference to a DLL file.

6. A reference to another project must always be within the same solution container.

7. Regression testing occurs only when you begin a new project and need to test code that you have imported from other projects.

8. Automated testing is used only when testing the user interface of an application.

9. A unit test is always an automated test.

10. White box testing implies that the tester has full access to the application's source code.

11. Unit tests can be written as black box tests.

12. Unit tests are supported by classes in the *Microsoft.UnitTesting namespace*.

13. In Visual Studio, it is possible to run a unit test in debug mode, and set breakpoints within the test code.

14. The Assert.AreEqual method has two versions: one for integers, the other for floating-point values.

15. When comparing floating-point numbers with Assert.AreEqual, you must supply a third parameter that indicates the size of the difference between the first two values.

16. When Assert.AreEqual fails, execution continues at the next line in the test method.

17. As a general rule, you should call Assert only once within a single test method.

18. Events provide a signaling system for messages that must be broadcast to whomever is listening.

19. The class that handles an event is usually the same class that raises the event.

20. When class A inherits from class B, we say that B is the *derived* class.

21. A *superclass* is the same thing as a derived class.

22. One class can inherit from multiple classes.

23. When a derived object is constructed, its base class constructors execute after the object's own constructor executes.

24. Although fields (variables) are inherited, properties and methods are not inherited by derived classes.

25. To overload a method is to replace a base class method with a derived class method having the same signature.

Short Answer

1. In terms of memory usage, how is a structure different from a class?

2. Under what circumstance would you need use the New operator when declaring a structure?

3. What is a *component*?

4. What is the primary advantage to using a component?

5. Which type of Visual Studio project is used when creating a component?

6. How do you add a component reference to a project in Visual Studio?

7. What main difficulty does a programmer face when the test/debug cycle is at the end of a project?

8. Define *continuous software testing*.

9. Define *regression testing*.

10. Define *unit test*.

11. How is a test engine used in Visual Studio?

12. Which .NET namespace supports unit testing?

13. Which .NET attribute identifies a class as one that contains unit tests?

14. Besides AreEqual, what other Assert class methods are listed in this chapter?

15. What does it mean for a class to raise an event?

16. What purpose does a delegate serve, in terms of class events?

17. When an object is declared, which qualifier must be used if the object will be permitted to raise events?

18. Define inheritance in terms of object-oriented programming.

19. How is the Protected access modifier different from Private?

20. If the Student class inherits from the Person class, explain how a downward cast would work.

21. Explain the term *overloading a method*.

Algorithm Workbench

1. Assuming that the Point structure has a constructor that receives two integer parameters (X, Y), write a statement that declares and initializes an array of two Points.

2. Create a class named File that contains the following properties: ID (string), Location (String), CreationDate (DateTime). Then derive a class named Document that has an additional property named Owner (String). Create constructors for both classes that use parameters to initialize all properties.

3. Show how to declare a test method, using the proper unit testing attributes for .NET.

Programming Challenges

1. **FlightSchedulerLib Component**

   Use the *Calculating Flight Times* exercise (Programming Challenge 5 in Chapter 2) as a starting point for this exercise. Create a component (class library) named *FlightSchedulerLib*. In this library, define a class named *Airport* that contains two properties: an airport code (such as *MIA* or *LAX*) and a UTC offset. (A UTC offset is a signed integer that represents the difference between the airport's local time zone and the Universal Coordinated Time zone.)

   Create a class named *Flight* that contains properties that hold a departure airport (an Airport object), arrival airport (an Airport object), the flight's departure date and time, and the flight's duration (in hours). The class must contain a method named *GetArrival* that returns the date and time of the flight's arrival, expressed in the local time zone of the arrival airport. This is its declaration:

   ```
   Public Function GetArrival() As DateTime
   ```

   Create a text file containing the following information. The Flight class should read this text file and save the information in variables inside the Flight class.

   ```
   MIA JFK HNL LAX DFW
   -5 -5 -10 -8 -6
   0 3 12 8 2.5
   3 0 14 8.5 3.5
   12 12 0 4.5 8.5
   8 8.5 4.5 0 3.5
   2.5 3.5 8.5 3.5 0
   ```

   The first line of the file contains the five airport codes; the second line contains the UTC offset of each airport; the next five rows contain a two-dimensional array of flight durations. For example, the duration of a flight from MIA to LAX is 8 hours. The durations of all flights leaving MIA are in the first row of the array. The flight duration from MIA to LAX is given in column 3 of the same row. (Column numbers start at 0.) Similarly, the duration of a flight from HNL to MIA is 12 hours (row 2, column 0).

   Add a Windows Forms project named *Flight Scheduler UI* to the same Visual Studio solution. Using the same interface shown in Programming Challenge 5 in Chapter 2, let the user select the departure and arrival airports and enter the departure date and time. When the user clicks a button, call the GetArrival method and display the flight duration and flight arrival time at the destination airport.

2. **Testing the FlightSchedulerLib Component**

   Use Programming Challenge 1 as a starting point for this application. Create a test project that tests the GetArrival method of the Flight class in the FlightSchedulerLib component. Create five unit tests that validate flights between different sets of airports. Be sure to include flights that begin before midnight and arrive the following day.

3. **GetSmallest Method**

   Add a method named *GetSmallest* to the IntArray class from Tutorial 6-5. The method should return the smallest element in an array of integers. Create a complete set of unit tests that test your method thoroughly. Create a test list in the Test Editor window for your new tests.

4. **GetMedian Method**

   Add a method named *GetMedian* to the IntArray class from Tutorial 6-5. The method should return a Double that contains the median value of a set of integers. Create a complete set of unit tests that test your method thoroughly. Create a test list in the Test Editor window for your new tests.

5. **RegistrationLib Changes**

   Once again, the college registrar has again changed the rules for determining the maximum credits a student can take. Let the RegistrationLib and Test RegistrationLib projects from Tutorial 6-6 be the starting point for this challenge. Using Table 6-6, modify all unit tests and corresponding code in MaxCredits to conform to the new criteria.

   Table 6-6 Second revision of the registration criteria in RegistrationLib

Academic Status	Year Level	Grade Average	Max Credits
Probation	LowerDivision		6
Probation	UpperDivision		3
Warning	LowerDivision	> 2.2	12
Warning	LowerDivision	≤ 2.2	6
Warning	UpperDivision	> 2.4	10
Warning	UpperDivision	≤ 2.4	8
	Graduate	< 3.0	6
	Graduate	≥ 3.0	12
Normal	LowerDivision	> 2.5	16
Normal	LowerDivision	≤ 2.5	12
Normal	UpperDivision		18
Honors		≥ 3.0	22
Honors		< 3.0	16

6. **Undergraduate and Graduate Students**

   Tutorial 6-8 presented classes named *Student* and *GradStudent*. In this programming challenge, you will build on that application. Create another class named *AuditStudent* that inherits from Student. Create a suitable constructor. Add a *CreditsEnrolled* property to the Student class, of type Double. Add a *TuitionAmount* property, of type Decimal.

   Audit students and undergraduate students pay the same tuition rate per credit hour. Graduate students pay a different rate. The two tuition rates should be initialized by assigning values to shared properties in the two classes. The TuitionAmount property calculates the amount due by multiplying the CreditsEnrolled by TuitionAmount. However, in the AuditStudent class, add an additional $100 to the TuitionAmount value. For graduate students, the total tuition amount is the same for nine credits as it is for any number of credits higher than that.

   Create a user input form that lets the user select a student by name from a list, input the number of credits enrolled, and view the student's tuition amount.

7. **Shapes Inheritance**

In this programming challenge, you will create three classes: Shape, Rectangle, and Circle. Shape is a base class, and Rectangle and Circle are derived classes. You will use the existing *Point* structure already defined in .NET, which has two properties named X and Y.

The Shape class has a single property named *Name*, a constructor with a Name parameter, and a MustOverride method named *GetArea* that returns a Double. It has a ToString method that returns the name of the shape.

The Rectangle class has two private members of type Point that represent the upper left and lower right corners of a rectangle. It has a constructor that initializes the two corner points of the rectangle. It overrides the GetArea method, which calculates the rectangle area as the length times width. It has a ToString method that displays the two point values.

The Circle class has two private members: the center of the circle, which is a Point object, and the radius of the circle, which is a Double. It has a constructor that initializes the center and radius values. It overrides the GetArea method by computing the area as *Math.PI* times the radius squared. It has a ToString method that displays the center point and the radius.

In the application's startup form, create Rectangle and a Circle. Display the contents of both shapes, as well as their calculated areas, rounded to two decimal places. A sample is shown in Figure 6-27.

Figure 6-27 Displaying shapes and their areas

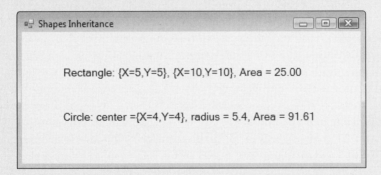

8. **Account Transactions**

Create a set of classes that permit you to keep track of savings accounts and transactions.

- Define an Enum type named *TransactionType* with two values: Deposit, Withdrawal.
- Create a class named *Transaction* with three properties: a transaction date, the type of transaction (using TransactionType), and the transaction amount. For example, a Transaction object could hold the values *#05/15/2011#, TransactionType.Deposit,* and *500.00.*
- The Transaction class must contain a constructor that initializes all property values.
- Create a class named *Account* with three properties: ID (String), Owner (String), and CashBalance (Double). For example, an Account object could hold the values *000123, Baker, James,* and *2140.55.*
- The Account class must contain a constructor that initializes all property values, a ToString method that displays all property values, and an Equals method that compares account ID numbers.

- Create a class named *TransactionHistory* that contains a single property named *Items*, whose type is Dictionary(Of Date, Transaction).
- Create a class named *SavingsAccount*, with two properties: InterestRate (Double), and TransHistory (a TransactionHistory object). This class inherits from the Account class.

Startup Form

- In the startup form, use a SplitContainer to divide the form in half. Insert a ListBox control in each panel. A sample is shown in Figure 6-28.
- In the Form_Load event handler, create two SavingsAccount objects. Add them to a *List(Of SavingsAccount)* object. For each account, create three different transactions and add them to the account transaction history.
- Display the account IDs, owner names and balances in the left-hand ListBox control. When the user selects an account, display the account transaction history in the right-hand ListBox control.

Figure 6-28 Displaying Account Transaction History

9. **Weather Station Summary**

   The purpose of this programming challenge is to show how events raised by a class can be broadcast to more than one class. Use the *Weather Station Events* application from Tutorial 6-7 as a starting point for this programming challenge. Create a *Summary* form, as shown in Figure 6-29, that keeps a running count of each type of event raised by the WeatherStation class. The Summary form's class contains an event handler for each type of event raised by the WeatherStation class. Just before showing the Summary form, the main form can pass to it a reference to the same WeatherStation object declared at the top of the main form. Use the Show (not ShowDialog) method to display the Summary form. As events appear on the main form, the summary form counts the number of each type of event that has been raised so far.

Figure 6-29 Weather Station Summary form and main form

CHAPTER 7 — LINQ to SQL

TOPICS

This chapter introduces LINQ for SQL, a powerful tool for querying and updating database data. LINQ for SQL offers the opportunity to use object-oriented programming (OOP) techniques to view and update databases. Essentially, you work with databases in the same way that you did with in-memory collections in Chapter 3. You will learn how to create entity classes that model database tables. You will create selection queries that join multiple entity classes, using common linking properties. You will learn how to insert, update, and delete table entries.

7.1 Using LINQ to Select Data

Language Integrated Query (LINQ) lets you work with objects and properties at the middle-tier level by writing code that performs queries on data collections. A variant of LINQ, named **LINQ to SQL**, translates object-oriented queries into SQL database syntax. LINQ lets you work with objects that represent database tables by providing a conversion process from one format to another. This conversion process is known as **database entity mapping**.

LINQ is implemented only by Microsoft .NET languages, so it is not found in Java or C++. Fortunately, similar tools for database entity mapping exist for these other languages. We think that once you learn how LINQ works in .NET, you will be able to learn to work with tools in other languages.

LINQ to SQL Object Model

When you use LINQ to SQL, you do not issue commands directly to a database. Instead, you use custom classes that represent database tables and the relationships between the tables. When you modify properties and call methods in the classes, LINQ translates your property and method calls into SQL commands. The following table lists some basic equivalencies between LINQ's object model and the relational data model used in databases.

LINQ to SQL	Relational Database
Entity class	Table
Entity property	Table column
Association	Relationship (foreign key)
Entity method	Stored procedure or function

An **entity class** is a class that contains properties that match the structure of a specific database table. An **entity property** is a member of an entity class that gets and sets the value of a class-level variable. It also raises events that signal the application before and after the property is modified. An **association** in an entity class is a reference to another class that corresponds to a relationship between two database tables. An **entity method** in an entity class contains code that executes a database-stored procedure or function.

The following is a declaration of an entity class. Every entity class must begin with a **table attribute**:

```
<Table(Name:="Members")> _
Public Class Member
  '...
End Class
```

In an entity class, you identify properties that represent database columns, using a **column attribute**:

```
<Table(Name:="Members")> _
Public Class Member
  <Column(IsPrimaryKey:=True)> _
  Public MemberId As String
    ' ...
  <Column()> _
  Public LastName As String
End Class
```

Only entity class members that are assigned a column attribute are saved when LINQ updates the underlying database. Column attributes have an optional Boolean property named *IsPrimaryKey*.

> **TIP:** Table attributes are defined by the .NET TableAttribute class, and column attributes are defined by the ColumnAttribute class. Both classes belong to the *System.Data.Linq.Mapping* namespace.

Connecting to a Database

To connect to a database, you need to create a **DataContext object**. This object provides methods that connect to the database, retrieve data, and submit updates to the database. The DataContext translates your requests for objects into SQL database queries. Also, it creates objects that return the results of SQL queries. The DataContext constructor is overloaded with different parameter lists, but the most common constructor receives a connection string, as follows:

```
Dim db As New DataContext(My.Settings.karateConnectionString)
```

Then you can call the DataContext's *GetTable* method to get a table containing the database table data. In the following example, one must already have defined an entity class named *Member*.

```
Dim Members As Table(Of Member) = db.GetTable(Of Member)()
```

We recommend, however, that you let Visual Studio create a strongly typed DataContext class that matches the database. In other words, Visual Studio creates a separate entity class for each database table, a specific DataContext class, and methods that use the entity classes.

Object Relational Designer

The **Object Relational Designer (O/R Designer)** is a Visual Studio design tool that lets you create LINQ to SQL entity classes. You also use it to design associations between the classes. To put it another way, the designer creates a system of objects that directly correspond to the objects in a database. Finally, the designer creates a strongly typed DataContext that is used to send and receive data between the entity classes and the database.

The following steps are required to create entity classes and a DataContext from an existing database:

1. In the Server Explorer window, add a connection to the database or database file.
2. Add a *LINQ to SQL Classes* item to your project, choosing a name that suggests the database, such as *KarateClasses.dbml*.
3. Drag one or more database tables from the Server Explorer window into the O/R Designer window. After doing this, you can see each table expressed as a class, as in the sample shown in Figure 7-1.

Pluralization: Entity class names in the O/R Designer are expressed as singular (by dropping the final *-s*) compared to the database table names. For example, *Member* is the entity class that represents one row of the *Members* table from the database. This naming approach is called *pluralization*, and it may be disabled from the Tools menu by selecting *Options, Database Tools, O/R Designer*, and *Pluralization of names*.

The arrows appearing between the classes are called *associations*. Any existing relationships between the database tables are expressed as associations in the O/R Designer.

Figure 7-1 Karate database entity classes in the O/R Designer

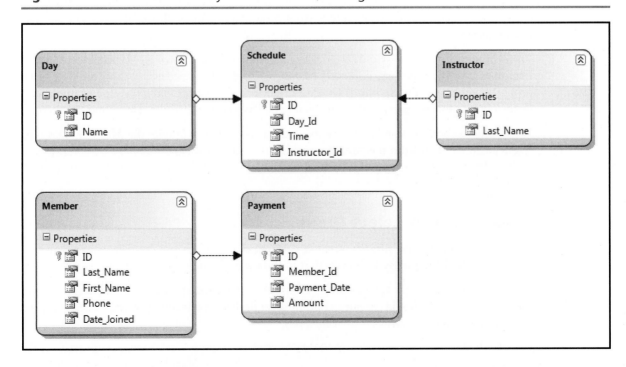

Creating an Association

If you want to create an association manually in the O/R Designer, right-click the name of the parent class, select *Add*, then select *Association*. Figure 7-2 shows an association being defined that links the Day.ID member to the Schedule.Day_Id member.

> **TIP:** When creating an association, the connecting members must be the same data type. In fact, their nullable properties must match, too. If one member is nullable, the other must be, too.

Figure 7-2 Creating an association between the Day and Schedule entity classes

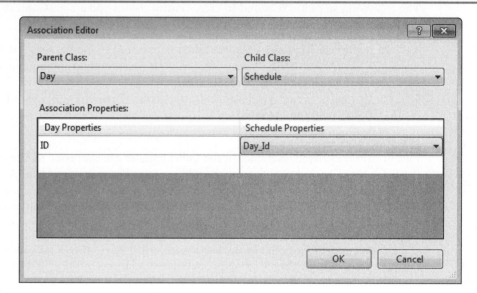

Table Property Names and Entity Class Names

It is helpful to understand how Visual Studio chooses names for table properties and entity classes when it creates a DataContext from a database. You will use these names in your LINQ queries.

Visual Studio chooses DataContext property names that identify strongly typed Table objects. Examples of table types are *Table(Of Member)*, *Table(Of Payment)*, and so on. The table property names are always plural (ending in -*s*). For the Karate database, for example, the DataContext table property names are Members, Payments, Schedules, Days, and Instructors.

Visual Studio chooses singular names for entity classes. For example, the *Member* class represents a single item from the Members table in the database, the *Payment* class represents an item from the Payments table in the database, and the *Schedule* class represents an item from the Schedule table in the database.

Constructing a Select Query

Assuming that you have already created a DataContext class for your database, you can begin to create LINQ to SQL queries that pull data from the database.

First, you must declare a DataContext object. Assuming that you have created one for the Karate database, it should already contain an initialized connection string. Therefore, we can call the default constructor as follows:

```
Dim db As New KarateClassesDataContext
```

Next, you write a query that selects each payment from the Payments table:

```
Dim query = From aPayment In db.Payments
    Select aPayment
```

This query is nearly identical to the LINQ queries we demonstrated in Chapter 3. At that time, the source of the data would have been a List(Of Payment) object. In the current context, *db.Payments* is a Table(Of Payment), which is almost the same. The difference is that the Table(Of Payment) class has a connection to the database.

You can assign the LINQ query directly to a DataGridView control's DataSource property:

```
dgvPayments.DataSource = query
```

or to a BindingSource object:

```
KarateBindingSource.DataSource = query
```

or you can iterate over the query, perhaps to accumulate the payments:

```
Dim total As Double = 0
For Each aPayment In query
    total += aPayment.Amount
Next
```

If you were interested in finding the average payment amount, you could rewrite the query to return only the payment amounts.

```
Dim query = From aPayment In db.Payments
    Select aPayment.Amount
```

Then a simple function call would return the average payment amount.

```
Dim avg As Double = query.Average()
```

Formatting a DataGridView Control

The primary disadvantage to using runtime data binding with a DataGridView control is that you cannot use format the grid columns in design mode. Although it is possible to format grid columns at runtime, it is not easy to do. But if you create an **Object data source** in Visual Studio, you can bind it to the grid and edit the grid in design mode. Here's how to create an Object data source:

1. In the Data Sources window, select *Add New Data Source*. The *Data Source Configuration Wizard* will appear, as shown in Figure 7-3. In the next step, shown in Figure 7-4, select one of the entity classes, such as Member. Click the *Finish* button to save the data source.

Figure 7-3 Creating an Object data source

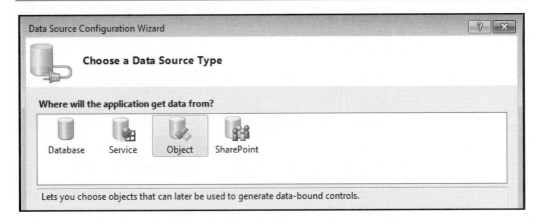

Figure 7-4 Selecting the Member entity class as a data source

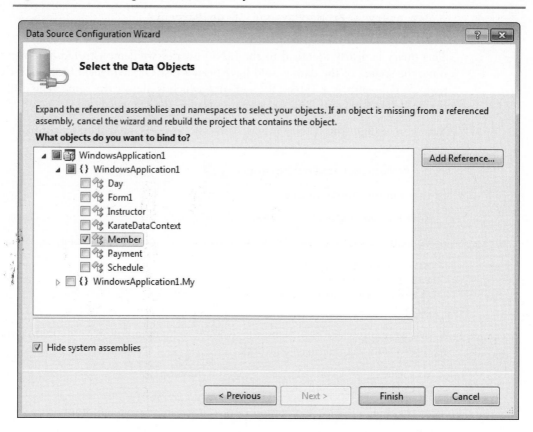

2. Open the *DataGridView Tasks* window and choose a data source for the grid. Select the data source you just created. As shown in Figure 7-5, a BindingSource object is automatically placed in the form's component tray and the table columns appear in the grid. Now you can edit the grid columns.

Figure 7-5 Binding source connects Member entity class to DataGridView control

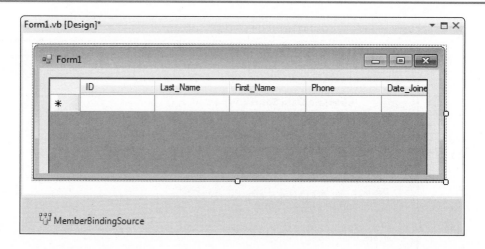

Summary

Runtime data binding offers great flexibility and is easily implemented in LINQ. At the same time, data binding with an Object data source lets you take advantage of Visual Studio's powerful design tools.

Tutorial 7-1:
Displaying the Karate Members table

In this tutorial, you will use Visual Studio to create an entity class named *Member*. Then you will create an Object data source based on the Member class and connect to a Data-GridView control. Finally, you will create a LINQ query that retrieves rows from the Members table in the Karate database.

Tutorial Steps

Step 1: Create a new Windows Forms application named *Karate Members Grid*.

Step 2: In the Server Explorer window, add a new connection to the *karate.mdf* database file. You can find a copy in the chapter examples directory.

Step 3: From the Project menu, select *Add New Item*, select the new *Link to SQL Classes* template, and name it *KarateClasses.dbml*.

Step 4: Drag the Karate.Members table from the Server Explorer window into the *KarateClasses.dbml* design window. Answer *Yes* when asked about copying the database file into the project directory. The *Member* class should appear in the window. Save your changes.

Step 5: In the Data Sources window, create a new Object data source. In the *Select the Data Objects* step, choose the *Member* class. Click the *Finish* button to save the data source.

Step 6: Open the startup form in Design view, add a DataGridView control named *dgvMembers*, and attach it to the *Member* entity class.

Step 7: Optionally, you can set the Dock property to *Fill*; set RowHeadersVisible to *False*; and disable adding, editing, and deleting.

Step 8: Create the following Form_Load event handler:

```
Private Sub Form1_Load() Handles MyBase.Load
   Dim db As New KarateClassesDataContext
   Dim query = From aPerson In db.Members
      Select aPerson
   dgvMembers.DataSource = query
End Sub
```

The KarateClassesDataContext class, created by Visual Studio, contains a *Members* property that is a *Table(Of Member)* object. That is why the LINQ query was able to use *db.Members* as its data source.

Step 9: Run the application. You should see the DataGridView output shown in Figure 7-6. Then stop the application.

Figure 7-6 Using a LINQ query to display the Members table

ID	Last_Name	First_Name	Phone	Date_Joined
1	Kahumanu	Keoki	111-2222	2/20/2002
2	Chong	Anne	232-3333	2/20/2010
3	Hasegawa	Elaine	313-3455	2/20/2004
4	Kahane	Brian	646-9387	5/20/2008
5	Gonzalez	Aldo	123-2345	6/6/2009
6	Kousevitzky	Jascha	414-2345	2/20/2010
7	Taliafea	Moses	545-2323	5/20/2005
8	Concepcion	Rafael	602-3312	5/20/2007
9	Taylor	Winifred	333-2222	2/20/2010

Step 10: Next, you will add a filter to the query that selects only members who joined after 1/1/2010. You will sort the rows by Date_Joined in ascending order. Change the query definition to the following:

```
Dim query = From aPerson In db.Members
   Where aPerson.Date_Joined > #1/1/2010#
   Select aPerson
   Order By aPerson.Date_Joined
```

Step 11: Run the application and verify that all Date_Joined column values are later than 1/1/2010 and are sorted in ascending order.

Summary

You learned how to display database tables in DataGridView controls in previous chapters, using TableAdapters and SQL queries. What makes the current example so different is that the underlying SQL query is hidden, making it possible for you to work completely in Visual Basic code.

Table Associations

As you know, an *association* in LINQ is the object-oriented equivalent of a database relationship. An association links two entity classes using properties that match foreign key relationships. Associations make it easy to create queries that combine columns from multiple database tables.

The Karate database contains the related Members and Payments tables. If you drag these two tables from the Server Explorer window into the Object Relational Designer window, as shown in Figure 7-7, an association is automatically formed between the Member and Payment entity classes.

When two entity classes contain an association, each class implicitly contains a property that references the other class. So it is with the Payment and Member classes in KarateClasses-DataContext. In the Payment class, the *Member* property links to the associated Member

Figure 7-7 Members and Payments tables in the DataContext Design window

object. For example, the following query selects the ID property from the Payment class and the Last_Name property from the Member class:

```
Dim query = From aPayment In db.Payments
    Select aPayment.ID, aPayment.Member.Last_Name
```

The output is shown in Figure 7-8. In the database, we know these values as the ID column from the Payments table and the Last_Name column from the Members table. But we are currently focusing on the classes in the DataContext rather than the database tables. The expression *aPayment.Member* provides the link to any property in the Member class.

Figure 7-8 Query that associates the Payment and Member entity classes

ID	Last_Name
1	Kahumanu
2	Chong
3	Kousevitzky
4	Kahane
5	Gonzalez
6	Hasegawa
7	Taylor

Karate Payments

The following query selects the ID, Payment_Date, and Amount properties from the Payment class, as well as the Last_Name property from the Member class:

```
Dim query = From aPayment In db.Payments
    Select aPayment.ID, aPayment.Member.Last_Name,
    aPayment.Payment_Date, aPayment.Amount
    Order By ID
```

The output from this query is shown in Figure 7-9. If you assign this query directly to the DataSource property of a DataGridView control, you can still format individual grid columns at runtime. Our query created four columns, so the following statement formats the Amount column to two decimal places:

```
dgvPayments.Columns(3).DefaultCellStyle.Format = "n2"
```

Figure 7-9 Selecting columns from both Members and Payments tables

ID	Last_Name	Payment_Date	Amount
1	Kahumanu	10/20/2009	48.00
2	Chong	11/20/2010	80.00
3	Kousevitzky	11/16/2010	75.00
4	Kahane	12/16/2009	50.00
5	Gonzalez	1/16/2009	65.00
6	Hasegawa	2/16/2009	75.00

Creating Aliases for Entity Class Properties

Sometimes you may want to rename some properties produced by a query. In a LINQ query, each alias name precedes the property name, followed by an equals (=) sign, in this format:

```
Alias = PropertyName
```

The *Alias* cannot contain any embedded spaces or punctuation, other than the underscore character. The following query contains aliases named *Date* and *Member*:

```
Dim query = From aPayment In db.Payments
Select Date = aPayment.Payment_Date,
   aPayment.Amount,
   Member = aPayment.Member.Last_Name
```

The most important use of aliases is in creating combined properties. For example, we might want to combine the first and last name of a member using an alias named *Member*. The following LINQ query does that:

```
Dim query = From aPayment In db.Payments
   Select aPayment.Payment_Date, aPayment.Amount,
   Member = aPayment.Member.First_Name + " " _
      + aPayment.Member.Last_Name
```

Sample output from this query is shown in Figure 7-10.

Figure 7-10 Combining columns with an alias

Payment_Date	Amount	Member
10/20/2009	48.0000	Keoki Kahumanu
11/20/2010	80.0000	Anne Chong
11/16/2010	75.0000	Jascha Kousevitzky
12/16/2009	50.0000	Brian Kahane
1/16/2009	65.0000	Aldo Gonzalez
2/16/2009	75.0000	Elaine Hasegawa
3/11/2010	77.0000	Winifred Taylor
2/27/2010	44.0000	Rafael Concepcion

Linking from the Parent Table to a Child Table

We have already seen how a child table (Payments) can link to a parent table (Members). You can also link in the reverse direction, from parent to child. The difference is that there might be multiple child rows that link to a single parent row.

Suppose we want to fill a grid with the name of each member, combined with a count of the number of payments made by the member. The following statements do that, using a grid named dgvPayments:

```
Dim query = From aMember In db.Members
   Select aMember.Last_Name, aMember.Payments.Count()
dgvPayments.DataSource = query
```

The query returns a list of Member objects. For each one of these, the expression *aMember.Payments* returns a list of payments made by the member. The code calls the *Count* extension method to count the number of items in the list. In Tutorial 7-2, you will put these techniques into effect by joining multiple tables.

Tutorial 7-2:
Displaying the Karate class schedule

In this tutorial, you will create entity classes for the Instructors, Schedule, and Days tables in the Karate database. Then you will create a LINQ query that uses associations among the three entity classes to display the class schedule. Essentially, you will create a SQL join query in the background, using LINQ techniques.

Tutorial Steps

Step 1: Create a new application named *Karate Class Schedule*.

Step 2: Add a connection to the Karate database inside the Server Explorer window.

Step 3: Add a *LINQ to SQL Classes* object to the project and name it *KarateClasses.dbml*.

Step 4: Drag the Days, Schedule, and Instructor tables from Server Explorer into the Object Relational Designer window. Verify that arrows appear between the classes, showing associations based on table relationships in the database.

Step 5: Add a DataGridView control to the startup form and name it *dgvSchedule*. Optionally, you can dock the grid to the form; set RowHeadersVisible to *False*; and disable adding, editing, and deleting.

Step 6: Create the following Form_Load event handler:

```
Private Sub MainForm_Load() Handles MyBase.Load
   Dim db As New KarateDataContext
   Dim query = From sched In db.Schedules
      Select sched.Day.Name, sched.Time.TimeOfDay,
      sched.Instructor.Last_Name
   dgvSchedule.DataSource = query
End Sub
```

There are some important things to notice about this code:
- The *sched* variable is a Schedule object, which represents one row of the Schedules table.
- We want to display the day name, so the expression *sched.Day.Name* uses the association between the Schedule and Day entity classes to locate the day name (such as *Tue* or *Wed*).
- The expression *sched.Time* would return a combined date/time object, so we change it to *sched.Time.TimeOfDay*, which gives us only the time portion.
- The expression *sched.Instructor.Last_Name* gets the Last_Name property from the Instructor entity class.

Step 7: Save and run the application. The output, shown in Figure 7-11, shows the class day, time, and instructor. The default column names are not too great, so add some aliases named *Day*, *Time*, and *Instructor* to the query:

```
Dim db As New KarateDataContext
Dim query = From sched In db.Schedules
  Select Day = sched.Day.Name,
  Time = sched.Time.TimeOfDay,
  Instructor = sched.Instructor.Last_Name
dgvSchedule.DataSource = query
```

Each alias name precedes the actual column name, followed by an equals (=) sign.

Figure 7-11 Class schedule, with columns from three entity classes

Step 8: Save and run the application. The revised output appears in Figure 7-12 with the new column headings.

Figure 7-12 Class schedule, with aliased column names

For extra practice, you may want to create an Object data source for this example. Once you have attached it to the DataGridViewControl, you can format the Time column to just hours and minutes.

Grouping Table Rows

The **Group By operator** is used in LINQ to group rows on one or more columns. For each group, you can use formulas to show the number of items in the group, the average value, total value, minimum, maximum, and so on.

For example, the following query groups the items in the Schedule table according to instructor last names, and counts the number of items in each group:

```
Dim query = From sched In db.Schedules
   Group sched By sched.Instructor.Last_Name
   Into InstructorGroup = Count()
dgvGrid.DataSource = query
```

Figure 7-13 shows the output from this code sample. The group is named *InstructorGroup*, and *Count* is a built-in LINQ function.

Figure 7-13 Instructor groups counts in the Schedule table

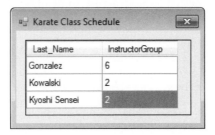

Counting the members of a group may be useful, but you may prefer to display the individual members of a group. To do that, you must use the *Group* keyword in the last line of the query:

```
Dim query = From sched In db.Schedules
   Group sched By sched.Instructor.Last_Name
   Into InstructorGroup = Group
```

Then you can loop through the query object and display the individual group members. The following code displays the Last_Name property of each group member in a list box:

```
For Each grp In query
   lstBox.Items.Add("Instructor = " & grp.Last_Name)
Next
```

The output from this query shows that the group names are automatically sorted in ascending order:

```
Instructor = Gonzalez
Instructor = Kowalski
Instructor = Kyoshi Sensei
```

Displaying the Items Inside Groups

Very often, you will want to display both the group names and the items belonging to each group in a hierarchical display. In Figure 7-14, for example, the list box groups by instructor and displays the day and time of each class. Also, it displays a footer for each group containing a count value. We can use the following query to generate the group information:

```
Dim query = From sched In db.Schedules
   Group sched By sched.Instructor.Last_Name
   Into InstructorGroup = Group
```

Figure 7-14 Displaying the items in each Instructor group

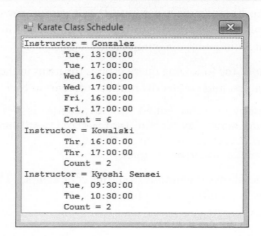

Then we use a nested loop structure to display all the information. The outer loop displays instructor names on line 2.

```
1:   For Each grp In query
2:       lstBox.Items.Add("Instructor = " & grp.Last_Name)
3:       For Each aClass In grp.InstructorGroup
4:         lstBox.Items.Add(vbTab & aClass.Day.Name _
5:             & ", " & aClass.Time.TimeOfDay.ToString)
6:       Next
7:       lstBox.Items.Add(vbTab & "Count = " & _
           grp.InstructorGroup.Count())
8:   Next
```

The inner loop, beginning on line 3, selects each class within an instructor group and displays the class day and time (lines 4–5). After this loop, line 7 counts the items in each group and displays a group footer line.

NOTE: The type of listing shown in Figure 7-14 is often called a *control-break report*. There are some great tools for creating reports that group items with headers and footers, and display totals and averages. In Chapter 12, you will learn how to use the Microsoft reporting tools.

There are other useful ways to group items in a table. In the Karate payments table, for example, you could group payments by Member ID, and calculate the number of payments or the total payments made by that member.

Summary

In this section, you learned about the LINQ to SQL object model, and how entity classes and DataContext objects are created. Then you learned how to create queries that select rows from one or more database tables, using associations among entity classes. You also learned how to group the rows.

It may take some time to become comfortable with the use of associations and table references in this example. The effort is well worth it because almost all nontrivial queries involve multiple tables. Remember, LINQ queries use objects and properties, not SQL server tables and columns.

 **Checkpoint**

1. LINQ translates your property and method calls into commands in which database language?

2. Which type of class contains properties that match the structure of a specific database table?

3. What is the purpose of the TableAttribute declaration?

4. What is the purpose of a DataContext object?

5. Which Visual Studio design tool lets you create LINQ to SQL entity classes?

7.2 Updating Tables

In this section, we will show you two basic approaches to updating database tables. The first is to use data binding, with an Object data source bound to a LINQ entity table. Almost no code must be written when you use this approach.

The second approach to updating tables is to write LINQ code statements to do the updating. This is more work than the data-bound approach, but it can be used in the middle tier of a multi-tier application.

Updating a Table Using a BindingSource

Perhaps the easiest way to update data on a form is to use a **BindingSource** component, which pulls data from a data source and assigns the data to controls on a form. It can also use data from the controls to update the data source.

You create a BindingSource by dragging a table or class from the Data Sources window onto a form. Or, you can add a BindingSource from the ToolBox window and set its DataSource property to the name of one of your LINQ entity classes.

To fill the BindingSource fields with data, you assign its DataSource property a LINQ query that selects table rows.

BindingNavigator

A **BindingNavigator** component appears as a ToolStrip control on a form, with buttons that navigate forward and backward through rows, insert rows, delete rows, and save changes, as shown here:

The navigator's BindingSource property can be assigned the name of an existing Binding-Source control. If you do that, the BindingNavigator and BindingSource work closely together to save you lots of time and effort. For example, if users click the *Delete* button (red X icon), the currently displayed item is deleted from the data-bound table. If users modify an entry and then move to a different entry, their changes are saved in the table.

By default, the *Save* button (floppy disk icon) is disabled. If you want to save changes to the underlying database, you can enable the *Save* button and write code that updates the database with changes made to the data-bound table. You just execute the *DataContext.SubmitChanges()* method. In Tutorial 7-3, you will learn how to use a binding source to update a table in the database.

Tutorial 7-3:
Using a BindingSource to update the Members table

In this tutorial, you will display rows from the Karate Members table in individual detail fields. You will use a BindingSource object to transfer the data from a LINQ query. The BindingSource will also let the user insert new entries, update existing entries, and delete entries from the table.

Tutorial Steps

Step 1: Create a new application named *Karate Member Details*.

Step 2: Add a connection to the Karate database inside the Server Explorer window.

Step 3: Add a *LINQ to SQL Classes* object to the project and name it *KarateClasses.dbml*.

Step 4: Drag the *Members* table from Server Explorer into the Object Relational Designer window. Verify that arrows appear between the classes, showing associations based on table relationships in the database.

Step 5: From the Data Sources window, add an Object data source to the project (Refer to Figure 7-3 for an example.). In the *Select the Data Objects* step, drill down into Karate_Member_Details and select the *Member* class. Click the *Finish* button to save the data source.

Step 6: In the Data Sources window, select the dropdown list next to *Member* and choose *Details*. Change the Date_Joined control type to *TextBox*.

Step 7: Drag the Member class into the design surface of the startup form. A ToolStrip and detail fields should be created for you. Notice that a MemberBindingSource object appears in the form's component tray. Rearrange the fields, using Figure 7-15 as a suggested layout.

Figure 7-15 Editing member details with a BindingSource

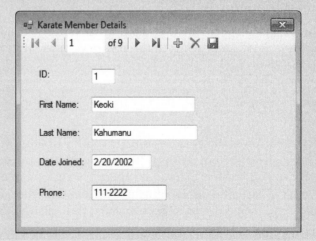

If you were to run the application, nothing would appear in the detail fields. You must write a query and assign it to the binding source.

Step 8: Open the form's code window and add the following to the class:

```
Private db As New KarateClassesDataContext

Private Sub Form_Load() Handles MyBase.Load
  Dim query = From aPerson In db.Members
    Select aPerson
  MemberBindingSource.DataSource = query
End Sub
```

The job of the MemberBindingSource is to provide two-way binding (read/write) from the individual Member object properties to the individual TextBox and Label controls.

Step 9: Save and run the application. Scroll forward and backward through the entries in the table. Click the *Delete* button (red X icon) on the ToolStrip and watch the entries disappear. Modify two of the entries and note the changes. Stop the application.

Step 10: Start the application and verify that no database entries were deleted or modified. Stop the application.

As you can see, changes made by the user affected only the table in memory, but not the underlying database. To change the database, you need to call the DataContext's SubmitChanges method.

Step 11: Enable the *Save* button on the ToolStrip (set its Enabled property to True). Create a Click event handler for the button, and insert the following code:

```
Private Sub MemberBindingNavigatorSaveItem_Click() _
  Handles MemberBindingNavigatorSaveItem.Click
  Try
    MemberBindingSource.EndEdit()
    db.SubmitChanges()
  Catch ex As Exception
    MessageBox.Show(ex.Message)
  End Try
End Sub
```

The call to EndEdit completes any editing that might be in progress on the currently displayed member.

Step 12: Experiment with inserting, updating, and deleting entries from the table. After clicking the *Save* button, close the application, restart the application, and verify that all changes you made were saved in the database.

Step 13: Build the application and run it again. Your database should return to its previous state.

Updating Tables Using LINQ Statements

Updating database tables with LINQ has two important advantages over writing update queries in SQL: You can step through your LINQ code in the debugger, and you can call functions within your own class.

LINQ works with strongly typed Table objects, which are defined with types such as Table(Of Member) or Table(Of Payment). When you delete, insert, or modify a row in a table, you can continue to display and update the table as long as the application is running.

The table is only in memory. From that point of view, tables have something in common with DataSet objects.

If you want to update the database represented by a DataContext, you must call the *SubmitChanges* method. Then all pending changes made to all tables within the DataContext are written to the database. After that, you can continue to make more changes to the tables, and call SubmitChanges again later, if you wish.

Deleting Table Rows

To delete a row from a list created by a LINQ query, call the *DeleteOnSubmit* method defined in the DataContext's Table class. For example, the KarateClassesDataContext class contains a property named *Payments*, which is a Table(Of Payment) object. The following statement would delete a row, assuming that *db* is a DataContext, and *aPayment* is a reference to the row we want to delete:

```
db.Payments.DeleteOnSubmit(aPayment)
```

If you want to delete the row from the underlying database, call the SubmitChanges method:

```
db.SubmitChanges()
```

Suppose that a variable named *selectedId* contains the ID of the payment we want to delete. The following code begins by finding the Payment object:

```
Dim db As New KarateClassesDataContext
selectedId = 5            ' we will delete payment #5
Dim query =
  From onePmt In db.Payments
  Where onePmt.ID = selectedId
  Select onePmt
```

The query returns a List(Of Payment) containing just one item. We can call the extension method named *First* to get a reference to the item and pass it to the *DeleteOnSubmit* method.

```
db.Payments.DeleteOnSubmit(query.First())
```

Finally, to submit our change to the database, we call the SubmitChanges method. It's a good idea to use exception handling to report possible database errors:

```
Try
  db.SubmitChanges()
Catch ex As Exception
  '(show error message)
End Try
```

Deleting from Related Tables

When you carried out SQL delete operations in Chapter 5, you found that deleting a row from a parent table in a foreign key relationship can violate a database referential integrity constraint. The same applies to associations between entity classes. You cannot, for example, delete a row from the Members table if it contains references to rows in the Payments table. Instead, you can delete all payments for the member and then delete the member.

Suppose we want to delete the member named Chong, whose ID = 2. We begin by deleting this person's payments:

```
Dim query = From aPayment In db.Payments
  Select aPayment
  Where aPayment.Member_Id = 2            ' Chong

For Each aPayment In query
  db.Payments.DeleteOnSubmit(aPayment)
Next
```

Having done that, we can now delete Chong from the Members table:

```
Dim query2 = From aPerson In db.Members
   Select aPerson
   Where aPerson.ID = 2              ' Chong

db.Members.DeleteOnSubmit(query2.First())
```

Finally, we submit our changes to the database:

```
Try
   db.SubmitChanges()
Catch ex As Exception
   '(show error message)
End Try
```

Inserting Table Rows

The **InsertOnSubmit** method inserts a new row in a LINQ DataContext table. You do this operation in two steps.

First, you construct the type of object that matches the table type. The Members table is type Table(Of Member), so the following code builds a Member object:

```
Dim mem As New Member With
   {.ID = 23,
   .First_Name = "Joe",
   .Last_Name = "Smith",
   .Date_Joined = #5/1/2011#,
   .Phone = 303-444-3333}
```

Notice that we use the recent VB syntax that lets us create objects by assigning values to properties. We no longer need a parameterized constructor.

Second, we call the InsertOnSubmit method, passing it the Member object:

```
Dim db As New KarateClassesDataContext
db.Members.InsertOnSubmit(mem)
```

Up to this point, the new row is only in the DataContext's table. To add it to the database, we call *SubmitChanges*:

```
Try
   db.SubmitChanges()
Catch ex As Exception
   '(show error message)
End Try
```

Updating Table Rows

To update a row in a DataContext's table, you first need to get a reference to the row or rows you plan to update. The following query, for example, finds the member with ID = 25:

```
Dim query =
   From aMember In db.Members
   Where aMember.ID = 25
   Select aMember
```

Then you can use a *For Each* loop to iterate through the object (or objects) returned by the query. You can modify one or more properties of the object. Here, we modify Date_Joined:

```
For Each person In query
   person.Date_Joined = #12/1/2011#
Next
```

Up to this point, only the DataContext's table has been modified. To write the changes to the database, we call the SubmitChanges method:

```
Try
   db.SubmitChanges()
Catch ex As Exception
   '(show error message)
End Try
```

In Tutorial 7-4, you will create an application that uses LINQ queries to insert, delete, and update rows in the Karate Schedule table.

Tutorial 7-4:
Using LINQ queries to add schedule entries

In this tutorial, you will create an application that lets the user add new entries to the Karate school schedule. A sample of the user interface is shown in Figure 7-16. In the upper half of the form, the current schedule is displayed in a DataGridView control. A splitter bar separates the upper half from the lower half, where input fields and a *Save* button are available for the user to input a new schedule item and save it in the table. The Day_Id and Instructor_Id columns are both assigned values when the user selects the day name and instructor name from combo boxes. Users should not be expected to remember ID values, so the combo boxes are in place to offer usable selections.

Figure 7-16 Karate Schedule Updates application

ID	Day	Time	Instructor
1	Tue	09:30:00	Kyoshi Sensei
2	Tue	10:30:00	Kyoshi Sensei
3	Tue	13:00:00	Gonzalez
4	Tue	17:00:00	Gonzalez
5	Wed	16:00:00	Gonzalez
6	Wed	17:00:00	Gonzalez
7	Thr	16:00:00	Kowalski

Add a New Class

ID [   ]   Day [▼]   Time [   ]   Instructor [▼]

[Save]

Tutorial Steps

Step 1: Create a new Application named *Karate Schedule Updates*. Change the Text property of the startup form to *Karate Schedule Updates*.

Step 2: Add a connection to the Karate database inside the Server Explorer window.

Step 3: Add a *LINQ to SQL Classes* object to the project and name it *KarateClasses.dbml*.

Step 4: Drag the Days, Schedule, and Instructor tables from Server Explorer into the Object Relational Designer window. Verify that arrows appear between the classes, showing associations based on table relationships in the database.

Step 5: Add a SplitContainer to the startup form and set its Orientation property to *Horizontal*. Its Dock property should automatically be set to *Fill*.

Step 6: Add a DataGridView control to the upper panel of the SplitContainer and name it *dgvSchedule*. Set its Dock property to *Fill*. Disable adding, editing, and deleting.

Step 7: Add the following code to the form's class:

```
 1: Private db As New KarateClassesDataContext
 2: Private selectedId As Short
 3:
 4: Private Sub Form_Load() Handles MyBase.Load
 5:    FillScheduleGrid()
 6: End Sub
 7:
 8: Private Sub FillScheduleGrid()
 9:    Dim query = From sched In db.Schedules
10:       Select sched.ID,
11:       Day = sched.Day.Name,
12:       Time = sched.Time.TimeOfDay,
13:       Instructor = sched.Instructor.Last_Name
14:
15:    dgvSchedule.DataSource = query
16: End Sub
```

When the form loads, line 5 calls FillScheduleGrid. The query on lines 9–13 was adapted from Tutorial 7-2, in which you combined properties from the Schedule, Day, and Instructor entity classes.

Step 8: Save and run the application, and verify that the schedule displays correctly. Close the application window.

Step 9: Add the controls listed in Table 7-2 to the form. They will help the user add a new class to the schedule.

Table 7-2 Essential controls in the Karate Schedule Updates application

Control Type	Name	Property Values
SplitContainer	(default)	Orientation = Horizontal
Label	lblTitle	Text = *Add a New Class*
		Font = Times New Roman 14.25 Bold
TextBox	txtId	
TextBox	txtTime	
ComboBox	cboDay	
ComboBox	cboInstructor	
Button	btnSave	Text = *Save*
DataGridView	dgvSchedule	Dock = Fill

Step 10: Next, you need to create LINQ queries that initialize the ID text box with the next available ID number. Add the PrepareInsertFields method.

```
 1: Private Sub PrepareInsertFields()
 2:   ' Choose the next ID number
 3:   Dim idQuery = From sched In db.Schedules
 4:     Select sched.ID
 5:   txtID.Text = (idQuery.Max() + 1).ToString
 6:
 7:   ' Fill combo box with days of the week
 8:   Dim dayQuery = From aDay In db.Days
 9:     Select aDay.ID, aDay.Name
10:   cboDay.DataSource = dayQuery
11:   cboDay.DisplayMember = "Name"
12:   cboDay.ValueMember = "ID"
13:
14:   ' Fill combo box with instructor names
15:   Dim instructorQuery = From aPerson In db.Instructors
16:     Select aPerson.ID, aPerson.Last_Name
17:     Order By Last_Name
18:   cboInstructor.DataSource = instructorQuery
19:   cboInstructor.DisplayMember = "Last_Name"
20:   cboInstructor.ValueMember = "ID"
21: End Sub
```

Lines 3–5 get the highest ID number from the Schedules table and add 1, thus generating the ID number we will use when inserting a new row. Lines 8–12 fill a combo box with the days of the week. They also set the ValueMember property so we can get the ID number of the user's selection when the user selects a day for the class. Lines 15–20 use a query to fill another combo box with all the instructor names. At runtime, when the user selects an instructor, we will take the ID from the combo box's SelectedValue property and insert it in the new Schedules table entry.

Step 11: Add a line to Form_Load that calls the PrepareInsertFields method.

```
Private Sub Form_Load() Handles MyBase.Load
  FillScheduleGrid()
  PrepareInsertFields()
End Sub
```

Step 12: Next, add the following Click handler for the *Save* button that creates a Schedule object from the user's entries and inserts it in the Schedules table.

```
 1: Private Sub btnSave_Click() Handles btnSave.Click
 2:   'Save the new class into the schedule
 3:   Try
 4:     Dim dt As Date = CDate(txtTime.Text)
 5:     Dim sched As New Schedule With {
 6:       .ID = CShort(txtID.Text),
 7:       .Day_Id = CShort(cboDay.SelectedValue),
 8:       .Time = Today.Add(New TimeSpan(dt.Hour,
          dt.Minute, 0)),
 9:       .Instructor_Id = CShort(cboInstructor.
          SelectedValue)}
10:     db.Schedules.InsertOnSubmit(sched)
11:     db.SubmitChanges()
12:     FillScheduleGrid()
13:     MessageBox.Show("Class saved into the schedule")
14:   Catch ex As Exception
```

```
15:        MessageBox.Show(ex.Message)
16:     End Try
17:  End Sub
```

Lines 5–9 use object initializers to create a new Schedule object, using values from the txtID, cboDay, txtTime, and cboInstructor controls. The Time property (line 8) is a special case because it must contain both a date and a time. We're not interested in the date, so we set to Today (current date), and add a TimeSpan object that was created on line 3. Line 10 inserts the Schedule object into the Schedules table, and line 11 saves the table changes to the database. Line 12 refills the DataGridView control with the updated contents of the Schedules table.

Step 13: Save and run the application. Add a new class to the schedule and verify that it appears at the bottom of the grid. Verify that the program cannot halt because of invalid input.

Summary

It requires a surprising amount of code to prepare the combo boxes in this example before the user can add a new row to the Schedules table, but the code is fairly straightforward. Fortunately, the code you would write to update an existing table row is almost identical to the code you just wrote for the *Save* button's click handler.

If You Want to Know More: A Close Look at the KarateClassesDataContext

You can learn many interesting things by looking at the source code of the KarateClassesDataContext we have been using in the tutorials. To see this code, select the *Show All Files* button in the toolbar at the top of the Solution Explorer window. Before examining this file, drag the Members table from the Server Explorer window into the Object Relational Designer window.

Open the *KarateClasses.designer.vb* file. You should not modify this file, but you can look at it. The following lines declare the KarateClassesDataContext class, which inherit from the DataContext class:

```
<Global.System.Data.Linq.Mapping.DatabaseAttribute(Name:="karate")> _
Partial Public Class KarateClassesDataContext
   Inherits System.Data.Linq.DataContext
```

The first line above is a special attribute that must be placed before any class that will be recognized by LINQ. The *DatabaseAttribute* property links this class to the karate database.

Next, an AttributeMappingSource object is declared. It is needed when you want to link up each database table column to a property in a class.

```
Private Shared mappingSource As System.Data.Linq.Mapping.MappingSource
   = New AttributeMappingSource()
```

Next are several constructors. One of the constructors receives a connection string argument. It passes the connection string and the mappingSource variable to the constructor in the DataContext class.

```
Public Sub New(ByVal connection As String)
   MyBase.New(connection, mappingSource)
   OnCreated
End Sub
```

The Members property returns a Table(Of Member) object, containing the rows from the Members table in the database.

```
Public ReadOnly Property Members() As System.Data.Linq.Table(Of Member)
    Get
        Return Me.GetTable(Of Member)
    End Get
End Property
```

Find the Member class, which represents a single member, or row from the Members database table. Notice that it uses a TableAttribute property to identify the database table.

```
<Global.System.Data.Linq.Mapping.TableAttribute(Name:="dbo.Members")> _
Partial Public Class Member
```

This is also declared as a partial class, which allows you to create a Member class in your own code and thus to add more features to the class. Then the compiler can join the two partial classes into a single class when the project is compiled.

Inside the Member class are private variables that match each column from the Members table.

```
Private _ID As Short
Private _Last_Name As String
Private _First_Name As String
Private _Phone As String
Private _Date_Joined As System.Nullable(Of Date)
```

Each variable is accompanied by a property procedure that does some fairly complicated work of updating the database field contents. Let's look at one of them:

```
 1:  Public Property Last_Name() As String
 2:     Get
 3:        Return Me._Last_Name
 4:     End Get
 5:     Set
 6:        If (String.Equals(Me._Last_Name, value) = false) Then
 7:           Me.OnLast_NameChanging(value)
 8:           Me.SendPropertyChanging
 9:           Me._Last_Name = value
10:           Me.SendPropertyChanged("Last_Name")
11:           Me.OnLast_NameChanged
12:        End If
13:     End Set
14:  End Property
```

When a new value is assigned to the property, line 6 checks to see if the new value being assigned is different from the existing value. Assuming that it is different, lines 7 and 8 raise events that indicate that the name property is about to change. Line 9 assigns the new value to the private variable, and lines 10–11 raise events indicating that the property has changed. You can inspect the SendPropertyChanging event code in this same file, if you wish.

Why, then, are these events raised? Sometimes you may want to write code that validates a value before it is assigned to a property. But you need to know when the change is about to take place, and that's where the events are useful. You can write an event handler that executes when one of the events is raised.

You could create your own DataContext class by hand, but it's a lot easier to let Visual Studio do it for you. The main thing is to understand what's in there and how to use it.

Summary

There's no doubt that expert SQL database programmers are in high demand in today's marketplace. If you are looking in that direction, you will have many opportunities. But many database application tasks are repetitive and time-consuming. LINQ provides an opportunity to spend your time on the more interesting, analytical, and design aspects of applications. To use an analogy, if you had spent your early years making cooking fires with wood sticks, imagine how much you would appreciate the invention of the barbecue grill!

Checkpoint

6. What is the purpose of a BindingSource component?

7. What is a BindingNavigator component?

8. If you want to update the database represented by a DataContext, which method must you call?

9. Which method deletes a row from a list or table created by a LINQ query?

10. Which method inserts a new row in a LINQ DataContext table?

Summary

7.1 Using LINQ to Select Data

- LINQ queries use objects and methods to view and update databases.
- LINQ queries are translated to SQL queries, which are executed against the database. When you use LINQ to SQL, you do not issue commands directly to a database. Instead, you use custom classes that represent database tables and the relationships between the tables.
- An *entity class* is a class that contains properties that match the structure of a specific database table.
- An *entity class property* is a member of an entity class that gets and sets the value of a class-level variable.
- An *association* in an entity class is a reference to another class that corresponds to a relationship between two database tables.
- A *method* in an entity class contains code that executes a database-stored procedure or function.
- To connect to a database, you need to create a DataContext object. This object provides methods that connect to the database, retrieve data, and submit updates to the database.
- The *Object Relational Designer (O/R Designer)* is a Visual Studio design tool that lets you create LINQ to SQL entity classes. The O/R Designer also creates strongly typed DataContext classes.
- An *Object data source* binds a LINQ entity class to controls such as DataGridView. A BindingSource object is added to the form's component tray.
- The Group By operator is used in LINQ to group table rows based on one or more columns. For each group, you can use formulas to show the number of items in the group, the average value, total value, minimum, maximum, and so on.

7.2 Updating Tables

- LINQ queries can be used to insert rows and delete rows from tables. They can also be used to modify existing table entries.
- The easiest way to update a table in LINQ is to use a BindingSource component (created as an Object data source).
- A BindingNavigator component appears as a ToolStrip control on a form, with buttons that navigate forward and backward through rows, insert rows, delete rows, and save changes.
- If you want to update the database represented by a DataContext, you must call the *DataContext.SubmitChanges* method. Then all pending changes made to all tables within the DataContext are written to the database.
- To delete a row from a list created by a LINQ query, you call the *DeleteOnSubmit* method defined in the DataContext's Table class.
- Deleting a row from the parent table in an association requires special care to avoid violating a referential integrity constraint.
- The InsertOnSubmit method inserts a new row in a LINQ DataContext table.
- To update a row in a DataContext's table, you first need to get a reference to the row or rows you plan to update. Then you can use a *For Each* loop to iterate through the objects returned by the query and modify their properties.

Key Terms

association	Group By operator
BindingNavigator	Language Integrated Query (LINQ)
BindingSource	LINQ to SQL
column attribute	Object data source
database entity mapping	Object Relational Designer (O/R
entity class	Designer)
entity method	pluralization
entity property	table attribute

Review Questions and Exercises

True or False

Indicate whether each of the following statements is true or false.

1. LINQ should be used in the data tier of a three-tier application.

2. LINQ is implemented only in Microsoft .NET languages.

3. A TableAttribute identifies a LINQ entity class.

4. The ColumnAttribute class belongs to the *System.Data.Mapping* namespace.

5. GetTable in the DataContext class returns a strongly typed DataTable object.

6. An *O/R Designer* file has an extension of .dbml.

7. Pluralization in LINQ is the practice of creating multiple classes from a single database table.

8. Associations between LINQ entity classes are always one to one.

9. Even if a relationship between two tables does not exist in the database, you can still create an association between two entity classes that represent the tables.

10. Table(Of Member) is an example of a strongly typed table class.

11. To assign a LINQ query to a DataGridView's DataSource property, you must call the ToList method.

12. You can assign a query to a BindingSource's DataSource property.

13. If you use runtime data binding with a LINQ query, you cannot format the grid columns.

14. To create an Object data source, you must run the Data Source Configuration wizard.

15. You cannot use an entity class association to link from a parent table to a child table.

16. Join queries are not supported by LINQ.

Short Answer

1. Which relational database object is represented by a LINQ entity class?

2. Which relational database object is represented by a LINQ entity property?

3. Which relational database object is represented by a LINQ association?

4. In the Karate database tutorials, what was the name of the strongly typed DataContext class?

5. What is the *O/R Designer*?

6. How are associations useful in LINQ queries?

7. What advantage does a BindingSource offer when used to fill a DataGridView from a LINQ query?

8. How do you create an alternate column name (an alias) when creating a LINQ query?

Algorithm Workbench

1. Write a LINQ query that selects all rows from the Karate Members table in which the phone number starts with the digit 3.

2. Write a LINQ query that selects all rows from the Karate Members table in which the Last_Name property contains the string "ha".

3. Write a query that groups the rows of the Schedule table in the Karate database by the instructor's last name.

4. Write a LINQ query that groups the rows of the Schedule table in the Karate database by the Day ID number. Within each group, display the day name and class time in a List-Box control.

5. Write a LINQ query that groups payments by Member_Id into a group named paymentGroup.

Programming Challenges

1. Adding New Payments

Create an application that lets the user add new payments to the Karate database. Use an Object data source, a LINQ query, and a BindingSource control. Do not use a MenuStrip control, but use a *Save* button to save the payments. Add a *Show Payments* button that displays the Payments table on a separate form in a DataGridView control. A sample main form is shown in Figure 7-17. Catch all exceptions and display a message box if an exception is thrown. Display a confirmation message when a row is added successfully. *Hint:* Be sure to initialize the BindingSource's DataSource property with a LINQ Select query when the form is loaded.

Figure 7-17 Adding a new payment to the Payments table

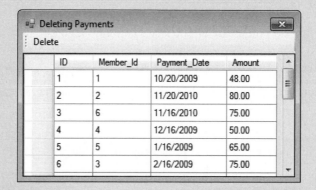

2. **Deleting Payments**

   Create an application that lets the user delete payments from the Karate database. Use an Object data source and a BindingSource control. Add a ToolStrip control containing a *Delete* button, as shown in Figure 7-18. Display all payments in a DataGridView control. When the user selects a payment and clicks the *Delete* button, LINQ queries that delete the payment and refresh the grid are executed.

Figure 7-18 Selecting and deleting payments

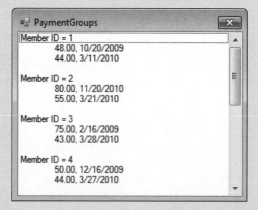

3. **Grouping Karate Payments**

   Use the Group By operator to group the Payments table by member ID. Display the member ID in the outside group, and display the individual payment dates and amounts within each group. Write the output to a ListBox control, as demonstrated in Figure 7-19.

Figure 7-19 Grouping payments by Member ID

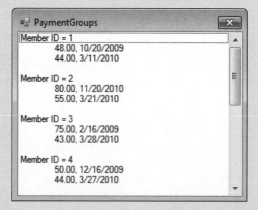

4. Grouping Payments by Member Name

Use the Group By operator to group the Payments table by the members combined first and last names. Display the member name in the outside group, and display the individual payment dates and amounts within each group. Write the output to a ListBox control, as demonstrated in Figure 7-20.

Hint: The Group By operator permits only a single key field, so you will have to create an anonymous type and assign it an alias name, called *MemberName* here:

```
Group aPayment By MemberName = New With {aPayment.Member.First_Name,
    aPayment.Member.Last_Name}
```

Figure 7-20 Grouping payments by member name

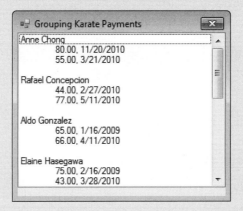

5. Students and Course Lists

In this programming challenge, you will use LINQ statements to display college courses taken by selected students. You will use a *CourseRegistration* database, which contains tables named *Students* and *Courses*.

- The *Students* table contains the following columns: Id (smallint, primary key), Last-Name (varchar(30)), Status (smallint), and Major (varchar(5)).
- The *Courses* table contains the following columns: Id (varchar(10)), Student_Id(smallint), Credits (smallint), and Grade (float). The primary key of the Courses table consists of two combined columns: Id and Student_Id.

Figure 7-21 shows a one-to-many relationship between the Students and Courses tables. You can find the *CourseRegistration.mdf* database file in the chapter examples folder.

Figure 7-21 Database relationship between the Students and Courses tables

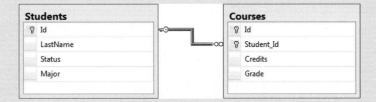

Use a LINQ query to fill a DataGridView with a list of Student objects. When the user selects a student in the grid, display all courses taken by the student in a separate grid. Use another LINQ query to fill the second grid. A sample is shown in Figure 7-22, in which Student 1001 (Charles) was selected by clicking the left side of his row. The grid on the right fills with the list of courses taken by the selected student. Notice that the rightmost column in the Student grid displays a count of the number of courses the student has taken. This column was not in the database, but it is calculated by the LINQ query. We showed how to do such a calculation in Section 7.1.

The two DataGridView controls should be inserted into panels belonging to a SplitContainer control. At runtime, the user will drag the divider between the two panels to adjust their size. To format the Grade column in the right-hand grid, set its DefaultCellStyle.Format property like this:

```
dgvCourses.Columns(2).DefaultCellStyle.Format = "n"
```

Figure 7-22 Displaying courses taken by a selected student

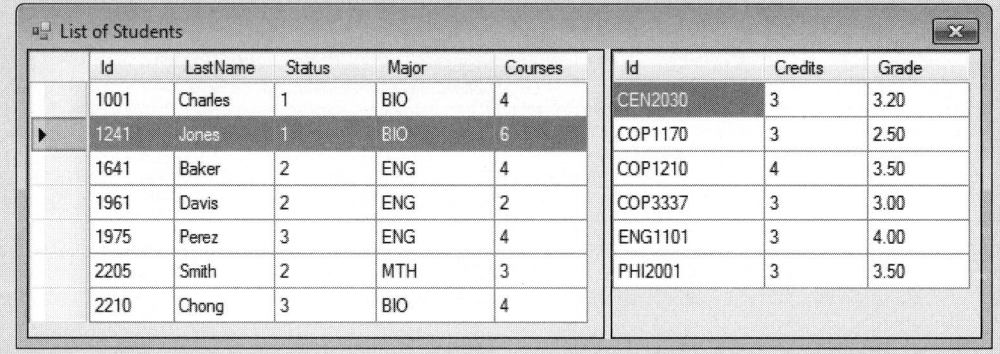

List of Students

Id	LastName	Status	Major	Courses
1001	Charles	1	BIO	4
1241	Jones	1	BIO	6
1641	Baker	2	ENG	4
1961	Davis	2	ENG	2
1975	Perez	3	ENG	4
2205	Smith	2	MTH	3
2210	Chong	3	BIO	4

Id	Credits	Grade
CEN2030	3	3.20
COP1170	3	2.50
COP1210	4	3.50
COP3337	3	3.00
ENG1101	3	4.00
PHI2001	3	3.50

8 Creating Web Applications

This chapter introduces the ASP.NET runtime environment, showing how to use Visual Studio to create Web sites. You learn what happens when an ASP.NET page is processed by a Web server. You learn about runtime events, the different categories of controls available in ASP.NET applications, and the differences between HTML controls and ASP.NET controls. The chapter describes application and configuration files required by ASP.NET applications. Finally, we show how to create a simple Web application containing various types of buttons, labels, headings, and text boxes.

8.1 Programming for the Web

Extended HyperText Markup Language (XHTML)

When the Web first became popular, **HyperText Markup Language (HTML)** was the only available markup language for creating pages with text, graphics buttons, and input forms. Later, **eXtended HyperText Markup Language (XHTML)** was created to meet a need for more advanced Web sites. XHTML not only describes the appearance of Web pages, it has the ability to embed commands that execute on the Web server.

Many Web sites today are fully functional, interactive applications. In past years, Web applications tended to be pasted together from a complicated combination of HTML, scripting languages such as JavaScript, and executable programs. But now you can create Web sites that integrate all of these elements in an easy and natural way, using Microsoft ASP.NET.

ASP.NET

ASP.NET is the name given to Microsoft's Web development platform. It provides development tools, code libraries, and visual controls for browser-based applications. ASP.NET applications run under Web browsers such as Internet Explorer, Netscape, and Mozilla Firefox. An application can run on the Web, on your own computer, or on a network (called a *network share*). ASP.NET provides a way to separate ordinary HTML from object-oriented program code. It also provides many powerful controls, which are similar to Windows Desktop controls. ASP.NET lets you transfer a lot of your Visual Basic knowledge to Web applications. Most important, ASP.NET uses a compiler to check for syntax errors before your program executes. Visual Basic code can be stored in a file separate from a page's text and HTML, making it easier for you to code and maintain program logic.

Web applications written for ASP.NET generally consist of the following parts:

- *Content*—Web forms, HTML code, ASP.NET controls, images, and other multimedia.
- *Program logic*—Code written in Visual Basic or C#.
- *Configuration information*—Stored in a file named *Web.config*.

Visual Web Developer

Visual Studio makes it easy to edit pages in Source view (XHTML markup), Design view, or Split view (both source and design). If you do not have Microsoft Visual Studio, you can download **Visual Web Developer,** a free Microsoft development tool that simplifies the way you create Web applications. It lets you do the following:

- Create powerful visual interfaces, with text boxes, color, images, buttons, list boxes, and calendars.
- Create connections to databases, with table adapters and datasets.
- Display database data in gridlike controls.
- Run and debug your programs in Visual Studio.
- Publish your applications to the Web so they can be enjoyed by everyone.

 TIP: Except where otherwise noted, everything we say about development tools, environment, editor, buttons, and so forth, applies equally to Visual Studio and Visual Web Developer.

How Web Applications Work

Web applications, which we define as Web sites containing executable code, are designed around a **client-server model,** which means that an entity called a *server* produces data consumed by another entity called a *client*. Put another way, clients make requests, which are satisfied by responses from servers.

When you use a Web browser to access a Web site, your browser is the client and the Web site provides the server. A program called a **Web server** runs on the computer hosting the Web site. Web browsers display data encoded in HTML. Web browsers connect to Web sites, causing HTML data to be sent to the client's computer. The browsers render the HTML, displaying the fonts, colors, and images from the pages in the browser windows.

Uniform Resource Locator (URL)

A **Uniform Resource Locator** (URL) is the universal way of addressing objects and pages on a network. It begins with a protocol such as http://, https://, or ftp://. It is followed by a domain name such as microsoft.com, gaddisbooks.com, or mit.edu. A specially defined domain name for your local computer is **localhost.** The URL may include a specific folder path and/or filename. The following are sample URLs:

```
http://localhost/Default.aspx
http://www.microsoft.com
http://www.kipirvine.com/vbnet/index.html
```

Displaying a Standard Web Page

When you navigate to a Web page in your Web browser, the browser must connect to a Web server. The Web server's job is to wait for connection requests, which occur in two steps:

1. A Web browser connects to the server by sending an **HTTP request** to the Web server. The request contains either an IP address such as 128.42.96.34 or, more commonly, a URL such as http://microsoft.com. The HTTP request may also contain the name of a Web page, such as Default.aspx.
2. The Web server translates the HTTP request into a directory and filename within the server computer's file system. The server reads the requested file, now called a **Web page.** The server sends the Web page back to the user's Web browser over the network. The browser renders (interprets) the HTML by displaying text, graphics, and sound and by executing scripting code.

After sending the Web page to the client, the server immediately breaks the connection. It becomes free to handle Web page requests from other clients.

After a Web page is displayed, the user may click a button or press the *Enter* key, causing the page contents to be sent back to the Web server. This action is called a **postback.** The server processes the page and resends a modified Web page to the browser. The processing might involve updating controls and executing functions in the application's compiled code.

ASP.NET Web Forms

Web applications written in ASP.NET use special Web pages called Web forms. A **Web form** can be identified by its aspx filename extension. A Web form contains text: **HTML tags, HTML controls** (such as buttons and text boxes), and special interactive controls called **server-side controls** (or **server controls**). These controls might be buttons, list boxes, and text boxes that execute on the server. They look like HTML controls but they are more powerful because they use event handler procedures to carry out actions based on user input. They behave a lot like Windows desktop controls.

The source code for a Web form is usually stored in a related file called a **codebehind file,** with the filename extension *aspx.vb*. This part of the application is also known as the **application logic.**

Configuration information is generally stored in two different files. A **Web.config file** contains required information about the runtime environment. Another optional file, called a **cascading style sheet (CSS)** file, contains style names that can be used to alter characteristics of the page, including colors, fonts, alignment, and spacing.

Web Servers

You can execute ASP.NET applications in three primary ways:

- The **ASP.NET Development Server** is installed automatically with Visual Studio and Visual Web Developer. It is easy to use and requires no special security setup, but it is invisible to all other computers on a network. You cannot, for example, run a Web site on one machine and use another machine to browse to the site.

- **Internet Information Services (IIS)** is a professional Web server that you can run on your own computer. It must be configured carefully to ensure proper security. It is visible across a network (or on the Internet), so you can use it to host a public Web site.
- A **remote Web server** is a Web site running on a computer somewhere else on a network. You can copy your application to the remote server before running it. Ordinarily, you must supply a username and password to publish on a remote server. Many companies offer Web site hosting services today.

HTML Designer

HTML Designer is an interactive tool in Visual Studio that you use to design and code Web pages. The designer generates HTML source code and embeds special codes that identify ASP.NET controls. It is possible to create Web forms using a plain text editor, but doing so requires considerable practice. HTML Designer offers three views of a Web page:

- *Design view:* You can visually edit Web pages, using the mouse to drag controls and table borders. This view most closely resembles Visual Studio's editor for Windows forms.
- *Source view:* Use this view to directly edit the HTML source code that makes up a Web form.
- *Split view:* The window is split between Design and Source panes. A change made in one pane will immediately change the contents of the other pane.

Web Browser Support

Several different Web browsers are popular today, each with their own capabilities and characteristics. To make it easier to adapt to different browsers, an ASP.NET-compatible Web server automatically detects the user's browser type and generates standard HTML that is appropriate for the user's browser.

> **TIP:** Before publishing a Web application for public usage, test it with several browsers, including Internet Explorer, Safari, Firefox, and Chrome.

Using Classes in Web Applications

You can create stand-alone classes such as Student, Person, or Account in Web applications. In fact, it's a good idea to do that so you can create multi-tier Web applications. You should always put these classes in a special folder within your project named *App_Code*. When the application starts, the Web server checks to see if any files in this folder have been modified since they were last compiled. If necessary, they are compiled before the applications startup form displays.

Classes must be declared Public for them to be accessible from other Web pages in your application.

Types of Controls

When you design Web forms in Visual Studio, the Toolbox window contains Web-related controls placed in the following groups:

- *Standard*—Also known as Web forms controls, this group contains the most commonly used controls on Web forms. Some are close relatives of Windows forms controls, including Label, Button, ListBox, CheckBox, CheckBoxList, and RadioButton. Others are unique to Web programming, such as the LinkButton and HyperLink controls.

- *Data*—Controls for connecting to data sources; displaying database tables and XML data in grids and lists.
- *Validation*—Controls for validating user input into controls such as text boxes.
- *Navigation*—Advanced controls for navigating between Web pages.
- *Login*—Controls related to authenticating users when they log into a Web site with usernames and passwords.
- *WebParts*—Controls that let a Web site's users modify the content, appearance, and behavior of Web pages directly from a browser.
- *AJAX Extensions*—Controls the use of server-side Ajax technology, a way to improve the user experience in a Web browser.
- *Dynamic Data*—DynamicControl, DynamicDataManager, etc.
- *Reporting*—ReportViewer control.
- *HTML*—Controls found on HTML Web pages, such as buttons, check boxes, radio buttons, lists, and text boxes. They are compatible with standard HTML and have a limited number of properties, no event handling, and no associated classes.
- *General*—Contains text that you may have dragged from the coding area onto the ToolBox window. (*Note:* For instructors especially, this is a good area to save code snippets when they are interactively building an application in class.)

 **Checkpoint**

1. Describe a Web application in your own words.
2. Describe the client-server relationship in a Web application.
3. What is a postback?
4. Why is ASP.NET called a platform?
5. In which files do you create *program logic* in an ASP.NET application?

 ## 8.2 Creating ASP.NET Applications

Types of Web Sites

Four types of Web sites, File System, Local IIS, FTP Site, and Remote Site, appear in the *Open Web Site* window, as shown in Figure 8-1. ASP.NET applications are also known as Web sites or Web applications. To reach this window, select *Open* from the File menu, and then select *Web Site*.

A **File System Web Site** runs directly under the ASP.NET Development Server supplied with Visual Studio and Visual Web Developer. The application files can be stored in any directory. The server is simple to use and does not leave the operating system open to security attacks. This type of Web site is best suited to college laboratory environments. We will use File System Web sites in this book.

A **Local IIS Site** runs under a Windows operating system utility named *Internet Information Services* (IIS). It is a professional-quality Web server with powerful security and configuration features, but it requires some expertise to set up and maintain. IIS requires you to have administrative rights on the computer running the server in order to test and debug Web applications.

FTP Site and **Remote Site** refer to existing ASP.NET Web sites located on remote computers (network or Web). You must supply a username and password to the remote site to upload a copy of your application to the site. Both sites are useful if you want to publish an application to a public Web site.

Figure 8-1 The *Open Web Site* window

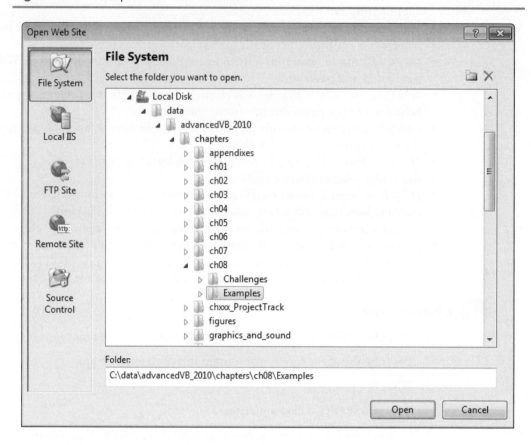

Creating a Web Application

To create a new Web application in Visual Studio, select *New* from the File menu, then select *Web Site*. The *New Web Site* window gives you a list of possible Web sites, as shown in Figure 8-2. Select *ASP.NET Empty Web Site*.

Figure 8-2 *New Web Site* window

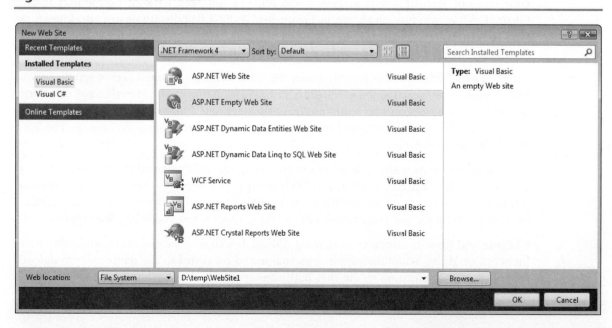

In the *Web location* dropdown list in the lower left corner of the window, select *File System*.

The edit box just to the right of the location lets you choose the path and folder name for your project. Suppose, for example, that you create an application named *Click* in the *c:\data\myWebs* folder. Then a project folder named *c:\data\myWebs\Click* is automatically created by Visual Studio.

The Web site name will appear in the Solution Explorer window. An empty ASP.NET Web site contains only a single file named *web.config*, known as a **Web configuration file**. Later, you will begin to modify this file.

Adding a Page to a Web Site

In any Web site, you will want to have at least one page (known as a *Web form* in ASP.NET). To add a page, right-click the Web site name in Solution Explorer, select *Add New Item*, and select *Web Form*. The window shown in Figure 8-3 will appear. For the first page you add to your site (your application's startup form), the name *Default.aspx* is the usual choice.

Figure 8-3 Adding a page to the Web site

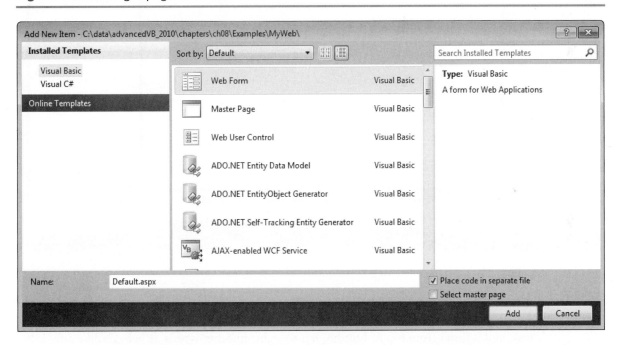

A second file named *Default.aspx.vb* (a *code behind* file) is also created automatically. It holds the Visual Basic code you write for event handlers and other program logic. Figure 8-4 shows the Solution Explorer window for a sample application named *MyWeb*. Our Web site is located inside a Solution container, but that is not required. Your Web site can exist by itself.

Figure 8-4 Files created for the *MyWeb* application

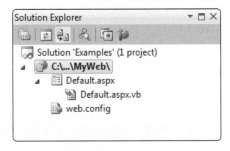

Source, Design, and Split Views

When you open a Web project or add a page to a new project, the page displays in its Source view. In Figure 8-5, near the bottom, notice the three tabs labeled *Design, Split,* and *Source.* These are the three views of, or ways of looking at a Web page. In Source view, two tool-bars are displayed below the menu: Standard and HTML Source Editing (on the right side). You can turn toolbars on an off from the *View / Toolbars* menu.

Figure 8-5 Displaying a page in Source view

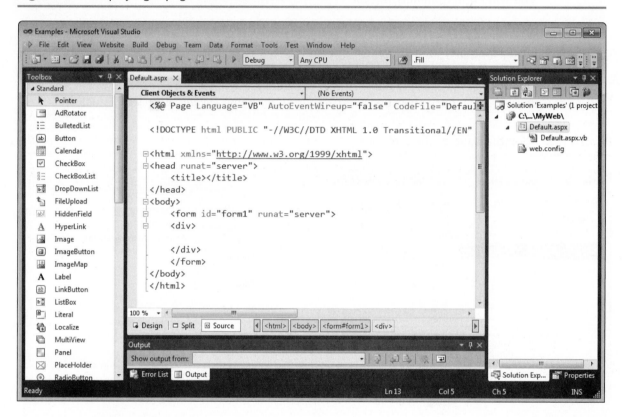

Design View

If you switch to Design view on a blank page, you will see nothing. But you can type text directly into a Web form when it is open in Visual Studio. The text you type is called **static text,** and it flows from top to bottom, left to right. In other words, it behaves like any ordinary text document. In Figure 8-6, for example, three lines of text were typed directly into a Web form in Design view.

Figure 8-6 Static text typed directly on a form in Design view

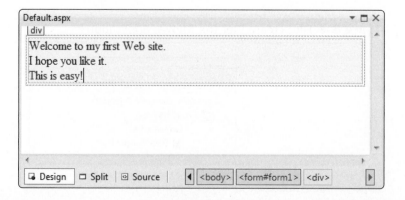

Source View

You can also view and type text into a form when it is in Source view. In that case, you must type the text between markers called HTML tags. In the following example, our text appears between the <div> and </div> tags:

```
<body>
  <form id="form1" runat="server">
    <div>
      Welcome to my first Web site.<br />
      I hope you like it.<br />
      This is easy!
    </div>
  </form>
</body>
```

Sections begin with a tag such as <body> and end with the same tag having a slash before its name, like </body>. Every Web form has a <form> tag. The optional <div> tag is inserted automatically in every new page created by Visual Studio. You can use <div> to assign font and color properties (called *styles*) that apply to all text following <div> until a </div> tag is found.

Each line of text in our example ends with a line break, expressed as <br />. There is another type of break you will often see, which is <p />, a paragraph break. To show the difference, we will modify our text:

```
<body>
  <form id="form1" runat="server">
    <div>
      Welcome to my first Web site.<p />
      I hope you like it.<p />
      This is easy!
    </div>
  </form>
</body>
```

Switching to design view in Figure 8-7, we can see that each line is a separate paragraph.

Most of your work can be done in the Design view. But you may want to gradually switch to working in the Source view, to give yourself more precise control over the page's output.

Figure 8-7 Each line ends in a paragraph break

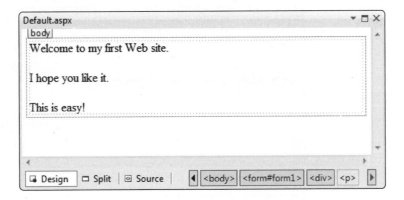

Split View

The Split view, shown in Figure 8-8, lets you see how text in the Design pane is translated into HTML in the Source pane. When you modify the contents of one pane, the other pane is updated automatically.

Figure 8-8 Split view

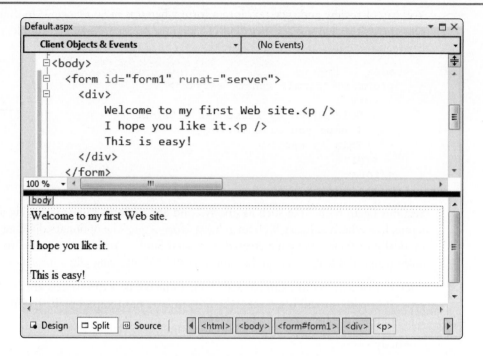

Running a Web Application

To run a Web application that is open in Visual Studio, right-click the name of the application's startup form in the Server Explorer window and select *View in Browser* from the popup menu. A default Web browser is selected for you, but you can select any browser on your computer. To see a list of available Web browsers, right-click the Web form in the Solution Explorer window and select *Browse With. . .* from the popup menu. The window, shown in Figure 8-9, also lets you select the default browser.

In Tutorial 8-1 you will create your first Web application.

Figure 8-9 Selecting a Web browser

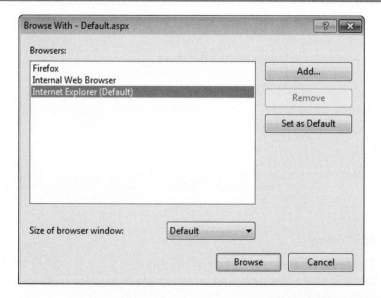

Tutorial 8-1:
Creating the Click application

In this tutorial, you create a Web application named *Click* that contains a Button control and a label that displays text when the button is clicked.

> **TIP:** When we show screen snapshots of Internet explorer, we often remove the Toolbar, status bar, and address bar. This is done only to save space on the printed page and focus your attention on the page's content. You can leave the Toolbar, address bar, and status bar visible in your own browser.

As a preparation step, decide which directory you will use to save Web projects.

Tutorial Steps

Step 1:   Start Visual Studio and, from the File menu, select *New,* then select *Web Site.* As in Figure 8-10, select *Empty ASP.NET Web Site* from the list of project types, name it *Click,* and click the *OK* button to close the window.

Figure 8-10 *New Web Site* window

Step 2:   You will add a new Web form named *Default.aspx* to the Web site. To do that, right-click the Web site name in Solution Explorer, select *Add New Item,* select *Web Form,* and name the form *Default.aspx.*

Step 3:   You are looking at the Source view of a blank Web form. Click the Design tab at the bottom to switch to Design view.

Step 4:   Next, you will create a title that displays in the title bar of the Web browser when the application runs. Select DOCUMENT in the Properties window and set its Title property to *Click Application*.

Step 5:   Switch to Source view and verify that the following text appears between the <title> and </title> tags:

```
<title>Click Application</title>
```

Return to Design view.

Step 6:   Look for the block format dropdown list on the left side of the formatting toolbar just above the Toolbox window (see Figure 8-11). This list contains a list of standard HTML formats that affect the font size, color, and other attributes. Select *Heading 1 <H1>*.

Figure 8-11 Block format pull-down list from the formatting toolbar

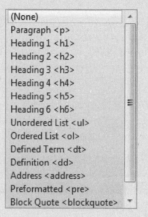

Step 7:   Click the mouse on the first line of the form and type *My Click Application*. Press *Enter* to move to the next line. Figure 8-12 shows a sample of your work so far.

Figure 8-12 After adding a heading in *Heading 1* style

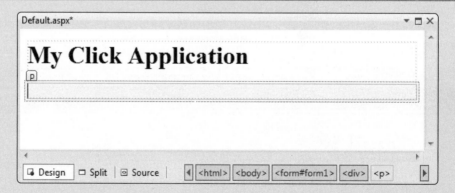

Step 8:   Drag a Button control from the Toolbox window onto your form. Use the mouse to make it wider. Set its Text property to *Click Here*. Set its ID property to *btnClick*.

NOTE: On Web pages, the ID property replaces the Name property used on Windows forms.

Step 9: Click the mouse just to the right of the Button and press *Enter* to move to the next line. Insert a Label control on the next line. Set its ID property to *lblMessage* and clear its Text property.

Step 10: Next, you will add code to the button's Click event handler. Double-click the Button and add the following statement to its Click event handler:

```
lblMessage.Text = "That was a great click!"
```

You have opened the file named *Default.aspx.vb*, which is the codebehind file for this Web page. Code written in this file is compiled by Visual Basic. It can contain classes and objects in the same way as Windows forms.

Step 11: Save the project. To open *Default.aspx* in the Web browser, right-click its name in the Solution explorer window and select *View in Browser*. When the Web browser opens your application, click the *Click Here* button. A message should appear below the button, as shown in Figure 8-13. Our example uses the Internet Explorer Web browser, but you can use a different one.

Figure 8-13 After clicking the button in the *Click* application

Step 12: Close the browser window.

Running in Debug Mode

You can start a program in Debug mode by selecting *Start Debugging* from the Debug menu. The first time you run a Web application in Debug mode, you will see the message box shown in Figure 8-14. When you click the *OK* button, a configuration file named *Web.config* is added to your project, containing an option that permits debugging.

```
<system.web>
  <compilation debug="true" targetFramework="4.0"/>
</system.web>
```

Figure 8-14 Debugging an application for the first time

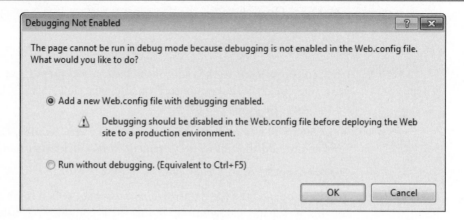

Useful Tips

Tip 1: Renaming the class behind a Web form

If you rename a Web form's class in the form's codebehind file, you must manually modify the first line of the Web form's XHTML code. Suppose the form's class is named *Default*.

```
public partial class _Default : System.Web.UI.Page
```

And you rename the class to *MainForm*.

```
public partial class MainForm : System.Web.UI.Page
```

Then you must open the form's aspx file and look for the *Page* directive on the first line.

```
<%@ Page Language="VB" AutoEventWireup="false" CodeFile="MainForm.aspx.vb"
    Inherits="_Default" %>
```

And change the *Inherits* property setting to the following:

```
<%@ Page Language="VB" AutoEventWireup="false" CodeFile="MainForm.aspx.vb"
    Inherits="MainForm" %>
```

Tip 2: Creating an HTTP Web Site

In the *Web location* option on the *Add New Web Site* window, if you select the *HTTP* option, your Web site will run under Internet Information Services (IIS). You enter the URL of your new Web site. The server must be running in one of two places:

- On your local computer. You must install and configure IIS in order to choose this type of Web site to run on your local computer. You must configure a base location for all your Web sites, using the configuration options in IIS.
- On a remote Web server where you have an account with an Internet service provider that supports ASP.NET. You use a domain name on the server as the base location for your HTTP site. For example, suppose your domain name were *mydomain.com*. You could create a new application named *MyWeb* by specifying the following URL:

```
http://mydomain.com/MyWeb
```

The Internet service provider would prompt you for a username and password.

 **Checkpoint**

6. Name four types of Web sites you can open in Visual Studio.

7. When you create a Web site, which tab must you click to switch from the startup page's Source view to Design view?

8. How do you select from a list of Web browsers when running a Web application in Visual Studio?

9. What is static text? How is it similar to or different from Label controls in Windows forms?

10. In the *Click* application, how did you specify the block format named Heading 1 for the first line of text in the Web form?

11. What special message appears the first time you run an ASP.NET application in Debug mode?

8.3 ASP.NET Controls

ASP.NET controls, also known as **Web server controls,** make Web applications dynamic and interactive. They are more powerful than standard HTML controls because each is defined by a class with a rich set of properties, methods, and events. The controls look and feel like Windows controls, making them easy to learn.

The following ASP.NET controls are the ones you are likely to use often. Except for those marked with an asterisk (*), all have counterparts among the controls used on Windows forms.

Button
ImageButton
LinkButton
Text Box
Label
RadioButton
RadioButtonList*
CheckBox
CheckBoxList*
ListBox
DropDownList (similar to the ComboBox control)
Image (similar to the PictureBox control)
Calendar (similar to the MonthCalendar control)

ASP.NET controls have similar properties to their Windows Forms counterparts. Examples of such properties are Text, Enabled, Visible, Font, BorderStyle, ReadOnly, and TabIndex. There are a few important differences, however, between ASP.NET controls and Windows controls:

- The ID property of ASP.NET controls is the counterpart to the Name property of Windows controls.
- ASP.NET controls have an important new property named AutoPostBack.
- ASP.NET controls lose their runtime values when the user moves away from the current page. Special programming techniques can overcome this disadvantage.

Web server controls are unique to ASP.NET. When a user connects to an ASP.NET Web page, a special process takes place, as shown in Figure 8-15. In Step (2), the Web server reads and interprets the ASP.NET controls on the page and executes Visual Basic statements in the application's codebehind file. In Step (3), the server creates a modified Web page consisting of standard HTML tags and controls. In Step (4), the modified Web page is sent back to the user and displayed in the Web browser.

Label Control

The ASP.NET **Label control** is almost identical to the Label control used in Windows applications. When displaying text, you need to use a Label only if its contents will change at

Figure 8-15 Connecting to ASP.NET Web pages

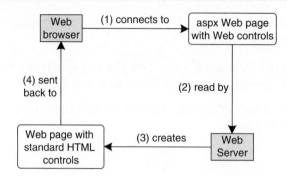

runtime, or if you need to change its Visible property. Assign a name to a Label's ID property if you plan to access it in code statements.

This is how a Label control is declared in the form's XHTML source code:

```
<asp:Label
   ID="Label1"
   runat="server"
   Text="This is a label">
</asp:Label>
```

Here are some important details to notice about the example:

- Attribute values are enclosed in quotation marks.
- There is no rule regarding indentation or line breaks. Programmers often prefer to arrange each property value on a separate line, as we have done, to make editing easier.
- ASP.NET controls always begin with the prefix *asp:*.
- All ASP.NET controls require the *runat="server"* attribute.
- A default value is assigned to the ID property, but you should rename it if you plan to refer to it in coding statements.
- The Text property holds a string that appears in the label at runtime.

Figure 8-16 shows how the label appears when displayed in a browser.

Figure 8-16 A Label control at runtime

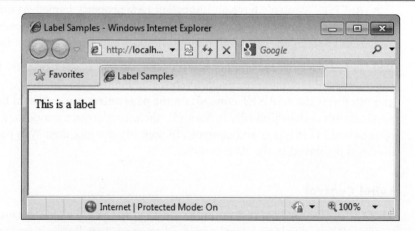

If you want to make a copy of a control, you can do it in Source view by copying the code to the clipboard and pasting it again. You just need to ensure that each control's ID property has a different value.

TextBox Control

The ASP.NET **TextBox control** is similar in many ways to the TextBox control for Windows applications. The *Text* property holds text that is entered by the user. The *MaxLength* property lets you limit the number of characters the user is permitted to type. The *TextMode* property has three possible values:

- SingleLine—Permits the user to enter only a single line of input.
- MultiLine—Permits the user to enter multiple lines of input in the box.
- Password—Characters typed by the user appear as asterisks.

Internet Explorer and other browsers behave differently when using the TextBox control. To be as compatible as possible with all Web browsers, you should use the *Columns* property to control the width of the TextBox. If you want the user to enter multiple lines of input, set the *Rows* property accordingly. In the following code, we declare two text boxes, a Single-Line and a MultiLine, with some static text in between:

```
TextMode = SingleLine:
<asp:TextBox
  ID="TextBox1"
  BorderWidth="1"
  runat="server">
  </asp:TextBox>
<p />

TextMode = Multiline:<br />
<asp:TextBox
  ID="TextBox2"
  runat="server"
  Columns="40"
  TextMode="MultiLine"
  BorderWidth="1"Rows="15">
  </asp:TextBox>
```

Notice that we also set the *BorderWidth* property of the text boxes to one pixel to make them easier for the user to see.

Figure 8-17 shows how these controls look in the user's browser.

Visual Studio does not provide a tool to set the Tab order on Web forms. By default, all controls have their TabIndex property set to 0, and the tab order at runtime will move sequentially down the page. If you want use a specific tab order, you must set the TabIndex for each control to a value greater than 0. If the browser's Address bar is visible, it will automatically consume one tab stop.

CheckBox Control

The ASP.NET CheckBox control is almost identical to the CheckBox in Windows applications. Use its Text property to set the visible text, and evaluate the *Checked* property at run time. The *TextAlign* property lets you position the text to the left or right of the box.

```
<asp:CheckBox
  ID="chkSavePassword"
  Text="Save my password"
  runat="server" />
```

Notice that an ending </asp:CheckBox> tag is not required.

Figure 8-17 TextMode examples: SingleLine and MultiLine

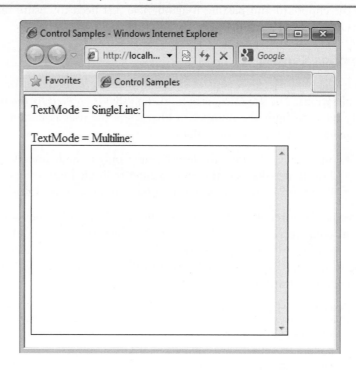

In Tutorial 8-2, you will create a Web form that uses labels, text boxes, a button, and a check box.

Tutorial 8-2:
Student Picnic application

In this tutorial, you will create an online sign-up application for a student picnic. Figure 8-18 shows how the application looks when it loads in the Web browser.

Figure 8-18 Picnic Signup application, on startup

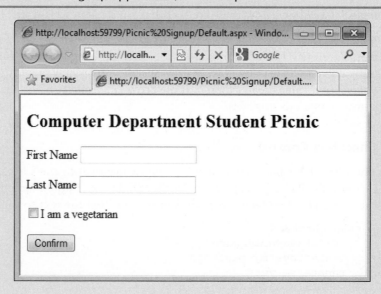

Tutorial Steps

Step 1: Create a new empty ASP.NET Web site named *Student Picnic* and add a Web form named *Default.aspx* to the site.

Step 2: Open *Default.aspx* in Source view and remove the <div> and </div> tags.

Step 3: Add the following code between the tags marked *<form id="form1" runat="server">*, and *</form>*:

```
<h2>Computer Department Student Picnic</h2>
First Name
<asp:TextBox
   ID="txtFirst"
   runat="server">
   </asp:TextBox>
```

The first line creates a level-two heading with the application title. The second line contains static text. Beginning on the third line, a TextBox control is named *txtFirst*.

Step 4: Add a second prompt and a text box for the last name. To save time, you may want to copy the first text box to the clipboard and paste a copy into the code editor.

```
<p />
Last Name
<asp:TextBox
   ID="txtLast"
   runat="server">
   </asp:TextBox>
```

The first line inserts a paragraph break.

Step 5: Add the following code, which inserts a paragraph break followed by a CheckBox control:

```
<p />
<asp:CheckBox
   ID="chkVegetarian"
   runat="server"
   Text="I am a vegetarian"/>
```

Step 6: Add the following paragraph break and Button control:

```
<p />
<asp:Button
   ID="btnConfirm"
   runat="server"
   Text="Confirm" />
```

Step 7: Add a Label control that will hold a response message to the user:

```
<p />
<asp:Label
   ID="lblMessage"
   runat="server">
   </asp:Label>
```

Next, you will write code in the form's codebehind file.

Step 8: Open the file named *Default.aspx.vb* and add the following *Page_Load* event handler:

```
Protected Sub Page_Load() Handles Me.Load
  txtFirst.Focus()
End Sub
```

This statement sets the input focus to the TextBox when the browser loads the page.

Step 9: Create the following Click event handler:

```
Protected Sub btnConfirm_Click() Handles btnConfirm.Click
  ' The user clicked the Confirm button.
  lblMessage.Text = "Thank you for signing up for the " _
    & "picnic, " & txtFirst.Text & " " & txtLast.Text & "."
  If chkVegetarian.Checked Then
    lblMessage.Text &= " You will be receiving a " _
    & "Vegetarian meal."
  End If
End Sub
```

This code may seem familiar because it is identical to how a Click handler would be written in a Windows Forms application. Microsoft's intent was to make the transition from desktop to Web programming as smooth as possible.

Step 10: View the Default.aspx page in your browser. Enter a person's name, select the check box, and click the *Confirm* button. The output should be similar to Figure 8-19. Notice that when you resize the browser window, the message at the bottom automatically wraps around to the next line.

Figure 8-19 The Student Picnic program, after clicking the *Confirm* button

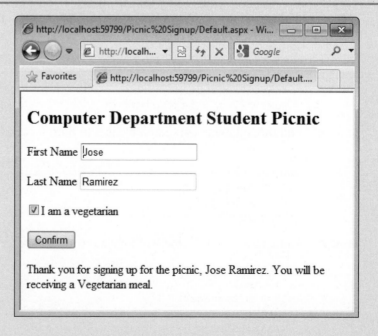

Step 11: Uncheck the check box and click the *Confirm* button again. The vegetarian portion of the message should disappear.

Web Form Events

Visual Basic programmers are usually pleased to find out that they can write code in ASP.NET pages in nearly the same way they write code in Windows applications. For example, every button generates a Click event.

```
Protected Sub btnOk_Click() Handles btnOk.Click
End Sub
```

Page_Load Event

Perhaps the most important Web form event of all is the Page_Load event, which is very similar to the Form_Load event in Windows Forms applications. The Page_Load event fires when a page is first loaded into the user's browser and posted to the server.

You typically put code in Page_Load that initializes controls and other class-level variables. In Tutorial 8-2, for example, you inserted code that set the initial input focus to the txtLastName TextBox.

```
txtFirst.Focus()
```

Page_Load also fires when a page is posted back to the server. This happens, for example, when the user clicks a Button control.

IsPostBack Property

Sometimes code must execute only once when a page is loaded but not each time the page posts back. For example, you might want to preselect a ListBox item when the form loads. There is a way to know if the page is being posted back and not loaded. The Page object has an **IsPostBack property** that equals *True* when the page is posting back rather than loading for the first time. The following code shows how you can selectively execute code either when the page is loaded for the first time or when it is posted back:

```
Protected Sub Page_Load() Handles Me.Load
   If IsPostBack Then
   ' Code in here only executes during postbacks.
   Else
   ' Code in here only executes when the page loads.
   Endif
   ' Code in this area executes when the page loads
   ' and when the page is posted back.
End Sub
```

Tutorial 8-3:
Tracking server events

In this Tutorial, you will create an application that tracks different server events as they happen on a Web page. The events you will track are Page_Load, Click (button), and TextChanged.

Events are fired in a different sequence in Web forms than they are in Windows forms. The Web form shown in Figure 8-20 inserts a message in the ListBox each time the Page_Load event fires. From the program display, we can see that Page_Load fired when the page was loaded in the browser.

Figure 8-20 Immediately after the Web form loads

Tutorial Steps

Step 1: Create a new empty ASP.NET Web site named *Event Demo* and add a Web form named *Default.aspx* to the site.

Step 2: Open *Default.aspx* in Source view and remove the <div> and </div> tags.

Step 3: Add the following code between the tags marked *<form id="form1" runat="server">*, and *</form>*:

```
<h1>Events</h1>
Enter your name:
<asp:TextBox
  ID="txtName"
  Columns="25"
  runat="server">
  </asp:TextBox>

<asp:Button
  ID="btnOk"
  runat="server"
  Text="OK" />

<p />
<asp:ListBox
  ID="lstEvents"
  runat="server"
  Width="250px"
  Height="109px">
  </asp:ListBox>
```

The ListBox control is empty at first, but it will be filled with the names of events.

Step 4: Open the form's codebehind file and insert the following code inside the class:

```
Protected Sub Page_Load() Handles Me.Load
  lstEvents.Items.Add("Page_Load")
End Sub
```

```
        Protected Sub txtName_TextChanged() Handles txtName.TextChanged
          lstEvents.Items.Add("TextChanged")
        End Sub

        Protected Sub btnOk_Click() Handles btnOk.Click
          lstEvents.Items.Add("Button Click")
        End Sub
```

The Page_Load, TextChanged, and Click events are all represented in this code. Each handler writes a line to the ListBox control that identifies the event name.

Step 5: Type in a name and click the *OK* button. As shown in Figure 8-21, the Page_Load event executes again because a postback event was fired. Then the TextChanged event handler executes, followed by the button's Click event.

Figure 8-21 After entering a name and clicking the *OK* button

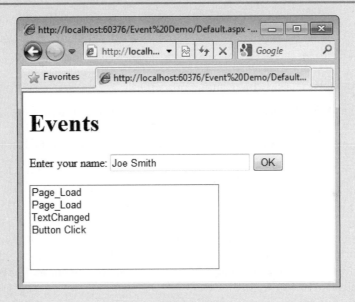

The sequence of events is different on Web forms compared to the sequence on Windows forms. Most notably, the TextChanged and Click events do not fire until after the page is reloaded.

8.4 List-Type Controls

The ListBox, DropDownList, CheckBoxList, and RadioButtonList can all be classified as **list-type controls**. They have the following common characteristics:

- All use the <ListItem> tag to identify items in their lists.
- All have an Items collection, and you can add items to it using the *ListItem Collection Editor* window, shown in Figure 8-22.
- All have a *ValueMember* property.
- All have a *SelectedIndexChanged* event.

Figure 8-22 ListItem Collection Editor window

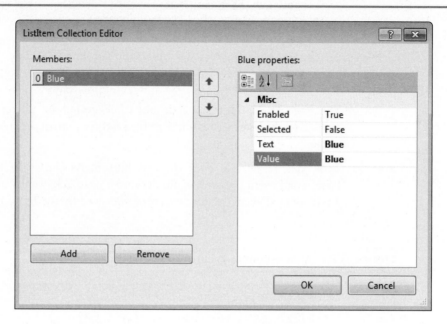

All have the following runtime properties:

- *SelectedIndex* returns the index of the selected item.
- *SelectedItem* returns the currently selected item, a ListItem object.
- *SelectedValue* returns the contents of the field identified by the *ValueMember* property.

The SelectedIndex property equals 0 when no item has been selected.

ListBox Control

In many ways, the ASP.NET **ListBox control** is similar to the ListBox control for Windows Forms applications. The main difference is that the first item (at index 0) is automatically selected when the Web page displays. This is how an empty ListBox named *lstColors* would be coded in XHTML:

```
<asp:ListBox
   ID="lstColors"
   runat="server"
   </asp:ListBox>
```

Another option would be to add Width and Height properties, measured in pixels, as follows:

```
<asp:ListBox
   ID="lstColors"
   runat="server"
   Width="150px"
   Height="50px">
   </asp:ListBox>
```

Adding ListBox Items

A ListBox has an Items collection, which can be filled in at runtime by calling the *Items.Add* method. Or in the page's Design view, you can open the *ListBox Tasks* window shown in Figure 8-23, and select *Edit Items*. This brings up the *ListItem Collection Editor* window.

Figure 8-23 ListBox Tasks window

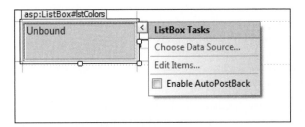

Or you can insert items directly into its XHTML code, as shown below. Each item is encoded as an ASP.NET ListItem control.

```
<asp:ListBox
  ID="lstColors"
  runat="server">
  <asp:ListItem>Blue</asp:ListItem>
  <asp:ListItem>Red</asp:ListItem>
  <asp:ListItem>Green</asp:ListItem>
  <asp:ListItem>Lavender</asp:ListItem>
</asp:ListBox>
```

SelectionMode

You can use the *SelectionMode* property to determine whether users can select only a single item or multiple items from a ListBox. The two possible choices are *Single* and *Multiple*. In Multiple mode, the user can hold down the *Ctrl* key to select multiple individual items or hold down the *Shift* key to select a range of items.

SelectedIndexChanged Event and the AutoPostBack Property

You can use a *SelectedIndexChanged* event handler to respond to selections by the user in any list-type control. There is one important consideration, however: the **AutoPostBack property** must equal *True* if you want the user's selection to be detected immediately. Otherwise, the SelectedIndexChanged event will not fire until the form is posted back to the server by some other control (such as a button). By default, Auto-PostBack equals *False*.

When AutoPostBack equals *True* for a list-type control, the user experiences a short delay each time he or she clicks on the list. Depending on the Web server's response time, the delay can be inconvenient for users. Most Web applications do not post back to the server each time users select items in lists. Instead, the sites use button controls to post all selections on the page back to the server at the same time.

AutoPostBack defaults to *False* for the CheckBox, CheckBoxList, DropDownList, ListBox, ListControl, RadioButton, RadioButtonList, and TextBox controls. Other controls, such as Button, LinkButton, and ImageButton automatically post the current page back to the server, so they have no need for an AutoPostBack property.

Control

The **CheckBoxList control** looks like a group of check boxes but works like a ListBox. In fact, the following code is identical to that of our previous ListBox, except that we changed *ListBox* to *CheckBoxList*:

```
<asp:CheckBoxList
  ID="lstColors"
  runat="server">
  <asp:ListItem>Blue</asp:ListItem>
  <asp:ListItem>Red</asp:ListItem>
  <asp:ListItem>Green</asp:ListItem>
  <asp:ListItem>Lavender</asp:ListItem>
</asp:CheckBoxList>
```

Like the Listbox, a CheckBoxList has *SelectedIndex*, *SelectedItem*, and *SelectedValue* properties. It has an *Items* collection, and each item has a *Selected* property (equal to *True* or *False*).

Figure 8-24 shows our CheckBoxList at runtime. You can iterate over the *Items* collection to find out which boxes have been checked. The following code is a sample:

```
For Each item As ListItem In lstColors.Items
  If item.Selected Then
  'do something
  End If
Next
```

Figure 8-24 CheckBoxList control

DropDownList Control

The **DropDownList control** permits the user to select a single item from a list. This is how a sample would be coded:

```
<asp:DropDownList
  ID="lstColors"
  runat="server">
  <asp:ListItem>Blue</asp:ListItem>
  <asp:ListItem>Red</asp:ListItem>
  <asp:ListItem>Green</asp:ListItem>
  <asp:ListItem>Lavender</asp:ListItem>
</asp:DropDownList>
```

Again, we just borrowed our earlier ListBox code and changed <asp:ListBox> to <asp:DropDownList> tag.

A DropDownList looks like a Windows ComboBox control, but there are two important differences. In a DropDownList, the initial value of SelectedIndex is 0, causing the first item to display. Also, users cannot enter an arbitrary string into the DropDownList, but they can do so in a ComboBox.

Figure 8-25 shows a simple expansion of a list by the user at runtime.

Figure 8-25 The user is expanding a DropDownList control

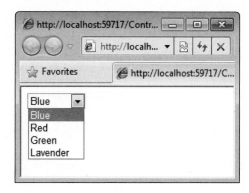

RadioButtonList Control

The **RadioButtonList control** displays a group of radio buttons, shown in Figure 8-26. You could create a set of individual RadioButton controls, but a single RadioButtonList is easier to use. As with any radio button list, only one item can be selected at a time. This is how we coded the control:

```
<asp:RadioButtonList
   ID="lstColors"
   runat="server">
   <asp:ListItem>Blue</asp:ListItem>
   <asp:ListItem>Red</asp:ListItem>
   <asp:ListItem>Green</asp:ListItem>
   <asp:ListItem>Lavender</asp:ListItem>
   </asp:RadioButtonList>
```

You can arrange the buttons horizontally or vertically, using the *RepeatDirection* property (the default is vertical).

Figure 8-26 RadioButtonList example

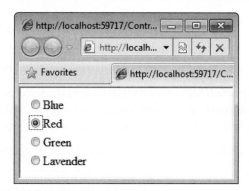

Calendar Control

The **Calendar control** lets the user select one or more dates from a monthly calendar grid. It is similar to the MonthCalendar control for Windows applications. Its default format is shown at runtime in Figure 8-27. Here is the code that created the sample control:

```
<asp:Calendar
   ID="Calendar1"
   runat="server">
   </asp:Calendar>
```

Figure 8-27 Calendar control in default format

≤		August 2010				≥
Sun	Mon	Tue	Wed	Thu	Fri	Sat
25	26	27	28	29	30	31
1	2	3	4	5	6	7
8	9	10	11	12	13	14
15	16	17	18	19	20	21
22	23	24	25	26	27	28
29	30	31	1	2	3	4

There are a number of predefined styles (fonts, colors) for this control. To select one, click on the control's Smart Tag in Design view, select *AutoFormat*, and choose from several standard formats. Figure 8-28 shows the result after choosing a format named *Professional 1*.

Figure 8-28 Calendar control, using the *Professional 1* format

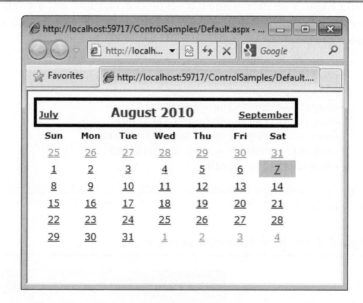

Some essential Calendar control properties are listed here:

- The *SelectedDate* property gets or sets the selected date—it defaults to the current date.
- The *VisibleDate* property determines which month is displayed.
- The *IsSelectable* property determines whether the user will be able to select dates.

The SelectionChanged event fires when the user selects a date. For example, the following code copies a Calendar's selected date into a Label control:

```
lblDate.Text = Calendar1.SelectedDate.ToString("d")
```

Selecting Weeks

By changing the *SelectionMode* property to *DayWeek*, you permit the user to select either a day or an entire week in the Calendar control, as shown in Figure 8-29. The *SelectedDate* property returns only the first day of the selected week. But you can iterate over the *SelectedDates* collection to get all dates in the range. The following statements display the list of selected dates to a Label control:

```
For Each dt As Date In Calendar1.SelectedDates
    lblDate.Text &= dt.ToString("d") & " "
Next
```

Figure 8-29 Selecting a week in the Calendar control

Tutorial 8-4:
Signing up for a Kayak Tour

The *Kayak Tour Scheduler* application lets a user sign up for kayak tours, as shown in Figure 8-30. The user selects the type of tour from a RadioButtonList, the type of kayak from a DropDownList, and optional equipment items from a CheckBoxList. The date is selected from a Calendar control. When the *Confirm* button is clicked, the user's selections are displayed in a Label control at the bottom of the window.

Figure 8-30 Kayak Tour Scheduler application

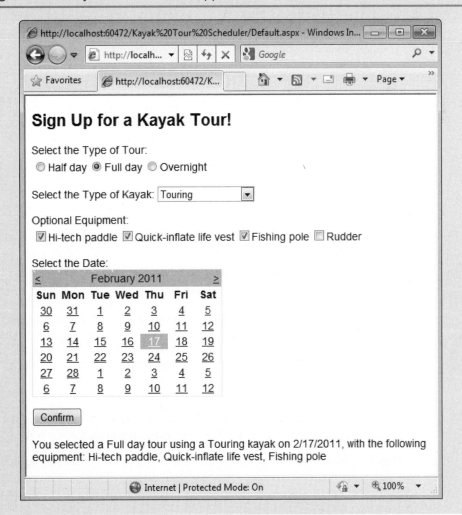

Tutorial Steps

Step 1: Create a new empty ASP.NET Web site named *Kayak Tour Scheduler* and add a Web form named *Default.aspx* to the site.

Step 2: Open *Default.aspx* in Source view and modify the <body> tag so it looks like this:

```
<body style="font-family:Arial;font-size:.9em">
```

The style property shown here sets the name of the font (Arial), and the font size (.9em, or 90% of the standard font size in the user's browser).

Step 3: On the next line following the <form> tag, add a level-two heading and a RadioButtonList control that holds different types of tours.

```
<h2>Sign Up for a Kayak Tour!</h2>
Select the Type of Tour:
<asp:RadioButtonList
  ID="lstTourType"
  RepeatDirection="Horizontal"
  runat="server">
  <asp:ListItem>Half day</asp:ListItem>
  <asp:ListItem>Full day</asp:ListItem>
  <asp:ListItem>Overnight</asp:ListItem>
  </asp:RadioButtonList>
<p />
```

Step 4: Add a DropDownList that holds a list of kayak types.

```
Select the Type of Kayak:
<asp:DropDownList
  ID="lstKayakType"
  runat="server">
  <asp:ListItem>Sit on top single</asp:ListItem>
  <asp:ListItem>Sit on top tandem</asp:ListItem>
  <asp:ListItem>Touring</asp:ListItem>
  <asp:ListItem>Sea Kayak</asp:ListItem>
  </asp:DropDownList>
<p />
```

Step 5: Add a CheckBoxList that lets users select optional equipment items.

```
<div>
Optional Equipment:
<asp:CheckBoxList
  ID="lstEquipment"
  RepeatDirection="Horizontal"
  runat="server">
  <asp:ListItem>Hi-tech paddle</asp:ListItem>
  <asp:ListItem>Quick-inflate life vest</asp:ListItem>
  <asp:ListItem>Fishing pole</asp:ListItem>
  <asp:ListItem>Rudder</asp:ListItem>
  </asp:CheckBoxList>
</div>
```

Above, a <div> tag groups the line of static text with the CheckBoxList control to prevent a blank line from appearing between them at runtime.

Step 6: Add a Calendar control that lets the user select the tour date. The VisibleDate property determines the first date displayed by the Calendar.

```
<p />
<div>
Select the Date:
<asp:Calendar
  ID="calTourDate"
  VisibleDate="2/1/2011"
  runat="server">
  </asp:Calendar>
</div>
```

Step 7: Add a *Confirm* button and a Label that will display information about the reservation.

```
<p />
<asp:Button
  ID="btnConfirm"
  runat="server"
  Text="Confirm" />

<p />
<asp:Label
  ID="lblComments"
  runat="server">
  </asp:Label>
```

Codebehind File

Step 8: Open the form's codebehind file and add the following Click handler for the *Confirm* button:

```
 1:  Protected Sub btnConfirm_Click() Handles btnConfirm.Click
 2:      ' The user clicked the Confirm button.
 3:      lblComments.Text =
 4:        "You selected a " _
 5:        & lstTourType.SelectedItem.ToString _
 6:        & " tour using a " _
 7:        & lstKayakType.SelectedItem.ToString _
 8:        & " kayak on " _
 9:        & calTourDate.SelectedDate.ToString("d")
10:
11:      ' Build the equipment list.
12:      Dim equip As String = String.Empty
13:      For Each item As ListItem In lstEquipment.Items
14:        If item.Selected Then
15:          equip &= item.ToString & ", "
16:        End If
17:      Next
18:      ' Display the equipment list.
19:      If equip.Length > 0 Then
20:        ' Remove the final comma and space.
21:        equip = equip.Remove(equip.Length - 2)
22:        ' Append to the Label.
23:        lblComments.Text &= ", with the following equipment: " _
24:          & equip
25:      End If
26: End Sub
```

Lines 3–9 build a string containing the user's selected items from the list of tours (lstTourType) and kayaks (lstKayakType), and the selected date from the

> calendar (calTourDate). Lines 13–17 loop through the *lstEquipment* Check-BoxList control and, for every selected item, add its name to a string. Line 19 checks to see if the string containing the list of equipment (named equip) is not empty. On line 23, the string is appended to the Label control.
>
> **Step 9:**   Save and view the page in a browser. As you change the values of controls, click the *Confirm* button, and observe that the page is posted back to the server and refreshed.
>
> It's important to see that much of the VB code you write for Web applications is the same as it would be for Windows Forms applications. We encourage you to learn about many of the other amazing controls that you find in the Visual Studio Toolbox.

 Checkpoint

12. Which ASP.NET control is the counterpart to the ComboBox in Windows forms?

13. Which ASP.NET control displays an image and fires a Click event?

14. Which ASP.NET control looks like a hyperlink (underlined text) and fires a Click event?

15. How can you find out which button in a RadioButtonList control was selected by the user?

16. How does setting AutoPostBack to *True* affect a ListBox control?

17. Which list-type control automatically initializes its SelectedIndex property to zero?

18. Which Calendar control property returns a single date selected by the user?

8.5 Designing Web Forms

Using Panels to Hide and Show Groups of Controls

One of the easiest to use and most powerful controls is the Panel. It is a blank container that can hold other controls as well as static text. It is defined like this:

```
<asp:Panel
  ID="Panel1"
  runat="server">
</asp:Panel>
```

Often, a Panel's *Visible* property will equal *False* when a page is first displayed, and you use runtime code to change Visible to *True*. To the user, the panel will seem almost like a popup window because it appears out of nowhere, anywhere on a page. In Design mode, all panels and controls are visible, regardless of the value of their Visible property.

You can use panels to control a user's sequence of inputs, much in the same way that a software wizard does so. Often, a selection made by the user at one stage will determine which Panel is displayed next.

College Advising Example

Suppose we have a Panel control named *pnlNewStudent* that contains information for newly admitted college students. Another Panel control named *pnlReturnStudent* has information for returning students. If an integer variable named *studentType* contains either 0 or 1, we can decide which panel to display.

```
Select Case studentType
   Case 0
      pnlNewStudent.Visible = True
   Case 1
      pnlReturnStudent.Visible = True
End Select
```

Or using best coding practices, we can declare an enumerated type for the two types of students.

```
Enum StudentStatus
   NewStudent
   ReturningStudent
End Enum
```

Then the Select Case statement can be coded like this:

```
Select Case studentType
   Case StudentStatus.NewStudent
      pnlNewStudent.Visible = True
   Case StudentStatus.ReturningStudent
      pnlReturnStudent.Visible = True
End Select
```

In Tutorial 8-5, you will create a short application that shows and hides Panels according to the user's actions.

TIP: Use a *nonbreaking space* character to force the browser to display a space. Normally, spaces within a page's XHTML markup are ignored by the browser unless they are enclosed in quotation marks. But if you insert the string * *; into the markup, the browser will display a space. In the following example, the Button controls are separated by two nonbreaking spaces:

```
<asp:Button ID="btnAdd" runat="server" Text="Add" />
 / 
<asp:Button ID="btnReplace" runat="server" Text="Replace" />
```

Tutorial 8-5:
College Advising Wizard

In this tutorial, you will create a short application that begins the process of online advising for college students. At the start, the student will be asked to make a selection, as shown in Figure 8-31. If the student clicks the *New student* button, the panel shown in Figure 8-32 is displayed. Notice that the initial question, which was also in a panel, has disappeared. If the student clicks the *Returning student* button when the page loads, the panel shown in Figure 8-33 is displayed.

Figure 8-31 College Advisor, initial question

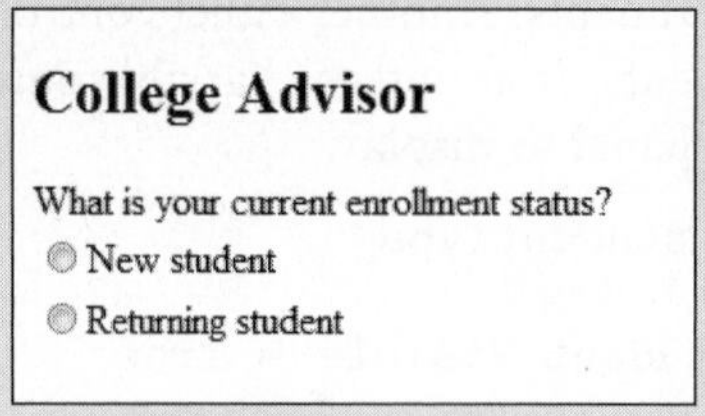

Figure 8-32 College Advisor, new student

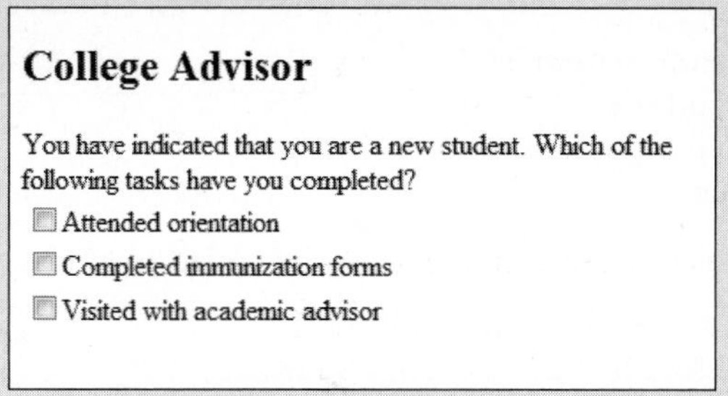

Figure 8-33 College Advisor, returning student

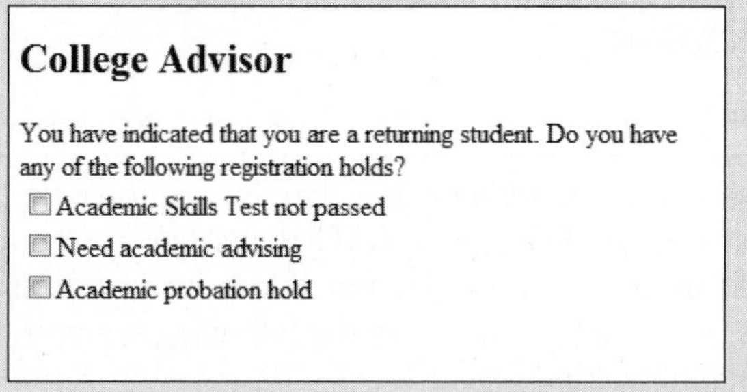

Tutorial Steps

Step 1: Create a new, empty ASP.NET Web site named *College Advising Wizard* and add a Web form named *Default.aspx* to the site.

Step 2: Add the following code to *Default.aspx*, in *Source* view. It creates a title (College Advisor) and a Panel control that contains the initial question and a RadioButtonList.

```
<h2>College Advisor</h2>
<asp:Panel ID="pnlStart" runat="server">
What is your current enrollment status?
  <asp:RadioButtonList ID="lstStudentType" runat="server"
    AutoPostBack="true">
    <asp:ListItem>New student</asp:ListItem>
    <asp:ListItem>Returning student</asp:ListItem>
  </asp:RadioButtonList>
</asp:Panel>
<p />
```

Step 3: Add the following code:

```
<asp:Panel ID="pnlNewStudent" runat="server" Visible="false">
You have indicated that you are a new student. Which of the
following tasks have you completed?
  <asp:CheckBoxList
    ID="lstNewStudentTasks" runat="server">
    <asp:ListItem>Attended orientation</asp:ListItem>
    <asp:ListItem>Completed immunization forms</asp:ListItem>
    <asp:ListItem>Visited with academic advisor</asp:ListItem>
  </asp:CheckBoxList>
</asp:Panel>
```

Step 4: Add the following code:

```
<asp:Panel ID="pnlReturnStudent" runat="server" Visible="false">
You have indicated that you are a returning student. Do you have
any of the following registration holds?
  <asp:CheckBoxList
    ID="lstRegistrationHolds"
    runat="server">
    <asp:ListItem>Academic Skills Test not passed</asp:ListItem>
    <asp:ListItem>Need academic advising</asp:ListItem>
    <asp:ListItem>Academic probation hold</asp:ListItem>
  </asp:CheckBoxList>
</asp:Panel>
```

Codebehind File

Step 5: Add the following VB code to the class in the form's codebehind file. As you can see, there's not much code to write:

```
 1:  Enum StudentStatus
 2:     NewStudent
 3:     ReturningStudent
 4:  End Enum
 5:
 6:  Protected Sub lstStudentType_SelectedIndexChanged() _
 7:     Handles lstStudentType.SelectedIndexChanged
 8:        pnlStart.Visible = False
 9:        Select Case lstStudentType.SelectedIndex
10:          Case StudentStatus.NewStudent
11:             pnlNewStudent.Visible = True
12:          Case StudentStatus.ReturningStudent
13:             pnlReturnStudent.Visible = True
14:        End Select
15:  End Sub
```

Step 6: View the Web form in the browser and test its operation.

If you were to add several more steps to this Wizard, each with its own panel, the Web form would soon become difficult to maintain. At some point, you would probably want to spread out the wizard among multiple Web forms. But for a simple set of choices, the Panel control is a great tool.

Using Tables to Align Text and Controls

The **HTML Table control** is an essential tool for designing the layout of Web forms. You can use it to align text, graphics, and controls in rows and columns.

The following HTML defines a table with one row (identified by <tr> . . . </tr>) and two cells within the row:

```
<table>
  <tr>
    <td>one</td>
    <td>two</td>
  </tr>
</table>
```

The tag used to define a cell within a row is <td>. If we were to view this table in a browser, it would just appear as two words side by side. However, we can add a border and widen the first cell by setting its style property.

```
<table border="1">
  <tr>
    <td style="width:150px">one</td>
    <td>two</td>
  </tr>
</table>
```

Now, this is what the table looks like at runtime:

Adding a border is useful when laying out controls because you can see the cell borders when looking at the page in Design view.

Using the Visual Studio Table Designer

Coding HTML tables by hand is a lot of work, so you will probably want to use the table designer in Visual Studio. You must be looking at the Design view of a page to use it. There are two ways to insert a table when viewing a form's design:

- Select *Insert Table* from the Layout menu. When you do so, the *Insert Table* window appears, letting you set various table layout options (see Figure 8-34).
- Select the Table control from the *HTML* section of the Toolbox window. A table with 3 rows and 3 columns is placed on the form, which you can resize by dragging the handles along its right and bottom sides.

Adjusting Row Heights and Column Widths

To adjust the width of a column, hover the mouse over the double bar along the column's right border. When the mouse cursor changes to a double vertical bar with arrows pointing left and right, hold down the mouse button and drag the border to its new location. As you do so, the column width (in pixels) displays inside the column. Often, the displayed number gives you a more accurate idea of the column width than the table's visual display.

To adjust the height of a row, hover the mouse over the row's lower border. When the mouse cursor changes to a double horizontal line with arrows pointing up and down, drag the mouse and the border up or down. As you do this, the column height (in pixels) displays inside the column. Often, the displayed number gives you a more accurate idea of the column height than the table's visual display.

Inserting Rows and Columns

To insert a new row or column in a table, click inside the table in Design view. Then select *Insert* from the *Table* menu, and select from the list of choices shown in Figure 8-35. In each

Figure 8-34 Insert Table window

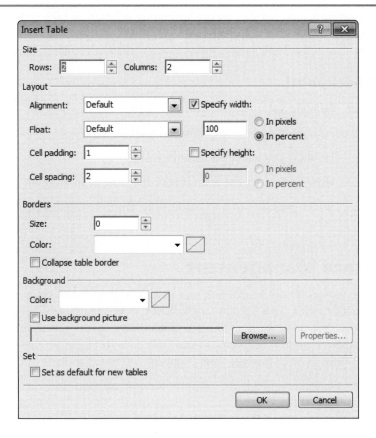

Figure 8-35 Inserting table rows and columns

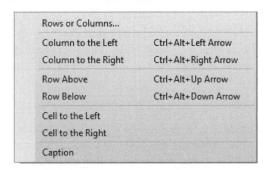

case, the inserted row or column will have the same attributes as the row or column that was selected when you issued the command.

Aligning Text Inside Cells

By default, static text typed into table cells is left justified. Each cell's Align property controls the placement of text and graphics in the cell. The possible values are center, char, justify, left, and right. You can also use the text alignment button on the Visual Studio formatting toolbar.

Merging Adjacent Cells

Sometimes, it is useful to merge, or combine, adjacent table cells into a single cell. The cells must be in the same column or row. To select a group of cells, drag the mouse over the cells. Then from the Table menu, select *Modify*, then select *Merge Cells*.

 Checkpoint

19. How do you merge several cells into a single table cell?

20. How do you select a column in a table?

21. How do you change a column width?

22. How do you set the default font for all cells in a table?

23. Which property of a CheckBoxList control contains the individual list items?

 ## 8.6   State Management

Web servers do not keep a link to a particular page active once the page has been sent to the user's browser. This presents a challenge when you have class-level variables in your Web forms that must keep their values. Similarly, when users move from one Web page to another, it is often necessary to transmit data from the first page to the second. Briefly, we will show how to manage state using the following tools:

- ViewState—Holds the runtime state of controls and variables when a page is posted back to the server.
- Session state—Holds data belonging to a single user's session that can be accessed from any Web form.

Page-Level State (ViewState)

Although Web pages are stateless, users expect controls to remember their settings when pages are posted back to the server. HTML controls cannot do this. An ASP.NET control retains its settings because of an extra step taken by the Web server: It encodes the control's state in a collection named **ViewState**. The ViewState data is rendered on the Web page sent back to the client as an encrypted, hidden field. Here is an example:

```
<input type="hidden" name="__VIEWSTATE" id="__VIEWSTATE"
value="/wEPDwUKMTkwNjc4NTIwMWRkbKFgfWrQ2DfhTDzQoPdyXJs3SKQ=" />
```

A simple comparison is shown in Figure 8-36, which has an HTML Input control and an ASP.NET TextBox control. On the left side, the user enters text into both boxes. The page just below the first page shows what happens when the user clicks the *Post* button. The TextBox control retains its data, but the HTML control does not.

The ViewState collection can contain only objects whose classes implement the ISerializable interface. Fortunately, that applies to almost all standard .NET data types.

Saving Values in ViewState

Although ASP.NET controls conveniently remember their values, class-level variables do not. Suppose you declare the following class-level variable in a Web page's codebehind file:

```
Private mTemperature As Double
```

And then you assign a value to *mTemperature* in one of the class methods:

```
mTemperature = 98.6
```

Figure 8-36 HTML and TextBox controls, before and after posting a page

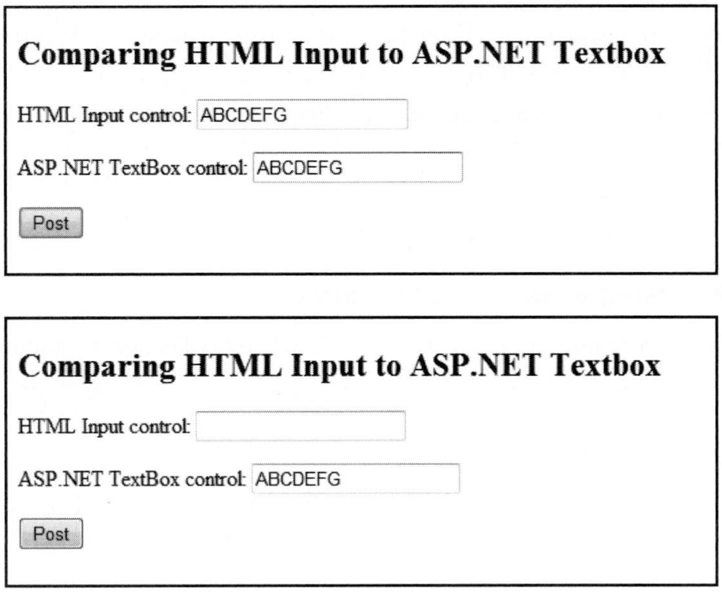

If the user clicks a button on the page, the page is posted back, and the contents of mTemperature are erased. This is very inconvenient, but there is a remedy. You can save mTemperature in the page's ViewState collection, using a name-value pair. Here's an example:

```
mTemperature = 98.6
Me.ViewState.Add("temperature", mTemperature)
```

The item's name is also called a *key* because it must be unique in the collection. No two entries in the ViewState collection can have the same key. Alternatively, you can use the ViewState.Item method to insert or replace a value, as shown here:

```
ViewState.Item("temperature") = mTemperature
```

Because Item is a default property, the preceding statement can be shortened to the following:

```
ViewState("temperature") = mTemperature
```

ViewState is the name of a property in the current Page object. It is a *StateBag* object, so you can see all of its methods and properties by looking up the StateBag class in the MSDN documentation.

Retrieving Values From ViewState

The *Item* property returns the collection entry that matches a key. Its return type is Object, so you must cast the object into its exact type. For example, mTemperature is a Double in the following line:

```
mTemperature = CDbl(ViewState.Item("temperature"))
```

Here is a shorthand version of the same operation:

```
mTemperature = CDbl(ViewState("temperature"))
```

If ViewState contains a List object, you must use the CType operator when assigning the item to a List variable. For example:

```
Dim nameList As List(Of String)
nameList = CType(ViewState("names"),List(Of String))
```

If you attempt to retrieve a value using a key that is not in the collection, the return value equals *Nothing*.

Restoring values from ViewState after a page postback is best done in the Page_Load event handler, as shown here:

```
Protected Sub Page_Load() Handles Me.Load
   If IsPostBack Then
      nameList = CType(ViewState("names"),List(Of String))
   End If
End Sub
```

Removing Values From ViewState

You can remove an entry from the ViewState collection by calling the Remove method:

```
ViewState.Remove("temperature")
```

Local Variables

Local variables and method parameters are not affected by page postbacks. Local variables exist on the runtime stack and are re-created each time their enclosing method is called.

Example: Counting Names

Let's look at a more complete example that involves ViewState. Suppose a program lets the user input names, and we want to keep track of how many names have been entered, as shown in Figure 8-37. In the figure, the count equals 2, so the application appears to work correctly.

Figure 8-37 Counting names that are input by the user

In a Windows Desktop application, a counter variable would be declared at the class level so it could keep its value each time the user added a name. But in a Web form, special care must be taken to achieve the same behavior. The following code shows our first attempt at a Web form that uses *nameCount* to count the names entered by the user. It does not retain the value of nameCount when the page is posted back to the server.

```
Partial Class NameList
   Inherits System.Web.UI.Page
```

```
      Private nameCount As Integer = 0

      Private Sub btnOk_Click() Handles btnOk.Click
         nameCount += 1
         lblCount.Text = CStr(nameCount) & " names have been entered"
      End Sub
   End Class
```

NameCount is reset to zero each time the page is posted back to the server, rendering the counting process useless. We can avoid this problem by saving the variable in the ViewState collection. The following statement associates nameCount with the collection key named *nameCount*:

```
   ViewState("nameCount") = nameCount
```

When the page is posted back and refreshed by the server, we retrieve the stored value and put it back in the same variable. The collection reference returns an Object, so we must cast it into the appropriate type. In this case, nameCount is an Integer:

```
   nameCount = CType(ViewState("nameCount"),Integer)
```

Following is the corrected version of the NameList class, using ViewState:

```
   Partial Class NameList
      Inherits System.Web.UI.Page

      Private nameCount As Integer

      Private Sub btnOk_Click() Handles btnOk.Click
         nameCount = CType(ViewState("nameCount"), Integer)
         nameCount += 1
         ViewState("nameCount") = nameCount
         lblCount.Text = CStr(nameCount) & " names have been entered"
      End Sub
   End Class
```

Objects Must Be Serializable

Any object stored in ViewState must be **serializable,** meaning that its class implements the ISerializable interface. Objects based on your own classes are not automatically serializable. This becomes an issue if we create, say, a List of custom object types. Here's an example:

```
   Dim myList As List(Of Student)
```

Although the List class implements ISerializable, chances are the Student class does not. Therefore, we cannot store myList in ViewState. We do not cover serialization in this textbook, but we will show you how to use Session state to save and restore your own objects.

Session State

Session state is the name of a collection that is associated with a particular user, across multiple Web forms. Session state is a great tool for saving data when a user browses from one Web page to another. When a user connects to an application, a unique session ID is created and saved as a temporary cookie by the user's Web browser. The session ID is used when saving and retrieving Session state information while the user's session is active. If the browser does not accept cookies, Session state can still be saved if the cookieless session option is specified in the application's Web.config file. A session remains active as long as the user's browser is open. If the user leaves the browser window open with no postbacks for a period of time, the session eventually expires.

> **TIP:** Limit the amount of data that you store in Session state. It is stored on the Web server, so a significant amount of server time can be spent transferring large amounts of data to users.

Session state items are stored in name-value pairs. The following example stores the string *A1234* in a session item named *customerId*:

```
Me.Session.Item("customerId") = "A1234"
```

The Session object is a property of the *System.Web.UI.Page* class. You can shorten the foregoing statement because Item is the default property:

```
Session("customerId") = "A1234"
```

When you retrieve an object from Session state, you must cast it into the appropriate type before assigning it to a variable. Here, for example, we cast the object into a String:

```
Dim customerId As String = CStr(Session("customerId"))
```

Saving and Restoring Objects

Any object can be saved in Session state. The object's class does not have to be serializable. For example, we can create a Student object and save it in a Session state item named *currStudent*:

```
Session("currStudent") = New Student(12345,"Smith")
```

When retrieving the Session object at another place on the page, we cast it into a Student.

```
objStudent = CType(Session.Item("currStudent"), Student)
```

Leaving out the implicit Item property name, the equivalent statement would be as follows:

```
objStudent = CType(Session("currStudent"), Student)
```

If Session state contains a List object, you must use the CType operator when assigning its item to a List variable. For example:

```
Dim nameList As List(Of String)
nameList = CType(Session("names"),List(Of String))
```

Verifying Session State Values

When you retrieve an object from Session state, use a cautious approach and consider that the object might not have been created yet. Suppose, for example, the following expression returns a value of *Nothing*:

```
Session.Item("currStudent")
```

If we try to cast the value *Nothing* into a Student object, an exception is thrown. A safer approach is to assign it to an Object variable, and then test it before casting to a specific type:

```
Dim S As Student = Nothing
Dim obj As Object = Session.Item("currStudent")
If obj IsNot Nothing Then
  S = Ctype(Session.Item("currStudent"), Student)
End If
```

From this point onward, S will either contain *Nothing*, or it will reference the object retrieved from Session state.

 **Checkpoint**

24. What important restriction applies to objects stored in the ViewState collection?

25. When a page is posted back to the server, how do TextBox controls avoid losing their contents?

26. Show an example of storing a string variable named mClientName in ViewState. Show an example also of retrieving the value and assigning it to a variable. Assume Option Strict is *On*.

27. When you save an object in Session state, when will the object be discarded?

28. Yes or no: If two users are running the same ASP.NET application, can they access each other's Session state collections?

29. Why is it important to be careful when casting Session state objects directly into specific types?

Summary

8.1 Programming for the Web

- Web applications are designed around a client-server model: An entity named a server produces data consumed by another entity called a client. Web applications must be run using a Web server.
- When the Web first became popular, HTML was the only available way to create pages with text, graphics buttons, and input forms.
- ASP.NET is Microsoft's platform for Web application development. It provides development tools, code libraries, and visual controls for browser-based applications.
- Web applications written for ASP.NET consist of the following parts: (1) Content, in the form of Web forms, HTML code, Web forms controls, images, and other multimedia; (2) program logic, in compiled Visual Basic (or C#) code; and (3) configuration information.
- Visual Web Developer is a Microsoft development tool with an editor that simplifies the way Web applications are created.
- A Uniform Resource Locator (URL) provides a universal way of addressing objects and pages on a network.
- Web applications written in ASP.NET use special Web pages called Web forms. A Web form, which can be identified by its .aspx filename extension, contains text, HTML tags, HTML controls (such as buttons and text boxes), and Web sever controls.

8.2 Creating ASP.NET Applications

- Using Visual Studio or Visual Web Developer, you can create a Web site in the local File System, HTTP (Web server), or FTP Site (remote location).
- A File System Web site runs directly under the ASP.NET Development Server supplied with Visual Studio and Visual Web Developer. An HTTP Web site runs under the Internet Information Services (IIS) Web server. An FTP Web site uses the FTP protocol to reference an existing ASP.NET Web site.
- ASP.NET applications are also known as Web sites or Web applications.
- You can start a program in Debug mode by selecting *Start Debugging* from the Debug menu. You will be prompted to create or modify a file named *Web.config* that contains a debugging option.

- The Calendar control lets the user scroll forward and backward through monthly date displays and select individual dates.
- The Kayak Tour Scheduler application shows how to use a Calendar control when scheduling tours.

8.3 Web Server Controls

- Web server controls make ASP.NET applications dynamic and interactive. The controls are more powerful than standard HTML controls because each is defined by a class with a rich set of properties, methods, and events.
- ASP.NET controls lose their runtime properties when the user moves away from the current page.
- The ASP.NET Label control is almost identical to the Label control for Windows applications. Use a Label only if its contents will change at runtime or if you plan to change its Visible property.
- The TextBox control in ASP.NET is similar in many ways to the TextBox control for Windows applications. The Text property holds text input by the user.
- The ASP.NET CheckBox control is almost identical to the CheckBox for Windows applications. Use the Text property to set the visible text. Evaluate the Checked property at runtime.
- Events are fired in a specific sequence in Web forms. The Page_Load event occurs when the page is first loaded into the user's browser, and again every time the page is posted back to the server. Page_Load executes before event handlers for other controls, such as the Button Click handler.
- When a control's AutoPostBack property equals *True*, clicking on the control causes the form to be posted back to the server.

8.4 List-Type Controls

- The ListBox, DropDownList, CheckBoxList, and RadioButtonList can all be classified as list-type controls. All use the <ListItem> tag to identify items in their lists, all have an Items collection, all have a ValueMember property, and all have a SelectedIndexChanged event.
- All list-type controls have SelectedIndex, SelectedItem, ValueMember, and Selected-Value properties.
- You can use the *SelectionMode* property to determine whether users can select a single item or multiple items from a ListBox.
- You can use a SelectedIndexChanged event handler to respond to selections by the user in any list-type control.
- The CheckBoxList control looks like a group of check boxes but works like a ListBox.
- In a DropDownList, the initial value of SelectedIndex is 0, causing the first item to display.
- The Calendar control is not a list-type control, but it does let you select a sequence of dates.

8.5 Designing Web Forms

- The HTML Table control is an essential tool for designing the layout of Web forms. Use it to align text, graphics, and controls in rows and columns.
- There are two ways to insert a table when viewing a form's Design: Select *Insert Table* from the Layout menu, or select the HTML Table control from the Toolbox window.
- To adjust the width of a column, hover the mouse over the double bar along the column's right border. To adjust the height of a row, hover the mouse over the row's lower border.

8.6 State Management

- Web servers do not keep a connection to a particular page active once the page has been sent to the client's browser. At the same time, programs often must preserve data when moving between pages.

- Web pages have a ViewState property that holds the contents of input controls when forms are posted back to the server.
- Any object stored in ViewState must be serializable, meaning that its class implements the ISerializable interface.
- Each user has a distinct collection named Session state that can be used to store objects and other data.
- The *SessionState Demo* program displays Session state properties and uses application state to save information about user connections.

Key Terms

application logic
ASP.NET
ASP.NET controls
ASP.NET Development Server
AutoPostBack property
Calendar control
CheckBoxList control
client-server model
codebehind file
Design view
DropDownList control
eXtended HyperText Markup Language (XHTML)
File System Web Site
FTP Site
HTML control
HTML Designer
HTML Table control
HTML tag
HTTP request
HyperText Markup Language (HTML)
Internet Information Services (IIS)
IsPostBack property
Label control

ListBox control
list-type controls
localhost
Local IIS Site
postback
RadioButtonList control
remote Web Server
serializable
server controls
Session state
Source view
static text
TextBox control
Uniform Resource Locator (URL)
ViewState
Visual Web Developer
Web application
Web.config file
Web configuration file
Web form
Web page
Web server
Web server control

Review Questions and Exercises

True or False

Indicate whether each of the following statements is true or false.

1. ASP.NET applications will work only if the user's Web browser is Internet Explorer Version 5.0 or above.

2. The DropDownList control permits the user to type text directly into the first line.

3. Session state can only hold objects whose classes implement the ISerializable interface.

4. The AutoPostBack property does not affect the ListBox control.

5. The ListBox control fires a SelectedIndexChanged event.

6. To create a Web site on your local computer, you must be running Internet Information Services.

7. The default value of SelectedIndex for a DropDownList control is 0.

8. The HyperLink control does not generate a Click event.

9. The ImageButton control generates a Click event and does not look like a button.

10. You can call the Add method or use the Item property to insert an item in the ViewState collection.

11. The best place to load a collection from ViewState is in the Page_Load event handler.

12. A Session ID is stored in a permanent cookie by the Web browser.

13. When adding text to a Web form, you can type static text directly onto the form.

14. Conventional Web pages contain tags based on the HyperText Markup Language.

15. The two ways to save state information are ViewState and ApplicationState.

16. URL stands for *Uniform Response Locator*.

17. ASP.NET controls are also known as *Web site controls*.

18. A powerful Web server used by Web developers is named *Internet Information Services*.

Short Answer

1. What are the three basic parts of an ASP.NET application?

2. What happens when an object is not found when you call the ViewState.Item property?

3. How are ASP.NET controls different from HTML controls?

4. What special requirement do remote Web servers have, compared to local Web servers?

5. What are the three ways to view a Web form in Visual Studio?

6. What command lets you choose the Web browser that will run your application?

7. How do you open an existing file-based Web application?

8. What happens the first time you try to run a Web application in Debug mode?

9. How is the DropDownList control different from the ComboBox control?

10. How are HyperLink and LinkButton controls different?

11. Which property in ASP.NET controls corresponds to the Name property in Windows controls?

12. When the user selects an item from a ListBox and then clicks a button to post the page back to the server (called a postback), which event executes first: Page_Load, or SelectedIndexChanged?

13. Which property in a ListBox governs whether the user's selection is posted back to the server immediately?

14. Which property lets you use program code to select a date in a Calendar control?

15. How can you make the Calendar control display date selections without allowing the user to make any selections?

16. How would you make the Calendar control display the month of April?

17. How can you permit the user to select either a day or an entire week in the Calendar control?

18. Which control displays a sequence of check boxes?

19. Which control displays a hyperlink and has a property named NavigateURL?

20. Which property of an ImageButton control holds the name of the image file?

21. Which property of a Label control can be used to make its border solid, dotted, or dashed?

22. Which property of a TextBox control determines whether the user can enter multiple input lines?

Algorithm Workbench

1. Write a statement that obtains a List(Of String) from the ViewState collection.

2. Write a statement that checks if the first button named *radButtons* in a RadioButtonList control has been selected by the user.

3. Write a statement that removes all items named *lstSummary* from a ListBox.

4. Write a loop that selects all check boxes named *chkOptions* in a CheckBoxList control.

5. Write a statement that makes February 10, 2011, visible in the Calendar control named *myCal*.

Programming Challenges

1. Stadium Seating

Suppose there are three seating categories at an athletic stadium. For a baseball game, Class A seats cost $15 each, Class B seats cost $12 each, and Class C seats cost $9 each. Create an application that allows the user to enter the number of tickets sold for each class. The application should display the amount of income generated from each class of ticket sales and the total revenue generated, as shown in Figure 8-38.

Figure 8-38 Stadium Seating form

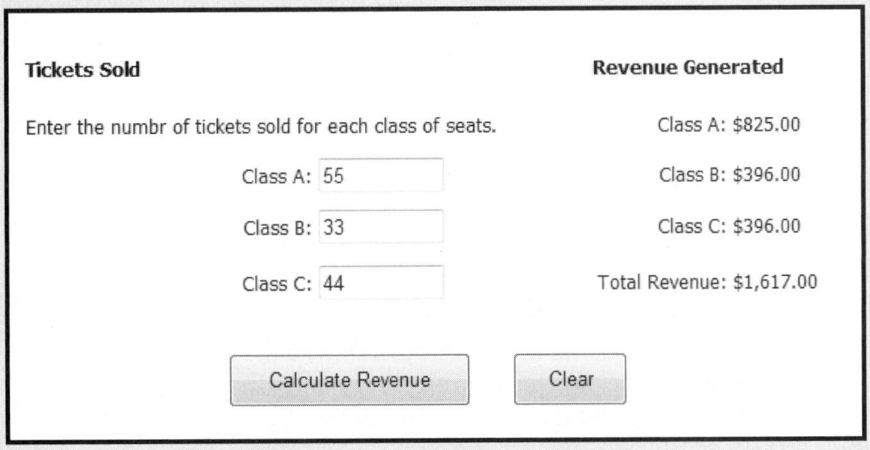

2. Room Charge Calculator

A customer staying at the Highlander Hotel may incur the following types of charges:

- Room charges, based on a per-night rate
- Room service charges
- Telephone charges
- Miscellaneous charges

Create an application that calculates the customer's total charges. Here are the basic operations, in sequence:

1. When the application starts, the user enters the number of nights and the nightly room charge. The user can also enter additional charges, in dollars.
2. When the user clicks on the *Calculate Charges* button, the application should multiply the nights by the nightly charge. Then it should add the additional charges, producing the subtotal.
3. Next, the application should multiply the subtotal by an 8 percent tax rate, producing the tax amount.
4. Finally, the application adds the tax amount to the subtotal, producing the total charges.

A sample is shown in Figure 8-39. Notice that the application displays the current date and time in the upper-right corner of the window.

Figure 8-39 Room Charge Calculator application

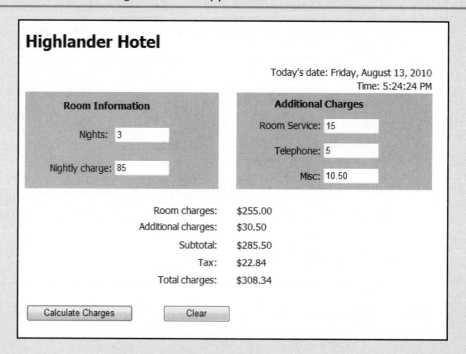

3. **Bank Charges**

A bank charges $10 per month, plus the following check fees, for a commercial checking account:

- $0.10 each for fewer than twenty checks
- $0.08 each for twenty through thirty-nine checks
- $0.06 each for forty through fifty-nine checks
- $0.04 each for sixty or more checks

Create a Web application that allows users to enter the number of checks they have written. The application should compute and display the bank's service fees for the month, as shown in Figure 8-40.

Input Validation

Do not accept a negative value for the number of checks written. Ensure that all values are numeric. Use the following test data to determine if the application is calculating properly:

Number of Checks	Total Fees
15	$11.50
25	$12.00
45	$12.70
75	$13.00

Figure 8-40 Bank charges

Bank Charges

Number of checks written: 22

Bank service fees: $11.76

Calculate Fees

4. **Long-Distance Calls**

A cellular phone provider charges the following rates for telephone calls:

Rate Category	Rate per Minute
Daytime (6:00 A.M. through 5:59 P.M.)	$0.07
Evening (6:00 P.M. through 11:59 P.M.)	$0.12
Off-Peak (12:00 A.M. through 5:59 A.M.)	$0.05

Create an application that allows the user to select a rate category (from a set of radio buttons) and enter the number of minutes of the call, and then displays the charges, as shown in Figure 8-41. Use the following test data to determine if the application is calculating properly:

Rate Category and Minutes	Charge
Daytime, 20 minutes	$1.40
Evening, 20 minutes	$2.40
Off-peak, 20 minutes	$1.00

Figure 8-41 Long-distance calls

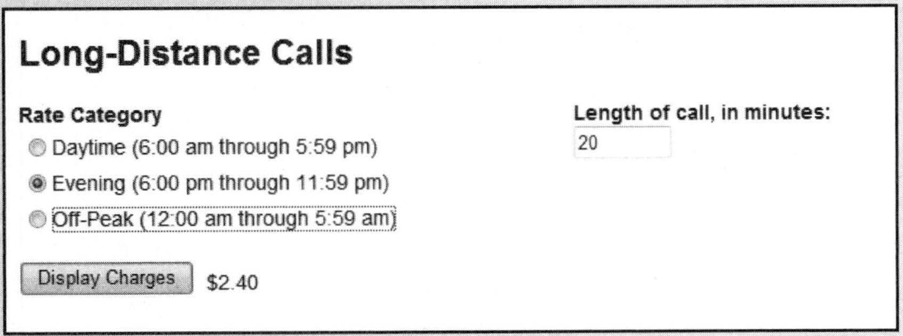

Long-Distance Calls

Rate Category
○ Daytime (6:00 am through 5:59 pm)
◉ Evening (6:00 pm through 11:59 pm)
○ Off-Peak (12:00 am through 5:59 am)

Length of call, in minutes:
20

Display Charges $2.40

5. **Accounts Dictionary**

Create an application that lists accounts from a Dictionary object. Create an *Account* class that contains an ID, name, and balance. Display the accounts in a ListBox, as shown in Figure 8-42. If the user enters new values, she can click on the *Add* button to add a new account to the dictionary. If she clicks the *Replace* button, she can replace a dictionary item. Use exception handlers to catch errors caused by invalid input values, or an attempt to add a duplicate Account ID to the dictionary. *Note:* Remember to save the Dictionary in Session state to avoid losing your changes when the page is posted back to the server.

Figure 8-42 Adding an Account to the dictionary

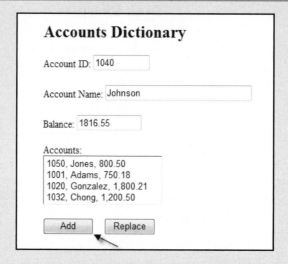

6. **Club Committee Organizer**

A student computer club needs to keep a record of which club members have joined committees. Your task is to write an application that will make the process easy. In Figure 8-43, the user is about to select the name of a committee from a combo box. In Figure 8-44, the

Figure 8-43 Club Committee Organizer, selecting a committee

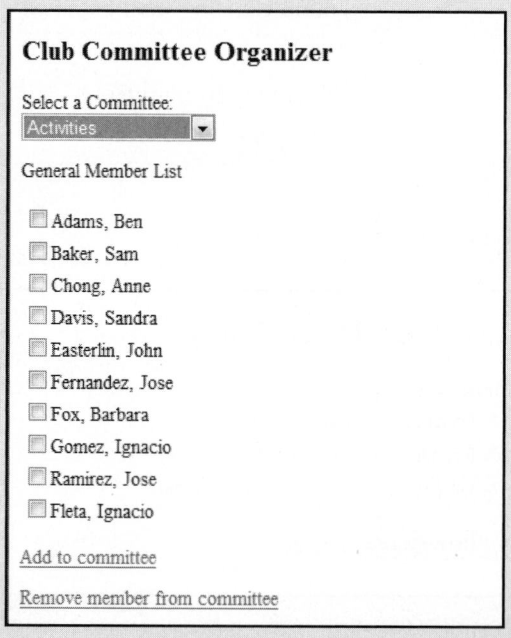

Club Committee Organizer

Select a Committee:

Activities ▼

General Member List

☐ Adams, Ben

☐ Baker, Sam

☐ Chong, Anne

☐ Davis, Sandra

☐ Easterlin, John

☐ Fernandez, Jose

☐ Fox, Barbara

☐ Gomez, Ignacio

☐ Ramirez, Jose

☐ Fleta, Ignacio

Add to committee

Remove member from committee

Figure 8-44 Club Committee Organizer, selecting several members

Club Committee Organizer

Select a Committee:
[Activities   ▼]

General Member List

☑ Adams, Ben

☑ Baker, Sam

☐ Chong, Anne

☐ Davis, Sandra

☑ Easterlin, John

☑ Fernandez, Jose

☐ Fox, Barbara

☐ Gomez, Ignacio

☐ Ramirez, Jose

☐ Fleta, Ignacio

Add to committee

Remove member from committee

user has selected several members from the general members list and is about to click the *Add to committee* link, which will copy the selected member names into the current members list. In Figure 8-45, the members have been copied into the current members, and they have been automatically unselected from the General Member list. If the user should try to select and copy a member who already belongs to the committee, nothing will happen. In Figure 8-46, the user is about to remove a selected committee member.

Figure 8-45 Club Committee Organizer, Activities committee

Club Committee Organizer

Select a Committee:
[Activities   ▼]

General Member List

☐ Adams, Ben

☐ Baker, Sam

☐ Chong, Anne

☐ Davis, Sandra

☐ Easterlin, John

☐ Fernandez, Jose

☐ Fox, Barbara

☐ Gomez, Ignacio

☐ Ramirez, Jose

☐ Fleta, Ignacio

Add to committee

Remove member from committee

Current Members:
Adams, Ben
Baker, Sam
Easterlin, John
Fernandez, Jose

Figure 8-46 One member is about to be removed from the committee

Add to committee
Remove member from committee
Current Members:
Adams, Ben
Baker, Sam
Easterlin, John
Fernandez, Jose

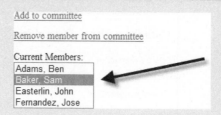

Insert the following list of committees into the combo box: Activities, Community Services, Executive, Membership, Programming Team, Scholarship, Sports, Travel, and Volunteer Tutoring. Make up your own list of at least ten names for the list box containing the general membership.

7. **Club Committee Collections**

   Using the solution program from Programming Challenge 6, make the following improvements:

   - Create a class named *Committee* that represents a single committee. It should contain a List(Of String) containing the names of students who are members. (Be sure to put it in the *App_Code* folder of your Web site.) The class should have a ReadOnly property that returns a reference to the class's internal List variable.
   - When the user selects different committees from the combo box, the application must remember which people were assigned to each committee. One way to do this is to store each list of names in another list. Suppose, for example, that the user adds Chong, Fernandez, and Fox to the Community Services committee, as in Figure 8-47. Then the user selects another committee and adds some people to that one. If the user

Figure 8-47 Club Committee Organizer: Community Services contains three people

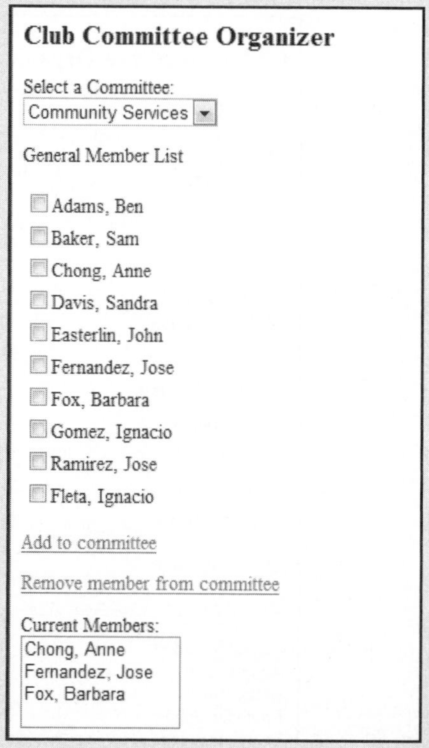

Club Committee Organizer
Select a Committee:
Community Services
General Member List
Adams, Ben
Baker, Sam
Chong, Anne
Davis, Sandra
Easterlin, John
Fernandez, Jose
Fox, Barbara
Gomez, Ignacio
Ramirez, Jose
Fleta, Ignacio
Add to committee
Remove member from committee
Current Members:
Chong, Anne
Fernandez, Jose
Fox, Barbara

then returns to the Community Services committee, she should see Chong, Fernandez, and Fox in the current list of members.

In the main form class, create a List(of Committee) object. (Don't forget to initialize this list with a loop in Page_Load.) When members are selected and copied into the committee list box, you must also add these members to the list in the appropriate Committee object. (Remember to retrieve the committee list from Session state and save it again after you have modified it.) Use the Committee list box's SelectedIndex property as a subscript in the list of Committee objects to access the appropriate Committee object. The DropDownList containing the committee names must have AutoPostBack set to *True* so you can refill the list of current members each time the user selects a different committee name.

9 Programming Web Forms

TOPICS

In this chapter, you will learn how to code directly in XHTML and how to use cascading style sheets (CSS) to control the spacing, alignment, color, fonts, and other visual properties. Then you will begin to use the rich set of controls that validate user input. Special tasks, such as uploading files to an application, sending email, and saving session information when moving between pages, are added benefits to this chapter.

9.1 Working in Source (XHTML) Mode

In the previous chapter, you were able to build applications with the built-in features of ASP.NET and the Visual Studio development environment. Microsoft did a good job of creating a first impression that Web programming can be done at a simple level with only minimal training. After the initial dip into the ASP.NET waters, however, people find that ASP.NET requires a basic understanding of the entire process that a Web page goes through from the user's initial request to the page's final rendering in a browser. Along the way, a fair amount of programmer training is required. Therefore, this chapter focuses on writing code for Web pages in ASP.NET to begin preparing you for what may be an exciting career as a Web programmer.

Let's clarify a few definitions of Web-based markup languages:

- **eXtensible Markup Language (XML)** is a general-purpose markup language that can be used to create other, more specific languages. XML files are usually used to share data across networks, particularly the Internet.
- **HyperText Markup Language (HTML)** is the standard publishing language of the World Wide Web. It is understood by all Web browsers. HTML was the first markup language for Web pages, and is a subset of XML.

- **eXtensible HyperText Markup Language (XHTML)** is an application of XML for Web pages. It has the same functions as HTML, but with a stricter syntax. It permits developers to define new tags (keywords). The World Wide Web Consortium (W3C) defines XHTML as a family of current and future document types and modules that reproduce, subset, and extend HTML 4.

If you load a typical HTML Web page into the Visual Studio source editor, you may see a few error messages. Errors are flagged when a Web page has malformed URLs, unknown properties, and overlapping tags that do not conform to XHTML rules. Fortunately, it is easy to learn how to write XHTML correctly, so your own pages should not contain errors.

An Inside Look at ASP.NET Code

The Visual Studio designer intentionally hides XHTML details when you look at a Web page in Design view. The designer approximates the way the page will look when shown in a Web browser. To adjust the page's visual details, however, you must work with the page's XHTML code directly. With practice, you will easily flip back and forth between Design view and Source view.

Before reading this section, you should have a basic working knowledge of HTML. If you need help, there are many excellent tutorials on the Web. For example, the W3C organization has a Tutorials page: *http://www.w3.org/2002/03/tutorials*. If this link changes, go to *http://www.w3.org*, view the site map, and look for *Tutorials*. (W3C stands for *World Wide Web Consortium*, the international governing body for Web standards.)

A Blank ASP.NET Page

Let's begin with a detailed description of a simple ASP.NET page. A new blank page generated by Visual Studio contains the XHTML shown in Figure 9-1. In the description that follows, each line of code will be followed by its explanation.

Figure 9-1 A blank ASP.NET page named *Default.aspx*

```
<%@ Page Language="VB" AutoEventWireup="false"
CodeFile="Default.aspx.vb" Inherits="_Default" %>

<!DOCTYPE html PUBLIC "-//W3C//DTD XHTML 1.0 Transitional//EN"
"http://www.w3.org/TR/xhtml1/DTD/xhtml1-transitional.dtd">

<html xmlns="http://www.w3.org/1999/xhtml">
<head runat="server">
  <title></title>
</head>
<body>
  <form id="form1" runat="server">
  <div>

  </div>
  </form>
</body>
</html>
```

The *Page* directive identifies the coding language (VB). *AutoEventWireup* determines whether page events (such as Load and Init) must use standard names. A value of False lets us choose any names we want for page event handlers. The *CodeFile* attribute names the visual basic source code file containing the event handlers for this Web page. The *Inherits* attribute defines the class name used by this page.

```
<!DOCTYPE html PUBLIC "-//W3C//DTD XHTML 1.0 Transitional//EN"
"http://www.w3.org/TR/xhtml1/DTD/xhtml1-transitional.dtd">
```

The DOCTYPE tag identifies the document type to the browser, along with the XHTML standard it follows. The URL given in the same line is a document that you can download from the W3C organization, which describes the syntax and keywords of this XHTML standard.

```
<html xmlns="http://www.w3.org/1999/xhtml">
```

The <html> tag identifies the beginning of the HTML document that makes up your Web page. The *xmlns* keyword identifies an XHTML namespace, which you can read about by following the URL given there.

```
<head runat="server">
<title>Untitled Page</title>
</head>
```

The area between the <head> and </head> tags defines the heading portion of the document. Sometimes this area contains program scripting code, keywords that hint at the document content, links to CSS files, and the document title.

```
<body>
```

The <body> tag defines the displayable area of the Web page.

```
<form id="form1" runat="server">
```

The <form> tag identifies the beginning of a Web form. The ID is optional. A form contains buttons, text boxes, and other controls that interact with the user. The runat="server" option indicates that the form must be posted back to the server and processed in some way.

```
<div>
</div>
```

The <div> and </div> tags mark a block of text that can be assigned style attributes. They are not required.

```
</form>
</body>
</html>
```

The </form> tag marks the end of the form, followed by the end of the document body, followed by the end of the HTML document.

In Tutorial 9-1, you will create a Web form in Source view.

Tutorial 9-1:
Designing a *Vacation Rentals* application

In this tutorial, you will create a simple vacation rentals application using XHTML code. *Source* view is activated when you click the *View* tab at the bottom of the page (when an *.aspx* Web page file is open). In the Source view, you work directly with HTML code. It is a good idea to view the Web page in a separate Web browser window so that you can see how the final page looks as you make changes.

> **TIP:** Some professional ASP.NET programmers prefer to build Web forms in Source view. Visual Studio's support for source XHTML editing is excellent, and we have seen people use it to create controls and text at lightning speed.

Tutorial Steps

Step 1: Create a new empty Web site and save it in a folder named *Vacation Rentals*.

Step 2: Add a Default.aspx page to the site. The page should appear in Source view. If it does not, switch to Source view now.

Step 3: Remove the <div> and </div> tags.

Step 4: Change the text between the <title> and </title> tags to *Vacation Rentals*.

Step 5: Change the <body> tag to the following, which sets the default font for the page:

```
<body style="font-family:Arial">
```

Step 6: On the next line after the <form> tag, type <h1>. Notice that the ending tag </h1> is inserted for you. Modify the line to be the following:

```
<h1>Vacation Rental Request</h1>
```

Step 7: Type the following text on the next line (it is not important where you break the line):

```
Please select a location, price range, number of people, and
starting date
```

Step 8: Drag a DropDownList control from the Toolbox into the next position in the *editor* window. Modify its ID property:

```
<asp:DropDownList ID="ddlLocation" runat="server">
</asp:DropDownList>
```

Step 9: Open a blank line before the </asp:DropDownList> tag and insert the following lines:

```
<asp:ListItem>London</asp:ListItem>
<asp:ListItem>Paris</asp:ListItem>
<asp:ListItem>Rome</asp:ListItem>
<asp:ListItem>Vienna</asp:ListItem>
```

As you start to type each item, the editor will display the ListItem control name. Press the *Tab* key to complete the automatic code insertion.

Step 10: Save the form. Start the application from the *Debug* menu. Keep the Web browser window open so you can use it as a reference.

Step 11: Begin editing the page's XHTML again. After the dropdown list, insert a paragraph tag, as follows:

```
<p />
```

Step 12: Add a RadioButtonList control to the form:

```
<asp:RadioButtonList ID="radPrices" runat="server"
  BorderColor="Navy" BorderStyle="Solid"
  BorderWidth="1px">
</asp:RadioButtonList>
```

Step 13: Insert the following items in the RadioButtonList:

```
<asp:ListItem>Less than $500 per week</asp:ListItem>
<asp:ListItem>$500 to $1000 per week</asp:ListItem>
<asp:ListItem>More than $1000 per week</asp:ListItem>
```

(ListItems are used in both DropDownLists and RadioButtonLists. They are also used in ListBox and CheckBoxList controls.)

Step 14: Save the form and refresh the browser. You should see the radio buttons now.

Step 15: Edit the form again, in Source view, and add the following lines:

```
<p />
Number of people:
```

Step 16: Add a TextBox control to the form:

```
<asp:TextBox ID="txtNumberOfPeople" columns="2"
  runat="server">
</asp:TextBox>
```

Step 17: Add the following text:

```
<p />
Number of weeks:
  <asp:TextBox ID="txtNumberOfWeeks"
  runat="server" Columns="2"></asp:TextBox>
```

Step 18: Add the following text:

```
<p />
Starting date:
```

Step 19: Add a Calendar control to the form:

```
<asp:Calendar ID="calStartDate" runat="server">
</asp:Calendar>
```

Step 20: Add the following text:

```
<p/>
```

Step 21: Add a Button control to the form:

```
<asp:Button ID="btnSubmit"
  runat="server"
  Text="Submit my Request" />
```

Step 22: Save the file and refresh the browser. Your output should look similar to that shown in Figure 9-2, with a different calendar month, of course.

Code Listing

The following is a complete listing of the form's HTML source, from the <head> tag onward:

```
<head runat="server">
  <title>Vacation Rentals</title>
</head>
<body style="font-family:Arial">
<form id="form1" runat="server">
<h1>Vacation Rental Request</h1>

Please select a location, price range, number of
people, and starting date
<p />
Location:
<asp:DropDownList ID="ddlLocation" runat="server">
  <asp:ListItem>London</asp:ListItem>
  <asp:ListItem>Paris</asp:ListItem>
  <asp:ListItem>Rome</asp:ListItem>
  <asp:ListItem>Vienna</asp:ListItem>
</asp:DropDownList>
<p />
Number of people:
<asp:TextBox ID="txtNumberOfPeople" columns="2"
  runat="server">
</asp:TextBox>
<p />
```

```
Price per week:
<asp:RadioButtonList ID="radPrices" runat="server"
  BorderColor="Navy" BorderStyle="Solid"
  BorderWidth="1px">
  <asp:ListItem>Less than $500 per week</asp:ListItem>
  <asp:ListItem>$500 to $1000 per week</asp:ListItem>
  <asp:ListItem>More than $1000 per week</asp:ListItem>
</asp:RadioButtonList>
<p />
Number of weeks:
<asp:TextBox ID="txtNumberOfWeeks"
  runat="server" Columns="2"></asp:TextBox>
<p />
Starting date:
<asp:Calendar ID="calStartDate" runat="server">
  </asp:Calendar>
<p />
<asp:Button ID="btnSubmit"
  runat="server"
  Text="Submit my Request" />
</form>
</body>
</html>
```

Figure 9-2 *Vacation Rental* Request form

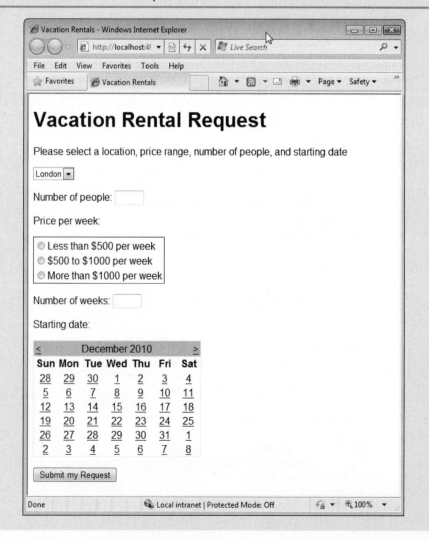

Coding ASP.NET pages in Source view is not difficult, given the excellent tools available in the Visual Studio editor. Tutorial 9-2 will show you how to arrange existing controls into HTML tables.

Tutorial 9-2:
Adding tables to the Vacation Rentals application

In this tutorial, you will continue the *Vacation Rentals* application by inserting an HTML table.

Tutorial Steps

Step 1: Open the *Vacation Rentals* application that you created in Tutorial 9-1, and open *Default.aspx* in Source view.

Step 2: Find the definition of the DropDownList control and add the Font-Size property:

```
<asp:DropDownList ID="ddlLocation" font-size="1em"
runat="server">
```

The default font size of this control is too small. By setting the Font-Size property to 1em, you will match the text of this control to that of the other elements.

Step 3: On the line following the </h1> tag, drag a Table control from the HTML area of the Toolbox. The editor will build a set of table tags for a table that has three rows and three columns. Each row begins with a <tr> tag. Each column within a row begins with the <td> tag.

Step 4: Change the <table> tag to <table border="1">. Each cell will have borders around it so you can see the rows and columns in *Design* view.

Step 5: Switch to the Design view so you can see the table. You should see the table outlines.

Step 6: Returning to Source view, change the first row to the following:

```
<tr>
  <td colspan="3">
    Please select a location, price range, number of
    people, and starting date
  </td>
</tr>
```

The colspan attribute permits the three columns in the first row to be merged into a single column.

Step 7: Insert second table row that is 10 pixels high:

```
<tr style="height:10px">
</tr>
```

Step 8: Move the DropDownList and TextBox into the third table row:

```
<tr>
  <td align="right">Location:</td>
  <td>
    <asp:DropDownList ID="ddlLocation" <cit>font-size="1em"
      width="100" runat="server">
      <asp:ListItem>London</asp:ListItem>
```

```
          <asp:ListItem>Paris</asp:ListItem>
          <asp:ListItem>Rome</asp:ListItem>
          <asp:ListItem>Vienna</asp:ListItem>
          </asp:DropDownList>
    </td>
    <td>Number of people:
      <asp:TextBox ID="txtNumberOfPeople" columns="4"
      runat="server">
      </asp:TextBox>
    </td>
  </tr>
```

Step 9:   Add the following table row:

```
<tr>
  <td align="right">Price per week:</td>
  <td>
    <asp:RadioButtonList ID="radPrices" runat="server">
      <asp:ListItem>Less than $500 per week</asp:ListItem>
      <asp:ListItem>$500 to $1000 per week</asp:ListItem>
      <asp:ListItem>More than $1000 per week</asp:ListItem>
    </asp:RadioButtonList></td>
  <td align="right">Number of weeks:
    <asp:TextBox ID="txtNumberOfWeeks"
      runat="server" Columns="2"></asp:TextBox></td>
</tr>
```

Step 10:   Save the file and switch to Design view to see your work. So far, so good!

Step 11:   Add a new row to the table. The first column contains *Starting date:*. The second column, which spans the width of two columns, contains the Calendar control:

```
<tr>
  <td>Starting date:</td>
  <td colspan="2">
    <asp:Calendar ID="calStartDate" runat="server">
    </asp:Calendar>
  </td>
</tr>
```

Step 12:   It's time to remove the table border. Remove the border attribute from the <table> tag.

Step 13:   Save the Web form. In Design view, it should look like Figure 9-3.

Step 14:   View the form in a Web browser. The rows are a bit jammed together right now, so one thing you can do to improve spacing is to insert some blank rows. Keep the browser window open.

Step 15:   In Source view, insert a new row above the row containing the RadioButton-List. The row does not need any columns, but it does need a height.

```
<tr height="10px">
<td></td>
</tr>
```

Refresh the browser and see if the spacing looks better. You can increase or decrease the height of this row one pixel at a time, giving you absolute control.

Step 16:   Insert ten-pixel rows above and below the row containing the Calendar control.

Figure 9-3 Using a table to format the *Vacation Rentals Request* form

Step 17: Insert another row just above the row containing the DropDownList.

> **TIP:** It is nearly impossible to drag table borders in Design view with any accuracy. You will find that you must work in Source view in order to make fine adjustments to row heights and column widths.

Step 18: Save the file and refresh the browser. The output should look like that shown in Figure 9-4.

Figure 9-4 Running the *Vacation Rentals* application

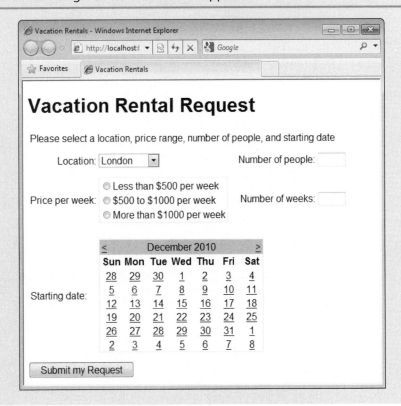

Step 19: Switch the default text size in your Web browser to a larger size. Did all the fonts resize, except for the Button control?

Step 20: In Source view, change the button definition to the following:

```
<asp:Button ID="btnSubmit" Font-Size="1em" runat="server"
Text="Submit my Request" />
```

Step 21: Save the file and close the Web browser. Run the application and resize the browser fonts. Now the button font should also resize.

We do not suggest that you design all Web forms at the source code level, but you will be able to solve problems more quickly if you understand the underlying code. We encourage you to continue to study HTML and even JavaScript if you plan to build Web sites.

Complete Source Code

Following is a listing of the Web page's source code that you created in this tutorial. We left out everything prior to the <head> tag:

```
<head runat="server">
  <title>Vacation Rentals</title>
</head>
<body style="font-family:Arial">
<form id="form1" runat="server">
<h1>Vacation Rental Request</h1>
<table>
  <tr>
    <td colspan="3">
      Please select a location, price range,
      number of people, and starting date
    </td>
  </tr>

  <tr style="height:10px">
  <td></td>
  </tr>

  <tr>
    <td align="right">Location:</td>
    <td>
      <asp:DropDownList font-size="1em" ID="ddlLocation"
        width="100" runat="server">
      <asp:ListItem>London</asp:ListItem>
      <asp:ListItem>Paris</asp:ListItem>
      <asp:ListItem>Rome</asp:ListItem>
      <asp:ListItem>Vienna</asp:ListItem>
      </asp:DropDownList>
    </td>
    <td>Number of people:
      <asp:TextBox ID="txtNumberOfPeople" columns="4"
        runat="server">
      </asp:TextBox>
    </td>
  </tr>
  <tr style="height:10px">
  <td></td>
  </tr>
```

```
<tr>
  <td align="right">
    Price per week:</td>

  <td>
    <asp:RadioButtonList ID="radPrices" runat="server">
      <asp:ListItem>Less than $500 per week</asp:ListItem>
      <asp:ListItem>$500 to $1000 per week</asp:ListItem>
      <asp:ListItem>More than $1000 per week</asp:ListItem>
    </asp:RadioButtonList>
  </td>
  <td align="right">Number of weeks:
    <asp:TextBox ID="txtNumberOfWeeks"
      runat="server" Columns="2"></asp:TextBox></td>
</tr>
<tr style="height:10px">
<td></td>
</tr>

<tr>
  <td>Starting date:</td>
  <td colspan="2">
    <asp:Calendar ID="calStartDate" runat="server">
    </asp:Calendar>
  </td>
</tr>
<tr style="height:10px">
<td></td>
</tr>
</table>

<asp:Button ID="btnSubmit" Font-Size="1em" runat="server"
Text="Submit my Request" Width="173px" />

</form>
</body>
</html>
```

Checkpoint

1. Which organization regulates Web standards, and what is its URL?

2. Which attribute in the <Page> directive identifies the file containing Visual Basic code?

3. In the Visual Studio designer *Source* view, how do you assign text to the title bar of a Web page?

4. Show a sample definition of a TextBox control, using HTML source code.

5. Which *HTML* tag inserts an item into a DropDownList control?

9.2 Cascading Style Sheets

Cascading style sheets (CSS) are XHTML style definitions that Web developers use to customize the appearance of fonts, tables, and other controls on Web forms. Rather than setting individual fonts and colors for every label or body of text, CSS styles define attributes that can be used over and over. Style sheets are based on industry standards from the *World Wide Web Consortium*, who also sets standards for XML, XHTML, and HTML.

If you want all elements within a table to have the same style, you can assign a style name to the table. The styles in a cascading style sheet file can be shared among all pages in an application. Cascading styles can be defined directly on a Web page (in XHTML). But we suggest defining the styles in a separate file, named a *cascading style sheet* file. You can add such a file to a Web project.

Setting Properties for an Entire Page

In Visual Studio, you can set style properties for an entire Web form. When the form is open in Design view, select DOCUMENT from the Object list in the *Properties* window. Any properties you set for the document apply to the entire Web page. Click the *Style* property and set characteristics like font name, font size, font color, background, and so on. All the text and objects that you add to the page will inherit the same style characteristics.

What you do *not* want to do is insert lots of specific, ad hoc text formatting into a Web page. This type of formatting results when you select a block of text and then start setting font types, font sizes, and such. The problem with that approach is that your Web page becomes a jumble of competing and overlapping HTML tags. At some point, it becomes nearly impossible to fix any formatting problems. Instead, you should create styles (known as style classes) and apply these styles to each of the objects on your Web pages. The accepted approach to Web page formatting parallels the way experienced *Microsoft Word* users create paragraph styles. They consistently apply the paragraph styles to all text in their document.

Creating a Cascading Style Sheet File

We recommend that you put all of your Web site's styles in a CSS file. To create a cascading style sheet (CSS) file, select *Add New Item* from the *Website* menu. Then select *Style Sheet* from the list of template icons. The default name for your file will be *StyleSheet.css*, but you can choose any name with a .css extension. The empty style sheet file will have only a single definition for the body tag, which defines the default appearance of all items on a Web form:

```
body
{
}
```

The elements that make up a style are inserted between the braces { .. }. The built-in editor makes it easy for you to see the possible tags, as shown in Figure 9-5. Just place the cursor between the braces and press the space bar. As an illustration, we will set the font family to Verdana, size = 1em, and weight to bold:

```
body
{
   font-family:Verdana;
   font-size:1em;
   font-weight:600;
}
```

Font sizes can be specified in different measurement units. The more common ones are listed here:

- *Em* units, which refer to the font size of the parent element.
- Relative names, such as small, smaller, medium, large, and larger.
- Percentage of the browser's default size, such as 75 percent.
- Fixed point heights, such as 8pt, 10pt, and 12pt.

When setting font sizes, we recommend using em units. This approach lets visually impaired users adjust the font size in their browsers. For example, if users set their default browser font to 20 points, then an em value of 1 produces a 20-point font. An em value of 2 produces a 40-point

Figure 9-5 Intellisense window while editing a CSS file

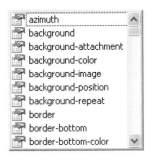

font. Do not use fixed-font sizes such as 10pt, because users will not be able to adjust the fonts. For more information about the *Web Accessibility Initiative*, visit *http://www.w3.org/WAI*.

Linking the CSS File to a Web Page

To make a CSS file active, you must link it to your Web form by switching to the page's Design view and dragging the *CSS* filename from the *Solution Explorer* window onto your Web form. If you're curious to see what happened, switch to the Source view and see that a <link> tag has been inserted into the <head> section of the page:

```
<head runat="server">
  <link href="StyleSheet.css" type="text/css" rel="stylesheet">
</head>
```

The *body* CSS style affects all text typed in the page. To demonstrate, we return to Design view and type some text, as shown in Figure 9-6. The new text matches the style we defined: Verdana font, weight = 600, and size = 1em.

Figure 9-6 Text in the form uses the body CSS style

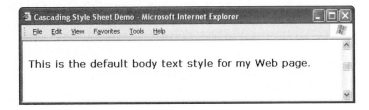

Here's the really good part: You can run an application and, while the browser is open, modify the *CSS* file. When you save the file and refresh the browser, the style changes appear immediately.

Modifying Other Styles

You can alter the look and feel of any standard HTML style tag. Suppose, for example, you want the h1 style to use a 2 em black Arial font, with spacing between letters of .3 em, and a solid border line below the text (thickness = .1 em). An example is shown in Figure 9-7. You can add the following definition to the CSS file:

```
h1 {
  font-family: Arial;
  font-size: 2em;
  letter-spacing: .3em;
  color: Black;
  border-bottom: solid .1em;
}
```

Figure 9-7 Redefining the Heading 1 style

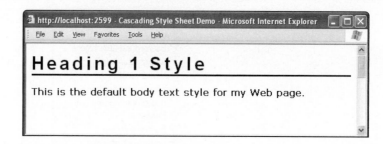

Needless to say, a large number of elements can be changed when determining the appearance of text. You can alter the appearance of all the standard HTML tags, including the following:

- Headings, such as h1, h2, h3, and h4
- Unordered lists (ul)—looks like a bullet list
- Ordered lists (ol)—looks like a numbered list
- Active hyperlink (a:active)
- Mouse hovering over a hyperlink (a:hover)

Line spacing is one of the most important factors in creating readable text on a Web page. The line-height property can be set to pixels, percentages, or ems. The latter two are best if the user wants to resize fonts in the browser. The following style, for example, redefines the *Unordered List (UL)* style (bullet list) with more spacing between lines, and square markers to the left of each item:

```
ul {
    line-height: 1.4em;
    list-style-type: square;
}
```

The corresponding output is shown in Figure 9-8. You can indicate images as part of the style. In the following UL definition, a red diamond icon is used as the bullet marker:

```
ul {
    line-height: 1.4em;
    list-style-image: url(diamond.gif);
    list-style-type: square;
}
```

A sample is shown in Figure 9-9. If the *diamond.gif* file is not found, square bullets are used instead.

Figure 9-8 Modified bullet list style

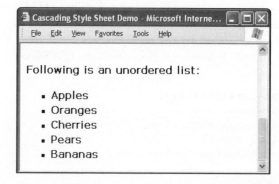

Figure 9-9 Unordered list with red diamond bullets

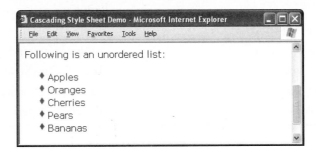

Defining Style Classes

When you select text in *Design* view with the mouse and apply style characteristics such as font, color, size, and boldface, Visual Studio inserts various HTML tags into the Web document. The results can be very messy. For example, suppose you inserted a Label control containing the following text. It uses a bold Arial font, size = 1.1em, color = blue.

This label contains text.

Here is the HTML generated for the Label control in the Web page:

```
<asp:Label ID="Label1" runat="server" Font-Bold="True"
  Font-Names="Arial" Font-Size="1.1em" ForeColor="Blue"
  Text="This label contains text.">
</asp:Label>
```

Suppose you had many such Labels with the same color and font characteristics throughout the application. Changing the characteristics at any time in the future would be very time consuming. Your best bet would be to define a style class in the CSS file as follows:

```
.blueLabel {
   font-family: Arial;
   font-weight: bold;
   font-size: 1.1em;
   color: Blue;
}
```

Once the style is defined, you can apply it to any control on the form.

In the CSS file, user-defined class names must begin with a period (.). To apply the style to a control, assign its name (without the period) to the CssClass property. Notice how much simpler the HTML for the Label control is now, compared to our previous version:

```
<asp:Label ID="Label1" runat="server" CssClass="blueLabel"
  Text="This label contains text.">
</asp:Label>
```

Later, if you want to change the appearance of all controls using the blueLabel style, just modify the style description in the CSS file. You should define a separate style for all the common elements in your Web application, including headers, footers, tables, ListBoxes, buttons, and so on. Your pages will have a consistent look and feel.

Applying CSS Styles

You can apply styles to nearly any HTML element, using the *class* keyword. Examples are shown in Table 9-1. To apply a CSS style to an ASP.NET control, select the control and look at the *Properties* window. Assign the style name to the *CssClass* property of the control.

Table 9-1 Examples of applying style names to document and table elements

Element	Example
Document (body)	\<body class="myStyle">
Table	\<table class="myStyle">
Table row	\<tr class="myStyle">
Table cell	\<td class="someStyle">
div blocks	\<div class="special">

To apply a style to an entire table, click inside the table until its *Select* icon (cross-shaped icon) appears in its upper-left corner. The *Properties* window will indicate that the table is selected. Assign the CSS style to the Class property of the table.

To apply a style to a table cell, click inside the cell. The \<TD> marker should be displayed in the top row of the *Properties* window. Assign the CSS style to the Class property.

> **TIP:** Sometimes when you are trying to select a table column with the mouse, you will see the \<p> tag rather than the \<TD> tag in the *Properties* window. The table cell contains a paragraph break, so you need to delete the \<p> (paragraph) tag before you can assign a CSS style to the table cell. Try to backspace over the line break. If that does not work, switch to the Source (HTML) view and delete the \<p> tag manually. Be careful not to delete anything else.

You can also assign a CSS class to an entire table row, but it can be done only in the Source (HTML) view of the page. Find the \<TR> tag and change it to \<TR class="classname">, where classname is your CSS class name. If you want to assign a CSS class to a block of text, use a \<span> tag. Text between \<span> and \</span> can be inserted side by side, creating the effect of a paragraph that changes styles. Here is an example:

This *is a rather curious* looking paragraph, **which contains different styles**

CSS Menu Demo Example

So that we can explore CSS styles further, let's look at a small *CSS Menu Demo* application. It displays a sliding bar menu, using an HTML table and several HyperLink controls. When the user hovers the mouse over a menu item, the item changes color. When the user clicks a menu item, the application transfers to a new Web page. Figure 9-10 shows the running program on the left and the page in design mode on the right. The menu is contained within an HTML table that has a blue border. The heading row of the menu has its own style. The detail rows use another style, which features an aqua background (which appears gray on the printed page). Each row holding a menu item contains a Hyperlink control, which uses yet another style that causes it to change color when the mouse hovers over the link.

The *CSS Menu Demo* application is located in the chapter examples folder. The CSS file named *StyleSheet.css* defines the styles used in the menu. The *h1* name defines the *Heading1* style:

```
h1 {
   font-family:Arial;
   font-size:2em;
   color:Blue;
}
```

Figure 9-10 Running the *CSS Menu Demo* application

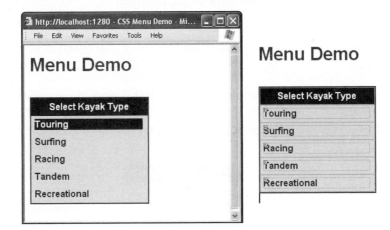

The *.menu* style is applied to the entire table. It specifies a standard-size bold Arial font and a solid blue border.

```
.menu {
  font-family:Arial;
  font-size:1em;
  font-weight:bold;
  border:solid .1em blue;
}
```

The menuHead style applies to the menu header row. It specifies white text on a navy blue background, centered.

```
.menuHead
{
  color:White;
  background-color:Navy;
  text-align:center;
}
```

The menuItem style applies to the individual menu items. It has an aqua background, and the text is padded (indented) on the left by .4 em units.

```
.menuItem {
  background-color:Aqua;
  padding-left:.4em;
}
```

The a (anchor) style defines the appearance of the Hyperlink control in each menu item's row. It specifies navy blue text on an aqua background. Because hyperlinks are underlined by default, the text-decoration:none specification removes the underlining.

```
.menuItem a {
  color:Navy;
  background:Aqua;
  text-decoration:none;
}
```

The a:hover (mouse hover) style indicates what happens when the user hovers the mouse over the Hyperlink controls in the menu items. The text becomes white on a navy blue background.

```
.menuItem a:hover {
  color:White;
  background:Navy;
}
```

In the Source (HTML) view of the startup page, the following line between the <head> and </head> tags connects the page to the *CSS* file:

```
<LINK href="StyleSheet.css" type="text/css" rel="stylesheet">
```

Figure 9-11 shows how each of the CSS styles is assigned to elements in the Web page.

Figure 9-11 CSS styles are applied to HTML and ASP elements

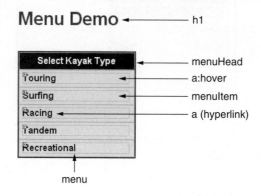

 Checkpoint

6. Which HTML table elements can be assigned style names?

7. Why should em units be used rather than points when setting font sizes?

8. Which property in the DOCUMENT object of a Web page would you use to set the font family name?

9. How do you connect a CSS file to a Web page?

10. In a CSS file, which tag defines default attributes for all items on the page?

9.3 Custom Error Handling

Custom error handling refers to the ability that ASP.NET programs have to configure the display of runtime error messages for both end users and program developers. You've encountered unhandled exceptions (runtime errors) on your Web pages by now. When running an application on the local machine, you can view detailed information about the error, including a stack trace. On the other hand, if you run your programs on a shared server, error information is usually restricted because security would be compromised by showing end users the names of variables, folder names, and other source code. We will show how to control the level of detail in error messages.

The *Custom Errors* setting determines the way in which error messages are displayed on Web pages. Three possible settings exist, and they are documented in the *Custom Error Messages* section of an application's *Web.config* file.

- On—Always display custom (friendly) error messages.
- Off—Always display detailed error information.
- RemoteOnly—Remote users see custom (friendly) error messages; meanwhile, users on the local machine see detailed error information.

Following are the default settings in *Web.config*:

```
<configuration>
  <system.web>
    <customErrors mode="RemoteOnly" />
  </system.web>
</configuration>
```

Additional entries in the system.web group are not shown here.

Example: Unhandled Exception

Suppose a program attempts to convert the contents of a text box to an integer and fails. Figure 9-12 shows the type of detailed information that a programmer needs to see. It includes line numbers and a stack trace. This level of detail is inappropriate for end users because it reveals sensitive information such as line numbers and source code.

Figure 9-12 Unhandled exception, viewed by the local user

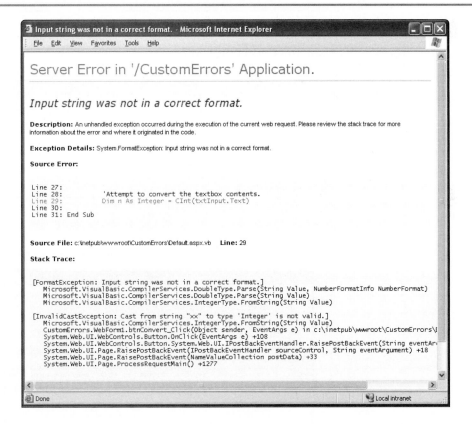

Figure 9-13 shows what happens when a remote user connects to the example program and generates the same error. The error window message hides secret information and tells the user nothing about what went wrong or what remedies are available.

A preferred approach to error handling is to create a custom error page similar to the one shown in Figure 9-14. The URL that loads this page includes a request parameter named *aspxerrorpath*, which is the path of the Web page that was executing when the error occurred. The custom error page displays *aspxerrorpath* and has an email link so the user can notify the support department about the error (see Figure 9-15).

Figure 9-13 Unhandled exception, viewed by the remote user

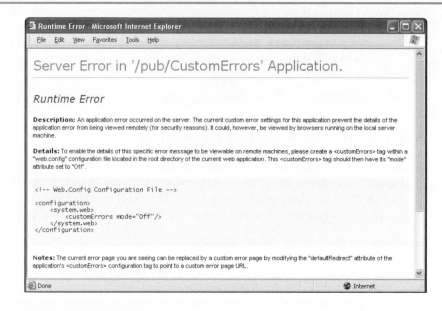

Figure 9-14 Custom Errors application

Figure 9-15 Sending an email report

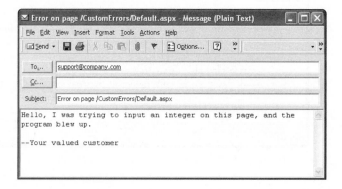

The following line in the *web.config* file lets us redirect the user to the custom error page named *error.aspx*:

```
<customErrors mode="RemoteOnly" defaultRedirect="error.aspx" />
```

You can test a redirected error handler on your local Web server without having to copy your program to a public Web server. Temporarily change the mode to On as follows:

```
<customErrors mode="On" defaultRedirect="error.aspx" />
```

Handling HTTP Errors

Most Web sites use custom error pages to handle **HTTP errors,** which are generated by the Web server. For example, error 404 is generated by a server when a requested Web page is not found. Rather than displaying a generic error page (which was shown in Figure 9-13), you can designate a specific page for error 404 in the *web.config* file. In the following example, the *notFound.aspx* file displays whenever error 404 occurs:

```
<customErrors mode="On" defaultRedirect="error.aspx">
  <error statusCode="404" redirect="notFound.aspx" />
</customErrors>
```

The error page used in the *Custom Errors* program appears in Figure 9-16.

Figure 9-16 Custom error page for 404 Not Found

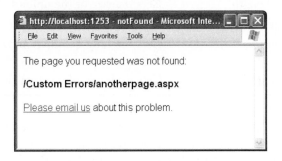

 Checkpoint

11. Which CustomErrors setting in *web.config* permits end users to see detailed error information when an unhandled exception is thrown?

12. What settings can you make in the *web.config* file that will allow remote users to see friendly error information and at the same time allow a user on the local machine to see detailed debugging information?

13. Which HTTP error is generated when the browser cannot locate a Web page?

9.4 Uploading Files and Sending Email

Allowing users to upload files to a Web site is often very useful. They can send email with attachments and upload pictures to online photo albums. Students can upload assignments, and groups of people collaborating on projects can share documents. The *FileUpload* control lets users upload any type of file, but you have the option of restricting the permitted file types and the maximum size of each file.

When the user uploads a file, it is held in server memory. When the file has finished uploading, the code in your Web page executes. The maximum file size that can be uploaded is set by the server's MaxRequestLength configuration setting. The default is 4MB.

FileUpload Control Properties

Table 9-2 lists a few commonly used properties of the FileUpload control. The *PostedFile* property, an *HttpPostedFile* object, represents the uploaded file. Table 9-3 lists the more

Table 9-2 FileUpload properties

Property	Description
FileBytes	A byte array containing the file's contents.
FileContent	A stream containing the file.
HasFile	Gets a Boolean value indicating whether the FileUpload contains a file.
PostedFile	An HttpPostedFile object that contains information about the file being uploaded.

Table 9-3 HttpPostedFile properties

Property	Description
ContentLength	Gets the size of the uploaded file, in bytes.
ContentType	Identifies the MIME content type of the uploaded file.
FileName	Gets the fully qualified name of the uploaded file (on the client computer).
InputStream	Gets a Stream object that points to the uploaded file's data.

common properties of the HttpPostedFile class. You can use the *ContentType* property to limit the types of files that can be saved. This helps to prevent users from uploading files containing malicious scripts and executable files. Table 9-4 lists a number of common **MIME types,** which are standardized descriptions of Web content.

Table 9-4 Common MIME types

MIME Type	Description
image/gif	GIF image file (.gif)
image/pjpeg	JPEG image file (.jpg, .jpeg)
image/*	any type of image file
text/plain	plain text file
application/octet-stream	Java source code file (.java)
application/java	Java class file (.class)
text/html	HTML file (.htm, .html)
application/x-zip-compressed	ZIP (compressed) file (.zip)
application/msword	Microsoft Word document (.doc)
application/rtf	Rich Text format file (.rtf)
application/pdf	Adobe Acrobat™ file (.pdf)
vnd.ms-excel	Microsoft Excel file (.xls)

Saving the File

After the user uploads a file, you are ready to save the file on the server. The *PostedFile.SaveAs* method receives an absolute path that determines the location of the saved file on the server. Here's a sample call, assuming the FileUpload control is named *btnSelectFile*:

```
btnSelectFile.PostedFile.SaveAs("c:\temp\picture.gif")
```

The filename might have been supplied by the user in a TextBox.

```
btnSelectFile.PostedFile.SaveAs("c:\temp\" & txtFileName.Text)
```

You might want to save the file in a folder that belongs to your Web application. Then you can use the *My.Request.PhysicalApplicationPath* property to get the absolute path of the Web application on the server. The path name always ends with a back slash character.

If a folder named *Uploads* exists inside the current project, the following statements assign its absolute path to the variable named *uploadPath*:

```
Dim uploadPath As String
uploadPath = My.Request.PhysicalApplicationPath & "Uploads\"
```

The following statement calls SaveAs, using the uploadPath variable:

```
btnSelectFile.PostedFile.SaveAs(uploadPath & txtFileName.Text)
```

Extracting the Client Filename

If you want to save the file under the same name as the uploaded filename, you must extract the filename and extension from the PostedFile property. The latter contains a fully qualified name (complete path), such as *c:\myStuff\files\recent\myfile.txt*. The easiest way to do this extraction is to call the System.IO.Path.GetFileName method, as follows:

```
With btnSelectFile.PostedFile
   fileName = System.IO.Path.GetFileName(.FileName)
End With
```

Now fileName contains just the filename and extension, such as *myfile.txt*.

Figure 9-17 shows a program that uploads a file to a Web site. The FileUpload control appears as a text box and button, side by side. When the user clicks the *Browse* button, the Web browser displays a file chooser window that browses their local computer. After a file is selected, its complete path appears in the text box on the Web form. The user also enters the name she or he wants to use when saving the file on the server. When the user clicks the *Upload Now* button, the file is transferred to the server.

Figure 9-17 *File Upload Demo*, just before uploading the file

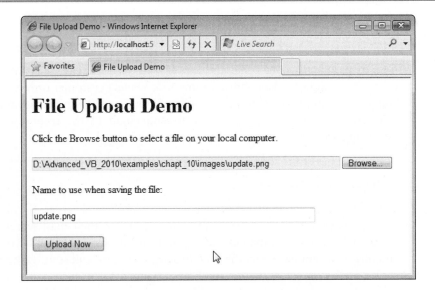

After the file is uploaded, the program displays a confirmation message (see Figure 9-18). The originally selected filename disappears from the FileUpload control. This may be good; if the user accidentally clicks the button twice in a row, the same file will not upload a second time.

Figure 9-18 *File Upload Demo,* after uploading the file

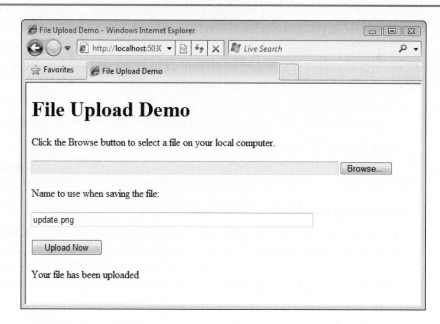

Implementation

Here is the source code for the *File Upload Demo* program:

```
Partial Class _Default
   Inherits System.Web.UI.Page

   Protected Sub btnUpload_Click() Handles btnUpload.Click
      Dim uploadPath As String
      uploadPath = My.Request.PhysicalApplicationPath & "Uploads\"
      btnSelectFile.PostedFile.SaveAs(uploadPath & txtFileName.Text)
      lblResult.Text = "Your file has been uploaded"
   End Sub
End Class
```

Sending Email

One of the most useful tasks an ASP.NET application can perform is to send email. For example, it might send a confirmation notice when a customer orders an item or when a person joins a club. It could use email to send time-sensitive information to users. Or if a run-time error occurs, an application can send email to the technical support department. Following are some suggestions on how to send email.

You must import the System.Net.Mail namespace at the top of a Web page:

```
Imports System.Net.Mail
```

You must know the name of your outgoing SMTP mail server. If you're working at home and you have an Internet service provider (ISP), use their mail server name. If you're in a college lab, check with the lab staff to find out the server name. If your Web application is running on a remote server, the Web hosting company will supply you with the name of the server. Here is an example of a mail server name:

```
Dim mailServerName As String = "mailhost.mycollege.edu"
```

The following statement declares an SmtpClient object using a sample mail server name:

```
Dim m_Client As New SmtpClient(mailServerName)
```

MailMessage Class

The **MailMessage class** provides all the necessary properties to define an email message. If you are sending mail to only one recipient, here is a simple way to create a MailMessage object. Pass the following parameters to the MailMessage constructor: sender email, receiver email, subject, and body. The following, for example, is a message from me@abc.com to you@xyz.com:

```
Dim message As New MailMessage("me@abc.com", "you@xyz.com",
   "Greetings", "This is the message body")
```

To send the message, call the SmtpClient.Send method, as follows:

```
m_Client.Send(message)
```

Use a Try..Catch block to catch exceptions. Exceptions are usually thrown when the name of the mail server is incorrect or the mail server does not respond.

File Attachments

The MailMessage class has a property named *Attachments*, which is a collection that holds the names of files attached to a message. First, you create an Attachment object by passing a fully qualified filename (path plus filename) to its constructor:

```
Dim attachedFile As New Attachment("c:\temp\myfile.txt")
```

Next, add the Attachment object to the Attachments collection, as follows:

```
Dim message As New MailMessage
message.Attachments.Add(attachedFile)
```

If you want users to be able to attach files to their messages, you might find it convenient to create a folder in your application to hold the files. Suppose a folder is named *Attachments*. The following statement gets the physical path of that folder:

```
Private ReadOnly attachPath As String =
   My.Request.PhysicalApplicationPath & "Attachments\"
```

When a file is uploaded (using a FileUpload control named *btnSelectFile*), we can get its filename and use the SaveAs method to save it in the *Attachments* folder.

```
btnSelectFile.PostedFile.SaveAs(
   attachPath & System.IO.Path.GetFileName(btnSelectFile.FileName))
```

(The System.IO.Path.GetFileName method removes path information from the file the user uploaded.)

MailAddress Class

The **MailAddress class** defines an object that can hold email addresses. The mail-sending example we showed earlier used a shorthand version for addresses of the sender and receiver. But if you want to store both the name of a recipient and their email address, you should construct a MailAddress object. Here are examples of its constructors:

```
new MailAddress("joe@anywhere.com")
new MailAddress("joe@anywhere.com", "Joe Smith")
new MailAddress("joe@anywhere.com", "Joe Smith",
   System.Text.Encoding.Unicode)
```

The first parameter must be in a correct email address format. Your mail server may check the domain name to see if it exists. The second constructor has a display name parameter, which shows in the message header when the message is received. The third constructor lets you select the encoding method for the address, an option used for international character sets.

In the following example, we create a MailMessage object. Then we create MailAddress objects and add them to the *From* and *To* properties of the message. The message is sent from Joe Smith to Sam Jones and Eric Chong.

```
Dim message As New MailMessage
With message
  .From = New MailAddress("joe@anywhere.com", "Joe Smith")
  .To.Add(New MailAddress("sam@sam.com", "Sam Jones"))
  .To.Add(New MailAddress("eric@xyz.edu", "Eric Chong"))
  .Subject = "This is the message subject"
  .Body = "This is the message body"
End With
```

MailMessage Properties

The MailMessage class has properties that configure messages and include attachments. Some of the more useful properties are shown in Table 9-5. The **Bcc** field is convenient when sending a message to multiple persons because each recipient cannot see the addresses of the other recipients. When a field contains a list of email addresses, each address must be separated by semicolons.

Table 9-5 Commonly used MailMessage properties

Property	Description
Attachments	Collection of MailAttachment objects that represent file attachments.
Bcc	A MailAddressCollection that contains a list of *blind carbon copy* recipients—recipients cannot see this field.
Body	Body of the message.
BodyEncoding	Gets or sets the encoding method used for the message body.
CC	A MailAddressCollection that contains a list of *carbon copy* recipients—recipients can see this field.
DeliverNotificationOptions	Options relating to how the message is delivered.
From	*Required:* The address of the message sender (MailAddress object).
Headers	Collection of headers used by the message.
IsBodyHtml	Gets or sets option to include HTML tags in the message body.
Priority	MailPriority enumeration. Choices are High, Normal, and Low.
ReplyTo	The *reply to* field of the message (MailAddress object).
Subject	Message subject.
To	*Required:* A MailAddressCollection that contains a list of recipients.

Messages Containing HTML Tags

You can embed HTML tags in a message body as long as you set the ***MailMessage.BodyFormat*** property to *HTML*. When the form is posted back, however, the HttpRequest class rejects HTML tags as being potentially harmful. Figure 9-19 shows the runtime error that results from inserting the <b> tag in the message body.

Figure 9-19 Request validation error message

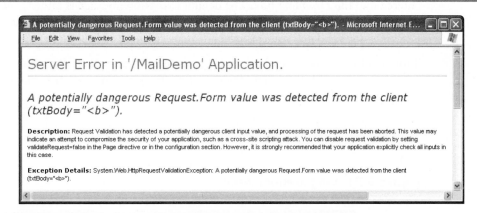

As the instructions in the error message explain, you can bypass this error by including the following assignment in the form's Page directive, which you can modify when the editor is in Source view:

```
ValidateRequest="false"
```

MailDemo Program

Figure 9-20 shows an ASP.NET application that sends mail to recipients using the MailMessage class. The program lets you send messages in either text or HTML format, depending on your choice in the dropdown list. If you select HTML, you can embed tags such as <b> or <h1> in your message.

 TIP: Before running this sample program, you must customize the *m_ServerName* variable in the program source code to make it match the mail server name on your system.

Figure 9-20 Sending a mail message

Figure 9-21 shows a sample error message that is generated when an invalid email address is entered into the *From* text box. The default exception message is rather general, so it's a good idea for you to perform validation on email addresses before sending a message. Use a RegularExpressionValidator control, which is demonstrated in Section 9.5.

Table 9-6 lists the controls used in the program. We set validateRequest= "false" in the Page directive of the Web form. The *StyleSheet.css* file contains one custom style definition:

```
.normal
{
  FONT-FAMILY: Verdana, Helvetica, sans-serif;
  FONT-SIZE: small;
}
```

Figure 9-21 Sample error message

Table 9-6 Controls used in the *MailDemo* program

Control Type	Name	Properties
<Table>	Table1	
<Table>	Table2	
TextBox	txtFrom	
TextBox	TxtTo	
TextBox	TxtCc	
TextBox	txtBcc	
TextBox	txtSubject	
TextBox	txtBody	TextMode: MultiLine
FileUpload	btnSelectFile	
Button	btnAttach	Text: *Attach*
Label	lblAttachedFile	
DropDownList	ddlFormat	Items: *Text, HTML*
Button	btnSend	Text: *Send*
Label	lblStatus	

Implementation

The following is a complete listing of the program source code:

```vbnet
Imports System.Net.Mail
Imports System.IO

Partial Class _Default
  Inherits System.Web.UI.Page
  'Change the following server name to your server:
  Private ReadOnly m_ServerName As String = "mail.bellsouth.net"
  Private ReadOnly m_AttachmentsPath As String = My.Request. _
    PhysicalApplicationPath & "Attachments\"

  Private Sub SetFormat(ByVal objMail As MailMessage)
    Select Case ddlFormat.SelectedValue
      Case "HTML"
        objMail.IsBodyHtml = True
      Case "Text"
        objMail.IsBodyHtml = False
    End Select
  End Sub

  Private Sub btnSend_Click() Handles btnSend.Click
    Dim fileName As String = String.Empty
    'If an attachment has been selected, upload
    'the file to the appropriate directory.
    With btnSelectFile.PostedFile
      If lblAttachedFile.Text.Length > 0 Then
        fileName = m_AttachmentsPath & lblAttachedFile.Text
        .SaveAs(fileName)
      End If
    End With
    Try
      ' Build a message object and set the HTML option.
      Dim objMail As New MailMessage
      SetFormat(objMail)
      With objMail
        .From = New MailAddress(txtFrom.Text)
        .To.Add(New MailAddress(txtTo.Text))
        .Subject = txtSubject.Text
        .Body = txtBody.Text

        ' send Carbon Copies.
        If txtCc.Text.Length > 0 Then
          .CC.Add(New MailAddress(txtCc.Text))
        End If

        ' send Blind Carbon Copies.
        If txtBcc.Text.Length > 0 Then
          .Bcc.Add(New MailAddress(txtBcc.Text))
        End If

        ' Add the file attachment, if any.
        If fileName.Length > 0 Then
          .Attachments.Add(New Attachment(fileName))
        End If
      End With

      ' Create the mail client and send the message.
      Dim client As SmtpClient = New SmtpClient(m_ServerName)
      client.Send(objMail)
      lblStatus.Text = "Mail message sent to " & txtTo.Text
```

```
        Catch ex As Exception
          lblStatus.Text = "Unable to send mail: " & ex.Message
        End Try
      End Sub

      Protected Sub btnAttach_Click() Handles btnAttach.Click
        With btnSelectFile.PostedFile
          If .FileName.Length > 0 Then
            lblAttachedFile.Text = Path.GetFileName(.FileName)
          End If
        End With
      End Sub
    End Class
```

Checkpoint

14. Which control makes it possible for users to upload files to a server from their browsers?

15. Why is the HttpPostedFile class important in a program that lets users upload files?

16. What is the name of the protocol used when sending mail?

17. Show an example of sending a mail message using an SmtpMail object.

18. Which class offers a rich set of properties that can be used to send mail with attachments?

9.5 Data Validation Controls

Data Validation controls check the contents of user input fields and produce error messages. They are located in the *Validation* section of the Visual Studio Toolbox and check for the following kinds of errors:

- An input field has not changed from its initial value.
- An input value is too small or too large.
- One input value does not correlate with the contents of another input value (a student, for example, might have entered a graduation date that is earlier than his or her initial enrollment date).
- An input value does not match a required format (a user, for example, might have entered a date that does not match the way dates are expressed in the geographical locale).

Validation controls can also perform custom error checking that involves logical rules. For example, a tax calculation program might have a number of rules that govern whether exceptions for dependents can be claimed. A custom validator could check those rules.

The names and descriptions of the validation controls are listed in Table 9-7. When you use these controls, you associate each one with a particular input field on a Web form.

Server-Side and Client-Side

Two basic types of validation work together: server-side and client-side.

- *Server-side validation* is activated when the user posts the page back to the server, typically by clicking a button. Validation error messages are displayed, and then the button's Click event handler executes.

Table 9-7 ASP.NET validation controls

Validation Control	Usage
RequiredFieldValidator	Alerts the user when an input field has not changed from its initial value.
RangeValidator	Checks a field's value against a predetermined range of values.
CompareValidator	Compares the value of one field with a constant or with the value of another field.
RegularExpressionValidator	Compares a field's value to a regular expression.
CustomValidator	Flexible validation performed by user-coded logic.
ValidationSummary	Displays a message for each validation control found to have an error.

- *Client-side validation* is performed when the user moves between input fields, using the *Tab* key or the mouse. ASP.NET generates Javascript code that executes directly on the user's browser, producing an effect similar to a Windows application. When the user fixes an error, the related error message disappears.

You have the option of disabling client-side validation for a particular validation control by setting its EnableClientScript property to *False*. But if you do so, you must manually check the control's *IsValid* property to find out if the control's contents are valid. We recommend leaving EnableClientScript set to its default value of *True*.

Client-side validation typically intercepts a button's Click event. If an error is found in a validated input field, the button's server-side Click handler never executes. When the user corrects all errors and clicks the button again, the Click handler is permitted to execute.

RequiredFieldValidator Control

The **RequiredFieldValidator** control alerts the user when the content of a particular input control has not changed from its initial value. Suppose a Web form has a text box that the user fills out before clicking the *OK* button. We will assume that the text box's initial value is empty, and a RequiredFieldValidator control is attached to the text box. In Figure 9-22, an error message displays if the user clicks the *OK* button without having entered a daily

Figure 9-22 RequiredFieldValidator example

rental rate. The properties of the RequiredFieldValidator in this example are assigned as follows:

Property Name	Value
ControlToValidate	txtRentalRate
InitialValue	*(empty)*
Text	*
ErrorMessage	Rental rate is required

The RequiredFieldValidator's Text property, which is usually assigned a single character, displays at the location where the validation control is located on the form. It is usually best to include a ValidationSummary control on the same form as other validation controls. A **ValidationSummary** displays all error messages generated by validation controls on the current form. When you assign a string to a validation control's ErrorMessage property, the string is displayed by the ValidationSummary control. Figure 9-23 contains a concept map that expresses the functional relationships among a TextBox being validated, a RequiredFieldValidator, and a ValidationSummary.

Figure 9-23 Communication relationships among the TextBox, RequiredFieldValidator, and ValidationSummary controls

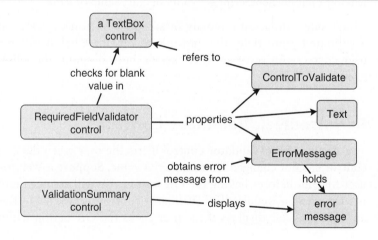

When the user corrects the error and clicks the *OK* button, the browser moves to the *Confirmation form*. In the example shown in Figure 9-24, the following Click handler is used for the *OK* button:

```
Protected Sub btnOk_Click() Handles btnOk.Click
    Response.Redirect("Confirmation.aspx")
End Sub
```

In Section 9.6, we will explain more details about the Response.Redirect statement.

Nonblank Values

If you assign a value to the RequiredFieldValidator control's *InitialValue* property, you can find out if the user has changed the contents of the control being validated. This feature is

Figure 9-24 After the user corrects the error

useful when validating a DropDownList control. You can set its default selection to something like *(none)*, with an associated value of –1. If the user does not make a selection at runtime, the RequiredFieldValidator displays an error because the value from the Drop-DownList is still equal to the InitialValue property of the RequiredFieldValidator control. Figure 9-25 shows such a situation. The Value property of the first ListItem in the Drop-DownList equals –1. Here are the validator control's settings:

Property Name	Value
ControlToValidate	*ddlRoomType*
InitialValue	–1
Text	*
ErrorMessage	Room type must be selected

Figure 9-25 DropDownList with a RequiredFieldValidator

CausesValidation Property

Any control that causes postback events has a *CausesValidation* property with a default value of *True*. Examples are Buttons and LinkButtons. Sometimes, however, you may not want any validation to occur when the user clicks a particular button. In Figure 9-22, we showed a LinkButton with the Text *Skip this page*. The CausesValidation property for that button was set to *False* to prevent the RequiredFieldValidator control from activating. Figure 9-26 shows the resulting page display.

Common Properties

A number of properties, shown in Table 9-8, are common to all validator controls.

Figure 9-26 User clicked the *Skip this page* LinkButton

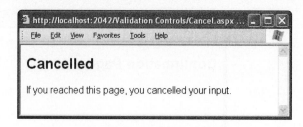

Table 9-8 Common validator control properties

Property Name	Description
ControlToValidate	Control whose contents are to be validated (called the *target control*).
Display	Determines how the message contained in the Text property is displayed (choices are Static, Dynamic, and None).
EnableClientScript	Enable or disable client-side validation.
Enabled	Enable or disable validation of the target control.
ErrorMessage	The message that is displayed by the ValidationSummary control when an error is detected.
IsValid	Equals *True* when the control's contents are valid (runtime property).
Text	Text displayed on the form at the location of the validator control when the validation check fails.

RangeValidator Control

The **RangeValidator** control checks the value of an input control, comparing it to a range of acceptable values. The *MaximumValue* and *MinimumValue* properties are used to set the range. This control becomes active only after the user enters some data into the input field. For example, Figure 9-27 shows an input form in which the user enters the number of occupants for a vacation rental. The range of acceptable values is 1 to 8. Table 9-9 shows the property settings used in this example. Ranges do not have to be numeric. For example, you can set the MinimumValue to *s* and MaximumValue to *x* if you want to require input strings to fall between these two letters of the alphabet.

Figure 9-27 Using the RangeValidator control

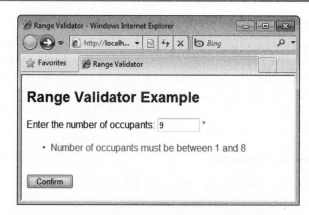

Table 9-9 Sample RangeValidator control settings

Property Name	Value
ControlToValidate	*txtOccupants*
Text	*
ErrorMessage	Number of occupants must be between 1 and 8
MaximumValue	8
MinimumValue	1

Multiple Validators

Input controls typically have more than one validator. A RequiredFieldValidator for each required input field is a starting point. Then you can add other validators to check the range, compare two fields, and so on. If an input field's contents are no different from its default value, only the RequiredFieldValidator is activated. Once the user modifies the field, the other validators become active.

CompareValidator Control

The **CompareValidator** control compares one input control's contents to either a fixed value or the value of another control. You identify the first control using the *ControlToValidate* property. If you are comparing to a fixed value, assign it to the *ValueToCompare* property. If you are comparing to another control, assign its name to the *ControlToCompare* property. This control has some unique properties, which are listed in Table 9-10.

Table 9-10 Unique CompareValidator properties

Property Name	Description
ValueToCompare	A constant value that is compared to the control's contents.
Operator	Used when comparing control contents to a constant value (select from a list of predefined operator identifiers: equal to, greater than, less than, and so on).
Type	The type of data used in the control being validated (select from String, Integer, Double, Date, or Currency).
ControlToCompare	A control whose contents will be compared to the control being validated.

Suppose we wanted to use the CompareValidator to check the values of starting and ending rental reservation dates. We would like to input the dates using Calendar controls, but they are not supported by the CompareValidator. Naturally, the return date must be greater than or equal to the rental date. In Figure 9-28, for example, the user has entered an invalid date range. Figure 9-29 shows the important property values in the CompareValidator control.

Comparing to Today's Date

Sometimes you may want to compare a date entered by the user to today's date. Although the standard *Today* property returns the current date, you cannot assign it to the ValueToCompare property in Design view. On the other hand, you can assign the property at runtime as follows:

```
cmpDate.ValueToCompare = CStr(Today)
```

Figure 9-28 CompareValidator Example

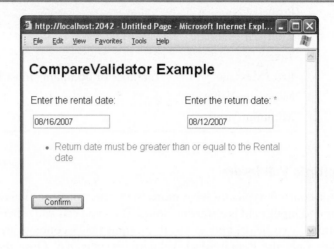

Figure 9-29 Property settings for the CompareValidator Example

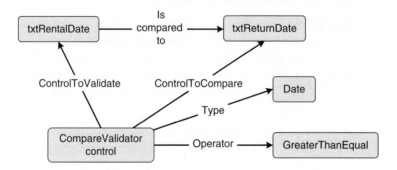

RegularExpressionValidator Control

The **RegularExpressionValidator** control performs string pattern matching against the contents of another control. Regular expression syntax is somewhat complex, but you can select from a dropdown list of predefined expressions when setting the *ValidationExpression* property. Here are some predefined regular expressions you can select:

- Internet URL
- Email address
- U.S. phone number
- U.S. Social Security number
- U.S. ZIP code

In Figure 9-30, a regular expression is used to validate an email address entered by the user. Table 9-11 lists the RegularExpressionValidator's property values used in this example.

Regular Expressions

Regular expressions are specification strings that conform to regular expression syntax. They are a powerful tool for pattern matching. You can match an expression against various input strings and accept or reject each string based on how it matches the expression.

Suppose a regular expression for a four-digit personal identification number (PIN) is encoded as \d{4}. This expression can be assigned to the *ValidationExpression* property of

Figure 9-30 Validating an email address

Table 9-11 Property values in the RegularExpressionValidator example

Property Name	Property Value
ControlToValidate	*txtEmail*
ErrorMessage	Invalid email format
Text	*
ValidationExpression	\w+([-+.]\w+)*@\w+([-.]\w+)*\.\w+([-.]\w+)*

a RegularExpressionValidator control. The following table shows the result of checking different strings against the sample expression:

String	Outcome
1234	accept
2222	accept
333	reject
999A	reject
11111	reject

A fairly large set of symbols are used in regular expressions. Although we cannot show them all here, some common symbols are listed in Table 9-12.

Table 9-12 Common regular expression symbols

Symbol	Description
\w	Matches digits 0 through 9, underscore, and any other characters classified as alphanumeric in the Unicode character properties database.
\d	Matches digits 0 through 9 only.
+	Matches any number of occurrences of the preceding character.
\	Escape: matches the next character following the backslash.
{*n*}	Specifies the number of occurrences *n* of the previous character.
( )*	Repeats sequence inside the parentheses any number of times.
[*aaa*]	The set of characters specified inside the brackets.
[^*aaa*]	All characters except the ones specified inside the brackets.

Table 9-13 lists a number of regular expression examples that you can modify and use in your own programs. If you are interested in learning more, look up *Regular Expressions* at the Microsoft MSDN Web site.

Table 9-13 Regular expression examples

Expression	Matches Strings Containing . . .	Sample Matching Strings
\d+	any number of digits	234249749875764392
\d*		1
(\d)*		
\d{5}	exactly five digits	98346
		11111
		00002
X(\d)*Y	strings beginning with X, ending with Y, containing any number of digits in between	X2Y
		XY
		X23423424234Y
\w*	any number of alphanumeric characters, including the underscore	sdjd6883sdfh_234AB
AB+	character A followed by any number of letter B's	AB
		ABBBBBBB
[123]{5}	any digit from the set {1,2,3}, repeated five times	11111
		11222
		13221
		33333
000\d{3}	three zeros followed by any three digits	000123
		000444
		000219
[A-Za-z]1	any number of capital or lowercase letters in the range A to Z	aBytXnp
		B
[a-z]:\\[a-z]+	lowercase letter, colon, backslash, followed by any number of lowercase letters	c:\xyz
		b:\z
[^aeiou]	any character not in the set of vowels	X
		Z
		M

Validating an Email Address

The validation expression used in our earlier example to validate an email address was \w+([-+.]\w+)*@\w+([-.]\w+)*\.\w+([-.]\w+)*. Table 9-14 breaks it into segments to make it more understandable. Examples of strings that match the first subexpression follow:

```
ben123
any_one
fred.jones
dan+miller
comp-sci
microsoft.com
```

Table 9-14 Email expression example

Subexpression	Description
\w+([-+.]\w+)*	Any number of alphanumeric characters can begin an email address (\w1) followed by a single occurrence of either minus, plus, or dot; this is followed by any number of alphanumeric characters
@	The @ symbol
\w+([-+.]\w+)*	Same as the first subexpression
\.	A period (.)
\w+([-+.]\w+)*	Same as the first subexpression

CustomValidator Control

The **CustomValidator** control can perform any validation not already covered by existing validation controls. The actual validation is performed by your own event handler. The event being handled is called *ServerValidate*.

Example: Evaluating Academic Status

In Figure 9-31, the user selects the academic status of a student who plans to register for classes and inputs the number of requested credits. When the *Verify* button is clicked, the program evaluates the request according to the following criteria:

- If the Advisor override box is checked, the student can register.
- If the Advisor override box is not checked, the status value must be checked:
  - If status = Satisfactory, the student may take no more than 18 credits.
  - If status = Warning, the student may take no more than 12 credits.
  - If status = Probation, the student may take no more than 8 credits.
  - If status = Not eligible, the student may not take any credits.

Figure 9-31 CustomValidator Example

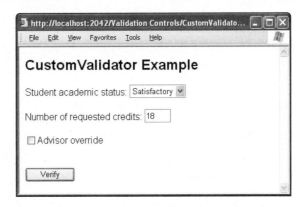

Suppose a student whose status equals *Satisfactory* tries to register for 19 credits. The result is shown in Figure 9-32.

A complete listing of the program's source code is shown in Figure 9-33. To enable a CustomValidator control, you must handle its *ServerValidate* event. The second parameter (args), has a property named *IsValid*, which you can set once you have applied your own validation logic, as follows:

```
Private Sub CreditsCustomValidate_ServerValidate(
   ByVal source As Object,
   ByVal args As ServerValidateEventArgs) _
   Handles CreditsCustomValidate.ServerValidate
```

Figure 9-32 Sample error message

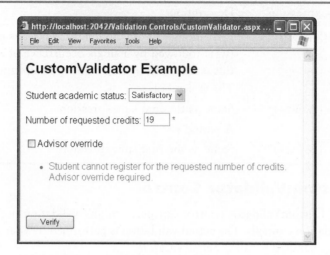

Figure 9-33 Listing of the CustomValidator Example

```vb
Partial Class CustomValidator
   Inherits System.Web.UI.Page

   Enum StatusType
      Satisfactory
      Warning
      Probation
      NotEligible
   End Enum

   Protected Sub CreditsCustomValidate_ServerValidate(
      ByVal source As Object,
      ByVal args As ServerValidateEventArgs) _
      Handles CreditsCustomValidate.ServerValidate

      args.IsValid = True
      ' If the advisor override box is checked, no further
      ' evaluation is necessary.
      If chkAdvisorOverride.Checked Then Return

      ' Determine the maximum number of credits the
      ' student can take.
      Dim maxCredits As Integer = 0
      Select Case ddlStatus.SelectedValue
         Case StatusType.Satisfactory
            maxCredits = 18
         Case StatusType.Warning
            maxCredits = 12
         Case StatusType.Probation
            maxCredits = 8
         Case StatusType.NotEligible
            maxCredits = 0
      End Select

      If CInt(txtCredits.Text) > maxCredits Then
         args.IsValid = False
      End If
   End Sub

   Protected Sub btnVerify_Click() Handles btnVerify.Click
      If CreditsCustomValidate.IsValid Then
         Response.Redirect("Confirmation.aspx")
      End If
   End Sub
End Class
```

This program uses the student's academic status and advisor setting to decide the maximum number of credits the student can take. Then it compares the requested number of credits to the maximum credits.

The Click handler for the *Verify* button has an important job—it checks the IsValid property of the CustomValidator control before displaying the Confirmation form.

Assigning Names to Validation Controls

There is no standard naming convention for Validation controls. An approach we suggest is to hint at the name of the control it validates, followed by the type of validation. Table 9-15 lists some examples of this naming scheme.

Table 9-15 Sample validation control names

Control Being Validated	Validation Control Type	Suggested Validation Control Name
txtDailyRate	RequiredFieldValidator	DailyRateRequiredValidator
txtRentalDate	CompareValidator	RentalDateCompareValidator
txtDailyRate	RangeValidator	DailyRateRangeValidator
txtEmail	RegularExpressionValidator	EmailExpressionValidator
txtCredits	CustomValidator	CreditsCustomValidator

 Checkpoint

19. Which validator control notifies a user that an input field should not contain its default value?

20. Which properties must be set when using the RangeValidator control?

21. Which validator control would be useful when verifying that an employee's promotion date is greater than or equal to her or his hire date?

22. Which validator control would be useful when verifying that an account number contains seven digits?

 9.6 ## Working with Multiple Web Forms

Before long, you will want to create Web applications having multiple pages. You might collect information on one page and display a summary on a second page. Or, you might display supplementary information on a third page, which the user can select at will.

Hyperlinks

A **hyperlink** is an image or text that acts as a transfer mechanism for the Web browser. When you hover the mouse over a hyperlink, the mouse changes shape. When you click the hyperlink, the browser transfers control to either a new place in the same Web page or a different Web page. Standard HTML Uses the <a> tag around a block of text to specify a hyperlink. Here is an example:

```
<a href="http://gaddisbooks.com>Tony Gaddis Books</a>
```

Within the <a> tag, the href property identifies a target URL. All text from the > character at the end of the <a> tag, until the closing </a> tag is a hyperlink. This is what the user would see if the page were set up to display underlined hyperlinks:

Tony Gaddis Books

Using style characteristics, you can make hyperlinks appear without underlining and in a specific color. Chapter 10 shows how to use CSS styles to change the appearance of hyperlinks.

To create a hyperlink in Visual Studio, select a block of text with the mouse; click the Hyperlink button on the Formatting toolbar, as shown in Figure 9-34; and enter the URL of the target URL. If the URL will point to a page in your project, you can click the *Browse* button to locate a file within your project, as shown in Figure 9-35.

Figure 9-34 Converting a block of text to a hyperlink

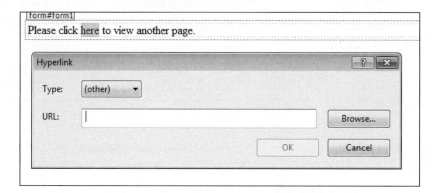

Figure 9-35 Selecting the target page for the hyperlink

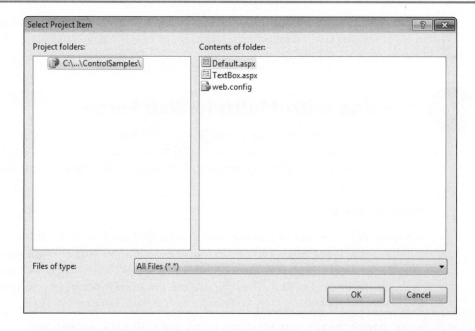

HyperLink, ImageButton, and LinkButton Controls

HyperLink Control

The **HyperLink control** is a programmable hyperlink that lets users navigate from the current page to another page. The link can appear as text or as an image. Here are the more commonly used properties:

- The *Text* property contains text to be displayed by the control. If you assign a value to this property, leave the ImageUrl property blank.
- The *ImageUrl* property contains the URL of an image to be displayed (rather than text). If you use this, leave the Text property blank.
- The *NavigateUrl* property contains the destination URL when the user clicks on the link. The property editor has a *Browse* button you can use to locate Web pages within your project.
- The *Target* property controls whether the new page will appear in the current browser window (the default) or in a separate window. To open in a separate browser window, set Target equal to *_blank*.

In XHTML, the hyperlinked text appears after the > character and before the closing </asp:HyperLink> tag. Here is a sample of a complete control definition:

```
<asp:HyperLink
   ID="lnkViewStudents"
   runat="server"
   NavigateUrl="ViewStudents.aspx">
   View the Student List
   </asp:HyperLink>
```

This is what the user would see, assuming that the page is configured to display underlined hyperlinks:

View the Student List

Alternatively, you can assign the hyperlinked text to the control's Text property, as follows:

```
<asp:HyperLink
   ID="lnkViewStudents"
   runat="server"
   NavigateUrl="ViewStudents.aspx"
   Text="View the Student List">
   </asp:HyperLink>
```

A HyperLink control has an ID that lets you access its properties at runtime. For example, the following VB code makes a hyperlink invisible:

```
lnkViewStudents.Visible = False
```

An HTML hyperlink (using the <a> tag), on the other hand, is not programmable because you cannot refer to it by name in runtime code.

 TIP: If you assign a value to a HyperLink control's ImageUrl property and display an image as the HyperLink, you cannot control the image size (the Height and Width properties are ignored).

ImageButton Control

Web pages typically use clickable images as an effective navigation tool. You can create the same effect with the ImageButton control. It does not look like or bounce like a typical button—instead, it simply shows an image. When the user hovers the mouse over the image, the mouse cursor changes shape. When the user clicks the image, a Click event is generated (which is probably why they call it a button).

You insert the image by placing an image's relative URL in button's *ImageUrl* property. Ordinarily, you copy the image file into your project folder. The button generates a Click event when the image is clicked by the user. An example of a relative URL is *Images/Tulips.jpg*, assuming that the image file is located in a project folder named *Images*. Here is a sample ImageButton control:

```
<asp:ImageButton
  ID="btnTulips"
  ImageUrl="Images/Tulips.jpg"
  Width="100"
  Height="80"
  runat="server" />
```

LinkButton Control

The LinkButton control looks and behaves like a HyperLink control, with one major difference: It generates a Click event. You can write an event handler that executes when the user clicks the button. Here is a sample:

```
<asp:LinkButton
  ID="btnContinue"
  runat="server">Click here to continue
  </asp:LinkButton>
```

The LinkButton control is implemented in a clever way: The Web server creates an ordinary hyperlink and then generates JavaScript code that posts the page back to the server when the hyperlink is clicked. To see this code when the page is visible in your browser, select the *View* menu, and then select *Source*.

Using Runtime Code to Load a Web Page

Applications often need the flexibility to navigate to another page without having to ask the user to click a hyperlink. Runtime VB code does this by calling the **Response.Redirect method**.

The following statement uses runtime code to navigate to a target page within the same Web application named *Students.aspx*:

```
Response.Redirect("Students.aspx")
```

If the page is inside a folder within the same Web site, you must include the folder name, as follows:

```
Response.Redirect("Members/Students.aspx")
```

The same page might be accessed from different places in an application, so it is best to precede any folder name with "~/", which is translated by the server into a path that starts from the root folder of the Web site. So we should rewrite the previous example as follows:

```
Response.Redirect("~/Members/Students.aspx")
```

If the target page is on another Web server, you must supply a fully formed URL.

```
Response.Redirect("http://anothersite.com/Students.aspx")
```

The Server.Transfer Method

If you want to use runtime code to go to another page on the same Web server, you can call the Server.Transfer method.

```
Server.Transfer("Page_two.aspx")
```

The user will not see any change to the URL in the Web browser's address bar. That feature can be useful if you do not want the user to bookmark individual pages in your Web site.

Server.Transfer is a little faster than Response.Redirect because it reduces the amount of data that must be passed back and forth between the browser and the server. However, Server.Transfer can be used only when the current page and the target page are located on the same Web server.

In Tutorial 9-3, you will write an application that transfers control between Web forms.

Tutorial 9-3:
Moving between Web forms

In this tutorial, you will experiment with different ways of moving between Web forms. The application begins with a form, shown in Figure 9-36, that displays a text box, a hyperlink, and a Button control. If the user clicks the hyperlink, she or he is taken to the second page, shown in Figure 9-37. The user can also use the Button control on the first page to navigate, but the button's Click handler has an If statement that requires the user to enter her or his name first.

Figure 9-36 Moving between forms, startup page

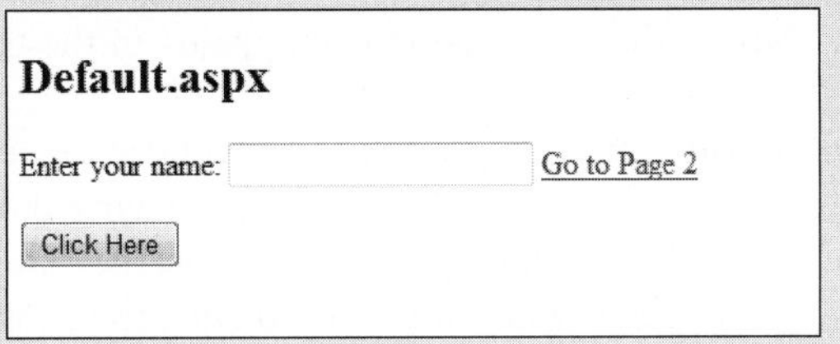

> **Default.aspx**
>
> Enter your name: [   ]   Go to Page 2
>
> [Click Here]

Figure 9-37 Moving between forms, second page

> **Page2.aspx**
>
> Return to Default.aspx

Tutorial Steps

Step 1: Create a new empty ASP.NET Web site named *Moving Between Forms*.

Step 2: Add Web forms named *Default.aspx* and *Page2.aspx* to the site.

Step 3: Add a level-two heading (<h2>) to each page that displays the page's filename.

Step 4: Add the following XHTML to *Default.aspx*; it contains a TextBox control and an HTML hyperlink:

```
Enter your name:
<asp:TextBox
   ID="txtName"
   runat="server">
   </asp:TextBox>
<a href="Page2.aspx">Go to Page 2</a>
```

Step 5: Add the following HyperLink control to *Page2.aspx*:

```
<asp:HyperLink
  ID="lnkReturn"
  runat="server"
  NavigateUrl="Default.aspx"
  Text="Return to Default.aspx">
  </asp:HyperLink>
```

The HyperLink control stores the target page location in its *NavigateUrl* property.

Step 6: Save the project and view *Default.aspx* in the browser. Enter your name into the text box and click the hyperlink to go to *Page2.aspx*.

Step 7: On *Page2.aspx*, click the HyperLink control to return to *Default.aspx*.

Have you noticed something interesting? When you returned from the second page to the first page, the name you typed on the first page disappeared. This happened because a fresh copy of *Default.aspx* was loaded from the Web server. (There are ways to reload controls when you move between pages, and we will demonstrate them in Section 9.7)

Step 8: On the *Default.aspx* page, type your name again and click the hyperlink to go to *Page2.aspx*. Now, click the browser's *Back* button (an arrow pointing to the left) to return to *Default.apx*.

Notice that your name still appears in the text box. But why? It turns out that your Web browser keeps the previous page in memory, so it does not have to reload *Default.aspx* from the Web server. You often see public Web sites that take advantage of this feature, relieving the programmer from having to preserve the previous page's data. On the other hand, more secure, professional Web sites do not allow you to click the browser's *Back* button when returning to a page. They want to verify your identity before reloading the previous page.

Step 9: Add a paragraph break and a Button control to *Default.aspx*.

```
<p />
<asp:Button ID="btnGo"
  runat="server"
  Text="Click Here" />
```

Step 10: Create a *Click* event handler for the *btnGo* button in the form's codebehind file. It calls the Response.Redirect method to move to *Page2.aspx*.

```
Protected Sub btnGo_Click() Handles btnGo.Click
  If txtName.Text.Length > 0 Then
    Response.Redirect("Page2.aspx")
  Else
    btnGo.Text = "Please type your name"
  End If
End Sub
```

This code will navigate to *Page2.aspx* only if the user remembered to type his or her name. Otherwise, a reminder is inserted directly into the button so the user can't miss it.

Step 11: Save the project and view *Default.aspx* in the browser. Leave the text box blank, and click the Button control. Did you notice how the button changes? Now type a name into the text box and click the button. You should see *Page2.aspx*.

Summary

In many situations, the HyperLink control is an efficient tool for navigating between pages. You can use it very effectively in a menu, for example, where you might want to modify the item's text or hide the menu item at runtime. But if you need to execute a conditional statement or perform other actions before navigating to another page, you'll probably want to use the Response.Redirect method.

Checkpoint

23. How do you set up a HyperLink control so that the user can navigate to a different Web page?

24. How do you convert a block of static text to a hyperlink?

25. Which method in the Response object navigates to a different Web page?

9.7 Focus on Problem Solving: *Vacation Rentals* Application

In Tutorials 9-1 and 9-2, you designed the user interface for an application named *Vacation Rentals*. We would now like to add some improvements that take advantage of techniques presented in this chapter. The user fills in a *Rental Request* form, as shown in Figure 9-38. In this new version, the radio buttons containing price ranges are determined at runtime.

Figure 9-38 *Vacation Rental Request* page

The user can enter the number of weeks for the rental. When the user clicks the *Submit my Request* button, she or he is taken to a Confirmation form, shown in Figure 9-39. If she or he returns to the *Rental Request* page by clicking the hyperlink, the existing inputs and selections are still visible.

Figure 9-39 *Confirmation form*

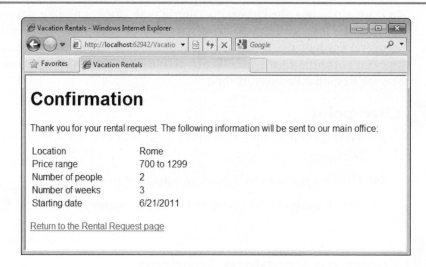

In a Windows application, passing information between pages and saving settings in controls are trivial. All values are automatically kept in memory. In a Web application, however, we have to do some extra work by saving data in the Session state collection. This application should give you a basic understanding of how we use page-level events to save and restore information.

Designing the Application's Web Forms

The Design view of the *Vacation Rental Request* form is shown in Figure 9-40. It has a DropDownList control holding vacation locations and TextBox controls for the number of people and number of weeks. An empty RadioButtonList is filled with price ranges at run-time. A Calendar control lets the user select a starting rental date. A button at the bottom collects the information from the form and sends the user to a Confirmation form. Table 9-16 contains a list of controls and properties for this form.

Figure 9-40 Design view of the *Vacation Rental Request* page, *Default.aspx*

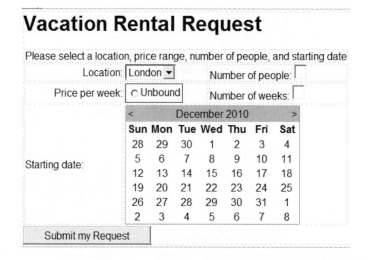

The Confirmation form displays information about the user's selections. This information is retrieved from Session state. (Session state was explained in Chapter 8.) A Design view of the form is shown in Figure 9-41. Nearly all its control names are visible in the Design view. The HyperLink control contains the Text: *Return to the Rental Request page*.

Table 9-16 Control names in the *Vacation Rental Request* page

Control Type	Control Name	Property Settings
DOCUMENT		Font-Family: *Arial* Title: *Vacation Rentals*
DropDownList	ddlLocation	Font.Size: *1em*
TextBox	txtNumberOfPeople	
TextBox	txtNumberOfWeeks	
RadioButtonList	radPrices	
Calendar	calStartDate	
Button	btnSubmit	Text: *Submit my Request*

Figure 9-41 Design view of the *Confirmation form*

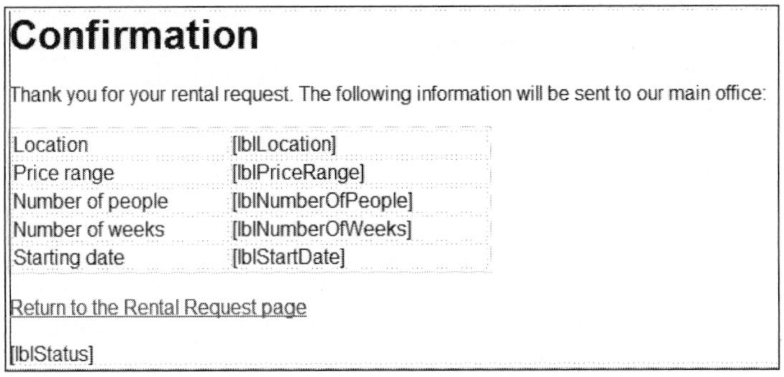

The DecimalRange Structure

The *Vacation Rentals* application defines a simple structure named DecimalRange. It is a container that holds two values, Min and Max, and it can be represented as a String.

```
Public Structure DecimalRange
  Public Min As Decimal
  Public Max As Decimal
  Public Sub New(ByVal mmin As Decimal, ByVal mmax As Decimal)
    Min = mmin
    Max = mmax
  End Sub
  Public Overrides Function ToString() As String
    Return Min.ToString() & " to " & Max.ToString()
  End Function
End Structure
```

DecimalRange could be useful in almost any program that deals with ranges of currency values.

RentalInfo Class

The **RentalInfo** class describes a container that holds the user's rental selections. A RentalInfo object is stored in Session state by the Rental Request form before it sends the user to the Confirmation form. It has a number of interesting details, as shown in Figure 9-42. First, it contains an Enum type named PriceCategory. Each value (Low, Medium, High) corresponds to an integer (0, 1, 2) that sets RadioButtonList values. The property named PriceRange is declared with the PriceCategory type.

Figure 9-42 The RentalInfo class

```vbnet
Imports Microsoft.VisualBasic

Public Class RentalInfo
  Enum PriceCategory
     Low
     Medium
     High
  End Enum

  Private Shared m_PriceCategories As DecimalRange() _
    = {New DecimalRange(0, 699), New DecimalRange(700, 1299),
    New DecimalRange(1300, 3000)}

  Public Property Location() As String
  Public Property PriceRange() As PriceCategory
  Public Property StartDate() As Date
  Public Property NumberOfPeople() As Integer
  Public Property NumberOfWeeks() As Integer

  Public Shared ReadOnly Property PriceCategoryStr(
    ByVal cat As PriceCategory) As String
    Get
      Return m_PriceCategories(cat).ToString()
    End Get
  End Property

  Public Shared ReadOnly Property PriceCategoryVals() As String()
    Get
      Dim temp(m_PriceCategories.GetUpperBound(0)) As String
      Dim j As Integer
      For j = 0 To m_PriceCategories.GetUpperBound(0)
        temp(j) = m_PriceCategories(j).ToString()
      Next
      Return temp
    End Get
  End Property
End Class
```

The m_PriceCategories array contains three DecimalRange objects. The PriceCategoryVals property uses this array to return an array of strings that can be used to initialize the RadioButtonList in the Rental Request form. The PriceCategoryStr property returns a string containing a single price category range, such as "700 to 1299." This method is useful when displaying the Confirmation form.

Rental Request Form

A complete listing of the code in the startup form (Default.aspx) appears in Figure 9-43. Each time this page is loaded, the RadioButtonList is filled with the price range from the RentalInfo class. This approach makes it easy to change the price ranges in the future. It is best not to hard-code the ranges in HTML.

```vbnet
' Initialize the RadioButtonList.
For Each str As String In RentalInfo.PriceCategoryVals
  radPrices.Items.Add(str)
Next
```

Figure 9-43 Code in the Startup form (Default.aspx)

```
Partial Class _Default
    Inherits System.Web.UI.Page

    Protected Sub Page_Load() Handles Me.Load
        ' The page might be loading for the first time, or loading
        ' when the user returns from the Confirmation form.
        If Not IsPostBack Then
            ' Initialize the RadioButtonList.
            For Each str As String In RentalInfo.PriceCategoryVals
                radPrices.Items.Add(str)
            Next
            Dim obj As Object = Session("rental")
            Dim rental As RentalInfo
            ' The Session state will contain an object when the user
            ' returns from the Confirmation.aspx page. The following
            ' code assigns the RentalInfo values to the controls.
            If obj IsNot Nothing Then
                rental = CType(obj, RentalInfo)
                With rental
                    ddlLocation.SelectedValue = .Location
                    radPrices.SelectedIndex = .PriceRange
                    txtNumberOfWeeks.Text = .NumberOfWeeks.ToString()
                    txtNumberOfPeople.Text = .NumberOfPeople.ToString()
                    calStartDate.SelectedDate = .StartDate
                End With
            End If
        End If
    End Sub

    Protected Sub btnSubmit_Click() Handles btnSubmit.Click
        ' Create and initialize a RentalInfo object,
        ' using the user's input in this form.
        Dim rental As New RentalInfo
        With rental
            .Location = ddlLocation.Text
            .NumberOfWeeks = CInt(txtNumberOfWeeks.Text)
            .NumberOfPeople = CInt(txtNumberOfPeople.Text)
            .StartDate = calStartDate.SelectedDate
            .PriceRange = radPrices.SelectedIndex
        End With
        ' Save rental info in Session state.
        Session("rental") = rental
        ' Go to the Confirmation form.
        Response.Redirect("Confirmation.aspx")
    End Sub
End Class
```

The btnSubmit_Click event handler collects all the user's input and control settings, and stores them in a new RentalInfo object. The object is then saved in Session state under a key named *rental*.

Page_Load Event Handler

If the user returns to this page via the Confirmation form, the Page_Load event handler reassigns settings to the controls. The first step is to look for a RentalInfo object in the Session state collection:

```
Dim obj As Object = Session("rental")
Dim rental As RentalInfo
```

If an object is found, it is cast into a RentalInfo object; the RentalInfo object retrieves the object's properties, and assigns them to controls on this form:

```
If obj IsNot Nothing Then
   rental = CType(obj, RentalInfo)
   With rental
      ddlLocation.SelectedValue = .Location
      radPrices.SelectedIndex = .PriceRange
      txtNumberOfWeeks.Text = .NumberOfWeeks.ToString()
      txtNumberOfPeople.Text = .NumberOfPeople.ToString()
      calStartDate.SelectedDate = .StartDate
   End With
End If
```

Without this step, the user would return to the startup form and find that all the settings had been erased.

Confirmation Form

Figure 9-44 lists all the source code in the Confirmation form. It looks for the rental item in Session state and, on finding it, gets a RentalInfo object. The object's properties are assigned to the controls on this form. The PriceCategoryStr property makes it easy to convert the PriceRange enumerated value into a string.

Figure 9-44 Listing of the Confirmation form source code

```
Partial Class Confirmation
   Inherits System.Web.UI.Page

   Protected Sub Page_Load() Handles Me.Load
      If Not IsPostBack Then
         Dim obj As Object = Session("rental")
         If obj Is Nothing Then
            lblStatus.Text = "Error: unable to receive Rental " _
            & "Request information"
         Else
            Dim m_Rental As RentalInfo = CType(obj, RentalInfo)
            With m_Rental
               lblLocation.Text = .Location
               lblNumberOfPeople.Text = .NumberOfPeople.ToString()
               lblNumberOfWeeks.Text = .NumberOfWeeks.ToString()
               lblStartDate.Text = .StartDate.ToString("d")
               lblPriceRange.Text = _
                  RentalInfo.PriceCategoryStr(.PriceRange)
            End With
         End If
      End If
   End Sub
End Class
```

Extending the Application

This application can be extended and improved in many ways. You could, for example, do a database search for all rental properties that match the criteria entered in the startup form. Then the Confirmation form could show a list of available properties. The user could select a rental property and make a reservation. A third-party credit card billing service could process the transaction, and our application could email a receipt to the customer.

 **Checkpoint**

26. How did the *Vacation Rentals* application restore the settings of the RadioButtonList when the user moved from the Confirmation form to the Vacation Rental Request page?

27. In the *Vacation Rentals* application, how do the user's selections in the Vacation Rental Request form get transmitted to the Confirmation form?

28. In the *Vacation Rentals* application, what utility class is used to hold the user's selection of minimum and maximum weekly rental prices?

29. In the *Vacation Rentals* application, show how items are inserted in the RadioButtonList control.

9.8 Browser Cookies

A **browser cookie** is a name-value pair stored on a user's computer by a Web browser. Cookies are appropriate for small amounts of data that can be expressed as strings. You cannot store a Student object, for example, but you can store the student's ID number. Browsers have the option to disable cookies, so your applications should be careful about assuming that you can use them. Cookies are not automatically encrypted, so do not store passwords, credit card numbers, or other sensitive information in a cookie unless you encrypt it yourself.

Cookies can be temporary, or they can be stored for days, months, or years at a time. Each cookie has an *Expires* property (set to a specific date) that controls its lifetime. If you leave the Expires property blank, the cookie is deleted when the user session ends.

Programs create and assign cookies using the **Response.Cookies** property. The **Request.Cookies** property, on the other hand, is used to retrieve cookie values.

You can see a list of cookies stored on your computer by looking in the directory named *<drive>:\Documents and Settings\<user>\Cookies*, where *<drive>* is your system drive letter, and *<user>* is your username. Each cookie is stored as a text file. For example, the following shows a cookie named *Name*, which is stored in a file named *kip@localhost[1].txt*:

```
Name
Kip Irvine
localhost/
1024
3984441856
29633514
3275258352
29633313
*
```

A **session cookie** is a cookie that expires as soon as the user closes the browser. A **persistent cookie** is stored in a file on the user's computer. To make a persistent cookie, you must set a cookie's expiration date to some time in the future.

Examples

The following statement declares an HttpCookie variable:

```
Dim aCookie As HttpCookie
```

The following statement creates a cookie named FirstName and assigns it a value of *Bill:*

```
aCookie = new HttpCookie("FirstName", "Bill")
```

The following statement retrieves the *FirstName* cookie from the Request object:

```
aCookie = Request.Cookies("FirstName")
```

The following statement assigns a cookie's value to a TextBox:

```
txtName.Text = aCookie.Value
```

The following adds a cookie to the Response object's *Cookies* collection:

```
Response.Cookies.Add(aCookie)
```

If you retrieve and modify the Value property of a cookie, the change is not permanent until you call the Cookies.Set method:

```
Response.Cookies.Set(aCookie)
```

The following assigns an expiration date of three days in the future:

```
aCookie.Expires = Now.AddDays(3)
```

To delete a cookie, set its Expires property to the current date and time. Then call the Cookies.Set method.

```
aCookie.Expires = Now
Response.Cookies.Set(aCookie)
```

Cookie Example Program

The *Cookie Example* program uses a persistent cookie to remember the name of the person who last logged in from the same user account on a particular computer. Figure 9-45 shows the program after the user has entered his name (Joe Smith) and checked the *Remember me the next time I visit* option. Clicking the *OK* button saves this information, hides the panel containing all the controls, and displays a closing message, as shown in Figure 9-46.

Figure 9-45 *Cookie Example* application

Figure 9-46 After the user has clicked the *OK* button

After closing the browser window, the user can open a new browser and run the example again. The program will look for the cookie and, if it is found, copy the person's name from the cookie to the TextBox.

Implementation

The TextBox control is named *txtName*. The CheckBox is named *chkRemember*. The Button control is named *btnOk*. These controls are located inside a Panel control named *mainPanel*. When we set the Panel control's Visible property to *False*, all controls within the Panel become invisible.

Figure 9-47 contains a complete listing of the program's source code. In the Page_Load event handler, the program looks for the *Name* cookie in the Cookies collection. If the cookie is found, it tells us that the cookie is currently stored on the user's computer. The program copies the user name from the cookie to the TextBox. In effect, the user has been remembered.

Figure 9-47 Listing of the *Cookie Example* application

```
Partial Class CookieExample
   Inherits System.Web.UI.Page
   Private m_NameCookie As HttpCookie

   Private Sub Page_Load() Handles MyBase.Load

     If Not IsPostBack Then
       m_NameCookie = Request.Cookies("Name")
       ' If the cookie was found, assign the name
       ' in the cookie to the TextBox.
       If m_NameCookie IsNot Nothing Then
         txtName.Text = m_NameCookie.Value
       End If
     End If
   End Sub

   Private Sub btnOK_Click() Handles btnOk.Click
     m_NameCookie = Request.Cookies("Name")
     ' Does the cookie exist?
     If m_NameCookie Is Nothing Then
       ' Does the user want to be remembered?
       If chkRemember.Checked Then
         ' Cookie not found. Create a 31-day cookie.
         m_NameCookie = New HttpCookie("Name", txtName.Text)
         m_NameCookie.Expires = Now.AddDays(31)
         Response.Cookies.Add(m_NameCookie)
       End If
     Else
       ' The cookie was found.
       If chkRemember.Checked = False Then
         ' Delete the cookie by making it expire immediately.
         m_NameCookie.Expires = Now
       Else
         ' Modify the existing cookie. Store the user name
         ' and set the expiration date 31 days from now.
         m_NameCookie.Value = txtName.Text
         m_NameCookie.Expires = Now.AddDays(31)
       End If
       ' Save it back in the Cookies collection.
       Response.Cookies.Set(m_NameCookie)
     End If
     mainPanel.Visible = False
     Response.Write("Thanks. Now close the browser window")
   End Sub
End Class
```

When the user clicks the *OK* button, the Click handler has a bit of work to do. First, it looks for the cookie. If the cookie is not found and the user has checked the *Remember me the next time* option, the code creates a cookie and assigns the name from the TextBox. The cookie is added to the Cookies collection:

```
If chkRemember.Checked Then
    m_NameCookie = New HttpCookie("Name", txtName.Text)
    m_NameCookie.Expires = Now.AddDays(31)
    Response.Cookies.Add(m_NameCookie)
End If
```

If the cookie already exists, the approach is a little different. If the user doesn't want to be remembered, the program sets the Expires property to the current date and time. If the user wants to be remembered, the program modifies the existing cookie. The name from the TextBox is assigned and the expiration date is moved forward. Finally, in both cases, the cookie is put back into the Cookies collection.

```
Response.Cookies.Set(m_NameCookie)
```

 **Checkpoint**

30. How do you set the lifetime of a browser cookie?

31. Show an example of getting the String value of a cookie named *myCookie*.

32. Show an example of deleting a cookie named *myCookie*.

33. Write a code statement that creates a cookie named *username*, and assigns it the Text property of the TextBox control named *txtUsername*.

Summary

9.1 Working in Source (XHTML) Mode

- The Visual Studio designer intentionally hides XHTML details when you work in its Web form *Designer* window. Occasionally you must work in the Source view to fine-tune the appearance of your Web forms.
- The Page directive identifies the coding language (VB). The AutoEventWireup property determines whether page events (such as Load and Init) must use standard names.
- The DOCTYPE tag identifies the document type to the browser, along with the standard it follows.
- The area between the <head> and </head> tags defines the heading portion of the document.
- The <body> tag defines the displayable area of the Web form.
- The <form> tag identifies the beginning of a Web form.
- The *Vacation Rental* application was created in source view, using ASP.NET controls and HTML tables.

9.2 Cascading Style Sheets

- Cascading style sheets (CSS) are definitions that Web developers use to customize the appearance of fonts, tables, and other controls on Web forms.
- We suggest defining CSS styles in a cascading style sheet file.
- To create a cascading style sheet file (*CSS file*), select *Add New Item* from the *Website* menu. Then select *Style Sheet* from the list of template icons.

- Use *em* units to specify font sizes, so users can adjust the font sizes in their Web browsers.
- The <link href> tag identifies the name of the linked *CSS* file.
- You can alter the look and feel of any standard HTML style tag in a *CSS* file.
- You can define style classes in a *CSS* file. Each class name begins with a period.
- You can apply styles to nearly any HTML element, using the class attribute.
- To apply a CSS style to an ASP.NET control, assign the style name to its CssClass property.
- The *CSS Menu Demo* application displays a sliding bar menu, using an HTML table and several HyperLink controls.

9.3 Custom Error Handling

- Custom error handling refers to the ability that ASP.NET programs have to configure the display of runtime error messages for both end users and program developers.
- The Custom Errors setting governs the way in which error messages are displayed on Web pages.
- Most Web sites use custom error pages to handle HTTP errors generated by the Web server.
- Programs often create custom error pages to handle common HTTP errors. The custom page references can be located in the *web.config* file.

9.4 Uploading Files and Sending Email

- The HTMLInputFile control lets users upload files to a Web site. Any type of file can be transferred, but you can limit which types of files are saved.
- The PostedFile property, an HttpPostedFile object, represents the uploaded file.
- Simple Mail Transfer Protocol (SMTP) is a service that responds to a standard set of commands for sending email.
- The simplest way to send an email message is to use the SmtpMail class. The Send method sends a message with few options.
- The MailMessage class has a rich set of properties that let you configure messages and include attachments.

9.5 Data Validation Controls

- The RequiredFieldValidator control alerts the user when an input field still contains its default (initial) value.
- The RangeValidator control checks minimum and maximum values against user input.
- The CompareValidator control compares one control's contents to that of another.
- The RegularExpressionValidator control performs string pattern matching against the contents of another control. Regular expressions are specification strings that conform to regular expression syntax. They are powerful tools for pattern matching.
- The CustomValidator control performs unique types of validation that are not available with existing validator controls.
- The ValidationSummary control displays error messages generated by other validation controls on the same Web form.

9.6 Working with Multiple Web Forms

- Most Web applications have multiple pages. You might collect information on one page and display a summary on another page. Or, you might display supplementary information on a second page.
- To permit your application to navigate from one Web page to another, you can use a HyperLink control, call Response.Redirect, call Server.Transfer, or convert a block of static text to an HTML hyperlink.

9.7 Focus on Problem Solving: *Vacation Rentals* Application

- The *Vacation Rentals* application asks the user to fill in the Rental Request form. The user selects a starting date, location, and price category, and enters the number of people and number of weeks.
- A support class named RentalInfo encapsulates the user's selections. The RentalInfo class has methods that return price category lists.
- The application uses Session state to save a RentalInfo object and pass it between pages.

9.8 Browser Cookies

- Cookies are name-value pairs stored on a user's computer by a Web browser. Such cookies are appropriate for small amounts of data, which can be expressed as strings.
- Cookies can be stored temporarily or for days, months, or years at a time. Each cookie has an Expires property (set to a date) that controls its lifetime.
- A session cookie is one that expires as soon as the user closes the browser. A persistent cookie is stored in a file on the user's computer.
- The *Cookie Example* program uses a persistent cookie to remember the name of the person who last logged in from the same user account on a particular computer.

Key Terms

browser cookie	HyperText Markup Language (HTML)
cascading style sheets (CSS)	MailAddress class
CompareValidator	MailMessage class
custom error handling	MIME types
CustomValidator	persistent cookie
eXtensible Markup Language (XML)	RangeValidator
eXtensible HyperText Markup Language (XHTML)	regular expressions
	RegularExpressionValidator
HTTP errors	RequiredFieldValidator
hyperlink	session cookie
HyperLink control	ValidationSummary

Review Questions and Exercises

True or False

Indicate whether each of the following statements is true or false.

1. Browser cookies can hold strings of limited length but not complex objects.

2. Browser cookies automatically remain on the client's computer for 24 hours.

3. A RequiredFieldValidator control displays a message only when the field it validates has the same value as the field's initial value.

Short Answer

1. What is the purpose of the DOCTYPE tag in HTML code?

2. What elements have been shown to appear between the <head> and </head> tags in this chapter?

3. Show the HTML encoding of a ListItem containing the word *Brussels* in a ListBox control.

4. Which ASP.NET controls contain the runat="server" attribute?

5. Which CSS style property governs the horizontal spacing between letters?

6. Which property in an ASP.NET control assigns a CSS style name to the control?

7. Which property in an HTML control assigns a CSS style name to the control?

8. In the *CSS Menu Demo* program, which CSS style name causes the menu items to change color when the mouse hovered over them?

9. In the *CSS Menu Demo* program, which type of control was used for each menu item?

10. How does the ValidationSummary control obtain the error message it needs from a RequiredFieldValidator control?

11. Which property of all the data validation controls identifies the control to be validated?

12. How is the ErrorMessage property different from the Text property in a CompareValidator control?

13. Which data validation control is best for checking the format of an email message?

14. If you wanted to compare a date entered by the user to today's date, which data validation control would be best?

15. How do you attach a file to an email message?

16. What kind of object needs to be added to the To property of a MailMessage object when the message has multiple recipients?

17. Show an example of a CSS style definition for a Tahoma font that is 1.5 times the size of the browser's default font and in bold.

18. Which HTML tag links a CSS file to a Web page, and where is this tag located?

19. Which setting in the *web.config* file lets you determine the way in which error messages are displayed on Web pages?

20. In a FileUpload control, which property provides information about the uploaded file?

What Do You Think?

1. Why does sending an HTML email message trigger a Request Validation error?

2. In what way(s) does the FileUpload control reveal information about the client's computer?

3. Does the Calendar control execute a postback every time the user selects a date?

Algorithm Workbench

1. Show the HTML encoding for a table containing a single row and three columns. Insert the letter A in the first column, the letter B in the second, and the letter C in the third.

2. Show the HTML encoding of a table cell that spans two columns.

3. Create a CSS style class named BigHead that uses a 2-em font size, font family = Tahoma, color = Red, a bold typeface, and line spacing equal to 2.3 ems.

4. Create a CSS style named SubHead that has an Arial font, a 1.2-em size, a solid line below the text, and width = .1 em.

5. Write a definition in the *Web.config* file that routes all HTTP error 403 instances to a Web page named *error403.htm*.

6. Write a statement that saves an uploaded file as *c:\temp\x.doc*, for the HTMLInputFile control named uplFile.

7. Write a single statement that sends an email message from me@fiu.edu to you@fiu.edu with the subject *Grades* and the body *Your grades are ready for viewing*.

8. Given a MailMessage object named *myMsg*, add a file attachment named *c:\classes\grades.htm*.

9. Write a code statement that transfers control to a Web page named *PageTwo.aspx* without changing the URL displayed in the address window of the user's browser.

Programming Challenges

1. **Computer Club Meeting**

   Write a Web application for a computer club that lets the user schedule a meeting by doing the following actions: Select a meeting date from a Calendar control, enter the meeting title as the message subject, and enter a list of email addresses for the message recipients. The title and recipient fields are required, so provide RequiredFieldValidator controls. Also, verify that the Recipient field contains a valid email address.

   Figure 9-48 shows a sample design for this application. The user has entered a title, selected a date, and entered one recipient's email address. The error message is displayed because the second email address (aaa) is not valid. The user must correct it and click the *Add Recipient* button again.

Figure 9-48 Computer Club Meeting Scheduler

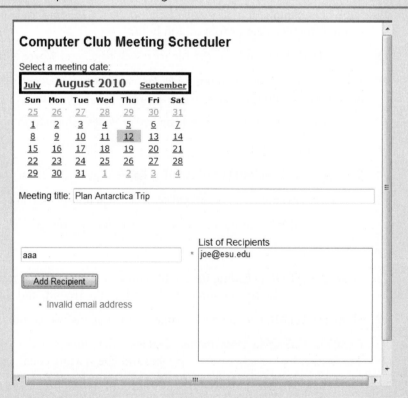

2. **Validating a DropDownList**

   When discussing the RequiredFieldValidator, we showed how you can remind users that they must select from a DropDownList control. In this programming challenge, show how you could do the same type of validation using the CompareValidator control. See Figure 9-49 for an example.

Figure 9-49 CompareValidator with DropDownList

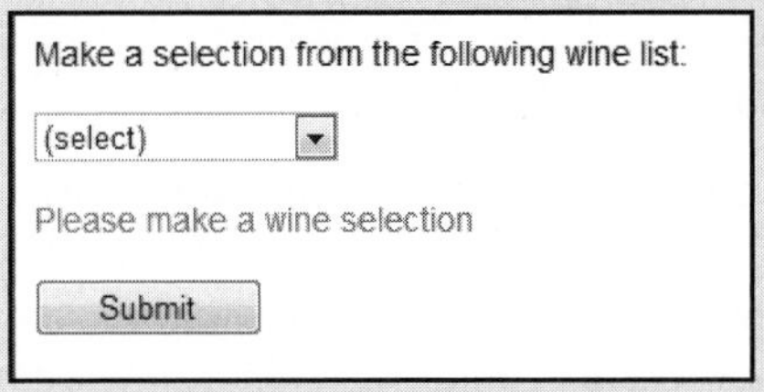

3. **Checking a Date with CompareValidator**

   The CompareValidator control can check an input field to make sure it contains a certain data type. You do this by setting its Type property. You also set the Operator property to *DataTypeCheck*. Write a short application that asks the user to input a birth date into a TextBox. Use the CompareValidator control to make sure the user enters a valid date. See Figure 9-50 for an example.

Figure 9-50 Checking a Date

4. **Validating a Date Range**

   In a project scheduling application, the user can schedule a project by entering a beginning date and an ending date. Your task is to use the RangeValidator control to make sure the two dates are no more than 100 days apart. *Hint:* You can modify the MaximumValue property at runtime and explicitly call the RangeValidator's Validate method. Write a short demonstration program. See Figure 9-51 for an example.

Figure 9-51 Validating a Date Range

5. **Vacation Rentals with Validation**

   Use the *Vacation Rentals* application presented in Section 9.7 as a starting point for this programming challenge. Add the following validation rules to the *Rental Request* page, using the ASP.NET validation controls:

   • All inputs are required.

- The number of people must be between one and eight.
- The number of weeks must be between one and twelve.
- The starting date must be at least three days from today but not greater than 120 days from today.

The default first item in the *Location* DropDownList should be *(select)*. Add an email input field to the *Vacation Rental Request* Web page. Use RequiredFieldValidator and RegularExpressionValidator controls to make sure the email is not blank and that it is a valid email address. Add a ValidationSummary control to the page. Use Figure 9-52 as a sample of the user interface, shown after the user has entered all inputs. You will need to add an email field to the RentalInfo class so the user's email can be preserved in Session state when returning from the Confirmation form to the Rental Request page.

Figure 9-52 Sample Vacation Rental Request form with email field

6. **Comparing Calendar Controls**

   The CompareValidator example we showed in this chapter let's the user input a rental date and a return date. The validator verified that the return date was greater than or equal to the rental date. In this programming challenge, you will use Calendar controls for the input, as shown in Figure 9-53. There's one slight problem: The CompareValidator control does not recognize the Calendar control. You will have to find a way around this restriction. Two CompareValidator members may prove useful:

   - The Validate method causes the CompareValidator to perform validation immediately.
   - The IsValid property returns *True* if the CompareValidator has validated the two inputs and found them to be correct.

Figure 9-53 Comparing *Calendar Controls* program

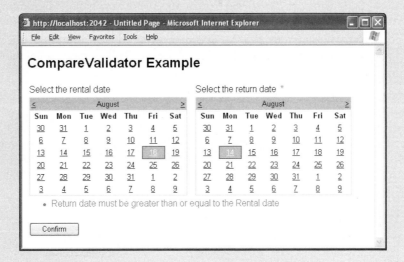

CompareValidator can compare TextBoxes, and you can copy a Calendar control's SelecteDate property into a TextBox. If the TextBox controls were not visible, the user might think that the Calendar controls were being compared.

7. *MailDemo* with Validation

Improve the *MailDemo* program from this chapter by adding validation controls. Specifically, make sure that the *From*, *To*, and *Subject* fields are not blank. Also, verify that all email fields are formatted correctly.

8. *Best Brew Coffee Shop*, Version 1

Write a program that displays several types of coffee and tea drinks in a list box (see Figure 9-54). When the user selects an item and clicks the *OK* button, the price is displayed in a Label control. You can put the prices into the Value property associated with the item when you build the Items collection from the *Properties* window. Display the price using a currency format.

Figure 9-54 *Best Brew Coffee Shop*, version 1

9. *Best Brew Coffee Shop*, Version 2

Start with the *Best Brew Coffee Shop Program* from Programming Challenge 8. Add a CheckBoxList control so the user can select extra items, such as chocolate and whipped cream (see Figure 9-55). Each item should have an add-on price, such as .25 cents for whipped cream. When the user clicks the *OK* button, display the basic price of the drink plus the price of the combined extras.

Figure 9-55 *Best Brew Coffee Shop*, version 2

10. *Best Brew Coffee Shop*, Version 3

Continue the *Best Brew Coffee Shop* program from Programming Challenge 9. When the user makes selections to order a drink, do not display the price on the same Web page. Instead, when the user clicks the *OK* button, display a separate Web page that contains a receipt. Figure 9-56 shows the user ordering a drink; Figure 9-57 shows the corresponding receipt. We have elongated the window so you can see that the order information was passed as a set of Request parameters appended to the URL. Assume that the sales tax rate is 7 percent.

Figure 9-56 *Best Brew Coffee Shop*, version 3

Figure 9-57 Displaying the receipt

10 Web Applications with Databases

TOPICS

This chapter introduces master-detail pages, which let you create a consistent look across a Web site. Next, we show how to use data binding to fill the GridView and DetailsView controls with database data. Then we introduce the popular JavaScript language for writing code that executes in the browser, and then we show how to use some common Microsoft Ajax controls.

10.1 Master-Detail Pages

In many Web applications, each page has common elements, such as a company logo, a menu, and navigation links. Duplicating these elements on each page requires a lot of work. If a change were made to the heading information at some time in the future, a lot of work might be required to make the same change to each page. Recognizing the need for common page elements, Microsoft uses a design technique called **master-detail pages.** An application contains one or more master pages that contain empty areas into which other pages may be inserted. Then, for each master page, you create one or more content pages that display inside the master page.

A **master page** contains empty areas called **content placeholders.** At runtime, the master page remains visible all the time, while different content pages are inserted into the content placeholders. Figure 10-1 shows a master page in Design view, with the empty content placeholder (the placeholder rectangle shows in lavender on the screen, and gray on the printed page).

Figure 10-1 Master page with a ContentPlaceHolder control

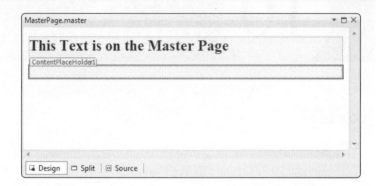

This is what the <head> and <body> sections of the sample master page contain:

```
<head runat="server">
  <title></title>
  <asp:ContentPlaceHolder id="head" runat="server">
  </asp:ContentPlaceHolder>
</head>
<body>
  <form id="form1" runat="server">
  <div>
    <h2>This Text is on the Master Page</h2>
    <asp:ContentPlaceHolder id="ContentPlaceHolder1" runat="server">
    </asp:ContentPlaceHolder>
  </div>
  </form>
</body>
```

You never explicitly put any text or controls directly inside a **ContentPlaceHolder control.** Instead, you create **content pages** (Web pages) that insert themselves inside the master page at runtime. Figure 10-2 shows the relationship between a master page and its content pages. A master page contains content placeholders. Each placeholder can be filled by a content page. Each content page has a reference to its master page. The user uses a Web browser to navigate to a content page. Users cannot directly open master pages in Web browsers.

Figure 10-2 Relationships among master page, content pages, and user

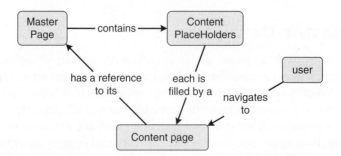

With a master-detail page design, a single master page is referenced by one or more content pages, but only one at a time. The master page, on the other hand, does not contain references to any content pages. When the user loads a content page, the Web server finds the

related master page and combines the two into a single HTML page. This final page is sent to the user's Web browser.

To add a content page to an application, select the master page filename inside the Solution Explorer window. Then select *Add Content Page* from the *Website* menu. Content page filenames have the usual *.aspx* extension.

Cascading style sheet (CSS) files can be linked to master pages, but not content pages. CSS styles can be used by content pages as long as their master pages have links to the styles.

Creating a Master Page

To create a master page in Visual Studio, select *Add New Item* from the Website menu. In the dialog window (see Figure 10-3), select *Master Page* and click the *Add* button. A master page has a special filename extension of .master.

Figure 10-3 Adding a Master Page

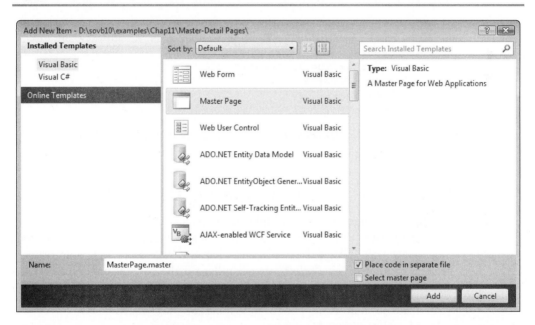

It is usually best to use an HTML table to control the position of the ContentPlaceHolders on a master page. A ContentPlaceHolder's width defaults to the width of its enclosing form. If it is located inside a table cell, however, the cell determines the ContentPlaceHolder's boundaries. The master page can contain any amount of text, controls, and components in addition to the ContentPlaceHolder.

Content Pages

It is always easiest to add a content page to an application if you have already created a master page. To add a content page, either select or open the master page file. Then select *Add Content Page* from the Website menu.

A content page does not contain any <body>, <form>, or <html> tags. This is a sample content page:

```
<%@ Page Title="" Language="VB"
  MasterPageFile="~/MasterPage.master"
  AutoEventWireup="false"
  CodeFile="Default.aspx.vb"
  Inherits="_Default" %>
```

```
<asp:Content ID="Content1"
  ContentPlaceHolderID="head"
  Runat="Server">
</asp:Content>

<asp:Content ID="Content2"
  ContentPlaceHolderID="ContentPlaceHolder1"
  Runat="Server">
</asp:Content>
```

Every content page has a *MasterPageFile* property in its Page directive that identifies the name and path of the master page file. In the example above, the master page filename is *MasterPage.master*.

By default, a content page has two **Content controls.** The first one matches up with the ContentPlaceHolder control that appears in the <head> area of a master page. The second Content control matches the ContentPlaceHolder in the <body> area of a master page. This is the control that normally contains other controls, text, and so on, that will be displayed on the content page. For example, the following Content control contains a level-three heading and a ListBox:

```
<asp:Content ID="Content2"
  ContentPlaceHolderID="ContentPlaceHolder1" Runat="Server">
  <h3>Events for This Month</h3>
  <asp:ListBox ID="lstEvents"
    runat="server">
  </asp:ListBox>
</asp:Content>
```

Notice how the *ContentPlaceHolderID* property identifies the ContentPlaceHolder control on the Master page that will hold the content declared here.

Setting the Master Page at Runtime

An application may contain multiple master pages, and you might want to use runtime code to switch master pages. For example, the choice of Master page might depend on whether the current user is logged in. You can alter the Page.MasterPageFile property at runtime inside a content page's **PreInit** event handler for the content page. In the following code, a different master file is selected just before the content page is displayed.

```
Protected Sub Page_PreInit() Handles Me.PreInit
  If UserIsLoggedIn Then
    Page.MasterPageFile = "~/MembersMaster.master"
  End If
End Sub
```

In Tutorial 10-1, you will create a master-detail application.

Tutorial 10-1:
Creating an application with a master page

In this tutorial, you will create a small application that has a master page and two content pages. The master page contains buttons that navigate to each of the content pages. The first content page, shown in Figure 10-4, has a single table cell containing text, a dropdown list of fruit types, a Button, and a Label (that cannot be seen in the figure). The second content page, shown in Figure 10-5, displays a simple heading. Users can click buttons on the master page to switch between the content pages.

Figure 10-4 Content Page 1

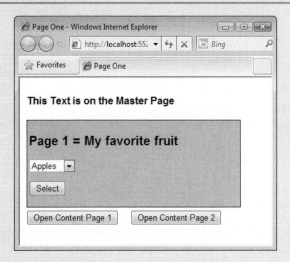

Figure 10-5 Content Page 2

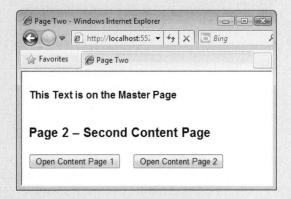

Tutorial Steps

Step 1: Create a new ASP.NET Empty Web Site named *Master-Detail Pages*.

Step 2: Add a master page named *MasterPage.master* to the application.

Step 3: In the master page's Source view, notice that a ContentPlaceHolder is placed in the <head> area (we will not be using it).

```
<head runat="server">
  <title></title>
  <asp:ContentPlaceHolder id="head" runat="server">
  </asp:ContentPlaceHolder>
</head>
```

Step 4: The <body> area of the page also contains a ContentPlaceHolder control. Remove the <div> and </div> tags. Modify the style of the body to be the following:

```
<body style="font-family:Arial; font-size:.85em">
```

Step 5: Add a table containing three rows to the <form> area and insert the heading as shown below in the first row. You may do this step in Design view if you wish:

```
<table style="width:90%">
  <tr>
    <td>
      <h3>This Text is on the Master Page</h3>
    </td>
  </tr>
  <tr>
    <td></td>
  </tr>
  <tr>
    <td></td>
  </tr>
</table>
```

Step 6: Move the ContentPlaceHolder control to the second table row and add two Button controls to the third row.

```
<table style="width:90%">
  <tr>
    <td>
      <h3>This Text is on the Master Page</h3>
    </td>
  </tr>
  <tr>
    <td>
      <asp:ContentPlaceHolder
        id="ContentPlaceHolder1"
        runat="server">
      </asp:ContentPlaceHolder>
    </td>
  </tr>
  <tr>
    <td>
      <asp:Button ID="btnPage1" runat="server"
        Text="Open Content Page 1" />
         
      <asp:Button ID="btnPage2" runat="server"
        Text="Open Content Page 2" />
    </td>
  </tr>
</table>
```

Notice that you inserted two nonbreaking spaces between the two buttons. In Design view, your page should look like Figure 10-6.

Step 7: Open the master page's codebehind file and add the following Click handlers. Each one displays a different content page.

```
Protected Sub btnPage1_Click() Handles btnPage1.Click
  Response.Redirect("Page1.aspx")
End Sub
Protected Sub btnPage2_Click() Handles btnPage2.Click
  Response.Redirect("Page2.aspx")
End Sub
```

Step 8: With the Master page still open, add a content page to the application and name it *Page1.aspx*. To add a content page, select (or open) the master page,

Figure 10-6 Master Page in Design view

usually named *MasterPage.master*. Then select *Add Content Page* from the Website menu.

> **NOTE:** From this point forward, you are editing the content page named *Page1.aspx*

Step 9: In *Page1.aspx*, directly edit the Title property in the Page directive to be the following:

```
Title="Page One"
```

Step 10: Insert the following CSS style definition inside the *head* area of the master page:

```
<style type="text/css">
.page1
{
   width:100%;
   background-color:Cyan;
   border:1px solid black;
}
</style>
```

Step 11: Insert an HTML table inside the *Content2* content control. Set the *class* property in the table to the CSS style named *page1*. The Content control with the table inside should be coded like this:

```
<asp:Content ID="Content2"
   ContentPlaceHolderID="ContentPlaceHolder1" Runat="Server">

   <table class="page1">
      <tr>
         <td>
             
         </td>
      </tr>
   </table>
</asp:Content>
```

Step 12: Insert some text, a DropDownList, a Button, and a Label inside the table cell (shown here as boxed text).

```
<table class="page1">
   <tr>
      <td>
```

```
              <h2>Page 1 = My favorite fruit</h2>
              <p />
              <asp:DropDownList ID="ddlFruitList"
                runat="server">
                </asp:DropDownList>
              <p />
              <asp:Button ID="btnSelect"
                runat="server"
                Text="Select" />
               
              <asp:Label ID="lblAnswer"
                runat="server">
                </asp:Label>
        </td>
      </tr>
</table>
```

Step 13: In the editor's Design view, insert several fruit names into the Items property of the DropDownList.

Step 14: In the page's codebehind file, create a Click handler for the *Select* button. It gets the item the user selected in the fruit list, and copies the item to the Label control.

```
Protected Sub btnSelect_Click() Handles btnSelect.Click
    lblAnswer.Text = "You chose " &
        ddlFruitList.SelectedItem.ToString
End Sub
```

Step 15: View *Page1.aspx* in the browser and verify that the master page, containing the first content page, is displayed. Select a fruit from the list and click the *Select* button.

NOTE: From this point forward, you are editing the content page named *Page2.aspx*.

Step 16: Add a second content page named *Page2.aspx* to the application, and insert the following text inside its Content control named *Content2*:

```
<asp:Content ID="Content2"
    ContentPlaceHolderID="ContentPlaceHolder1" Runat="Server">

    <h2>Page 2 — Second Content Page</h2>
</asp:Content>
```

Step 17: Modify the Web form's Title property inside the Page directive:

```
Title="Page Two"
```

Step 18: Save the Web form, and view *Page1.aspx* in the browser. Click both buttons, to alternate between Page1 and Page 2.

Notice that if you select a fruit on page 1 (and click *Select*), go to Page 2, and return to Page 1, the fruit selection has disappeared. This is normal because we have not saved the fruit selection in Session state.

More Advanced Use of Master and Content Pages

Web.config File

In the <configuration> section of a project's web.config file, you have the option of specifying the default master page for every content page in the application.

```
<configuration>
  <system.web>
    <pages masterPageFile="~/MasterPage.master" />
  </system.web>
</configuration>
```

Even if you do this, you can still override the default by identifying a specific master page filename inside the Page directive of a content page.

Handling Events

Buttons and other controls on a master page pass their events to the currently displayed content page. There can be a button on a master page with a Click handler that navigates to another page. The following Click event handler, located in the codebehind file of a content page, transfers control to *Page2.aspx*:

```
Protected Sub btnPage2_Click() Handles btnPage2.Click
    Response.Redirect("Page2.aspx")
End Sub
```

References to Content Controls

To access controls such as buttons and text boxes on the currently displayed content page, you can write code in the master page that calls the ContentPlaceHolder's *FindControl* method. The following example hides a Button control named *btnCancel* that is located in the Web page currently displayed by ContentPlaceHolder1:

```
Dim btn As Button = ContentPlaceHolder1.FindControl("btnCancel")
If btn IsNot Nothing Then
    btn.Visible = False
End If
```

Changing the Class Name of a Master Page's Class

If you rename the class in a Master Page's codebehind file, you must also assign the new class name to the Inherits property of the Master page's Master directive. For example, suppose you had just renamed a Master page class to the following in its codebehind file:

```
Partial Class MasterPage
    Inherits System.Web.UI.MasterPage
```

Then the Master directive in the *MasterPage.master* file should be as follows:

```
<%@ Master Language="VB" CodeFile="MasterPage.master.vb"
Inherits="MasterPage" %>
```

Referencing the Master Page

To reference the master page from a content page, use the Me.Master property. It returns a general Web.UI.MasterPage object, but you can cast it to your specific master page class type. For example, suppose a master page's class is named *MyMasterPage*. The following statement, located in a content page, gets a reference to the master page:

```
Dim tmaster As MyMasterPage = CType(Me.Master, MyMasterPage)
```

Once your code contains a reference to the master page, it can access individual controls on the page. To do that, call the *FindControl* method, passing the control's ID. In the following example, we get a reference to a Label control named *lblStatus* on the master page:

```
Dim ctrl As Label = CType(tmaster.FindControl("lblStatus"), Label)
```

Then we modify the control's Text property:

```
ctrl.Text = "The Content page says Hello!"
```

Any controls on the master page modified in this manner revert to their default values when another content page is loaded into the content pane. If FindControl fails to find the control ID, it returns a value of *Nothing*. One final point: The content page's Load event fires before the same event in the master page.

 Checkpoint

1. Which control on the master page holds data from a content page?

2. Which control on a content page holds data that will be displayed on the master page?

3. How does a content page identify its related master page?

4. How can all pages in an application use the same master file without having to specify the master file name on every page?

 Using the GridView Control

In ASP.NET applications, the **GridView control** is the counterpart to the DataGridView control in Windows Forms applications. The two grids have many of the same capabilities, but their underlying structure is very different. The GridView control is specified in XHTML on a Web form. Then the grid is turned into a standard HTML table when the server sends the containing Web page back to the user's browser.

Web forms applications use a different model for accessing databases than do Windows forms. Rather than using a DataSet, Web forms use a type of control named **DataSource control.** Actually, you can select between different controls, depending on the type of database being used. One control is named **AccessDataSource control,** for Microsoft Access databases. The other is named **SqlDataSource control,** for SQL Server databases. **DataSource controls** directly update the underlying database because no dataset is kept in memory.

There is a third type of DataSource control named *ObjectDataSource* that binds to a class. It automatically calls Select, Insert, Update, and Delete methods from a middle-tier class. In every other way, it functions just like an SqlDataSource control.

GridView Control

The GridView control offers the ideal way to display a database table by binding to a data source. It lets you sort on any column, select the column order, and format the data within columns. You can also edit, insert, and update database rows in the grid.

The GridView control is located in the Data section of the Visual Studio Toolbox window. An example is shown in Design view in Figure 10-7. When you click the smart tag, the *GridView Tasks* menu pops up, as in Figure 10-8. You can use it to set various grid properties and connect a data source.

The XHTML code for a GridView is simple when displayed in Source view:

```
<asp:GridView
  ID="GridView1"
  runat="server">
</asp:GridView>
```

There are a large number of GridView properties that can be used to control alignment, colors, fonts, borders, and so on. It is easiest to select one of the predefined *AutoFormat* styles from the GridView Tasks window. In Figure 10-9, for example, we have selected the *Oceania*

Figure 10-7 GridView control in design mode

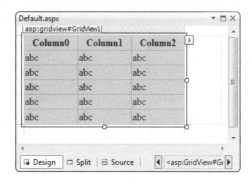

Figure 10-8 GridView tasks popup menu

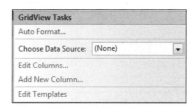

Figure 10-9 GridView, using the *Oceania* autoformat

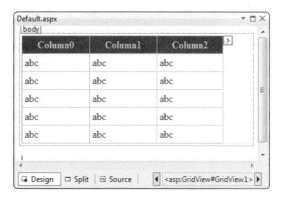

autoformat, where the column headings are dark blue (appearing in gray on the printed page). After selecting this format, the XHTML code for the control is more complicated:

```
<asp:GridView ID="GridView1" runat="server" BackColor="White"
  BorderColor="#3366CC" BorderStyle="None" BorderWidth="1px"
  CellPadding="4" Height="156px" Width="325px">
  <FooterStyle BackColor="#99CCCC" ForeColor="#003399" />
  <HeaderStyle BackColor="#003399" Font-Bold="True"
    ForeColor="#CCCCFF" />
  <PagerStyle BackColor="#99CCCC" ForeColor="#003399"
    HorizontalAlign="Left" />
  <RowStyle BackColor="White" ForeColor="#003399" />
  <SelectedRowStyle BackColor="#009999" Font-Bold="True"
    ForeColor="#CCFF99" />
  <SortedAscendingCellStyle BackColor="#EDF6F6" />
  <SortedAscendingHeaderStyle BackColor="#0D4AC4" />
  <SortedDescendingCellStyle BackColor="#D6DFDF" />
  <SortedDescendingHeaderStyle BackColor="#002876" />
</asp:GridView>
```

You can see from this code that formatting is accomplished by various tags such as <Footer-Style> and <HeaderStyle>. Many developers prefer to create a separate CSS class for each of these tags to make the source code easier to read and modify.

SqlDataSource Control

When you create a connection to an SQL Server database on a Web form, you need to use an SqlDataSource control. It appears in Design view as a gray rectangle, with the control's name inside, as in Figure 10-10. The following is the XHTML encoding of an SqlDataSource control that connects to the Karate database:

```
<asp:SqlDataSource ID="MembersDataSource"
  runat="server"
  ConnectionString="<%$ ConnectionStrings:karateConnectionString %>"
  SelectCommand="SELECT ID, Last_Name, First_Name, Phone,
    Date_Joined FROM Members ORDER BY Last_Name">
</asp:SqlDataSource>
```

Figure 10-10 SqlDataSource control in Design view

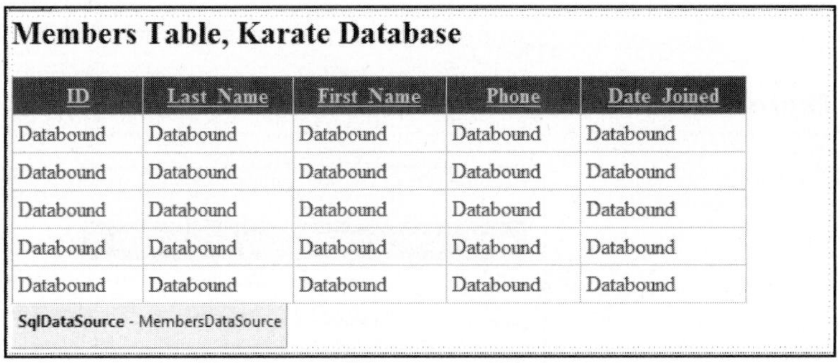

Members Table, Karate Database

ID	Last Name	First Name	Phone	Date Joined
Databound	Databound	Databound	Databound	Databound
Databound	Databound	Databound	Databound	Databound
Databound	Databound	Databound	Databound	Databound
Databound	Databound	Databound	Databound	Databound
Databound	Databound	Databound	Databound	Databound

SqlDataSource - MembersDataSource

The *ConnectionString* property identifies the name of a specific database connection string from the ConnectionStrings area of the application's configuration file. The *SelectCommand* property contains an SQL query that retrieves rows from the database.

Meanwhile, the actual connection string is in the Web site's *web.config* file. Notice the *name* property:

```
<connectionStrings>
  <add name="karateConnectionString"
    connectionString="Data Source=.\SQLEXPRESS;
    AttachDbFilename=|DataDirectory|\karate.mdf;
    Integrated Security=True;
    Connect Timeout=30;
    User Instance=True"
    providerName="System.Data.SqlClient" />
</connectionStrings>
```

The *AttachDbFilename* parameter is important because it identifies the database file location. It could contain a complete disk directory path, which would have to be corrected if we moved the Web site to a new computer or directory. Instead, our example uses the *DataDirectory* keyword (with vertical bars on either side) as the root of the database path. This keyword asserts that the database is located inside the Web site's *App_Data* folder.

In Tutorial 10-2, you will display a GridView control, using an SqlDataSource control to provide the database connection.

Tutorial 10-2:
Displaying the Karate Members table in a GridView control

In this tutorial, you will create an application that connects to the Karate database and displays the Members table in a GridView control. A sample of the running application is shown in Figure 10-11.

Figure 10-11 Running the Karate Member Grid application

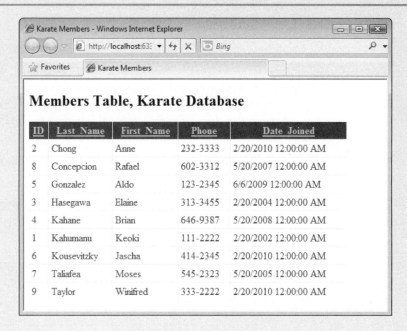

Tutorial Steps

Step 1: Create a new empty Web site named *Karate Member Grid*.

Step 2: Add a folder to the project named *App_Data*.

Step 3: In Windows Explorer, copy the *karate.mdf* database file from the chapter examples folder into your project's App_Data folder.

Step 4: In Visual Studio, right-click the App_Data folder and select *Refresh Folder* from the popup menu. (The database filename should appear.)

> **TIP:** If you refresh the App_Data folder after copying a database to this folder, Visual Studio will be able to create a correct connection string when you create a database connection. To verify later that you did it correctly, open the *web.config* file and examine the database connection string. The AttachDbFileName property must begin with **|DataDirectory|** rather than an absolute database path.

Step 5: Add a new Web form named *Default.aspx* to the project. It must be located in the project's root folder. Open this form in Source view.

Step 6: In the <head> area of the form, set the title to *Karate Members*.

Step 7: Inside the <form> area, add a level-two heading.

```
<h2>Members Table, Karate Database</h2>
```

Step 8: Add the following GridView control:

```
<asp:GridView ID="gvMembers"
  style="width:90%"
  runat="server">
</asp:GridView>
```

Step 9: Switch to the form's Design view, open the *GridView Tasks* window, and select *New Data Source* under the *Choose Data Source* entry.

Step 10: In the *Data Source Configuration Wizard*, select *SQL Database*, change the ID value to *MembersDataSource*, and click the *OK* button to continue.

Step 11: In the *Choose Your Data Connection* step of the wizard, select the *karate.mdf* file from the dropdown list of existing connections. (The database filename appears in this list because you copied the database file to the Web site's *App_Data* folder and refreshed the folder in Solution Explorer.) Click the *Next* button to continue.

Step 12: In the *Save the Connection String* step, click the *Next* button to continue.

Step 13: In the *Configure the Select Statement* step, select the Members table, as shown in Figure 10-12. Place a check in the check box next to each of the columns.

Figure 10-12 Configuring the SELECT statement

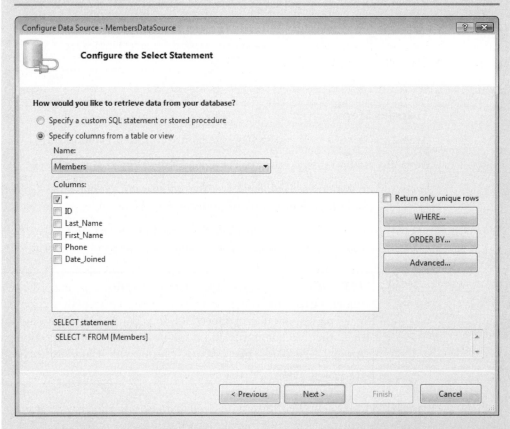

Step 14: Click the *ORDER BY...* button. In the dialog box shown in Figure 10-13, sort by the Last_Name column. Click the *OK* button to close the dialog box.

Figure 10-13 Adding an ORDER BY clause to the query

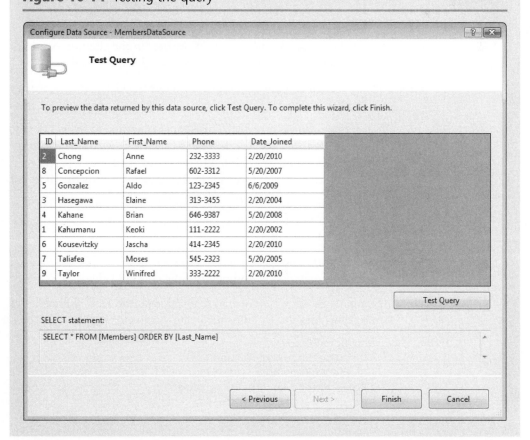

Step 15: Returning to the *Configure the Select Statement* dialog box, click the *Next* button, which takes you to the *Test Query* dialog. Click the *Test Query* button. If the displayed columns match those shown in Figure 10-14, click the *Finish* button to close the window.

Figure 10-14 Testing the query

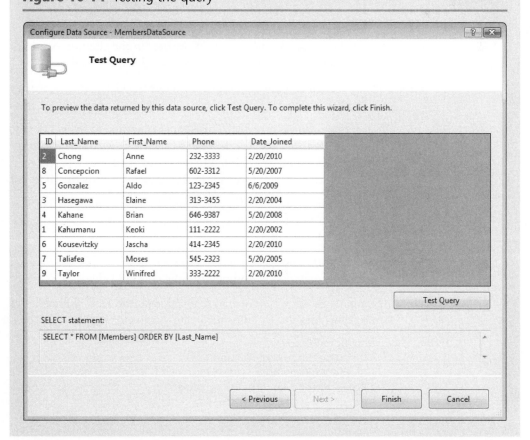

Step 16: Click the GridView's smart tag again and check the *Enable Sorting* option.

Step 17: Select *AutoFormat* from the GridView Tasks window and select the *Oceania* format.

Step 18: Save the project and view *Default.aspx* in the browser. You should see the display shown earlier in Figure 10-11, although some data in the rows may be different.

Step 19: Sort on each column by clicking its column header. If you click the same column header twice in a row, the column sorts in descending order.

Summary

You will find that, with a small amount of practice, you can put together a form like this with a data-bound grid in a very short time—perhaps 2 minutes or less. The tools Microsoft has provided are the product of years of refinement and many user suggestions! You probably noticed that the Date_Joined column did not appear in the best possible format in the GridView control. In Tutorial 10-3, you will learn how to alter the alignment and formatting of any column in the grid, with a few simple commands.

Tutorial 10-3:
Formatting the Karate Members columns

In this tutorial, you will format one of the columns in the *Karate Member Grid* application. You will also modify a column heading and find out what happens when you incorrectly set the DataField property of a column.

Tutorial Steps

Step 1: Open the *Karate Member Grid* Web site. (In the chapter examples folder, the solution program for this tutorial is named *Karate Member Grid 2*.)

Step 2: In the Design view of *Default.aspx*, select the GridView control and open the Properties window.

Step 3: Select the *Columns* property. This should cause the *Fields* window to appear, as in Figure 10-15. In the *Selected fields* list, select *Date_ Joined*. In the properties list for this column, enter {0:d} into the DataFormatString property. The notation {0:d} is called a *format specifier*. In this case, it specifies the short date format.

Step 4: Expand the entries under the Date_Joined column's ItemStyle property. Change the HorizontalAlign subproperty to *Center*. Click the *OK* button to close the dialog box.

Step 5: Save the form and view it in the browser. Observe that the dates are now formatted in *mm/dd/yyyy* format, and the column values are centered.

Step 6: Examine the form's source code and locate the Date_Joined column. Notice that it includes the DataFormatString parameter that you just created:

```
<asp:BoundField
   DataField="Date_Joined"
   HeaderText="Date_Joined"
   SortExpression="Date_Joined"
   DataFormatString="{0:d}">
```

Figure 10-15 Modifying the GridView columns

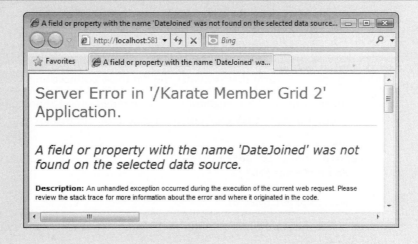

Step 7: In the source code, change the *HeaderText* parameter to *Join Date* and save the form. This will change only the name displayed in the column heading.

Step 8: View the page in the browser and verify that your change appears. (If the browser was already open, you can just refresh the page.)

What if you were to change the name of the *DataField* property? Let's find out.

Step 9: Change the DataField property for the *Date_Joined* column to *DateJoined*. When you save the form and view the page in the browser, you should see the error shown in Figure 10-16, although your application will be named as *Karate Member Grid*.

Figure 10-16 Using the wrong column binding name

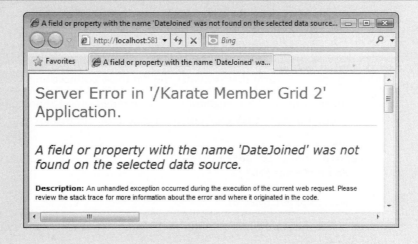

> Errors like this are fairly common, and it is important for you to know how the error was caused. If you examine the SQL query in the SqlDataSource control, it lists the column names:
>
> ```
> SelectCommand="SELECT ID, Last_Name, First_Name, Phone,
>    Date_Joined FROM Members ORDER BY Last_Name"
> ```
>
> And it is clear that DateJoined is not a column name.
>
> **Step 10:** Change the DataField property for the *DateJoined* column to *Date_Joined*. Save the form and view it in the browser. Verify that the grid displays correctly.
>
> As you can see, there are a lot of details to learn about the GridView control. We encourage you to experiment on your own with different properties, formats, and alignments in the grid you used for this tutorial. It's the best way to learn, and you can always undo your changes if you make a mistake.

✅ Checkpoint

5. How do you edit the columns in a GridView?

6. In this chapter, what type of control was used as the data source for the GridView control?

7. How do you select one of the predefined GridView formats?

8. Which property in an SqlDataSource control identifies the database connection?

10.3 Using the DetailsView Control

The **DetailsView control** lets the user add, view, edit, and delete database table rows. If you connect it to a DataSource control, it displays one table row at a time. No programming is required. Microsoft has been working hard to automate as many menial tasks as possible, and database table editing is high on the list of tasks most programmers would prefer not to code by hand.

The DetailsView control is found in the Data section of the Toolbox window. When you place it on a Web form, use its *DetailsView Tasks* window to attach it to a data source.

Properties

The *DataSourceID* property of the DetailsView control contains a reference to a DataSource control on the same form that provides the database connection.

Each member of the *Fields* collection is a *BoundField* object. For example, in the following XHTML code for a DetailsView control, the BoundField displays the ID database column:

```
<Fields>
  <asp:BoundField DataField="ID"
    HeaderText="ID"
    ReadOnly="True"
    SortExpression="ID" />
```

You can select the *AutoFormat* link in the DetailsView Tasks window to select from a set of predefined formats.

The *DataKeyNames property* is a collection of strings that identifies the columns from the data source that make up the primary key.

The *DefaultMode property* selects the starting state of the control when it first becomes visible. The default setting is *ReadOnly*, but you can set it to *Edit* or *Insert* if you want the user to begin editing or inserting items immediately.

In Tutorial 10-4, you will update the Members table from the Karate database, using a DetailsView control.

Tutorial 10-4:
Karate member details

In this tutorial, you will create an application that lets the user view, edit, insert, and delete individual rows in the Members table in the Karate database. You will connect a DetailsView control to an SqlDataSource.

Figure 10-17 shows the application at runtime. The underlined words *Edit, Delete*, and *New* are built-in LinkButton controls. In Figure 10-18, the user has clicked the *New* button and entered data for a new member. When the user clicks the *Insert* button, the row is saved in the database. If the user tries to add a row having an ID number equal to an existing ID in the table, an error page displays. When the user clicks the *Edit* button, she can modify any of the member fields, as shown in Figure 10-19. When the user clicks the *Update* button, changes to the record are saved in the database.

Figure 10-17 DetailsView control showing the Members table at runtime

Tutorial Steps

Step 1: Create a new empty Web site named *Karate Member Details*. Add a folder named *App_Data*, and add a Web form named *Default.aspx*.

Step 2: In Windows Explorer, copy the *karate.mdf* file from the chapter examples folder to your project's App_Data folder.

Step 3: Change the page's <title> value to *Members Table Details*.

Figure 10-18 About to insert a new member

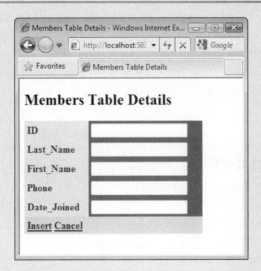

Figure 10-19 After clicking the *Edit* button

Step 4: On the first line of the <form> section, insert the following:

```
<h2>Members Table Details</h2>
```

Step 5: Add a DetailsView control to the page, and set its ID property to *dvAddMember*. Widen it to about 300 pixels.

Step 6: In Design view, select the smart tag in the upper-right corner of the dvAdd-Member control. Under *Choose Data Source*, select *New data source*. The *Data Source Configuration Wizard* window will appear.

Step 7: Name the data source as *MembersDataSource* and connect it to the *karate.mdf* database file. Select all columns of the Members table. Order the rows by Last_Name in ascending order.

Step 8: Before moving to the next window, click the *Advanced* button. In the *Advanced SQL Generation Options* window, select the *Generate INSERT,*

UPDATE, and DELETE statements option, as shown in Figure 10-20. Click the *OK* button, and then click the *Next* button.

Figure 10-20 Selecting advanced SQL generation options

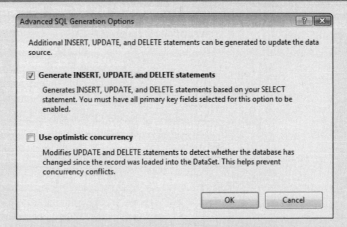

Step 9: Click the *Finish* button to close the *Configure Data Source* window. Back in the Design view of the form, open the Tasks menu for dvAddMember and select the check boxes to enable inserting, editing, and deleting. The form should now appear in Design view, as in Figure 10-21. Notice that the control includes LinkButton controls named *Edit*, *Delete*, and *New*.

Figure 10-21 DetailsView control in design mode

Step 10: Save the form and view the page in the browser. It should look like Figure 10-22.

Step 11: Select the grid in Design view and open the *Fields* property. (Or, you can select *Edit Fields* from the control's Tasks menu.) In the *Fields* window, select the Date_ Joined field (from the *Selected Fields* list) and set its *DataFormatString* property to {0:d}. You may recall this is the same short date format specifier you used in the GridView control.

Step 12: Save the form and view the page in the browser. The Date_Joined field format should be correct.

Figure 10-22 Initial view of the DetailsView in the browser

Step 13: In the Tasks window for the control, select *AutoFormat*, and select *Classic*. Try other formats as well.

Next, you will test the control by inserting, editing, and deleting members. All the changes you make will be permanent. The "rollback" capability you had in Windows Forms applications is not available here. Of course, you can always make a fresh copy of the database file in the chapter examples folder.

Step 14: View the form in a browser and click the *New* button. The fields will clear. Enter the following data: *14, Baker, Eric, 654-3210, 3/1/2011*. Then click the *Insert* button. The display should now show the member you inserted.

Step 15: Try to insert a second new record, using the same ID number. You should see an error message saying that the changes you requested for the table were not successful. Click the browser's *Back* button, change the ID to 15, and click the *Insert* button.

> **TIP:** To verify changes to a database table, select the database inside the Server Explorer window, open the *Tables* group, right-click the table name, and select *Show Table Data*.

Step 16: Click the *Delete* button. The record you inserted should disappear, and the first person in the table (probably Anne Chong) should display.

Step 17: Click the *Edit* button, change any one of the fields except for the ID, and click the *Update* button. The changes should be saved.

Summary

We think you'll agree that the DetailsView control is a great convenience. You could create all the necessary code yourself, but this control frees you up to do more meaningful things (like going to the beach). If you want to customize the control, you can select *Edit Templates* from the control's Tasks menu. We do not have space to talk about custom templates, but there's lots of help at the Microsoft MSDN Web site.

Tutorial 10-5:
Selecting members by ID

In this tutorial, you will add a parameterized query to the SelectCommand property of the SqlDataSource of the *Karate Member Details* application. The user will be able to edit any row of the table. When the application starts (see Figure 10-23), users are prompted to enter a member ID number. When they do so and click the *Go* button, the appropriate member displays, as shown in Figure 10-24. User can enter any ID number and move to a different row.

Figure 10-23 On startup, the user enters an ID number

Figure 10-24 Displaying the member with ID = 2

Tutorial Steps

Step 1: If it is not already open, open the *Karate Member Details* Web site.

Step 2: Just below the DetailsView control, insert the text: *Select ID to view*.

Step 3: Insert a TextBox control to the right of the text. Set its ID property to *txtFindId*.

Step 4: Insert a Button control to the right of the TextBox. Set the following properties: ID = btnGo, Text = *Go*. Refer again to Figure 10-24 as a guide.

Next, you will modify the query in the SqlDataSource control by adding a query parameter. The parameter will be bound to the TextBox control you just added.

Step 5: Click the smart tag of the *MembersDataSource* control and select *Configure Data Source*.

Step 6: Click the *Next* button, keeping the same connection.

Step 7: In the *Configure the Select Statement* panel, the table and columns should already be selected, as shown in Figure 10-25.

Figure 10-25 Configuring the Select Statement

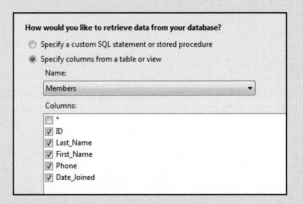

Step 8: Click the *WHERE* button. The *Add WHERE Clause* window appears.

Step 9: Select the ID column, and select Control in the dropdown list entitled *Source*. Select *txtFindId* from the dropdown list labeled *Control ID*. The form values should appear as shown in Figure 10-26.

Step 10: Click the *Add* button. A new entry should appear in the box at the bottom of the window.

Step 11: Click the *OK* button to close the window, which takes you back to the *Configure the Select Statement* window.

Step 12: Click the *Next* button, and then click the *Finish* button.

Step 13: Save the page and view it in the browser.

Step 14: Enter an ID (usually between 1 and 9) in the TextBox and click the *Go* button. The DetailsView control should fill with the matching member's data. Experiment with different ID values.

Figure 10-26 Adding a WHERE clause with a query parameter

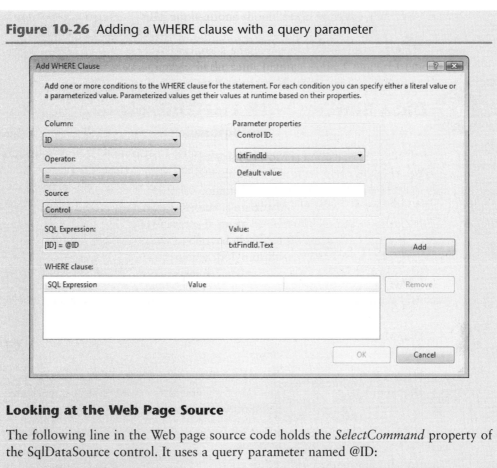

Looking at the Web Page Source

The following line in the Web page source code holds the *SelectCommand* property of the SqlDataSource control. It uses a query parameter named @ID:

```
SelectCommand="SELECT [ID], [Last_Name], [First_Name], [Phone],
   [Date_Joined] FROM [Members] WHERE ([ID] = @ID)
   ORDER BY [Last_Name]"
```

It is interesting to see how the ID entered into the text box by the user is assigned to the SQL query parameter at runtime. The SqlDataSource control has a *SelectParameters* collection, into which you inserted a single *ControlParameter* object:

```
<SelectParameters>
  <asp:ControlParameter
    ControlID="txtFindId"
    Name="ID"
    PropertyName="Text"
    Type="Int16" />
</SelectParameters>
```

The ControlParameter was created when you specified the Control ID, shown previously in Figure 10-26. In the figure, the ControlID property is assigned to *txtFindId*, the name of the TextBox control that held the ID entered by the user. At runtime, the Web server finds this ControlID value and uses it to get the contents of the txtFindId text box, and plugs that value into the query parameter.

Checkpoint

9. Which property in a DetailsView control permits you to modify the formatting of a column containing a date?

10. Which property of an SqlDataSource control holds the SQL SELECT query?

11. What type of object is inserted into the SelectParameters collection?

12. How do you enable the *Edit* button in a DetailsView control?

 ## 10.4 Data Binding with ListControls

In Web applications, the ListBox, DropDownList, CheckBoxList, and RadioButtonList controls all inherit from a common class named **ListControl.** If you understand its properties and methods, you automatically understand how to use the classes that inherit from it. Table 10-1 lists the properties of the ListControl class. The ones marked with an asterisk (*) can be accessed only at runtime.

Table 10-1 ListControl properties

Property	Description
AutoPostBack	Determines whether a postback will occur when the user selects an item.
DataMember	The specific table in the data source that will be bound to the control.
DataSource	The data source that fills the Items collection.
DataSourceID	The ID of a DataSource control; it automatically binds to the DataSource control at runtime.
DataTextField	The field within the DataSource that provides the visible list of items.
DataTextFormatString	A format string that is applied to the displayed items.
DataValueField	The field in the DataSource that provides the value of each list item.
Items	The collection of items in the list control (read-only).
SelectedIndex*	The lowest index of the selected items in the list.
SelectedItem*	The selected item with the lowest index (read-only).
SelectedValue*	Gets the value that is associated with the selected item in the list control, or selects the item associated with the specified value.

*Property is available only at runtime.

Static Data Binding

The technique of binding a control to a data source in design mode is known as **static data binding.** First, open the control's *Tasks* popup window and select *Choose Data Source.* The *Data Source Configuration Window* (see Figure 10-27) appears. Select the SqlDataSource control name, the field to display, and the data field.

Suppose we want a ListBox to display a list of names from the Customers table in the RepairServices database. The following XHTML code accomplishes the binding:

```
<asp:ListBox ID="lstCustomers"
  runat="server"
  DataSourceID="CustomersDataSource"
  DataTextField="Name"
  DataValueField="CustId">
  </asp:ListBox>
```

Figure 10-27 Binding a Control to a data source

CustomersDataSource refers to an SqlDataSource control on the same form. The *DataSourceID* property points to the SqlDataSource control. The *DataTextField* property identifies the database column to be displayed in the list box. The *DataValueField* identifies the database column that will supply a value at runtime when the user uses code to obtain the contents of the SelectedValue property.

Runtime Data Binding

Sometimes, you may want to bind ListControls at runtime, using Visual Basic code. This approach is known as **runtime data binding.** It gives you the flexibility of calling a middle-tier method (in this case, named *GetCustomers*) that returns a DataTable.

```
With lstCustomers
   .DataSource = GetCustomers()
   .DataTextField = "Name"
   .DataBind()
End With
```

Notice that you must also call the DataBind method.

You can also use runtime code to assign the ID of an SqlDataSource control to the ListBox's DataSourceId property. You do not have to call DataBind:

```
With lstCustomers
   .DataSourceID = CustomersDataSource.ID
   .DataTextField = "Name"
   .DataValueField = "CustId"
End With
```

The DataSourceID and DataSource properties of a control cannot both contain values. For example, if you assign a value to DataSource using runtime code, you must erase any value that is currently in the DataSourceID property. The converse is also true.

Checkpoint

13. Which types of controls inherit from the ListControl class?

14. Which ListControl property identifies the DataSource control that provides data?

15. Which ListControl property identifies the field within the DataSource that provides the visible list of items?

16. Which common ListControl property gets the runtime value of the selected item in the list control?

10.5 Interacting with the GridView Control

The GridView control is easy to use tool for displaying data. But it is also an enormously rich control, with many properties and capabilities. Most often, users like to interact with the control and carry out operations on the grid data. They might select one or more rows, delete rows, edit row data, or insert new rows. In this section, we introduce the use of command buttons in the GridView. We also show how an SqlDataSource control can use grid selection information to filter data in a related query.

The Campus.mdf Database

Throughout this section, we will use a database named *Campus.mdf*, which contains hypothetical college courses, student data, and a table that tracks students enrolling in the courses. First, we will display the *courses* table from this database, which contains the following columns (CourseId is the primary key):

Field	DataType	Sample Values
CourseId	int	33333
YearSem	varchar(10)	2010-01
CourseNum	varchar(10)	COP4338
Credits	int	3

Figure 10-28 lists sample rows from the *courses* table.

Figure 10-28 Courses table data

CourseId	YearSem	CourseNum	Credits
33333	2010-01	COP4338	3
11111	2010-01	COP2210	4
22222	2010-01	ENC1101	3
20000	2010-02	ENC1102	3
12121	2010-01	MTH1011	3
22333	2010-02	COP2210	4
32323	2010-02	COP3337	3

Later, we will use the *students* table, which contains the following columns (StudentId is the primary key):

Field	DataType	Sample Values
StudentId	varchar(4)	1010
FirstName	varchar(50)	James
LastName	varchar(50)	Smith
Gpa	float	3.2
Birthdate	smalldatetime	5/1/1990
Status	int	2

Finally, we will use an *enroll* table that keeps track of which students have enrolled in which courses:

Field	DataType	Sample Values
CourseId	Int	33333
StudentId	varchar(4)	1010
RegistrationDate	Smalldatetime	5/15/2011

The three tables contain the relationships shown in Figure 10-29. A one-to-many relationship exists between *courses* and *enroll*. Another one-to-many relationship exists between *students* and *enroll*.

Figure 10-29 Class relationships in the Campus database

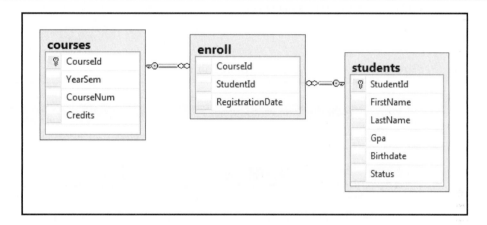

Inserting Command Buttons in a GridView

Figure 10-30 shows a Web form in design mode with GridView and SqlDataSource controls. The latter connects to the Courses table in the *Campus.mdf* database file. The LinkButtons along the left side of the grid are automatically generated when you select the *Enable Selection*, *Enable Editing*, and *Enable Deleting* options in GridView Tasks window. These

Figure 10-30 Web form with GridView and SqlDataSource controls, in Design view

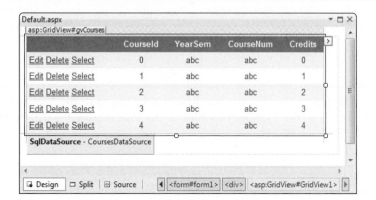

buttons are collectively known as *GridView commands*. The color scheme you would see in the figure if it were printed in color was produced by selecting *Auto Format* in the GridView Tasks window.

> **TIP:** When you open the *Configure Data Source* window, you can click the *Advanced* button to generate queries that join multiple tables. The table used in the data source must have a primary key before you can generate Insert, Delete, and Update queries.

When the user clicks the *Delete* button in a GridView control, the corresponding row is immediately deleted from the database. There is no in-memory DataSet. When the user clicks the *Edit* button, the grid displays an editing template containing TextBox controls, as shown in Figure 10-31. After making changes, the user clicks the *Update* button to save the changes, or the *Cancel* button to discard the changes. No other rows can be selected until one of these buttons is clicked.

Figure 10-31 GridView control in Edit mode

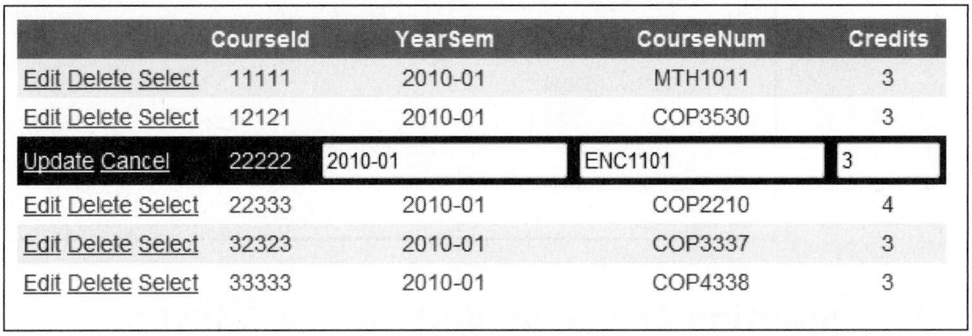

	CourseId	YearSem	CourseNum	Credits
Edit Delete Select	11111	2010-01	MTH1011	3
Edit Delete Select	12121	2010-01	COP3530	3
Update Cancel	22222	2010-01	ENC1101	3
Edit Delete Select	22333	2010-01	COP2210	4
Edit Delete Select	32323	2010-01	COP3337	3
Edit Delete Select	33333	2010-01	COP4338	3

You can customize the appearance and operations of the GridView control by changing the text of the Cancel, Delete, Edit, and Update links. To do that, edit the *Columns* property, select the *CommandField* column, and change the CancelText, DeleteText, EditText, and UpdateText properties.

You can also use image buttons rather than text to carry out operations on each grid row. In Figure 10-32, for example, we set ButtonType = *Image,* and assigned image filenames for the *DeleteImageUrl*, *EditImageUrl*, and *SelectImageUrl* properties.

> **TIP:** Some of images used here can be found in the *VS2010 Image Library* collection, located in the *Common7* folder of the Visual Studio 2010 installation.

In Tutorial 10-6, you will create a Web site that displays a GridView with buttons.

Figure 10-32 GridView using image buttons

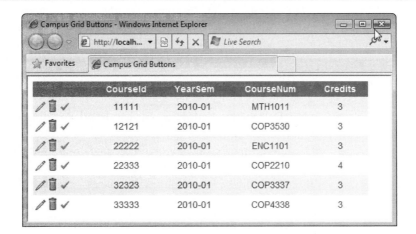

 Tutorial 10-6:
Displaying the Courses table in a GridView

Tutorial Steps

Step 1: Create a new empty ASP.NET application named *Campus GridButtons*.

Step 2: Add a form named *Default.aspx* to the project.

Step 3: Create an *App_Data* folder.

Step 4: Copy the *Campus.mdf* database file from the chapter examples folder to the App_Data folder of your project.

Step 5: Refresh the *App_Data* folder in Solution Explorer.

Step 6: In the Source view of *Default.aspx*, change the <body> tag to:

```
<body style="font-family:Arial;font-size:.85em">
```

Step 7: Insert a GridView control on the form and name it *gvCourses*.

Step 8: In the *GridView Tasks* window, create a new data source named *CoursesDataSource*. It should connect to the Courses table in the *Campus.mdf* database. Sort the rows on the CourseId column.

Step 9: When creating the data source, click the *Advanced* button. Select the option to create INSERT, UPDATE, and DELETE statements. Finish the DataSource configuration.

Let's take a moment to examine the SqlDataSource in Source view:

```
<asp:SqlDataSource ID="CoursesDataSource" runat="server"
  ConnectionString="<%$ ConnectionStrings:CampusConnection-
  String %>"
  DeleteCommand="DELETE FROM [courses] WHERE [CourseId] =
  @CourseId"
  InsertCommand="INSERT INTO [courses] ([CourseId],
  [YearSem], [CourseNum] [Credits]),
    VALUES (@CourseId, @YearSem, @CourseNum,  @Credits)"
```

```
          SelectCommand="SELECT [CourseId], [YearSem], [CourseNum],
          [Credits] FROM [courses] ORDER BY [CourseId]"

          UpdateCommand="UPDATE [courses] SET [YearSem] = @YearSem,
            [CourseNum] = @CourseNum, [Credits] = @Credits
            WHERE [CourseId] = @CourseId">

          (etc.)
      </asp:SqlDataSource>
```

In the DataSource definition, notice the four command objects: DeleteCommand, InsertCommand, SelectCommand, and UpdateCommand. Each is an SQL query that executes when activated by a control attached to this data source. The GridView control is connected, so these commands execute when the grid is filled (SelectCommand), when the user clicks the *Delete* button (DeleteCommand), and so on.

Step 10: Select the grid and verify that its *DataKeyNames* property is set to *CourseId*.

Step 11: Select the grid's *Columns* property and center each column, using the *ItemStyle* property of each column.

Step 12: Select the grid's smart tag and enable the *Selection, Editing,* and *Deleting* options.

Step 13: Save the project and run the application. It should display a list of courses. Experiment with selecting, editing, and deleting rows. In Tutorial 10-7, you will substitute graphical buttons for the grid commands.

Tutorial 10-7:
Using graphical command buttons in the Courses grid

In this tutorial, you will continue the Campus GridButtons application by associating icons with the *Edit, Delete, Select, Update,* and *Cancel* buttons in the GridView control.

Tutorial Steps

Step 1: Open the *Campus GridButtons* Web site.

Step 2: Copy the following files from the *images* folder inside the chapter examples folder to your project folder: *cancel.jpg, delete.gif, edit.png, select.png,* and *update.png*.

Step 3: Refresh the project name inside Solution Explorer. The image filenames should appear.

Step 4: Select the GridView in Design view and open the *GridView Tasks* window. Select *Edit Columns*.

Step 5: In the *Fields* window, select *CommandField* from the *Selected fields* box (lower left corner of the window).

Step 6: Set the ButtonType property to *Image*. Set the following properties:

Cancel ImageUrl	cancel.jpg
DeleteImageUrl	delete.gif
EditImageUrl	edit.png
SelectImageUrl	select.png
UpdateImageUrl	update.png

Step 7: Save the form and view it in the browser. Verify that the icons appear as shown in Figure 10-33.

Figure 10-33 GridView using image buttons

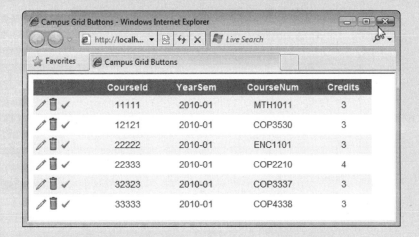

Step 8: Click the *Delete* (🗑) icon and verify that the row is deleted.

Step 9: Click the *Select* (✓) icon and verify that the row is selected.

Step 10: Click the *Edit* (✐) icon. Verify that a blue check mark and a red **X** appear in the two command fields, as shown in Figure 10-34. Experiment with updating and canceling the current edit.

Figure 10-34 Editing a row in the GridView

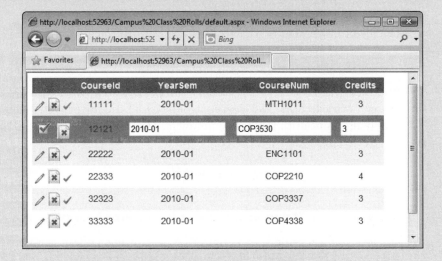

As you can see, it's fairly easy to substitute icons for text in the command buttons.

Filling Query Parameters from Different Sources

When you configure a DataSource control with an SQL query that contains query parameters, you have some choices about how the parameters will be assigned values. In the *Define Parameters* step (see Figure 10-35), the Parameter source entry contains a dropdown list that lets you select from some useful choices. Here are the parameter values that you are likely to use:

- *Cookie*—Gets the parameter value from a HttpCookie object. You must supply the cookie name.
- *Control*—Another control on the same page. You can use the default property of the control, or you can specify a property from the control.
- *Form*—Gets the value of an HTML form field, identified by name.
- *QueryString*—Gets the value from a QueryString (passed on the line at the end of the URL).
- *Session*—Gets the value from an object in the Session state collection. You must supply the key value.

Figure 10-35 GridView using image buttons

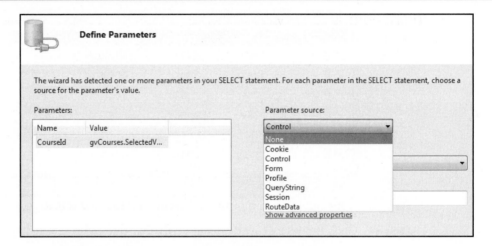

Using a GridView as the Control Parameter Source

A GridView control makes a great parameter source as long as it is configured correctly. First, you must create a DataSource from a query that includes the primary key field of one of your database tables. Second, the ***DataKeyNames*** property in the grid must contain the column name(s) that comprise the table's primary key. In the Courses table of the Campus database, the column is *CourseId*.

Once you have these two items in place, you can include a WHERE clause in your data source that compares the query parameter to the primary key field:

```
WHERE (enroll.CourseId = @CourseId)
```

And then when you get to the *Define Parameters* step (when you are configuring the data source), you select the GridView control by its ID and the property name in the grid that will supply the value at runtime. The following code becomes part of the DataSource control:

```
<SelectParameters>
  <asp:ControlParameter ControlID="gvCourses" Name="CourseId"
    PropertyName="SelectedValue" />
</SelectParameters>
```

Using a Query String as a Control Parameter Source

Suppose you want to fill a grid on a Web page, using a query string (part of the URL) as the input value. For example, if you type the following string into the address bar of a Web browser, you'll see a list of links to Web sites relating to snow:

```
http://www.google.com/search?q=snow
```

So, *q=snow* is known as a **query string.** You can assign a query string value to an SQL query parameter. To do this for the Campus database, for example, we would initialize the *CourseId* query parameter with a query string named *ID*. All we need to do is insert the following QueryStringParameter object into the SelectParameters collection of an SqlData-Source control:

```
<SelectParameters>
  <asp:QueryStringParameter
    Name="CourseId"
    QueryStringField="ID" />
</SelectParameters>
```

Then a statement like the following can pass an ID value to the Web page containing the Sql-DataSource:

```
Response.Redirect("DisplayRoll.aspx?ID=11111")
```

If you prefer to hide the query string from the user for security purposes, call *Server.Transfer*:

```
Server.Transfer("DisplayRoll.aspx?ID=11111")
```

Then the URL in the browser's address bar will not change when the new page appears. The user will not be able to see the query string.

Identifying GridView Selections at Runtime

When a GridView row is selected by the user, a SelectedIndexChanged event is fired. Assuming that the grid's DataKeys collection contains the primary key of the underlying dataset, you should be able to get the selected key value from the SelectedValue property. Here, for example, we get the course ID from the gvCourses grid:

```
Dim courseId As Integer = gvCourses.SelectedValue
```

The grid's *SelectedRow* property returns a reference to the grid row selected by the user. It returns a GridViewRow object.

```
Dim row As GridViewRow = gvCourses.SelectedRow
```

Once you have a GridViewRow object, you can index into its *Cells* collection and obtain a TableCell object.

```
Dim cell as TableCell = row.Cells(2)
```

The *Text* property of a TableCell object contains the cell's contents. The following statement copies the cell's contents into a Label control:

```
lblCourseNumber.Text = row.Cells(2).Text
```

In Tutorial 10-8, you will display a list of students who are enrolled in a course when the user selects the course from a GridView control.

Tutorial 10-8:
Displaying class rolls

When the user selects a row in a GridView control, you can write code statements to find out which row was selected. Then you can use that information to filter rows in a second grid. In this tutorial, you will display a class roll in a GridView control filled from tables in the Campus database. The *courses* table contains a list of courses offered by the college, the *students* table contains a list of students, and the *enroll* table shows which students have enrolled in which courses. Sample rows from the enroll table are shown in Figure 10-36.

Figure 10-36 Sample enroll table data

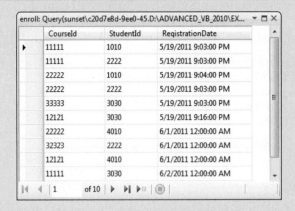

The application shows a list of classes when the application starts (Figure 10-37). When the user selects a class, another GridView control displays the list of students who are enrolled in the class, sorted by last name and first name. An example appears in Figure 10-38.

Figure 10-37 Application startup, with list of classes

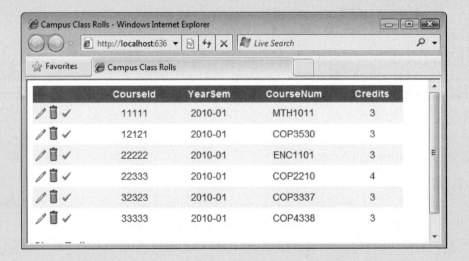

Preparation Step

Open the *web.config* file in the Campus GridButtons project and examine the database connection string. The AttachDbFileName property must equal *|DataDirectory|\Campus.mdf*. Having this correct value will enable you to copy the project and retain a usable database connection.

Tutorial Steps

Step 1: Make a copy of the *Campus GridButtons* Web site from Tutorial 10-7 and rename the copy *Campus Class Rolls*. If you deleted any rows from the classes table when testing the previous tutorial, get a fresh copy of the *Campus.mdf* database file.

Figure 10-38 Displaying the class roll for a selected class

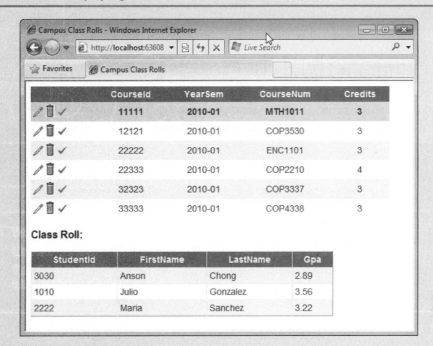

Step 2: Insert the following line in the form's Source view, just below the SqlData-Source control:

```
<h3>Class Roll:</h3>
```

Step 3: Switch to Design view and insert another SqlDataSource control on the form. Name it *EnrollDataSource*. Use the existing connection to the Campus database file. Configure the data source so it joins the *courses*, *enroll*, and *students* tables. Here's the query:

```
SELECT students.StudentId, students.FirstName,
students.LastName, students.Gpa
FROM enroll INNER JOIN students ON enroll.StudentId =
students.StudentId
WHERE (enroll.CourseId = @CourseId)
ORDER BY students.LastName, students.FirstName
```

You can use the Query Builder tool to create this query, as you did in Chapter 5. In the *Define Parameters* step (shown in Figure 10-39), select *Control* as the parameter source and select *gvCourses* as the ControlID. This will ensure that the SQL query parameter is filled at runtime with the course ID selected by the user in the gvCourses GridView control. Notice that the *SelectedValue* property was selected automatically by Visual Studio.

Step 4: After saving the data source, switch to the form's Source view and verify that EnrollDataSource is defined like this:

```
1:  <asp:SqlDataSource ID="EnrollDataSource" runat="server"
2:     ConnectionString="<%$ ConnectionStrings:
       ConnectionStrings:CampusConnectionString %>"
3:     SelectCommand="SELECT students.StudentId,
       students.FirstName,
```

```
4:        students.LastName, students.Gpa FROM enroll INNER JOIN
5:        students ON enroll.StudentId =
6:        students.StudentId WHERE (enroll.CourseId = @CourseId)
7:        ORDER BY students.LastName, students.FirstName">
8:    <SelectParameters>
9:      <asp:ControlParameter ControlID="gvCourses"
           Name="CourseId"
10:          PropertyName="SelectedValue" />
11:    </SelectParameters>
12: </asp:SqlDataSource>
```

Figure 10-39 Defining the query parameter

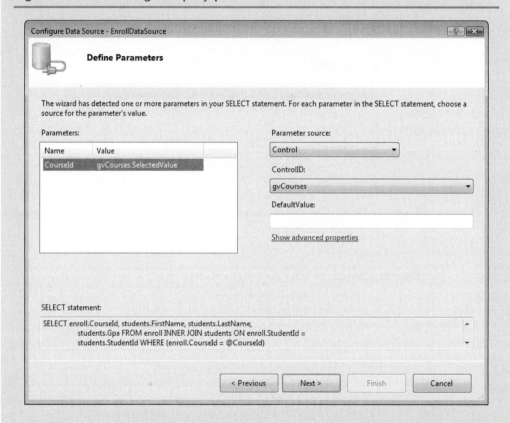

On line 2, your connection string name might be different. On line 9, a ControlParameter links the gvCourses grid to the CourseId query parameter. The PropertyName value identifies SelectedValue as the property in the gvCourses grid that will return the Course ID that we need.

Step 5: Add a second grid to the bottom of the form and name it *gvClassRoll*. Set its Width to 80 percent. Open its GridView Tasks window and select *EnrollDataSource* as its data source.

Step 6: Save the page and view it in the browser. Click the check mark icon next to each course in the grid, and watch the lower grid appear with a list of students enrolled in the course.

You did not have to write a single line of code in this application. But if you want the class roll to appear on a different Web page, you would have to do a little more work. In Tutorial 10-9, you will find out how this works.

Tutorial 10-9:
Displaying the class roll on a separate page

In this tutorial, you will modify the *Campus Class Rolls* application. The user will select a course in the GridView control on the startup page shown in Figure 10-40 and click a link to continue. Then the browser will navigate to a second Web page (shown in Figure 10-41) that displays the class roll for the selected course.

Figure 10-40 The user selects a course and clicks a link to view the class roll

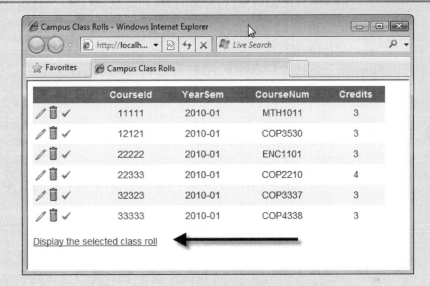

Figure 10-41 The class roll appears on a second page

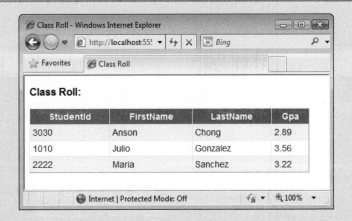

Tutorial Steps

Step 1:   Close Visual Studio, make a copy of the *Campus Class Rolls* application, and rename the copy *Campus Class Rolls 2*. If you have deleted any rows from the database, get a fresh copy of the *Campus.mdf* database from the chapter examples folder.

Step 2: Add a Web form named *DisplayRoll.aspx* to the Web site. Open the form in Design view.

Step 3: Cut the *gvClassRoll* GridView control in *Default.aspx* to the Windows Clipboard and paste it into *DisplayRoll.aspx*.

Step 4: Cut the *EnrollDataSource* control in *Default.aspx* to the Windows Clipboard and then paste it into *DisplayRoll.aspx*.

Step 5: In Source view, modify the *SelectParameters* section of the EnrollDataSource control so it looks like this:

```
<SelectParameters>
  <asp:QueryStringParameter
    Name="CourseId"
    QueryStringField="ID" />
</SelectParameters>
```

Step 6: Move the following heading from *Default.aspx* to *DisplayRoll.aspx*:

```
<h3>Class Roll:</h3>
```

Step 7: Add the following paragraph break and LinkButton control to the bottom of *Default.aspx*:

```
<p />
<asp:LinkButton ID="btnShowRoll"
  runat="server">Display the selected class roll
  </asp:LinkButton>
```

Step 8: In the same page's codebehind file, create the following Click handler for the btnShowroll control that allows the user to navigate to the *DisplayRoll.aspx* page:

```
Protected Sub btnShowRoll_Click() Handles btnShowRoll.Click
  Response.Redirect("DisplayRoll.aspx?ID=" _
    & gvCourses.SelectedValue.ToString)
End Sub
```

Notice that the statement passes a query string (*?ID=*) to the new page, getting the *CourseId* value from the grid's SelectedValue property.

Step 9: Save both pages and view *Default.aspx* in the browser. Select a course in the grid and click the link to view the class roll. To return to the previous page, click the browser's *Back* button.

You're done. As an alternative approach, you could use a Session state value as the query parameter.

⊘ Checkpoint

17. Which options in the GridView Tasks panel cause *Edit* and *Delete* buttons to appear in each row of a GridView?

18. When the user clicks the *Edit* button in a GridView, which buttons appear in the current row?

19. What is a CommandField column?

20. Which GridView property contains an array of primary key values?

10.6 Using JavaScript

Two general types of code execute on Web pages: server-side script and client-side script. The first, **server-side script,** executes on the server after a page is posted back to the server. The second, **client-side script,** refers to computer programs that execute on the user's Web browser. The user's browser is known as the client.

JavaScript is the most common client-side scripting language. It is not just for ASP.NET pages; it also works on all types of Web pages. Code that runs in a user's browser does not need to wait for the page to be posted back before it executes. Client-side script includes both JavaScript and VBScript.

You may have noticed how some Web sites display a popup window as soon as you hover the mouse over an object on the page. To do that, they must execute client-side scripts. Also, Web pages that display graphical animations are using client-side scripts.

Our focus in this chapter will be on JavaScript. It can access built-in browser objects such as the document and window objects, which have large sets of properties and methods. In fact, to get the most out of JavaScript, you should learn the Web browser's complete object model.

JavaScript is often mistaken for the *Java* programming language because of its similar name. The two languages have some minor similarities in syntax, such as IF statements, math expressions, and loops. But they are different in some fundamental ways: In JavaScript, variables and function parameters have no types whereas JavaScript code is interpreted, Java is compiled.

Although you may not have realized it, ASP.NET validation controls such as RequiredField-Validator use JavaScript to flag errors without requiring a round trip to the server. They can also respond when the user tabs from one field to the next.

Writing JavaScript

You can insert JavaScript directly into a Web page by enclosing it between <script> and </script> tags. The script executes as soon as the page is loaded or posted back to the server. Here's an example that calls the *alert* function:

```
<script type="text/javascript">
  alert('Welcome to my Web site!')
</script>
```

This function, which is predefined, displays a small popup window called an **Alert dialog** containing a string and an *OK* button. Figure 10-42 shows the alert dialog displayed by our example.

Figure 10-42 Showing an alert dialog with JavaScript

Executing JavaScript from ASP.NET Controls

You can attach a client-side script to a Button control by assigning it to the button's *OnClientClick* property. The script executes immediately when the user clicks the button and before the page is posted back to the server. Here is an example:

```
<asp:Button ID="btnConfirm"
  runat="server"
  Text="Confirm"
  OnClientClick="alert('You clicked the Confirm button')"
  Width="74px" />
```

Double quotes must enclose any control property, which in this case contains JavaScript code. Therefore, within the JavaScript code, single quotes must be used to surround the string literal. In our example, when the page loads and the user clicks the button, the alert dialog box pops up, as shown in Figure 10-43.

Figure 10-43 Alert dialog displayed by JavaScript in the OnClientClick property

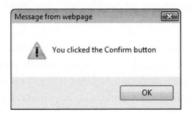

 TIP: If an ASP.NET contains a client script in its OnClientClick property and also has a Click event handler, the client script executes before the postback. Then after the page is posted back, the Click event handler executes.

You can embed a script in a hyperlink, using the *javascript:* prefix. The following HTML code, for example, causes the Web browser to show a Print dialog for the current page:

```
<a href="javascript:window.print()">Print this page</a>
```

You can also insert a javascript statement in a HyperLink control's *NavigateURL* property.

```
<asp:HyperLink
  ID="hypPrint"
  NavigateUrl="javascript:window.print()"
  runat="server">Print this page
  </asp:HyperLink>
```

If your embedded script contains multiple JavaScript statements, they must be separated by semicolons(;). The following example pops up an Alert dialog box. When the user clicks the *OK* button, the Alert dialog closes and the Print dialog appears.

```
<a href="javascript:alert('About to print'); window.print()">
  Print this page</a>
```

Script Debugging

Errors in your JavaScript code are often difficult to detect when your Web browser is configured to ignore JavaScript errors. You can change that. In Internet Explorer, for example, open the *Internet Options* dialog from the Tools menu, click the *Advanced* tab, and unselect the two options that begin with the phrase *Disable script debugging*. Then, when you browse to the Web page and encounter a script error, you will be given the option of opening the debugger. In Figure 10-44, for example, a script error was found on line 12. The right-hand side of the window shows an execution trace.

Figure 10-44 Internet Explorer script debugger, showing the location of an error

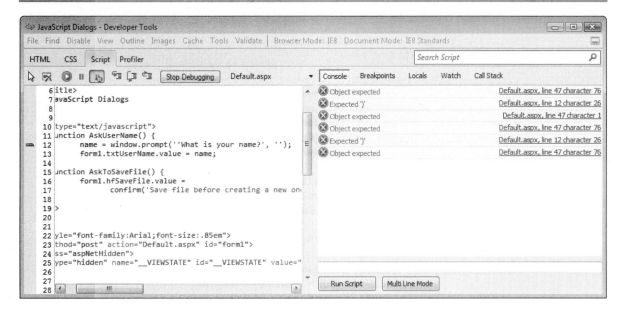

Accessing Form Fields

When it receives a Web page from a server, the Web browser displays a **document object** that encapsulates the contents of the page. For example, it contains an array named *forms*. There is only one form on an ASP.NET page, so your JavaScript code can refer to the form using *document.forms[0]* or document.form1, assuming that it was defined like this in the page:

```
<form id="form1" runat="server">
```

Within a form, each input control has an ID property. To refer to an ASP.NET TextBox whose ID equals txtName, for example, you would use the following expression:

```
form1.txtName
```

JavaScript statements use a property named *value* to refer to the Text property of ASP.NET controls. The following statement, for example, assigns a person's name to the Text property of a TextBox control named txtName:

```
form1.txtName.value = "Joe Smith"
```

Why the *value* property? Because when a TextBox is rendered by a Web browser, it becomes a standard HTML input control on the page sent to the user's browser:

```
<input name="txtName"
  type="text"
  id="txtName"
  value="Joe Smith" />
```

You can also access the value property of a HiddenField control:

```
form1.hfSaveFile.value = true
```

You cannot access a Label control in JavaScript because Labels are not form fields. But you can, in the codebehind file, assign the contents of a HiddenField control to a Label. You will see how to do this in Tutorial 10-10.

JavaScript Functions

To execute more than one JavaScript statement at a time, it's best to call a function containing the statements. A function definition begins with the *function* keyword, followed by a parameter list, followed by a block within braces { . . . }. Here is a simple JavaScript function that returns the sum of two integers:

```
function addTwo( v1, v2 )
{
   return v1 + v2;
}
```

Parameters are declared without types, and the function has no specific return type. The following JavaScript statement shows how the *addTwo* function is called:

```
sum = addTwo(10, 20)
```

The following statements call a function and pass its return value to a TextBox control:

```
X = form1.txtValueX.value
Y = form1.txtValueY.value
form1.txtSum.value = addTwo(X, Y)
```

The window.open Function

JavaScript uses the window.open function to display popup browser windows. A popup can display a calendar, as in Figure 10-45; a photo; or an appointment book. When calling window.open, pass it the name of a Web page that supplies the content. Here is an example:

```
window.open('Calendar.aspx')
```

Figure 10-45 Sample popup calendar window

A popup browser window is a fully functioning Web browser window, in contrast to an alert dialog, which is a predefined dialog window with no customizable properties. On the other hand, a popup browser window can be configured so that it restricts the user. It can hide the menu, the address input field, the status bar, and even the title bar.

Although many Internet users configure their Web browsers to block popup windows, a window that is displayed without any configuration parameters is usually not blocked.

As another option, you can pass a window title and a number of options that set the window size, the toolbar visibility, and so on.

```
window.open('calendar.aspx','Calendar','width=400,height=300,
resizable=yes')
```

Popups that set the window size and perform other customizations are more likely to be blocked because they may be hidden windows containing malicious scripting code.

Generating JavaScript at Runtime

In server-side code, you can add JavaScript to a Web form while an application is running. To do this, call the **RegisterClientScriptBlock method** and pass to it the following arguments:

- A reference to the current form's type, obtained by calling the GetType method
- A string that uniquely identifies the script block on the current page
- The JavaScript code

The following statement causes an alert dialog to display:

```
ClientScript.RegisterClientScriptBlock(Me.GetType(), "alertWelcome",
    "<script>alert('Welcome to my JavaScript page')</script>")
```

If you put this code in a Button.Click event handler, the page posts back to the server when the user clicks the button; the server then creates a Web page and passes it to the client's browser. This page includes the JavaScript code you have inserted. As the user's browser renders the page, the alert window appears.

The main advantage to generating JavaScript at runtime is that you can configure the script by including the values of variables and controls.

In Tutorial 10-10 you will write a short application that displays popup windows.

The *confirm* and *prompt* Functions

The *confirm* function in JavaScript displays a *Confirm* dialog, as shown in Figure 10-46.

```
confirm('Save file before creating a new one?')
```

Figure 10-46 Displaying a Confirm dialog

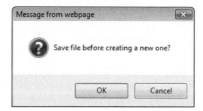

If the user clicks the *OK* button, the function returns *True*. If the user clicks the *Cancel* button, the function returns *False*. It is possible to convey this information back to your server-side Visual Basic code by assigning the return value of the function to a control. Here, for example, we use a HiddenField control to hold the return value:

```
form1.hfSaveFile.value = confirm('Save file before creating a new one?')
```

The *window.prompt* function displays an input dialog and returns a string. An example is shown in Figure 10-47.

Figure 10-47 Prompting the user for a string

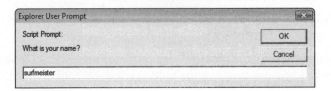

 Tutorial 10-10:
Receiving user input in JavaScript

In Tutorial 10-10, you write a short application that displays the following dialogs and windows:

- A dialog that asks a question.
- A dialog that inputs a string from the user.
- A popup window that displays a Calendar control.

Tutorial Steps

Step 1: Create a new Web application named *JavaScript Dialogs*. Add a Web form named *Default.aspx* to the project.

Step 2: Using Figure 10-48 and Table 10-2 as guides, build the controls and text on the page.

Figure 10-48 Design view of the *JavaScript Dialogs* page

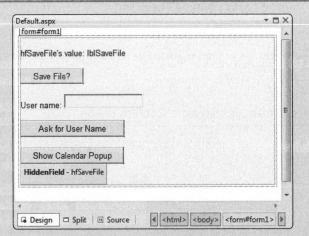

Step 3: In Source view, insert the following JavaScript functions anywhere between the <head> and </head> tags. Be careful not to change the capitalization. The second argument to the prompt function is an empty string.

```
<script type="text/javascript">
  function AskUserName()
  {
    name = window.prompt('What is your name?', '');
    form1.txtUserName.value = name;
  }
```

Table 10-2 Controls in the *JavaScript Dialogs* application startup page

Control Type	Control Name	Control Values
DOCUMENT		Title: *JavaScript Dialogs*, Style: *font-family:Arial;font-size:.85em*
HiddenField	hfSaveFile	Value: *False*
Label	lblSaveFile	
Button	btnSaveFile	OnClientClick: *AskToSaveFile()* Text: *Save File?*
TextBox	txtUserName	
Button	btnUserName	OnClientClick: *AskUserName()* Text: *Ask for User Name*
Button	btnCalendar	OnClientClick: *window.open('calendar.aspx')* Text: *Show Calendar Popup*

```
   function AskToSaveFile()
   {
     form1.hfSaveFile.value =
     confirm('Save file before creating a new one?')
   }
</script>
```

The *AskUserName* function displays a popup dialog with an input field. Its return value is the string typed by the user, which is assigned to the txtUser-Name TextBox control.

The *AskToSaveFile* function displays a popup dialog with a question. It returns a Boolean value, which is assigned to the HiddenField control named *hfSaveFile*.

Step 4: Open the form's codebehind window and insert the following statements inside the Page_Load event handler:

```
If IsPostBack Then
   lblSaveFile.Text = hfSaveFile.Value
End If
```

This code executes only during a page postback; it assigns the HiddenField control's value to the Label control. As we mentioned earlier, a Label control cannot be assigned a value directly by JavaScript, so we use the HiddenField control as a helper.

Step 5: Add another Web form to the application and name it *Calendar.aspx*.

Step 6: Add a Calendar control to the form, using Table 10-3 as a guide.

Table 10-3 Controls in the Calendar.aspx page

Control Type	Control Name	Control Values
DOCUMENT		Title: *Calendar*, Style: *font-family:Arial*
Calendar	(default)	

Step 7: In the *Default.aspx* form, set the btnCalendar button's OnClientClick property to the following:

```
window.open( 'calendar.aspx' ).
```

Step 8: Save the page and view it in a browser. Click the *Save File?* button, click *OK*, and notice that the Label changes when the dialog closes.

Step 9: Click the *Ask for User Name* button, enter a name, and close the dialog. Notice that the name appears in the text box.

Step 10: Click the button that opens the calendar.

We have touched upon only a few basic JavaScript techniques in this tutorial. JavaScript can be tricky to debug, and is prone to unexpected runtime errors. Fortunately, a new user interface technology named *Ajax* reduces the need for JavaScript programming. You will learn about this in Section 10.7.

 Checkpoint

21. Which group of ASP.NET controls mentioned in this section uses client-side JavaScript?

22. Show how to use JavaScript to display *Hello* in a popup dialog window.

23. Which section(s) of an HTML document can contain JavaScript statements?

24. How do you cause JavaScript to execute directly when an ASP.NET Button control is clicked?

25. How does a JavaScript statement access the contents of a TextBox control named *txtName*?

 Using Microsoft Ajax Controls

Ajax technology provides a richer user experience on Web sites by handling many actions within the Web browser. The letters in its name refer to *Asynchronous JavaScript and XML*. The Microsoft implementation of Ajax is a synthesis of the following different Web technologies:

- *HTML*—HyperText Markup Language.
- *Cascading style sheets (CSS)*—Used to define appearance styles on Web pages.
- *JavaScript*—The client-side scripting language whose code is executed by Web browsers.
- *Document Object Model (DOM)*—Lets you access directly Web page elements and events using JavaScript.
- *Extended Markup Language (XML)*—Customizable markup language for objects and other data.
- *XMLHttpRequest*—A technology that permits direct communication between elements on a Web page with a Web server.

Ajax controls are able to update individual components on Web pages. Ordinarily, when you click a non-Ajax page, the browser posts the entire page to the server. The server executes code embedded in the page's codebehind file and sends back a complete new copy of the page. But Ajax controls circumvent this process and communicate directly with the Web server.

 NOTE: The Microsoft online documentation at *http://msdn.microsoft.com* uses the capitalizations Ajax and AJAX interchangeably.

Microsoft Ajax Controls

The basic controls in the *AJAX Extensions* section of the Visual Studio toolbox are Script-Manager, ScriptMangagerProxy, UpdatePanel, Timer, and UpdateProgress. Here are brief descriptions of each:

- The **ScriptManager control** is required on every page that uses other Ajax controls. It provides a connection to a standard Microsoft library of JavaScript functions. It enables partial-page rendering and calls to Web services.
- The **ScriptManagerProxy control** enables nested components such as content pages and user controls to add script and service references to pages when a ScriptManager control is already defined in a parent element.
- The **UpdatePanel control** allows applications to refresh only selected parts of a Web page, without having to post an entire page back to the server. This technique is known as *partial-page update*.
- The **Timer control** performs postbacks at defined time intervals. You can use it to post back an entire page or just the part of a page that is located inside an UpdatePanel control.
- The **UpdateProgress control** lets the user know the ongoing status of a partial page update. For example, the user might initiate a database operation that takes some time to execute. The UpdateProgress control can let the user know that the operation is in progress.

Microsoft Ajax Control Toolkit

In addition to its basic set of Ajax controls, Microsoft produces a set of advanced controls called the **Ajax Control Toolkit.** You can use these advanced controls to create highly interactive Web pages, with a variety of advanced features. The controls are fairly easy to use, and they are provided with examples and documentation. Currently, they are a free download from *http://ajaxcontroltoolkit.codeplex.com*. After downloading the set of controls, install them in your copy of Visual Studio. To give you a general impression of their capabilities, we list a few examples here:

- *Accordion Control*—Contains text panels that expand and collapse when selected by the user. Each panel has a heading and a content area that can be customized with style sheets.
- *AlwaysVisible Control*—Lets you define a text area that floats above the other contents of a page.
- *AnimationExtender Control*—Adds animation capabilities to a page. It can start an animation (such as a fading panel) when the user clicks a button, hovers the mouse, and so on.
- *AsynchFileUpload Control*—Lets the user upload a file as a background operation while he or she continues to interact with the Web page.
- *AutoComplete Control*—Displays a list of choices for a text box. It looks much like the desktop ComboBox control because the user can select from the list.
- *CalendarExtender Control*—Displays a popup calendar from which the user can select a date.
- *CascadingDropDownControl*—Displays a series of dropdown lists. When the user selects from the first list, the second list is populated accordingly. When that selection is made, the next list in the series is populated.
- *CollapsiblePanel Control*—Adds collapsible sections to a Web page, each defined as panels.
- *ColorPicker Control*—Lets you display a popup color picker when a specified control receives the focus.

There are too many toolkit controls to describe here. But you can read the complete documentation for these controls online at *http://www.asp.net*.

Ajax Timer and UpdatePanel Controls

The Ajax *Timer control* is an ideal tool for refreshing the contents of individual controls or sections of a Web form. You might like to check for the latest sports scores, check to see if someone has sent you an instant message, or obtain the latest data from a database. The Timer control has an Interval property, measured in milliseconds, that determines how often it will generate a *Tick event*. Then you can create a Tick event handler in your codebehind file that carries out any operation you want.

If you were to use only the Timer control, every Tick event would cause the enclosing page to post back to the server. Therefore, it is best to combine the Timer with an Ajax *UpdatePanel control*. With this control on the form, the only part of a Web page that is posted to the server is that which is located inside the panel. Suppose, for example, that your page used a ListBox control to hold a set of news headlines. You could place the ListBox and Timer controls inside an UpdatePanel. Then each time a Tick event fired, you could either add new entries to the ListBox or refill the ListBox completely.

The UpdatePanel control contains two sections. The *<ContentTemplate>* section is required. It contains the text and controls that will be posted back to the server and therefore will be updated. Another section named *<Triggers>* is optional. It can be used when you want the control generating the postback to be located outside the UpdatePanel control. In Tutorial 10-11, you will experiment with the Timer and UpdatePanel controls.

Tutorial 10-11:
Displaying the Web server time with Ajax controls

In this tutorial, you will display the Web server's current date and time. You will use an Ajax Timer control to refresh the portion of the Web page that is located inside an UpdatePanel control. A ScriptManager control will be used to enable the other Ajax controls to function properly. A sample of the output is shown in Figure 10-49.

Figure 10-49 Displaying the Web server time with Ajax controls

> **Ajax ScriptManager, Timer, and UpdatePanel Controls**
>
> Current Web Server date and time: 10/30/2010 7:29:40 PM

Tutorial Steps

Step 1: Create a new empty ASP.NET Web site named *Ajax Example*.

Step 2: Add to the Web site a single Web form named *Default.aspx*, and open it in Source view.

Step 3: Insert a ScriptManager control from the *AJAX Extensions* section of the Toolbox onto the form immediately following the <form> tag.

```
<asp:ScriptManager ID="ScriptManager1" runat="server">
</asp:ScriptManager>
```

Step 4: Add a level-two heading to the form on the next line.

```
<h2>Ajax ScriptManager, Timer, and UpdatePanel Controls</h2>
```

Step 5: Insert an Ajax UpdatePanel control in the next line.

```
<asp:UpdatePanel ID="UpdatePanel1" runat="server">
</asp:UpdatePanel>
```

Step 6: Insert a ContentTemplate section inside the UpdatePanel control.

```
<asp:UpdatePanel ID="UpdatePanel1" runat="server">
  <ContentTemplate>
  </ContentTemplate>
</asp:UpdatePanel>
```

Step 7: Insert the following text, and a Label control named *lblTime* inside the ContentTemplate, followed by a blank line. The entire template is shown here:

```
<ContentTemplate>
  Current Web Server date and time:
  <asp:Label ID="lblTime" runat="server" Text=""></asp:Label>

</ContentTemplate>
```

Step 8: Insert an Ajax Timer control into the form where you left a blank line inside the ContentTemplate. Set the Timer properties as shown here:

```
<asp:UpdatePanel ID="UpdatePanel1" runat="server">
  <ContentTemplate>
    Current Web Server date and time:
    <asp:Label ID="lblTime" runat="server" Text=""></asp:Label>
    <asp:Timer ID="UpdateTimer"
      Enabled="true"
      Interval="1000"
      runat="server">
    </asp:Timer>
  </ContentTemplate>
</asp:UpdatePanel>
```

Step 9: Switch to Design view and double-click the Timer control to create a *Tick* event handler. Edit the content of the handler (in the codebehind file) as follows:

```
Protected Sub UpdateTimer_Tick() Handles UpdateTimer.Tick
  ' Get the date and time from the Web server.
  lblTime.Text = DateTime.Now.ToString()
End Sub
```

The Label control is assigned the Web server's date and time. This event handler executes each time the Time control generates a Click event.

Step 10: Save the project and open *Default.aspx* in the browser. After a one-second delay, you should see the date and time, and the time should update itself once per second. Notice that the rest of the page is not posted back to the browser.

Step 11: In Source view, move the lblTime Label control just above the UpdatePanel control and save the form. Open the page in the browser, and notice that the date and time are never displayed. This is because the Timer control posts back only the contents of the UpdatePanel control. It does not update any page areas outside the UpdatePanel.

Step 12: Move the lblTime Label back into the ContentTemplate area, save the form, and view it in the browser again.

UpdateProgress Control

The UpdateProgress control is an ideal tool for those situations when the user might have to wait for an operation to finish. For example, a large database table might be loading into a GridView control. Or, the browser might be waiting for a credit card service to respond with a payment authorization.

The UpdateProgress control always activates when one or more UpdatePanel controls are in the process of communicating with the Web server. To use it, add an UpdateProgress control to the form, and indicate some text that you want to display, such as *Please wait*. Or, you can use a graphic image that has built-in animation.

In Tutorial 10-12, you will create a Web site that uses the UpdateProgress control.

Tutorial 10-12:
Using the UpdateProgress Control

In this tutorial, you will create an application containing an update panel with a LinkButton control. When the user clicks the button, there will be a short delay, which you will use to simulate the time it might take to read a large file. While the user is waiting, the UpdateProgress control will display an animated image and a message that says, "Please wait. . . ." As soon as the delay ends, the UpdatePanel is refreshed and the message and animated image disappear.

Tutorial Steps

Step 1: Create a Web site named *UpdateProgress Demo*.

Step 2: Copy the file named *ajax-loader.gif* from the *images* folder in the chapter examples directory to your Web site directory.

Step 3: Add a new form to the site named *Default.aspx*, and open it in Source view.

Step 4: Add a ScriptManager control to the form.

Step 5: Insert the following UpdatePanel below the ScriptManager, containing a LinkButton control inside its ContentTemplate area:

```
<asp:UpdatePanel ID="UpdatePanel1" runat="server">
  <ContentTemplate>
    <asp:LinkButton ID="lnkRead" runat="server">
      Read a large file</asp:LinkButton>
  </ContentTemplate>
</asp:UpdatePanel>
```

Step 6: Add the following UpdateProgress control to the form:

```
<asp:UpdateProgress id="PageUpdateProgress"
  runat="server" >
  <ProgressTemplate>
    <asp:Image ImageUrl="~/ajax-loader.gif" runat="server" />
    Please wait...
  </ProgressTemplate>
</asp:UpdateProgress>
```

The ProgressTemplate section displays some text on the page during the time that the LinkButton's click event takes place. In addition, there is an Image control that displays an animated GIF file.

Step 7: Create a Click handler for the LinkButton control. Modify its code so that it calls the Thread.Sleep method, telling the program to pause for 4,000 milliseconds:

```
Protected Sub lnkRead_Click() Handles lnkRead.Click
    System.Threading.Thread.Sleep(4000)
End Sub
```

Step 8: Save the page and view it in the browser. Click the *Read a large file* button, and watch the animated image (balls moving in a circle) and the *Please wait . . . .* message appear on the page for 4 seconds. They disappear automatically when the Click handler finishes.

Summary

10.1 Master-Detail Pages

- Master-detail pages let you create a consistent appearance for a set of Web pages by giving them common page areas (such as headers and footers).
- A master page contains empty areas called *content placeholders*. At runtime, the master page remains visible all the time, while different content pages are inserted into the content placeholders.
- You never explicitly put anything inside the ContentPlaceHolder control. Instead, you must create *content pages* that insert themselves inside the master page at runtime.
- With a master-detail page setup, a single master page is referenced by one or more content pages, but only one at a time. When the user loads a content page, the Web server finds its matching master page and combines the two into a single HTML page sent to the user's browser.
- Buttons and other controls on a master page pass their events to the currently displayed content page.
- To access controls such as buttons and text boxes on the currently displayed content page, a master page calls the ContentPlaceHolder's *FindControl* method. Conversely, to reference the master page from a content page, use the *Me.Master* property.

10.2 Using the GridView Control

- Similar to the Windows control named DataGridView, a GridView control binds to a data source. It lets the user sort on any column, select the column order, and format the data within columns. The user can also edit, insert, and update database rows in the grid.
- When you create a connection to an SQL Server Database on a Web form, Visual Studio automatically inserts an SqlDataSource control on the form.
- You format the contents of a grid column by selecting its ItemStyle property.

10.3 Using the DetailsView Control

- The DetailsView control makes it easy for the user to add, view, edit, and delete database table rows. If you connect it to a DataSource control, it displays one table row at a time.
- You can create customized templates for the DetailsView control that affect its appearance when displaying or editing a single table row.
- Use the Fields property of the DetailsView control to modify the appearance of each field.

10.4 Data Binding and ListControls

- In Web applications, the ListBox, DropDownList, CheckBoxList, and RadioButton-List controls all inherit from a common class named ListControl. If you understand its properties and methods, you automatically understand how to use the classes that inherit from it.
- The ListBox control has a property named SelectionMode that is not part of the List-Control class. If you set it to Multiple, the user can select multiple items at run time.
- The DropDownList control is almost identical in function to a ListBox control, except that it uses only one line on a Web page, and only one item may be selected at a time.
- The RadioButtonList control is almost identical in function to a CheckBoxList control, except that only one item can be selected.

10.5 Interacting with the GridView Control

- The GridView control can display command buttons in each row. You can customize the text and appearance of buttons such as *Select*, *Edit*, *Cancel*, *Update*, and *Delete*.
- In Web applications, the SqlDataSource control reads and writes databases.
- The GridView control's DataKeys property contains a collection of values that represent the primary key of each row.
- The GridView control has event handlers and properties that you can use to your advantage when the user selects a row.
- If you include a database table's primary key column when filling a GridView control, your program code can uniquely identify rows selected by the user at runtime.

10.6 Using JavaScript

- JavaScript is a client-side scripting language that you can put into ASP.NET pages. When added to a Web page, JavaScript code executes directly on the user's Web browser.
- Although JavaScript looks superficially like Java, it is fundamentally different. For example, variables and function parameters have no types; the code is interpreted, not compiled.
- You can insert JavaScript directly into a Web page by enclosing it between <script> and </script> tags.
- The RegisterClientScriptBlock method inserts a block of JavaScript into a Web page at runtime.
- You can insert client-side JavaScript code into the OnClientClick property of a Button control.
- JavaScript code can refer to individual controls on a form.
- The JavaScript window.open function opens a popup window. The confirm function in JavaScript displays a popup dialog that asks a yes or no question. The window.prompt function displays a popup dialog and inputs a string from the user.

10.7 Microsoft Ajax Controls

- Ajax technology provides a rich user experience on a Web site by handling many actions within the Web browser. The letters in its name refer to Asynchronous JavaScript and XML.
- Ajax is a synthesis of different Web technologies: HTML, cascading style sheets, JavaScript, Document Object Model, Extended Markup Language, and XMLHttpRequest.
- In addition to a basic set of Ajax controls, Microsoft produces a set of advanced controls named the *Ajax Control Toolkit*. You can use the toolkit to create highly interactive Web pages, with a variety of advanced features.
- The Ajax Timer control refreshes an UpdatePanel or an entire page at regular time intervals.

- The Ajax UpdatePanel control lets you post only part of a Web page back to the server, while leaving the rest of the page unchanged.
- The Ajax UpdateProgress control is useful for situations in which the user might have to wait for an operation to finish. It displays a wait message or icon until an UpdatePanel is refreshed.

Key Terms

AccessDataSource control
Ajax technology
Ajax Control Toolkit
AccessDataSource control
Alert dialog
client-side script
Content control
content page
content placeholder
ContentPlaceHolder control
DataSource
Details View control
document object
GridView control
JavaScript

ListControl class
master-detail pages
master page
query string
RegisterClientScriptBlock method
runtime data binding
ScriptManager control
ScriptManagerProxy control
server-side script
SqlDataSource control
static data binding
Timer control
UpdatePanel control
UpdateProgress control

Review Questions and Exercises

True or False

Indicate whether each of the following statements is true or false.

1. A master page can contain only one ContentPlaceHolder in the <form> section.

2. You always navigate to a content page, never a master page.

3. Cascading style sheets can be linked to a content page only.

4. If a master page is currently open in the editor, you can find the *Add Content Page* selection in the Website menu.

5. The *MasterPageFile* property of the Page directive in a content page identifies the filename of the master page.

6. You can set the default master page filename in *web.config*.

7. The FindControl method cannot be used by code in a content page to reference a control on its master page.

8. The Load event for a content page occurs before the Load event for its master page.

9. You select a GridView auto format from the GridView Tasks window.

10. When you create a connection to an SQL Server Database on a Web form, Visual Studio automatically inserts an SqlDataSource control on the form.

11. In a connection string in *web.config*, the FileName property shows the path to the database file.

12. If you place a database file in any folder belonging to your Web site, you can use the *DataDirectory* keyword to identify the database path in a connection string.

13. In the *Configure Data Source* wizard, click the *Advanced* button to let Visual Studio generate insert, update, and delete queries.

14. To change the horizontal alignment of a column in a GridView, navigate to the ItemStyle property.

15. The DetailsView control displays only one data source row at a time.

16. The StartingMode property of a DetailsView control selects its starting state when it first becomes visible.

17. The DataValueField property of a ListControl identifies the column that will be displayed in the list.

18. Client-side script waits for a Web page to be posted back before it executes.

19. The OnClientClick method always executes before a server-side Click handler.

20. You can embed JavaScript in the NavigateUrl property of a Hyperlink control.

21. If a form has an ID property, you can refer to it by name in JavaScript code.

22. The window.open function always opens a full-size window.

23. The RegisterClientScriptBlock method adds JavaScript to the Web page when it is posted back to the server.

24. The window.prompt function returns an integer.

Short Answer

1. How does the end user know that a master-detail page combination was used?

2. If you have a master page open in the Design window, how do you create a content page?

3. Where is the MasterPageFile attribute defined?

4. How can you specify the default master page filename for an entire application?

5. In the codebehind file, how can a master page get a reference to a Button control inside the currently displayed content page?

6. In the codebehind file, how can a content page get a reference to its master page?

7. Which page Load event fires first: master page or content page?

8. Which properties must you set when binding a ListBox to an SqlDataSource control?

9. In a multiselect ListBox, how do you identify all selected items?

10. What is the default SelectedIndex value of a DropDownList control?

11. How do you make a CheckBoxList control display three columns of items?

12. How do you get the contents of the first cell in the currently selected row of a GridView control?

13. Which GridView property contains the index of the currently selected row?

14. Which GridView event occurs when the user clicks on a row's *Select* button?

15. What is the ASP.NET equivalent to the DataBindingSource in a Windows Forms application?

16. Buttons containing a long Text value should be displayed by which type of ASP.NET control?

17. Which three properties of a ListControl are available only at runtime?

18. If you want to control the formatting of a GridView's column, which property must you set?

19. Using JavaScript, show how to obtain the Text property of a Button control named btnOk. The form's ID property equals *form1*.

20. Which .NET method adds JavaScript to a Web page at runtime?

21. Write a JavaScript statement that asks the user to answer a yes or no question.

22. Write a JavaScript statement that displays a popup dialog that asks for a project name.

23. Define a JavaScript function named *calculate* that returns the first parameter divided by one-half of the second parameter.

24. Write a JavaScript statement that opens a popup window and displays a file named *Schedule.aspx*.

25. Which method does a master page use to locate a reference to a control on its content page?

Programming Challenges

1. **Karate Master Pages**

   Create a Web application that uses a Master page and several content pages to display lists of members and payments from the Karate database. The master page contains a top-level menu, and some of the content pages have menus that show immediately below the master page menu. The result is a two-level menu system that helps the user to navigate easily between the two subsystems: Members and Payments. The master page should contain a heading, a club logo as an image, and a menu with three selections (Home, Members, Payments). An example is shown in Figure 10-50. When the user clicks the *Members* menu selection, she or he is taken to the Members page (Figure 10-51). Notice that this content page contains a submenu (*List All, Delete Selected*). Figure 10-52 shows the result when the user selects *List All* from the menu. If the user selects *Payments* from the top-level menu, the Payments page appears, as shown in Figure 10-53. Notice that this page also contains a menu.

Figure 10-50 Master Page, showing the homepage

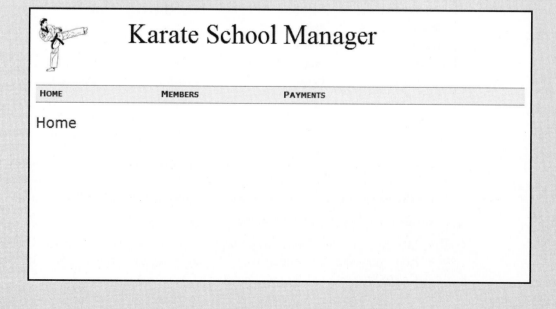

Figure 10-51 Members page

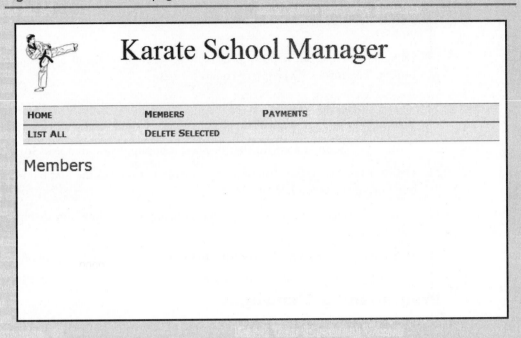

Figure 10-52 Gridview listing of all members

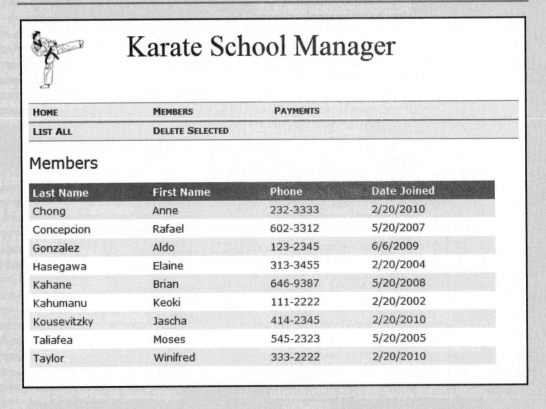

On the Payments page, you only need to implement the *List All* menu item.

Create the following content pages:

- Members—On this content page, display a menu containing: *List All* and *Delete Selected*.
- Payments—On this content page, display a menu containing: *List All*, *Date Range*, *Delete Selected*, and *By One Member*.

Figure 10-53 Payments page

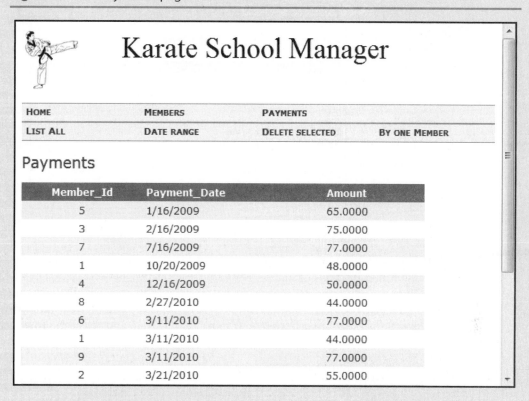

The following are suggested CSS style classes for the main menu. The second style becomes active when the user hovers the mouse over the menu.

```
.MainMenu
{
  background-color:#ebf5fc;
  padding-top:3px;
  padding-bottom:5px;
  border-bottom:solid 1px #00a8ec;
  border-top:solid 1px #00a8ec;
  font-size:.8em;
  font-weight:bold;
  font-variant:small-caps;
}
.MainMenu a:hover
{
  color:#ebf5fc;
  color:White;
  background-color:Navy;
}
```

2. **Karate Payments Grid**

   Write an ASP.NET application that displays the first name, last name, date, and payment amounts made by members in the Karate database. Permit the user to display payments, but not modify the data. Sort the rows by last name. Center the payment dates in short date format. For each column except the payment date, left-justify the heading by setting the HeaderStyle.HorizontalAlign property to Left. Put a blue, one-pixel-wide border around the grid. Use the grid's HeaderStyle property to give the headings white text on a dark blue background. A sample is shown in Figure 10-54.

Figure 10-54 Grid showing member names, dates, and payments

Payments by Karate Students

First_Name	Last_Name	Payment_Date	Amount
Anne	Chong	11/20/2010	$80.00
Rafael	Concepcion	2/27/2010	$44.00
Aldo	Gonzalez	1/16/2009	$65.00
Elaine	Hasegawa	11/16/2010	$75.00
Brian	Kahane	12/16/2009	$50.00
Keoki	Kahumanu	10/20/2009	$48.00
Jascha	Kousevitzky	2/16/2009	$75.00
Moses	Taliafea	3/11/2010	$77.00
Winifred	Taylor	3/11/2010	$77.00

3. **Karate Schedule Details**

The Schedule table in the Karate database contains the following columns: ID, Day, Time, and Instructor_Id. The Day value is an integer between 0 and 6, where 0 indicates Monday and 6 indicates Sunday. Display the table in a DetailsView control, as shown in Figure 10-55. Permit the user to add, remove, and update table rows. Include a TextBox control that lets the user enter an ID value and select the row to be displayed.

Figure 10-55 Showing Karate schedule details

Karate Schedule Details

Enter Schedule ID: 4 [Go]

ID	4
Day	1
Time	5:00 PM
Instructor_Id	2
Edit Delete New	

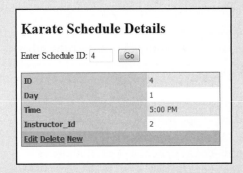

4. **Campus GridButtons Application**

Use the Campus GridButtons application you wrote for Tutorial 10-2 as a starting point for this programming challenge. When the user clicks the *Edit* button on a grid row, as shown in Figure 10-56, text boxes automatically appear in the row. When the user clicks

Figure 10-56 The user has entered an invalid number of credits

Courses Table, Campus Database

	ID	Year/Sem	Course Num	Credits
Update Cancel	11111	2010-01	MTH1011	3
Edit Delete	12121	2010-01	COP3530	3
Edit Delete	22222	2010-01	ENC1101	3
Edit Delete	22333	2010-01	COP2210	4
Edit Delete	32323	2010-01	COP3337	3
Edit Delete	33333	2010-01	COP4338	3

the *Update* button, a *RowUpdating* event is fired. Inside the event handler, you must implement error-checking code that checks the value entered in the Credits column. If the user enters a value less than 1 or greater than 5, display an error message below the grid, and cancel the update operation. The text boxes remain open. In the grid's RowUpdating event handler, the expression *e.NewValues.Item ("credits")* returns the contents of the TextBox containing the credits. If you find it to be out of range when you check the value, display an error message and set e.Cancel to *True*.

5. **Bug-Tracking Application**

   Using what you have learned about databases, ASP.NET controls, CSS styles, and master-detail pages, create an application that helps a development team track software bugs. Use the SQL Server database file *BugTrack.mdf*, located in the chapter examples folder. Study the database structure and match the data in the tables to the screen images shown in this description.

   When the application runs, as shown in Figure 10-57, the master page displays the bar along the top and the menu on the left. The content area with the program title is supplied by a page named *About.aspx*. It is the same page displayed when the user clicks the *About* menu item on the left. The content area on the bottom is a GridView control located directly in the master page.

Figure 10-57 Running the BugTrackAW application

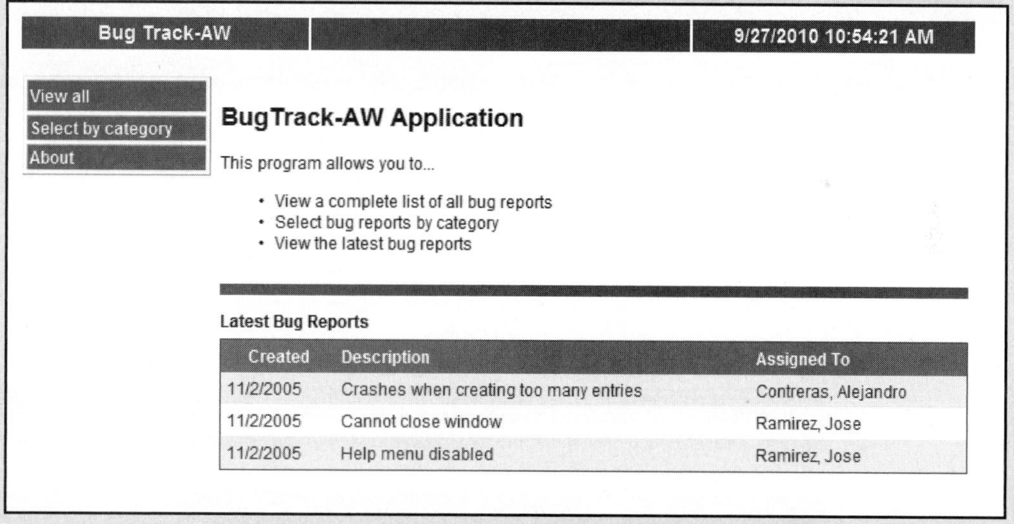

Figure 10-58 shows the master page in Design view. The ContentPlaceHolder at the bottom of the page contains a GridView control that displays default content. In other words, when the user navigates to the content pages, the contents of the lower ContentPlaceHolder (*Latest Bug Reports*) stay the same.

When the user selects *View all* from the menu, the upper pane displays a list of all bug reports, as shown in Figure 10-59. When the user chooses *Select by category* from the menu, the upper content pane displays a list of categories, as shown in Figure 10-60. When the user selects a category and clicks the *Go* button, the upper grid displays a list of matching bug reports.

6. **Home Repair Services—Adding Appointments (Extra Challenging)**

   In Section 5.4 of Chapter 5, you learned how to create a Windows Forms application named *Home Repair Services*. In this (extra challenging) programming challenge, you

Figure 10-58 Bug TrackAW master page, in Design view

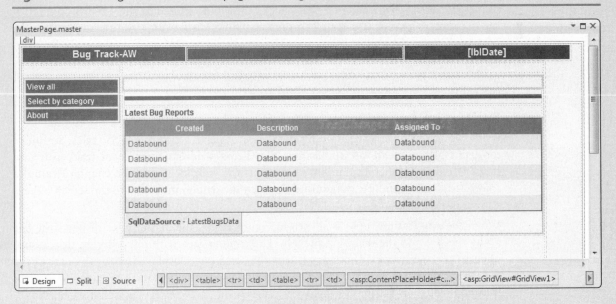

Figure 10-59 Executing the *View all* command (ViewAllBugs.aspx)

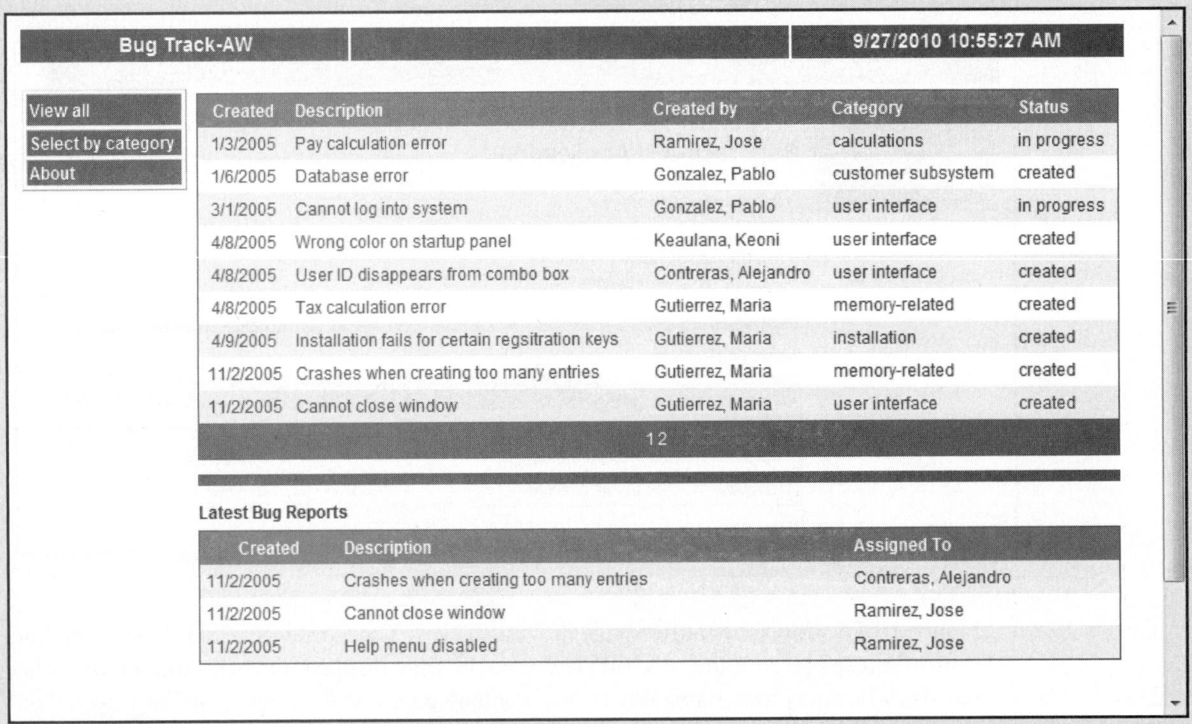

will convert that program to a Web application and then implement the *New Appointment* window, as shown in Figure 10-61.

The data-tier and middle-tier classes should be put into a component (class library) named *RepairServicesLib*. This is a more advanced assignment, so you may have to consult with your classroom instructor on the details of getting the DataSet set up in your project. Here are the general steps, in the order that we used when creating the solution:

1. Using Windows Explorer, copy the following files to your component: Customers.vb, Appointments.vb, RepairTypes.vb, and RepairServices.mdf. Refresh the

Figure 10-60 Executing the *Select by category* command

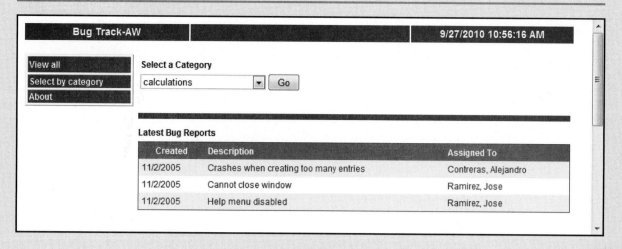

Figure 10-61 Adding a new repair appointment

New Repair Appointment

Date
5/20/2011

Time
9:30 AM

Customer
Johnson, David

Repair type   Carpentry   ☐Must be licensed

Description (0-100 chars)
Add hand rails to shower.

Save

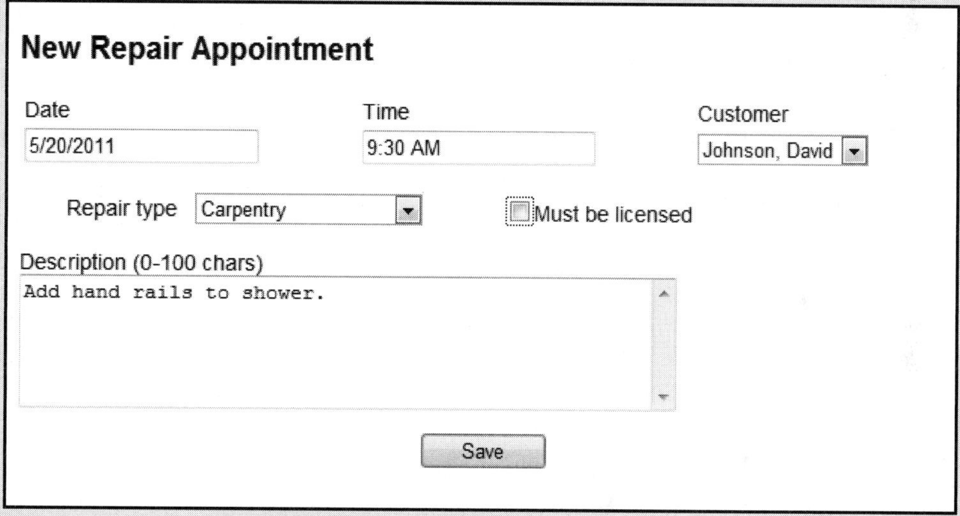

component's project name inside Visual Studio. (*Note:* This copy of the database is needed only while creating the DataSet definitions.)

2. Right-click the project name and add a DataSet component to the project. Drag the Appointments, RepairTypes, and Customers tables from the ServerExplorer window onto the surface of the editor window for *RepairServicesDataSet.xsd*.

3. Within the same Visual Studio solution, create a separate Web site that references the RepairServicesLib component.

4. Create an App_Data folder in your Web site, and copy the *RepairServices.mdf* file into that folder. This is the database file that will be updated when your application executes.

5. Right-click the Web site name in Server Explorer, select *Add Reference*, and select *RepairServicesLib*.

Other Details

Fill the dropdown list controls from the Page_Load event handler when the IsPostBack property equals *False*. Use a TextBox for the appointment date. Use a Label control to display a message that tells the user whether adding the Appointment was successful.

11 Web Services and Windows Presentation Foundation

TOPICS

This chapter will help you understand the basic technologies behind Web services and the types of applications that use them. You will learn how to create and consume Web services. Next, the chapter introduces Microsoft's exciting new Windows Presentation Foundation (WPF). WPF programs can be run from both the desktop and the Web. We show how to use ClickOnce technology, which greatly simplifies application deployment and installation.

11.1 Introducing XML Web Services

XML Web Services is a valuable technology that permits computers to share data and methods across networks, particularly across the Internet. Applications can be built that collect data and perform useful operations from a wide variety of sources. Web services are strongly supported by the .NET Framework.

In general, a **Web service** is a component that is compiled and stored on a Web site. It has no visual interface, but it exposes methods and properties that may be accessed by other programs on a network. The *XML* part of the name says that the data transferred over the network is in Extended Markup Language (XML) format.

When an application wants to use a Web service, it creates a local object that acts as a representative, or proxy, for the Web service. It then uses the object to call Web service methods. We say that the application *consumes* the Web service. Web services can be consumed by Windows applications and Web applications. Web services make it convenient for programs to acquire and distribute data across the Internet.

Web Service Technology

Some Web sites let users compare prices of consumer items sold by different online stores. The user searches for an item by category, views a list of matching items, and selects an item for price comparisons. Behind the scenes, the Web application consumes Web services provided by each online store that return the item's price, shipping information, and so on. The Web application builds a Web page from all this information that lets the end user view store names and prices.

Here are a few ways Web services are useful:

- Credit card transactions are processed in the background.
- Manufacturers and distributors provide prices and inventory availability on demand.
- Stores provide product and pricing information. Amazon.com, for example, has a Web service that lets you search for books by keyword and retrieve detailed information about individual titles.
- Government agencies provide weather and satellite information.
- Real-time stock market data is sent to subscribers.
- Sports events results are obtained on demand.
- Companies embed functions in their desktop software that permit users to order products from other companies.

Initially, background communication on the Web was accomplished by custom-designed communication programs. Because of a lack of standardization, data produced by one program was not compatible with other software. Web services make it possible for Web sites to standardize the interactions between programs on the Web. Web services incorporate the following enabling technologies and specifications:

- **eXtensible Markup Language (XML)**—A text markup language for the exchange of structured documents and data across the Internet. Web services use XML to store and transmit objects and other data.
- **Simple Object Access Protocol (SOAP)**—An industry-standard protocol for handling requests and responses. It includes class names, method names, and parameters. SOAP, like XML, is represented as plain text and can pass through Internet firewalls. A **firewall** is a software barrier set up by a person or organization to limit or filter communications between their internal network and the Internet.
- **Web Services Description Language (WSDL)**—Specifies the formatting of calls to Web service methods. In ASP.NET, a WSDL file is created in the Web References folder of a program that consumes (calls) the Web service. For each method exposed by the Web service, the WSDL file shows the method name, parameter list, and return type.
- **Universal Description, Discovery, and Integration (UDDI)**—A directory service that makes information about Web services public. You can use it to search for Web services on a network or on the Internet.

Windows Communication Foundation (WCF)

Microsoft created **Windows Communication Foundation (WCF)** as a unified programming model and runtime support for building Web services applications. Using the .NET framework, WCF lets you build secure, reliable Web services. It integrates very nicely into other Microsoft technologies, such as Enterprise Services and System.Messaging. We say that a **WCF service** is a Web service that was built using Windows Communication Foundation.

Attribute Classes

The .NET framework uses **attribute classes** to identify important elements of a WCF service. The most important classes are:

- ServiceContractAttribute

- OperationContractAttribute
- DataContractAttribute
- DataMemberAttribute

We will discuss details about these classes in a moment. But what you need to know is that attribute classes associate predefined system information or custom information with a target element. Examples of such elements are classes, fields, methods, interfaces, and events. In Visual Basic, attributes are special markers inserted in your source code just before the elements they affect. You may recall from Chapter 6, for example, that each Unit test method was preceded by the *<TestMethod()>* attribute. Attributes are often referred to as *metadata*.

In the following discussions, we will refer to the ServiceContractAttribute class as simply a *service contract*. The same is true for the other attribute classes.

Service Contract

In .NET terms, a **service contract** is an interface that defines which methods can be called from a specific WCF service. The service contract is defined as a Visual Basic interface. You may recall from Chapter 3 that an interface defines a set of methods and properties that can be implemented by other classes. The classes that implement the interface are guaranteed to contain these methods and properties. At that time, you learned how to create a CompareTo method, which was part of the IComparable interface. The <ServiceContract()> attribute must be inserted just before the declaration of an interface.

```
<ServiceContract()>
Public Interface IService
```

The name *IService* can be any name you select and that defines your WCF service. For example, you could call it *IBookService* if the service returns information from a bookstore.

Operation Contract

Within an Interface that has been identified as a ServiceContract, you create methods and properties named operation contracts. An **operation contract** is a method that exists within a service contract. It can also be called a *WCF service method*.

The following shows a sample operation contract in which the exported method named Get-Data receives a String input parameter and returns a Book object. The <OperationContract()> attribute must appear just before the function declaration.

```
<OperationContract()>
Function GetData(ByVal ID As String) As Book
```

Data Contract

A **data contract** is a class type that will be used by the WCF service. The type is implicitly *serializable*, meaning that it can be converted to and from a stream of bytes. This is an essential quality for all data types used by WCF services because only by serializing an object can you pass it across a network. The *<DataContract()> attribute* must appear just before the class declaration. The class must be declared Public. Following is an example of a data contract:

```
<DataContract()>
Public Class Book
  <DataMember()>
  Public Property ISBN() As String
  <DataMember()>
  Public Property Title() As String
  <DataMember()>
  Public Property Price() As Double
End Class
```

By creating this data contract, we show that we intend to pass Book objects between clients and the WCF service. Notice that each property in this class contains a <DataMember()> attribute.

Data Member

In the current context, a **data member** is a member of a data contract. Within a data contract, the <DataMember()> attribute identifies fields, properties, and events that hold values you want to serialize. Any member not having this attribute will be invisible to client applications that call the WCF service.

Creating a WCF Service in Visual Studio

You create a WCF service in Visual Studio by selecting *File*, and then *New Web Site* from the File menu. Select *WCF Service* from the list of templates, as shown in Figure 11-1.

Figure 11-1 Creating a WCF Service Web site

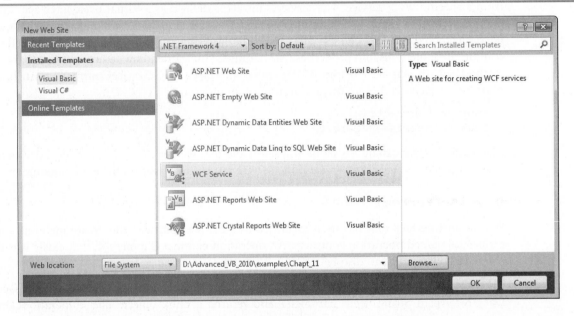

The following files are created automatically:

- Service host file (Service.svc)
- Service contract file (IService.vb)
- Service implementation file (Service.vb), also known as a *CodeBehind file*
- Web configuration file (Web.config)

The **service host file** contains just one line, the ServiceHost directive, written as follows in XHTML:

```
<%@ ServiceHost
   Language="VB"
   Debug="true"
   Service="Service"
   CodeBehind="~/App_Code/Service.vb" %>
```

The *Language* property identifies the programming language used in the service implementation (CodeBehind) file. The *Debug* property enables or disables debugging. The *Service* property names the Visual Basic class that implements the WCF service (named Service in this example). Finally, the *CodeBehind* property contains the path of the service implementation file.

The **service contract file** (IService.vb) defines an interface that is passed to all client programs so they know what they can use from the Web service.

A **service implementation file** contains the Visual Basic code that implements all methods defined in the interface for the WCF service.

A **Web configuration file** looks very much like a configuration file for a normal ASP.NET Web site. It contains a section named *<system.serviceModel>,* however, that defines attributes relating only to WCF services.

Consuming a Web Service

If you imagine a Web service to be a kind of server of information and services, then **consuming a Web service** means to act as its client. A Web service consumer can be a Windows Forms application, a Web site, a class library, or even another Web service.

Suppose we want our client to be an ASP.NET Web site. After creating the site, we must add a Web reference to the Web service. A **Web reference** is information added to an application's web.config file that permits a Web application to locate a Web service. Here is an example:

```
<add key="localhost.BookService"
   value="http://localhost:61796/Book Service/BookService.svc"/>
```

Visual Studio lets you add four types of Web references:

- A Web service within the same Visual Studio solution container.
- A Web service running on the same computer, using the Internet Information Services (IIS) Web server.
- A Web service running on the local network (using a UDDI server).
- A Web service running on the Internet.

To add a reference to an existing Web service, select the client project's name in the Solution Explorer window and select *Add Web Reference* from the context menu.

Figure 11-2 shows the list of choices within the *Add Web Reference* dialog window. Of these four types, the first is easiest to use, so you should create your client application(s) within the same solution container as the WCF service. When you click the *Web services in this solution* hyperlink, you will see a list of services, as in Figure 11-3. Select one of the services, causing the window in Figure 11-4 to appear. Notice on the right side that the default Web reference name is *localhost.* You use this identifier as a namespace when writing code that refers to Web service classes and methods.

Figure 11-2 Adding a Web Reference to a client application

Start Browsing for Web Services

Use this page as a starting point to find Web services. You can click the links below, or type a known URL into the address bar.

Browse to:

- **Web services in this solution**

- **Web services on the local machine**

- **Browse UDDI Servers on the local network**
  Query your local network for UDDI servers.

Figure 11-3 About to select a Web service

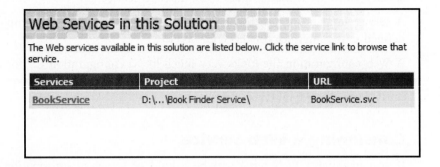

Figure 11-4 After selecting a Web service

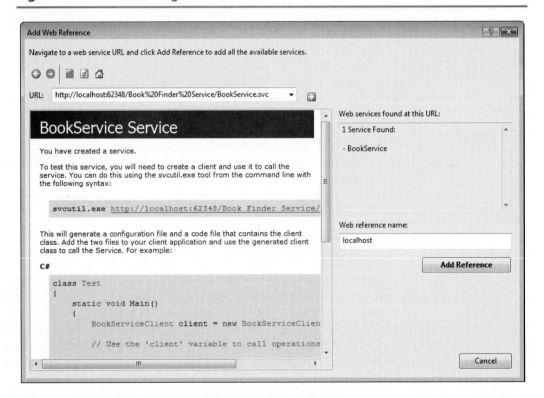

Writing Code That Calls Web Service Methods

Once you have added a Web Reference to your client Web site, you can open the CodeBehind window of a Web form in your site and add an *Imports* statement for the Web reference name (localhost):

```
Imports localhost
```

Then you must create an instance of the WCF service:

```
Dim client As New localhost.BookService
```

Then you can call a service method. The following statement, for example, calls GetBookList, which returns a list of Book objects.

```
Dim bookList As List(Of Book)
bookList = client.GetBookList()
```

We assume that the Book class was defined inside the WCF service interface, with the <Data-Contract()> attribute class. Because the WCF service has already defined the Book class, we do not need to redefine it in the client Web application. You will create your own Web service in Tutorial 11-1.

 ## Checkpoint

1. How does a Web service transmit objects across a network?

2. What does WSDL stand for?

3. What function does UDDI provide?

4. What is the name of Microsoft's implementation of Web services?

5. When a Web service declares a class, which attributes are required for the class to be serializable?

6. What purpose do *attribute classes* serve in WCF services?

 ## BookService Web Service

The easiest way to learn about Web services is to create one of your own. Aside from the few attribute classes explained in Section 11.1, the implementation of a Web service is just like programming a Web site. First, we will show you how to create a simple Web service that lets the user display a list of books and search for books by ISBN number. Then you will create a Web site that consumes your Web service. Finally, you will create a Windows Forms application that consumes the same Web service.

 ### Tutorial 11-1:
Creating the *BookService* Web Service

In this tutorial, you will create a WCF Service Web site named *BookService*. In its implementation, the service contains a list of books, with titles, ISBN numbers, and prices. The service will let callers get the complete book list or an individual book. Figure 11-5 shows a simple client application that consumes the ***BookService Web service***. The ListBox control contains the entire list of books. The Label just above the ListBox contains the title and price of the book that was returned when the user searched for ISBN 1000555.

Figure 11-5 Consuming the *BookService* Web service

Tutorial Steps

Step 1: From the *File* menu, select *New*, and then select *Project*. Under *Other Project Types* in the left-hand pane, select *Visual Studio Solutions*. Choose the *Blank Solution* template and name it *BookService Example*.

Step 2: Next, you will add a WCF Service Web site named *BookService* to the solution. To do that, right-click on the solution name in the Solution Explorer window, select *Add*, select *New Web Site*, and select *WCF Service* from the list of templates.

Step 3: Rename the service host file (Service.svc) to *BookService.svc*. Change its contents to the following:

```
<%@ ServiceHost
   Language="VB"
   Debug="true"
   Service="BookService"
   CodeBehind="~/App_Code/BookService.vb" %>
```

Step 4: Rename the service contract file (IService.vb) to *IBookService.vb*. Open the file and replace the ServiceContract definition with the following code:

```
<ServiceContract()>
Public Interface IBookService
   <OperationContract()>
   Function GetBookList() As List(Of Book)

   <OperationContract()>
   Function FindBook(ByVal ISBN As String) As Book
End Interface
```

The IBookService interface contains two methods: *GetBookList* returns a List of Book objects. *FindBook* searches for a book with a matching ISBN number and either returns the book or it returns null (*Nothing*).

Step 5: In the same file, replace the existing DataContract definition with the following code that defines the *Book* class:

```
<DataContract()>
Public Class Book
   <DataMember()>
   Public Property ISBN() As String
   <DataMember()>
   Public Property Title() As String
   <DataMember()>
   Public Property Price() As Double
End Class
```

Step 6: Rename the service implementation file (*Service.vb*) to *BookService.vb*. Open the file and replace its code with the following lines. Notice that the class has been renamed as *BookService*.

```
1:  Public Class BookService
2:     Implements IBookService
3:
4:     Private bookList As New Dictionary(Of String, Book)
5:
6:     Public Sub New()
7:        bookList.Add("1000021", New Book With {.ISBN =
           "1000021",
8:           .Title = "Starting out with C++", .Price = 92.0})
```

```
 9:        bookList.Add("1000034", New Book With {.ISBN =
           "1000034",
10:          .Title = "Starting out With Visual Basic", .Price
             = 95.0})
11:        bookList.Add("1000555", New Book With {.ISBN =
           "1000555",
12:          .Title = "Starting out With Java", .Price = 85.0})
13:        bookList.Add("1000786", New Book With {.ISBN =
           "1000786",
14:          .Title = "Assembly Language", .Price = 97.0})
15:        bookList.Add("1001029", New Book With {.ISBN =
           "1001029",
16:          .Title = "Starting out With C#", .Price = 89.5})
17:    End Sub
18:
19:    Public Function GetBookList() As List(Of Book) _
20:        Implements IBookService.GetBookList
21:
22:        Return bookList.Values.ToList()
23:    End Function
24:
25:    Public Function FindBook(ByVal ISBN As String) As Book _
26:        Implements IBookService.FindBook
27:      If bookList.ContainsKey(ISBN) Then
28:        Return bookList(ISBN)
29:      Else
30:        Return Nothing
31:      End If
32:    End Function
33: End Class
```

Line 4 defines a Dictionary object that will contain all the books. Each book is indexed by a string containing its ISBN number. Lines 6–17 use the class constructor to initialize and insert several books into the list. The GetBook-List method on line 19 returns the Values property of the dictionary (as a list). The FindBook method on line 25 searches for a book that matches the given ISBN number and returns a book if one is found.

Step 7:   View the BookService.svc file in a browser. You will see the message shown in Figure 11-6, which explains that you must create a client application to test the service.

Figure 11-6 Viewing the BookService.svc file in a browser

BookService Service

You have created a service.

To test this service, you will need to create a client and use it to call the service. You can do this using the svcutil.exe tool from the command line with the following syntax:

```
svcutil.exe http://localhost:61796/Book Service/BookService.svc?wsdl
```

This will generate a configuration file and a code file that contains the client class. Add the two files to your client application and use the generated client class to call the Service. For example:

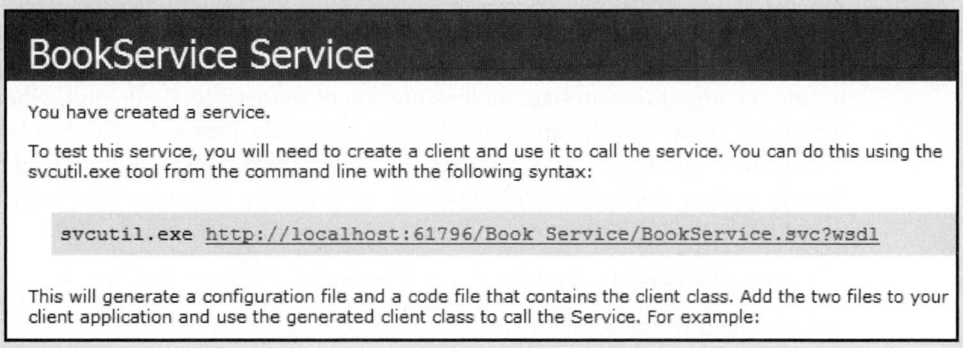

Step 8: Click on the hyperlink. You should see a large amount of XML code that defines the Web service. Specifically, this XML code is written in *Web Services Description Language (WSDL)*. Look at the excerpt from this file shown in Figure 11-7. Notice how the GetBookList method has been encoded as two values: (1) IBookService_GetBookList_InputMessage, which is sent from the client to the Web service, and (2) IBookService_GetBookList_OutputMessage, which represents the message sent back from the Web service to the client.

Figure 11-7 Excerpt from BookService.svc file

```
– <wsdl:message name="IBookService_GetBookList_InputMessage">
    <wsdl:part name="parameters" element="tns:GetBookList" />
  </wsdl:message>
– <wsdl:message name="IBookService_GetBookList_OutputMessage">
    <wsdl:part name="parameters" element="tns:GetBookListResponse" />
  </wsdl:message>
– <wsdl:message name="IBookService_FindBook_InputMessage">
    <wsdl:part name="parameters" element="tns:FindBook" />
  </wsdl:message>
– <wsdl:message name="IBookService_FindBook_OutputMessage">
    <wsdl:part name="parameters" element="tns:FindBookResponse" />
  </wsdl:message>
```

Summary

An explanation of WSDL is beyond the scope of this book, but you can read about it from many sources on the Web. We encourage you to read the article *Understanding WSDL,* which is available at http://msdn.microsoft.com.

Creating a simple Web service is surprisingly easy, given the excellent tools available in Visual Studio. In Tutorial 11-2, you will create a client Web site that consumes Book-Service.

TIP: If you modify a WCF service that is referenced by a client application, the client must refresh the Web reference to see the modifications. To do that, select the Web reference in the client's Solution Explorer window and select *Update Web/Service References.*

Displaying Web Service Exception Information

Like other methods, Web service methods can throw exceptions. For security reasons, they don't automatically convey details about of the thrown exception. If they did, a dishonest programmer could call the service method in a way that would generate an exception, just to find out about the internal implementation of the service. By default, when a Web method throws an exception, the output in the client program looks like Figure 11-8, assuming that a Web client application is consuming the Web service. The instructions on the page explain how to modify the *web.config* file in the Web service project if you want to display more information. All you have to do is find the following line:

```
<serviceDebug includeExceptionDetailInFaults="false"/>
```

and change it to the following:

```
<serviceDebug includeExceptionDetailInFaults="true"/>
```

Figure 11-8 Unhandled exception when the book ISBN is not found and no debugging information is generated by the Web service

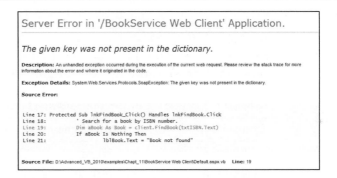

Then, if you enable debugging in the Web client application, an uncaught exception looks like Figure 11-9. In this example, the message says: *The given key was not present in the dictionary*, and you can see the location in the client source code where the FindBook method was called.

In any event, when you write code that consumes a Web service method, remember to use Try Catch statements to catch possible exceptions.

Figure 11-9 Unhandled exception when the ISBN is not found, with debugging enabled

---

Tutorial 11-2:
Consuming *BookService* from a Web application

In this tutorial, you will create a simple Web site that consumes the BookService Web service. The user interface for this Web site was shown previously in Figure 11-5.

Tutorial Steps

Step 1: Using the same Visual Studio Solution that contains the BookService Web service, add a new empty ASP.NET Web site named *BookService Web Client*.

Step 2: Right-click the Web site name in the Solution Explorer window and select *Add Web Reference*. In the window that appears, click on *Web services in this solution*. Select *BookService*, and click the *Add Reference* button to close the window.

Notice that a new folder named *App_WebReferences* was added to your site. Another folder within it is named *localhost* and it includes several files:

- BookService.disco—Here, you can find the Web path to the BookService.svc, known as the service host file.

- BookService.wsdl—A file written in Web Services Discovery Language (WSDL), which matches the file you examined at the end of Tutorial 11-1.
- BookService.xsd—Called a *schema definition file*, which defines the Web service methods and return values. It can be displayed in the *XML Schema Explorer* window, as shown in Figure 11-10. (To display this window, double-click the filename, which opens a design window. In that window, click the hyperlink phrase *XML Schema Explorer*.)

Figure 11-10 BookService.xsd file, displayed in the XML Schema Explorer

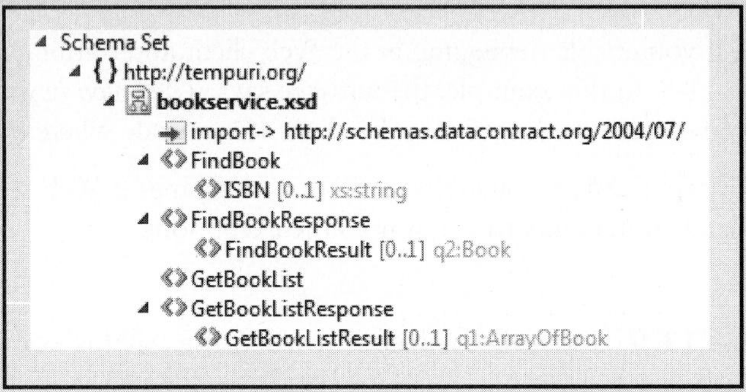

- BookService0.xsd and BookService1.xsd—Additional schema definitions for the *Book* and *ArrayOfBook* serializable types.

Step 3: Add a Web form named Default.aspx to the Web site and insert the controls shown in Table 11-1. (Refer back to Figure 11-5.)

Table 11-1 Controls in the BookService Client application page

Control Type	Control Name	Property Values
LinkButton	lnkGetList	Text: *Get complete book list*
LinkButton	lnkFindBook	Text: *Find book by ISBN:*
TextBox	txtISBN	
Label	lblBook	
ListBox	lstBooks	

Step 4: Add the following Imports statement to the top of the form's CodeBehind file. This is necessary to reference the Web service interface.

```
Imports localhost
```

Step 5: Add the following code to the form's class. First, a BookService object named client is declared.

```
 1:  Private client As New localhost.BookService
 2:
 3:  Protected Sub lnkGetList_Click() Handles lnkGetList.Click
 4:     With lstBooks
 5:        .Items.Clear()
 6:        For Each bk As Book In client.GetBookList
 7:           lstBooks.Items.Add(bk.Title)
 8:        Next
 9:     End With
10:  End Sub
```

Line 1 declares a BookService object named *client*. Line 3 declares a Click handler for a LinkButton control. Line 6 iterates through the list of books returned by the Web service's *GetBookList* method. The method returns a List(Of Book) object. Line 7 adds each book title to the ListBox named *lstBooks*.

Step 6: Add the following code to the class:

```
 1: Protected Sub lnkFindBook_Click() Handles lnkFindBook.Click
 2:    ' Search for a book by ISBN number.
 3:    Dim aBook As Book = client.FindBook(txtISBN.Text)
 4:    If aBook Is Nothing Then
 5:       lblBook.Text = "Book not found"
 6:    Else
 7:       lblBook.Text =
 8:       String.Format("Book found: {0}, on sale for " _
 9:          & "{1:c}", aBook.Title, aBook.Price)
10:    End If
11: End Sub
```

Line 1 declares a Click handler for the other LinkButton, which searches for a book. Line 4 calls the Web service's *FindBook* method, passing the ISBN number entered by the user into the text box. Line 4 checks for a return value of *Nothing*, in case the ISBN number was not found. If the book was found, line 8 builds a string containing the book's title and price. Note that HTML tags are embedded inside the string so the fields can be displayed in a bold font.

Step 7: Save the form and view in a Web browser. Experiment with searching for the following ISBN numbers: 1000021, 1000034, 1000555, 1000786, and 1001029.

Summary

In general, creating and consuming Web services is not overly different from ordinary Web application programming. The main issues you must deal with are practical—for example, the client might not be able to connect to the service in a timely manner. Also, the Web service may require some authentication of the client in the form of a name and password.

In Tutorial 11-3, you will consume the same BookService Web service from a Windows Forms application.

Tutorial 11-3:
Consuming *BookService* from a Windows Forms application

In this tutorial, you will create a simple Windows Forms application site that consumes the BookService Web service. The running application appears in Figure 11-11. The user can click a link to get the complete book list, which appears in the list box. Or, they can enter an ISBN number and click another link to find a matching book, which appears in a Label control just above the list box.

Figure 11-11 Running the BookService WinForms client

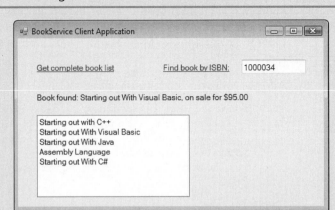

Tutorial Steps

Step 1: Open the Solution container that you used when creating the BookService Web service. Add a new Windows Forms project to the solution and name it *BookService WinForms Client*.

Step 2: Using Figure 11-11 as a guide, add the controls listed in Table 11-2 to the form.

Table 11-2 User interface controls

Control Type	Name	Property Settings
Form	(default)	Text: *BookService Client Application* FormBorderStyle: *FixedSingle*
TextBox	TxtISBN	
LinkLabel	lnkGetList	Text: *Get complete book list*
LinkLabel	lnkFindBook	Text: *Find book by ISBN:*
ListBox	lstBooks	
Label	lblBook	

Step 3: Right-click the project name in Solution Explorer and select *Add Service Reference*. In the window that appears, click the *Discover* button. Expand the entry entitled *BookService/BookService.svc*. A sample is shown in Figure 11-12. Click on *IBookService* to display its operations (FindBook and GetBookList). Rename the Namespace entry at the bottom to *LocalServices*. Click the *OK* button to save the reference.

 TIP: There is nothing special about the name *LocalServices*. We chose it for the namespace because the Web service we're calling is located on your local computer.

Figure 11-13 shows that the *LocalServices* namespace has been added to the *Service References* section of the Solution Explorer window.

Figure 11-12 Adding a Service Reference

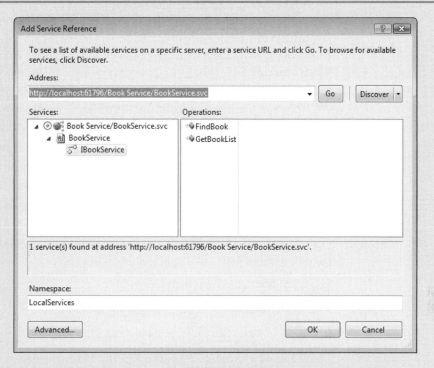

Figure 11-13 Service References entry in Solution Explorer

Step 4: Double-click *BookService_WinForms_Client.LocalServices* in the Solution Explorer window. This will display the namespace in the Object Explorer window, as shown in Figure 11-14.

Figure 11-14 Displaying the LocalServices namespace in Object Explorer

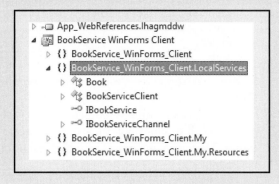

Notice that the LocalServices namespace contains two classes, BookService-Client and Book. The *Book* class was imported directly from the Web service definition. The *BookServiceClient* class was created by Visual Studio when you added the service reference in Step 3 of this tutorial. Your application communicates directly with this class, which is often called a *client proxy*. When you call its methods, the proxy relays the calls to the Web service. If you would like to see the source code for this class, select the *Show All Files* toolbar button at the top of the Solution Explorer window, and then open the file named *Reference.vb*, which is displayed when you expand the entry named *Reference.svcmap*.

Step 5: Click on *BookServiceClient* in the Object Browser window.

Notice that BookServiceClient contains the FindBook and GetBookList methods. These methods match the name and parameter lists of the BookList Web service exactly.

Step 6: Open the startup form's code window and add the following Imports statement, which imports the *LocalServices* namespace:

```
Imports BookService_WinForms_Client.LocalServices
```

Step 7: Add the following declaration to the top of the class:

```
Private client As New BookServiceClient
```

The BookServiceClient class contains the methods you will be calling when you invoke the Web services.

Step 8: Add the following code to the class:

```
Protected Sub lnkGetList_Click() Handles lnkGetList.Click
   With lstBooks
      .Items.Clear()
      For Each bk As Book In client.GetBookList
         lstBooks.Items.Add(bk.Title)
      Next
   End With
End Sub
```

Step 9: Add the following Click method for the link button that searches for books:

```
Protected Sub lnkFindBook_Click() Handles lnkFindBook.Click
   ' Search for a book by ISBN number.
   Try
      Dim aBook As Book = client.FindBook(txtISBN.Text)
      lblBook.Text =
         String.Format("Book found: {0}, on sale for " _
         & "{1:c}", aBook.Title, aBook.Price)
   Catch ex As Exception
      lblBook.Text = "Book not found"
   End Try
End Sub
```

Notice that the code above catches exceptions. In the Web client version (Tutorial 11-2), we were able to check for a return value of *Nothing* when calling FindBook. In a Windows Forms application, which we have written here, the call to FindBook throws an exception when the ISBN number is not found. Therefore, we must catch the exception and display a *Book not found* message.

> **Step 10:** Save and run the application. Experiment with searching for the following ISBN numbers: 1000021, 1000034, 1000555, 1000786, and 1001029.
>
> **Step 11:** Enter an ISBN number that cannot be found. The application should say *Book not found*.

Services That Return Database Data

One of the most useful tasks a Web service can perform is to return database data. Suppose you want to populate a DataGridView control in a client application, using data from a Web service. Getting service contracts in .NET to return DataTable and DataSet objects can be tricky. But you can easily return a strongly typed collection such as List(Of *Type*). First, you will need to define a DataContract for the type of object you want to insert in the list and then copy the rows from a DataTable into the list. To illustrate this concept, let us adapt an example from the *Home Repair Services* application in Chapter 5. The following Data-Contract defines a class named *Appointment*. It contains a constructor and a set of public properties. Each property is labeled with the DataMember attribute.

```
<DataContract()>
Public Class Appointment

   Public Sub New(ByVal apptIdv As Short, ByVal typeIdv As Short,
      ByVal Descriptionv As String,ByVal Licensedv As Boolean,
      ByVal CustIdv As Short, ByVal Scheduledv As DateTime)
      ApptId = apptIdv
      TypeId = typeIdv
      Description = Descriptionv
      Licensed = Licensedv
      CustId = CustIdv
      Scheduled = Scheduledv
   End Sub

   <DataMember()>
   Public Property ApptId As Short
   <DataMember()>
   Public Property TypeId As Short
   <DataMember()>
   Public Property Description As String
   <DataMember()>
   Public Property Licensed As Boolean
   <DataMember()>
   Public Property CustId As Short
   <DataMember()>
   Public Property Scheduled As DateTime
End Class
```

The DataContract is usually located in the same file as the ServiceContract. A typical filename would be *IRepairService.vb*.

Next, our Web service contract can include a method named *AllAppointments*, which returns a strongly typed List of Appointment objects. This is how we can implement the method in the service implementation file:

```
1:  Public Function AllAppointments() As List(Of Appointment) _
2:     Implements IRepairService.AllAppointments
3:
4:     Dim appts As New Appointments
5:     Dim table As RepairServicesDataSet.AppointmentsDataTable
6:        = appts.AllAppointments
```

```
 7:    Dim aList As New List(Of Appointment)
 8:    For Each row As RepairServicesDataSet.AppointmentsRow In table
 9:       aList.Add(New Appointment(row.ApptId, row.TypeId,
10:         row.Description, row.Licensed, row.CustId, row.Scheduled))
11:    Next
12:    Return aList
13: End Function
```

Line 4 creates an instance of a middle-tier class named Appointments, which is not shown here. Line 5 calls AllAppointments on that object, which returns a DataTable. Line 7 creates a List object; line 8 iterates through the DataTable. Line 9 creates a new Appointment object, using data from the current table row, and adds it to the List object (named aList). Finally, Line 12 returns the List object. You will have a chance to implement this application in Programming Challenge #3 at the end of this chapter. After compiling the Web service, you can build a Web or desktop application that consumes the service.

Connecting an ObjectDataSource to a Web Service

The ObjectDataSource control in a Web application connects easily to Web services. When you add this control to the form, select *Configure Data Source* from its tasks window, then select localhost.*ServiceName*, where *ServiceName* is the name of the Web service. An example is shown in Figure 11-15, using the RepairService Web service.

Figure 11-15 Connecting a Web service to an ObjectDataSource control

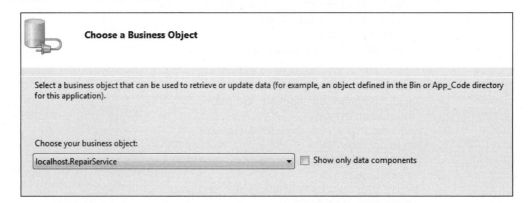

In the next panel, select the Web service method that you want to use for the *Select* operation of the data source, as shown in Figure 11-16. If you bind a GridView control to the ObjectDataSource, you will notice that extra columns have been created. When you edit the grid's columns collection as shown in Figure 11-17, delete the extra columns ending with the suffix *Specified*.

As an alternative, you can always fill a GridView control using dynamic binding by calling the Web service method and assigning its return value to the grid's DataSource property. Here is an example:

```
Dim service As New localhost.RepairService
gvwAppointments.DataSource = services.AllAppointments()
gvwAppointments.DataBind()
```

This approach prevents you from modifying the grid columns in Design view.

Figure 11-16 Selecting a Web service method (ObjectDataSource control)

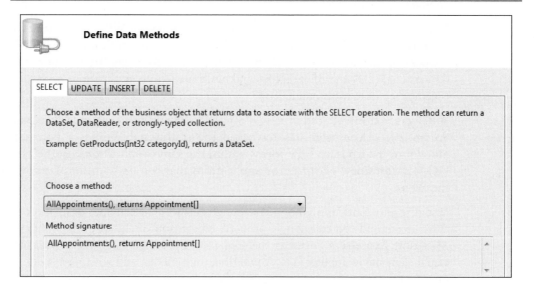

Figure 11-17 Editing the columns collection of a GridView control

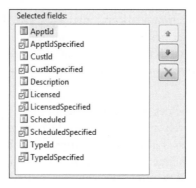

 **Checkpoint**

7. Yes or no: Does a Web service display a Web page by itself?

8. What is the term for actions by an application that calls Web service methods?

9. What was contained in the service host file for the BookService Web service?

10. Which two methods were exposed by the BookService Web service?

11.3 Windows Presentation Foundation (WPF)

Imagine a single application that has the usual set of menus and controls, along with rich text displayed in columns, a three-dimensional (3D) bar chart, and live video. Imagine being able to combine all these elements on the same page. These capabilities are available to advanced developers using Microsoft's **Windows Presentation Foundation (WPF)**. In the past, developers with a wide variety of specialties and skills would be required to create such an application. They would have to integrate different toolkits and spend a lot of time testing and debugging. To make matters worse, they might have to redo these applications completely for the Web.

Microsoft created the Windows Presentation Foundation (WPF) technology for a number of reasons: (1) They wanted developers to be able to create applications that could run both on the desktop and the Web, and (2) they wanted to make it easy to incorporate advanced two-dimensional (2D) and 3D graphics and multimedia into applications without having to link together separate tools manually.

WPF was first introduced in Visual Studio 2008 and has been greatly expanded in Visual Studio 2010. Microsoft has reworked the traditional Windows Forms technology to allow it to incorporate WPF forms within the same applications. In the future, WPF will be Microsoft's new platform for applications that run on both the Windows desktop and the Web.

Visual Studio contains an interactive design surface that provides drag-and-drop support for WPF layout and controls, a new property editor, and Intellisense support for source editing. **Microsoft Expression Blend** is the tool used by designers to create advanced interactive visual elements in applications. Animation, multimedia, and advanced styles are often developed in this way.

eXtensible Application Markup Language (XAML)

eXtensible Application Markup Language (XAML) is an XML-based markup language that describes visual elements in WPF applications. In some ways, it resembles the XHTML markup used in ASP.NET Web applications. Pronounced as *Zamel*, XAML it can be generated by both Expression Blend and Visual Studio. It can be referenced by coding statements at runtime.

In the past, artistic designers and programmers had great difficulty working together unless they were extensively trained to do so. The designer might create a graphic design for a Web page and then pass it along to the programmer to add functions needed by the application. But the designer might not know whether his or her design vision could be implemented by the programmer. Once the programmer started to add code, it was nearly impossible to make any changes or improvements to the visual design.

By creating XAML and WPF, Microsoft allowed designers and programmers to work together, each taking advantage of his or her special skills. The same project can be passed back and forth between the designer and the programmer as it gradually takes shape. Using XAML, the designer can create rich visual interfaces that easily lend themselves to coding by a programmer.

Layout and Controls

A WPF application controls its layout through the user of containers named *panels*. Each panel can contain child elements, such as controls like buttons and check boxes, or other panels. There are three types of panels:

- DockPanel—Allows child elements to be positioned along the edges of the panel.
- Grid—Allows child elements to be positioned in predetermined rows and columns, similar to a table.
- Canvas—Allows child elements to be positioned anywhere in the panel.

All of the standard controls are available, such as TextBox, CheckBox, and ComboBox. More advanced controls are also available, including DocumentViewer, MediaElement, and ViewPort3D.

Types of Applications

Stand-Alone WPF

A **stand-alone WPF application** runs like any other Windows application. You do not need to use a Web browser to run it. This type of program runs with the same privileges as the current user, so it can access the computer's hard drive, use network sockets, and so on. It can be installed from a local disk, a network server, or in a third way named *ClickOnce*. Using ClickOnce technology, a Web browser connects to a page containing a button that downloads and installs the WPF application on a user's computer.

There is a clear advantage to creating ClickOnce applications. You can publish an application to a Web server for others to use. Later, when you have made improvements to the program, you can republish the application. This makes it easy for users to get the latest version of your work.

XAML Browser Applications (XBAPs)

A **XAML browser application (XBAP)** runs inside Internet Explorer. It can use most of the capabilities of WPF in a browser application.

An XBAP is silently loaded via ClickOnce and looks just like a Web page. It is given only a limited amount of trust, so it does not have all the privileges normally given to desktop applications. For example, it cannot create other windows, display dialog boxes, access the full file system of the computer, or execute user interface code created with Windows Forms.

In Tutorial 11-4, you will begin to create your first stand-alone WPF application.

Tutorial 11-4:
Creating the *Kayak Tour Reservations* application

In this tutorial, you will begin to create a stand-alone WPF application named *Kayak Tour Reservations* that lets the user sign up for a kayak tour. By the time you finish the tutorials in this chapter, your application will let users select the type of kayak they want to use, the tour location, and the tour date.

Tutorial Steps

Step 1: On the File menu, select *New Project*. Select *WPF Application* from the list of application templates. Name the project *Kayak Tour Reservations* and click the *OK* button.

Step 2: Select *Save All* from the File menu. When the *Save Project* dialog appears, choose a folder location for your project and click the *Save* button.

Step 3: The *MainWindow.xaml* Design window should appear, as shown in Figure 11-18. You should also see another tab, labeled *MainWindow.xaml.vb*. When you click this tab, you see the code file for MainWindow, where you will write event handler procedures.

Step 4: Using the mouse, drag the slider in the upper-left corner of the Design window to zoom the form display in and out, making it appear larger and smaller. This adjustment does not change the actual size of the window object. Look

Figure 11-18 Design window, immediately after creating a new WPF project

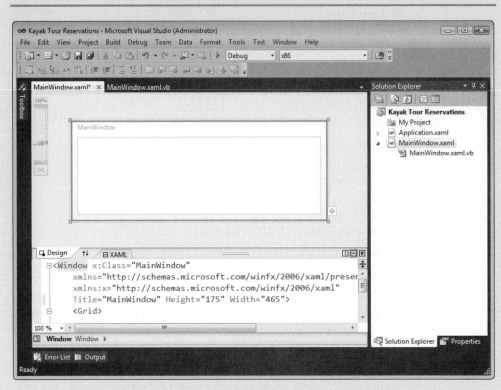

for its Height and Width properties in the Properties window to verify that their values do not change.

Step 5: Using the mouse to drag the corner of the window, expand the window's size to about 380 units high and 600 units wide. Now you can see that Height and Width properties have changed.

Step 6: Set the window's Title property to *Register for a Kayak Tour*.

 TIP: The design surface automatically contains a single Grid control. The advantage to using a grid is that you can use the mouse to drag controls from the Toolbox onto the grid and position them anywhere you want. In some applications, you will insert additional rows and columns into the grid to help you align the different controls.

Step 7: Open the Toolbox window and expand the *Common WPF Controls* section.

Step 8: Drag a Label control from the Toolbox into the middle of the grid, near the top. Set the following properties for the Label: FontSize = 30; Content = *Our Featured Kayak Tours*. Drag the borders of the label with the mouse so that all the text in the label is visible. A sample is shown in Figure 11-19.

Step 9: Drag a Label control onto the grid near the left side and set its Content property to *Select a Type of Kayak*.

Figure 11-19 A Label containing the application title

Step 10: Drag a ListBox control onto the grid, just below the label on the left side. At the very top of the Properties window, set the ListBox's Name property to *lstKayaks*. Select its Items property, and click the *Add* button to add three items to the box, as shown in Figure 11-20. For each item, you need to enter a value into its Content property. The values are as follows:

```
Solo recreational
Tandem recreational
Solo sea kayak
```

Figure 11-20 Adding items to the lstKayak ListBox

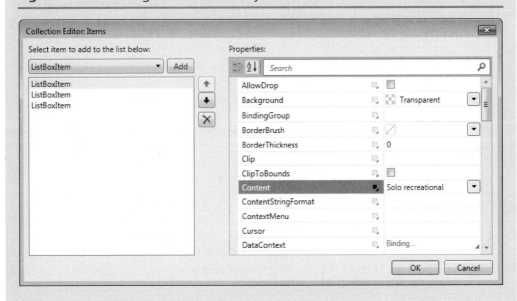

Click the *OK* button to close the dialog. Figure 11-21 shows the design of the form after adding the ListBox. It also includes ComboBox and DatePicker controls that you will add during the next few steps.

Figure 11-21 Kayak Tours window in design mode

Step 11: Add another label to the right side of the form and set its Content property to *Select a Kayak Tour*.

Step 12: Add a ComboBox control to the right side of the form and name it *cboTour*. Select its Items property and add three items. Set the Content properties of the three items to the following:

```
Na Pali Coast tour
Hanalei Bay tour
Wailua River tour
```

Step 13: We would also like to let the user select the date of his or her tour. Just below the ComboBox control, add a Label that says *Tour Date:*. Next to it, add a DatePicker control, and set its Content property to Show Calendar. In the following figure, you can see the ComboBox control, with the DatePicker just below it:

Step 14: Save the project and run the application by selecting *Start Debugging* from the Debug menu. Verify that you can select kayak types from the list box and that you can select tour names from the ComboBox. Click the DatePicker control, which causes the month calendar to appear, as shown in Figure 11-22. When you select a date, the calendar closes and the date appears in the text box.

Figure 11-22 KayakTourWPF application at runtime

Step 15: Close the application window and return to Design mode.

Tutorial 11-5:
Adding Images to the *Kayak Tour Reservations* application

Most customers who go on kayak tours for the first time are not familiar with the various types of kayaks that they might be able to use. Therefore, a well-designed reservation system should display a picture of each kayak type to help the user make a selection. In this tutorial you will add three kayak images to the *Kayak Tour Reservations* application. The pictures will be displayed by a WPF Image control. When the user selects each type of kayak in the ListBox, the appropriate image will display at the bottom of the window.

 TIP: Adding an image to a WPF application is a little different from the way it's done in Windows Forms. You must first add the image file to the project, using the Solution Explorer window. Then, when you want to display the image in an Image control, select the image name from a list of images belonging to the project.

Tutorial Steps

Step 1: Copy three image files from the chapter examples folder into your application's directory (the directory containing the file named *MainWindow.xaml*). The image filenames are *rec_kayak.jpg*, *sea_kayak.jpg*, and *tandem_rec_kayak.jpg*.

Step 2: Right-click the project name in Solution Explorer, select *Add*, and select *Existing Item*. In the *Add Existing Item* dialog window, select *Image Files* in the *file type* dropdown list in the lower corner of the window, as shown here:

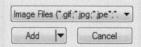

Select the three image files from your project directory. Then click the *Add* button. The three filenames should appear in the list of files in your Solution Explorer window.

Step 3:   Add three Image controls to the form, positioned near the bottom. Each Image control should be about 2 inches long and 1.5 inches high. For each, set its Stretch property to *None*, and set its Visibility property to *Hidden*. The image controls should occupy the same general position on the form.

> **TIP:** When you have elements stacked on top of each other in a WPF form, you can select the top one with the mouse and move it to the back. Here's how: Select the item with the mouse; then, from the Format menu, select *Order*, and select *Send to Back*.

Step 4:   Using Table 11-3 as a guide, assign names and images to the three Image controls on the form. As you assign each image filename to the Source property, adjust the displayed size of the image on the form by dragging its handles with the mouse.

Table 11-3 Kayak Tour form property settings

Control Type	Control Name	Property Settings
Image	imgRecKayak	Source: *rec_kayak.jpg*
Image	imgRecTandem	Source: *tandem_rec_kayak.jpg*
Image	imgSeaKayak	Source: *sea_kayak.jpg*

> **TIP:** If you experience difficulties when trying to set control properties in the editor, rebuild the application and try setting the properties again.

If you were to run the application now, the images would not appear because the Image controls are hidden. Instead, the images should pop out and become visible when the appropriate type of kayak is selected in the ListBox control. To make that happen, you need to create a SelectionChanged event handler for the ListBox.

Step 5:   Select click the lstKayaks ListBox control with the mouse. At the top of the Properties window, click the lightning bolt icon (events) to display all the ListBox event types. Double-click the box to the right of the SelectionChanged event in the Properties window. You should now see the code window editor for *MainWindow.xaml.vb*, containing the *lstKayaks_SelectionChanged* event handler procedure. Modify it as follows:

```
Private Sub lstKayaks_SelectionChanged() _
    Handles lstKayaks.SelectionChanged
```

```
      imgRecKayak.Visibility = Windows.Visibility.Hidden
      imgRecTandem.Visibility = Windows.Visibility.Hidden
      imgSeaKayak.Visibility = Windows.Visibility.Hidden

      If lstKayaks.SelectedIndex = 0 Then
         imgRecKayak.Visibility = Windows.Visibility.Visible
      ElseIf lstKayaks.SelectedIndex = 1 Then
         imgRecTandem.Visibility = Windows.Visibility.Visible
      ElseIf lstKayaks.SelectedIndex = 2 Then
         imgSeaKayak.Visibility = Windows.Visibility.Visible
      End If
End Sub
```

Depending on the SelectedIndex of the kayak selected in the ListBox in the code above, we set one of the Image controls to *Visible*. The other two images remain set to *Hidden*.

Step 6: Save the project and run the application by selecting *Start Debugging* from the Debug menu. Test the application by selecting each of the kayak types from the ListBox. As you do so, a different kayak image should appear. Figure 11-23 shows a sample of the application at runtime.

Figure 11-23 Viewing the kayak photos while running the application

ClickOnce Deployment

ClickOnce refers to the Microsoft application deployment technology that permits applications to be installed just by clicking a link or a button that starts the installation. The installation can be from the desktop, from a network share (a directory on an organization's network), or on the Web. It is offered as an alternative to the standard Microsoft Windows Installer program.

A ClickOnce application is any Windows Presentation Foundation, Windows Forms, or console application published using ClickOnce technology. A ClickOnce application can be published in three different ways:

- From a Web page

- From a network file share
- From external disk-type media such as a USB or CD-ROM

A ClickOnce application can be installed on an end user's computer, or it can be run from the network without being installed on the user's computer.

Comparing Windows Installer to ClickOnce

Windows Installer has been the standard installation program used by many Windows desktop applications for several years. It requires the user to have administrative rights, because it makes a number of important changes to the system. Also, the user must install an entire application, even when the application has been updated in only a minimal way. Finally, Windows Installer has the potential to affect other installed programs that use the same shared components.

ClickOnce technology simplifies the process of installing and updating applications. Installation does not require the user to have administrative privileges because the application runs in a restricted environment. ClickOnce applications are isolated and self-contained, so they do not affect any other installed applications. When a ClickOnce application automatically detects that it has been updated by its author, it downloads just the changed parts of the application to users' computers.

How It Works

ClickOnce Deployment is based on two XML files, both of which are created by the *Publish Wizard* in Visual Studio. These two XML files are:

- **Application manifest**—Describes the application, including the assemblies, dependencies, and files that make up the application; the required permissions; and the location where updates will be available.
- **Deployment manifest**—Describes how the application is deployed. This includes the location of the application manifest and the version of the application that clients should run.

If you have administrative rights on the computer where you plan to deploy a ClickOnce application, the deployment manifest can be deployed right after it is created by Visual Studio. This is also true also if you have read/write permissions for a Web folder that will hold the manifest. If you do not have administrative rights, then the computer administrator must run a tool that digitally signs the manifest using a command-line tool. (The use of this tool is beyond the scope of our discussion here.)

After the two manifests are copied to a deployment location, users can download and install the application by running a small setup program or by navigating to a Web location. For example, you can install the sample application from this chapter by browsing to this location on the Web:

```
http://kipirvine.com/KayakTour/KayakTourWPF.application
```

 TIP: For more information on ClickOnce deployment, we encourage you to read the article entitled *ClickOnce Deployment Overview* at *http://msdn.microsoft.com*.

In Tutorial 11-6, you will publish the *Kayak Tour Reservations* application, using ClickOnce deployment. In Tutorial 11-7, you will see how the same application can be published on a Web site.

Tutorial 11-6:
Publishing the *Kayak Tour Reservations* application

In this tutorial, you will publish the *Kayak Tour Reservations* to a folder on your computer. The files in this folder could be given to anyone to install and run the application on their computer.

Tutorial Steps

Step 1: Select *Publish Kayak Tour Reservations* from the *Build* menu. The *Publish Wizard* window appears, as shown in Figure 11-24. Enter *publish*.

Figure 11-24 Selecting a folder to hold the published files

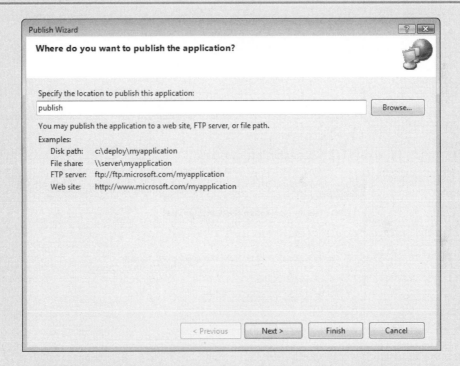

Another option is to enter a complete path, such as *c:\data\Kayak Tour*. Or if you enter just a folder name, such as *publish*, the application will be published in a folder inside your WPF project folder.

Step 2: Click the *Next* button to continue. As shown in Figure 11-25, the *Publish Wizard* asks which location users will access when they want to install the application. Click the *Next* button to continue.

Step 3: The Publish Wizard then asks where the application will go to check for updates. Select *The application will not check for updates,* as shown in Figure 11-26, and click the *Next* button to continue.

Step 4: The final step of the Publish Wizard is shown in Figure 11-27. It shows the directory path of the location where the application will be installed. Click the *Finish* button.

Figure 11-25 Selecting the method of installation

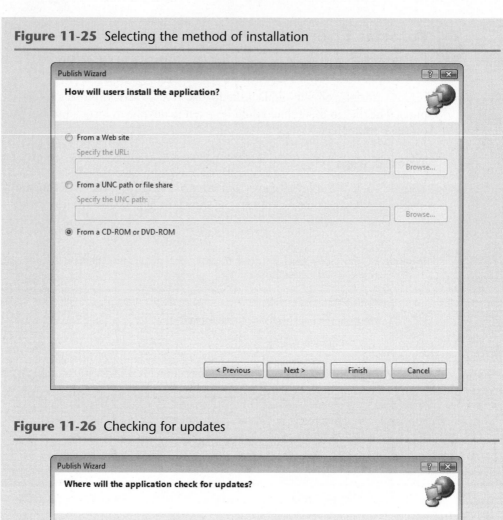

Figure 11-26 Checking for updates

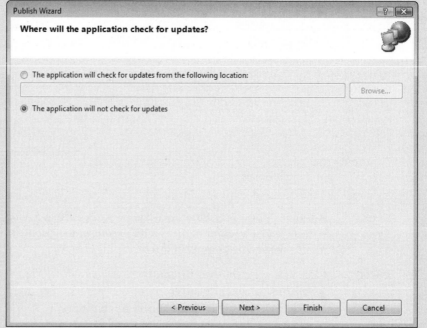

Step 5: Open Windows Explorer and browse to the folder in your project named *publish*. In this folder, you should find the following files:

```
Application Files (a folder)
autorun.inf
Kayak Tour Reservations.application
setup.exe
```

Figure 11-27 Final step of the Publish Wizard

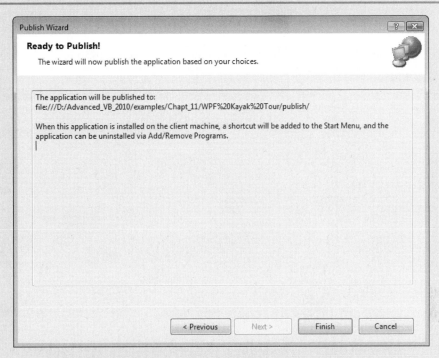

Step 6: Double-click on *setup.exe* to install and run the application. It will briefly check for required components, as in Figure 11-28. It may then display a security warning, similar to that shown in Figure 11-29, which shows a slightly different application name.

Figure 11-28 Launching the application

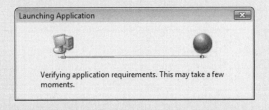

Figure 11-29 Security warning on installation (Windows 7)

Step 7: Click the *Install* button, and in a moment you will see the application window shown in Figure 11-30.

Figure 11-30 The *Kayak Tour Reservations* application window

Step 8: (Optional) Open the computer's Control Panel, go to the list of installed programs, and look for the *Kayak Tour Reservations* application.

Step 9: Click the Windows *Start* menu and run the application from this menu.

If you modify the application, you can publish it again and update the files in the *publish* folder.

Tutorial 11-7:
Publishing the *Kayak Tour Reservations* application to the Web

If you have access to a Web server, you can easily publish your WPF application to the server. From Visual Studio, you identify the Web site where the application will be published. When users navigate to the site using a Web browser, they will be able to install your application just by clicking a button.

This tutorial is designed as a demonstration. We will use a Web site named *http://kipirvine.com* for this demonstration. If you wish to reproduce the steps, you will need to substitute the URL of your own Web site.

Tutorial Steps

Step 1: Select *Publish Kayak Tour Reservations* from the *Build* menu. The *Publish Wizard* window appears, as shown in Figure 11-31. Enter the Web address of a folder on our Web site, and click the *Next* button.

Step 2: Next, shown in Figure 11-32, the *Publish Wizard* asks which location users will access when they want to install the application. We have selected a folder named *Install* on the same Web site.

Figure 11-31 Selecting a location where the *Kayak Tour Reservations* application will be published

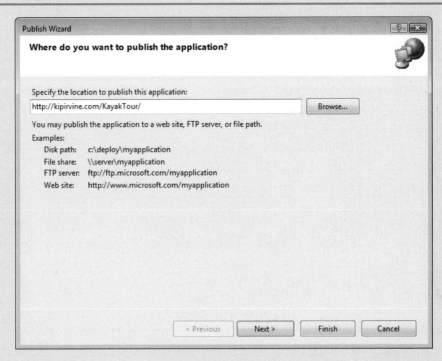

Figure 11-32 Selecting the Install location

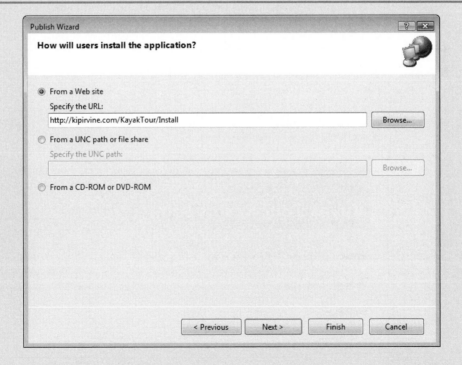

Step 3: The *Publish Wizard* then asks if the application will be available online only (see Figure 11-33), or whether it should be added to the *Start* menu of the user's computer. We do not wish to install any software on the local computer, so we select the Web-only option.

Figure 11-33 Choosing to make the application available online only

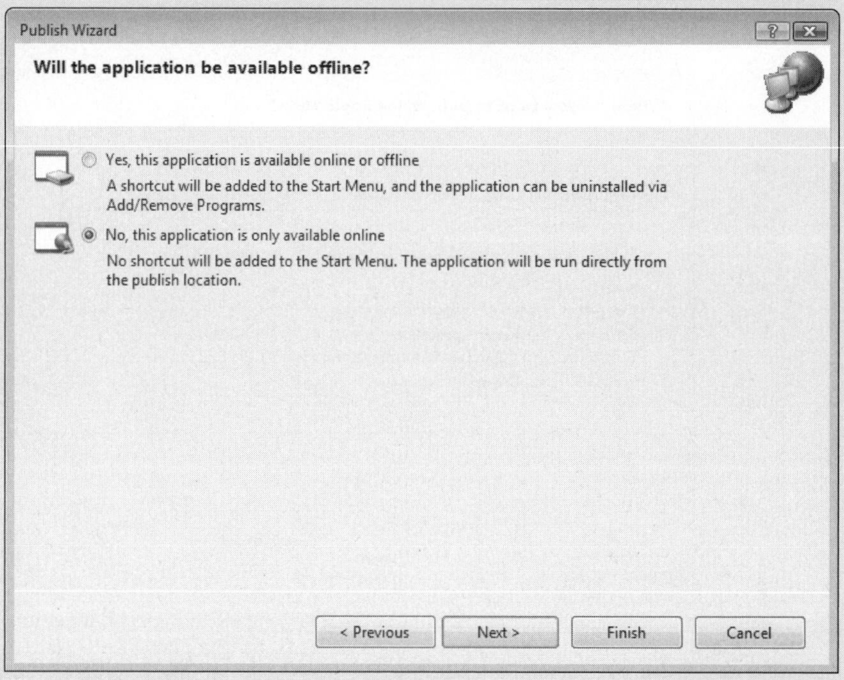

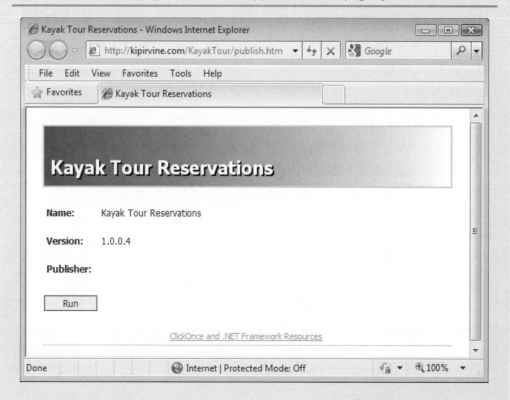

Step 4: Next, Visual Studio opens the Web site and asks for user authentication (user-name and password). After a brief pause, during which Visual Studio copies the application to the remote Web site, the application's published Web page (named *publish.htm*) appears. This is shown in Figure 11-34.

Figure 11-34 Displaying the published application Web page (publish.htm)

If the user's local computer were missing any required components, he or she would have to click the *Run* button and wait for the components to be installed directly from Microsoft's Web site. In our sample, however, there are no missing components.

Step 5: The user clicks the *Run* button. A dialog window, shown in Figure 11-35, appears briefly, while Windows verifies that all required software components exist on the user's computer. Then the application window, shown in Figure 11-36, appears.

Figure 11-35 Launching the application

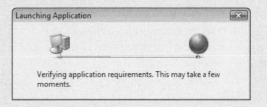

Figure 11-36 The *Kayak Tour Reservations* application window

Our WPF application does not run in a Web browser window. It runs what might be called a *desktop application* mode, on the local computer. The Web browser is used only when launching the application.

You can run the application by browsing directly to its application file. For the *Kayak Tour Reservations* application, the direct execution URL on the Web is: *http://kipirvine.com/KayakTour/KayakTourWPF.application*

 **Checkpoint**

11. What important feature (other than graphics and multimedia) does WPF have over Windows Forms applications?

12. What is XAML?

13. What two general types of WPF applications can you create?

14. How can ClickOnce deployment be used with a Web browser?

15. What are the two types of manifests in a ClickOnce deployment?

Summary

11.1 Introducing XML Web Services

- *XML Web Services* is a valuable technology that permits computers to share data and methods across networks.
- A *Web service* is a component class that is compiled and stored on a Web site. It has no visual interface, but it exposes methods and properties accessed by other programs across a network.
- *Extensible Markup Language (XML)* is the standard protocol used to represent data on the Web.
- *Simple Object Access Protocol (SOAP)* is an industry-standard protocol for handling requests and responses. It includes class names, method names, and parameters.
- *Web Services Description Language (WSDL)* specifies the formatting of calls to Web methods.
- *Universal Description, Discovery, and Integration (UDDI)* is a directory service that makes information about Web services publicly available.
- Microsoft created *Windows Communication Foundation* (WCF) as a unified programming model and runtime support for building Web services applications.
- In Visual Studio, when creating a client program that consumes a Web service, you must add a Web reference to the project that identifies and locates the Web service.
- The .NET framework uses attribute classes to identify important elements of a WCF service. The most important classes are ServiceContractAttribute, OperationContractAttribute, DataContractAttribute, and DataMemberAttribute.

11.2 BookService Web Service

- The *BookService* Web service returns a list of books and lets calling programs search for books by ISBN number.
- *BookService* is implemented as a Windows Communication Foundation (WCF) Web site.
- WCF service methods, like other methods, can throw exceptions. For security reasons, they don't automatically convey which type of exception was thrown.
- You can modify the *<serviceDebug>* attribute in the WCF service's web.config file to permit it to convey detailed exception information to client programs.
- We create both Windows Forms and ASP.NET applications that consume the Book-Service service.

11.3 Windows Presentation Foundation (WPF)

- Microsoft created the Windows Presentation Foundation (WPF) technology for a number of reasons: (1) They wanted developers to be able to create applications that could run on both the desktop and the Web, and (2) they wanted to make it easy to incorporate advanced 2D and 3D graphics and multimedia into applications without having to link together separate tools manually.
- eXtensible Application Markup Language (XAML) is used to describe the visual elements in a WPF application. By creating XAML and WPF, Microsoft allows designers and programmers to work together, each taking advantage of their special skills.

- A WPF application controls its layout through the use of containers named *panels*. Each panel can contain child elements, such as controls like buttons and check boxes, or other panels.
- A stand-alone WPF application runs like any other Windows application. You do not need to use a Web browser to run it.
- A XAML browser application (XBAP) runs inside Internet Explorer. It can use most of the capabilities of WPF in a browser application.
- *Click-Once Deployment* refers to the Microsoft technology that permits applications to be installed just by clicking a link or a button that starts the installation.
- ClickOnce technology simplifies the process of installing and updating applications. Installation does not require the user to have administrative privileges because the application runs in a restricted environment.
- ClickOnce applications are isolated and self-contained, so they do not affect any other installed applications.
- ClickOnce applications can automatically detect when an application has been updated by its author, and then it downloads only changed parts of the application to users' computers.

Key Terms

application manifest
attribute classes
ClickOnce technology
consuming a Web service
data contract
data member
deployment manifest
eXtensible Application Markup Language (XAML)
eXtensible Markup Language (XML)
firewall
Microsoft Expression Blend
operation contract
service contract
service contract file
service host file
service implementation file

Simple Object Access Protocol (SOAP)
stand-alone WPF application
Universal Description, Discovery, and Integration (UDDI)
WCF Service
Web configuration file
Web service
Web Services Description Language (WSDL)
Windows Communication Foundation (WCF)
Windows Presentation Foundation (WPF)
XAML browser application (XBAP)
XML Web Services
Web reference

Review Questions and Exercises

True or False

Indicate whether each of the following statements is true or false:

1. A Web service can be consumed only by an ASP.NET application.

2. A Web service is a component class, which is compiled and stored on a Web site. It has no visual interface, but it exposes methods and properties accessed by other programs across a network.

3. The <MethodContract()> attribute is required for WCF service methods.

4. A WPF application can run only on the Web.

5. A stand-alone WPF application runs with full administrative privileges.

6. With ClickOnce installation, the user can use a Web browser to connect to a page containing a button that downloads and installs the WPF application on his or her computer.

7. A XAML browser application runs inside Internet Explorer, but it cannot use all of the WPF controls.

8. An XBAP application is given only a limited amount of trust, so it does not have all the privileges normally given to desktop applications.

9. A ClickOnce application cannot be installed from a network file share.

10. Windows Installer does not require the user to have administrative privileges.

11. ClickOnce does not require the user to have administrative privileges.

12. A ClickOnce installation is not able to verify that the user's computer has the right components (also known as application requirements).

13. WPF applications can automatically check for updates.

Short Answer

1. What does XML stand for?

2. When a Visual Studio project calls Web service methods, how does it know which methods to call?

3. Describe *Single Object Access Protocol*.

4. Which language specifies the formatting of calls to Web service methods?

5. Which directory service is helpful when you want to locate available Web services?

6. What do the letters WCF stand for in a WCF service?

7. What is the attribute tag used just prior to the class name in a WCF service?

8. Which attribute tag is used just before a class defined inside a WCF service?

9. What is the attribute tag used just prior to a method name in a WCF service?

10. What is a service host file?

11. What is a service contract file?

12. What is a service implementation file?

13. In which file does the <system.serviceModel> tag appear?

14. What does WPF stand for in Microsoft .NET?

15. What is the name of the .NET development tool used by designers to create advanced interactive visual elements in application?

16. What does XAML stand for?

17. Which WPF control allows child elements to be positioned along the edges of the panel?

18. What is the name of the Microsoft technology that permits applications to be installed just by clicking a link or a button that starts the installation?

19. What is the name of the WPF file that describes the application, including the assemblies, dependencies, and files that make up the application; the required permissions; and the location where updates will be available?

20. What is the name of the WPF file that describes how the application is deployed and includes the location of the other manifest and the version of the application that clients should run?

21. What is the name of the tool that lets the developer deploy a WPF application?

Programming Challenges

1. **Currency Conversion Web Service**

   Create a Web service that converts currency values between U.S. dollars and several other world currencies. Consumers can pass each currency code as a two-character or three-character string. One method, named GetDollarValue, returns the amount in U.S. dollars corresponding to the amount parameter.

   ```
   Public Function GetDollarValue(ByVal Country As String,
     ByVal amount As Decimal) As Decimal
   ```

   The other method, named GetCurrencyValue, returns the value in a foreign currency that corresponds to the dollars parameter.

   ```
   Public Function GetCurrencyValue(ByVal Country As String,
     ByVal dollars As Decimal) As Decimal
   ```

   Client Program

   Create a client application (Windows or Web) that lets the user select a currency type from a ComboBox and then input a U.S. dollar amount or a foreign currency amount. In Figure 11-37, the user clicks the button with the arrow pointing right to convert $55 U.S. into the equivalent amount in euros. If the user enters the foreign currency amount in the right-hand text box and clicks the arrow pointing left, the equivalent amount in dollars should appear.

   Figure 11-37 Currency Conversion Web service, client program

2. **Asynchronous Message Web Service**

   Create a Web service that permits users to send short text messages to other users and receive messages from other users. The Web service is termed asynchronous because messages are not received as soon as they are sent; users decide when they want to receive messages.

   When a user logs in with a name and password, the Web service authenticates him by searching a database table. If the user is accepted, a unique ID number is created and sent to the user. The Web service uses this ID number to identify the user in all subsequent calls to Web methods.

   A user sends a message by calling a Web service method and passing a user ID, the name of the recipient, and the message text. A user receives her messages by passing a user ID to a Web method that returns an array of message strings.

When the user logs out, the unique ID assigned to the user is discarded. Here are the suggested method declarations:

```
'Logs into the message service with a username and password.
'Returns a unique integer to be used in subsequent transmissions.
Public Function Login(ByVal user As String,
  ByVal passwd As String) As Integer
```

```
'Sends a message to a specific user. Parameters:
'userId: unique identifier returned by Login method.
'recipient: username of the receiver of the message
'msg: the text of the message
'Returns True if the userId is recognized, or False if it is not.
Public Function Send(ByVal userId As Integer,
  ByVal recipient As String,
  ByVal msg As String) As Boolean
```

```
'Gets all messages addressed to the current user.
'If the userId is recognized, an Array of String containing
'the messages is returned; otherwise, an empty array is returned.
Public Function GetMessages(ByVal userId As Integer) As String
```

```
'Logs out of the mail service. Discards the unique user ID.
Public Sub Logout(ByVal userId As Integer)
```

3. **RepairServices Web Service—Appointments**

The Home Repair Services database was introduced in Chapter 5. Create a Web service that returns the contents of the Appointments table from the database as a strongly typed List of Appointment objects. Then create a Web site that consumes your Web service client and displays the list of appointments in a GridView control (see Figure 11-38). Use an ObjectDataSource control to bind the return value of the WebMethod to the grid.

Figure 11-38 Web client for the RepairServices Web service

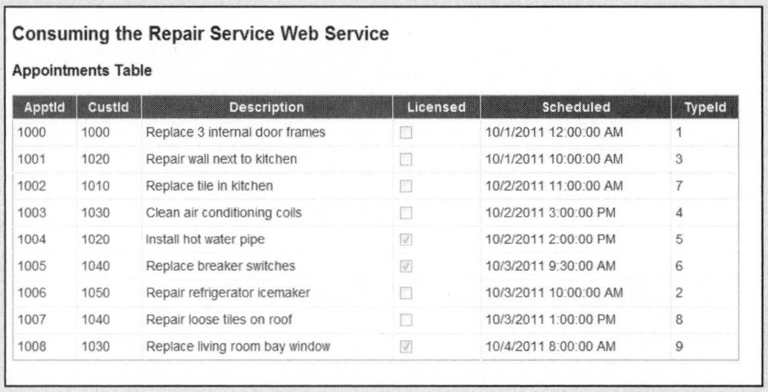

Consuming the Repair Service Web Service

Appointments Table

ApptId	CustId	Description	Licensed	Scheduled	TypeId
1000	1000	Replace 3 internal door frames	☐	10/1/2011 12:00:00 AM	1
1001	1020	Repair wall next to kitchen	☐	10/1/2011 10:00:00 AM	3
1002	1010	Replace tile in kitchen	☐	10/2/2011 11:00:00 AM	7
1003	1030	Clean air conditioning coils	☐	10/2/2011 3:00:00 PM	4
1004	1020	Install hot water pipe	☑	10/2/2011 2:00:00 PM	5
1005	1040	Replace breaker switches	☑	10/3/2011 9:30:00 AM	6
1006	1050	Repair refrigerator icemaker	☐	10/3/2011 10:00:00 AM	2
1007	1040	Repair loose tiles on roof	☐	10/3/2011 1:00:00 PM	8
1008	1030	Replace living room bay window	☑	10/4/2011 8:00:00 AM	9

4. **Customers and Appointments—Web Service**

The Home Repair Services database was introduced in Chapter 5. Create a Web service named CustomerRepairServices that reads the database and creates a List of Customer objects. Each Customer object should contain the customer Name, ID, Phone, and a list of Appointments for which the customer is scheduled. Next, create a Web site that consumes your Web service and displays the list of Customers in a GridView control. When the user selects a customer, display the person's list of appointments in a second Grid-View on the same page.

5. **Winter Sports Rentals WPF**

   A winter sports rentals store needs an application that will let the store clerk enter information about each customer's rental. The store clerk should be able to select multiple equipment items, a rental duration, and insurance (see Figure 11-39). The detailed description appears in Programming Challenge 3 in Chapter 2. Your task is to implement it as a WPF application, except that you may eliminate the Weather Forecast form.

Figure 11-39 Winter Sports Rentals application

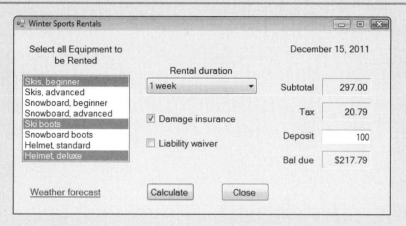

12 Reports, MDI, Interfaces, and Polymorphism

CHAPTER

TOPICS

This chapter introduces several important topics. First, it shows how to create reports for the desktop and Web, using Microsoft Report templates and the ReportViewer control. Next, we show how to create Multiple Document Interface (MDI) applications, which manage multiple client windows under a single parent window. Then we introduce advanced topics in object-oriented programming (OOP): interface types, abstract classes, and polymorphism. Although these topics are not heavily emphasized in Visual Basic applications, they can be important as your programs grow in size and complexity.

12.1 Creating Microsoft Reports

Microsoft Reports consist of Visual Studio templates, a definition language, and tools that make it easy for you to create printable reports in Visual Studio for Windows Forms and ASP.NET applications. You use a designer tool to create **report definition files.** The contents of these files are based on Microsoft's **Report Definition Language (RDL).** This language is completely specified as an XML file, which can be customized and extended by individual developers.

Figure 12-1 shows an example of a report based on a sample Microsoft database named *AdventureWorks*. This report has a page heading and column headings, and the report detail lines are grouped according to the product name. The report can be viewed in a Windows Forms or ASP.NET application.

Figure 12-1 After adding a page heading to the report

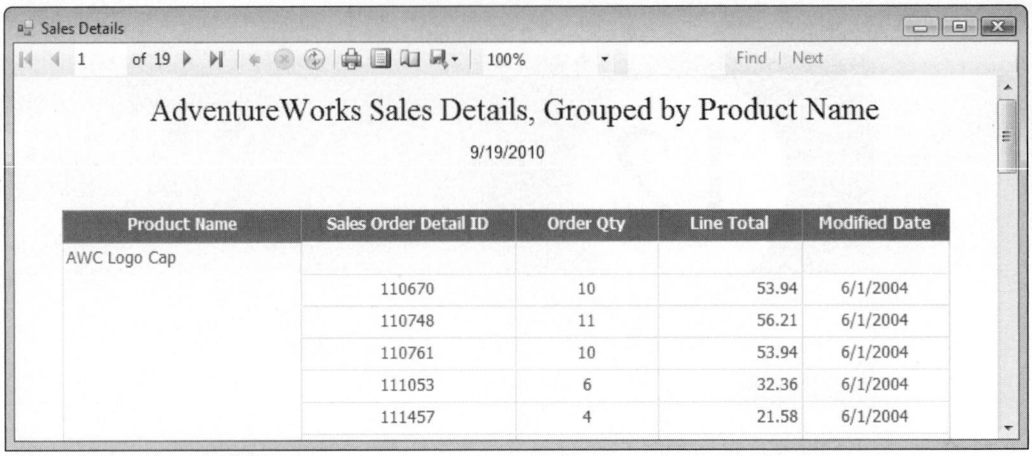

Report Designer

Visual Studio **Report Designer** is a powerful built-in tool for creating and modifying reports. A report can contain ordinary text, data-bound fields, graphic images, and charts. A report must be bound to a data source. In our examples, the data source will be a DataSet.

Tablix Data Region

Microsoft reports use a **Tablix data region** as the basis for report designs. It is a general layout item that displays report data as rows and columns, much like an electronic spreadsheet. You can insert detail data from a database query into a Tablix data region, or you can aggregate the data into groups. A Tablix data region has four main areas, each containing Tablix cells:

- The corner
- The row group area
- The column group area
- The body

Tablix cells in each area have a distinct purpose. You can display detail data and grouped data by adding cells to the Tablix body area. You can display group headings by adding cells to the Tablix row group area. You can also create headings that repeat on each page.

Detail Data and Grouped Data

Detail data consists of all the rows returned by a query from a data source. It might contain fields from multiple tables as well as calculated values.

Grouped data is detail data that is organized by a value that you specify in the group definition, for example, *Product Name*. You display grouped data on group rows and columns by using simple expressions that aggregate the grouped data. Referring back to Figure 12-1, for example, you might want to calculate the sum of all values in the *Order Qty* column.

ReportViewer Control

The **ReportViewer control** provides a convenient way to display report files on Windows and Web forms. This control reads data from a data source and renders the data according to the design of a Microsoft Report file. The control contains a toolbar at the top, with buttons that perform a number of basic operations on the report. These buttons let you print the report; zoom in and out; modify the print layout and page setup; and export the report to Excel, PDF, and Word formats.

The ReportViewer control displays a toolbar with navigation buttons that let you do the following tasks:

- Print the report.
- Zoom in and out.
- Modify the print layout.
- Modify the page setup.
- Export the report to Excel, PDF, and Word formats.
- Search for text inside the report.

The toolbar is shown in Figure 12-2.

Figure 12-2 ReportViewer toolbar

The AdventureWorks Databases

The AdventureWorks databases are recommended by Microsoft for training materials, and they are used in many of their tutorials. They contain tables of products sold by a fictitious company that sells sporting equipment for outdoor adventures. In addition, there are tables of customers who buy the products, and sales orders. There are two primary versions of the database—the larger is named *AdventureWorks*, and the smaller is named *AdventureWorks LT*. It is the smaller database that we will use in this chapter because it can be downloaded and installed on student computers more easily. The database is ideally suited to generating reports.

The Product table, shown in Figure 12-3, is one of the most important tables in the database. We will display some of its columns on our reports. Sample rows from this table are shown in Figure 12-4.

Figure 12-3 Product table, AdventureWorks LT database

Figure 12-4 Sample rows from the Product table

Produ...	Name	ProductNumber	Color	StandardCost	ListPrice	Size
680	HL Road Frame - Black, 58	FR-R92B-58	Black	1059.3100	1431.5000	58
706	HL Road Frame - Red, 58	FR-R92R-58	Red	1059.3100	1431.5000	58
707	Sport-100 Helmet, Red	HL-U509-R	Red	13.0863	34.9900	NULL
708	Sport-100 Helmet, Black	HL-U509	Black	13.0863	34.9900	NULL
709	Mountain Bike Socks, M	SO-B909-M	White	3.3963	9.5000	M
710	Mountain Bike Socks, L	SO-B909-L	White	3.3963	9.5000	L
711	Sport-100 Helmet, Blue	HL-U509-B	Blue	13.0863	34.9900	NULL
712	AWC Logo Cap	CA-1098	Multi	6.9223	8.9900	NULL
713	Long-Sleeve Logo Jersey, S	LJ-0192-S	Multi	38.4923	49.9900	S
714	Long-Sleeve Logo Jersey, M	LJ-0192-M	Multi	38.4923	49.9900	M
715	Long-Sleeve Logo Jersey, L	LJ-0192-L	Multi	38.4923	49.9900	L

Creating a Report Application

Visual Studio Report Designer is a built-in tool for creating and modifying reports. It shows a blank report template, onto which you can add report fields, text, and graphics. A report is saved as a *Client Report Definition* (.rdlc) file. To add an empty report to a project or Web site, perform the following steps:

1. Select *Add New Item*.
2. In the Installed Templates pane, select *Reporting*.
3. In the Templates pane, select *Report*.

A blank .rdlc file is added to the project.

Report Wizard

When you are learning to create reports, we recommend using the **Report Wizard,** which guides you through the following steps when creating a report:

- DataSet Properties—You are asked either to select an existing project data source or to create a new data source.
- Arrange Fields—You arrange the report fields into row groups, column groups, and detail rows.
- Choose the Layout—You design the overall report layout, add grand totals and subtotals to group data, and decide on the placement of the totals.
- Choose a Style—You select a style template to affect the style properties such as colors and fonts.

To start the Report Wizard and add a report to an existing project or Web site, do the following steps in sequence:

1. Right-click the Web or project name in Solution Explorer, and select *Add New Item*.
2. In the Installed Templates pane, select *Reporting*.
3. In the Templates pane, select *Report Wizard*, then select *Add*.

To create a new Windows Forms report application, select the *Reports Application* template, as shown in Figure 12-5. The Report Wizard will start automatically.

To create a new ASP.NET Reports Web site, select the *ASP.NET Reports Web Site* template, as shown in Figure 12-6. The Report Wizard will start automatically.

In Tutorial 12-1, you will create a Sales Order Detail report based on two tables from the AdventureWorks LT database.

Figure 12-5 Creating a Reports Application

Figure 12-6 Creating an ASP.NET Reports Web Site

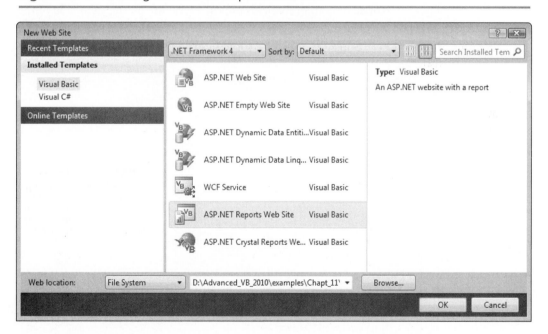

Tutorial 12-1:
Creating a Sales Order Detail Report

In this tutorial, you will create a Windows Forms application with a report that displays rows from the SalesOrderDetail and Product tables of the AdventureWorks LT database.

Tutorial Steps

Step 1: Create a new Windows Forms application named *Sales Details*.

Step 2: Create a new Data Source that links to the *AdventureWorksLT_Data.mdf* file as the data source. In doing so, select the SalesOrderDetail table. Name the dataset *SalesDetailsDataSet* and click the *Finish* button. You can find the database file in the chapter examples folder.

Step 3: Open the DataSet Designer window. Right-click *SalesOrderDetailTableAdapter*, and select *Configure*.

Step 4: Open the Query Builder window. Unselect all the SalesOrderDetail columns, and add the Product table to the query. Select the following fields in any order, and save your changes:

- Product.Name
- SalesOrderDetail.SalesOrderDetailID
- SalesOrderDetail.OrderQty
- SalesOrderDetail.LineTotal
- SalesOrderDetail.ModifiedDate

Step 5: From the Project menu, select *Add New Item*, and select the Report Wizard template from the *Reporting* category. Name it *SalesDetails.rdlc*.

Step 6: The Report Wizard will begin with the *DataSet Properties* step. From the *Data source* dropdown list, select *SalesDetailsDataSet*, as shown in Figure 12-7. Notice that all of its fields appear in the list on the right side of the window.

Figure 12-7 Choosing the data source in the Report Wizard window

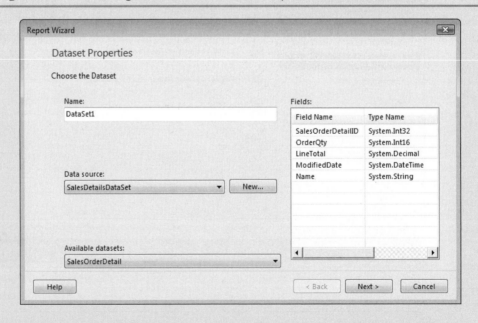

Step 7: Click the *Next* button, taking you to the *Arrange fields* step, shown in Figure 12-8. Drag field names from the *Available fields* box on the left into the *Values* box on the right.

Step 8: Notice that the SalesOrderDetailID field is marked as a Sum calculation. Select the field, and remove the check mark next to the Sum option. We do not want to accumulate this column.

Figure 12-8 Arranging the Report fields

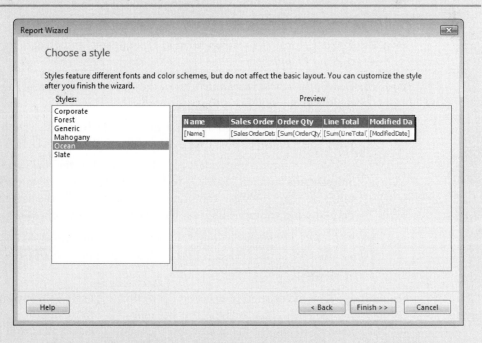

Step 9: Click the *Next* button, taking you to the *Choose the layout* step. You will not make any changes to this panel, so click the *Next* button again.

Step 10: In the step named *Choose a style*, which is shown in Figure 12-9, select any of the available styles and click the *Finish* button to save the report.

Figure 12-9 Choosing a report style

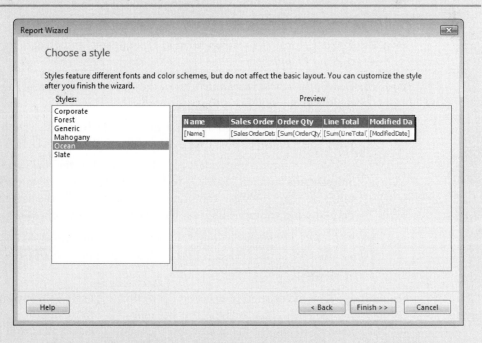

Step 11: The SalesDetails report will appear in the Design window. Drag the report handles with the mouse until the report fills the available area, as shown in Figure 12-10. You may want to drag the edge of the report border and widen it a bit.

Figure 12-10 Report layout, in Design view

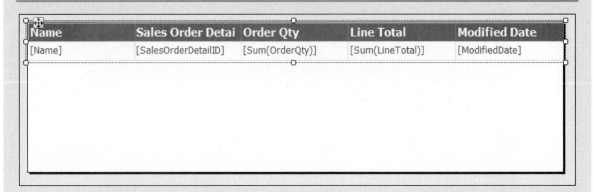

Name	Sales Order Detai	Order Qty	Line Total	Modified Date
[Name]	[SalesOrderDetailID]	[Sum(OrderQty)]	[Sum(LineTotal)]	[ModifiedDate]

 TIP: To select the report, click anywhere inside it and then click the gray square in the upper-left corner of the report, as shown in Figure 12-11.

Figure 12-11 Selecting the entire report

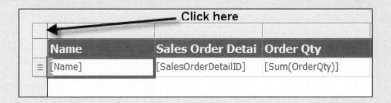

Click here

Name	Sales Order Detai	Order Qty
[Name]	[SalesOrderDetailID]	[Sum(OrderQty)]

Step 12: Change the report's font size to 9pt.

Next, you will add a ReportViewer control to the application's startup form, and link it to your report.

Step 13: Open the project's startup form in Design view and change its Text property to *Sales Details*.

Step 14: Drag a ReportViewer control from the Reporting section of the Toolbox onto the form. Set its Dock property to *Fill*.

Step 15: Click the report's smart tag and display the ReportViewer Tasks window. From the *Choose Report* dropdown list, select the SalesDetails report.

Notice that three components have been added to the form's component tray: SalesDetailsDataSet, SalesOrderDetailBindingSource, and SalesOrderDetailTableAdapter. These components work in exactly the same manner as the data-binding components used with DataGridView controls.

Step 16: Save and run the application. You should see the report shown in Figure 12-12. As you can see, the report columns could use some formatting, which can easily be fixed.

Step 17: Click the navigation buttons on the toolbar and scroll through all pages of the report. Use the buttons to print the report; zoom in and out; modify the print layout and page setup; and export the report to Excel, PDF, and Word formats.

Step 18: Type *Racing Socks* into the text box next to the *Find* button on the toolbar, and then click the *Find* button. Notice that the report display jumps to the first product name that matches this string. Then you can use the *Next* button to move to the rest of the matched names.

Figure 12-12 Viewing the Sales Details report without formatted columns

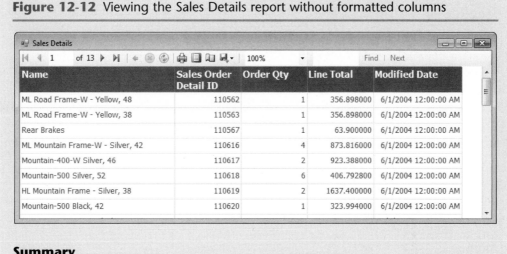

Summary

In this tutorial, you have created the simplest of detail reports. Although you have used only a small fraction of the capabilities of the Microsoft Reporting tool, we hope you can see that it simplifies many tasks. In Tutorial 12-2, you will format the report columns and add report totals.

Modifying a Report

When modifying existing reports, it helps to know how reports are constructed. A report is comprised of individual text boxes, which can be bound to static text, detail fields, totals, and custom formulas. To modify a single text box in a report, right-click on it and select *Text Box Properties* from the popup menu. You will see the window shown in Figure 12-13. You

Figure 12-13 Modifying the properties of a single report text box

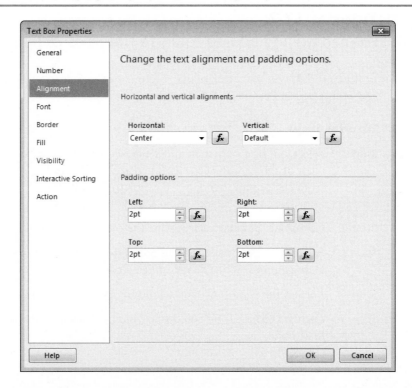

can modify the number formatting, text alignment, fonts, borders, and other properties in this window. If you select Number formats, Figure 12-14 shows the available options.

Figure 12-14 Number formatting in a text box

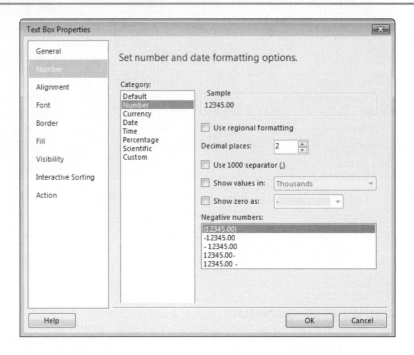

In Tutorial 12-2, you will modify the *Sales Details* report.

Tutorial 12-2:
Formatting and adding totals to the Sales Details report

In this tutorial, you will format the columns in the Sales Details report, and you will add report totals. Let's begin by formatting the report.

Tutorial Steps

Step 1: Select the text box that holds the heading for the Name column. Click the edge of the box to select it. Then right-click and select *Text Box Properties* from the popup menu. Set the horizontal alignment to *Center*. Also, set the Font size to *9pt*. Click *OK* to save your changes.

Step 2: Carry out the same changes for the other headings.

Step 3: Select the text boxes for the SalesOrderDetailID, OrderQty, and Modified-Date columns. Center each of these columns.

Step 4: Format the ModifiedDate column in short date format (mm/yy/dddd).

Step 5: Format the LineTotal column in Number format with two digits after the decimal point.

Step 6: Save the report and run the application. The report should appear as in Figure 12-15, with formatted columns.

Figure 12-15 Viewing the *Sales Details* report with formatted columns

Sales Details
1 of 13
100%
Find | Next
Name
Sales Order Detail ID
Order Qty
Line Total
Modified Date
ML Road Frame-W - Yellow, 48 110562 1 356.90 6/1/2004
ML Road Frame-W - Yellow, 38 110563 1 356.90 6/1/2004
Rear Brakes 110567 1 63.90 6/1/2004
ML Mountain Frame-W - Silver, 42 110616 4 873.82 6/1/2004
Mountain-400-W Silver, 46 110617 2 923.39 6/1/2004
Mountain-500 Silver, 52 110618 6 406.79 6/1/2004
HL Mountain Frame - Silver, 38 110619 2 1637.40 6/1/2004
Mountain-500 Black, 42 110620 1 323.99 6/1/2004
LL Mountain Frame - Black, 48 110621 1 149.87 6/1/2004
HL Mountain Frame - Black, 42 110622 1 809.76 6/1/2004

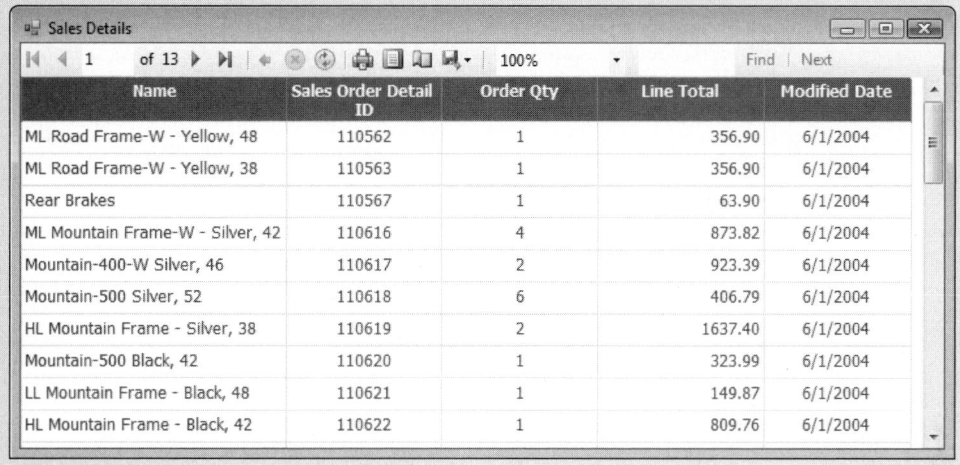

Next, you will add final totals to the report.

Step 7: Find the orange Details bar (appears in gray in Figure 12-16) at the bottom of the report designer, and click the dropdown arrow on the right side of the bar, as shown in the figure. Click on *Add Total* in the popup menu, and select *After*. You should immediately see another line added to the report design, as shown in Figure 12-17. This line defines the final totals, which will appear at the bottom of the last page of the report at runtime. This type of total is often called a *report total.*

Figure 12-16 Adding a final totals line to the *Sales Details* report

Row Groups
(Details)
Add Group
Add Total
Delete Group
Group Properties...

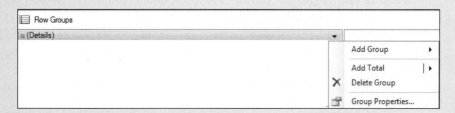

Figure 12-17 After adding a final totals line to the design

Name
Sales Order Detail ID
Order Qty
Line Total
Modified Date
[Name]
[SalesOrderDetailID]
[OrderQty]
[LineTotal]
[ModifiedDate]
[Sum(OrderQty)]
[Sum(LineTotal)]

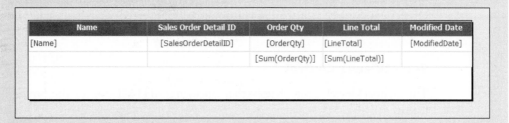

Step 8: Insert the following text into the leftmost column of the report total line: *Report Totals:*. Use a bold font.

Step 9: Save the report and run the application. Go to the last page of the report and view the report totals, which should appear as in Figure 12-18.

Figure 12-18 Viewing the *Sales Details* report, with final totals

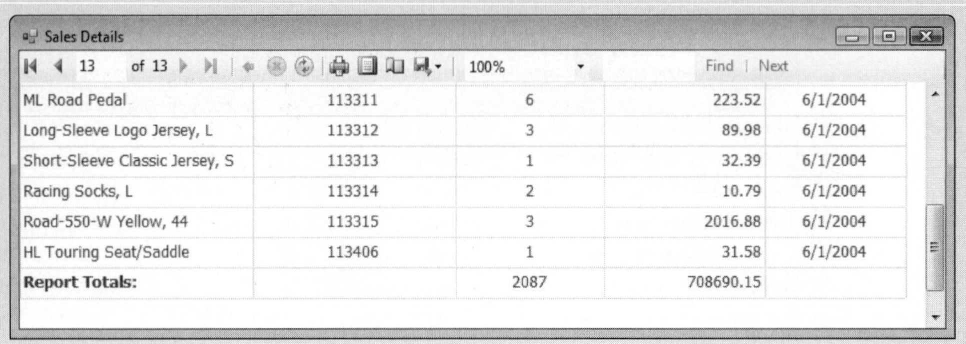

ML Road Pedal	113311	6	223.52	6/1/2004
Long-Sleeve Logo Jersey, L	113312	3	89.98	6/1/2004
Short-Sleeve Classic Jersey, S	113313	1	32.39	6/1/2004
Racing Socks, L	113314	2	10.79	6/1/2004
Road-550-W Yellow, 44	113315	3	2016.88	6/1/2004
HL Touring Seat/Saddle	113406	1	31.58	6/1/2004
Report Totals:		2087	708690.15	

Displaying Reports on Web Pages

Once you have displayed a report in a Windows Forms application, you may be pleased to discover that the same report can easily be displayed on a Web form. Only a few steps are involved. First, you must add a DataSet to the Web site, which is done by selecting from a list of predefined templates. Then, in the DataSet Designer window, you create one or more table adapters. The easiest way to do this is to drag a table from the Server Explorer window onto the designer surface. After doing that, you can customize the TableAdapter by modifying its SELECT query.

A Web form that displays a report must contain the following three components:

- A ***ScriptManager control,*** which is a server component located in the AJAX section of the Visual Studio Toolbox.
- An ***ObjectDataSource control,*** which uses a TableAdapter object to execute SQL queries against the database. The ObjectDataSource passes the query data to the ReportViewer control.
- A ***ReportViewer control,*** which is used to render the Report file and display a toolbar at the top of the report.

It is usually convenient to place a ScriptManager control on the form first. Then, when you place a ReportViewer control on the form and open its Tasks window by clicking on the smart tag, you will select a report file from the project. At that moment, an ObjectDataSource control is automatically inserted on the form and linked to the ReportViewer.

ReportViewer Control

The ReportViewer control uses the following XHTML tag in the Source view of a Web form:

```
<rsweb:ReportViewer ID="ReportViewer1" runat="server">
```

The ***ReportPath*** property identifies the name and file path of the report definition file. The ***DataSourceId*** property identifies the name of the ObjectDataSource control that supplies the data for the report. The following XHTML code shows how these properties are used:

```
<rsweb:ReportViewer ID="ReportViewer1" runat="server">
  <LocalReport ReportPath="SalesDetails.rdlc">
    <DataSources>
      <rsweb:ReportDataSource
        DataSourceId="SalesDataSource" Name="DataSet1" />
    </DataSources>
  </LocalReport>
</rsweb:ReportViewer>
```

You can modify the ReportPath and DataSourceId properties at runtime if you want to let the user select from a list of available reports.

In Tutorial 12-3, you will use a ReportViewer control on a Web form to display the Sales Details report.

Tutorial 12-3:
Displaying the *Sales Details* report in a Web page

In this tutorial, you will display the *Sales Details* report on a Web form. A sample is shown in Figure 12-19.

Figure 12-19 Sales Details report in a Web application

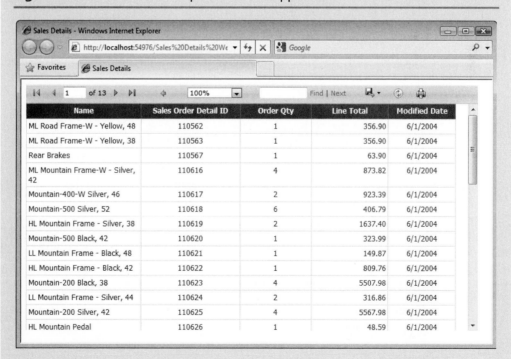

Tutorial Steps

Preparation Step: Close Visual Studio to release any lock it may have on the database file. Then open Visual Studio again.

Step 1: Create an empty ASP.NET Web site named *Sales Details Web*.

Step 2: Add both an App_Code folder and an App_Data folder to the project.

Step 3: In Windows Explorer, copy the *AdventureWorksLT_Data.mdf* file into the App_Data folder. Then in Visual Studio, right-click the folder and select *Refresh Folder*.

Step 4: Right-click the App_Code folder, select *Add New Item*, and select the DataSet template. Name it *SalesDetailsDataSet.xsd* and click the *Add* button. The DataSet Designer window should open.

Step 5: Open the Server Explorer window, select the *AdventureWorksLT_Data.mdf* file, open its *Tables* folder, and drag the SalesOrderDetail table onto the DataSet Designer's editing area.

Next, you will modify the TableAdapter query.

Step 6: Right-click the SalesOrderDetailTableAdapter and select *Configure*.

Step 7: Click the *Query Builder* button to open the Query Builder window. Unselect all the SalesOrderDetail columns, and add the Product table to the query. Select the following fields in any order, and save your changes:

- Product.Name
- SalesOrderDetail.SalesOrderDetailID
- SalesOrderDetail.OrderQty
- SalesOrderDetail.LineTotal
- SalesOrderDetail.ModifiedDate

Step 8: In Windows Explorer, locate the *SalesDetails.rdlc* report file from the *Sales Details* project you created in Tutorial 12-1 and copy it into the current Web site's folder.

Step 9: Refresh the project folder in Solution Explorer so you can see the report filename.

Step 10: Add a *Default.aspx* Web form to the site and set its Title to *Sales Details*.

Step 11: In the Web page's Design view, drag a ScriptManager control from the AJAX Extensions section of the Toolbox onto the beginning area of the form.

Step 12: Drag a ReportViewer control from the Reporting section of the Toolbox onto the form. Place it immediately after the ScriptManager.

Step 13: In the ReportViewer Tasks popup window, select the *SalesDetails.rdlc* report. Notice that an ObjectDataSource control was automatically added to the form.

Step 14: Set the report's Width property to 98 percent.

Step 15: View the Web form in a browser, and experiment with the buttons on the toolbar.

Summary

As you learned in this tutorial, the same report file can be used interchangeably in Windows Forms and Web applications.

Creating a Report with Groups

Report groups make it easy to join together detail rows according to a common column value. For example, in the Sales Details report, we could group together all rows having the same product name, as shown in Figure 12-20. Notice that we can suppress the printing of the product name on each detail line because the group header displays the name anyway. Creating this type of grouping involves two steps. First, you insert a group header line into the report and configure the header to display the group name. Second, you remove the existing display of the group name from each detail line.

Figure 12-20 Grouping Sales Details by product name

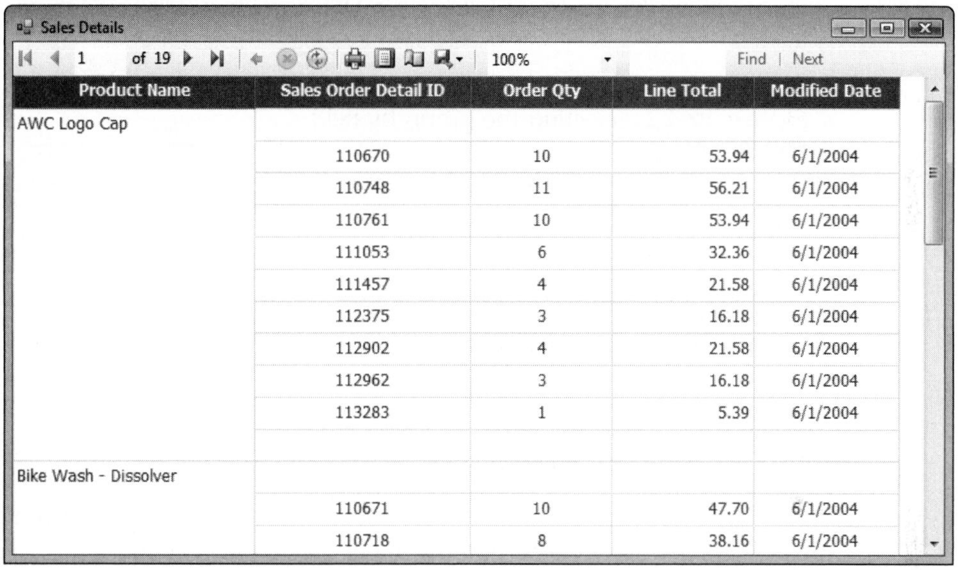

Product Name	Sales Order Detail ID	Order Qty	Line Total	Modified Date
AWC Logo Cap				
	110670	10	53.94	6/1/2004
	110748	11	56.21	6/1/2004
	110761	10	53.94	6/1/2004
	111053	6	32.36	6/1/2004
	111457	4	21.58	6/1/2004
	112375	3	16.18	6/1/2004
	112902	4	21.58	6/1/2004
	112962	3	16.18	6/1/2004
	113283	1	5.39	6/1/2004
Bike Wash - Dissolver				
	110671	10	47.70	6/1/2004
	110718	8	38.16	6/1/2004

You can also display group summary information, such as counts, totals, and averages. In Tutorial 12-4, you will modify the Sales Details report so that it displays rows grouped by product name.

Tutorial 12-4:
Grouping the *Sales Details* report by product name

In this tutorial, you will modify a copy of the *Sales Details* report so that it displays rows grouped by product name.

Tutorial Steps

Step 1: Open the *Sales Details* project that you last modified in Tutorial 12-2.

Step 2: Copy the *SalesDetails.rdlc* file and rename the copy to *GroupSalesByName.rdlc*. Open the report file in the Design window.

Step 3: Click inside the cell that displays the *Name* detail field, as shown in Figure 12-21.

Figure 12-21 Selecting the Name detail cell

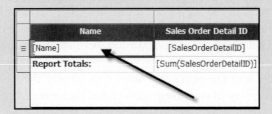

Step 4: Right-click the gray button just to the left of the Name field, select *Add Group*, and select *Parent Group*. In the Tablix group window that appears (see Figure 12-22), select the Name field, and select *Add group header* and *Add group footers*. Click the *OK* button to save the selections.

Figure 12-22 Selecting the group by field

Step 5: Right-click the gray button just above the *Name* column heading, and select *Delete Columns* from the popup menu. The column should disappear.

Step 6: Change the *Group1* heading name to *Product Name*, and widen the column. Insert *Report Totals:* into the page footing. The report should now appear as in Figure 12-23.

Figure 12-23 Report with group header and footer lines

Step 7: Save the report. Open the startup form and open the ReportViewer Tasks popup window. Select the *GroupSalesByName.rdlc* report from the drop-down list.

Step 8: Save your changes and run the application. The report should appear just as in Figure 12-20, shown earlier.

Tutorial 12-5:
Adding group totals to the *Sales Details* report

In this tutorial, you will add group totals to the Sales Details report.

Tutorial Steps

Step 1:   Open the *Sales Details* project that you last modified in Tutorial 12-4.

Step 2:   Open the *GroupSalesByName.rdlc* report file in the Design window.

Step 3:   Right-click the cell in the group totals line just below the cell marked [OrderQty] and select *Expression* from the popup menu.

Step 4:   In the Expression window, select and expand *Common Functions* in the *Category* box, select *Aggregate Functions*, and then double-click on *Sum*, as shown in Figure 12-24. You will see an expression begin to build in the upper pane.

Figure 12-24 Expression editor window, creating a group total

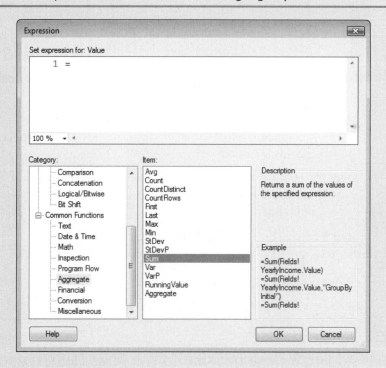

Step 5:   Select Fields in the *Category* box, and double-click on *OrderQty* in the Values box. You should see the following expression appear in the upper pane:

```
=Sum(Fields!OrderQty.Value
```

Add a closing parenthesis.

```
=Sum(Fields!OrderQty.Value)
```

Step 6: Click the *OK* button to save the expression. Notice that [Sum(OrderQty)] now appears in the report cell just below the OrderQty detail field.

Step 7: Insert the text *Group Totals:* into the cell immediately to the left of the expression you just created. Highlight the text in bold.

Step 8: Save the report and run the application. You should see a totals line appear after each group, as shown in Figure 12-25.

Figure 12-25 After adding a group total for Order Quantity

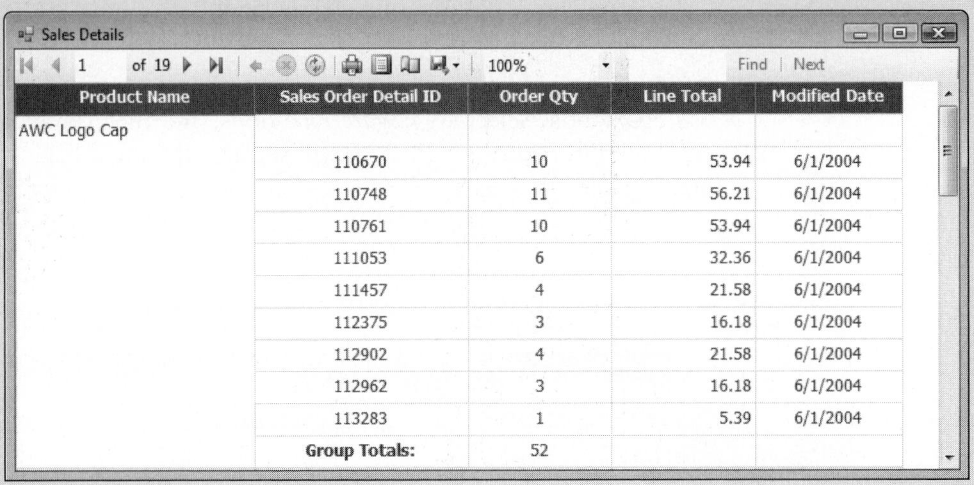

Product Name	Sales Order Detail ID	Order Qty	Line Total	Modified Date
AWC Logo Cap				
	110670	10	53.94	6/1/2004
	110748	11	56.21	6/1/2004
	110761	10	53.94	6/1/2004
	111053	6	32.36	6/1/2004
	111457	4	21.58	6/1/2004
	112375	3	16.18	6/1/2004
	112902	4	21.58	6/1/2004
	112962	3	16.18	6/1/2004
	113283	1	5.39	6/1/2004
	Group Totals:	52		

Step 9: Add another total that shows the sum of the *Line Total* column. Format the column to two decimal places by modifying the properties of the text box that holds the total.

Step 10: Highlight all cells in the group totals line with a bold font. Select a fill color for each cell (from the Properties popup window) that highlights the line.

Step 11: Save the report and run the application.

Tutorial 12-6:
Adding a page heading to the *Sales Details* report

Page headings may contain images, text, and other basic report controls. They are repeated at the top of each report page. In this tutorial, you will add a page heading that contains a title and the current date to the Sales Details report.

Tutorial Steps

Step 1: Select the report by clicking on its border with the mouse. Then use the mouse to move the report and create a ¼-inch blank border around the table.

Step 2: Right-click the area at the top of the report. From the popup menu, select *Insert*, and select *Page Header*. A page heading area should appear.

Step 3: Drag a TextBox control from the Toolbox into the report header area. Expand it to fill three-quarters of the area, and center it on the page. Enter the following text: *AdventureWorks Sales Details, Grouped by Product Name*.

Step 4: Center the text by clicking the text alignment tool on the toolbar.

Step 5: Select the header text with the mouse and change its size to 18pt, and change its font to Times New Roman.

Step 6: Just below the title, insert a smaller text box. Set its text alignment to centered. Right-click inside the box, select *Expression*, and enter the following formula:

```
=Today().ToString("d")
```

Step 7: Save the report and run the application. You should see a heading similar to the one shown in Figure 12-26 at the top of each page. The date, of course, will be different.

Figure 12-26 After adding a page heading to the report

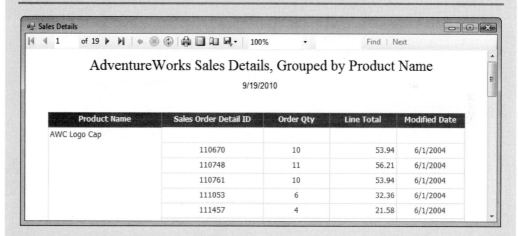

You might want to find an image of some outdoor activity, such as biking or kayaking, and add it to the report page heading.

Checkpoint

1. What is the RDL language used in report files?

2. What is the name of the Visual Studio tool for creating report files?

3. What name is given to a general layout item that displays report data as rows and columns, much like an electronic spreadsheet?

4. Which control displays reports on Windows forms?

5. How do you change the formatting of a TextBox in a report?

Multiple Document Interface (MDI)

Multiple Document Interface (MDI) is the term used for applications in which child windows are retained with the boundaries of an enclosing parent window. In fact, the terms **MDI child** and **MDI parent** apply to the two types of windows. The MDI parent is also known as an **MDI container.** When the MDI parent closes or is minimized, the child windows do the same. A single application can contain multiple MDI parent windows, although a single MDI parent is more common.

There are two ways to create an MDI form:

- An existing form can be made into an MDI container by setting its IsMdiContainer property to *True.*
- You can select the *MDI Parent Form* template when adding a new form to a Windows Forms application. A sample is shown in Figure 12-27. The form is automatically assigned a menu, toolbar, and status line, as shown in Figure 12-28.

Figure 12-27 Adding an MDI Parent form to an application

When Visual Studio generates the MDI form, quite a bit of code is added to the form, including methods that show new forms and that display the *Open File* and *Save As* dialogs. You can just customize the menu and toolbar, and add extra event handlers. Figure 12-29 shows what happens when you run the application after creating an MDI parent from the template. The user has selected *New* from the *File* menu four times and has selected the *Cascade* command from the *Windows* menu.

Creating Your Own MDI Child Forms

You probably will not want to use the default child forms generated by the menu commands in the automatically generated MDI parent forms. The forms have no controls on them. Let's assume that you want to create customized MDI child forms. Just design each form the way

Figure 12-28 Default MDI parent form at runtime

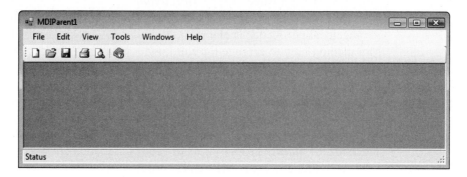

Figure 12-29 MDI Parent with cascading child windows

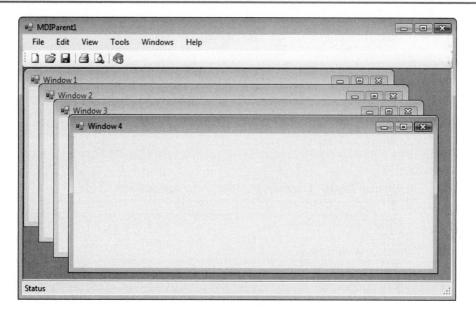

you always do, and set its MdiParent property to the name of the MDI parent form at runtime. The following code, located in the parent form, displays a child form:

```
Dim childForm As New RegisterForm
childForm.MdiParent = Me
childForm.Show()
```

Form Class

The following list contains Form class properties, methods, and enumerations related to MDI windows. Some of these have been mentioned before.

- The *ActiveMdiChild* property returns a reference to the child form that has the focus or was most recently active.
- The *ActiveControl* property of a form returns a reference to the control that has the focus.
- The *MdiChildren* property returns an array of forms that represent the children of the MDI parent. It is a read-only property.

- The *LayoutMdi* method arranges the MDI child forms within the parent form. When calling it, pass it a value of type *MdiLayout*.
- The *MdiLayout* enumeration consists of four constants with the following names: ArrangeIcons, Cascade, TileHorizontal, and TileVertical. The values tell the Layout-Mdi method how to arrange the child windows.
- The *MdiParent* property identifies the form that acts as an MDI parent container for this form. The property may be set only at runtime.
- The *MergedMenu* property returns a MainMenu object that represents the merged menu for the form.
- The *IsMdiChild* property returns *True* if the form is an MDI child. It is read-only.
- The *IsMdiContainer* property gets or sets a value indicating whether the form is currently a container for any MDI child forms.

Tutorial 12-7:
Creating the Class Registration MDI interface

In this tutorial, you will create the user interface for a simple MDI application that lets the user select a college course by name, view the scheduled time, and confirm the course selection. The application will display a summary of the courses selected by the user. Figure 12-30 shows a sample of the application at runtime, when the user is in the process of selecting courses.

Figure 12-30 Class Registration MDI application

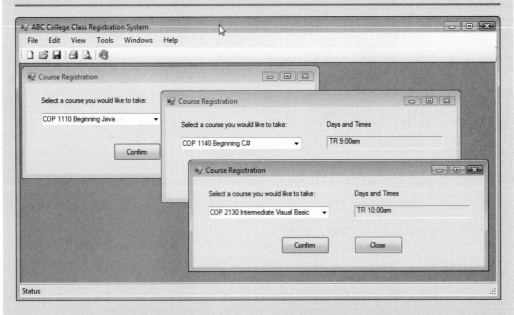

Why, one might ask, should this be an MDI application? In response, we can say that users might like to display and select multiple courses at the same time before confirming their choices. Users might want to juggle their schedules a bit to avoid time conflicts and get exactly the right courses. If they should be interrupted by an instant message from a friend, they can just minimize the MDI parent window. The child windows will automatically disappear. When the parent window is restored, the child windows are restored to their original locations and contents.

Tutorial Steps

Step 1: Create a new application named *Class Registration MDI*.

Step 2: Rename the existing form to *RegisterForm.vb*.

Step 3: Add an MDI Parent form to the application. Its filename will be MDIParent1 by default, so rename it MdiMain.vb.

Step 4: Set the MDI Parent form's Text property to *ABC College Class Registration System*.

Step 5: In the Project Designer, set the startup form to *MdiMain.vb*.

Step 6: In MdiMain, open the code window and change the ShowNewForm method to the following:

```
Private Sub ShowNewForm() Handles NewToolStripMenuItem.Click,
   NewToolStripButton.Click, NewWindowToolStripMenuItem.Click

   ' Create a new instance of the child form.
   Dim childForm As New RegisterForm

   ' Make it a child of this MDI form before showing it.
   childForm.MdiParent = Me
   childForm.Show()
End Sub
```

Step 7: Add the following code to the beginning of the class. The m_Registered-Courses variable is a collection that holds course names and times of courses selected by the user. The AddCourse method permits methods in other classes to add to the collection.

```
Private m_RegisteredCourses As New Collection

Public Sub AddCourse(ByVal courseInfo As String)
   m_RegisteredCourses.Add(courseInfo)
End Sub
```

Step 8: Delete the OpenFile and SaveAsToolStripMenuItem_Click methods.

Step 9: Verify that the ExitToolStripMenuItem_Click procedure contains the following line:

```
Me.Close()
```

From this point forward, you will edit the *RegisterForm.vb* file.

Step 10: Add the following controls to RegisterForm, using Figure 12-31 as a guide:
- cboCourses, a ComboBox
- lblDateTime, a Label, positioned to the right of the combo box, at the same level
- btnConfirm, a Button
- btnClose, a Button

Step 11: Add the two additional descriptive labels, using default names.

Figure 12-31 The Course Registration form

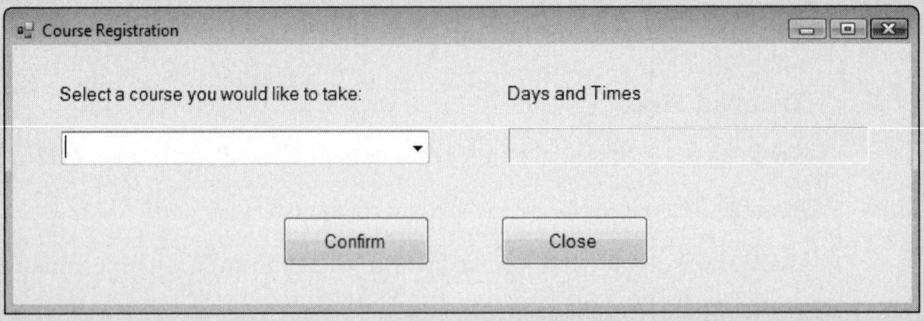

Step 12: Add the following values to the Items property of the combo box:

```
COP 1110 Beginning Java
COP 1120 Beginning C++
COP 1130 Beginning Visual Basic
COP 1140 Beginning C#
COP 2210 Intermediate Java
COP 2120 Intermediate C++
COP 2130 Intermediate Visual Basic
COP 2140 Intermediate C#
```

Step 13: Insert the following code near the beginning of the RegisterForm class:

```
Dim m_CourseDaysTimes() As String = {"MW 8:00am", "MW 11:00am", _
   "TR 8:00am", "TR 9:00am", "MW 9:00am", "MW 12:00pm", _
   "TR 10:00am", "TR 11:00am"

Private Sub cboCourses_SelectedIndexChanged() _
   Handles cboCourses.SelectedIndexChanged
   lblDateTime.Text = m_CourseDaysTimes(cboCourses.SelectedIndex)
End Sub
```

The m_CourseDaysTimes array contains the days and times for courses in the cboCourses combo box. When the user selects a course, the ComboBox's SelectedIndex property is used as a subscript into the m_CourseDaysTimes arrray. The day and time that results is displayed in the Label control named lblDateTime.

Step 14: Create the following Click handler for the *Confirm* button:

```
Private Sub btnConfirm_Click() Handles btnConfirm.Click
   CType(Me.MdiParent, MdiMain).AddCourse( _
      cboCourses.SelectedItem.ToString() & " [" _
      & lblDateTime.Text & "]")
End Sub
```

The MdiParent property returns a reference to the MDI parent form. The property returns type System.Windows.Forms.Form, so we must use the CType function to cast it into an MdiMain object before calling the Add-Course method:

```
CType(Me.MdiParent, MdiMain).AddCourse(...
```

The AddCourse method adds the course name and course day and time information to a collection. We pass to it the course name (from the combo box) and the course day and time information from the Label named lblDateTime.

Step 15: Write an event handler for the *Close* button that closes RegisterForm.

Step 16: Add a new form to the project and name it *RegisteredCoursesForm.vb*. Add a ListBox to the form and name it *lstCourses*. Add a button named *btnClose*. Set the form's Text property to *Selected Courses* and set the Font.Size property to *9pt*. Add a Click event handler to the *Close* button. A sample of the form (at runtime) is shown in Figure 12-32.

Figure 12-32 The Selected Courses form

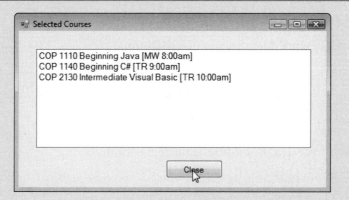

Step 17: Return to the design view of MdiMain and add a new entry to the View menu: &*Registered courses*. Write a Click event handler for the menu item and insert the following code:

```
Private Sub RegisteredCoursesToolStripMenuItem_Click() _
  Handles RegisteredCoursesToolStripMenuItem.Click

  With RegisteredCoursesForm
    .lstCourses.Items.Clear()
    For Each course As String In m_RegisteredCourses
      .lstCourses.Items.Add(course)
    Next
    .MdiParent = Me
    .Show()
  End With
End Sub
```

In this code, you iterate through the m_RegisteredCourses collection and add each course that the user has selected to the ListBox named lstCourses (in RegisteredCoursesForm). After setting the MdiParent property, you show the form. You do not have to create an instance of RegisteredCoursesForm.

Step 18: Save the project and run the application. Open several Course Registration windows and select a course in each one. Click the *Confirm* button just once in each window.

Step 19: Minimize the parent window. Notice that all child windows vanish. Restore the parent window, and watch the child windows reappear.

Step 20: Select *Registered courses* from the View menu. You should see names, days, and times for the courses you selected.

Step 21: Close the application.

Summary

This application presents at least two weaknesses that should provide interesting challenges. What happens if the user clicks the *Confirm* button two or three times for the same course? What if the user selects the same class in two different windows and confirms both? In the Programming Challenges at the end of this chapter, we ask you to prevent duplicate classes from being selected.

 Checkpoint

6. What does the acronym MDI stand for?

7. Which property identifies a Windows form as an MDI parent form?

8. Which property in a Windows form identifies the form serving as the form's MDI parent?

9. How does an MDI parent form identify the child form that currently has the focus or was the most recently active form?

10. Which property may be assigned values such as ArrangeIcons, Cascade, TileHorizontal, and TileVertical?

12.3 Interfaces

An interface defines specific behaviors for a set of classes that have a set of common properties and methods. Those classes are said to *implement* the interface.

Interfaces are very important in the real world. For example, a robotic vehicle might support operations such as TurnRight, TurnLeft, GoForward, GoBackward, and Stop. With that in mind, we could create an interface named IRobotVehicle that would describe the actions of a certain group of robot-related classes. Figure 12-33 shows the operations we have suggested.

Figure 12-33 The IRobotVehicle interface

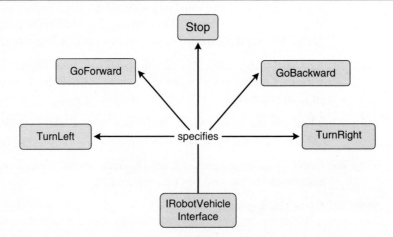

How does the interface concept relate to programming? We would create classes that implement the IRobotVehicle interface. The Interface definition, shown below, lists every method that our classes would be required to contain:

```
Interface IAutomobile
    Sub TurnLeft(ByVal degrees As Integer)
    Sub TurnRight(ByVal degrees As Integer)
    Sub GoForward(ByVal speed As Integer)
    Sub GoBackward(ByVal speed As Integer)
    Sub Stop()
End Interface
```

Interface names in .NET always start with a capital letter I, so we follow that naming convention.

Implementing an Interface

After creating an interface, the next step is to create one or more classes that *implement* the interface. In other words, the classes must contain the same methods and properties that were specified in the interface. In addition, these implementing classes can contain other variables, properties, and methods.

Figure 12-34 shows the relationship between an interface and a class that implements the interface. The interface specifies, but does not implement, a set of methods and properties. A class can implement the interface by providing implementations of all the properties and methods in the interface. Finally, other classes are free to implement the same interface.

Figure 12-34 A class implements the methods specified by an interface

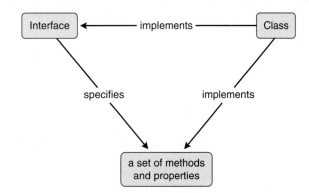

TIP: You cannot create an instance of an interface. The following, for example, is incorrect, assuming that IRobotVehicle is an interface:

```
Dim myCar As New IRobotVehicle
```

The .NET library already contains many important interfaces. The IList interface, for example, specifies method names such as Add, Remove, IndexOf, and Contains, which you have already seen used in Collection objects. The IComparable interface contains a method for comparing objects.

Defining an Interface

An interface is defined much the same way as a class, except it uses the Interface keyword:

```
Interface identifier
   property-definition
   method-definition
   event-definition
   type-definition
End Interface
```

Interfaces can contain properties, methods, events, and type definitions. Method and property definitions appear as prototypes, each consisting of a return type, name, and parameter list. All members are implicitly public, so you cannot use a Public or Private modifier.

For example, payroll software for an organization might use an interface named IPayable that defines properties and methods related to paying people salaries.

```
Interface IPayable
   Function CalculateTax() As Decimal
   ReadOnly Property NetPay() As Decimal
End Interface
```

CalculateTax returns the amount of withholding tax for the current pay period. NetPay returns the person's biweekly pay after subtracting taxes.

Tutorial 12-8:
Defining and Implementing the IPayable Interface

In this tutorial, you will create an application that defines an IPayable interface that applies to employees at a company who would be paid a salary. You will also create a class that implements IPayable.

Tutorial Steps

Step 1: Create a new application named *IPayable Example*.

Step 2: From the *Project* menu, add a new item, select the *Code* tab, and select the *Interface* template. Name it *IPayable.vb*. Enter the following code in the editor:

```
Interface IPayable
   Function CalculateTax() As Decimal
   ReadOnly Property NetPay() As Decimal
End Interface
```

Step 3: Create an Employee class, and input the following code:

```
Public Class Employee
   Implements IPayable

   Private ReadOnly mTaxRate As Decimal = 0.1D
   Public Property Name As String
   Public Property Salary As Decimal

   Sub New(ByVal pName As String, ByVal pSalary As Decimal)
      Name = pName
      Salary = pSalary
   End Sub
```

```
    Public ReadOnly Property NetPay() As Decimal _
       Implements IPayable.NetPay
       Get
          Return (Salary / 26D) - CalculateTax()
       End Get
    End Property

    Public Function CalculateTax() As Decimal _
       Implements IPayable.CalculateTax
       Return Salary * (mTaxRate / 26D)
    End Function

    Public Overrides Function ToString() As String
       Return Name & " (Employee), Salary = " &
       Salary.ToString("c")
    End Function
End Class
```

> **TIP:** When you type *Implements IPayable* and press *Enter* in Visual Studio, the editor automatically creates empty shells for CalculateTax and NetPay. In other words, all properties and methods declared in the interface are generated for you.

Adding a Consultant Class

An interface would not be very useful unless you were to implement it in more than one class. An interface only tells you what properties and methods *should be* used in all classes that implement the interface. Therefore, your next step will be to create a *Consultant* class that implements the IPayable interface. Consultants are often paid by the hour, so you will implement the CalculateTax and NetPay interface methods in a manner that is appropriate for hourly consultants.

Step 4: Add a new class to your project and name it *Consultant.vb*. Enter the following code:

```
 1: Public Class Consultant
 2:    Implements IPayable
 3:
 4: Public Property Name As String
 5: Public Property Hours As Single
 6: Public Property HourlyRate As Single
 7: Private Const TAX_RATE As Decimal = 0.1D
 8:
 9: Sub New(ByVal pName As String, ByVal pHours As Single,
10:    ByVal pHourlyRate As Decimal)
11:    Name = pName
12:    Hours = pHours
13:    HourlyRate = pHourlyRate
14: End Sub
15:
16: Public ReadOnly Property GrossPay As Decimal
17:    Get
18:       Return CDec(HourlyRate * Hours)
19:    End Get
20: End Property
21:
```

```
22: Public Function CalculateTax() As Decimal _
23:    Implements IPayable.CalculateTax
24:    Return GrossPay * TAX_RATE
25: End Function
26:
27: Public ReadOnly Property NetPay() As Decimal _
28:    Implements IPayable.NetPay
29:    Get
30:       Return GrossPay - CalculateTax()
31:    End Get
32: End Property
33:
34: Public Overrides Function ToString() As String
35:    Return Name & " (Consultant), Hourly rate = " _
36:       & HourlyRate.ToString("c") & ", Hours = " & Hours
37: End Function
38: End Class
```

Line 16 begins a readonly property named *GrossPay* that multiplies the hourly pay rate by the number of hours worked. This property is called from two places: lines 24 and 30. On line 24, the tax is simply the gross pay multiplied by the tax rate. On line 30, the net pay is found by subtracting the tax from the gross pay.

Creating the User Interface

Step 5: Edit the project's startup form in Design view and insert the controls listed in Table 12-1. Also, use Figure 12-35 as a guide when designing the form.

Table 12-1 Controls in the IPayable Example form

Control Type	Name	Property Settings
Form	(default)	Text: *IPayable Example*
Button	btnEmployee	Text: *Create Employee*
Button	btnConsultant	Text: *Create Consultant*
ListBox	lstShow	Anchor: Top, Bottom, Left, Right

Figure 12-35 Output from the IPayable Example program

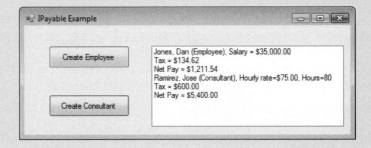

When a method parameter is declared using an interface type, any object implementing the interface can be passed as an argument when calling the method. It is useful to create a method that can be passed both Employee and Consultant objects. Therefore, you will create a method named ProcessPayroll that has an IPayable parameter.

Step 6: Create the ProcessPayroll method, which displays the calculated tax and net pay of any type of Payable object.

```
Sub ProcessPayroll(ByVal P As IPayable)
  lstShow.Items.Add(P.ToString())
  lstShow.Items.Add("Tax = " & P.CalculateTax().ToString("c"))
  lstShow.Items.Add("Net Pay = " & P.NetPay.ToString("c"))
End Sub
```

Step 7: Create a Click handler for the btnEmployee button, which creates an Employee and passes the object to ProcessPayroll.

```
Dim emp As New Employee("Jones, Dan", 35000D)
ProcessPayroll(emp)
```

Step 8: Create a Click handler for the btnConsultant button, which creates a Consultant object and also passes it to ProcessPayroll.

```
Dim cons As New Consultant("Ramirez, Jose", 80, 75D)
ProcessPayroll(cons)
```

Step 9: Save and run the application. Figure 12-35 (shown earlier) shows the expected output.

IComparer Interface

In Chapter 3, you learned about the IComparable interface, which a class must implement if arrays and lists of the class objects are to be sorted. To compare two Student objects, for example, you have to create a CompareTo method that defines which property (or properties) will participate in the comparison.

On the other hand, what if Student objects must be compared in different ways? You might want to sort a Student array first by student ID numbers, then later by last names, and finally by grade point averages. Unfortunately, the CompareTo method cannot be written all three ways. Instead, you can create a separate class that implements an interface named IComparer.

The **IComparer interface** declares a single method named ***Compare***. It compares two objects and returns an integer in the same manner as the CompareTo method. This is the IComparer interface definition:

```
Interface IComparer
  Function Compare(ByVal x As Object, ByVal y As Object) _
    As Integer
End Interface
```

Unlike CompareTo, the Compare method is not declared in the class it compares. It is declared in its own class, one that implements the IComparer interface. The following lines show a general template for this type of class, in which *className* and *methodName* are replaced by programmer-chosen names:

```
Class className
  Implements IComparer

  Public Function methodName(ByVal A As Object,
    ByVal B As Object) As Integer _
    Implements IComparer.Compare
  End Function
End Class
```

When an IComparer object is created using the New operator, we call it a **comparator.** For example, the following code calls the Array.Sort method, passing to it an array of Point objects, and a comparator:

```
Array.Sort(pArray, new PointComparer)
```

Employee Example

The following Employee class contains two properties (ID and Salary), which could each be used when comparing Employee objects:

```
Class Employee
  Public Property Salary() As Double
  Public Property ID As Integer
  Public Sub New(ByVal pId As Integer, ByVal pSalary As Double)
    ID = pId
    Salary = pSalary
  End Sub
  Public Overrides Function ToString() As String
    Return ID & ", " & Salary
  End Function
End Class
```

We've also added a constructor and a ToString method to this class. Next, let's define a comparator class that compares two employees by their ID numbers.

```
 1: Class CompareByID
 2:    Implements IComparer
 3:
 4:    Public Function Compare(ByVal emp1 As Object,
 5:      ByVal emp2 As Object) As Integer _
 6:      Implements IComparer.Compare
 7:      Dim e1 As Employee = CType(emp1, Employee)
 8:      Dim e2 As Employee = CType(emp2, Employee)
 9:      Return e1.ID.CompareTo(e2.ID)
10:    End Function
11: End Class
```

Lines 4–6 are standard for every comparator. Lines 7 and 8 cast the object parameters into the types we want to compare (Employee). Line 9 calls the CompareTo method, using the ID properties of the two employees. Fortunately, the CompareTo method is implemented for all standard .NET types, and it returns the same values that our Compare needs to return.

To test the comparator, we can create an array of Employee objects and call the Array. Sort method.

```
Private empArray(3) As Employee
empArray(0) = New Employee(1005, 50000.0)
empArray(1) = New Employee(1002, 40000.0)
empArray(2) = New Employee(1001, 60000.0)
empArray(3) = New Employee(1004, 35000.0)
Array.Sort(empArray, New CompareByID)
```

Now the array contains objects that are sorted in ascending order by ID number. The following code creates a second comparator for salaries:

```
 1: Class CompareBySalary
 2:    Implements IComparer
 3:
```

```
 4:    Public Function Compare(ByVal emp1 As Object,
 5:      ByVal emp2 As Object) As Integer _
 6:      Implements IComparer.Compare
 7:      Dim e1 As Employee = CType(emp1, Employee)
 8:      Dim e2 As Employee = CType(emp2, Employee)
 9:      Return e1.Salary.CompareTo(e2.Salary)
10:    End Function
11: End Class
```

Comparators give you the flexibility to sort arrays and other collections in different ways. You can compare not only individual class properties but calculated values and combinations of values. Comparators are one of the most powerful tools for sorting that you can imagine.

Summary

Interfaces are an essential part of the .NET library because they define standard behaviors for many classes. Essentially, if you understand how an interface works, you then understand how to use all classes that implement the interface. If you want to become a proficient programmer in .NET, learn how to design your own interfaces. For further study, read about the IList, IComparable, and IDictionary interfaces in the online .NET library documentation.

When a class implements multiple interfaces, it takes on the behaviors (operations) of all the interfaces it implements. The following declaration says that we can call CalculateTax and NetPay using Employee objects, as well as the CompareTo method:

```
Class Employee
   Implements IPayable, IComparable
```

 **Checkpoint**

11. What is an interface?

12. Yes or no: Can a class implement an interface by providing implementations of only some of the properties and methods in the interface?

13. Which common .NET interface contains a method for comparing objects using the CompareTo method?

14. Which common .NET interface contains a method named Compare?

15. Yes or no: Can a method parameter be declared as an interface type?

12.4 Abstract Classes and Polymorphism

Abstract Classes and Methods

A class declared with the **MustInherit** keyword is known as an **abstract class.** You cannot create an instance of an abstract class, but it's a great place to put fields, properties, and methods that will be common to all of its derived classes.

A method declared as **MustOverride** is an **abstract method.** It contains a method prototype with no implementation. It must be overridden and implemented in a derived class before instances of the derived class can be created.

In the following code, the Base class is declared MustInherit, making it an abstract class. It contains a MustOverride method named Print.

```
MustInherit Class Person
   MustOverride Sub Print()
End Class

Class Employee
   Inherits Person

   Public Overrides Sub Print()
      MessageBox.Show("Employee.Print was called")
   End Sub
End Class
```

If you want to be able to create an instance of the Employee class, the class must override the Print method, as we have done above. The following statements create an instance of the Employee class and call the Print method:

```
Dim emp As New Employee
emp.Print()
```

If we removed Print method from the Employee class, a compiler error would say that the Employee class must be declared as MustInherit, or it must override the Print method.

You cannot create an instance of an abstract class. Instead, think of it as a class inside which elements are defined so that they can be used by derived classes.

Employee Classes Example

The Employee class in Figure 12-36 is an abstract class (using the MustInherit keyword) that implements the IComparable interface. Combining inheritance with interfaces is common because it combines a rich set of attributes and behaviors. Note the following:

- The GrossPay property is declared *MustOverride* because the Employee class does not contain enough information to calculate a person's pay.
- NetPay and CalculateTax are implemented in Employee because their calculations may work for some types of employees. At the same time, NetPay and CalculateTax are declared *Overridable* in case derived classes need to calculate the net pay and taxes differently.
- The ToString method is not declared Overridable because it inherits this attribute from the Object class.
- CompareTo relaxes the type-checking rules by allowing the input parameter to be any type of Employee. The TypeOf operator returns *True* if the input parameter's class is derived from Employee.

SalariedEmployee and HourlyEmployee Classes

The SalariedEmployee and HourlyEmployee classes are shown in Figure 12-37. Each class must override the GrossPay method and calculate the employee's pay in a manner appropriate to the class. We assume that a SalariedEmployee receives one twenty-sixth of his or her annual salary every two weeks, and an hourly employee receives hours worked multiplied by the hourly pay rate.

Derived class constructors should always call their base class constructors. The SalariedEmployee constructor demonstrates the way to do it by calling MyBase.New.

```
Sub New(ByVal empId As Integer, ByVal name As String,
   ByVal salary As Decimal)
   MyBase.New(empId, name)
   Me.Salary = salary
End Sub
```

Figure 12-36 Abstract Employee class

```
MustInherit Class Employee
  Implements IComparable

  Private ReadOnly m_TaxRate As Decimal = 0.1D
  Public Property Name As String
  Public Property EmpId As Integer
  Public MustOverride ReadOnly Property GrossPay() As Decimal

  Public Sub New(ByVal empIdp As Integer,
      ByVal namep As String)
    EmpId = empIdp
    Name = namep
  End Sub

  Public Overridable Function CalculateTax() As Decimal
    Return GrossPay * m_TaxRate
  End Function

  Public Overridable ReadOnly Property NetPay() As Decimal
    Get
       Return GrossPay - CalculateTax()
    End Get
  End Property

  Public Function CompareTo(ByVal obj As Object) As Integer _
    Implements IComparable.CompareTo

    If obj Is Nothing Then Return 1
    If Not TypeOf (obj) Is Employee Then
      Throw New ArgumentException
    End If
    Return Name.CompareTo(CType(obj, Employee).Name)
  End Function

  Public Overrides _
  Function Equals(ByVal obj As Object) As Boolean
    If obj Is Nothing Then Return False
    If Not obj.GetType Is Me.GetType Then Return False
    Return EmpId.Equals(CType(obj, Employee).EmpId)
  End Function

  Public Overrides Function ToString() As String
    Return EmpId & ": " & Name
  End Function
End Class
```

Similarly, the ToString method should call the same method in its base class.

```
Overrides Function ToString() As String
  Return MyBase.ToString() & " " & m_Salary.ToString("c")
End Function
```

Testing the Classes

The following code creates both salaried and hourly employees and executes the payroll calculations for each:

```
Dim S As Employee
Dim H As Employee
```

Figure 12-37 SalariedEmployee and HourlyEmployee classes

```
Class SalariedEmployee
   Inherits Employee

   Public Property Salary As Decimal

   Public Sub New(ByVal empId As Integer,
      ByVal name As String, ByVal salary As Decimal)
         MyBase.New(empId, name)
         Me.Salary = salary
   End Sub

   Public Overrides ReadOnly Property GrossPay() As Decimal
      Get
         Return (Salary / 26D)
      End Get
   End Property

   Public Overrides Function ToString() As String
      Return MyBase.ToString() & " " _
         & Salary.ToString("c")
   End Function
End Class

Class HourlyEmployee
   Inherits Employee

   Public Property Hours As Decimal
   Public Property PayRate As Decimal

   Public Sub New(ByVal empId As Integer,
      ByVal name As String, ByVal hours As Decimal,
      ByVal payRate As Decimal)
         MyBase.New(empId, name)
         Me.Hours = hours
         Me.PayRate = payRate
   End Sub

   Public Overrides ReadOnly Property GrossPay() _
      As Decimal
         Get
            Return Hours * PayRate
         End Get
   End Property

   Public Overrides Function ToString() As String
      Return MyBase.ToString() & " Hrs/Rate = " _
         & Hours & "/" & PayRate
   End Function
End Class
```

```
S = New SalariedEmployee(1001, "Johnson, Cal", 57000)
H = New HourlyEmployee(2002, "Ramirez, Ben", 85, 35.5D)

MessageBox.Show(S.ToString() & ": " & _
   S.GrossPay.ToString("c") & " - " & _
   S.CalculateTax().ToString("c") & " = " & _
   S.NetPay.ToString("c"))

MessageBox.Show(H.ToString() & ": " & _
   H.GrossPay.ToString("c") & " - " & _
   H.CalculateTax().ToString("c") & " = " & _
   H.NetPay.ToString("c"))
```

The following two images show the output generated by the given code:

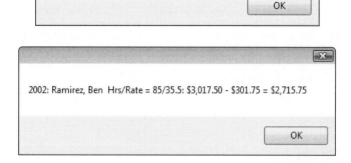

Polymorphism

Webster's dictionary defines the term *polymorphic* as "having, occurring, or assuming various forms, characters, or styles." In the world of object-oriented design, the definition of **polymorphism** is a bit more concrete: It expresses a base object type's ability to reference derived object types. For example, if we declare a variable of type Employee, we can assign it a reference to an object of a derived type, such as SalariedEmployee. Polymorphism lets us do this:

```
Dim emp As Employee
emp = New SalariedEmployee(1001, "Johnson, Cal", 57000)
```

At a later point in the program's execution, we might assign an HourlyEmployee to the same variable:

```
emp = New HourlyEmployee(2002, "Ramirez, Ben", 85, 35.5D)
```

This type of assignment is permitted because it gives programs the flexibility to create arrays and collections of various employee types. A program can use the same method to handle objects of different types, as long as the types are related by inheritance.

Using the recently shown Employee, SalariedEmployee, and HourlyEmployee classes, let us create a method that calculates and displays the pay and taxes for all types of employees:

```
Sub DoCalculations(ByVal emp As Employee)
   MessageBox.Show(emp.ToString() & ": " & _
      emp.GrossPay.ToString("c") & " - " & _
      emp.CalculateTax.ToString("c") & " = " & _
      emp.NetPay.ToString("c"))
End Sub
```

The input parameter for DoCalculations is type Employee, but we can pass any derived type as an argument. In the future, if new types of employees were added to the inheritance hierarchy, they could also be passed as arguments to the DoCalculations method. Having a method that works for all types of employees can greatly reduce the amount of duplicate code. We could add new types of employees to our application without having to revise and rewrite existing methods that handle employees.

Suppose we call DoCalculations with the following code:

```
Dim emp As Employee
emp = New SalariedEmployee(1001, "Johnson, Cal", 57000)
DoCalculations(emp)
```

During the program's execution, the .NET runtime examines *emp* and, upon discovering that it references a SalariedEmployee object, calls the GrossPay property method in the SalariedEmployee class.

Checkpoint

16. A class declared with the _____ keyword is known as an *abstract class*.

17. A method declared with the _____ keyword is an *abstract method*.

18. Yes or no: Can you create an instance of an abstract class?

19. In the Employee abstract class example, which property must be overridden by derived classes?

Summary

12.1 Microsoft Reports

- You use the Visual Studio *Report Designer* to create report definition files. The contents of these files are based on Microsoft's *Report Definition Language (RDL)*.
- Microsoft reports use a *Tablix data region* as the basis for report designs. It is a general layout item that displays report data as rows and columns, much like an electronic spreadsheet.
- Detail data consists of all the rows returned by a query from a data source. It might contain fields from multiple tables, as well as calculated values.
- The ReportViewer control provides a convenient way to display report files on Windows and Web forms. This control reads data from a data source and renders the data according to the design of a Microsoft Report file. You can use the same report file in both Windows Forms and Web applications.
- The Web form we used to display a report contained a ScriptManager control, an ObjectDataSource control, and a ReportViewer control.
- Grouped data is detail data that is organized by a value that you specify in the group definition. To create a report group, insert a group header line into the report and configure the header to display the group name.
- The AdventureWorks databases contain tables of products sold by a fictitious company that sells sporting equipment for outdoor adventures.

12.2 Multiple Document Interface (MDI)

- *Multiple Document Interface (MDI)* is the term used for applications in which child windows are retained with the boundaries of an enclosing parent window.
- An existing form can become an MDI container form by setting its IsMdiContainer property to *True*. Or, you can create an MDI Parent form using the template that shows up in the Add New Item window.
- From an MDI parent form, you can find out which child form is active, you can close all child windows, and you can change the layout and arrangement of the child forms.

12.3 Interfaces

- An interface defines specific behaviors for a set of classes that have a set of common properties and methods. Those classes are said to *implement* the interface.
- The Interface keyword is used to define an interface, much in the way the Class keyword defines a class.

- Interface names in .NET applications should begin with the letter I, such as IComparable, IPayable, and IList.
- The IComparer interface declares a single method named Compare. It compares two objects and returns an integer in the same manner as the CompareTo method from the IComparable interface. When an IComparer object is created using the New operator, we call it a *comparator*.

12.4 Abstract Classes and Polymorphism

- A class declared with the *MustInherit* keyword is known as an *abstract class*. You cannot create an instance of an abstract class, but it's a great place to put fields, properties, and methods that will be common to all of its derived classes.
- A method declared *MustOverride* is an *abstract method*. It contains a method prototype with no implementation. It must be overridden and implemented in a derived class before instances of the derived class can be created.
- In object-oriented programming, polymorphism expresses a base object type's ability to reference derived object types.

Key Terms

abstract class
abstract method
comparator
IComparer interface
MDI child
MDI container
MDI parent
Multiple Document Interface (MDI)

polymorphism
report definition file
Report Definition Language (RDL)
Report Designer
Report Wizard
ReportViewer control
Tablix data region

Review Questions

True or False

Indicate whether each of the following statements is true or false.

1. A report file created for a Windows Forms application cannot be displayed by an ASP.NET application.

2. You can use the ReportViewer toolbar to zoom a report view in and out.

3. You can use the ReportViewer toolbar to export the report to a Microsoft Word file but not to a PDF file.

4. You can use the ReportViewer toolbar to search for text inside a report.

5. The ScriptManager control is located in the Reports section of the Toolbox.

6. A ReportDataSource control uses a TableAdapter object to execute SQL queries against the database.

7. The ObjectDataSource control is used only in Windows Forms applications.

8. To add a group to a report, right-click the gray button just to the left of a detail field and select *Add Group*, then select *Parent Group*.

9. You cannot make a form into an MDI parent by setting its IsMdiContainer property.

10. A child form cannot identify its MDI parent form at runtime.

11. The read-only MdiChildren property returns an array of forms that represent the children of the MDI parent.

12. The CurrentControl property on an MDI parent form returns a reference to the control that has the focus.

13. In an MDI application, all child windows are retained within the boundaries of a parent window.

14. An Interface can contain methods but not properties.

15. The methods in an Interface contain no implementations.

16. A class that implements an interface need not contain all the methods specified by the interface.

17. The *Implements* keyword is optional in each method that implements an interface method.

18. Derived class constructors should never call their base class constructors.

19. You can assign an object of a derived type to a variable of a base type, assuming that base and derived are related by inheritance.

20. You can assign an object of a base type to a variable of a derived type, assuming that base and derived are related by inheritance.

Short Answer

1. How do you select an entire table in the Report Designer?

2. Which supplementary controls are required by the ReportViewer control on Web pages?

3. Which tables from the AdventureWorks LT database are used in this chapter?

4. Which project component must already exist before your start the Report Wizard?

5. How do you change the alignment of text inside a report TextBox?

6. In this chapter, how did the Employee and Consultant classes vary in the way they implemented the IPayable interface?

7. What is the primary advantage to defining an interface type in an application?

8. Suppose you want to sort a collection of BankAccount objects, and the BankAccount class CompareTo method compares account numbers. How could you sort the collection on a different BankAccount property, such as Balance, without modifying the CompareTo method?

9. Suppose an MDI parent form needs to close all its child forms. What is the easiest way to do this?

10. To be called an abstract class, what special keyword is required in a class definition?

11. To be called an abstract method, what special keyword is required in a method definition?

12. What keyword is used with a method in a base class to indicate that derived classes can override the method?

Programming Challenges

1. **Karate Payments Report**

   Create a printable report that displays all rows in the Karate Payments table. Include page headings, and a final totals line that displays the total amount of payments by all members, as well as the largest and smallest payments. Format the *Payment Date* column in short date format.

2. **College Registration MDI**

   Use the College Registration MDI program from Tutorial 12-7 as a starting point for this project. Make the following improvements:

   - The AddCourse method in the MDI parent window must not permit the same course to be added twice.
   - If the *Selected Courses* window is open and the user clicks the *Confirm* button in one of the *Course Registration* windows, update the ListBox in the *Selected Courses* window immediately.
   - Let the user remove courses from the *Selected Courses* window.

3. **SalesEmployee Class**

   Create a component named *EmployeeLib*. Include in it the abstract Employee class from Figure 12-36. Also, create a SalesEmployee class that inherits from Employee. The class will contain properties that hold the employee's base pay, sales quota, sales amount, and commission rate. Use the following formula to calculate the employee's gross pay:

   ```
   base pay + ((sales amount – sales quota) * commission rate)
   ```

   If the sales amount is less than the sales quota, however, the gross pay should just equal the base pay.

   Add a Windows Forms application to the Visual Studio solution. Its startup form must let the user input the employee name, base pay, sales quota, sales amount, and commission rate. Then when a button is clicked, the application must display the person's name, gross pay, tax, and net pay.

4. **Employees and Managers**

   Using the IPayable interface presented in this chapter as a starting point, make the following modifications:

   1. The Employee class should implement both the IPayable and IComparable interfaces.
   2. Add a CompareTo method to the Employee class that compares the values of the Net-Pay properties of each pair of Employee objects.
   3. Add a class named *Manager* that inherits from the Employee class. It has two new properties: (1) Title (String), containing values such as *VP Research*, or *Evening Shift Supervisor*, and (2) ExpenseAccountBalance (Decimal). Create a constructor for this class that permits the new fields to be initialized, as well as the parameters required by the Employee constructor. (Our discussion about inheritance in this chapter explained that a derived class constructor must call MyBase.New, passing to it all required parameters for the base class constructor.) The ToString method in the Manager class should display the same fields as Employee.ToString, as well as the manager's title.
   4. In the startup form's Load event handler, fill an array with six Employee and Manager objects. Display the array in a list box, as shown in Figure 12-38. Note that the same array can hold both Employee and Manager objects because the two classes are related by inheritance.

Figure 12-38 Employees and Managers list, before sorting

5. When the user clicks the *Sort by Net Pay* button, your code should sort the array and redisplay it in the list box. A sample is shown in Figure 12-39.

Figure 12-39 Employees and Managers, after sorting

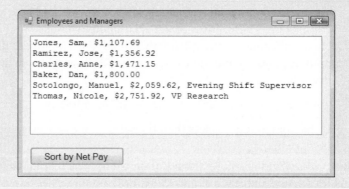

Suggestions

You can resize an array without losing its elements, using the *Redim Preserve* statement. The following statement, for example, resizes an array named *Names* so its upper subscript equals 30:

```
ReDim Preserve Names(30)
```

The *Array.Sort* method sorts an array. You can pass the starting index position and the number of items to sort as second and third parameters. The following statement sorts the first twenty elements of an array named Names, starting at index position 0:

```
Array.Sort(Names,0,20)
```

The ordering of the elements in the Employee is controlled by code that you write inside the *CompareTo* method of the Employee class.

Chapter 1

1. A class is a program structure that defines an abstract data type.
2. class instance
3. method
4. value
5. Both variables reference the same object, so a change to one variable will cause a change to the other. This is known as a side effect.
6. Private, Public
7. A class-level variable is declared outside any of the methods in a class.
8. The information hiding principle dictates that most variables and even some methods must be hidden inside classes. Effectively, the hidden variables and methods can be accessed only by other methods in the same class.
9. ReadOnly property
10. Get and Set
11. default constructor
12. presentation, middle, data access
13. It makes the program code more understandable and self documenting.
14. yes, using the CType function
15. yes, using the CInt function
16. Because you can list each possible enumerated value in a way that is easy to read
17. manual testing
18. automated testing
19. It is a complete description of the behavior of an application. It should include a description of inputs and actions by the user, and how those inputs and actions affect the program's behavior.
20. testing plan

Chapter 2

1. 16
2. Chars
3. IsLetterOrDigit
4. Call Char.ToUpper
5. Call IsControl
6. Unhandled exception
7. It throws an exception.

8. It may continue if it catches the exception.
9. No, the variable is optional.
10. yes
11. It lets the user check the item as soon as it is clicked.
12. SelectedIndices
13. SelectionMode
14. Items.AddRange
15. Items. RemoveAt
16. Format
17. MinDateTime and MaxDateTime
18. AddDays
19. Dim duration as New TimeSpan(2, 30, 5)
20. Button, Label, SplitButton, DropDownButton, Separator, ComboBox, TextBox, ProgressBar.
21. DisplayStyle
22. Image
23. ImageScaling
24. ToolStripDropDownButton
25. Navigate
26. GoBack
27. Document
28. DocumentCompleted
29. SplitContainer

Chapter 3

1. The subscript is 0.
2. ArrayList
3. no
4. Item
5. IndexOutOfRangeException
6. A *For Each* loop
7. Equals
8. IComparable
9. True
10. By the Student ID number
11. A collection that does not restrict the types of items inserted into it.
12. A class that implements a strongly typed collection, by taking on a specific data type only when an instance of the class is created.
13. List, Dictionary, SortedDictionary, and KeyValuePair.
14. It must implement the Equals method.
15. It permits you to sort a List in a nonstandard way, different from the ordering implied by the class's CompareTo method.
16. Language Integrated Query
17. From, Where, Select
18. The variable is not given a type, but it is known as IOrderedEnumerable(Of Type), where Type depends on the data being queried.
19. It is a method that can be applied to the results of a LINQ query.
20. When its results are assigned to a collection, or you use a loop to iterate through the query's values

Chapter 4

1. A database can contain multiple tables.
2. Employee ID
3. Boolean
4. Maintenance would be difficult if the department name changed in the future.
5. A foreign key identifies a field that matches the primary key of some other table. There can be multiple instances of the same foreign key value in the same table.
6. SELECT pay_rate, employee_id, hours_worked FROM Payroll ORDER BY hours_worked DESC
7. SELECT pay_rate AS Rate_of_Pay FROM Payroll
8. SELECT gross_pay AS pay_rate * hours_worked FROM Payroll
9. SELECT * FROM Payroll WHERE pay_rate > 20000 AND pay_rate <= 55000
10. SELECT * FROM Payroll WHERE employee_id LIKE 'FT%'
11. Select Columns, select the Salary column, select DefaultCellStyle, select Format, and select Currency.
12. Data binding
13. TableAdapter component
14. It is not affected.
15. DataGridView control
16. BindingSource component
17. Structured Query Language
18. The SQL language is standardized and has been adopted by nearly all database vendors.
19. SELECT First_Name, Last_Name FROM Employees
20. Right-click the TableAdapter, select Add Query, and enter the appropriate SQL statement.
21. WHERE Salary <= 85000
22. Data Sources
23. Data Source
24. Drag the table from the Data Sources window onto the form.
25. Drag the column from the Data Sources window onto the form.
26. DateTimePicker
27. From the Data menu, select *Add New Data Source*.
28. Members
29. Members and Payments
30. Columns
31. The ID is found in the ComboBox's SelectedValue property.
32. LIKE

Chapter 5

1. Server Explorer
2. Create a database diagram, add the tables to the diagram, and drag the mouse between the linking columns in both tables.
3. One-to-many, with Customers as the parent table
4. TypeId field
5. To create a many-to-many relationship between the Employee and Appointments tables.
6. GetData
7. DefaultView
8. DataColumn
9. DataSource

10. INSERT INTO
11. UPDATE
12. all rows

Chapter 6

1. class library
2. Libraries make it easier to create reusable code, and for applications to share the same code.
3. References page
4. Imports
5. automated test
6. unit test
7. regression testing
8. white box testing
9. black box testing
10. raises
11. delegate
12. WithEvents
13. Normal, Raining, Snowing, Lightning
14. yes
15. yes, except when the methods are declared *Private*
16. Inherits
17. override

Chapter 7

1. SQL
2. entity class
3. A TableAttribute identifies a LINQ entity class
4. A DataContext provides methods that connect to a database, retrieve data, and submit updates to a database.
5. Object Relational Designer
6. It can also use data from the controls to update the data source.
7. It appears as a ToolStrip control on a form, with buttons that navigate forward and backward through rows, insert rows, delete rows, and save changes.
8. SubmitChanges
9. DeleteOnSubmit
10. InsertOnSubmit

Chapter 8

1. Functional description: A Web browser opens a Web site. The Web server opens the page, interprets the server-side code, executes functions and creates objects. It then renders (creates) a Web page, which is sent to the client's browser.
2. The client-server relationship means that a Web site (the server) produces data consumed by clients, which are users running Web browsers.
3. When a page is sent back to the server for processing

4. ASP.NET is called a platform because it provides development tools, code libraries, and visual controls for browser-based applications

5. In codebehind files, having an .aspx.vb filename extension

6. File system, local IIS, FTP, and Remote

7. Design tab

8. Right-click the project name in the Solution Explorer window and select *Browse With . . .* from the context menu.

9. Static text is typed directly into a document. It does not require any type of control. Windows applications require a Label control to display text.

10. Look for the Block format dropdown list on the left side of the formatting toolbar just above the Toolbox window. Select Heading 1 <H1>.

11. The message asks if you want to enable debugging, and explains that if you approve, the application's Web.config file will be modified.

12. DropDownList

13. ImageButton

14. LinkButton

15. Examine the SelectedIndex property.

16. The page posts back as soon as the user selects an item.

17. DropDownList

18. SelectedDate

19. The cells must be in the same column or row. To select a group of cells, drag the mouse over the cells. Then select Merge Cells from the Layout menu.

20. Select the table and click the arrow tag at the top of the column.

21. Grab and drag the column's right-hand border with the mouse.

22. Select the table in its upper-left corner and open the table's Style property.

23. Items property

24. Objects stored in ViewState must be serializable.

25. Their contents are automatically stored in ViewState.

26. Code examples:

```
ViewState("clientName") = mClientName
mClientName = CType(ViewState("clientName"),String)
```

27. When the user closes the Web browser, or after a period of inactivity (usually 20 minutes)

28. no

29. Their values might be null (VB keyword *Nothing*), so casting can cause an exception to be thrown.

Chapter 9

1. World Wide Web Consortium, at www.w3.org

2. CodeFile attribute

3. Insert the text between the <title> and </title> tags.

4. Code example:

```
<asp:TextBox ID="TextBox1" runat="server"></asp:TextBox>
```

5. The <asp:ListItem> tag

6. Table, TR, TD

7. Because they allow the user to resize the fonts in his or her browser

8. Style property

9. Drag the CSS filename from the Solution Explorer window on to the form, in Design view.

10. body

11. Off

12. `<customErrors mode="RemoteOnly">`
13. Error 404 (file not found)
14. FileUpload control
15. The PostedFile property of the FileUpload control is an HttpPostedFile object.
16. SMTP
17. Code example:

```
SmtpMail.Send( me@myCollege.edu, you@somewhere.com,
    "this is my subject", "this is my message")
```

18. MailMessage class
19. RequiredFieldValidator
20. ControlToValidate, MaximumValue, MinimumValue
21. CompareValidator
22. RegularExpressionValidator
23. Assign the target page name to the NavigateUrl property.
24. Highlight the block with the mouse, and select the hyperlink button on the toolbar.
25. The Redirect method
26. We obtained the RentalInfo object from Session state and assigned its PriceRange property to the SelectedIndex property of the RadioButtonList.
27. The selections are stored in a RentalInfo object, which is placed in the Session state collection.
28. DecimalRange class.
29. The values are obtained from the PriceCategoryVals property of the RentalInfo class.

```
For Each str As String In RentalInfo.PriceCategoryVals
    radPrices.Items.Add(str)
Next
```

30. By placing a date in its Expires property
31. Code example:

```
Dim temp As String = Request.Cookies("myCookie")
```

32. Code example:

```
myCookie.Expires = Now
Response.Cookies.Set(myCookie)
```

33. Code example:

```
Response.Cookies.Add(New HttpCookie("username",
        txtUsername.Text))
```

Chapter 10

1. ContentPlaceHolder control
2. Content control
3. MasterPageFile attribute of the Page directive
4. In the System.web section of Web.config, you can identify the name of the master page file.
5. Select *Edit Columns* from GridView tasks, or select *Columns* from the Properties window.
6. SqlDataSource control
7. Select AutoFormat from the GridView Tasks window.
8. ConnectionString
9. DataFormatString
10. SelectCommand
11. ControlParameter

12. First, you must enable updates in the SqlDataSource control connected to the DetailsView. Then you must select the *Enable editing* check box in the DetailsView Tasks window.
13. ListBox, DropDownList, CheckBoxList, and RadioButtonList
14. DataSourceID
15. DataTextField
16. SelectedValue
17. Enable Editing and Enable Deleting
18. Update and Cancel
19. A column that contains some combination of *Select*, *Edit*, and *Delete* buttons
20. DataKeyNames
21. ErrorProvider
22. alert('Hello')
23. <head> and <body>
24. Insert it in the OnClientClick property.
25. document.forms(0).txtName.value (or form1.txtName.value).

Chapter 11

1. By encoding the objects in XML
2. Web Services Description Language (WSDL)
3. UDDI is a directory service that makes information about Web services public. You can use it to search for Web services on a network, or on the Internet.
4. Windows Communication Foundation (WCF)
5. DataContractAttribute, DataMemberAttribute
6. They identify important elements, such as the service class name, method names, data types, and data members.
7. no
8. consuming the Web service
9. Language (VB), Debug, the service name, and the codebehind filename
10. GetBookList and FindBook
11. WPF applications can run on the desktop or on the Web.
12. eXtensible Application Markup Language (XAML) is used to describe the visual elements in a WPF application.
13. Stand-alone WPF application, and XAML Browser application
14. Using ClickOnce, the user can use a Web browser to connect to a page containing a button that downloads and installs the WPF application on her or his computer.
15. Application manifest, and Deployment manifest

Chapter 12

1. Report Definition Language (RDL)
2. Report Designer
3. Tablix data region
4. ReportViewer
5. Right-click in the box and select Text Box Properties.
6. Multiple Document Interface
7. IsMdiContainer
8. MdiParent
9. ActiveMdiChild property

10. MdiLayout
11. An interface defines specific behaviors for a set of classes that have a set of common properties and methods.
12. No, it must implement all of the interface properties and methods.
13. IComparable
14. IComparer
15. yes
16. MustInherit
17. MustOverride
18. no
19. GrossPay

B Optional Reference Topics

TOPICS

Appendix B contains a collection of useful reference topics. It shows how to calculate TimeSpan objects and how to format dates and times. It shows how to use the ListView control, which displays rows and columns in the same manner as Windows Explorer. Next is a handy guide to SQL Queries (SELECT, INSERT, DELETE, and UPDATE). Finally, we show how to write messages to the application log file. Log files can be very useful for producing diagnostic messages that monitor the health and performance of an application.

B.1 TimeSpan and DateTime Formatting

TimeSpan Class

The TimeSpan class holds time and date ranges. The constructor is overloaded with four versions:

- TimeSpan(Int64)—Initializes a new TimeSpan to the specified number of ticks.
- TimeSpan(Int32, Int32, Int32)—Initializes a new TimeSpan to a specified number of hours, minutes, and seconds.
- TimeSpan(Int32, Int32, Int32, Int32)—Initializes a new TimeSpan to a specified number of days, hours, minutes, and seconds.
- TimeSpan(Int32, Int32, Int32, Int32, Int32)—Initializes a new TimeSpan to a specified number of days, hours, minutes, seconds, and milliseconds.

The TimeSpan class has a number of useful properties, including Days, Hours, Minutes, Seconds, and Milliseconds. Here are some of the more interesting methods:

- The *Add* method adds two TimeSpan objects.
- The *Subtract* method subtracts two TimeSpan objects.
- The *FromDays* method converts a specific number of days to a TimeSpan.
- The *FromHours* method converts from hours to a TimeSpan.

- The *FromMinutes* method converts from minutes to a TimeSpan.
- The *Equals* and *CompareTo* methods compare TimeSpan objects.

Calculating a Future Date

Quite a few applications require the use of date calculations. The *DateTime* class in .NET is very powerful, yet it is rarely understood by many intermediate programming students. For example, you can easily subtract one date from another to find out the number of days between the dates. If you need to calculate a future date, you can create a *TimeSpan* object with a given duration, passing it a number of days, hours, minutes, and seconds. Then you add the TimeSpan object to a DateTime object.

Suppose that you want to calculate the date 133 days from today. First, you create a TimeSpan containing 133 days. Then you add the TimeSpan object to the current date, which is returned by the Today() method. The following statement does all of this:

```
Dim newDate As Date = Today() + New TimeSpan(133, 0, 0, 0)
```

Airplane Flight Example

An airplane flight on April 11, 2007, leaves at 10:30 P.M. The flight is expected to take 5 hours and 22 minutes. Assuming that the plane does not fly through a different time zone, when will it arrive? First, a Date object with the takeoff time and date is constructed.

```
Dim takeoff As New Date(2007, 4, 11, 22, 30, 0)
```

Next, the flight duration is stored in a TimeSpan object.

```
Dim duration As New TimeSpan(5, 22, 0)
```

Finally, the duration is added to the takeoff time, producing the arrival date and time.

```
Dim arrival As Date = takeoff.Add(duration)
```

The sample flight will arrive April 12, 2007, at 3:52 A.M.

Project Duration Example

Suppose a project began on July 1, 2006, and ended on April 5, 2007. We would like to find the length of the project, in days. First, DateTime objects for the starting and ending dates of the project are constructed.

```
Dim projStart As DateTime = New DateTime(2006, 7, 1)
Dim projEnd As DateTime = New DateTime(2007, 4, 5)
```

Next, the Subtract method is called, producing a TimeSpan object.

```
Dim duration As TimeSpan = projEnd.Subtract(projStart)
```

The *Days* property of the TimeSpan object produces the answer we seek.

```
Dim days As Integer = duration.Days
```

In this instance, the project lasted 278 days.

Coordinated Universal Time

Coordinated Universal Time (UTC) identifies a single time zone as the reference point for all other world times. (Although the letters in *UTC* seem to be out of order, they represent a compromise between the wording of the phrase in different languages.) You may think of UTC time as roughly equivalent to GMT (Greenwich Mean Time). UTC offsets of cities and countries change, depending on whether daylight savings time is in effect.

When you do time calculations that involve crossing time zones, you use UTC encoding. The DateTime class has methods for performing conversions.

- The *ToLocalTime* method converts from UTC time to local time; the local time is based on the time zone in which the user's computer is located.
- The *ToUniversalTime* method converts from local time to UTC time.

The only problem with these methods is that they work with time zones in which the computer is located. That presents a problem for Web applications because their servers and end-users are often located in different time zones. You can take control of time conversion by understanding the process: Each time zone has a value known as a *UTC offset*, measured in hours, that is added to the UTC time to produce an equivalent time in the local time zone.

When converting from local time to UTC time, wrap the UTC offset in a TimeSpan object and subtract it from the local time. Here is an example:

```
Dim localTime As DateTime= #10/1/2011 12:00 PM#
Dim utcTime As DateTime
Dim utcOffset As Integer = -5
utcTime = localTime.Subtract(New TimeSpan(0, utcOffset, 0, 0))
```

When converting from UTC time to local time, add the UTC offset:

```
localTime = utcTime.Add(New TimeSpan(0, utcOffset, 0, 0))
```

Sometimes, adding to a time value will move the date forward one day. Subtracting from a time may cause the date to move backward one day. For example, Malaysia has a UTC of 8 hours. If their local time is 3:00 A.M. on July 2, the equivalent UTC Time is 1900 on the previous day:

```
0300 - 0800 = -0500
2400 + (-0500) = 1900 the previous day
```

To convert a negative time to positive time, add it to 2400.

Formatting Dates and Times

Applications written for .NET use standard DateTime formats. In many cases, you can select the format by entering a DateTime formatting string. Table B-1 contains most of the common DateTime format strings. The output examples are based on the *en-US* (United States of America) culture format. If you would like to learn more about the available formats, look for *standard date time format* in the online MSDN documentation.

Table B-1 DateTime format strings

Format String	Description	Example
d	short date	5/10/2006
D	long date	Wednesday, May 10, 2006
t	short time	7:00 A.M.
T	long time	7:00:00 A.M.
f	long date + short time	Wednesday, May 10, 2006 7:00 A.M.
F	long date + long time	Wednesday, May 10, 2006 7:00:00 A.M.
g	short date + short time	5/10/2006 7:00 A.M.
G	short date + long time	5/10/2006 7:00:00 A.M.

B.2 ListView Control

One of the most commonly used controls, the ListView control stands out for its flexibility and power. The effort you take to master the ListView is well rewarded because it gives your applications a distinctly professional appearance. It offers a number of useful features:

- The user can switch between display formats: large icons, small icons, list, or details.
- Data can easily be aligned in columns, without the need for tabs.
- The user can resize columns by dragging the column headings with the mouse.
- Column widths can be set at runtime by programming statements.
- Column headers can respond to click events.
- Text appearing in columns can be centered, left justified, or right justified.
- List items are stored in a collection, making it easy to find individual items.
- List items can be edited by the user at runtime.

An example of the ListView control is shown in Figure B-1.

Figure B-1 ListView Control example

The ListView control stores each row of its display in a ListViewItem object. The ListViewItem objects belong to a collection named Items. Each column heading belongs to a collection named Columns. Because of the complexity of the ListView, we will show only the most common techniques here.

Creating Column Headings

If a ListView is to display data in a tablelike format (called the Detail view), it must have column headings. You can create column headings in design mode by clicking on the *Columns* entry in the ListView control's properties window. The property page is reasonably self-explanatory.

You can also create column headings at runtime by calling the ***Columns.Add*** method, passing the column title, its width (in pixels), and the type of alignment. The possible alignment values are HorizontalAlignment.Left, HorizontalAlignment.Center, and HorizontalAlignment.Right. The following code, for example, creates a column heading named *Name*, which is 150 pixels wide and left-aligned. The column is added to the ListView.

```
lvwContacts.Columns.Add("Name", 150, HorizontalAlignment.Left)
```

A more detailed way to add the column is as follows:

```
Dim column As New ColumnHeader()
With column
   .Text = "Name"
   .Width = 150
   .TextAlign = HorizontalAlignment.Left
End With
lvwContacts.Columns.Add(column)
```

The following code demonstrates a nice trick you can use to calculate column header widths as percentages of the ListView's Width property:

```
With lvwContacts
   .Columns.Add("Name", CInt(.Width * 0.3),
```

```
      HorizontalAlignment.Left)
   .Columns.Add("Phone", CInt(.Width * 0.3),
      HorizontalAlignment.Left)
   .Columns.Add("Email", CInt(.Width * 0.4),
      HorizontalAlignment.Left)
End With
```

Each calculated expression returns a Double, so it must be cast into an Integer argument when passed to the Add method.

ListViewItem Class

The *ListViewItem* class defines the appearance, behavior, and data associated with each row in a ListView control. Depending on which view is selected, the items may appear in a table-like format, or as large icons, small icons, or a list of items.

If a ListView is to display icons, they must be stored in an ImageList control associated with the ListView. Each ListViewItem contains an *ImageIndex* property that identifies the index of the item's icon in an ImageList. You can construct a ListViewItem in a number of different ways, shown by the following definitions:

```
new ListViewItem( )
new ListViewItem( itemText As String )
new ListViewItem( itemArray As String() )
new ListViewItem( itemText As String, imageIndex As Integer )
```

Following are examples of each:

```
Dim item As ListViewItem
item = New ListViewItem()                     '1
item = New ListViewItem("John Smith")         '2
Dim strArray As String() = {"Tennis Racket",
   "10.25", "40.50", "200.00", "15"}
item = New ListViewItem(strArray)             '3
item = New ListViewItem("John Smith", 0)      '4
```

Creating and Inserting a ListViewItem

To insert a new row in a ListView, you can create a ListViewItem using the text you want to display in the first column. To add more columns to the item, pass their values to the item's *SubItems.Add* method. Finally, call the Items.Add method to add the complete ListViewItem to the ListView control. The following statements, for example, create a ListViewItem containing a person's name, phone number, and email address:

```
With lvwContacts
   Dim item As ListViewItem
   item = New ListViewItem("John Smith")
   item.SubItems.Add("305-222-3333")
   item.SubItems.Add("smithj@mydomain.com")
   item.ForeColor = Color.White
   item.BackColor = Color.DarkBlue
   .Items.Add(item)
End With
```

(You can set individual item colors.) When you are ready to display a ListView containing multiple columns, set the View property to show all column details:

```
lvwContacts.View = View.Details
```

Other possible values for the View property are related to the same view options available in Windows Explorer: View.LargeIcon, View.List, and View.SmallIcon.

Changing Font Styles

You can set font styles such as bold and italic for ListViewItem objects by creating a Font object and passing to it the existing font and the desired font style. For example, the following lines create a ListViewItem and set its font style to Bold:

```
Dim item As New ListViewItem("John Smith")
item.Font = New Font(item.Font, FontStyle.Bold)
```

FontStyle is a standard Enum type that includes the following types: bold, italic, regular, strikeout, and underline.

ListViewItem Properties

Table B-2 contains descriptions of ListViewItem properties that you are most likely to use.

Table B-2 ListViewItem properties

Property	Description
BackColor	Background text color
Checked	Boolean: indicates whether the item is currently checked
Font	Font object: defines a format for text, including font face, size, and style attributes
Selected	Boolean: indicates whether the item is currently selected
ForeColor	Foreground text color
ImageIndex	Index of the image associated with the item (the image is stored in an ImageList control)

TIP: If you forget to define column headings for a ListView and set the View property to Details, the ListView will appear empty when the application runs.

Tutorial B-1 will show you how to fill a ListView control.

Tutorial B-1:
Filling a ListView control with contact information

This tutorial takes you through the steps to fill a ListView control containing employee contact information. There are three columns and two employees, as shown in Figure B-2. The item data is inserted by code in the form's Load event handler.

Figure B-2 ListView Contacts example

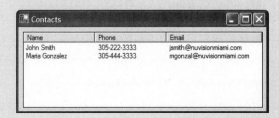

Tutorial Steps

Step 1:   Create a Windows application project named *ListView Contacts*. Rename the startup form ContactsForm.

Step 2:   Add a ListView control to the form and name it *lvwContacts*. Size the ListView so that it fills the entire form, and set its Anchor property to (top, bottom, left, right). Another option is to change the BorderStyle property to *FixedSingle*.

Step 3:   Insert the following code into the form's Load event handler:

```
With lvwContacts()
    .Columns.Add("Name", CInt(.Width * 0.3), _
      HorizontalAlignment.Left)
    .Columns.Add("Phone", CInt(.Width * 0.3),
      HorizontalAlignment.Left)
    .Columns.Add("Email", CInt(.Width * 0.4),
      HorizontalAlignment.Left)
    .Width += 2
    .View = View.Details              'show all column details
    Dim item As ListViewItem
    item = New ListViewItem("John Smith")
    item.SubItems.Add("305-222-3333")
    item.SubItems.Add("jsmith@nuvisionmiami.com")
    .Items.Add(item)
    item = New ListViewItem("Maria Gonzalez")
    item.SubItems.Add("305-444-3333")
    item.SubItems.Add("mgonzal@nuvisionmiami.com")
    .Items.Add(item)
End With
```

Step 4:   Set the ListView's FullRowSelect property to *True*. This will permit the user to select a row by clicking on any column within the row.

Step 5:   Save the project. Run the application and confirm the output shown earlier in Figure B-2. Try selecting rows with the mouse to verify that the row selection feature works.

Useful ListView Techniques

Responding to ItemCheck

The ItemCheck event fires when the user clicks a ListViewItem's check box. The Index property of the parameter e indicates the row index checked by the user. The following code displays the contact name of the person whose check box was clicked:

```
Private Sub lvwContacts_ItemCheck(ByVal sender As Object,
  ByVal e As System.Windows.Forms.ItemCheckEventArgs) _
  Handles lvwContacts.ItemCheck
  MessageBox.Show(lvwContacts.Items(e.Index).Text _
    & " was checked/unchecked")
End Sub
```

The Text property of an item contains the contents of the first column. Row indexes begin at zero.

Selecting Items

When the user clicks on a single list item, the item reference is stored at index 0 in the SelectedItems collection. The following code displays the item:

```
Private Sub lvwContacts_Click() Handles lvwContacts.Click
   MessageBox.Show(lvwContacts.SelectedItems.Item(0).Text _
     & " has been selected")
End Sub
```

If multiple items have been selected (by clicking and holding down the *Ctrl* or *Shift* key), you can iterate through the SelectedItems collection. The following code concatenates a list of all selected items into a string:

```
Private Sub lvwContacts_Click() Handles lvwContacts.Click
   Dim temp As String
   Dim item As ListViewItem
   For Each item In lvwContacts.SelectedItems
     temp = (item.Text & ", ")
   Next item
   MessageBox.Show(temp, "Selected Contacts")
End Sub
```

Removing Items

You remove an item from a ListView control by calling the Items.Remove method. Pass it an object that matches the one to be removed from the collection. The following code removes a single selected item:

```
Dim item As ListViewItem = lvwContacts.SelectedItems(0)
   .
   .
   .
lvwContacts.Items.Remove(item)
```

The CheckedItems collection contains references to all items in the ListView that are currently checked. You can use it in the same way as the SelectedItems collection.

Properties and Methods

In this section, we feature some of the more common properties, methods, and events of the ListView control. Table B-3 displays a list of ListView properties you would commonly use in design mode or at runtime. Table B-4 contains a list of properties that can be accessed only at runtime. Table B-5 contains a list of commonly used ListView events at runtime. Table B-6 contains descriptions of common ListViewItem properties.

Table B-3 ListView design mode / runtime properties

Property	Description
AllowColumnReorder	When set to *True*, the user can rearrange columns by dragging his or her headers with the mouse (the altered column order is not saved).
CheckBoxes	When *True*, every item will have a check box.
CheckedIndices	Gets the indexes of the currently checked items.
CheckedItems	Gets a collection of the currently checked items.
Columns	Gets the collection of ColumnHeader objects, each describing a column heading when the Details view is active.

Table B-3 (*continued*)

Property	Description
FullRowSelect	Gets or sets a value indicating whether clicking an item selects all of its subitems.
GridLines	Gets or sets a value indicating whether horizontal and vertical grid lines appear between rows and columns.
Items	Gets the collection of ListViewItems.
LabelEdit	Gets or sets a value indicating whether the first column of each item can be modified by the user (or by program code).
LargeImageList	Gets or sets an ImageList holding large icons associated with the Items collection.
MultiSelect	If set to *True*, permits the user to select more than one item at a time.
SmallImageList	Gets or sets an ImageList holding small icons associated with the Items collection.
Sorting	Gets or sets the sort order for the items.
View	Determines how the items are displayed; values are Large-Icon, SmallIcon, List, and Details.

Table B-4 ListView runtime properties

Property	Description
CheckedIndices	Returns a collection containing the indexes of the currently checked items (ListViewItem objects).
CheckedItems	Returns a collection of the currently checked items.
SelectedIndices	Gets the collection of indexes of the currently selected items.
SelectedItems	Gets the collection of the currently selected items.
TopItem	Returns the first visible item in the control (useful when the user scrolls the items).

Table B-5 ListView events

Property	Description
AfterLabelEdit	Occurs when the user has finished editing the label of an item.
BeforeLabelEdit	Occurs when the user starts editing the label of an item.
ColumnClick	Occurs when the user clicks on a column header.
ItemActivate	Occurs when an item is activated.
ItemCheck	Occurs when the check state of an item changes.
SelectedIndexChanged	Occurs when the index of the selected item in the list view control changes.

Table B-6 ListViewItem properties

Property	Description
BackColor	Background text color.
Checked	Boolean: indicates whether the item is currently checked.
Font	Font object: defines a format for text, including font name, size, and style attributes.
ForeColor	Foreground text color.
ImageIndex	Index of the image associated with the item (the image is stored in an ImageList control).
Selected	Boolean: indicates whether the item is currently selected.

B.3 Guide to SQL Queries

Structured Query Language (SQL) was developed as a universal language for creating, updating, and retrieving data from databases. In this section, we introduce the most important of all SQL statements, called SELECT. It is used to retrieve rows from database tables.

SELECT Statement

The SELECT statement retrieves rows from one or more database tables. The most basic format for a single table is as follows:

```
SELECT column-list
FROM table
```

The members of *column-list* must be table column names separated by commas. The following statement selects the ID and Salary from the SalesStaff table:

```
SELECT ID, Salary
FROM SalesStaff
```

There is no required formatting or capitalization of SQL statements or field names. The following queries are equivalent:

```
SELECT ID, Salary FROM SalesStaff
select ID, Salary from SalesStaff
Select id, salary from salesstaff
```

As a matter of style and readability, you should try to use consistent capitalization. If field names contain embedded spaces, they must be surrounded by square brackets, as in the following example:

```
SELECT [Last Name], [First Name]
FROM Employees
```

The * character in the column list selects all columns from a table.

```
SELECT *
FROM SalesStaff
```

Aliases for Column Names

Column names can be renamed using the AS operator. The new column name is called an *alias*, as in the following example that renames the Hire_Date column to Date_Hired:

```
SELECT
   Last_Name, Hire_Date AS Date_Hired
FROM
   SalesStaff
```

Renaming columns is useful for two reasons. First, you may want to hide the real column names from users for security purposes. Second, column headings in a report can be more user-friendly if you substitute descriptive names for the columns in the query that fills the report.

Creating Alias Columns from Other Columns

A query can create a new column from existing columns. For example, we might want to combine Last_Name and First_Name from a table named *Members*. We can insert a comma and space between the columns, as follows:

```
SELECT Last_Name + ', ' + First_Name AS Full_Name
FROM Members
```

Notice that we assigned a name (Full_Name) to the new column. In general, when strings occur in queries, they must always be surrounded by single quotes (apostrophes). The + operator concatenates strings.

Calculated Columns

You can create new columns whose contents are calculated from existing column values. Suppose a table named Payroll contains columns named employeeId, hoursWorked and hourlyRate. The following statement creates a new column named *payAmount* using hoursWorked and hourlyRate:

```
SELECT employeeId, hoursWorked * hourlyRate AS payAmount
FROM PayRoll
```

Setting the Row Order with ORDER BY

The SELECT statement has an ORDER BY clause that lets you control the display order of the table rows. In other words, you can sort the data on one or more columns. The general form for sorting on a single column is the following:

```
ORDER BY columnName [ASC | DESC]
```

ASC indicates ascending order (the default), and DESC indicates descending order. Both are optional, and you can use only one at a time. The following clause orders the SalesStaff table in ascending order by last name:

```
ORDER BY Last_Name ASC
```

We can do this more simply, as follows:

```
ORDER BY Last_Name
```

The following sorts the data in descending order by Salary:

```
ORDER BY Salary DESC
```

You can sort on multiple columns. The following statement sorts in ascending order first by last name; then within each last name, it sorts in ascending order by first name:

```
ORDER BY Last_Name, First_Name
```

For a more complete example, the following SELECT statement returns the first name, last name, and salary, sorting by last name and first name in the Members table of the Karate database:

```
SELECT
   First_Name, Last_Name, Date_Joined
FROM
   Members
ORDER BY Last_Name, First_Name
```

Selecting Rows with the WHERE Clause

The SQL SELECT statement has an optional WHERE clause that you can use to *filter*, or select zero or more rows retrieved from a database table. The simplest form of the WHERE clause is:

```
WHERE columnName = value
```

In this case, *columnName* must be one of the table columns, and *value* must be in a format that is consistent with the column type. The following SELECT statement, for example, specifies that Last_Name must be equal to Gomez:

```
SELECT First_Name, Last_Name, Salary
FROM SalesStaff
WHERE Last_Name = 'Gomez'
```

Character comparisons are case-insensitive, so the following WHERE clause is equivalent to the previous one:

```
WHERE Last_Name = 'gomeZ'
```

Because Last_Name is a varchar column, it must be assigned a string literal enclosed in single quotes. If the person's name contains an apostrophe (such as O'Leary), the apostrophe must be repeated:

```
SELECT First_Name, Last_Name, Salary
FROM SalesStaff
WHERE Last_Name = 'O''Leary'
```

Relational Operators

Table B-7 lists the operators that can be used in WHERE clauses. The following expression matches last names starting with letters B..Z.

```
WHERE Last_Name >= 'B'
```

The following expression matches nonzero salary values:

```
WHERE Salary <> 0
```

Table B-7 SQL relational operators

Operator	Meaning
=	equal to
<>	not equal to
<	less than
<=	less than or equal to
>	greater than
>=	greater than or equal to
BETWEEN	between two values (inclusive)
LIKE	similar to (wildcard match)

Bit Field (Boolean) Values

SQL Server stores Boolean values in columns that use the Bit type. You can compare this type of column to bit constants such as 1, 0, 'True', and 'False'. A value of 1 indicates True, and 0 indicates False. Here are examples:

```
WHERE Full_Time = 1
WHERE Full_Time = 'True'
WHERE Full_Time = 0
WHERE Full_Time = 'False'
```

Numeric and Date Values

Numeric literals do not require quotes. The following expression matches all rows in which Salary is greater than $30,000:

```
WHERE (Salary > 30000)
```

Date and time values must be delimited by single quotation marks:

```
WHERE (Hire_Date > '12/31/2009')
```

The following expression matches rows containing hire dates falling between (and including) January 1, 2002, and December 31, 2009:

```
WHERE (Hire_Date BETWEEN '1/1/2002' AND '12/31/2009')
```

Following is a complete SELECT statement using the WHERE clause that selects rows according to Hire_Date and sorts by last name:

```
SELECT First_Name, Last_Name, Hire_Date
FROM SalesStaff
WHERE (Hire_Date BETWEEN '1/1/2002' AND '12/31/2009')
ORDER BY Last_Name
```

> **TIP:** Microsoft Access databases use a slightly different syntax for SQL. For example, dates are delimited by the number sign (#) character. The WHERE clause we just looked at would be written as follows:
>
> WHERE (Hire_Date BETWEEN #1/1/2002# AND #12/31/2009#)

LIKE Operator

The LIKE operator can be used to create partial matches with Text column values. When combined with LIKE, the underscore character matches a single unknown character. For example, the following expression matches all Account_ID values beginning with X and ending with the digit 4:

```
WHERE Account_ID LIKE 'X_4'
```

The percent (%) character matches multiple unknown characters. We also call % a *wildcard* symbol. For example, the following matches all last names starting with the letter A:

```
WHERE Last_Name LIKE 'A%'
```

You can combine wildcard characters. For example, the following matches all First_Name values in the table that have the letters *dr* in the second and third positions:

```
WHERE First_Name LIKE '_dr%'
```

The character comparisons are case-insensitive.

Compound Expressions (AND, OR, NOT)

SQL uses the NOT, AND, and OR operators to create compound expressions. In most cases, you should use parentheses to clarify the order of operations.

The following expression matches rows in which the person was hired after 1/1/2005 and her or his salary is greater than $40,000:

```
WHERE (Hire_Date > '1/1/2005') AND (Salary > 40000)
```

The following expression matches rows in which the person was hired either before 2005 or after 2008:

```
WHERE (Hire_Date < '1/1/2005') OR (Hire_Date > '12/31/2008')
```

The following expression matches two types of employees: (1) those hired after 1/1/2005 and whose salary is greater than $40,000, and (2) part-time employees:

```
WHERE (Hire_Date > '1/1/2005') AND (Salary > 40000)
   OR (Full_Time = 'False')
```

The following expression matches rows in which the hire date was either earlier than 1/1/2005 or later than 12/31/2009:

```
WHERE (Hire_Date NOT BETWEEN '1/1/2005' AND '12/31/2009')
```

The following expression matches rows in which the last name does not begin with the letter A:

```
WHERE (Last_Name NOT LIKE 'A%')
```

Inserting Table Rows

The SQL statement INSERT INTO inserts a new row into a table, using the following syntax:

```
INSERT INTO target
[(field1[,field2[,...]])]
VALUES(value1,[,value2[,...])
```

Target is the table name. Field (column) names must be specified unless you are willing to assign values in exactly the same order as they occur in the database's table structure.

The following query, for example, inserts a row into the Payroll table of the Karate database; all column names are specified:

```
INSERT INTO Payroll (SSN, PaymentDate, HoursWorked, HourlyRate)
   VALUES('400-33-2555', '1/15/1998', 47.5, 17.50)
```

Text (string) values and dates must be enclosed in single quotation marks.

Query Parameters

Generally, INSERT INTO statements do not contain literal column values. More often, parameterized queries are the best tools for updating a database. The following statement, for example, inserts a row in the Payments table using query parameters:

```
INSERT INTO Payments( Amount, MemberId, PaymentDate )
   VALUES (@amount, @memberId, @paymentDate)
```

Updating Table Rows

The SQL UPDATE statement modifies the contents of one or more rows in a database table. It has the following basic syntax:

```
UPDATE table
SET fieldname = newvalue
[ SET fieldname = newvalue ] ...
WHERE criteria
```

The UPDATE statement has the potential to modify every row in a table. For example, the following query increases the hourly pay rate in all rows of the Payroll table by 5 percent:

```
UPDATE Payroll
SET HourlyRate = HourlyRate * 1.05
```

If you want to update only some of the rows in a table, use a WHERE clause with selection criteria. The following query, for example, increases the hourly pay rate for employees who were paid after a given payment date:

```
UPDATE Payroll
SET HourlyRate = HourlyRate * 1.05
WHERE PaymentDate > '05/01/1999'
```

If you want to update a single row, the WHERE clause must uniquely identify the selected row. Ordinarily, you would use an expression containing the table's primary key. For example, the following increases the hourly pay rate for a single employee:

```
UPDATE Payroll
SET HourlyRate = HourlyRate * 1.05
WHERE SSN = '111223333'
```

Karate Database Example

The following query updates the Payments table of the Karate database; it sets Amount to $60 for the row in which the payment ID equals 23:

```
UPDATE Payments
SET Amount = 60
WHERE PaymentId = 23
```

Deleting Table Rows

The DELETE FROM statement removes rows from a table. The WHERE clause can be used to select the rows. The following format is used when deleting from a single table:

```
DELETE FROM table
WHERE criteria
```

Once a row has been deleted, it cannot be recovered. It is also possible to delete from multiple tables. When you're deleting a single row from a table, the WHERE clause must uniquely identify the row you want to delete. The usual thing to do is to specify a value for the primary key field.

Examples

The following statement, for example, deletes all rows from the Payroll table in which the payment date is before January 1, 1998:

```
DELETE FROM Payroll
WHERE PaymentDate < '1/1/1998'
```

The following command deletes all rows from the Payroll table and retains the empty table in the database:

```
DELETE FROM Payroll
```

The following statement deletes a single row from the Payments table, identified by Payment ID 19:

```
DELETE FROM Payments
WHERE PaymentId = 19
```

B.4 Writing to the Application Log File

Writing Messages to the Application Log File

Application developers like to keep a record of all the errors that occurred when their software was running. Sometimes an end user will call to complain about an error but will not be able to describe the error very well. The developer can then inspect the log file, which will contain the exception messages along with supporting information. Fortunately, .NET makes this process very easy. The key to making this happen is to use the *My.Application.Log* class, which has two methods:

1. The *WriteEntry* method receives a string and writes it to the log file:

   ```
   My.Application.Log.WriteEntry( ByVal message As String )
   ```

2. The *WriteException* method writes an exception object to the log file, along with an optional message string:

   ```
   My.Application.Log.WriteException( ByVal ex As Exception,
      ByVal type As TraceEventType, ByVal message As String )
   ```

The complete path of the log file can be found at runtime in the following property:

```
My.Application.Log.DefaultFileLogWriter.FullLogFileName
```

For example, the log file for an application named *Exception_Test*, with a Windows 7 account named *sam*, has this path:

```
C:\Users\sam\AppData\Roaming\Exception_Test\My\1.0.3814.17463\
Exception_Test.log
```

Payroll Example

Suppose the HoursWorked property in a class named Payroll throws an exception if it receives an invalid value. We might want to write a Click handler for a button that assigns a value to HoursWorked. The following example code catches any thrown exception and writes the exception information to a log file along with the current date and time:

```
Private Sub bntOk_Click() Handles bntOk.Click
  Try
    myPayRoll.HoursWorked = CDbl(txtHours.Text)
  Catch ex As Exception
    My.Application.Log.WriteException(ex,
       TraceEventType.Error, Now.ToString())
  End Try
End Sub
```

Then, if the user enters an out-of-range value into the txtHours text box, the following two lines are written to the log file:

```
DefaultSource Error 2 Must be between 0 and 80
  Parameter name: HoursWorked 6/11/2010 11:44:30 PM
```

Any message can be written to the log file. For example, when the main form loads, we could write a note, like the following, to the log indicating the date and time when the application starts to run:

```
Private Sub PayrollForm_Load() Handles MyBase.Load
  My.Application.Log.WriteEntry("Application started at " & Now)
End Sub
```

The resulting string in the log file looks like this:

```
DefaultSource Information 0 Application started at 6/12/2010
12:01:12 AM
```

Index